The Chaucer Bibliographies

Chaucer's
Romaunt of the Rose and *Boece*, *Treatise on the Astrolabe*, *Equatorie of the Planetis*, Lost Works, and Chaucerian Apocrypha

AN ANNOTATED BIBLIOGRAPHY

1900 TO 1985

Russell A. Peck

Published in Association with the University of Rochester by

UNIVERSITY OF TORONTO PRESS

Toronto   Buffalo   London

© University of Toronto Press 1988
Toronto Buffalo London
Printed in Canada
ISBN 0-8020-2493-9

Canadian Cataloguing in Publication Data

Peck, Russell A.
Chaucer's Romaunt of the rose and Boece, The
treatise on the astrolabe and The equatorie of
the planetis, the Lost works, and the Chaucerian
apocrypha

(The Chaucer bibliographies ; 2)
Includes index.
ISBN 0-8020-2493-9

1. Chaucer, Geoffrey, d. 1400 – Bibliography.
I. Title. II. Series.

Z8164.P43 1988   016.821'1   C88-093599-5

To Nathan Russell Peck
Master of Earth and Planetary Science

For out of olde feldes, as men seyth,

Commeth al this newe corn from yer to yere,

And out of olde bokes, in good feyth,

Cometh al this newe science that men lere.

Contents

Part IV: The Equatorie of the Planetis

Part V: The Lost Works

Part VI: The Chaucer Apocrypha

🐦 Preface

This second volume of the *Chaucer Bibliographies* includes Chaucer's longer, independent translations, those which stand without incorporation into some other literary enterprise, that is, the *Romaunt* and *Boece*; his scientific writings, namely *The Treatise on the Astrolabe* and, on the chance that it is Chaucer's, *The Equatorie of the Planetis*; and the Lost Works and the Chaucerian Apocrypha. Such material is less heterogeneous than it at first seems. Several of the lost works were apparently independent translations. Moreover, some of the Chaucerian translations which we possess, namely the *Romaunt*, may be apocryphal. In his translations Chaucer makes significant forays into those diverse areas of science, philosophy, and French courtly rhetoric which combine in his own poetry to make it uniquely Chaucerian. To a considerable extent this bibliography is an index to Chaucer's intellectual sources and literary influences. Apart from Chaucer's individual genius, more than anything else it is his fertile mastery of French literary traditions devolving from the *Roman de la Rose*, his intimate knowledge of the *Consolation of Philosophy* and its potentialities as a seed-bed for poetry, and the practical empirical disposition of his scientific endeavors which filter into his poetry and set it profoundly apart from that of English writers before him. It is, moreover, these same three areas of intellectual and rhetorical pursuit that Chaucer's subsequent admirers single out for comment and which, even in his own lifetime, they imitate. For them he was the great translator, the philosophical poet, the master rhetorician, the learned mathematician and man of science.

Chaucer's closest followers, many of whose works become confused with Chaucer's own during the next two hundred years, write within the literary tradition of the *Roman de la Rose*, which they see embodied in Chaucer's poetry like some shining *aetas prima* for English poetry. They imitate his versification, his stanzas, his courtly personifications and rhetoric, even his phrasing. More than *Troilus* or the *Canterbury Tales*, Chaucer's lyrics and dream visions, written in the French vein, are the texts that attract a fifteenth-century audience. Even Charles of Orleans, who was himself of the French court and knew its poetry even better than did Chaucer, turns to Chaucer for models in writing his English poetry. Chaucer showed England how to be French in English, or at least so it seemed to fifteenth-century poets. His early translation of the *Romaunt* marked for English literature a primary departure in that direction.

For a more talented few, Chaucer also taught, as Jean de Meun had taught him, the possibilities of philosophical poetry, a poetry whose structural subtleties, themes, and rich philosophical vocabulary are largely indebted to Boethius. In this area the debt of subsequent Chaucerians is even more specifically to Chaucer than the influence of French rhetorical tradition had been, for it is usually Chaucer's very translation of the *Consolatio* which they cite. Just as he used Jean's translation of *Boece* in the making of his own, fifteenth- and sixteenth-century English translators of the treatise used Chaucer. The influence of his work far exceeds that of other translators, however. From Usk's *Testament of Love* to the *Kingis Quair* and Henryson's *Testament of Cresseid*, Chaucer's *Boece* provided literary inspiration.

Unlike the rhetorical and philosophical Chaucer, the scientific Chaucer is more revered than imitated, at least by literary men. He was after his death esteemed as a mathematician and astronomer. Some of the Chaucerian poets use astronomical material in a Chaucerian manner. But astronomy involved technicalities beyond the capacities of most subsequent poets, who simply marvel that Chaucer could have mastered the art. His *Astrolabe* remained for hundreds of years *the* English treatise on the subject. Its influence was more with civil engineers than men of letters, though its impact upon the myth of the learned Chaucer was awesome, and justly so. Chaucer pursued and did what few other poets have been able to do in any age, whether as poet, philosopher, or scientist.

One unforeseen effect of including these several works and the Chaucer Apocrypha in the same volume is the highlighting of their interrelatedness, not simply in terms of sources and literary influences, but in other ways as well. It is amazing to discover how frequently the scholarship on these individual works converges, sometimes unwittingly, sometimes with shrewd intent. I have attempted in the indexing of the volume to indicate something of the interrelatedness of topics and studies in the diverse sections of the volume. Each section of the bibliography poses its own unique problems. The most nebulous area is the Chaucerian Apocrypha, which tends, because of Chaucer's overwhelming influence, to become a survey of fifteenth-century literature. I have tried to include all studies which deal specifically with the Apocrypha as a topic, but only selected studies on works once thought to be by Chaucer or which were once included with Chaucer's works but which now are studied as independent poems.

Other gray areas where I have found myself being inconsistent and arbitrary occur in the sections on *Boece* and the *Romaunt*. I have tried to be thorough in ferreting out discussions of the translations themselves; but these are not the kinds of studies students concerned with the *Romaunt* and *Boece* are likely to be seeking. So I have included selected studies of the influence of the originals behind Chaucer's translations upon his writings in general. The indices to the annotated bibliographies on *Troilus*, the *Knight's Tale*, *Wife of Bath's Tale*, *Book of the Duchess*, and so on in the other volumes of this series will reveal the full extent of the influence of Boethius and the *Romance of the Rose* on Chaucer, though the annotations there will not share the peculiar slant of this volume.

I apologize to any whose work I have misrepresented or inadvertently ignored. That I have made blunders and omissions seems inevitable. I have tried to be objective and balanced, but undoubtedly my prejudices and enthusiasms have interfered. The annotations attempt to indicate the scope of the work under consideration as it pertains to the purview of this volume and to provide a summary of pertinent matter. When it has been practical to do so, I have quoted phrases or passages which characterize the tone or thesis of the work. I have also tried, within reasonable limits, to include exact quotation of material appearing in influential studies which is frequently quoted by subsequent studies. I have annotated some reviews — those which offer astute appraisal of the work under consideration or which advance the topic in a substantive way. I have also included some unpublished doctoral dissertations.

Any bibliography of Chaucer studies in recent years owes a primary obligation to Dudley David Griffith, *Bibliography of Chaucer: 1908-1953* (Seattle: University of Washington Press, 1955); William R. Crawford, *Bibliography of Chaucer: 1954-1963* (Seattle and London: University of Washington Press, 1967); and Lorrayne Y. Baird, *A Bibliography of Chaucer, 1964-1973* (Boston: G.K. Hall, 1977). In my researches for Chaucer material in compiling this volume I always began with these three volumes. This present volume does not, however, displace them. Baird especially remains valuable for her comprehensive listing of reviews and such unusual material as musical adaptations, phonograph recordings, films, and filmstrips. And all three of the earlier volumes include dissertations and some items I was unable to obtain, as well as reviews which I ignored. I also have made use of the *New Cambridge Bibliography of English Literature*, which led me to a few items not found in Griffith, Crawford, or Baird. And, of course, I am indebted to the annual bibliography of the Modern Language Association, and, recently, to the annual bibliography in *Studies in the Age of Chaucer*. Because of the peculiar range of topics

included in this volume I have found some material in places not
normally examined by Chaucer students in their general preparations
— histories of science, studies in prosody, histories of literature,
studies in Catholicism, studies in *translatio*, and studies in writers
other than Chaucer. Also, footnotes in various studies have yielded
important items which have not previously been noted in published
bibliographies. And sometimes I simply came across material by luck.

A word about the arrangement of this volume. I have divided the
sections into those categories that reflect the most likely ways in which
a user of the bibliography might be working. Editions are arranged
chronologically, since that is the way scholars usually think of editions.
Critical discussions of the works, on the other hand, are arranged
alphabetically according to author, since we generally think of such
material in terms of who wrote it. If, however, an author is reponsible
for more than one entry in a section, then the works are listed
chronologically, again since that is the way we customarily think about
a single author's canon. Reviews appear chronologically immediately
following the work being reviewed.

In the annotations themselves I have followed the spelling of
proper names used by the authors of the work cited. Thus one finds
some variation in the volume in the spelling of proper names,
particularly names in French or Latin. I have restricted use of ellipsis
to indicate material omitted within the quotation. In such quotations I
have adjusted capitalization and end punctuation to suit the new
context. Numbers in bold face type indicate main entries of items
located elsewhere in the bibliography.

I am indebted to Alfred David for helpful comments on the
Romaunt chapter, to Traugott Lawler, Ralph Hanna III, and Tim
Machan for thoughtful comments on the *Boece* sections, to Chauncey
Wood and Laurel Braswell for their several suggestions on the
Astrolabe and *Equatorie* sections, and to Rossell Hope Robbins for his
careful perusal of a draft of the material on the Chaucerian
Apocrypha. A.J. Colaianne and R.M. Piersol oversaw the early
progress of most portions of this volume with tolerance and good
cheer. I am grateful to the John Simon Guggenhiem Foundation for
funding my researches on the philosophical Chaucer, some of which
research went into the making of this bibliography. At the University
of Rochester, Thomas Hahn has proven a patient counsellor and
faithful friend to the project and recently has served as general editor
of the volume. I owe special thanks to Marjorie C. Woods, whom I
consulted on various matters, and to the staff of the Rush Rhees
Library at the University of Rochester, especially to Phyllis Andrews
in the Reference Department and to Carol Cavanaugh and Sally
Morsch of Interlibrary Loan, all of whom endured with good spirit

numerous odd requests and helped me track down out-of-the-way references. Sheila Robertson, Cindy Warner, and Kay Strassner of the University of Rochester English Department have been helpful in the xeroxing of materials and in the arranging of a meeting of all the editors in the series of annotated bibliographies at Rochester in October 1981. I am especially grateful to Claire Sundeen, who typed the manuscript, to James Meador, who initially put it on tape at Virginia Polytechnic Institute and State University, and, especially, to Mary Heinmiller at the University of Rochester for help in the editing of the text. And finally, I wish to thank Carol Wilkinson Whitney and Sandra Bernhard, who assisted me with the checking of references and in proofreading.

Both Virginia Polytechnic Institute and State University and the University of Rochester have made considerable investment in the scripting of the volume. Robert Taylor of the University of Rochester Computing Center has been particularly valuable in facilitating various program conversions which the producing of the book has required. The office of the Dean of Arts and Science at the University of Rochester has provided financial support for the moving of the project to Rochester and for its continuance. I and my colleagues in the project are grateful for the trust of both universities in the scholarly worth of the project and for their encouragement and institutional support.

Abbreviations

LITERARY WORKS CITED

AA	*Anelida and Arcite*
ABC	*An A B C*
Adam	*Chaucers Wordes unto Adam, His Owne Scriveyn*
AL	*Assembly of Ladies*
Astrolabe	*A Treatise on the Astrolabe*
AWU	*Against Women Unconstant* (also called *Newfanglenesse*)
BC	*A Balade of Complaint*
BD	*Book of the Duchess*
Beryn	*Tale of Beryn*
Boece	*Boece de Consolacione*
Bukton	*Lenvoy de Chaucer a Bukton*
CA	*Confessio Amantis*
CBK	*Complaint of the Black Knight*
CD	*Complaynt D'Amours: An Amorous Complaint Made at Windsor*
CL	*Court of Love*
ClerkT	*Clerk's Tale*
CMF	*Complaint to my Mortal Foe*
CML	*Complaint to my Lodesterre*
CN	*Cuckoo and the Nightingale* (*Book of Cupid*)
CT	*Canterbury Tales*
CYT	*Canon Yeoman's Tale*
EP	*Equatorie of the Planetis*
FA	*The Former Age*
FC	*Flower of Courtesy*
FL	*Flower and the Leaf*
Fortune	*Fortune: Balades de Visage sanz Peinture*
FriarT	*Friar's Tale*
FrankT	*Franklin's Tale*
Gamelyn	*Tale of Gamelyn*
Gent	*Gentilesse: Moral Balade of Chaucier*
GP	*General Prologue to the Canterbury Tales*
HF	*House of Fame*

IL	Isle of Ladies (sometimes called Chaucer's Dream)
JU	Jack Upland
KnT	Knight's Tale
KQ	Kingis Quair
Lady	A Complaint to his Lady (also called A Balade of Pity)
LBD	La Belle Dame Sans Merci
LGW	The Legend of Good Women
MancT	Manciple's Tale
Mars	The Complaint of Mars
MB	Merciles Beaute
Mel	Tale of Melibee
MerchT	Merchant's Tale
MilT	Miller's Tale
MLT	Man of Law's Tale
MonkT	Monk's Tale
NPT	Nun's Priest's Tale
OM	Ovide moralisée
PardT	Pardoner's Tale
ParsT	Parson's Tale
PF	Parliament of Fowls
PhysT	Physician's Tale
Pity	The Complaint unto Pity
PlowT	The Plowman's Tale
PriorT	Prioress's Tale
Prov	Proverbs
Purse	The Complaint of Chaucer to his Purse
Retr	Chaucer's Retraction
Romaunt	The Romaunt of the Rose
Ros	To Rosemounde
RR	Le Roman de la Rose
ReeveT	Reeve's Tale
Scogan	Lenvoy de Chaucer a Scogan
ShipT	Shipman's Tale
Siege	The Siege of Thebes
SNT	Second Nun's Tale
SqT	Squire's Tale
Sted	Lak of Stedfastnesse: Balade
SumT	Summoner's Tale
T&C	Troilus and Criseyde
TC	Testament of Cresseid
Thop	Tale of Sir Thopas
TL	Testament of Love
Truth	Truth: Balade de Bon Conseyl
Venus	The Complaint of Venus

WBT	*Wife of Bath's Tale*
WN	*Womanly Noblesse: Balade That Chaucier Made*

JOURNALS, REFERENCE WORKS, AND INSTITUTIONS

AB	*Anglia Beiblatt*
ABR	*American Benedictine Review*
Acad	*Academy*
AJP	*American Journal of Philology*
AJPh	*American Journal of Physics*
AHR	*American Historical Review*
Ang	*Anglia*
AnM	*Annuale Mediaevale*
BM/BL	British Museum (British Library)
BN	Bibliothèque Nationale
BJRL	*Bulletin of the John Rylands Library*
CBEL	*Cambridge Bibliography of English Literature*
CE	*College English*
ChauR	*Chaucer Review*
CHEL	*Cambridge History of English Literature*
CL	*Comparative Literature*
Crit	*Criticism*
CR	*Critical Review*
DA	*Dissertation Abstracts*
DAI	*Dissertation Abstracts International*
DNB	*Dictionary of National Biography*
E&S	*Essays and Studies*
EETS	*Early English Text Society*
EIC	*Essays in Criticism*
EigoS	*Eigo Seinen* [The Rising Generation] Tokyo
ELH	*Journal of English Literary History*
ELN	*English Language Notes*
EM	*English Miscellany*
ES	*English Studies*
ESt	*Englische Studien*
Expl	*Explicator*
FCS	*Fifteenth Century Studies*
JEGP	*Journal of English and Germanic Philology*
JHA	*Journal for the History of Astronomy*
JHI	*Journal of the History of Ideas*
JMRS	*Journal of Medieval and Renaissance Studies*
MA	*Le Moyen Age*
MAE	*Medium Aevum*
M&H	*Medievalia et Humanistica*

MLN	*Modern Language Notes*
MLQ	*Modern Language Quarterly*
MLR	*Modern Language Review*
MP	*Modern Philology*
MRS	*Medieval and Renaissance Studies*
MS	*Mediaeval Studies*
Neophil	*Neophilologus*
NM	*Neuphilologische Mitteilungen*
NQ	*Notes and Queries*
NED/OED	*Oxford English Dictionary*
PLL	*Papers on Language and Literature*
PMLA	*Publications of the`Modern Language Association*
PQ	*Philological Quarterly*
PRO	*Public Record Office*
RES	*Review of English Studies*
RF	*Romanische Forschungen*
Rom	*Romania*
RPh	*Romance Philology*
RomR	*Romanic Review*
SAC	*Studies in the Age of Chaucer*
SATF	*Société des Anciens Textes Français*
SB	*Studies in Bibliography*
ScLT	*Scottish Literary Journal*
SELit	*Studies in English Literature* (English Literary Society of Jap
SHR	*Scottish Historical Review*
SN	*Studia Neophilologica*
SP	*Studies in Philology*
Spec	*Speculum*
SSL	*Studies in Scottish Literature*
TLS	*London Times Literary Supplement*
TSL	*Tennessee Studies in Literature*
TSLL	*Texas Studies in Literature and Language*
UCTSE	*University of Cape Town Studies in English*
UMSE	*University of Mississippi Studies in English*
UTQ	*University of Toronto Quarterly*
YFS	*Yale French Studies*

Chaucer's *Romaunt, Boece,*
Scientific Works,
Lost Works, and Apocrypha

✹ Part I: Romaunt of the Rose

Introduction

It is certainly true, as Legouis **130** pointed out long ago, that the
Roman de la Rose was 'the one poem which had the most constant
hold on Chaucer' (p 54). From *The Book of the Duchess* and the
earliest lyrics of the 1360s to the marriage group of the *Canterbury
Tales* in the 1390s, the *Roman* remained for Chaucer 'a sort of poetic
Bible' (Legouis, p 54) from which he drew stylistic and rhetorical
techniques, social situations, psychological insights, and literary
modes. Guillaume de Lorris instructed Chaucer in the possibilities of
personification-allegory and the rich flexibilities of dream vision. To
Guillaume and later French poets who thrived on his inspiration,
Chaucer owed most of his knowledge of craftsmanship. Jean de Meun,
on the other hand, opened to Chaucer the doors to sophisticated social
criticism, intricate layers of irony, and the rich possibilities of
philosophical poetry. In Jean he discovered the compatibility of
Boethian ideas and literary methodology. It is understandable that
Chaucer would not only draw upon the vast French poem for subject
matter but that he would train himself in its literary techniques and
sensibilities through the rigorous exercise of direct translation.
Moreover, it is not surprising that he would take pride in having made
his translation, for it enabled him the better to introduce a stylish wit
and literary manner to his English audience, a wit and manner he
would soon be able to claim as his own. He even makes inverted boasts
and jokes about his effort in the Prologue to his *Legend of Good
Women*. But precisely what he is alluding to when Cupid accuses
Geoffrey of heresy for having made the translation is not clear:

'Thou maist yt nat denye,
For in pleyn text, withouten nede of glose,

Thou has translated the Romaunce of the Rose,
That is an heresye ageyns my lawe,
And makest wise folk fro me withdrawe.'
LGW, F 327-31

The history of what that translation might in fact be is fraught with apparently unsolvable problems.

Only one ms of a Middle English translation of the *Romaunt* survives — Glasgow, Hunterian Museum, MS V.3.7 — and that in a fragmented condition, with the first leaf missing and ten others displaced as well. Skeat **2** (vol 1, p 13) dates it ca 1440. In the Glasgow ms the *Romaunt* is followed by *Troilus and Criseyde*, so although the heading, which might have had information about the scribe's view of the poem's authorship, is missing, its context is definitely Chaucerian. A second authority is Thynne's printed edition of 1532. Ronald Sutherland **8** reasons that the scribe of the Glasgow ms used two other mss as sources and that Thynne must have worked from a different one still, which would suggest the existence of at least four mss of the *Romaunt* at some point, though all apparently shared the same mixture of dialects and combination of materials as the two examples that survive. James Blodgett **23**, on the other hand, argues that Thynne used as his copy text the very Glasgow ms that survives. (See also Kaluza **1**.) But even with additional hypothetical mss the number of copies of the *Romaunt* is miniscule compared to the vast number of French mss of the *Roman*. We have noted in discussing Chaucer's lyrics (*Chaucer's Lyrics and Anelida and Arcite* [Toronto, 1983], pp 5-6) that it is the Chaucer of the French courtly manner who appealed most strongly to men of letters in the fifteenth and sixteenth centuries. That manner is as much derived from the *Roman de la Rose* as it is from Chaucer, or, if the dominant influence is Chaucer, it is the Chaucer of the *Roman de la Rose*. Why then is the translation about which he playfully boasted so obscure? It must be that although Chaucer set the fashion (a fashion which germinated in the *Roman*), that work continued to exert its own influence and continued to be read in French. Perhaps the language barrier was a means of keeping the court exclusive — as exclusive as *fine amor* itself. Many of the fifteenth-century mss of the French poem are indeed grand showpieces, as ornate in their illustrations and ornamentation as Books of Hours and Psalters. And many are of English provenance.

There are doubtless other reasons for the paucity of mss of the English *Romaunt*. Scholars are unable to determine just how much of the poem Chaucer in fact translated. The most curious fact about the two surviving witnesses is that they represent the work of no one person. Rather, the *Romaunt* apparently consists of three fragments by different translators, which some editor has conjoined. The A-fragment (lines 1–1705) is based upon the French text, 1–1678. The B-fragment (1706–5810) is a bit more diffuse (see 2), covering the French text, 1679–5169. The C-fragment (5811–7698) leaps over five thousand lines of Jean de Meun's narrative to present the account of the friars and False-seeming (French text, 10716–12564). It can hardly be true that the C-fragment was originally intended to follow the B-fragment. The splicing between the A- and B-fragments is straightforward. The A-text may have been longer; so too the B-text. The editor has simply shifted from one to the other at a matching couplet. Thus there was no need whatsoever for a transition; the slight shift in dialect and style is likely to go initially unnoticed even by an alert reader who knows in advance that the change is coming.

Between them, the A- and B-fragments include all of Guillaume de Lorris' poem and the beginning of the Lover's renewed dialogue with Reason in Jean de Meun's addition. The C-fragment reads more like a satire against current abuses within the church. But why the Middle English *Romaunt* should consist of these portions of the original in these particular fragments remains a mystery, especially since Chaucer's favorite passages from Jean de Meun (and there were many) do not fall within the compass of any of the fragments. Recent scholars seem to agree that the A-fragment is the only part of the translation which could be by Chaucer; it constitutes less than eight percent of the entire French poem. Nor does it include the 'heretical' matter to which Cupid, in *LGW*, might object; that appears in the B-fragment. Has part of Chaucer's translation been lost? Or was part of it retranslated into the Northern dialect by the B-scribe? That might seem an appropriate explanation in view of the provenance of the Glasgow ms. But it would not easily account for the different ways in which the B-translator handles proper names and French vocabulary or the diffuseness of his translation. It is hard to imagine that a work which would have been so attractive to an English courtly audience — even if by a youthful Chaucer, who had not yet established his literary reputation — could simply have disappeared. Perhaps 'translated' as Cupid uses the term has a more general meaning than we are accustomed to and implies not only line-by-line translation such as we find in the *Romaunt* but also such adaptations of matter from the *Roman* as we find in the Wife of Bath's *Prologue*, where Chaucer takes off on Jean de Meun's loquacious old duenna. The context of Cupid's statement in *LGW*, which links the *Romaunt* and *Troilus*, implies no reference to the *Canterbury Tales*, however. Indeed, any allusion to the Wife of Bath in the courtly *LGW* would be decidedly misplaced as well as chronologically impossible, for the marriage group, which would include the Wife's *Prologue*, is usually dated about half a dozen years to a decade after the *F-Prologue*. Cupid seems to be referring to the *Romaunt*, not some other adaptation of the *Roman*. Was Chaucer's *Romaunt* one of the works Eustache Deschamps had in mind when he referred to Chaucer as 'grant translateur'? What text might he have known? We simply do not know.

When Thynne printed the *Romaunt* in 1532, he did so unhesitatingly believing it to be entirely Chaucer's work. Not until the latter part of the nineteenth century was its authenticity called into question. Henry Bradshaw was one of the first to notice disparities in style and prosody in the *Romaunt*. By indexing rhymes, which he then compared with other Chaucerian poems, Bradshaw concluded that there was 'no so strong internal evidence in the poem ... as to rebut the evidence of the false rhimes' (F.J. Furnivall, *Temporary Preface* [London, 1868], p 108). Furnivall lists some of the 'rhimes' Bradshaw found to be un-Chaucerian (pp 108–10) and admonishes scholars to prepare themselves by independent work 'to accept or contest Mr. Bradshaw's argument and conclusions when they appear. They will not be of the pooh poohable kind, as they are the result of careful and honest hard work by a man with a pair of eyes and a head' (p 110). But Furnivall, whose good instincts were always strong, adds that he himself is 'not prepared to give up the *Romaunt* as Chaucer's without a fight.' The fight did indeed ensue, and in the end both sides had their victories, though Bradshaw, who was always reluctant to publish his findings, left the siege-work to others.

For the next several decades — indeed, for the remainder of Furnivall's life — the *Romaunt* enjoyed the limelight of Chaucer criticism, as the Chaucer Society, which Furnivall had begun, attempted to work out the corpus and chronology of the Chaucer canon. In fact, before the debacle was over, Furnivall would find himself editing the poem. It was the American scholar F.J. Child who first picked up the hue and cry from Bradshaw: 'It will take a great deal more than the fact that the *Romaunt of the Rose* is printed in old editions, to make me believe that it is Chaucer's. The rhymes are not his, and the style is not his, unless he changed both extraordinarily as he got on in life. The translation is often in a high degree slovenly. The part after the break, from v 5814 on, seemed to me, on a recent comparison with the French, better done than the middle; and as the Bialacoil of the earlier portion is here called Fair-welcomyng, *perhaps* this part belongs to a different version' (*Athenaeum*, Dec. 3, 1870, p 721). Child's observation calls attention to several crucial considerations: the possibility of multiple authorship; the differences in translating proper names in different parts of the text; and the fact that there is a great break in the narrative after the first five thousand lines, a break which omits the second five thousand lines of the French text entirely. Then Skeat entered the fray.

Skeat's initial investigations (*NQ* [1874], p 185) followed Bradshaw in casting doubt on the translation's authenticity; further reflection led him to reject the *Romaunt* altogether as a Chaucerian work. Re-editing Bell's *Poetical Works of Chaucer* (first published in 1854–6 in eight volumes, revised in 1878 as four volumes), Skeat concluded decisively that the *Romaunt* could not be by Chaucer because of the 'clear and consistent evidence' of Northern dialect in the translation. He relegated it to a separate volume of spurious poems, along with *Court of Love, Cuckoo and Nightingale, Flower and Leaf*, and *Complaint of a Lover's Life*, all of which Bell had printed as Chaucer's works. In addition, the volume included *Isle of Ladies, Mother of Nurture, Proverbs, Roundel, Virelay*, and *Mother of God*, which Bell had also thought to be spurious. It was a sad blow for the *Romaunt* to be demoted to such scraggly company, and when ten Brink (*Anglia* 1 [1878], 533) lent his considerable authority to Skeat's position, the blow seemed decisive.

Furnivall, with his favorite warriors now vigorously attacking the Chaucer claim, silenced whatever nostalgic sentiments he may have formerly felt for the piece. Watching Zeus-like over his Chaucer Society, he expressed admiration for Skeat's vigorous moves. Using the *Academy* as his forum, he praised Skeat's good service of 'putting all the spurious poems, once wrongly attributed to Chaucer, in an Appendix'; his praise then turned into an admonition to the whole of his court, especially an unnamed scholar — 'that chief sinner in this matter, who, in a well-known London College and many provincial lecture-rooms, still confuses his pupils' minds to the wonder of the best-informed among them, by giving them "mixtelyn" [rye and wheat ground together], for the pure flour of Chaucer's brain.' Perhaps Skeat can convert such sinners. 'If only all professors of English literature and writers of articles on Chaucer could be endowed with Mr. Skeat's clear common-sense, critical power, and knowledge of the English language in all its stages from Beowulf to Shakespeare, Chaucer's memory and genius would soon be cleared from all the rubbish which old printers and editors heaped round it.' The metaphor becomes even more definitive as Furnivall concludes that in putting the spurious poems in a separate bin Skeat has 'knocked the last nail into the coffin of superstition that has hitherto defended them' ('Skeat and Bell's Chaucer,' *Academy*, April 27, 1878, p 365). For most of the poems in the appended volume, Furnivall's metaphor proved, alas, to be deadly accurate. Not only were the poems nailed away; until very recently most of them were forgotten. But the *Romaunt* still had some champions bold enough to address even the formidable Skeat.

T. Arnold ('The Date of the "Court of Love" and the "Romaunt of the Rose," ' *Academy*, July 20, 1878, pp 66–7) challenged Skeat's placing of the *Court of Love* in the reign of Henry VIII (it is surely an earlier work which, though not Chaucer's, is indeed Chaucerian in its idiom and phrasing), and reviewed the controversy over the *Romaunt* to make it appear less lopsided. On the side of Chaucer's authorship Arnold placed the following arguments: 1) Chaucer claims to have made such a translation, and Lydgate reiterates the claim; 2) there is only one known *Romaunt*, and no other poet's name has been associated with it; 3) Thynne claims to have searched long to obtain correct copies of Chaucer's works that had been already printed and to have found diverse others that were almost unknown and in oblivion: presumably the *Romaunt* is one of the latter; 4) the language of the *Romaunt* is definitely Chaucerian in point of date; 5) Chaucer's phrases and turns of expression occur frequently. Against Chaucerian authorship are the following arguments: 1) Skeat believes that the *Romaunt* can be shown to have been originally composed in a dialect much more Northern than that of London; 2) off-rhymes of the *generaly-curtesye* type have made ten Brink, Bradshaw, and others doubt the poem's authenticity; 3) other rhymes, like *thore-more* (lines 1830–1), Chaucer never employs. Arnold concludes: 'That one rule as to rhymes is observed in the *Canterbury Tales*, and another in the *Romaunt*, must be freely granted. But till it is shown that the discrepancy might not have been due to Chaucer's own varying practice at different periods of his life, the fact will not have all the importance that is claimed for it' (p 67).

But such peas on the deck were nothing to Skeat, who immediately replied (*Academy*, Aug. 10, 1878, pp 143–4) that his dialect analysis suggested that the *Romaunt* may even have been written as early as 1350. For a rare moment he bends, even admiring the poem: 'It is also well written, and will always remain a standard authority for many interesting forms, as well as being of considerable literary interest. Yet none of these things proves its identity with the translation made by Chaucer; and it so happens that the internal evidence against this is decisive and complete' (p 143). He then cites numerous rhymes and Northern forms which could not possibly be Chaucerian, eg, *sittand-hand* (vv 2262–3) and *fand-doand* (vv 2706–7). Arnold has noted that the poem is 'tinged' with Northern forms, but that, says Skeat, is too weak an observation: 'it must be remembered that the tinge is a deep one, and not to be easily washed away' (p 144). The dialect is a puzzle, however, a mixture of Midland and Northern forms, many of which are similar to those of *Havelock* and Barbour's *Bruce*. And such off-rhymes as *annoy/away* (2675) and *bothoms/sesouns* (4011) could not be Chaucer's.

For a time it seemed the battle was over. Skeat summarized the material more fully with detailed lists of Northern forms and bad rhymes in his third edition of *The Prioress' Tale* (London, 1880) and in 'Why the *Romaunt of the Rose* is not Chaucer's,' *Essays on Chaucer* (Chaucer Society, 1884), pp 437–51. Only a few distant rumblings in defense of Chaucer's association with the *Romaunt* continued on the horizon. Across the sea, W. Fick ('Zur Frage von der Authenticität der Mittel-Englischen Übersetzung des Romans von der Rose,' *ESt*, 9 [1886], 161–7) pointed out verbal parallels between the *Romaunt* and other poems by Chaucer — *LGW, BD, T&C, Fortune*, and several of the *CT* — to reaffirm the likeliness that the *Romaunt* was Chaucer's. Skeat replied (p 506): 'I think Herr Fick cannot have seen my Essay on the Romaunt of the Rose which has been pronounced conclusive by many whose judgement I much value. It is printed in the *third* edition of Chaucer's Prioresses Tale ... I need say no more.' The scholar from Kiel (same page) replied that he had not had access to Skeat's note, but that he still thinks the *Romaunt* is Chaucer's. It must be remembered that it has the character of a translation by a young poet who was not yet the 'perfect rhymer.' Albert S. Cook's ' "The Romaunt of the Rose" and Professor Skeat's "Vocabulary Test," ' *MLN*, 2 (1887), 285–91, likewise called into question Skeat's methods of determining authorship. Skeat had emphasized in the Prioress edition and the Chaucer Society *Essays* the large number of unusual words in the *Romaunt*. Cook shows that a large proportion of the peculiar words are from the French original and that the translator used them because of 'some exigency of his verse' (p 286). Cook pointed out that several of the 'peculiar' words occur elsewhere in Chaucer. Moreover, he argued, vocabulary study tends to be a weak means of determining authorship because it usually ignores the unique requirements of the individual work in which the words occur. Skeat made no reply whatsoever to the American scholar.

Then two more German philologists appeared on an unexpected flank. F. Lindner ('Die Englische Übersetzung des Romans von der Rose,' *ESt*, 11 [1888], 163–73) returned to a simple observation that scholars had made from the beginning of the dispute, namely that the poem consists of more than one fragment. He contrasted the rhymes, proper names, quality of translation, and adaptation of French forms between the first part (ie, the narrative prior to line 5810) and the second part (5811 to the end), to conclude that the two parts are not by the same translator and that he could not say which might be Chaucer's. Skeat ('A Further Note on the "Romaunt of the Rose," ' [*Academy*, Sept. 8, 1888, pp 153–4]), mildly irritated that the old issue was still kicking, agreed that the independence of the two fragments is 'glaringly obvious, now that it has once been pointed out' (p 153). But the first part cannot be Chaucer's for the reasons he had so often rehearsed. He then took a different approach, as further proof: 'Chaucer is extremely fond of borrowing his own language, and often repeats himself word for word' (p 153). (Cf *Mars*, line 61, and *NPT*, line 340.) If Chaucer *did* translate the *Romaunt*, we may be sure that he would occasionally repeat his own lines. The repetitions should agree word for word if the translation is his, and if not, not. 'Well', says Skeat, 'they do *not*' (p 153). He admitted, however, that in some instances the parallel passages come close, as in *BD*, lines 424 ff and *Rom*, 1396 ff; *BD*, 410 ff and *Rom*, 59 ff; and *BD*, 283 ff and *Rom*, 7ff. But wherever we compare, 'we invariably find a difference and never a coincidence. This is surely remarkable, when we observe how constantly Chaucer borrows from his own lines, and never hesitates to give the same words over again' (p 154). This argument was picked up many years later by the great German scholar John Koch 45, who refused to the end to readmit the *Romaunt* to the Chaucer canon.

Meanwhile, Max Kaluza was editing the Glasgow MS for the Chaucer Society. He proved to have a pair of eyes and a head that would make Furnivall proud. In 1890 he wrote of his findings to Furnivall, who published the heart of the letter in *Academy* (July 5, 1890, pp 11–12). Kaluza argued that the so-called first part of the *Romaunt* was really two parts (A_1 and A_2) and that lines 1–1704 were Chaucer's translation, as were lines 5814–7964. The middle lines belong to 'another man.' Chaucer's translation follows the original almost word for word, as his *Boece* does not. Moreover, all phrases, rhymes, metrical and dialectal peculiarities in these first and last sections are 'quite the same as in Chaucer's genuine works' (p 11). Skeat's objections, outlined in his *Essays on Chaucer*, all pertain to the middle part. As a final point Kaluza noted that the A-fragment regularly uses the word 'knoppe' for *bud*, while the B-fragment uses the word 'bouton.' Kaluza developed his views fully in *Chaucer und der Rosenroman* (Berlin, 1893).

In the face of this new approach Skeat capitulated (*Academy*, July 19, 1890, pp 51–2), acknowledging that Kaluza made 'a really important discovery' (p 51). He took strong issue with the notion that the third part could be Chaucer's, however. 'I think I can undertake to prove, to utter demonstration, that Chaucer had no hand in fragment B' (ie 5811–7698). Some difficulties remain in accepting the A_1 fragment as Chaucer's, but 'without considering this question as quite settled, we may at least admit that it has entered upon a new and more satisfying phase. It is much to Dr. Kaluza's credit' (p 52). In scarcely more than a year, even before Kaluza had time to publish his conclusions, the indomitable Skeat turned the new flanking operation into his own front line. In 'The Three Fragments of "The Romaunt of the Rose" ' (*Academy*, Aug. 15, 1891, p 137), he begins, 'If I had nothing new to say about "The Romaunt of the Rose," I should not be writing this letter. But I have so much to propose, in the way of a new theory, that I can only give the *outline* of my scheme.' First he corrects Kaluza's division of the A-fragment at line 1704, and notes that the division should occur at 1705, since 1705–6 do not properly rhyme: 'I claim for him [Chaucer] *one more line.*' Moreover, he also notes a difficulty of syntax at the break: 'That we can now *see* the gap, is really a great gain. It separates fragment A from fragment B quite definitely.' (Skeat relabels the fragments A, B, and C rather than A_1, A_2, and B.) He then compares the Glasgow ms and Thynne, pointing out transpositions in both witnesses by which he is able to determine that the C-fragment was copied from an original ms that usually had 24 lines to a page. The A-fragment, on the other hand, was copied from a ms that had 25 lines to a page. Thus there is a high probability that the A and C sources were from different mss. 'Fragment C is most decidedly not Chaucer's. That Chaucer's piece should come *at the beginning* is precisely what we should expect.'

Skeat reviewed the history of the debate in his introduction to the *Romaunt* in the *Oxford Chaucer* (**2**, vol 1, pp 1–14). In one further note, 'Lydgate's Testimony to "The Romaunt of the Rose" ' (*Athenaeum*, June 6, 1896], p 747), he argues that not only does Lydgate imitate passages of the *Roman de la Rose* in his *Complaint of the Black Knight* (lines 36–114), but that 'it is a remarkable fact that he must have had before him ... that very English version of "The Romaunt of the Rose" which I have called Fragment A.' Skeat demonstrates the point by noting that Lydgate's 'velvet' and 'soft' to describe 'brass' appear in the *Romaunt*, but without equivalents in the *Roman*.

In one way the drama of the *Romaunt* comes to a satisfying conclusion. Chaucer's authorship of at least part — certainly the best part — remains a defensible possibility (but see Koch **45**); virtually everyone agrees that the whole of the *Romaunt* could not be his. True, Thomas Lounsbury, with characteristic eccentricity, rejected Skeat's skeptical proofs and ignored Furnivall's report on Kaluza's findings to conclude: 'the weight of evidence is overwhelmingly in favor of Chaucer's authorship' of the whole of the *Romaunt* (*Studies in Chaucer*, 1892, II, 164). And Louise Pound (' "The Romaunt of the Rose": Additional Evidence that it is Chaucer's,' *MLN* 11 (1896) 193–204, offers a statistical comparison of sentence structures in Chaucer and non-Chaucer poems to conclude that the *Romaunt* fits into the Chaucerian patterns. But most scholars seem to have accepted the Kaluza three-part division and followed Skeat in affirming the authenticity of the A-fragment. In his last years Furnivall undertook the editing of Thynne's edition of the *Romaunt*. He died before completing the task. Skeat wrote the introduction for him and saw it through the press. (He always had the last word!) Their edition marked the end of what was perhaps the most lively chapter in the history of Chaucer scholarship.

But in another way the conclusion has not been satisfactory, for, once tarnished, the *Romaunt* has fallen into a kind of limbo. It appears as a questionable work — a fragmentary translation — tucked in at best at the end of volumes which profess to be complete works of Chaucer. Hammond **36** discusses it under the heading 'Works Printed as by Chaucer,' where it appears between 'Remedy of Love' and 'Sayings of Dan John.' And it may well be that Koch is right, that none of the translation is Chaucer's. To recent scholars no longer interested in territorial claims, the *Romaunt* seems hardly worth the time of perusal when there is so much bounty elsewhere in Chaucer at which to marvel. Perhaps at this juncture we should recall once again the words of Skeat, who found artistic merit in the poem even when he was most convinced that it was not Chaucer's and stressed its felicity of manner and its historical significance both in matters of taste and technique.

Editions of the *Romaunt*

See also **15**.

1 Kaluza, Max, ed. *The Romaunt of the Rose from the unique Glasgow Ms, parallel with its original, Le Roman de la Rose.* The Chaucer Society, 1st ser., no. 83. London: Kegan Paul, Trench, Trübner, 1891. Edited from the English fragments of the Hunterian Museum ms V.3.7. The French original is from M. Michel's edition of *Le Roman de la Rose* (Paris, 1864), which Kaluza has collated with other mss. The edition does not mark the fragments, but rather sets the text as it is found in the ms. It is 'not a critical text but an attempt at restoring the text that was in the hands of the Englisher or Englishers' (Hammond **36** p 451). Kaluza's introduction was published separately as '*The Romaunt of the Rose* from the unique Glasgow MS,' *ESt*, 18 (1893), 106–11, where he argues that Thynne used G or G's copy text, supplying missing lines by referring to a French text.

2 *The Complete Works of Geoffrey Chaucer.* Ed. W.W. Skeat. London: Oxford University Press, 1894. *The Oxford Chaucer*, in six volumes with a supplementary vol. 7. *Chaucerian and Other Pieces*, 1897. Rpt 1899. Introduction, I, 1–20; text, I, 93–259.

Skeat places the *Romaunt* with the Minor Poems. His edition marks the fragments and for Fragment A places the French text at the bottom of the page. His introduction reviews briefly the discussion of the translation's authenticity, explains the three fragments, measures the diffuseness of each (A-frag: English, 1705 lines; French, 1678; ratio 101.6 to 100. B-frag: English, 4105 lines; French, 3491; ratio 117.5 to 100. C-frag: English, 1888 lines; French, 1849; ratio 102.1 to 100) (vol I, p 4), and discusses his dialect and rhyming tests whereby he rejects the B-fragment. Skeat's edition principally follows the Glasgow ms, but has been collated with Thynne throughout. Skeat alters *-id*, *-is*, and *-ith* suffixes to 'the more usual' *-ed*, *-es*, and *-eth*, and in general has 'made the text more like the usual texts of Chaucer in appearance. But in Fragments B and C such changes have been made more sparingly' (vol I, p 15).

3   *The Works of Geoffrey Chaucer* [The Globe Chaucer]. Ed. Alfred W. Pollard, H. Frank Heath, Mark H. Liddell, and W.S. McCormick. London: Macmillan, 1898/rev 1928. *Romaunt* edited by Mark H. Liddell: Introduction, pp liv–lv; text, pp 659–744.
Liddell's text is based almost solely upon the Glasgow ms, although he makes some emendations based upon consultation with the French original. Textual notes compare Thynne's and Skeat's variations. 'The chief interest that attaches to *The Romaunt of the Rose* is due to the possibility of its being wholly or in part the work of Chaucer. Its felicity as a translation, making anew, as it were, the French poem, the beauty and ease of its versification, the fact that Chaucer did translate Jehan de Meung's French poem, and that a large part of this version offers little to hang an objection to as far as Chaucerian grammar is concerned, have combined to enable it to resist most successfully all attempts to fix it among the spurious Chaucer pieces' (p liv). The horrible slander that Cupid objects to in *LGW* occurs in lines 4252–66. Liddell does not mark the fragments.

4   *The Works of Geoffrey Chaucer and Others, Being a Reproduction in Facsimile of the First Collected Edition 1532* [Thynne]. Introduction by Walter W. Skeat. Oxford: Oxford University Press, 1905.
Skeat's introduction discusses both William and Francis Thynne and all early editions and their contents. Skeat prints in full Sir Brian Tuke's preface to the 1532 edition (pp xxii–xxiv). Of the twenty-two new works never before printed which Thynne includes, only six are Chaucer's. But he is the first to print the *Romaunt, LGW, BD, Pity, Sted,* and the *Astrolabe.* Moreover, his edition of the *Romaunt* is sole authority for a good portion of the text. He also includes *Boece,* first published by Caxton. Besides the genuine Chaucerian works, Thynne includes: *TC, FC, LBD, AL, CBK, A Praise of Women, TL,*

Lamentation of Mary Magalene, Remedy of Love, Letter of Cupid, A Balade in Commendation of Our Lady, To My Soverain Lady, Gower to Henry IV, CN, Envoy to Alison, Scogan to the Lords, Go Forth King, A Balade of Good Counsel, Epitaphum Galfridi Chaucer.

5 Furnivall, Frederick J., ed. *The Romaunt of the Rose: A Reprint of the First Edition by William Thynne.* Chaucer Society, 1st ser., no. 82. London: Kegan Paul, Trench, Trübner, 1911.
A posthumous publication, with introduction by W.W. Skeat. 'The chief use of this reprint lies in the fact that there are *only two* authorities in existence for the text of this poem, viz, the Glasgow MS. no. V.3.7, and Thynne's text of 1532' (p v). Glasgow is on the whole a slightly better authority, but it has lost several leaves (approx. 539 lines) for which Thynne is the sole authority (ll. 1–44, 333–80, 892, 1387–1432, 1553, 1892, 2395–2442, 3136?, 3490, 3595–3690, 4856, 6688, 6786, 7092, 7109?, 7383–7574, and 7692–96). Skeat summarizes his views on the fragments in **64**.

6 *The Romaunt of the Rose Rendered out of French into Anglise by Geoffrey Chaucer,* illustrated by Keith Henderson and Norman Wilkinson. London: Chatto and Windus (Florentine Press), 1908.
A fine edition of 512 copies printed in quarto. Colored frontispiece and colored plates, with plates mounted. Uses the text of the Globe edition (**3**). Reissued in popular edition, London: Chatto and Windus; New York: Henry Holt, 1911.

7 *The Poetical Works of Chaucer.* Ed. F.N. Robinson. Cambridge, Mass.: Houghton Mifflin, 1933. Text, pp 663–739; explanatory notes, pp 988–1000; textual notes, pp 1043–48. Rev 1957 (New Cambridge Edition). Text, pp 564–637; explanatory notes, pp 872–82; textual notes, pp 924–28.
Text based on Glasgow ms, completed and corrected by Thynne. 'The two authorities are independent, but closely similar' (p 924). Robinson uses Langlois **13** for his French citations, but notes that Langlois does not provide 'enough data to fix with certainty even the place of the ms in his classification. Kaluza printed Michel's French text in parallel columns with the English, substituting for many of Michel's readings variants which corresponded more closely to the translation. Of the readings in which the English is there shown to depart from Michel a large number are not registered at all by Langlois' (p 924). Robinson incorporates notes and emendations by Lange **48**. In his Explanatory Notes he reviews the controversy over authorship of the fragments. 'Professor Brusendorff's hypothesis of a transmitter by memory is a rather desperate measure to save the Chaucerian authorship of the whole poem' (p 872 [cf **25**]). In his Introduction Robinson points out that the A-fragment contains nothing that would justify Cupid's

accusation against Chaucer in *LGW*. On Jean's continuation of the poem he observes: 'The interest of Jean de Meun, like that of his readers, lay less in finishing the tale than in expounding the philosophy which has gained him the name, not without appropriateness, of "the Voltaire of the thirteenth century" ' (p 564).

8 Sutherland, Ronald, ed. *The Romaunt of the Rose and Le Roman de la Rose: A Parallel Text Edition.* Oxford: Blackwell, 1967; Berkeley: University of California Press, 1968.

'By indicating how appropriate readings were found and key manuscripts selected from the more-than-300 existing *Roman* codices, this edition is intended to show in what way and by how many authors the extant *Romaunt* was created' (p v). The poem as we have it comes from no one source but has been artificially constructed. Different portions were translated from different originals by different men. The A-fragment corresponds to the H family of Langlois' Group I of mss (see **13**); the remainder of the *Romaunt* corresponds to the R family of Group II. A third person who possessed a ms of the G/B type patched A and B together and made some revisions. 'Failure to speculate on the possible activity of a reviser ... was undoubtedly the reason why Brusendorff did not carry his investigations to a more plausible conclusion than that of the scribe with a faulty memory' (p xvi; [cf **25**]). Robert de Becchys may have been the translator of the B-Fragment (p xxviii). 'There is ... no reason to doubt that Fragment A ... save for a few revisions, is Chaucer's genuine work' (p xxxiv). Sutherland uses Thynne as his basic text rather than the Glasgow ms. Neither the Glasgow ms nor its immediate ancestor 'was as satisfactory a codex as that employed to produce the 1532 edition' (p vi). Sutherland does use Glasgow and the French for emendation of Thynne, however.

- Review by Alfred David, *Spec,* 44 (1969), 666–70: Though the Glasgow ms is 'no model of Chaucerian or fifteenth-century usage,' it is 'still a safer guide' than Thynne's edition (p 667). David cites numerous instances where the wording in G is closer to the French. Sutherland makes 'extravagant claims' for the French mss he works with and errs in thinking that the mss can be classified into more or less homogeneous families. 'He is evidently unaware of the extent of contamination possible in the case of a poem as popular as the *Roman de la Rose*' (p 669). 'The editor and the publisher owe the reader a sheet of *errata*' (p 670).

9 *Chaucer: Lyric and Allegory.* Ed. James Reeves. London: Heinemann, 1970; New York: Barnes and Noble, 1971.

Selections include excerpts from the A-fragment of the *Romaunt.*

10 *Geoffrey Chaucer. The Works, 1532, with supplementary material*

from the editions of 1542, 1561, 1598, and 1602. A facsimile edition, ed. with introduction by Derek S. Brewer. London: Scolar Press, 1969. Rpt 1974.

Brewer's introduction comments on all early printings from Thynne's 1532 edition to the 1687 reissue of Speght. As well as providing a facsimile of the 1532 edition, he prints in facsimile all new material added after 1532. He discusses the contents of each volume item by item: first the forty-four entries in Thynne's 1532 edition; then the additions of 1542, especially the *Plowman's Tale*; then the twenty-six new items in Stowe's 1561 edition; then the seven new items of Speght's 1598 edition, including *FL*, for which Speght is sole authority; then eight new items from Speght's 1602 edition, including the first printing of *ABC*, *Jack Upland*, and Speght's expanded glossary of 'Old and Obscure Words,' which incorporates annotations from the 1598 edition; and, finally, the 1687 edition, the last of the black letter editions, which, along with an edition ca 1550, Brewer comments on but does not represent in facsimile text, since neither includes new material. Speght (1598) is the first to add an introductory argument to the *Romaunt*, which I print here in full and juxtapose with Urry's argument (1721) to illustrate how accretions in the black letter editions were passed on and embellished by subsequent editors, a practice which continued into the nineteenth century. Speght writes:

> This booke was made in French by Iohn Clopinell, alias Iohn Moone, borne at Mewen vpon the riuer of Loyer not farre from Paris, and translated into English meetre by Geffrey Chaucer, but not finished. It is entituled, the Romaunt of the Rose; or, The Arte of Loue: wherein is shewed the helpes and furtherances, as also the lets and impediments that Louers haue in their sutes. In this booke the Authour hath many glaunces at the hypocrisie of the Clergie; whereby hee got himselfe such hatred amongst them, that *Gerson* Chauncellour of Paris, writeth thus of him: saith hee, There was one called *Iohannes Meldinensis*, who wrote a booke called, The Romant of the Rose: which booke if I only had, and that there were no more in the world, if I might haue 500. pound for the same, I would rather burne it then take the mony. He saith more, That if he thought the Authour thereof did not repent him for that booke before he dyed, he would vouchsafe to pray for him no more then he would for Iudas that betrayed Christ.

(Brewer facsimile addenda
for 1598, unpaginated)

Urry's 1721 version (see **525**, p 215) is as follows:

> This Book was begun in French verse by *William de Lorris,*
> and finished 40 Years after by *John Clopinell,* alias John
> Moone, born at *Mewen* upon the River of *Loyer,* not far
> from *Paris* as appeareth by *Molinet* the French author upon
> the morality of the Romaunt, and afterwards translated for
> the most part into English Metre by *Geoffrey,* but not
> finished. It is entituled the Romaunt of the Rose [etc,
> verbatim to the end].

11 *The Complete Poetry and Prose of Geoffrey Chaucer.* Ed. John H.
Fisher. New York: Holt, Rinehart, and Winston, 1977. Pp 709–811.
Fisher uses Thynne as his copy text and takes his French references
from Sutherland's composite French text (**8**) which is closer to the
English than Kaluza **1**, Langlois **13**, or Lecoy **14**. Fisher dates the
Glasgow ms 'first quarter of the fifteenth century' (p 970).

11a Hira, Toshinori. '*The Romaunt of the Rose* (Fragment A). Translated
into Japanese.' Bulletin of the Faculty of Liberal Arts, Nagasaki
University, Humanities, 21, 2 (1981), 75-88.

Selected Editions and Concordance of the French text

12 Danos, Joseph R. *A Concordance to the Roman de la Rose of
Guillaume de Lorris.* North Carolina Studies in the Romance
Languages and Literatures: Texts, Textual Studies, and Translations,
no 3. Chapel Hill: Publication of the Department of Romance
Languages UNC, 1975.
A concordance based on Langlois' edition (**13**), 'which has not been
supplanted by the more recent diplomatic edition by Lecoy' (p i). The
concordance follows a chronological distribution. Four appendices: I.
Alphabetized Word-Frequency List; II. Word-Frequency List,
Arranged in Descending Order of Frequency; III. Reverse-Alphabetized
Word List; IV. Verse Numbers in the Langlois and Lecoy Editions.

12a *Le Roman de la Rose dans la version attribuée à Clément Marot,* ed.
Silvio F. Baridon. *Testi e documenti di Letteratura Moderna,* ed. A.
Viscardi and S.F. Baridon. 2 vols. Milan: Instituto Editoriale
Cisalpino, 1954.
Volume I includes an introduction tracing the history of *RR* in the
14th and 15th centuries leading up to Marot's redaction of 1526, and
his revision of Guillaume's text. Volume II is the redaction of Jean de
Meun's part.

13 Langlois, Ernest, ed. *Le Roman de la Rose.* 5 vols. Paris: SATF, 1914–24.
On the basis of 116 of 215 mss studied in **128**, Langlois reconstructs an 'archetypal' text, using ms BN fr. 1573 as his base text, which he normalizes and corrects according to other good mss. This edition has remained the preferred text of many subsequent scholars, partly because of its extensive scholarly notes. See **14**, however.

14 Lecoy, Felix, ed. *Le Roman de la Rose.* Les Classiques français du moyen âge. 2 vols. Paris: Champion, 1965–70.
Using ms BN fr. 1573 as his basic text, Lecoy provides a diplomatic text based on the best surviving manuscript. He discusses the two authors in his introduction as well as the success of the poem (pp xxviii–xxxv) and his choice of mss. His notes offer some commentary as well as information on the sources, but they are not as extensive as Langlois' **13**. According to Luria **136**, this edition is 'now widely considered to have supplanted Langlois' as the standard edition' because of Lecoy's editorial decision to keep as close as possible to the 'best manuscript' and to avoid normalization (p 23).

15 Nichols, Stephen G., Jr. *Le Roman de La Rose, par Guillaume de Lorris.* New York: Appleton-Century-Crofts, 1967.
A student edition based on Langlois' text, with modern French glosses, appended to which is the A-fragment of the *Romaunt* (pp 147–97). In his French introduction Nichols discusses the psychology of love as Guillaume presents it through personifications and the progression of allegorical events. '*Le Roman* n'est pas qu'une simple histoire d'amour' (p 2). Through the youth, Guillaume explores the 'humeurs intérieures' which are given 'la représentation concrète' (p 5). The Rose symbol represents 'la dame prise dans sa totalité, avec toute sa splendeur et son secret, ou bien représenter ce que sa beauté neuve et sa virginité ont de plus éphémère. La Rose est à la fois plus importante que toutes les figures allégoriques du caractère de la dame et plus délicate. Dans ce sens, elles existent seulement pour la protéger contre la victoire prématurée de son amant, et c'est dans ce sens qu'elles contrôlent sa destinée ... eternellement bouton: symbole de l'anticipation et de la promesse' (p 6). The success of *RR* rests mainly in the personality of the lover in such scenes as the episode of 'la Fontaine Perilleuse,' with its narcissistic implications. Of the *Romaunt*, Nichols observes: 'We know that medieval and Renaissance poets considered it part of their craft to translate important works into the language and idiom of their own day. They did not look upon this activity as in any way inferior to their own creative work. Translations provided opportunity for experimenting with new techniques, and this in itself was a challenge to engage a large measure

of their poetic skill' (p 150). Though Chaucer had already
experimented with the decasyllabic line in *ABC*, in the *Romaunt* he
'gracefully maintains the four-beat octosyllabic meter of Guillaume's
original' (p 150). His translation lacks the succinctness of the French,
though Chaucer tends to abbreviate catalog lists of trees, flowers, and
birds which Guillaume found pleasing. His meter is more irregular
than the French and with such embellishment as alliteration, of which
there is nothing in the French.

Selected Translations into a Modern Language of the *Roman de la Rose*

16 *The Romance of the Rose*, by W. Lorris and J. Clopinel. Englished
and edited by F.S. Ellis. The Temple Classics. 3 vols. London: Dent
and Sons, 1900.
A somewhat bowdlerized translation into octosyllabic couplets, divided
into 105 chapters. The English does not follow the French beyond line
21504 (ie, the consummation scene is omitted). An appendix contains
the French version from line 21505 to the end. The story of
Pygmalion, in that section, is translated, however.

17 Lanly, André, trans. *Le Roman de la Rose, traduction en français
moderne*. 2 vols in 4. Paris: H. Champion, 1971–76.
According to Luria **136**, 'the most reliable French modernization' (p
232). Line by line translation based on Lecoy **14**.

18 Mary, André, trans. *Le Roman de la Rose*. Paris: Payot, 1928. Rpt
1960.
A modern French translation of the poem based on Langlois' text.
Some passages are omitted or summarized.

19 Robbins, Harry W., trans. *The Romance of the Rose*, by Guillaume de
Lorris and Jean de Meun, ed., with Introduction by Charles W. Dunn.
New York: Dutton, 1962.
Robbins' blank verse translation divides the poem into one hundred
chapters, with a six-beat line at the end of each chapter. The edition
includes fifteen plates from three *RR* manuscripts in the Pierpont
Morgan Library, and a selective bibliography. The translation is based
on the Langlois edition (**13**). Robbins includes a translation of the
seventy-eight line anonymous conclusion which appears at the end of
Guillaume's poem in some mss. Dunn's introduction comments on
Guillaume's and Jean's perceptions of the poem, and also on the
poem's great popularity.

20 Dahlberg, Charles, trans. *The Romance of the Rose*, by Guillaume de Lorris and Jean de Meun. Princeton: Princeton University Press, 1971. A prose translation, based on Langlois' edition (13). Includes plates of sixty-four mss illustrations, extensive notes and commentary, excellent bibliography, a table of concordances coordinating line-numbering in Langlois and Lecoy 14. Dahlberg's introduction discusses the unity of the two parts of *RR*, techniques of irony and style, the love theme, and philosophical matter. 'Much of the irony of the poem depends upon the imagery, and it was partly in the hope of maintaining such imagery for its iconographic significance that the present translation was undertaken' (p 26).

Discussions of the *Romaunt* and Selected Discussions of the *Roman de la Rose*

See also **191, 670, 679**.

21 Ando, Shinsuke. 'The Language of *The Romaunt of the Rose* (Fragment A), with Particular Reference to Chaucer's Relationship to Middle English Provincial Poetry.' *Studies in English Literature* (English Literary Society of Japan), Engl. no. (1970), 63–74.
Though critics have frequently emphasized Chaucer's debt to French literature, Ando shows that there is a debt to the English tradition as well. To illustrate his thesis he examines the A-Fragment of *Romaunt*, which he takes to be an early work definitely in the French tradition, to show how English tag phrases, words from the common stock of alliterative poetry, and English idioms are used whereas Guillaume de Lorris did something else or nothing at all. Ando gives special attention to Chaucer's use of *lemman, doughty, ywis*; the rhyming of *comen/nomen*; and rhyme tags with *of prys*.

22 Baskervill, Charles R. 'English Songs on the Night Visit.' *PMLA*, 36 (1921), 565–614.
Features of the night visit lie behind *Romaunt* lines 2640–80, where the God of Love tells the lover how it will be at night 'without rest, in payne and wo' (pp 569–70).

23 Blodgett, James E. 'Some Printer's Copy for William Thynne's 1532 Edition of Chaucer.' *The Library*, sixth series, 1 (1979), 97–113.
Demonstrates that the Glasgow ms of the *Romaunt* was the copy-text from which Thynne's edition was printed. Discrepancies between G and Th sometimes may be accounted for by Thynne's use of other mss,

though Thynne often made emendations of his own. G has marginal marks that lay out the copy in columns which correspond to the columns in Th. Similar marks may be found in ms 258 at Longleat House [Lg], which contains *PF, AA, Mars, Pity, LBD*, and *AL*, and in a copy of Caxton's *Boece*. Thynne used Lg for only the last six stanzas of *LBD*. Its column markings for *AA* suggest that *AA* was printed from Lg but in a different place than originally planned. The Longleat copy of Caxton's *Boece* also is marked apparently by the same hand that marked G and Lg; it was marked off twice before the compositer set up the type. (See also Blodgett, 'William Thynne and His 1532 Edition of Chaucer.' *DAI*, 36 [1976], 5311A. Indiana University Dissertation, 1975. Dir. Alfred David.)

24 Brewer, D.S. 'The Ideal of Feminine Beauty in Medieval Literature, Especially "Harley Lyrics," Chaucer, and Some Elizabethans.' *MLR*, 50 (1955), 257–69.
After commenting on Guillaume's use of stock conventions of beauty in *RR* (pp 259–60), Brewer notes various instances of Chaucer's variations on the tradition, even in the *Romaunt* where he praises *Beaute* for *not* plucking her eyebrows (p 268).

25 Brusendorff, Aage. *The Chaucer Tradition*. London: Oxford University Press, 1925; Copenhagen: V. Pio and Povl Branner, 1925. Ch 5, 'The Romance of the Rose,' pp 296–426, compares the Glasgow ms with Thynne's edition to note that Thynne's source is not a sister codex to the one surviving ms, that it is a genuine source; and that Thynne frequently prints preferable readings. [But see **23**.] In considering the arguments on the text, dialect, and suggested emendations of Skeat, Liddell, and Kaluza, Brusendorff finds Kaluza's division of the ms into A, B, and C fragments (**1**), which scholars have generally come to accept, to be 'based on curiously weak evidence' (p 320), and comes up with an 'extraordinary explanation' for the 'extraordinarily unsatisfactory' state of the text (p 326), an explanation which preserves Chaucer's original authorship of the whole *Romaunt*. Comparing the Middle English fragment with the French text Brusendorff notes that expansions and corruptions 'which are of rather rare occurrence in the first 1700 lines, greatly increase during the following 2000 lines and still more so during the next 2000 ones, while in the last 1900 lines there is a return to the comparatively good order of the first 1700' (p 378). The middle 4000 lines are dominated by Northern forms. Many of the mistakes in this section are 'eye mistakes,' but 'at the same time there is an astonishingly large number of mistakes which can only be explained as errors of the ear' (p 378). It would seem then that the *Romaunt*, 'originally composed in the standard English of the late fourteenth century ... has only been

preserved in a version, written down in the beginning of the fifteenth
century by some person from the North Midlands, who had once
learned the translation by heart, and who still knew its first 1800 lines
or so almost perfectly; during the next 4000 lines, however, his memory
constantly kept failing him, so that at last he had to break off abruptly
and start again at an episode which occurred nearly 6000 lines further
on in the translation, but which he remembered better, until after
some 1900 lines he had to break off finally, still almost 10,000 lines
from the end' (p 382). Brusendorff finds several 'striking verbal
parallels' between the *Romaunt* and other works by Chaucer, though
not in *BD* which, though it draws often on *RR*, must have been
written before the *Romaunt* translation (p 396). Despite the many
corruptions the *Romaunt* 'remains a decidedly creditable, in parts even
a brilliant piece of work, well worthy of Chaucer as a whole, while the
detailed evidence given above seems to me to put his ultimate
authorship practically beyond any doubt' (pp 414–15). It is impossible
to give the reviser a name, but his local habitat must have been North
Midlands, and he appears to have been 'a person of a rather Puritan
turn of mind' (p 415). Brusendorff concludes by discussing faulty
rhymes and expansions (pp 416–24). (For assessment of Brusendorff's
theory see **7** and **8**. On the relative merits of G and Th see **23**.)

26 Caie, Graham D. 'An Iconographic Detail in the *Roman de la Rose*
and the Middle English *Romaunt*.' *ChauR*, 8 (1973–4), 320–23.
The sleeve-basting at the beginning, an iconographic sign of foolish
love, implies a deliberate choice by Amant. Well-sewn sleeves are a
mark of lecherous vanity (cf St Jerome and scripture on Christ's
seamless gown). 'Amant's sleeve-basting symbolizes his search for *fol
amour*' (p 322).

27 Carruthers, Mary. *The Search for St. Truth: A Study of Meaning in
Piers Plowman*. Evanston: Northwestern University Press, 1973. Pp
37–40.
Uses *RR* in Chaucer's translation to demonstrate the versatility of
personification allegory. 'It is precisely because personification reveals
meaning through the structural design of its narrative that it is such
an excellent device for exploring meaning: a personification enlarges
the concept it signifies every time it moves from one place to another'
(p 37). Dangier, who 'moves both temporally and spatially,' behaves
differently in four different contexts; his 'significance changes from
situation to situation. This is not simply a process of accreting
different meanings ... [He] has a degree of fluidity and flexibility
which the exemplary figure of Hate, frozen on the wall, cannot
possibly have' (p 39). 'Personification gives a definite narrative shape
to language; the word becomes a character in a story, which is the

vehicle for the expression of its meaning(s)' (p 39).

28 Cook, Albert S. 'Two Notes on Chaucer.' *MLN*, 31 (1916), 441–42.
'Fryse' (*Romaunt*, line 1093), interpreted by Skeat as 'Friesland,' refers
to Phrygia, Midas, the Pactolus, and embroidery in gold. Cf *Roman de
Thebes*, 6630 — 'nel donast per tot l'or de Frise' (p 442).

29 — 'Chaucer and Venantius Fortunatus.' *MLN*, 39 (1924), 376–8.
Langlois **127** suggests Matthew of Vendôme as the source of *RR*
67–68, 74–75. Cook suggests instead an Easter poem of Fortunatus.
Chaucer may have drawn upon it also in *NPT*, lines 30–2 (p 377, n. 3).

30 Donaldson, E.T. *Speaking of Chaucer*, New York: W.W. Norton, 1970.
In his discussion of 'Idiom of Popular Poetry in the *Miller's Tale*,'
Donaldson mentions Chaucer's appropriation of 'the conventional
vocabulary of poetry' in the A-fragment of *Romaunt* where, as in all
Chaucer's indisputable works, he transmutes 'perfectly simple English
words with extraordinary ease into genuinely poetic language of a kind
that makes the phrase "poetic diction" seem entirely too high-flown to
be apt' (p 14). Elsewhere in the essay Donaldson uses phrases from
Romaunt to show how courtly language is given an ironic twist.

30a Eckhardt, Caroline D. 'The Art of Translation in *The Romaunt of the
Rose*.' *SAC*, 6 (1984), 41–63.
'One would like to think that *The Romaunt of the Rose*, as a poem
about dreaming in the springtime, was itself a springtime production,
a new English text for the new year' (p 61). The English translation
has a greater sense of intimacy than the French. 'The narrator is
somewhat more distinctly present; the images tend to be a little
clearer and more precise; the language is slightly more natural. For
these gains there is a corresponding loss of the special *courtoisie* of the
Roman. The difference is not to be exaggerated, however. It is merely
a small shift along a broad spectrum. The predominant quality of the
Romaunt remains its fidelity to its source ... It is difficult to imagine
how Guillaume de Lorris could have been more appropriately
transferred into courtly English language of the time' (pp 61–62).
Eckhardt analyzes only the A-fragment.

31 Fansler, Dean Spruill. *Chaucer and the Roman de la Rose*. New York:
Columbia University Press, 1914. Rpt Gloucester, Mass: Peter Smith,
1965.
Ch 1, 'Influence of the *Romance de la Rose* on Chaucer's Reading,' pp
11–23. It is evident that even before 1369 Chaucer was familiar with
RR as a whole, not just what is reflected in the *Romaunt*. Ch 2,
'Allusions to Historical and Legendary Persons and Places,' pp 24–47.
RR provides a source for legendary and historical characters in
MonkT, *PhysT*, *BD*, *LGW*, *HF*, and *WBT*. Ch 3, 'Mythological

Allusions', pp 48–72, discusses the encyclopedic quality of *RR* — 'an amazing jumble of heathen divinities, allegorical vices and virtues, realistic duennas and hypocrites — so confusing that one well-nigh loses his way in the bewildering labyrinth. Everything, in fact, is there' (p 48). But such plenitude makes it a treasury of source material, especially of the mythological kind. Ch 4, 'Chaucer's Style as Affected by the *Roman*,' pp 73–122. 'One must proceed cautiously, even skeptically, in a search for the sources of Chaucer's style' (p 73). Indirect influence of *RR* comes through Boccaccio, Dante, Machault, Froissart, and Deschamps. Direct influence is seen in 1) picturesque negation, such as 'nat worth a boterflye' — Chaucer's predilection for the trick is like Jean de Meung's; 2) exclamations and imprecations; 3) figures of speech, eg, allegory or personification, similes, metaphors, anaphora, rhymes and vocabulary; 4) serial devices for emphasis, eg, series of contrasts, lists of birds, trees, spices, musical instruments; 5) transitional and summarizing sentences. Ch 5, Situations and Descriptions, pp 123–74. Fansler uses examples from *Romaunt* as well as *RR*, covering a wide range throughout Chaucer's dream visions, *T&C*, and *CT*, with occasional references to the lyrics. Ch 6, Proverbs and Proverbial Expressions, pp 175–202, with some examples traced even to *Boece* (pp 180–82). Ch 7, Influence of *RR* on Chaucer's Philosophical Discussions, pp 203–34. *RR* influences most of Chaucer's favorite topics, but especially fortune, destiny, free will, and necessity; alchemy and astrology; dreams and their significance; habit and natural instinct; true nobility or gentilesse; apology for plain speaking; the former age (p 223); attitudes toward marriage and celibacy. Fansler's conclusion stresses Chaucer's 'undeniable sympathetic relationship' with Jean de Meung which reflects itself 'unmistakably in their critical, inquiring attitude toward life and its problems, in their tendency to visualize abstractions, in their significant blending of medievalism and modernism, of romanticism and realism' (p 234).

32 Fleming, John V. 'Chaucer's Squire: The *Roman de la Rose* and the *Romaunt*.' *N&Q*, 14 (1967), 48–9.
Compares *CT* A lines 94–9, on the Squire's riding, singing, flute playing, painting, dancing, and writing abilities to *Romaunt* 2321 ff, lines perhaps influenced by Chaucer's phrasing in *GP*. The lines in *Romaunt* must come from Langlois' Ra variant group of *RR* mss rather than the text Langlois prints. 'If so, it is clear that the translator of the *Romaunt* was working from a French text different from that on which Chaucer relied' (p 49).

33 French, Robert Dudley. *A Chaucer Handbook.* New York: Appleton-Century-Crofts, 1927/rev 1947.
French briefly comments on the history of *RR*, then summarizes the

controversy over the text of *Romaunt* (pp 75–82).

34 Geissman, Erwin William. *The Style and Technique of Chaucer's Translations from French.* Yale University Dissertation, 1952. Dir. Helge Kökeritz.

Geissman excludes *Boece* because of unavailability of necessary materials. His study includes chapters on the art of translation, medieval translations contemporary with Chaucer, *Melibee*, the *Romaunt*, miscellaneous translations from French, Chaucer's use of doublets, and a conclusion. Also, five appendices: on *Romaunt A* and Langlois' variants, in which Geissman catalogs readings in mss which are closer to Chaucer than those in Langlois' edition; on *Romaunt C*, with a catalog of ms variants that are closer than Langlois'; on Chaucer's Borrowed Rhyme-Words, with lists for *Romaunt A* of romance rimes and direct borrowings; on borrowed words in the *Mel*; and on borrowed words in *Romaunt A* other than the direct rhyme borrowings. In Ch 4 Geissman gives a detailed review of the authorship controversy (pp 147–54). He follows Skeat and Robinson in accepting Fragment A as a genuine Chaucerian piece, commenting on the paucity of ME texts of *Romaunt* — a striking contrast to the abundance of French mss. *Romaunt A* seems closer to Langlois' group 2 mss, though variants from both groups appear in the ME text. Mersand 51 shows something of the romance vocabulary in *Romaunt*, but does not reveal 'the amazing extent to which Chaucer actually borrows words from his original' (p 159). Geissman counts 758 cases in *Romaunt A* where Chaucer translates a French word by its English derivative. Even so, the direct borrowing is less extensive in *Romaunt* than in *Mel*. The heaviest borrowing occurs with rhyme words. Of the 1705 rhyme words, 569 are of romance origin; more than half — 286 — are directly descended from French source words. The main difficulty for the translator comes in maintaining octosyllabics, because the English form often is a monosyllable or dissyllable, where the French original is longer. Still Chaucer succeeds in translating literally with a skill which does not destroy the music of the verse or the character of his own language (p 162). His translation lacks 'the epigrammatic sharpness of the French.' In his translation of the dance passage in Mirth's garden, eg, 'Chaucer's description is accurate and charming in its own right, but has lost something of the sportiveness of the original' (p 177). Yet there are places where Chaucer improves the original: 'Where the French is general and commonplace, the English is often more concrete and arresting' (p 178). Perhaps the greatest significance of the translation is that it brought Chaucer early in his career 'into intimate contact with one of the great medieval storehouses of learning, allusive reference, poetic imagery, and courtly atmosphere. The French poem may have introduced him to the ideas of Boethius, whose *De Consolatione* shares the place with the *Roman* as the two principal literary influences on Chaucer's work' (p 188). The C-translator seems to be an imitator of Chaucer.

35 Getty, Agnes K. 'Chaucer's Changing Conceptions of the Humble Lover.' *PMLA*, 44 (1929), 202–216.
Getty sees a continuous development in Chaucer's treatment of the lover, from the humble lover of the French poetry in the early works to the satire and ironic poses of the late works. In the *Romaunt* 'Chaucer consistently follows the formal concept of the humble lover throughout. In Fragment A ... the theme and treatment are strictly those of conventional love, built about the French devices of the love vision and the court of love' (p 203).

36 Hammond, Eleanor Prescott. *Chaucer: A Bibliographical Manual.* Boston: Macmillan, 1908. Rpt New York: Peter Smith, 1933.
Hammond provides a detailed summary of investigations into the fragments of the *Romaunt* and into the question of its authenticity (pp 450–54).

37 Herben, Stephen J. 'Arms and Armor in Chaucer.' *Spec*, 12 (1937), 475–87.
Discusses styles of armor in Chaucer's day and armor references throughout Chaucer's writing, especially Sir Thopas' arming, two references in *Mars*, one in *FA*, one in *ABC*, and about a dozen in *Romaunt*. Eg, *Rom* 7559, the phrase 'with spear in thyne arest alwaye,' is a metaphor for alertness, being on guard. Comments on 'Turke bowes' p 485.

38 Hinckley, Henry Barrett. 'Chaucer and *Ywaine and Gawin*.' *Academy*, 71 (1906), II, 640–41.
Ywaine and Gawin influenced Chaucer's *KnT* and the *Romaunt*. It may be that all three fragments of the *Romaunt* are by Chaucer; the northern forms in the 'so-called B fragment' are 'prompted by intimacy with *Ywaine and Gawin*' (p 640) as Chaucer makes 'the restless experiments of a youth hampered by a dearth of English models, and by the necessity of choosing, and to some extent even constructing, his very dialect. Two centuries later Spenser faced the same difficulties, and solved them in a far more artificial way' (p 641).

39 Reply to Hinckley **38** by W.W. Skeat, *Academy*, 71 (1906), II, 647.
Skeat is doubtful of the early date of *Iwain and Gawin*. 'But I altogether repudiate the alleged influence of this poem on the *Romaunt*.' 'The arguments which I adduced ... to show that fragment B, and that fragment only, is written in the Northern dialect, have never been answered.' Skeat points out that there are no Northern

traces in the A-Fragment, where Chaucer begins his training. That some forms like *their* do occur in the Glasgow ms proves nothing other than that it's a Glasgow ms: 'How very remarkable! Well, *her* occurs in the other copy.'

40 Hinckley's reply to Skeat **39**. 'Chaucer Again.' *Academy*, 72 (1907), I, 99.
Hinckley objects to the tone of Skeat's reply which 'anathematises' anybody who refuses to admit to Skeat's emendations, thus making it impossible to quarrel. He reasserts his tentative suggestions, adding to them the *Reeve's Tale*, the Northern features of which 'would not have occurred had not Chaucer at an early age become familiar with the Northern dialect, whether through his residence at Hatfield or through the study of "Ywayne and Gawin," or through both.'

41 Huppé, Bernard F. 'The Translation of Technical Terms in the Middle English *Romaunt of the Rose*.' *JEGP*, 47 (1948), 334–42.
Noting Jean de Meun's conversance with scholastic terminology Huppé examines the *Romaunt* to see how its translators deal with the following technical terms: *conclue le peeur; consequence; sentence* and *letter; determine; demonstrate; lire* (cf *lectio*); *respondre, distinter, elenches; le meien.* The C-translator seems more aware of technical innuendoes than the B-translator. Huppé's sampling is sufficient 'to indicate the difficulty encountered by the Middle English translators in finding words of sufficient exactness in English to convey the precise meanings of the technical terms in French' (p 342). The translators are often careless, but when aware of technical problems, they take pains to find the nearest English equivalents. But often their mistakes are more 'a matter of training, not of language' (p 342).

42 Hussey, S.S. 'The Minor Poems and the Prose.' In *The Middle Ages*. Ed. Whitney Frank Bolton. Sphere History of Literature in the English Language. London: Barrie and Jenkins, 1970. Pp 229–62.
Hussey comments on the importance of the *Romaunt* as an early Chaucer translation (pp 231–33), a work which probably preceded *BD*. Chaucer must have known Boethius' *Consolation* well before he translated it, for parts of the *Romaunt* owe a good deal to it (p 247).

43 Kaluza, Max. *Chaucer und der Rosenroman: Eine litterargeschichtliche studie*. Berlin: E. Felber, 1893.
Kaluza explains in full the conclusions he arrived at during the editing of the Glasgow ms. The *Romaunt* consists not of two fragments, but three, with the first break occurring after line 1705. He concludes that the A and C fragments are both by Chaucer.

44 Kittredge, George Lyman. 'The Authorship of the English *Romaunt of the Rose*.' *Harvard Studies and Notes in Philology and Literature*, 1

(1892), 1–65.
Kittredge refutes T.R. Lounsbury's claim that Chaucer wrote the
whole *Romaunt* (*Studies in Chaucer* [1892] II, ch 6). 'We must
therefore be allowed to prefer the theory that is in accordance with all
the facts to the theory that is strongly opposed to the most significant
of them, and to believe that the *Romaunt* is not Chaucer's, with the
possible exception of the first seventeen hundred lines' (p 65).

45 Koch, John. 'Alte Chaucerprobleme und neue Lösungsversuche,' *ESt*,
55 (1921), 161–225.
Koch attempts solutions to the problem of authorship and the
fragments of the *Romaunt* (pp 161–74), the two prologues of *LGW*
(pp 174–96), the Palamon and Arcite poem (pp 196–209), Quene
Anelide and fals Arcite (pp 209–215), and a crux in *PF* (pp 215–25).
Koch does not accept the conclusions of Kaluza or Skeat that Chaucer
is author of the A-fragment. He recognizes five points in support of
Chaucer's claim, which he rejects one by one. 1. *LGW* indicates that
Chaucer translated *RR*. Probably he did; but that is no proof that the
Romaunt is his translation. 2. Lydgate seems to have known the
Romaunt in that he draws upon it in *CBK* and *Resoun and
Sensuality*. And he says in *Fall of Princes* that Chaucer translated
RR. His reference to Chaucer's translation may in fact be a reference
to Chaucer's reference, however. 3. Thynne indicates that the
Romaunt is Chaucer's. But Thynne is unreliable (unzuverlässigkeit) —
enough said! 4. Chaucer frequently draws upon *RR*, as Fansler **31** and
others have noted. Koch finds several parallel passages between the
A-and B-fragments which are close to Chaucerian works like *BD*,
LGW, and *PF*, but even so insists that such comparisons are not
proof: first of all because they are *not* word for word; nor are those
from the A-fragment closer than those from the B-fragment, which
nobody thinks is Chaucer's. Besides, Chaucer draws on *RR* from
memory when he is composing, rather than following a specific text. 5.
Some argue that the A-fragment is much more like Chaucer's usual
language than either of the other fragments. In exploring likenesses
and dissimilarities of idiom between the fragments and Chaucer, Koch
raises several issues. He does not think the break between the A- and
B-fragments occurs at line 1705. The bad rhyme there which Skeat
took to be an indicator of the new section is a scribal error, as a look
at the original French makes clear. Moreover, the 'dide' in line 1705
which troubled Skeat should be 'filde.' Koch would divide the
fragments at line 1714, where an idea is concluded; in line 1715, then,
we find the first instance of *bouton* instead of *knoppe*, for bud, which is
a mark of the B-translator. The B-fragment is in Lydgate's dialect. Its
rhyming and alliterative mannerisms, which many have called

unChaucerian, however, often appear in the A-fragment, especially in the Glasgow ms. In his editing of the text Skeat has removed many of these 'irregularities' from the A-fragment, making it look more Chaucerian than it is. There are many peculiarities of vocabulary in the A-fragment. One might say that that is because the translator (ie, Chaucer) is very young. But that is a weak argument since the differences are there; moreover, it seems likely that the *Romaunt* that he translated was done about the time he was working on *T&C*, at a time when he had written many books. But the most telling point is that all of the fragments reflect Northern features. Koch would associate the *Romaunt* with Lydgate's Bury St Edmunds and remains unconvinced that even the A-fragment is Chaucer's: 'Jedenfalls bin ich nach wie vor überzeugt, dass Chaucer nicht der Verfasser des ersten Bruchstücks der mittelenglische Übersetzung des Rosenromans war' (p 174). For previous comments by Koch as he developed his argument against Chaucerian authorship of the *Romaunt*, see: 'Werden abschnitte des me. Rosenromans mit recht Chaucer zugeschrieben?' *ESt*, 27 (1900), 61–73, which reviews Liddell's position on authorship of *Romaunt* in the Globe Chaucer **3**; 'Nochmals der mittlengl. Rosenroman,' *ESt*, 27 (1900), 227–34, with further comments; Review of Skeat's *Chaucer Canon* **64**, *ESt*, 30 (1902), 450–58, which challenges Skeat's argument for Chaucerian authorship of A, but which likes the affiliation of B with Lydgate; and 'Neuere Chaucer-Literatur,' *ESt*, 46 (1912), 98–114, which reviews once more the positions of Kaluza, Skeat and J.H. Lange on the authorship of *Romaunt* (pp 103–09) to cast doubt on all theories in favor of Chaucer.

46 Kuhl, E.P. 'Chaucer and the Red Rose.' *PQ*, 24 (1945), 33–38. Chaucer colors his roses red in *Romaunt* lines 1680 and 907, where no color is cited in the French. The red rose was the badge of Blanche, Duchess of Lancaster. Gaunt took a red rose as his device in 1362 out of the dignity held by his father-in-law. Nor did the red rose belong to any other house (p 33). Noting the strong influence of *RR* on *BD*, which is part of the compliment to Blanche's memory, Kuhl suggests that the *Romaunt* was translated in honor of Blanche and that Chaucer broke off translating at line 1705, at the time of Blanche's death. Red and white allegorical imagery also occurs in the G text of *LGW* and in *HF*. Chaucerians need to be more alert to the political overtones of Chaucer's poetry. Such a view might modify our conceptions of Chaucer's whole philosophy of composition and free us from 'the preoccupation with Chaucer's technique.' Once aware of his political involvement we might face squarely the possibilty that *CT* is more than 'escape' literature and instead a 'grappling with affairs of state' (p 38). Chaucer's model for this kind of writing is in Jean de

Meun's satire.

47 Kunstmann, John G. 'Chaucer's "Archangel".' *MLN*, 55 (1940), 259–62.
Thompson's theory (70) for the derivation of 'archangel' as a bird name in *Romaunt* line 915 is too ingenious to be convincing. Kunstmann proposes instead that Chaucer, looking for a word to rime with 'aungell,' chose the name of a bird known today as the red-backed shrike, whose Middle English name is 'wariangel' (cf *FriarT* D 1408). 'Wariangel' was copied as 'ariangel'; this in turn was corrupted to 'archangel.'

48 Lange, Hugo. 'Rettungen Chaucers: Neue Beitrage zur Echtheitsfrage von Fragment A des mittelenglischen Rosenroman.' *Anglia*, 35 (1911), 338–46; 36 (1912), 479–91; 37 (1913), 146–62.
Lange identifies numerous verbal echoes between *Romaunt A* and Lydgate's *Reson and Sensualyte*. It appears that Lydgate had a thorough knowledge of Fragment A; but he also seems to have known the B-fragment, from which he borrows imagery as well as phrasing. Lange suggests that Lydgate used both the *Romaunt* and the Old French poem [35 (1911), 338–46]. In his sixteen 'rescues' (*rettungen*) of the A-fragment as a genuine Chaucerian work, Lange challenges Koch and enlarges upon several points made by Skeat on the probability of Chaucer's authorship. He notes the limitations of Skeat's efforts to determine genuineness (*echtheit*) by rhyme tests and regularity of stress, however. Lange cites numerous instances in works known to be Chaucer's, where stress within a word varies, depending upon the exigencies of the line in which Chaucer places it. He also gives examples of rhymes in the A-fragment that differ from those of Lydgate but which could be from Chaucer [37 (1913), 159–61].

49 — 'Zur Datierung des mittelenglischen Rosenromanfragments A.' *Anglia*, 38 (1914), 477–90.
Lange reasserts the likelihood of Chaucer's authorship of the A-fragment and dates it after 1377 because of a cross reference with the B-text of *Piers Plowman*, which Lange thinks Chaucer knew, but before *Boece* and *PF*, which appear to draw on the *Romaunt*.

49a Lange, J.H. 'Lydgate und Fragment B des *Romaunt of the Rose*.' *ESt*, 29 (1901), 397–405.
Reviews Skeat's suggestion that B-Fragment might be by Lydgate, adding supporting evidence.

50 Mathew, Gervase. 'Ideals of Friendship.' In *Patterns of Love and Courtesy: Essays in Memory of C.S. Lewis*. Ed. John Lawlor. London: Arnold; Evanston, Ill.: Northwestern University Press, 1966. Pp 45–53.
Friendship finds its expression in action (cf Aquinas). Mathew

compares the behavior of 'Franchise' and 'Bel Accuiel' in the *Romaunt:* 'Franchise' slowly takes the place of 'debonneirete' in the early *roman courtois.* In the *Romaunt* 'it is the arrow winged by courtesy and by courage' (p 50). 'Bel Accuiel' is Courtesy's son, a kind of friendliness based on 'the recognition of the essential connaturality of all men' (p 51). This attitude toward friendship derives from Boethius, Isidore, and Bede, though especially (and explicitly) from Cicero. 'There seems very little divergence between the theories of friendship current in vernacular and in Latin; perhaps precisely because vernacular and Latin texts interpenetrate and derive from the same sources. The medieval culture of which we have literary record seems homogeneous' (pp 52–3).

51 Mersand, Joseph. *Chaucer's Romance Vocabulary.* Brooklyn: Comet Press, 1937.
Ch 6, 'Romance Words in the Romaunt of the Rose,' pp 58–61, considers fifty-seven words that make their first appearance in written English in *Romaunt A.* 'Chaucer's manipulation of his foreign originals gives us revealing insight into his mental processes. We can almost re-live his own experience in discovering the peculiar merits of this or that particular French, Latin, or Italian word, and his desire to naturalize it into English' (p 58). Most often Chaucer borrows nouns, especially nouns that denote concrete objects and are visual in appeal. He also borrows adjectives, not necessarily because they are vivid or precise, but for sound rather than meaning. Fifty-three percent of his new words are used as rhymes: 'their appeal to the poet's ear cannot ... be overlooked' (p 61).

52 Morgan, Gerald. 'The Self-Revealing Tendencies of Chaucer's Pardoner.' *MLR,* 71 (1976), 241–55.
Morgan studies the limitations of modern psychological approaches to medieval literature, using *Romaunt* and *PardT* as his exemplary texts. C.S. Lewis' psychological interpretation of the poem (see **132**) 'raises insurmountable problems at the fictional level' (p 246). Morgan discusses Jelousy, Bialacoil, Daunger, and Shame as objectifications of moral categories rather than as particular manifestations of personality. Fals-Semblant shares much in common with Chaucer's Pardoner. The medieval poet is fully aware of the incongruity between action and intention as Fals-Semblant is ignorant of his falseness. 'The dislocation at the psychological level is dependent on the need for an objective account and ... the nature of hypocrisy of itself involves a corresponding moral dislocation. It should be evident, too, that a modern psychological perspective is in direct conflict with the very assumption upon which the convention of the dramatic monologue is based' (p 250). Like *Romaunt, PardT,* especially, is a 'test-case for

modern critics who assert the primacy of psychological principles' (p 250).

53 Nathan, Leonard E. 'Tradition and Newfangleness in Wyatt's *They Fle From Me*,' *ELH*, 32 (1965), 1–16.
The main influences on Wyatt's poem are the *Romaunt*, *T&C*, and such fifteenth-century courtly poetry as that of Charles of Orleans, who had the *Romaunt* 'at his elbow' when composing Ballade #38 (p 3). 'The poet of the "Ballade" lives comfortably in the world of *The Romaunt*: a fantasy world in which the relationship of love analyzes into a static complex, in which subtle and transitory feelings transform into slow-moving personifications obeying automatically, as in a dream, the laws of the love code and of a simplified and ritualized faculty psychology' (p 7). It is most revealing that literary conventions in the *Romaunt* can be 'so mechanically detached from the whole and served up as lyrics' (p 5). The *Romaunt* goes beyond the Ballade in providing 'dictional analogues' for Wyatt's poem (p 10), though many of Wyatt's touches break with convention, especially the aggressiveness of the women, the lack of ideal aristocratic love service, and the insistence that 'it was no dreme.' 'Much of Wyatt's poignancy ... derives from just such "confusion" ' (p 14).

54 Nordahl, Helge. '*Ars fidi interpretis:* Un Aspect rhetorique de l'art de Chaucer dans sa traduction du *Roman de la Rose*.' *Archivum Linguisticum: A Review of Comparative Philology and General Linguistics*, 9 (1978), 24–31.
In view of the unique lexical structures of different languages, 'les tautologies représent, pour le traducteur, une difficulté considerable' (p 24). Nordahl discusses various ways in which Chaucer conserves tautologies within his metrical line, transforms grammatical components (eg, adverbs into prepositional phrases), amplifies tautologies, deletes them, or shifts the emphasis within them.

55 Norton-Smith, John. *John Lydgate: Poems, with Introduction, Notes, and Glossary*. Oxford: Clarendon Press, 1966.
Twelve selections from Lydgate, including 'Letter to Gloucester,' 'On the Departing of Thomas Chaucer,' 'Balade Sente to the Shirrefs Dyner,' 'An Exclamacioun of the Deth of Alcibiades' (*Fall of Princes* III. 3655–82), 'A Tale of Froward Maymond,' 'The Rebuilding of Troy' (*Troy Book* II. 479–710), 'As a Mydsomer Rose,' 'A Balade in Commendation of Our Lady,' 'A Defence of Holy Church,' 'Life of Our Lady' (II. 519–903), 'A Complaynt of a Loveres Lyfe,' and 'The Temple of Glas.' Smith's notes to 'Complaynt of a Loveres Lyfe' and 'Temple of Glas' are rich in cross references to the *Romaunt* and also to *Boece*. 'Tale of Froward Maymond' derives its poetic texture from Chaucer's *Cook's Tale* and thus qualifies as one of several fifteenth-

and sixteenth-century poems, like Lydgate's *Siege of Thebes* and Book IV of Spenser's *Faerie Queene*, which attach themselves in some way to the unfinished *CT*.

56 Ord, Hubert W. *Chaucer and the Rival Poet in Shakespeare's Sonnets*. London and Toronto: J.M. Dent, 1921.
Ord attempts to prove the direct influence of Chaucer's *Romaunt* on Shakespeare's sonnets.

57 Pollard, Alfred William. 'Chaucer.' *Encyclopedia Britannica*. Eleventh edition. Cambridge, 1910. Vol. VI, pp 13–17.
Chaucer 'knew the *Roman de la rose* as modern English poets know Shakespeare, and the full extent of his debt to his French contemporaries ... is only gradually being discovered. To be in touch throughout his life with the best French poets of the day was much for Chaucer. Even with their stimulus alone he might have developed no small part of his genius' (p 14). His translation of the *Romaunt* was an important part of that development.

58 Preston, Raymond. *Chaucer*. London and New York: Sheed and Ward, 1952.
Praises the musical qualities of the *Romaunt* (pp 17–18) and stresses the Englishness of the rhythm in Chaucer's lyrics and the *Romaunt* (pp 21–4).

59 Rattenbury, Arnold. 'Geoffrey Chaucer: The Poet in Society.' *Our Time*, 4 (1944), 7.
'Chaucer's first writings were strongly influenced by the France in which he had been fighting and spying, and by the Court that employed him, which culturally at any rate was a little France in itself' (p 7). *BD* is 'little more than a restatement of the chivalry-in-love theme' of the French poets, and the *Romaunt* is 'sheer copy book' from the French.

60 Reeves, W.P. '*Romance of the Rose*, 1705.' *MLN*, 38 (1923), 124.
Skeat misreads *dide* as an auxiliary verb in *Romaunt* line 1705. It means *dyed*. 'The rose not only illumined, but it also fragrantly dyed the place all about. Skeat's dash after the line is wholly gratuitous. Dogmatism about phonology or inconsistent rhymes in a ms. so late as Glasgow, to say nothing of the text of the First Folio, bears a heavy burden of proof' (p 124). [But see Koch 45 who says *dide* should read *filde*.]

61 Root, Robert Kilburn. *The Poetry of Chaucer: A Guide to its Study and Appreciation*. Boston: Houghton Mifflin, 1900/rev 1922. Pp 45–56.
The *Romaunt* was Chaucer's 'first serious undertaking in literature ... Surely no better exercise than that of translation could have been

found to develop a technical mastery of poetic form' (p 45). *RR* offered Chaucer a broad and varied scope which was thoroughly congenial to his tastes and sympathies. Its influence is so great on Chaucer that it should be studied in its entirety by every Chaucer student. Without *RR*, 'Chaucer would not have been Chaucer, and English literature would have followed a different channel' (p 49). Root concurs with Kaluza **43** that the A and C texts are genuine. 'Though the portions of the work which may be attributed to Chaucer are of a high degree of excellence, easy and spirited, they have not the power of his maturer work. The translation is a good one, but not a great one' (p 56).

62 Saintsbury, George. 'Chaucer.' In *The Cambridge History of English Literature*. Ed. A.W. Ward and A.R. Waller. Cambridge: Cambridge University Press; New York: G.P. Putnam's Sons, 1908. Vol 2, pp 179–224.
Saintsbury concurs with theories that the A-fragment is an early work by Chaucer: 'There is no verse translation which approaches this in the combined merits of fidelity, poetry and wit' (p 194).

63 Schoch, A.D. 'The Differences in the Middle English "Romaunt of the Rose" and Their Bearing upon Chaucer's Authorship.' *MP*, 3 (1906), 339–58.
Kaluza's theory that Chaucer never translated more than the A- and C-fragments conflicts with the statement on Chaucer's heretical translation in *LGW*. The A-fragment contains nothing against the law of love, and C is directed against hypocrisy and begging friars and is decidedly favorable to the lover and Cupid. It is the B-fragment which contains the enumeration of the woes of lovers, the harangue of Reason, and the lover's mistreatment by 'Wikked Tunge,' 'Daunger,' and 'Ielousye.' Whether the extant B-fragment is the one Chaucer translated is not the question, though the methods of determining the fragments are inconsistent and based on slim evidence. B shows more variation simply because it is longer (p 343). Moreover, there is much variation within B. Should it be divided into two parts? The question implies 'the hint to be a little skeptical as to there being even three fragments' (p 354). Anyone proposing a linguistic theory of authorship should be consistent; he must decide how much latitude he will allow the author in varying the usage of his other undisputed works. Kaluza and Skeat, who would save some part for Chaucer, are inconsistent in their method. Lounsbury, who says it is all Chaucer's, and Koch, who says none of it, seem too extreme. 'Perhaps no entirely satisfactory solution of the difficulty will ever be reached, unless another manuscript of the *Romaunt* should be found with some indication of the author's identity' (p 358).

64 Skeat, W.W. *The Chaucer Canon*. Oxford: Clarendon Press, 1900.

On the basis of *SqT*, a work known for certain to be Chaucer's, Skeat sets up grammatical and rhyming tests against which he checks the authenticity of other works. Chs 6–8 (pp 65–93) are devoted to the three fragments of the *Romaunt*. Skeat finds no difficulty in accepting the A-fragment as genuine (p 66). 'The riming words can always be depended on, not only throughout the Canterbury Tales, but everywhere else in the genuine works of Chaucer, for yielding trustworthy grammatical results' (p 67); in this respect the A-fragment is 'immaculate' (p 69). The *NED* assigns 1366 as the date for the A-fragment: 'this must be very near the truth' (p 74). The very completeness of the case for the A-fragment is fatal to the pretensions of the B-fragment, which 'fails to satisfy nearly every test that exists' (p 75). Skeat finds evidence that the author of *Kingis Quair* was acquainted with Chaucer's version of the *Romaunt* and was capable of translating it into a mixed jargon of Northern and Chaucerian English (pp 88–9). The fragment is definitely by a Northern imitator. Skeat sees no reason against ascribing it to James I: 'Indeed, there is much to be said in favour of that supposition' (p 89). The C-fragment is definitely different from B. But unlike A it does not satisfy the -y/-ye rhyme test. There are several other unsatisfactory rhymes as well. The translator was not interested in translating the whole poem — only the episode on False Semblant or Hypocrisy (p 92). 'All that we can say is that he was one who was attracted rather by religious satire than by romance, one who sympathized, probably, with the author of *The Plowman's Tale* ... The author was not in the position of a continuator, but assumed an independent attitude of his own' (p 93). Skeat would date the fragment as early as 1390.

65 Smith, Merete. 'Literary Loanwords from Old French in the *Romaunt of the Rose:* A Note.' *ChauR*, 17 (1983), 89–93.
Of the thirty-nine Old French loan words in *Romaunt* pertaining to dress and fabrics, only six are found (according to *MED*) in *Romaunt* for the first time: *camelyne, chapelet, cheuesayle, mourdant, suckeny,* and *tyssue.* Of the six only two gain currency in English (*chapelet* and *tyssue*).

66 Snyder, Edward D. 'The Wild Irish: A Study of Some English Satires against the Irish, Scots, and Welsh.' *MP*, 17 (1919–20), 687–725.
B-fragment, lines 3807–11, derives 'Wikkid-tunge' from 'an Irish woman,' a reference to the popular belief that 'the Irish were especially liable to be sharp of tongue' (p 712).

67 Speirs, John. *Chaucer the Maker.* London: Faber and Faber, 1951.
Chaucer begins his literary career as a translator of *RR*, which remained his primary literary source throughout his life. 'The new music is ... what first enchants those who attend to the Chaucerian

Romaunt of the Rose, the new music, heard for the first time sustainedly in English' (p 36). Elements of Chaucer's mature art are present from the beginning, though conventional figures and types become more particularized and individualized with each successive poem. Speirs contrasts Ydelness in the *Romaunt* with the Prioress, emphasizing the vividness of Chaucer's description and his developing preference for 'the more vigorous realism of Jean de Meung' when he came to write the Tales, where we see 'the disenchanting spirit' of Jean (p 39). In poems written more immediately after the *Romaunt* 'the allegorical designs remain ... but what we may observe is a deepening humanization of the designs and a developing dramatic genius' (p 40).

68 Sutherland, Ronald. 'The *Romaunt of the Rose* and Source Manuscripts.' *PMLA*, 74 (1959), 178–83.
By comparing fragments A, B, and C with ms classes of two hundred French originals catalogued by Langlois, Sutherland demonstrates that the sources of the A-fragment differ from those of B and C, to conclude: 'we may securely maintain on the basis of separate and different ms originals that whoever composed Fragment A of the ME *Romaunt* was not responsible for B and C, even before they were tampered with. Not only is this view in happy accord with the fruits of close stylistic analysis, it also explains the reason why there should be a difference of styles among the various fragments of the *Romaunt*. Moreover, there is every indication to believe Chaucer was the author of Fragment A ... Accordingly, Fragments B and C cannot be considered in any way the work of Geoffrey Chaucer' (p 183).

69 Tarlinskaja, Marina. *English Verse: Theory and History*. The Hague: Mouton, 1976.
Tarlinskaja uses the *Romaunt* as a primary source in discussing problems of Middle English word stress, of non-correspondence between word stress and ictus, of the saturation of verses with words occupying positions of metrical non-correspondence, and in the study of morphology and sound structure of native English disyllabic nouns in the positions of metrical correspondence and non-correspondence.

70 Thompson, D'Arcy W. ' "Archangel" as a Bird-Name in Chaucer.' *NQ*, 175 (1938), 332.
The French source for *Romaunt* line 915 has *mesenge*, which is usually translated 'titmouse.' Perhaps Chaucer used the Latin name for goldfinch or siskin, ie, *acanthalis* or *acanthyllis*, which was shortened to *acanthal*, then easily mistaken for *acangal*, for which *arcangal*, then *archangel* were substituted. What Chaucer wrote was: 'With finch, with lark, with acaunthyl, / He semed as he were an aungel.' [See 47 and 75.]

71 Thompson, Neste M. *A Furthur Study of Chaucer and The Romance*

of the Rose. Stanford University Doctoral Dissertation, 1926.
Thompson argues that the present ME version of the *Romaunt* is not
the work of Chaucer.

72 Vyvyan, John. *Shakespeare and the Rose of Love: A Study of the
Early Plays in Relation to the Medieval Philosophy of Love.* London:
Chatto and Windus; New York: Barnes and Noble, 1960.
Ch 3, pp 68–97, is devoted to the *RR*, with Thynne's 1532 edition of
Romaunt as the primary source. Vyvyan suggests that Guillaume's
part of the story 'would make a delightful ballet' (p 73). 'It is
necessary to remember that the lover is dreaming. The garden of the
Rose is not a place, but a state of mind. It is what every imaginative
youth discovers when he has the leisure to dream; but it cannot be
explored by a young man in a hurry' (p 75). In a sense the Lady 'is
being psycho-analysed, and her inner life presented as a play; we never
meet her as a complete person, but her emotions are introduced to us
individually. From the point of view of literary technique, this type of
allegory is of great importance; by imitation and development it was
perpetuated; no later medieval poet escaped its influence' (p 80).
'What Guillaume de Lorris bequeathed to his successors was, in fact,
an extremely subtle form of character analysis' (p 82). The printing of
the *Romaunt* in 1532 'kept its memory green' (p 82) into the
Renaissance. Its influence appears in *Love's Labour's Lost, Two
Gentlemen of Verona*, and *Romeo and Juliet* (pp 84–97). 'There is one
element in Shakespeare's heroines that is not to be found in the Rose:
it is the Platonic conception of Beauty, which the Middle Ages had
forgotten, and which the Renaissance translators revived' (p 97).

73 Walter, J.H. *'Astrophel and Stella and The Romaunt of the Rose.'*
RES, 15 (1939), 265–73.
Though Sidney does not follow the allegorical method of *Romaunt*, he
does use its personifications, especially at the beginning of the
sequence — the words and actions of Daunger, Bialacoil, Pity,
Franchise, etc — in presenting Stella. The plot is also similar, first
attraction and partial success, then a separation which provokes bitter
lament. Reason appears twice in the *Romaunt*; so too on two main
occasions in *Astrophel and Stella*. 'Sidney was almost certainly
acquainted with *The Romaunt*, and as a model it had the advantages
of a high chivalric morality. The passages in the older poem which
have parallels in *Astrophel and Stella* all occur in the English fragment
... There is no hint that Sidney used the French ... [If he did draw
upon the *Romaunt*,] his aims and methods as a poet, the consistency of
his practice with his precept [cf his theory of imitation in the *Apology*],
and his final rank as a poet become the more clearly defined' (p 273).

74 Webster, C.M. 'Chaucer's Turkish Bows.' *MLN*, 47 (1932), 260.

The phrase 'turkish bows' occurs in *KnT* A 2895 and *Romaunt* 923–30. Guillaume and Chaucer wished to describe a very strong bow. The turkish bow was very powerful and made of layered horn, wood, and sinew. A far-shooting weapon, it even surpassed the famed English long bow, which Chaucer probably had in mind.

75 Whitteridge, Gweneth. 'The Word *Archaungel* in Chaucer's *Romaunt of the Rose.*' *English and Germanic Studies*, 3 (1950), 34–6.
There may have been an error in the French text comparable to an error in the Crawford ms of *RR*. *Mesenges* was corrupted to *arcanges*. 'Being impressed by the list of birds, Chaucer may have failed to recognize *arcanges* as an error on the part of the French scribe and thought it another pleasantly-named bird. Hence he translated it quite simply as *archaungel* enriching the language with an imaginary bird to the confusion of later critics' (p 36). [See **70** and **47**.]

Selected Discussions of the *Roman de la Rose* and its Influence on Chaucer

76 *Le Roman de la Rose* (Film in color). Introduction and Commentary by Brian Merrilees. 1981. Media Centre and Centre for Medieval Studies. University of Toronto.
A retelling of *RR* using over one hundred illustrations from Bodleian ms Douce 195 (late fifteenth-century), perhaps the most splendid of *RR* mss. English version 32 minutes long; French version, 37 minutes.

77 Allen, Judson B. *The Friar as Critic: Literary Attitudes in the Later Middle Ages*. Nashville: Vanderbilt University Press, 1971.
Uses *RR*, 'next to Dante's, the most important allegorical poem of the later Middle Ages' (pp 13–14), to exemplify the intricacy of spiritual sense and literal sense through extended metaphor. See esp pp 18–20.

78 Badel, Pierre-Yves. *Le Roman de la Rose au XIVe siècle: Étude de la Réception de l'Oeuvre*. Publications Romanes et Françaises. Genève: Librairie Droz, 1980.
Badel's focus is on *RR* in France among French readers, poets, and commentators. His chapter on fourteenth-century readers discusses the great output of *RR* mss and lists thirty whose owners are known (pp 56–62). Badel comments on allusions to and derivations from other works besides *RR* by Jean de Meun, noting his status as a sort of legendary hero in the fourteenth century, then focuses attention on 'Gilles li Muisis et la Tradition Satirique' (pp 74–82), 'Machaut et la poésie de cour' (pp 82–94), 'Eustache Deschamps: amour et moralité'

(pp 94–114). Ch 3, 'La Forge de Nature,' pp 115–33, discusses responses to the subject matter and moral issues of *RR*, from Jean de Condé's *Messe des Oiseaux* and his *Dit de l'Ipocresie des Jacobins* to 'grivoiseries' (smutty stories) such as Brasdefer's *Pamphile et Galatée*. Ch 4, 'Culte et Mépris de la Femme,' pp 135–205, surveys courtly literature with attitudes derived from *RR* as various as *fine amor*, the celebration of marriage, or lamentations against women's wiles. Ch 5, 'Le Chapitre de Faux Semblant,' pp 207–62, discusses *RR*'s relationship to *Le Roman de Fauvel*, *Le Livre de Mandevie*, *Le Dit de l'Evêque et de Droit*, *Renard Le Contrefait* and *Le Roman d'Alexandre*. Ch 6, 'Miroir de Vie Humaine,' pp 263–330, considers the relationship of *RR* to *Les Echecs d'Amour* and *Les Echecs Amoureux*, pp 263–315, and to *Le Chevalier Errant*, pp 315–30. Ch 7, 'Songes et Apparitions,' pp 331–409, discusses 'songe allégorique' as genre, outlining definitive elements and contrasting them with features of vision poetry. Badel comments on 'songe autobiographique,' 'récit personnel,' 'personnification,' and Jean's role in the evolution of 'songe,' then gives special attention to *La Voie de Povreté et de Richesse*, *Liber Fortunae*, the three *Pélerinages* of Guillaume de Deguilleville, *Le Roman de Deduis*, and various political songs. Ch 8, 'La Querelle du Roman de la Rose,' pp 411–89, offers a brief chronology of the exchanges between Christine de Pizan, Jean de Montreuil, Gautier and Pierre Col, and Jean Gerson, summarizes their positions, and discusses the origins of the debate. Badel includes separate sections on 'Opinion et science chez Christine de Pizan,' pp 436–47, 'Gerson et l'hérésie,' pp 447–61, 'Humanistes ou clercs lettrés,' pp 462–82, and 'Jean de Meun vengé: Laurent de Premierfait,' pp 482–9. An appendix, pp 507–11, lists 106 works written between 1414 and 1640 which mention *RR* or its authors. Useful bibliography, pp 513–21.

79 Baird, Joseph L. and John R. Kane, eds. *La Querelle de la Rose: Letters and Documents*. North Carolina Studies in the Romance Languages and Literatures, no. 199. Chapel Hill: University of North Carolina Press, 1978.

In 1399 Christine de Pisan attacked Jean de Meun harshly in her *L'Epistre au Dieu d'Amours*. Subsequently a *débat littérairre* developed between Christine, Jean de Montreuil, and others in an exchange of informal letters questioning the moral worth of *RR*. 'This controversy, however, should not be viewed merely as a kind of lofty exchange of views among a small group of the sophisticated albeit rather moralistic *litterati* of the time. The evidence seems to indicate that the debate was quite a live issue of real and earnest moral interest to a large number of people ... The notable Jean Gerson addressed himself to the subject in a series of sermons ... preached to the populace in the vernacular' (pp 11–12). This debate, referred to as *La Querelle de la Rose*, is sometimes seen as a first phase of the later more voluminous sixteenth-century *débat, La Querelle des Femmes*. Baird and Kane include excerpts in English translation from Christine's *Epistre* and six of her letters (one a dedicatory letter addressed to the Queen of France), seven letters by Jean de Montreuil, two by Gontier Col, two by Pierre Col, and four entries from sermons, essays, and letters by Jean Gerson. Baird and Kane's introduction discusses Christine as a fourteenth-century feminist (pp 15–28). A representative sample of her condemnation of *RR* may be seen in her letter of October 1401 to Gontier Col: 'I say that it [*RR*] can be a source of wicked and perverse encouragement to disgusting conduct, although it does contain some good things ... This book can be, for many people, a supporter of the dissolute life; a doctrine full of deceit; the road to damnation; a public defamer; a source of suspicion, mistrust, shame, and, perhaps, of heresy. And in several places a most loathsome book! All this I choose and dare to hold and maintain everywhere and before everyone, and I can prove it by reference to the book itself' (pp 63–64).

80 Baker, David Jeffrey. 'Allegory and Exegesis in Jean de Meun's *Roman de la Rose*.' Yale University Dissertation, 1978. See also *DAI*, 39 (1978), 2312-A.
Attempts to define Jean de Meun's theory of allegory in the context of his general poetics and to determine his relationship to post-classical and medieval traditions. Focuses on passages of literary commentary in *RR* and on rhetorical terminology.

81 Baker, Denise N. 'The Priesthood of Genius: A Study of the Medieval Tradition.' *Spec*, 51 (1976), 277–91.
Baker compares the role of Genius in Alain de Lille's *De planctu Naturae*, Jean de Meun's *RR*, and John Gower's *CA*. Jean affirms the same moral position of Alain, where Genius is both the tutelary spirit inherent in each individual as reason and also the god of generation, but he does so through the mode of comic irony. Jean emphasizes Genius' role as priest, 'but, ironically, Genius's claim to sacerdotal authority has been undermined by Natura's disassociation from her function as moral instructor. Genius, as Natura's "other self," is qualified to share in her work as *procreatrix*; but because she no longer has jurisdiction over man's rational faculties, his activities as spiritual advisor are absurd. And Jean de Meun makes it hilariously clear that Genius is a false priest' (p 285). Gower fuses the two meanings of Genius he found in Alain and Jean, carefully distinguishing between law of *kinde* and law of *reson*. In Gower Genius 'is not an inconsistent figure but rather a complex and sophisticated assimilation of his two precursors in the literary tradition ... [which demonstrates] the

limitations of natural concupiscence as a moral guide' (p 291).

82 Barney, Stephen. *Allegories of History, Allegories of Love.* Hamden, Connecticut: Shoe String Press, 1979.
Part One, 'Marking Time: Allegories of History,' considers Prudentius' *Psychomachia,* Langland's *Piers Plowman,* Book One of the *Faerie Queene,* and Melville's *The Confidence-Man.* Part Two, 'The Reflex of the Heart: Allegories of Love,' considers *RR,* Books Three and Four of the *Faerie Queene,* Hawthorne's *Rappaccini's Daughter,* and Kafka's *The Castle.* Ch 6, 'Adornment: *The Romance of the Rose,*' pp 179–215, explores the relation of rhetorical structures to allegory and the theme of love. The allegory in *RR* is of several kinds — mainly personification, but also typological, the allegorization of classical myth, and reification. 'Guillaume presents the traditional language surrounding love in an emphatically rhetorical form and rationalizes the rhetoric in allegorical form; Jean criticizes the view of love presented by his predecessor, both by demolishing the rhetorical structure which underpins it, and by presenting his own, parodic hyperallegorical version of love in terms of cosmic theosophy' (p 194). Barney comments on Jean's use of mirrors and of the Pygmalion and Narcissus myths (pp 201–10) and appends a bibliographical note which devotes special attention to these items.

83 – 'Chaucer's Lists.' In *The Wisdom of Poetry: Essays in Early English Literature in Honor of Morton Bloomfield.* Ed. Larry D. Benson and Siegfried Wenzel. Kalamazoo: Medieval Institute Publications, Western Michigan University, 1982. Pp 189–223.
Cites *RR* as source and rhetorical model for 'lists' in Chaucer.

84 Batany, Jean. *Approches du Roman de la Rose: Ensemble de l'oeuvre et verse 8227 a 12456.* Paris: Bordas, 1973.
'A student's guide, which surveys *Roman's* place in the history of love, poetry, allegory, and marriage satire' (Luria **136**, pp 237–38).

85 Bloomfield, Morton. 'A Grammatical Approach to Personification Allegory.' *MP,* 60 (1963), 161–71.
Personification allegory and symbolism are modes of understanding expressed through different grammatical means. Personification allegory is not the opposite of symbolism in any fundamental sense, only in its clarity of subject; the subject is unveiled, usually for didactic purpose, while the predicate is the most veiled part. With symbolism the subject is veiled as well.

86 Bourdillon, Francis William. *The Early Editions of the Roman de la Rose.* The Bibliography Society Illustrated Monographs, no 14. London: Chiswick Press, 1906.
A general bibliographical account of the mss, early printed editions,

folios, quartos, Clément Marot's recension, and Molinet's prose
version, with a description of the twenty-one editions. Describes in
Part II the illustrations in early printed editions and prints samples of
the eight series of special illustrations and the *Mathéolus* woodcuts.

87 Brumble, Herbert D. 'Genius and Other Related Allegorical Figures
in the *De Planctu Naturae*, the *Roman de la Rose*, the *Confessio
Amantis*, and the *Faerie Queene*.' University of Nebraska Dissertation,
1970. Dir. Paul A. Olson. See also *DAI*, 31 (1971), 4113-A.
The Genius formulated by Alanus as a figure for natural inclination
was the real source of the allegorical tradition of Genii in Jean de
Meun, Gower, and Spenser. Brumble analyzes the Shepherd's Park
episode to show that Jean 'was religiously more orthodox than many
other critics have assumed.'

88 Cherniss, Michael D. 'Irony and Authority: The Ending of the *Roman
de la Rose*.' *MLQ*, 36 (1975), 227–38.
'No one ... can seriously take the opinions and example of the
narrator-hero Amant, as he emerges at the end of the poem, as the
embodiment of Meun's conception of perfect *amor*' (p 227). Nor does
the poet's figure of authority lie with Reson (pp 230–31), Nature (pp
229–30), or Genius (pp 231–33, 238). 'Ultimately, no figure emerges to
provide an authoritative, valid definition of *amor*, because none can be
drawn ... from the realm of post-lapsarian Nature' (p 230). Spiritual
love is hinted at through the carefully circumscribed allegory, but it
never appears in an openly recognized form in the Garden of Deduit.
'The final, pervasive irony of the *Roman* is that the reader learns
about love by learning what it is not' (p 233). 'Through Genius's
evocation of the park of the Lamb, which exists beyond Deduit's
garden and is infinitely superior to it, and through the finally negative,
ironic view of temporal, erotic love which emerges from his narrative,
Meun succeeds in pointing his reader toward a source of resolution and
harmony standing counterpoised against the problems, paradoxes,
inadequacies, and chaotic activity of the *Roman*' (p 238).

89 Chesterton, G.K. *Chaucer*. London: Faber, 1932. Rpt 1965.
Chesterton does not talk specifically about *Romaunt*, but rather about
the reasons why Chaucer would have translated *RR*. *RR* is like the
Briar Rose of pre-Raphaelite legend — half roses, half thorns.
Guillaume offers a graceful allegory, like a tapestry in the background
of the medieval mind: Jean de Meung, on the other hand, 'seems to
have declined to accept the medieval convention that everything in the
garden was lovely; with the result that everything in the garden
became considerably more lively' (p 121). It is the two kinds of poems,
with their different tones, which appealed to Chaucer.

90 Cipriani, Lisi. 'Studies in the Influence of the *Romance of the Rose*

upon Chaucer.' *PMLA*, 22 (1907), 552–95.
Cipriani locates specific lines in Chaucer's canon which are taken from
RR. Discussion concentrates on *BD*, *PF*, *T&C*, and *LGW*, with
comments also upon *FA*, *Fortune*, *Gent*, *ABC*, and *AA*.

91   Cohn, Norman. *The World-view of a Thirteenth-Century Parisian
Intellectual: Jean de Meun and the Roman de la Rose.* Durham: The
University of Durham, 1961. Inaugural lecture of the Professor of
French (22 pages).
'Jean de Meun claims to be continuing a story ... left unfinished; but
this is the merest pretence. There is no evidence that Guillaume
regarded his work as unfinished and it certainly makes the effect of a
complete and rounded work of art. And in any case Jean de Meun
should have been the last man to undertake to finish any story, for
there never was a writer with less gift for narrative' (p 6). What
interests Jean is the opportunity of presenting his view of the world.
He was 'an eminent free-lance intellectual' with a restless inquiring
mind who believed 'it is good to know everything' (p 7). He lived in
the midst of an intellectual adventure which had all the excitement of
novelty: 'there never was a university more rapturously awake than
the University of Paris in the days of Jean de Meun' (p 9), as it
rediscovered the literature and thought of Graeco-Roman antiquity.
Cohn summarizes the discoveries in the humanities and sciences of the
day along with the exuberance of free thinking which stimulated Jean.

92   Dahlberg, Charles Raymond. 'The Secular Tradition in Chaucer and
Jean de Meun.' Princeton University Dissertation, 1953. Dir. D.W.
Robertson, Jr. See also *DA*, 14 (1954), 121.
Chaucer's favoring of parish priests over friars stems less from
Wycliffite sympathies than from *RR*. His antipathy to friars 'reflects
an attitude toward poetry and life which is characteristic of a
deeply-rooted medieval tradition.'

93   — 'Macrobius and the Unity of the *Roman de la Rose*.' *SP*, 58
(1961), 573–82.
Dahlberg challenges Gunn's assessment (**116**) of the flawed ending of
RR: 'The conclusion that the poem fails because of the inadequacy of
the allegorical method is based upon the mistaken assumption that
allegory consists of personifications' (p 573). In the medieval
understanding, allegory had little to do with literary forms as forms.
Rather it simply deals with hidden meanings. *Trope* (St Augustine's
term) is a more useful concept than *personification* in understanding
how allegory works through structures of images with a progressive
effect, stage by stage, as the perennial fall of man is repeated in each
sin. In the latter part of *RR*, more than ever because of this
progressive effect, 'the comedy is a fundamental part of the poem's

meaning, for the very blasphemy of the mock religiosity of the lover's quest, figured in terms of an aberration of the celestial pilgrimage, shows the depth and extent, as well as the ridiculousness of the full and final overthrow of reason, where everything is turned upside-down and black seems white. The futility of such a perversion is hinted at in the closing lines of the poem — "straitway it was day, and I awoke" — which suggest that the dream of the lover is fleeting and insubstantial' (p 582).

94 — 'Love and the *Roman de la Rose.*' *Spec*, 44 (1969), 568–84.
In *RR*, language pertaining to love, the lady, and beauty is ambiguous, a religious vocabulary appropriate to charity as well as cupidity. The beautiful lady may be understood, 'from the Lover's point of view, as his sweetheart, but that does not make her Guillaume's or Jean's, that is, the poet's' (p 568). Phrases like 'the one' (*cele*) or 'the beautiful lady' (*la bele*) could easily refer to the Virgin Mary. The ambiguities serve to remind the reader of the Lover's perversion of the idea of natural love, to point to his lack of reason, and to develop the theme of his ludicrous and cupidinous love. 'Study of the imagery of the poem and of the iconography of some of the early miniatures tends strongly to confirm this conclusion and to support the view that the entire work is structured in stages characteristic of the pattern of the Fall' (p 584).

95 — 'First Person and Personification in the *Roman de la Rose*: Amant and Dangier.' *Mediaevalia*, 3 (1977), 37–58.
'The *Roman de la Rose* is probably the first major French narrative poem that uses a first-person narrator to control the point of view from beginning to end' (p 37). The device has antecedents in interior monologues of earlier OF romances, courtly lyrics, Latin narratives of Ovid, Macrobius, Boethius, Andreas Capellanus, Alanus de Insulis, and in St Augustine's *Confessions*. The voice, in both Latin and vernacular traditions, is often deliberately ambiguous — both the voice of the subjective lover and the objective poet. The narrator's encounters and responses, which initially seem 'secular,' may turn out to be deliberate highlighting of images and events of worldly life ironically set 'against an implied background of extra-mundane values' (p 40). Jean de Meun stretches the double voice to 'audacious lengths,' as the personification of Dangier whom Amant encounters well demonstrates. Dahlberg first examines Dangier as a linguistic phenomenon, then from the familiar perspective argued by C.S. Lewis of Dangier as a psychological aspect of the Lady's personality which gets in Amant's way, then as a moral category manifested in psychological restraint, as Fleming **109** argued. By examining ms illuminations Dahlberg shows representations of Dangier which present him as a guardian of the narrator (whom the narrator sees as his

enemy). But regardless of point of view, irony is generated along with wit and provocative ambiguity. 'Amant's devils are Dangier's saints and *vice versa*' (p 51). The unlikenesses and likenesses remind the reader of hierarchical modes of thought which relate to the structure of the poem. 'The image of Amant's amusing and antic pursuit of the rose, when it is set up in apparent opposition to the repellant image of Dangier's correction, creates a resonating set of discords that reminds us of the harmony that is characteristic of the image of God in man' (p 52).

96 David, Alfred. 'How Marcia Lost Her Skin: A Note on Chaucer's Mythology.' In *The Lerned and Lewed: Harvard English Studies for B.J. Whiting*. Cambridge Mass.: Harvard University Press, 1974. Pp 19–29.
   Chaucer's source for *HF*, lines 1229–32, seems to be a ms related to a branch of the B family of *RR* mss in which Marsyas is presented as a female and the event of her piping and flaying given a comic tone. David prints and translates a forty-line interpolation from the ms group (pp 22–24). The *HF* treatment thus helps pinpoint our knowledge of at least one kind of *RR* which Chaucer knew and chastens claims of Chaucer's vast knowledge of the classics.

97 Defourney, Michel. 'Le *Roman de la Rose* à travers l'histoire et la philosophie.' *Marche Romane*, 17 (1967), 53–60.
   A brief review of responses to *RR* from the Querelle and Jean Molinet's redaction of 1483 to the twentieth-century editions of Lecoy and André Mary.

98 Eberle, Patricia J. 'The Lovers' Glass: Nature's Discourse on Optics and the Optical Design of the *Romance of the Rose*.' *UTQ*, 46 (1977), 241–62.
   The key to Jean de Meun's design lies in the speculum tradition — not that of Vincent of Beauvais, but rather Nigel Longchamps' *Speculum Stultorum*, where the glass distorts the image for multiple effects. Eberle discusses Grosseteste's optical treatise on rainbows and mirrors and the prominence of optics as a thirteenth-century topic, which she relates to discussions of Narcissus and the poet. Jean says the poet copies nature 'like a monkey'; Jean's technique is akin to that of a Cubist painter who creates 'the illusion of simultaneous perceptions from a multiplicity of perspectives,' the work being confusing 'until one has learned to "see" it with the artist's multiple perspectives in mind' (pp 255–56). Seneca tells of the scandalous Hostius Quadra, who contrived a chamber of mirrors which distorted the size of things to enhance his sexual pleasures; the mirrors may enhance pleasures, but they may also enhance moral insights, through their same distortions. Jean's *Mirouer aus Amoureus* 'is a complex glass through

which all aspects of Guillaume's love-vision are revealed so fully that nothing whatever remains hidden. The result is a poem that is not a unity in traditional terms, but one that is cohesive and complex, an optical glass of poetry that gives to the mind's eye of any reader who understands the instrument's design a multiplicity of perspectives on that oldest and newest of subjects, endlessly fascinating to man in all ages, love' (p 260).

99 Economou, George D. 'Januarie's Sin Against Nature: The *Merchant's Tale* and the *Roman de la Rose.' CL*, 17 (1965), 251–57.
Argues that the comparison of Januarie's 'heigh fantasy' to a polished mirror set in a market place (lines 1577–88) reflects narcissistic mirrors in *RR* rather than (as Robinson suggests) *Boece*.

100 — 'The Character of Genius in Alan de Lille, Jean de Meun, and John Gower.' *ChauR*, 4 (1970), 203–10.
We cannot fully understand the Genius figures in these poems unless we consider them in light of the tradition of the Goddess Natura. In Alan, Genius is a kind of double to Natura insofar as he shares with her 'those features which pertain to her as *procreatrix* of the sublunary world' (p 205). Jean expands Genius' role to that of confessor as well as priest and official spokesman of Natura. 'The Christian cosmological and moral conception of sexual love as it is expressed in Alan is assigned to the character Reason rather than to Natura and Genius ... [Moreover] Natura and Genius in the *Roman* represent the procreative instinct without reference to the institution of marriage or a thorough awareness of Christian morality' (p 206). No apologies are necessary for Jean, however. 'It makes just as good sense for a Genius who is almost obsessed with unrestrained sexuality to fear chastity as it does for the same Genius who is the advocate of a Natura stripped of her traditional association with reason to fail to see that the real enemy is not man's chastity but his cupidity, his desire to enjoy sex as an end in itself rather than as a means to the divinely ordained end that Genius and his mistress serve' (p 207). Gower follows Jean's placement of Genius in the service of Venus.

101 — *The Goddess Natura in Medieval Literature*. Cambridge, Mass.: Harvard University Press, 1972.
Ch 1, 'Philosophical Background,' pp 1–27; Ch 2, 'Boethius and the Poetic Background,' pp 28–52, with subsections on Pseudo-John Scotus Eriugena and William of Conches, The Poetic Natura in the *Consolatio*, the Orphic Hymn to Physis, Statius, and Claudian (see also **301**); Ch 3, 'The Latin Middle Ages: Bernardus Silvestris and Alan of Lille,' pp 53–103; Ch 4, 'Jean de Meun,' pp 104–24, emphasizing links with Alan of Lille; Ch 5, 'Chaucer's *Parlement of Foules*,' pp 125–50, with an Appendix summarizing Bernard Silvestris'

De Mundi Universitate; and a bibliography. Economou surveys the
scholarship on the subject of Nature in *RR*, and emphasizes that Jean
takes two qualities of Alan's Nature and divides them between his
Natura, who becomes exclusively a personification of the God-given
reproductive power, and Raison, who teaches a doctrine of natural
love. 'Jean de Meun's vision of Natura as procreatrix who gives man
his sexual but not his rational power, who struggles against Death in
order to ensure continuity to God's creatures in the mutable world,
who finds man's unwillingness to obey her law regrettable and
offensive, and who regards chastity and abstinence with suspicion and
fear, is the result of the poet's careful and deliberate modification of
the figure handed down to him by Alan and other writers. In
humanizing the august goddess of the twelfth-century poet and in
limiting her moral sphere to demand for fruitful procreation, Jean
produces a strikingly novel figure of Natura' (p 123).

102 — 'The Two Venuses and Courtly Love.' In *In Pursuit of Perfection:
Courtly Love in Medieval Literature*. Ed. Joan M. Ferrante and George
D. Economou. Port Washington, New York: Kennikat Press, 1975. Pp
17–50.
Poets like Alanus de Insulis and Bernardus Silvestris depict original
man enjoying sexual love without harm in his state of innocent
perfection. After the fall such innocence is possible only through
divine grace. Nonetheless, 'sexual or earthly love was not simply sinful
luxuria or *cupiditas*; no matter how far it might have departed from its
original dignity and nobility, this love — like every aspect of man's
nature — had its purpose under providence and credentials from Eden'
(p 19). This duality in love is reflected in the double Venus figure of
medieval mythology. The idea is not exclusively medieval, however: cf
Ovid's *Fasti* and Pythagorean writings of antiquity. John Scotus was
one of the first medieval authors to write on the subject: 'There are
two Venuses, one the goddess of pleasure, ie, a lustful one, whose son is
Hermaphroditus, and another chaste one who was Vulcan's wife. Thus
there is a love that is chaste and one that is shameful' (p 21).
Economou discusses the double tradition in poetry of the twelfth
through fourteenth centuries: *RR, PF, CA*, Chretien's *Yvain*,
Wolfram's *Parzival*, Gottfried's *Tristan*, and *T&C*. The anticourtly
attitudes in *RR* stem in part from Alanus (p 25) and are shared by
Chaucer. 'From the outset, the *Roman de la Rose* is a poem about
adulterous love, which means that only one Venus will play an active
role, a fact which Guillaume makes clear by making Jocus and Amor
the lords of the Garden of Deduit' (p 29).

103 Elliot, Ralph W.V. 'Chaucer's Reading.' In *Chaucer's Mind and Art*.
Ed. Arthur C. Cawley. London and Edinburgh: Oliver and Boyd,

1969. Pp 46–68.

'To one nurtured, as Chaucer was, on the *Roman de la Rose* and the love-visions of other medieval poets, the dream was the obvious portal into the world of courtly allegory in which the whole traditional "machinery" of *fine amour* could be brought to life in settings both sufficiently close to, and sufficiently removed from, the world of real love and sex and *harlotrie*, for the connexions between them to remain palpable without being too insistent' (p 57).

104   Faral, Edmond. '*Le Roman de la Rose* et la pensée française au XIIIe siècle.' *Revue des deux mondes*, 35 (1926), 430–57.
Sees Jean as a philosophical poet whose ideas are pervaded by the naturalism of Bernardus Silvestris and Alain de Lille and the school of Chartres. Jean is not a skeptic but a Christian of the faith who preaches ' une sort de religion étrange' with 'un enthousiasme de prophète qu'il le rappelle de ses égarements pour lui remettre en mémoire la volonté de la nature. Et cette attitude a sa grandeur' (p 443). Comments on Jean's antifeminism and the 'querelle' a century after Jean's death.

105   Fenley, G. Ward. 'Faus-Semblant, Fauvel, and Renart le Contrefait: A Study in Kinship.' *RR*, 23 (1932), 323–31.
Jean de Meun establishes a literary type with his religious hypocrite Faus-Semblant, who culminates, after many permutations, in Tartuffe. Faus-Semblant set the fashion to be copied closely by Fauvel and Renart, 'a trio created for the special task of fighting the wrongs of their time' (p 331).

106   Ferster, Judith Ilana. 'Chaucer and l'Art Véritable: The Epistemology of Art in Two Early Dream Visions and Two of their French Sources.' Brown University Dissertation, 1974. Dir. Elizabeth Kirk. See also *DAI*, 35 (1975), 7253A–7254A.
Ferster examines *BD* and *PF* in conjunction with *RR* and Alanus' *De Planctu Naturae* to show that Chaucer uses his sources not merely to borrow individual wordings and conventions, but to develop poetic theory and practice based on the subjectivity of perception, the idea that all perceived nature is 'artful' in that it is ordered through the process by which it is perceived, observed, and described. Chaucer plays off various perceptions of art works from the literary tradition that preceded him. Such a theory of fiction implied by *BD* and *PF* 'must make critics wary of naive description of Chaucer's naturalism.'

107   Fisher, John H. 'Chaucer and the French Influence.' In *New Perspectives in Chaucer Criticism*. Ed. Donald L. Rose. Norman, Oklahoma: Pilgrim Press, 1981. Pp 177–91.
Reviews the question of Chaucer's Frenchness as opposed to his Englishness. 'Chaucer could not have written the poetry he did or

have had the influence he has had were it not that he naturalized in English a new poetic mode and language' (p 178). Fisher comments on Chaucer's prosody, rhythms, and French vocabulary. 'Chaucer's idiom and music are based upon the French model. Whether or not he ever wrote poetry in French, he must have understood very well the principles both of the French language and of French prosody, and he was able to create on the same principles a completely harmonious and idiomatic equivalent in English' (p 191). Comments on *RR* in conjunction with persona and dream vision.

108 Fleming, John V. 'The Moral Reputation of the *Roman de la Rose* Before 1400.' *RPh*, 18 (1965), 430–35.
Fleming supports Pierre Col's view in the early fifteenth century *Querelle* on the morality of *RR* by arguing that it escaped reproach for a hundred years before its alleged evils were exposed. The initial publication of Jean's poem caused no furor. Even Étienne Tempier, who was 'a liberal condemner,' does not mention the *Roman*. 'On the other hand, there is significant evidence to show that his work was warmly approved in morally conservative circles throughout the 14th century' (p 435).

109 — *The Roman de la Rose: A Study in Allegory and Iconography.* Princeton: Princeton University Press, 1969.
To exemplify 'that interpretation of the *Roman de la Rose* enjoyed by its urbane readers at the apex of its popularity in the fourteenth century' (p 3), Fleming explores the work's 'moult noble doctrine,' rooted in Boethius, Jean's own *Testament*, and various classical and patristic writers. 'A wealth of neglected manuscript materials,' particularly marginal glosses and illuminations, add to a 'medieval reading' of the poem. 'In many illuminated manuscripts of the Middle Ages the illustrations are more than merely decorative. There is an intimate relationship between the painted picture and the written text' (p 12). The illuminations 'form a gloss in pictures even as the Latin commentary is a gloss in words' (p 12). Fleming thus comments on visual puns as well as verbal ones. He makes frequent references to Chaucer's use of *RR*, though offers nothing specifically on his translation of the poem. Fleming's argument considers 'Text and Glose,' 'The Hortus Deliciarum,' 'Love's Preceptors,' and 'Natural and Unnatural Nature'; he includes forty-two plates of mss illuminations of the poem, many of which are English in provenance.

- Review by Alfred David, *ELN*, 9 (1971), 134–39. Questions the congruence of significant detail that Fleming sees between illuminations and the poetic text. Argues that readers of *RR* like Froissart and Machaut are more 'urbane' than the occasional reader who added moralistic glosses to ms margins. 'To rely on this sort of unimaginative "moral paraphrase" is not the best way to understand a great poem' (p 138). Finds Fleming's sense of the poem's irony to be heavy-handed. Amant is a foolish lover, but not to be taken seriously as a seducer or candidate for hell. 'He is neither a Lancelot nor a Socrates, but he sincerely loves his rose as most ordinary men set their hearts on a mortal object. Without finding anything heretical or particularly modern, one can read Jean's conclusion as showing the lover following not the path of deadly sin but the way of all flesh' (p 138). David would emphasize the poem's comic, Rabelaisian spirit.

110   — 'A Poetic Gambit in the *Roman de la Rose*.' *RPh* 33 (1980), 518–22.
Fleming discusses Jean de Meun's borrowing of a chess-fortune metaphor from Henry of Septimellos' *Elegia*, a metaphor which Chaucer in turn uses in his writing.

110a   — *Reason and The Lover*. Princeton: Princeton University Press, 1984.
Fleming defends Reason as the one voice within the poem to which the reader can confidently listen for the moral adjudication of the poem's doctrine. In Ch 1, 'The Lineage of Lady Reason,' pp 3–63, Fleming wittily rebukes the 'Ithacan heretics' (Michael Cherniss, Winthrop Wetherbee, Carol Kaske, and Thomas Hill), who emphasize the comic limitations of Reason's powers of understanding, to insist instead that Lady Reason, 'the image of the sapiential Christ in man, and the mirror of *sapientia* in the created world' (p 30), provides (or could provide) the Lover with what he needs if he is to maintain himself in his proper paradise. Jean's characterization of Reason differs from Alain's. She is the inventress of language. Her literary lineage derives from Boethius, the first three thousand lines of Jean's poem being 'an extended "parody" of the *Consolatio*, with Reason cast as Philosophia and Amant as Boethius' (p 40). Although there are parallels with the rich twelfth-century tradition of Old Girls such as Natura, Phronesis, and Theologica, Jean's Raison is a *Ratio* figure, similar in conception to Peter Compostella's *De Consolatione Rationis*, a fourteenth-century Boethian redaction which blends ideas from Augustine's *De libero arbitrio* in presenting Reason. In assessing Jean's Raison, we should look to books which inspired Boethius, not simply those which he influenced. Fleming discusses in detail the Christian context of Boethius' *Consolatio* (pp 41–63); 'Boethius fairly reeks of Augustine' (p 47), particularly with the ideas and rhetoric of *De Soliloquia*. Ch 2, 'Looking for Love in Carthage,' pp 64–96, links *RR* directly with Augustine's dialogues in the Ciceronian mode, a mode which demands strenuous readers who are willing to discover truth through reading (p

66). *RR* is 'a poem of contexts; every part of it explains, qualifies, illuminates another part' (p 67). 'Supertexts' like Boethius' *Consolatio*, Cicero's *De amicitia*, and various writings of Augustine perpetually hover about it. In this respect Jean is like Chaucer who is *always* translating an anterior text. 'Jean's French *Boece* is one way he "handles" the *Consolatio*; the central metaphor of the *Roman de la Rose* is another. Chaucer's actual translation of the *Roman* we do not have, yet we see him "translating" Jean de Meun on virtually every page he wrote' (p 70). In savoring the ironies of Jean's treatments of friendship Fleming discusses Aelred of Rievaulx's Ciceronian *De spirituali amicitia*, a humanistic text translated by Jean. Jean's allusions to *amor sauvage* and Carthage (*RR*, Lecoy 5346–48) derive from Augustine's *Confessions*, which shares an 'overarching generic kinship' with *RR*. 'Carthaginian love' might be a better term than the procrustean 'courtly love' to explain 'the amatory mysteries of medieval poems' (pp 95–96). Ch 3, 'Words and Things,' pp 97–135, explores the gap between Reason's ability to deal with facts as opposed to the Lover's, all of which is tied up with sign theory on the nature of language. Jean uses Guillaume's rules on pure speech as grafting staddle for more subtle issues. The exchange on language between Reason and the Lover is orchestrated around central themes of Jean's 'silent supertext, the *De magistro* of St. Augustine' (p 103). Fleming discusses the amusing incongruities of the Lover's literalism, his confusion of evil deeds with words, and Jean's practice of mislabeling, whether in the interplay of notions of *voluptas, concupiscentia, libido, cupiditas*, or *delit*, the distorting of Virgil or Ovid, or, like Lactantius, the quoting of the Bible and calling it Cicero, or the amusing dragging of 'Socrates' swan' into the discussion of dreams, dream images, and the understanding of figural revelations to show that 'a *cigne* is a *signe*' (pp 128–29). Ch 4, 'Augustinus and Franciscus,' pp 136–83, speculates on the intertextuality of *RR* and Petrarch's *Secretum*, a dialogue which is really 'a spiritual autobiography, classical dialogue, essay in ascetical theology, and emblem of Petrarch's lifelong quarrel with himself' presented as 'a debate between Reason and the Lover' (p 145). The common denominator between *RR* and the *Secretum* is Augustine, along with Boethius, whom Petrarch claimed he read 'not once but a thousand times' (p 175). But despite the debts to Boethius and Augustine, 'I cannot think that the *Secretum* would be as it is were it not for Jean de Meun' (pp 175–76).

11 Frank, Robert Worth, Jr. 'The Art of Reading Medieval Personification-Allegory.' *ELH*, 20 (1953), 237–50.
Differentiates between Dante's 'symbol-allegory' and Langland's 'personification-allegory.' *RR* is personification-allegory, though it uses

symbols. Frank considers various kinds of personification in *RR* (pp 246–48) and the weakness of the case for imposing fourfold interpretation upon personification-allegory (p 249). 'If the reader ... will remember that personification-allegory is primarily designed to make the meaning explicit and is very close to the literal in its statement, the form *as form* will cause him little difficulty' (p 250).

112 Friedman, Albert B. 'Jean de Meun an Englishman?' *MLN*, 65 (1950), 319–25.
Early literary historians — Leland, Bale, Pits, Oldmixon, Rymer, Warton — confuse Jean de Meun and John Moon, thus making the author of *RR* an Englishman who was a student at Paris.

113 Friedman, Lionel J. ' "Jean de Meung," Antifeminism, and "Bourgeois Realism," ' *MP*, 57 (1959), 13–23.
After demonstrating that the antifeminist and bourgeois sentiments of jealous husbands in *RR* are commonplaces in Ovid and the stock characters of romances and patristic writings, Friedman concludes that it is doubtful that such material reflects Jean's personal opinions. The common misconception that it does is 'homage to the remarkable comic talent of Jean de Meung and his extraordinary capacity for incarnating abstractions and revitalizing moral precepts in so personal a form that modern scholars have been deceived to "maken ernest of game" ' (p 23).

114 — 'Gradus Amoris.' *RPh*, 19 (1965), 167–77.
Friedman traces five successive stages of the medieval love process — *visus, alloquium, contactus, asculum,* and *factum* — from Horace and Ovid to the Latin elegiac comedies of the twelfth and thirteenth centuries, noting variations in the scheme by Matthew of Vêndome (six stages) and Andreas Capellanus (four stages), who is followed by Drouart la Vache, Baudouin de Condé, and others. 'Thus, to flatter Guillaume de Lorris as the inventor of the "psychological" novel, to extol him for a fine, minute analysis of the genesis and evolution of the feeling of love, to wax ecstatic over the delicacy of his insights' may be misguided; 'without wishing to detract from a merited reputation, I submit that the basic progression of the psychologic narrative in his portion of the *Roman de la Rose* is anything but original. He merely leads the lover up four or five of the steps already analyzed' (p 174).

114a Giamatti, A. Bartlett. *The Earthly Paradise and the Renaissance Epic.* Princeton: Princeton University Press, 1966.
'The image of the earthly paradise haunts the *Roman de la Rose*, and the *Roman* haunts the literature of the succeeding centuries. Its allegories, its landscapes, its visions of love earthly and divine, left an indelible mark upon the imagination of the West' (p 66). The two gardens of *RR* forecast the situations of most later Medieval and

Renaissance literary gardens which combine philosophic and courtly traditions (pp 60–66). Though the second, recalled by Genius at the end, is the true Garden of Eden, in the first, the dreamer only *thinks* he is in paradise. 'That the garden of the Rose even resembles the earthly paradise only makes it more misleading and ultimately more worthy of condemnation' (p 66).

114b Gilson, Étienne. *Dante the Philosopher.* New York: Sheed & Ward, 1949.
'When people tell us that "the *Roman de la Rose* ought to be studied here as Dante Alighieri is studied in the institutes of Rome and Tuscany," they are simply and solely confusing art with philology. When Jean de Meun chances to tell us of Charlemagne, Abelard and Heloise, we fall greedily upon these drops of water in his desert of allegories, but Slander, Giving-Too-Much and Mad Bounty soon reassert their rights, and Jean's few profoundly human lines on Guillaume de Lorris and on himself are quickly buried beneath the chatter of Fear, Shame, Danger, and Hypocrisy. The adventures of these proper names leave us cold and we no longer read what they say because it is completely and utterly insipid, but we shall always read Dante because the *Divine Comedy* is the story of a living being in the midst of other living beings and, among these living beings, there is none more real than Beatrice' (p 73).

115 Goldin, Frederick. *The Mirror of Narcissus in the Courtly Love Lyric.* Ithaca: Cornell University Press, 1967.
Discusses Narcissus in *RR* (pp 52–68). Why does the dreamer escape the fate of Narcissus in *RR?* 'The answer is precisely that he knows the story of Narcissus' (p 54), and that it is necessary for him to love another. Still he falls victim to love at the *miroers perilleus,* which leaves the beholder with nothing but 'the irresistible desire to love' (p 56). Courtly love begins in the Fountain of Narcissus (p 58). Goldin comments on similarities of treatment of Narcissus by Jean de Meun and *OM.*

116 Gunn, Alan M.F. *The Mirror of Love: A Reinterpretation of the Romance of the Rose.* Lubbock, Texas: Texas Tech Press, 1951.
Gunn argues the essential unity of the two parts of *RR* in terms of the basic goodness of natural love. The purpose of the entire work is to create a mirror of love. Its theme is love and all its ramifications, from copulation to cosmic principles. For Guillaume the lore is an art and a discipline; for Jean it is a duty to God and Nature. Gunn sets his argument in opposition to that of C.S. Lewis **132**, to praise Jean de Meun's achievement in developing a medieval psychology of love by means of the rhetorical device of amplification. Gunn divides his argument as follows: *Bk I. The Critics and the Allegory*: i. Chaos or

Cosmos? ii. The Theme is Love. *Bk II. The Rhetoric of the Rose*: i.
The Two-fold Design; ii. 'Toute est pour enseignement'; iii. The
Branching Tree of Rhetoric; iv. Guillaume's Garden of Delight; v. The
'Lay Process' of Jean de Meun. *Bk III. The Unity of the Rose*: i.
Discourses of Love; ii. The Quest of the Rose. *Bk IV. The Fount of
Generation*: i. The 'Significatio' of Jean de Meun; ii. The Philosophy
of Plenitude; iii. The Regeneration of Man; iv. Youth's Entelechy; v. A
World of Myth and Symbol. *Bk V. The Grand Debate*: i. Symposium
of Love; ii. Masters of Love's Art and Theory; iii. The Clash of
Doctrine; iv. The Judgment of Nature. *Bk VI. The Sources of
Conflict*; i. Of Many Minds about Love; ii. 'Questions D'Amour'; iii.
Youth's 'Psychomachia'; iv. The Medieval 'Conflictus.' *Bk VII. The
Judgment of the Rose*: i. For a Reversal of Judgment; ii. The Final
Issues. Appendix: Figures of Amplification.

- Review by C.S. Lewis, *MAE*, 22 (1953), 27–31: 'This long, but
  never tedious, book has the charm of being written by an
  enthusiast. Professor Gunn loves the *Roman de la Rose*' (p 27).
  Lewis finds the argument on unity to be the weakest feature of
  the book, though its thesis 'that all the apparent ramblings of
  Jean de Meun conform to the rules of *amplificatio*' is strong and
  'in my opinion' successful (p 27). The same might be said of
  Dante's *Commedia*, though the end result is very different.
  'Gunn's case [for unity] depends mainly on connexions which Jean
  de Meun has never mentioned ... He believes that Jean de Meun
  "makes use of suggestion and indirection, of symbolic rather than
  logical reference, of foreshadowing and repetition and variation
  and contrast of significant images and apologues" ... in fact, of a
  method rather like that of the symphony' (p 29). Lewis wonders
  if Jean could really have been quite so like a modern *symboliste* as
  Gunn's theory demands, or even have understood the theory
  Gunn propounds. Most objectionable, however, is Gunn's
  proposition that Jean is wholly serious about the 'doctrine of
  copulation' as chief duty and obligation of every human, a chief
  concern of God, and chief manifestation of the goodness, love,
  and overflowing bounty of God. What of the divine bounty of the
  Passion? Lewis asks. 'That any man of European stock could
  have thought thus before the twentieth century is to me
  incredible. Such ideas seem to me to belong wholly to a modern
  monistic outlook in which biological values are primary. But Jean
  de Meun is not monistic: his Nature herself tells us that there is a
  part in every man which is not of her making' (p 30).

- Review by Urban Tigner Holmes, Jr, *MLQ*, 14 (1953), 465–67:
  Holmes emphasizes the value of Gunn's theory of *amplificatio*,

which incorporates such devices as *ratiocinatio, occupatio, expeditio, translatio,* and *gradatio.* When these principles of medieval rhetoric are taken fully into account it will be discovered that Jean de Meun did not willfully introduce irrelevant material. 'We wish for Dr. Gunn that he could have possessed that beautiful style and limpid prose of his intellectual adversary, C.S. Lewis. The importance of this book for medieval thought in general will be considerable' (p 467).

117 Hill, Thomas D. 'La Vieille's Digression on Free Love: A Note on Rhetorical Structure in the *Romance of the Rose,*' *Romance Notes,* 8 (1966), 113–15.
La Vieille tells the story of Venus and Mars to the point where the lovers are trapped, then digresses on the virtues of free love. The digression suggests an ironic parallel between Venus and La Vieille. Venus is one who binds but who also is bound, who catches otherwise rational persons in her chain yet is herself caught. Such is the pattern of La Vieille's life as she tells it to Bel Acueil. That she repeats the pattern as she digresses in her own autobiography suggests that the pattern is significant and that Jean's poem is less disorganized than some have argued.

118 — 'Narcissus, Pygmalion, and the Castration of Saturn: Two Mythological Themes in the *Roman de la Rose.*' *SP,* 71 (1974), 404–26. The Narcissus and Pygmalion exempla are complementary in a crucial way: the lover in *RR* is both an example of lust and folly and a man who achieves the good and natural end of sexuality, that is, the conceiving of a child. Sexuality in the course of the poem is thus 'a profoundly paradoxical and ambivalent phenomenon' (p 426). The castration of Saturn is linked with the fall (p 418). Venus also represents fallen human sexuality, though she remains 'a necessary aspect of the post-lapsarian world, since Venus enables man to perpetuate himself' despite the fact that she is 'autonomous and irrational' (p 420). *Raison* is not *sapientia,* though she is 'created by God for man, and man's highest gift' (p 421). All are employed by Jean to define human sexuality, which is the subject of his poem.

118a Ineichen, G. 'Le Discours linguistique de Jean de Meun.' *Romanistiche Zeitschrift für Literaturgeschichte,* 2 (1978), 245–53. 'The most illuminating treatment of Jean's "linguistics" ' (Fleming, 110a, p 104, n. 4).

119 Jauss, Hans Robert, with Uda Ebel. 'Entstehen und Strukturwandel der allegorischen Dichtung.' In *La Littérature didactique, allégorique, et satirique.* Ed. Hans Robert Jauss. *Grundriss der romanischen Literaturen des Mittelalters.* Vol 6, tome 1. Heidelberg, 1968. Bibliography, Vol 6, tome 2. Heidelberg, 1970.

'The full bibliography ... should be the starting point for any investigation of medieval French allegory' (Barney 82, p 212).

120 Jauss, Hans Robert. 'La Transformation de la forme allégorique entre 1180 et 1240: D'Alain de Lille à Guillaume de Lorris.' In *L'Humanisme Médiéval dans les Littératures Romanes du XIIe au XIVe Siècle*. Ed. Anthime Fourrier. Actes et Colloques, 3. Le Centre de Philologie et de Littératures romanes de Université de Strasbourg, 1962. Paris: C. Klincksieck, 1964. Pp 107–44.

Using twenty-six allegorical poems, arranged chronologically from Bernardus Silvestris' *De Universitate Mundi* to Richart de Fournival's *Le Bestiaire d'Amour*, Jauss traces changes in allegorical forms deriving originally from Prudentius' *Psychomachia*, with special reference throughout to Guillaume de Lorris' *RR*.

121 Jung, Marc-René. 'Der Rosenroman in der Kritik seit dem 18. Jahrhundert.' *RF*, 78 (1966), 203–52.

An introductory essay on main currents in twentieth-century *RR* criticism, with an annotated bibliography of 82 items.

122 — *Études sur le poème allégorique en France au moyen âge*. Berne: A. Franke, 1971.

An historical preface to Guillaume's *RR*, with discussions of the terminology of allegory; Prudentius' *Psychomachia*; Martianus Capella; Bernard Silvestris and Alain de Lille; adaptations of the *Anticlaudianus*; troubadour lyrics; Boethius' *Philosophia*; twelfth-century personification and monologue dialogues; God of Love debate poems like *Phillis et Flora, Le Concile de Remirement, Le Jugement d'Amour, Hueline et Aiglantine, Blancheflour et Florence, Melior et Ydoine, Le Fable du dieu d'Amour, De Venus la deesse d'Amour*; religious allegorical poems, the four daughters of God poems, and the poetry of Guillaume le Clerc, Guiot de Brevins, Raoul de Houclenc, the *Songe de Paradis*, the recluse of Molliens, and Huon de Méry. In the final chapter, 'L'allégorie de l'amour,' pp 290–325, Jung discusses such features of Guillaume de Lorris' *RR* as 'allégorie statique' and 'allégorie dynamique,' 'l'innamoramente,' 'les commandements d'amour,' and 'l'allégorie du château,' with concluding remarks on Thibaut's *Roman de la Poire* and the anonymous *La Complainte d'amour* of BN ms fr 837.

123 Kelly, Douglas. *Medieval Imagination: Rhetoric and the Poetry of Courtly Love*. Madison, Wisconsin: University of Wisconsin Press, 1978.

The cognitive function *vis imaginativa* is 'an explicit feature of invention and composition for the Chartrian poets, the medieval arts of poetry, and medieval French literature from the thirteenth century on' (p ix). Imagination 'governs the invention, retention, and expression of Images in the mind; it also designates the artist's Image, projected as it were into matter' (p xii). Invention is both a *skille* and *demonstracion* of Imagination. *RR* is one of Kelly's principal texts for exemplifying medieval Imagination. Ch 4, 'Guillaume de Lorris and Imagination in the *Roman de la Rose*,' pp 57–95, discusses medieval dream theory and image making with special attention given to the Images on the wall and inside the Garden of Deduit and to the poet's use of amplification as a compositional device to realize the potential within the Images through *interpretatio, expolitio, oppositio* and other subforms of amplification. 'The garden is ... neither narrative nor psychological analysis. The purpose of the amplification is entirely rhetorical: the evocation of joy through the qualities prerequisite to noble love ... The reader is not expected to analyze the joy or to appreciate a presumptive psychoanalysis of the author or anyone else. Rather he should open himself to the topical suggestiveness of the Image, by anticipation desire the joy and the qualities that are its essence, and, figuratively, seek out the source of the joy that animates the personifications during and after the carol' (p 82). The latter part of the chapter (pp 85 ff) is devoted to 'the Allegorical Narrative: the Fountain of Narcissus and the Rose.' Other chapters in Kelly's discussion include 'Guillaume de Machaut and the Sublimation of Courtly Love in Imagination,' 'Imagination in the Writings of Jean Froissart,' 'Verisimilitude and Imagination: The Crisis in Late Courtly Poetry,' and 'Imagination in the Poetry of Charles d'Orléans and René d'Anjou.'

124 Knopp, Sherron. 'Chaucer and Jean de Meun as Self-Conscious Narrators: The Prologue to the *Legend of Good Women* and the *Roman de la Rose*, 10307–10680.' *Comitatus*, 4 (1973), 25–39.
Better than any of the French love poems, *RR* 'explains the distinctive character and temper of Chaucer's Prologue' (p 27). Both Jean and Chaucer 'violate courtly expectations about the art of love. Both insist on viewing love in its broadest dimensions, unlimited by a restricting code ... Jean transcends the courtly while Chaucer undermines it, but they meet on the same planes of meaning. And it is the self-conscious narrative voice which constitutes the focal point and creates the comedy in both works' (p 37).

125 Koeppel, E. 'Jehan de Meung.' *Anglia*, 14 (1891–92), 238–67.
Identifies parallel passages between *RR* and *BD, AA, KnT, T&C, HF, FA, Boece, Fortune, Gent, LGW, GP, ReeveT, WBP, WBT, FriarT, SumT, MerchT, SqT, FrankT, PhysT, MonkT, MancT*. Also cites parallels between *Le Testament de Maistre Jehan de Meung* and *ReeveP, WBP, MonkP, SumT, PhysT, T&C*, and *MLT*.

125a Köhler, Erich. 'Narcisse, la Fontaine d'Amour et Guillaume de Lorris.'

Journal des Savants. Paris: Klincksieck, 1963. Pp 86–103. Rpt. in *L'Humanisme Médiéval dans les Littératures Romanes du XIIe au XIVe Siècle,* Ed. A. Fourrier. Paris: C. Klincksieck, 1964. Pp 147–66. Köhler explores the magic of the Lover's encounter with the fountain of Narcissus, a fountain of love where the two crystals suggest not simply his own eyes but the transforming power of the lady's eyes. The scene differs from Jean de Meun's garden with its single carbuncle of Divine Love. In Guillaume the two crystals are like mirrors through which an illusion of self, self-knowledge, innocence, and the courtly bliss of a golden age seem temporarily true, albeit defined through the other and still in the dying world. Guillaume utilizes knowledge of medieval crystalmancy and hydromancy for powerful effect in his fusing of mirror, crystal, fountain, Narcissus, and love concepts to establish a motif Dante will draw on in the eyes of Beatrice, whose magical streams help purify the one they bless. ' "Les vrais paradis sont les paradis perdus," a dit quelque part Marcel Proust. Guillaume de Lorris les a retrouvés, ces paradis de l'enfance innocente de l'humanité, du moins dans le rêve et dans la poésie indéniable de son oeuvre' (p 103).

126 Kuhn, Alfred. 'Die Illustration des *Rosenromans.*' *Jahrbuch der Kunsthistorischen Sammlungen der allerhöchsten Kaiserhauses,* 31 (Vienna, 1913–14), 1–66.
I have not seen this item. According to Luria (**136**, p 245) it is 'a pioneering study (though flawed by errors) of the ms illustrations, containing fifteen plates and forty-five text figures.'

127 Langlois, Ernest. *Origines et Sources du Roman de la Rose.* Bibliothèque des écoles françaises d'Athènes et de Rome, 58. Paris: Ernest Thorin, 1891.
Langlois approaches the sources of *RR* topically, culturally, and by rhetorical catagories as well as through specific authors. He treats first Guillaume (pp 1–92), then Jean de Meun (pp 93–190).

128 — *Les manuscrits du Roman de la Rose, description et classement.* Travaux et mémoires de l'Université de Lille. Nouvelle série, I. Droit et lettres, vol 7. Lille: Tallandier, 1910.
Part I catalogs and describes 215 mss which are arranged by location (pp 1–212). Langlois also lists other works included in the mss (pp 213–18) and identifies known copyists (p 219) and owners of mss (pp 219–27). Part II discusses the classification of *RR* mss and on the basis of 116 mss sets out two main groups with several variants (pp 235–523).

129 Lazar, Moshé. *Amour Courtois et Fin' Amors dans la littérature du XIIe siècle.* Bibliothèque française et romane. Series C, VIII. Paris: C. Klincksieck, 1964.

A useful background study of *l'amour courtois* in troubadour lyrics, *Tristan*, the romances of Chrétien de Troyes, the *lais* of Marie de France, and in Andreas Capellanus.

130 Legouis, Emile. *Geoffrey Chaucer*. Trans. L. Lailavoix. London: J. Dent and Sons, 1913. Rpt New York: Russell and Russell, 1961. Originally published Paris, 1910.

Ch 2, 'Making of Chaucer as a Poet,' pp 48–61: After discussing the state of the English Language ca 1360, Legouis turns to Chaucer at the school of the French trouvères. 'The influence which the *Roman de la Rose* had on Chaucer should certainly not be reduced to a mere stylistic training. This romance ... was really the one poem which had the most constant hold on Chaucer'; it was 'a sort of poetic Bible' for him (p 54) which helped him but also hindered him: 'It led him to adopt and to retain for many years the allegorical style' (p 55).

131 Leonard, Frances McNeely. *Laughter in the Courts of Love: Comedy in Allegory, from Chaucer to Spenser*. Norman, Oklahoma: Pilgrim Books, 1981.

Ch 2, 'Chaucer's Comic Visions,' pp 27–56, discusses *RR* as 'a model for Chaucer' (pp 30–3). 'The *Roman* is an extravagant comedy about man triumphing in his belief that he can disturb the universe to gratify his own desires, a triumph he achieves by casting out his own reason and impiously conferring a spiritual significance upon his lust' (p 32). Leonard comments on Jean's use of parody, satire, and farce. Chaucer finds in *RR* character types, ways to turn anticlerical sentiment into poetry, techniques of unconscious self-revelation, and ways of using dream vision as a framework for structuring the contents of his poetry.

132 Lewis, C.S. *The Allegory of Love*. Oxford: Oxford University Press, 1936.

Ch 3, 'The Romance of the Rose,' pp 112–56, remains one of the most influential discussions of *RR*. Lewis emphasizes the 'real life' qualities of Guillaume's allegory. In explaining Guillaume's method Lewis notes its utility: 'A man need not go to the Middle Ages to discover that his mistress is many women as well as one, and that sometimes the woman he hoped to meet is replaced by a very different woman ' (p 118). Lewis explores setting, character, and progress of plot. Of the Middle English translation of Guillaume's portion he writes: 'We are fortunate to have a complete text of it —in part possibly by Chaucer — in fourteenth-century English; a version which lacks, to some extent, the plashing fluidity of the original, and which makes the poem in places racier and more pointed, less gentle and equable, than it really is. There is a quality in the best Old French which Gower alone among the English has approached. No poetry could be more tranquil, more pellucid. It has a winning and unobtrusive way which the harder-hitting style and deeper-chested voice of English cannot reproduce. Ours is "all instruments"; theirs is the "lonely flute." I labour the point because it is this side of the original which necessarily escapes my analysis. While we talk of psychology and of the conduct of the story, the reader must try to remember that all this story is conveyed in a medium that is nearly perfect; that the bright beauty of the scenes depicted and the wistfulness (it is hardly pathos) of many speeches would make the poem worth reading for their sakes alone. And few poets have struck better than Guillaume de Lorris that note which is the peculiar charm of medieval love poetry — that boy-like blending (or so it seems) of innocence and sensuousness which could make us believe for a moment that paradise had never been lost' (p 135). The sentimental novel originates in Guillaume. More than Boccaccio he is the source of Chaucer's Criseyde. Lewis cares less for Jean's contribution. 'One thing that he is not is an allegorist' (p 137). 'His *significacio* is hardly worth the finding' (p 138). His great digression lacks unity not because it is medieval but because it is not well-constructed. 'It was the misfortune of Jean de Meun to have read and remembered everything and nothing that he remembered could be kept out of his poem' (p 151). Lewis notes the philosophic relationship of Jean's poem with Boethius and finds his blending of materials useful and pleasant. Jean is 'profoundly dissatisfied with the erotic tradition' (p 146). He shows himself most a true poet 'when he touches on the idea of eternity — of all metaphysical ideas the richest in poetic suggestion' (p 153). Yet 'Jean has no final view of love or anything else.' His ideas were 'capable of fusion, but he could not fuse them' (p 154). In his 'formlessness' he remains a subject only for professional scholars, and not very many of them (p 155).

133 Longo, John Duane. 'Literary Appropriation as *Translatio* in Chaucer and the *Roman de la Rose*.' Princeton University Dissertation. Dir. John V. Fleming. See also *DAI*, 42 (1982), 4444A.
Chaucer's literary appropriations are acts of literary interpretation. Ch 1 'focuses on the concept of *translatio*, the rhetorical means of effecting it, its influence on vernacular French literature, and its presence in the twelfth-century *Narcisus* and Guillaume de Lorris's *Roman*.' Ch 2 views Jean de Meun as translator and considers his method of oblique allusion and irony. Ch 3 deals with the Prologue to *LGW*; ch 4, with *BD* and its sources, including *RR*; ch 5, with *T&C*; ch 6, with *FrankT* as a 'reading' of sources in Boccaccio and *RR*, 'a *translatio* of Jean's critique of Amis and La Vieille.'

134 Louis, René. *Le Roman de la Rose: Essai d'Interprétation de l'Allégorisme Érotique*. Paris: Honoré Champion, 1974.
After introductory remarks on the respective designs of the poem's

two authors, Louis explores 'La jeune fille, object idéal de l'amour,' 'Le jardin clos, image de la jeune fille,' 'Personnalité de la jeune fille oiseuse,' 'L'allégorie comme procédé d'analyse psychologique,' 'La fontaine d'amour et le buisson de roses,' 'La crise: irruption de Danger et de ses compagnons,' 'Le baiser à la Rose et le Chateau de Jalousie,' 'La prophétie du Dieu d'Amour ou présentation de Jean de Meun par lui-même,' 'Esquisse d'une biographie de Jean de Meun,' 'Une conception dépoètisée et dépersonnalisée de l'amour,' 'Le discours insidieux d'Ami et sa misogynie,' 'Un changement radical dans la structure et l'ésprit du poême,' 'Jean de Meun dénigre l'all substitue de nouveaux symboles,' and 'L'assaut donne au chateau et la cueillette de la rose.'

134a Lowes, John Livingston. *Geoffrey Chaucer and the Development of His Genius.* Boston: Macmillan, 1934. Rpt. Bloomington, Indiana: Midland Book, 1958.
'I am inclined to think that there is, on the whole, no book so thoroughly typical of the Middle Ages as the *Roman de la Rose* — of their strange contradictions, and their conflicting ideals; of their blind reverence for authority, and their rebellious skepticism; of their worship of woman, and their contempt for women; of their ethereal idealism and their brute realism; of their deadly monotony and their surging variety. The *Divine Comedy* is typical, too, but every detail in it has passed through the alembic of Dante's personality; the Middle Ages are there, but they are moulded by the compelling power of a supreme selective artist. In the *Roman de la Rose* the elements are present in something of their own warring chaos, yet pregnant with the poems of the next two centuries. It is one of the great germinal books of the Middle Ages' (p 83/66–67).

135 Luria, Maxwell. 'A Sixteenth-Century Gloss on the *Roman de la Rose.*' *MS*, 44 (1982), 333–70.
After a concise discussion of fifteenth-century glossing of *RR* mss, Luria transcribes the glosses in a fifteenth-century ms of *RR* in the Philadelphia Museum of Art (Collins Collection 45-65-3), a beautifully illuminated ms of 202 leaves, 150 of which contain over 200 marginal inscriptions in an early sixteenth-century hand. Forty-three of the more substantial of these glosses are included in English translation in Luria 136, pp 207–17.

136 — *A Reader's Guide to the Roman de la Rose.* Hamden, Conn.: Archon Books, 1982.
Intended for readers at all levels of sophistication, Luria's *Guide* provides the best general introduction to *RR* and its scholarship available in English. Part One, 'In Search of the Rose,' pp 1–84, surveys critical issues surrounding the poem and its history, with

liberal excerpts from English and French sources (in English translation). Considers the poem and its authors, mss, editions, translations, the art of love as topos, allegory, satire, the poem's reception, the Quarrel, and 'Chaucer, the *Roman*, and the *Romaunt*' (pp 75–84). 'Practically speaking, as Chrétien de Troyes had in the twelfth century invented the Arthurian romance, so Guillaume de Lorris in the first half of the thirteenth century invented the medieval dream vision of love, and both inventions were to have a copious and sometimes brilliant progeny' (p 9). 'By the latter half of the fourteenth century, the *Roman de la Rose* had provided Western European poetry with an allegorical locus, a set of allegorical personifications, and an archetypal fable through which the period might project its abiding interest in the varieties of love and their relation to the inherited values of humanistic Christian culture' (pp 62–63). Luria summarizes the quarrel over *RR* beginning at the end of the fourteenth century, led by Christine de Pisan and Jean Gerson, and responded to by Pierre Col and Jean de Montreuil and others (pp 63–67, 183–202). 'Of all the medieval poets whose works provide evidence that they read the *Roman de la Rose* none used the poem with more conspicuous success than Chaucer' (p 75). Discusses the relationship of the A-fragment to Chaucer's youthful complaint poems, not simply in terms of allegorical personifications but in subtler ways as well — manipulation of perspective; irony; mixing of *ernest* and *game* and of playful surfaces with serious content; the posings of a first-person narrator and the use of psychological motives, especially in poems like *BD* and *PF*. Considers also the borrowing of topics and literary types. Part Two, 'Mapping the Garden,' pp 85–118, provides two analytic outlines of *RR*, one based on narrative and thematic development and the second based on constituent episodes and dialectical elements. A narrative summary paraphrases the major contents of the poem in terms of the two schemes. Part Three, 'Personifications and Allusions,' pp 119–151, consists of two glossaries. Part Four, 'Some Useful Texts,' pp 153–221, working from the premise that *RR* is 'an intensely literary poem' (p 155), traces echoes and quotations which 'fertilized our poets' imaginations' to four basic passages in Macrobius, Alanus de Insulis, and Andreas Capellanus, then adds five further texts of criticism which *RR* provoked, from the Quarrel of 1400 to the revival of interest in *RR* in 1735, the latter group including Pierre Col's letter to Christine de Pisan (mid-1402), the Prologue of Jean Molinet (1433–1507) to *Romant de la rose moralisie*, the Preface of Clement Marot (1495–1544), selections from the Collins ms Gloss (ca 1500–1520), and Lenglet du Fresnoy's Preface of 1735. Part Five consists of an intelligently arranged and judiciously chosen 'Select Research Bibliography' (pp 223–265), with sections on Bibliographies

and Concordances to *RR* and *Romaunt,* Scholarship on mss of *RR,*
French Printed Editions, French Modernizations, Translations,
Scholarship and Criticism before the Twentieth Century, Scholarship
and Criticism of the Twentieth Century, Materials and Scholarship
Relating to the Quarrel, Ancillary Materials for Study of the *Roman,*
Special Topics (Alanus, Andreas, Boethius, Jean de Meun, 'Echecs
Amoureux,' 'Il Fiore' and Italian Literature, Controversy concerning
the Friars), and the *Romaunt* and its Relation to *RR.*

137 Magoun, F.P., Jr. 'Chaucer and the *Roman de la Rose,* vv.
16096–105.' *RomR* 17 (1926), 69–70.
Suggests that in *SqT,* F. 253–60, Chaucer borrows the illustration on
'the wonder of glass-making' and 'the reference to the cause of thunder
and mist' from Jean de Meun.

138 Muscatine, Charles. 'The Emergence of Psychological Allegory in Old
French Romance.' *PMLA,* 68 (1953), 1160–82.
Guillaume comes upon psychological allegory in such Old French
romances as *Voie de Paradis, Galeran de Bretagne, Eneas,* and
Guillaume de Palerne, which utilize rhetorical self-address,
dialogue-in-monologue, and personifications of desires, impulses, and
even doctrines that love brings to the lover's consciousness, and which
thus prepare the way 'for our first full-scale psychological novel' (p
1182).

139 — *Chaucer and the French Tradition: A Study in Style and Meaning.*
Berkeley: University of California Press, 1957.
Chaucer's most fundamental traits are medieval. His literary matrix is
not English, Latin or Italian, but rather French of the twelfth and
thirteenth centuries, whence Chaucer derives his 'new style' from a
mixture of courtly and bourgeois traditions. Muscatine draws
extensively on *RR* and Chrétien in accounting for settings, rhetorical
descriptions, and various forms of dialogue and monologue in Chaucer.
In *RR* 'the clarity and precision with which the allegory is handled
testify to the medieval audience's astounding capacity to see the
subjective as objective, as real; and the particular organization of this
allegory, around a conception of character, and the finesse with which
the emotional life is thereby explored, show us literary convention at
its best. Here, faced with the problem of describing an invisible world,
and attacking it directly through convention, the poet yet makes his
strongest claim to dealing with reality' (p 36). From Guillaume,
Chaucer learns a 'symbolic' style. 'There is a paradox inherent in the
very terms we use in describing the poetry [of Guillaume]: earthly
paradise, sensuous, even sensual idealism. We can broadly see the
same paradox in other areas of medieval culture. The individual soul
was replacing the cosmos, in mystical theology, as the battleground of

good and evil. The limited introspective individualism thus fostered is similarly poised between human and cosmic claims. For literature, the conflict inevitably becomes one of styles. The courtly style is not equipped to sustain a radical alteration in point of view. For this another style was fashioned, finally to become an implement of attack on the courtly position itself' (p 41). Muscatine places Jean de Meun in a scholarly rather than a courtly or bourgeois tradition. Jean is able to move within both, a master of irony and stylistic manipulation (pp 96–97). Muscatine makes little explicit comment on the *Romaunt*, though he uses it whenever possible as his gloss on the French. He usually refers to it as 'the Middle English translation,' thus avoiding the problem of authorship, though once he does speak of the lines bringing out 'the best in the translator Chaucer' (p 32).

139a Ott, Karl August. *Der Rosenroman.* Darmstadt: Wissenschaftliche Buchgesellschaft, 1980.
A general introduction to *RR* in its time and in subsequent criticism. Considers such matters as its sources, structure, irony and allegory, originality, and problems with 'christlichen' interpretations of the poem.

140 Paré, Gérard M. *Les Idées et les Lettres au XIIIe Siècle: Le Roman de la Rose.* Université de Montréal Bibliothèque de Philosophie. Montréal: Le Centre de Psychologie et de Pédagogie, 1947.
Jean de Meun's thought and vocabulary is profoundly influenced by scholasticism. Ch 1, 'Vocabulaire Scholaire et Scholastique,' pp 15–52, discusses in the context of scholastic thought Jean's use of such terms as aucteur, auctorité, authentique; lire, congié de lire; glose, gloser, espondre, integumenz; sentence, doner sentence, determiner; moele, escorce; question, despute, desputer, querele; obicier, oposer, respondre, soudre; distinter, deviser; otreier, neier; accidenz, sustance; diffinicion, defenir, especiaus, diferences, contraires; argumenz, conclusion, conséquence, sofime, aparence; raison; conclure le peeur; elenches; demonstraison, science, opinion, creance; convertibilité, convertible; simplement, necessité simple, necessité en regart; possible, chose possible, verité possible; generaument, en generalité, en especialité; violence, violent; fantasie; sen comun, sen particulier; diter, ditié; usure, prester a usure; religion; ignorance desierrée; theme; converser; qualitez; and proprement. Ch 2, 'Thèmes Scholastiques,' pp 53–80, considers in conjunction with Plato's *Timaeus*, Aristotle, Bernard Silvester, St Thomas Aquinas, Albert the Great, etc, Jean de Meun's use of scholastic topoi such as 'individus et espèces,' 'génération et corruption,' 'forme et matière,' 'l'art imite la nature,' 'l'art d'alchimie,' 'in medio stat virtus,' 'microcosme et mégacosme,' and 'l'homme, image de Dieu.' Ch 3, 'Le Discours de Raison,' pp

81–135, examines Raison's great address to the Lover, with special attention to her discussion of the nature of love and lovers, social and political morality, and fortune. Paré draws parallels with Boethius, St Augustine, and Albert the Great. Ch 4, 'Autour de la Prison de Bel-Accueil,' pp 136–202, is devoted to 'Un art d'aimer,' 'Le mari jaloux,' and 'Faux-semblant,' that is, that portion of *RR* between the departure of Raison and the appearance of Dame Nature. Ch 5, 'La Confession de Nature,' pp 203–78, gives special consideration to 'La présentation de Nature,' 'La science des corps célestes,' 'Le monde sublunaire,' 'Liberté humaine et prescience divine,' and 'Mystères Chreteins.' Ch 6, 'Le Message de Génius,' pp 279–97, summarizes Genius' argument, noting Jean's departures from Alain which verge on heresy in their criticism of chastity and continence. Ch 7, 'La Philosophie du Roman de la Rose,' pp 298–345, summarizes the scholastic points which Paré's analysis has assembled, pointing out that Jean's deity is not only the God of the Chartrian philosophers or that of Boethius but also the God of the Bible. *RR* is 'un riche syncrétisme' (p 345) of medieval thought, encyclopedic in its range from classical sources in Cicero, Horace, Virgil, Juvenal, Livy, Ovid, and Boethius to Jean's near contemporaries, whether Alain de Lille, Andreas Capellanus, John of Salisbury, or St Thomas Aquinas. 'Si Aristote y est exploité au degré que nous avons vu, la raison en est que ses principaux traités étaient alors au programme à la Faculté des Arts de Paris, et que même à la Faculté de Théologie, certains maîtres comme Thomas d'Aquin s'en inspiraient largement pour leurs constructions théologiques' (p 346). Jean combined the scholasticism of Paris with the rhetoric and dialectic of Orleans.

40a   Patterson, Lee. ' "For the Wyves love of Bathe": Feminine Rhetoric and Poetic Resolution in the *Roman de la Rose* and the *Canterbury Tales*.' *Spec*, 58 (1983), 656–695.
The language of poetry and the reading and glossing of texts is habitually conceived in the Middle Ages in sexual and specifically feminine terms. 'The voice of the poet is inescapably aligned with that of women,' the voice of the go-between, the *entrematteuse* (p 659). As background to the principles in *RR* and Chaucer, Patterson explores feminine rhetoric in Rutebeuf's *Dit de l'herberie*, the *Liber lamentationum Matheoluli*, the pseudo-Ovidian *De vetula*, Jean Lefevre's *La vieille*, and Roger de Collerye's *Sermon pour une nopce*. Jean de Meun's Vieille is both *entrematteuse* and rhetorician, her erotic autobiography a *dilatio* organized to match the rose's floral dilation. Its interlocking box structure delays the lover from attaining his goal at the same time that it lures him (*emboîtement* and *prolangance*). 'Jean's achievement ... is not merely to exploit the

meanings contained in the rhetorical term *dilatio*, a process that
Chaucer will carry even further in the Wife of Bath's discourse. In a
larger sense he manages to translate the central Ovidian principle of
amorous delay into stylistic terms, and to show with impressive
specificity how rhetorical structure can bear erotic value' (p 671).
Patterson applies this poetic of dilation to the Wife of Bath's role in
the Tales as interrupter of the Parson (ML Endlink) to prolong the *CT*
through her own dilations.

141 Payen, Jean-Charles. 'A Semiological Study of Guillaume de Lorris.'
YFS, 51 (1974), 170–84. [Translated by Margaret Ann Leff.]
Payen sets forth an inventory of forms in *RR* — allegory, tropology,
anagoge, semiology — and then juxtaposes a 'naive reading' (one we
must not reject) of the poem as 'autobiography' with tropological and
anagogic readings. 'The anagogic reading must not fall into the trap of
system-building' (p 178). In Guillaume's *RR* the anagoge is 'a
non-systematic and profane one ... The author invents his figures of
speech as his narration requires them, without worrying about the
internal coherence or rigor of his work' (p 180). The poem reveals
'only an existential semiology, so to speak' (p 181). There is 'a series
of semiological ruptures' throughout *RR* 'which allow the gradual
passage from the narration to the unambiguous dogmatic statements.
But these ruptures compromise the relevance of a rigorous reading, as
much on the vertical axis of the meaning as along the horizontal axis
of the story's coherence' (pp 183–84).

142 Poirion, Daniel. 'Narcisse et Pygmalion dans *Le Roman de la Rose*.'
In *Essays in Honor of Louis Francis Solano*. Ed. Raymond J. Cormier
and Urban T. Holmes. University of North Carolina Studies in the
Romance Languages and Literatures, 92. Chapel Hill: University of
North Carolina Press, 1970. Pp 153–65.
Compares Guillaume's use of Narcissus with Jean's use of Pygmalion
to show their relatedness and the skill of the poets in focusing major
ideas and narrative sections of their poems around mythological
figures. The Narcissus and Pygmalion passages are not isolated
rhetorical ornaments. The artistry of the two poets is distinctly
modern, as is their attitude toward art.

142a — *Le Roman de la Rose*. Paris: Natier, 1973.
A critical analysis of the poem in two parts. Part I provides a cursory
reading of the psychological and courtly allegory and the literary
contexts out of which Guillaume developed his marvellous story; it
consists of three chapters: *Songe et allégorie, Le conte merveilleux*,
and *L'art d'amour*. Part II consists of chapters 4–6, on Jean de
Meun's part of the poem. Ch 4, *L'amplification de l'allégorie*, breaks
Jean's narrative down into sections of narration, discourse, and

dialogue, demonstrating how Jean uses *emboîtement* (interlocking box structures) to organize and develop his material, especially in the discourses of Ami and La Vieille, but also in the long section of Nature's discourse. Guillaume's simpler allegory is displaced by a wide configuration of topoi geometrically arranged. 'L'esthétique de la digression nous monstre ... le mouvement le plus profond de la pensée, ce qui se situe au plus près de la vie personnelle et de la réalité concrète. C'est ce qui fait équilibre au conceptualisme un peu excessif, à l'arbitraire de l'ordre scholastique. Car en face des constructions arithmétiques, géométriques, ou plus simplement classificatrices, il y a place pour ce que nous appellerions aujourd'hui l'inspiration' (p 124). Such a mosaic, parenthetical style reflects the interlocking boxes of Jean's intellectualized culture (p 127). Ch 5, *L'enseignement ironique*, explores Jean's ironic instruction through satire, burlesque, paradox, logical perversion, etc. 'La perfection de ce style ironique est sans doute à chercher dans la profession de foi de Faux Semblant dont le nom, à lui seul, évoque l'archetype de l'ironie' (p 153). Indeed, the whole sexual process is ironic (p 173). The amusing incongruities enable Jean to develop serious matter by means of the humor. Ch 6, *Le dévoilement poétique*, demonstrates how philosophical content from Boethius, Alain de Lille, and school matter from Paris and Chartres is veiled throughout Jean's narrative, especially in the discourses of Nature and Genius and in the abundant classical mythology.

43 Quilligan, Maureen. 'Words and Sex: The Language of Allegory in the *De planctu naturae*, the *Roman de la rose*, and Book III of the *Faerie Queene*.' *Allegorica*, 2 (1977), 195–216.
Alain's discussion of sex through analogies with grammar, Jean's discussion of *coilles* which turns into a debate about language, and the House of Busyraine passage of *FQ* with its attack on courtly and Petrarchan terminology all resolve the problem of language and sexuality through actions organized around the character of Genius. 'Jean's Genius is a lewd humorist after his author's heart. Yet Jean makes serious as well as comic use of him. Genius retells the same myth of the birth of Venus, and has a problem with the same word that stymied Raison. This Genius, a direct parody of Alain's, understands the word 'coilles' so literally that he digresses for forty-five lines on the evils of emasculation — completely neglecting to mention, therefore, the birth of Venus, or what *coilles* might mean allegorically; he gets side-tracked by what has become an all-important word in the poem' (p 205). Genius' literalism is quintessentially unallegorical. In the end of the poem 'Jean demonstrates the necessarily unallegorical results of a strict adherence to courtly euphemism' (p 206).

44 — *The Language of Allegory: Defining the Genre*. Ithaca: Cornell

University Press, 1979.
Quilligan explores not only ways in which allegories signal their
membership in a generic class, but the way those signals guide the
reader's response. The first two chapters, on 'Text' and 'Pretext,'
focus on 'what texts themselves say about the genre.' The chapter on
'context' considers the historical milieu out of which the author may
write allegory.' The last chapter, 'The Reader,' 'demonstrates its own
historical theory, for currently the "reader" has been experiencing a
revival in literary criticism for the same reasons that allegory has
recently become again a privileged genre. From structuralism to
affective stylistics, the reader has once again become the producer of
meaning' (p 21). Quilligan draws extensively on *Piers Plowman* and
the *Faerie Queene* for exemplary material. In setting up her definition
of allegory as a genre of wordplay she compares *HF, RR*, and
Pynchon's *The Crying of Lot 49* as 'a class of literature very much
"hung up with words, words" ' (p 14) — a phrase which defines the
core of the genre.

145 — 'Allegory, Allegoresis, and the Deallegorization of Language: the
Roman de la rose, the *De planctu naturae*, and the *Parlement of
Foules.*' In *Allegory, Myth, and Symbol*. Ed. Morton W. Bloomfield.
Harvard English Studies 9. Cambridge, Mass.: Harvard University
Press, 1981. Pp 163–86.
Following the theoretical premises of her earlier study (**144**), Quilligan
differentiates between allegory and allegoresis: allegory is a species of
text which announces itself by a number of blatant signals (eg,
personification and wordplay) to be 'about the magic signifying power
of language'; allegoresis is a critical procedure for making any text,
'whatever its manifest literal meaning, appear to be about language, or
any other (latent) subject' (pp 163–4). In *PF* Chaucer has
'deallegorized his two sources,' *RR* and the *De planctu naturae*, by
transforming 'the silent, unvoiced textuality of his allegorical sources
into a dramatic, mimetic fiction of audible, voiced sound. Quite
simply, he takes the static, embroidered birds of Alain's *Complaint*
and in the *Parlement* makes them sing ... Because allegories, in effect,
"deconstruct" themselves they leave no room for externally imposed
interpretations. Unallegorical Chaucer is most vulnerable to that
invasive interpretive force' (p 164). Chaucer learned much about
language from Jean and Alain. In the elaborate joke about testicles in
RR 'Jean shows that to speak about sexuality in euphemisms is simply
to limit the nonliteral meaning of language to the carnal, the merely
erotic; to lift the veil of such metaphoric language is merely to lift up
skirts. When, however, one uses the flesh itself as a veil — as Reason
had tried to do in telling the myth of Venus — one may incarnate

spiritual truths which reveal the connection between flesh and spirit, between the world and the Word of God' (p 170). In the first part of *PF*, the narrator is in an allegorical world which he observes silently. But in the second part, as he enters the crowded landscape of noisy birds (so different from the birds on Nature's cloak in Alain), he becomes a listener rather than a reader, denying himself the opportunity for writing allegory. 'If this makes Chaucer a precursor of Shakespeare rather than Spenser in the English Renaissance, it also indicates what Spenser had to do to Chaucer to turn his master's narratives back into allegory. What is one of the most wonderful, oral style jokes in the *Canterbury Tales*, the tale of Sir Thopas, Spenser takes with a wonderful genius of his own and makes the basic fiction of *The Faerie Queene*' (p 181). In *RR* Reason is the namer of all things. When her voice is silenced the poem becomes vulnerable to the Lover's 'fallacious attitude toward language, an attitude which insists (like allegoresis) on a polite disjunction between word said and meaning meant ... The last episode of the *Roman* is a self-conscious parody of allegoresis by means of which Jean warns the reader that to translate the real facts of physical sexuality into metaphoric terms is a form of idolatry' (p 185). Quilligan compares Reason's assumption of a critical authority in *RR* to the role critics like Paul de Man 'would need to appropriate for themselves'; 'right reading is ethical action' (pp 184–5).

146 Rand, E.K. 'The Metamorphoses of Ovid in *Le Roman de la Rose.*' *Studies in the History of Culture: The Discipline of the Humanities.* Manosha, Wisconsin: Banta, 1942. Pp 103–21.
After considering the teaching of the classics in the thirteenth century, Rand discusses Jean's love of the ancient authors, especially Boethius and Ovid. He also relates Ovid to Guillaume's portion of the poem and comments on scholarly work done on *RR*.

147 Robertson, D.W., Jr. 'The Doctrine of Charity in Medieval Literary Gardens: A Topical Approach through Symbolism and Allegory.' *Spec*, 26 (1951), 24–49. Rpt in D.W. Robertson, Jr. *Essays in Medieval Culture*. Princeton: Princeton University Press, 1980. Pp 21–50.
After discussing biblical gardens and patristic lore pertaining to them Robertson brings exegetical lore on such figurae as the *hortus conclusus* and the *hortus deliciarum*, trees, fruit, wells, streams, wisdom, and charity or cupidity to bear on *Beowulf*, Andreas' *de Amore*, Chrétien's *Cligés*, *RR*, and Chaucer's *MerchT*. In *RR* the garden of Deduit is an obverse to that of the *Canticum*, where fleshly delights only seem spiritual to the Lover as his idleness awakens *concupiscentia carnis* and his narcissistic dream. Jean de Meun, 'who was in a much better position than we are to understand Guillaume's garden' (p 43), juxtaposed to Guillaume's *hortus deliciarum* with its well of Narcissus

and barren pine tree, the vision of another garden, with a fountain of Living Waters and a fruitful olive tree, a garden of *Deus caritas* which clarifies the inverted typologies elsewhere in the poem.

148 — *A Preface to Chaucer: Studies in Medieval Perspectives.* Princeton: Princeton University Press, 1962. Pp 91–104, 195–207, 361–65.
Although Robertson includes no specific discussion of *Romaunt*, he comments extensively on the Narcissus and Pygmalion passages of *RR* as elaborate poetic integuments on *luxuria, phantasia,* and the danger of *delectatio cogitationis* (pp 91–104). 'Characters' in *RR* within their narrative framework serve the poet as a vehicle for the development of ideas (pp 195–205). 'The organization of Jean de Meun's continuation is ... far from being discursive or haphazard. The main themes are set by Raison, and the rest of the poem is an elaborate, but not a digressive account of what happens to those who disobey Raison's counsels' (p 202). Robertson discusses tensions between Platonists and anti-humanistic Aristotelians in the late Middle Ages. 'The controversy over the *Roman de la rose* affords an excellent means of describing the issues that were at stake in the defense of allegory as a humanistic device' (p 361). In his intricate discussion of the principles of Romanesque and Gothic aesthetics and style, Robertson comments on eighteen *RR* illuminations, along with other examples from medieval art.

148a Saintsbury, George. *A Short History of French Literature (From the Earliest Texts to the Close of the Nineteenth Century.)* 6th edn. Oxford: Clarendon Press, 1901.
Ch 7, 'Serious and Allegorical Poetry,' reviews the scope of *RR* and its influence: 'The real secret of its vogue, as of all such vogues, is that it faithfully held up the mirror to the later middle ages. In no single book can that period of history be so conveniently studied. Its inherited religion and its nascent free-thought; its thirst for knowledge and its lack of criticism; its sharp social divisions and its indistinct aspirations after liberty and equality; its traditional morality and asceticism, and its half-pagan, half-childish relish for the pleasures of sense; its romance and its coarseness, all its weakness and all its strength, here appear' (p 71).

148b Schless, Howard H. *Chaucer and Dante: A Revaluation.* Norman, Oklahoma: Pilgrim Books, 1984.
In his introductory chapter Schless contrasts the kind of influence *RR* had on Chaucer with the influence of Dante (pp 15–18).

149 Snell, F.J. *The Age of Chaucer.* London: Bell 1901/rev 1906. Pp 137–42.
Snell reviews problems of who translated what (pp 137–38). Quite evidently Chaucer's study of *RR* was an education in itself. 'The

Romance of the Rose, in its later extension, so far exceeds its primitive limits as to anticipate the Reformation, and frankly avow Jacobinical principles' (p 142).

150 Stone, Donald, Jr. 'Old and New Thoughts on Guillaume de Lorris.' *Australian Journal of French Studies*, 2 (1965), 157–70.
By examining the figures within and without the garden, the fountain of Narcissus, the speech of Love, and the speech of Reason, Stone entertains the possibility of a courtly ending to Guillaume's poem rather than the moralistic ones proposed by C.S. Lewis and D.W. Robertson, Jr. 'The more one penetrates into Lorris' text, the more difficult it is to be categorical about any projected ending. What stands out in Lorris is the art of "balanced pressures," that consummate skill with which the poet bent an iconographic tradition to meet his own ends, yielding, however, in the end to a faithful presentation of the psychology of his age, even to the point of reproducing its impasses and contradictions' (p 170).

151 Strohm, Paul. 'Guillaume as Narrator and Lover in the *Roman de la Rose.*' RomR, 59 (1968), 3–9.
Suggests that Guillaume abandoned his projected ending: 'the complaint with which his lines end is really the conclusion of a finished poem' (p 4). 'If Guillaume's poem lacks the conventional ending of a dream vision, it has the conventional ending of a lover's complaint, and the final mingling of the worlds of the Narrator and the Lover gives this ending greater significance and more finality than most readers have seen' (p 9).

152 Tatlock, J.S.P. *The Mind and Art of Chaucer*. Syracuse: Syracuse University Press, 1950.
'Chaucer never grew beyond the influence of French literature; to the end of his life he cites and quotes it, but in his early years it was the sole contemporary influence on him' (p 21). Of all French influences *RR* is the greatest. 'The expert Chaucerian is constantly startled when reading either the *Roman* or Chaucer to find how many passages even in his late poems are filched from the *Roman*, though it lacks his raciest and most human manner' (p 22). Chaucer outgrew Guillaume, though never Jean. 'There is no ground for stating that Guillaume wrote for the upper class and Jean for the bourgeois' (p 24).

153 Tuve, Rosemond. *Allegorical Imagery: Some Mediaeval Books and their Posterity*. Princeton, N.J.: Princeton University Press, 1966.
'Allegory is supremely fitted to examine closely the nature of great abstractions as they touch men's lives, and this generalized quasi-philosophical interest is asked of readers, while the method remains, in great writers, stubbornly literary' (p 160). Tuve explores several great medieval allegories, including *RR* and its redactions, to

show how traditional imagery and allegorical techniques were
transmitted to the English Renaissance and Spenser. Renaissance
authors often drew material from medieval mss. Eg, Thomas Lodge
got *Gamelyn*, from which he made his *Rosalynde*, from Chaucer mss (it
was not printed until 1721); moreover, large portions of his *Catharos*
come from a ms of the French Franciscan Jean Benedicti's *Somme des
Pechez*. Renaissance iconography often goes directly back to mss
which have illustrations that clarify the imagery. Tuve's study includes
110 pictorial illustrations, which she frequently uses to demonstrate
how allegory works. Ch 1, 'Problems and Definitions,' pp 3–55, draws
especially on Christine de Pizan's *Epistle of Othea to Hector* and the
Queste del Saint Graal in defining characteristics of allegorical
imagery. Ch 2, 'Allegory of Vices and Virtues,' pp 57–143, considers
Frère Lorens' *Somme le roi* and the *Moralium dogma philosophorum*
by William of Conches (?), along with numerous other moral treatises,
out of which the allegorical imagery of Spencer's Vices and Virtues
sprang. Ch 3, 'Guillaume's Pilgrimage,' pp 145–218, analyses the
language and illustrations in the numerous mss of Guillaume de
Deguileville's *Pèlerinage de la vie humaine*; many of the illustrations
in the *Pèlerinage* bear similarity to *RR* illustrations. Ch 4, 'Imposed
Allegory,' pp 219–333, explores moralized redactions of *RR*, especially
Jean Molinet's *Romant de la rose moralisie cler et net* (ca 1482),
which went through three printed editions in the first quarter of the
sixteenth century. 'Molinet got himself deeply into ... difficulties when
he made *this* [*RR's*] God of Love "nostre Seigneur" ' (p 240). Molinet's
greatest difficulties arise 'when his allegory forces him to get both
Amis and La Vieille "on the right side," since both instruct the Lover
in how to secure the Rose, and "the Rose" is ... axiomatically a good'
(p 241). 'Molinet's wildest infelicities are the fruit of disregarding
literary decorum, and this is typical of bad allegory' (p 243). 'Jean de
Meun's method is very risky, as is amply clear from the obloquy he has
received from critics who speak of his paraded learning, his large
undigested chunks of interpolated encyclopaedic materials, his
digressions. This is an unhappy and undeserved fate for an author who
shows such extreme subtlety in using juxtapositions for ironic point, in
making the arrows of his satiric points all face in the same direction,
or in choosing just such details for his long monologues as will nail the
speaker to a monstrous inadequacy, and pierce through him to nail his
interlocutor to an equally monstrous acceptance' (p 259). Jean is not
easily understood, as is evident in the diverse misrepresentations of his
work. He defines love by negatives and 'the ironic presentation of
unrelieved inadequacies and deceptions and rationalizations and errors'
(p 256). It is readers like Molinet, who ignore the allegory, who have
the 'truly shocking taste' (p 263). Molinet unsuccessfully tries to

translate *RR* 'into a potpourri of images with Christological meanings ... He does not study morals; instead, he reads everywhere one great figure of allegory — Christ's loving pursuit and final salvation of the human soul' (p 265). Jean de Meun had been careful to avoid such a radical solution to moral issues. His Dame Nature is 'a poor faulty female, not overbright' (p 269); but her confusions are mild compared to those provided by her confessor Genius, with his 'naturalistic misreading of the whole image of the Garden of Heavenly Love' (p 277). The complexities and ambiguities of *RR* were bound to teach craftsmanship to intelligent readers. Spenser was one who learned much about the potentialities of allegory and the pleasure of wit from Jean. Ch 4 concludes with discussion of illustrations in *RR*, *Othea*, and *OM* (pp 315–33), with warnings against turning allegories into 'moralizations' (p 333). Ch 5, 'Romances,' pp 335–436, considers the imagery of chivalry, historical allegory, and the quest (entrelacement and web-structures) in various French and Arthurian romances, but especially in Spenser. 'I think it appears from Spenser's practice that he could still read mediaeval allegorical romances allegorically without stumbling into [the common] pitfalls, as an interpreter; hence he does not make similar pitfalls for us by writing an allegorical romance with such abuses of allegory written into it' (p 410).

154 Vitz, E.B. 'The *I* of the *Roman de la Rose*.' *Genre*, 6 (1973), 49–75. [Translated by Barbara Di Stefano]
Because of the underlying split between the identity of the hero of the narrative and the narrator, 'autobiography as a literary form has a very definite tendancy to irony' (p 49). Medieval writers have little interest in 'the specific individuality of the writer. When speaking of himself, the writer was expected to transform himself, both esthetically and morally, into a symbol of humanity as a whole, or, at the very least, of an entire class of men ... Human experience is presented in its archetypal aspect, not as an individualized sequence of actual events' (p 51). Focussing on Guillaume's part of the poem, Vitz differentiates between four '*I*' figures in *RR*: 1) The Dreamer who 'had' the dream, who is twenty years old (an age both exact and vague), 'a symbol, if not of Everyman, at least of every young aristocrat' (p 52); 2) the hero of the dream — *jolis* (charming, graceful, beautiful, dainty, joyful, well-adorned), who is the same age as the Dreamer; 3) the real life hero who looks back on the events after they happened; 4) the Narrator who remembers all the past events, recognizing that his memory may be faulty, who struggles to present a 'semblaunce' of what happened over the period of five years and more. The 'mixture of preterite and present seems to have constituted a technique used deliberately as a means of dramatization rather than

for logical considerations, a technique obviously linked to oral tradition. Its main advantage lay in the fact that it allowed an author constantly to change his point of view' (p 64). Perhaps there is a fifth 'I' as well, the 'implicit author' hidden unobtrusively behind the narrator. The multiplicity of I's, rather than tearing the poem apart, make it the more 'intensely harmonious and unified' (p 69).

155 Warren, F.M. 'On the Date and Composition of Guillaume de Lorris' *Roman de la Rose*,' *PMLA*, 23 (1908), 269–84.
Jean de Meun says he picked up the ms some forty years later. If he wrote ca 1271–77 that would place Guillaume's composition ca 1229–36. The rose metaphor on which the poem rests had appealed to another mind (Gautier of Arras) 'long before it was elaborated by the talent of Guillaume de Lorris,' however (p 284).

156 Wetherbee, Winthrop. 'The Literal and the Allegorical: Jean de Meun and the *De Planctu Naturae*.' *MS*, 33 (1971), 264–91.
Working from Platonic traditions anchored in Alanus, Wetherbee examines Jean's personifications in *RR* as they move beyond tradition into 'the depths of the anti-allegorical world' of pragmatism, skepticism, and self-interest. 'It is important to realize that Raison is *only* "reason," that her high court of appeal is the will of Nature' (p 271). Moreover, like Nature, she is incapable of conceiving of the Lover's problem in theological terms. 'She can think only in terms of an allegorically coherent universe where the *integumenta* of human behavior are reflected in a harmony with cosmic processes which man has now lost' (p 274). But Ami, who usurps Raison's place, is little more successful in answering the Lover's real concerns. Raison and Ami come together in the barren Vieille, 'at best an eloquent ruin like Rochester's Maim'd Debauchee. But we sense in her profound humanity and in the history of her life the working of forces more simply natural than those which galvanize the world depicted by Faus Semblant' (p 278). Wetherbee follows the plot closely with his analysis, exploring tensions in Jean's section between the allegorical and the literal, his argument culminating in his discussion of Genius. 'That Genius, ostensibly no more than the patron of procreative instinct, should presume to draw together so many diverse strands of the allegory, and offer to account for what transcends Nature and confounds Raison, is of course highly ironical, but it is also appropriate' (p 283). Genius knows that Adam, had he not fallen, would have merited eternal life *per naturalia*; 'he knows the Good Shepherd and the Lamb, but not the Incarnation, and is unaware that Grace is a necessary supplement to those innate capacities which are his only resource. He is, in short, a symbol of all that is best in human nature, with the capabilities and limitations which the fact implies.

The limitations, of course, are severe: Genius must exert his influence through the sexual nature of a corrupt and irrational humanity obedient unconsciously, if at all, to laws which it can never strictly know' (pp 284–85). But the conquest of the Rose is not the sole result of Genius' exhortation. 'Sexuality in the *Roman* is a symptom of the minimal survival of man's original dignity, but it is not a metaphor for that dignity' (p 287). Jean uses a complex of mythological analogues — Narcissus, Adonis, Pygmalion, Orpheus — to illustrate how 'depravity, cupidity, all the perils of love in a fallen world become necessary means to the end of human survival' (p 287). Wetherbee compares Vulcan in Martianus Capella to Jean's Genius figure, both comical, but still maintaining 'their essential dignity by a vision which sees beyond the accidents of experience' (p 289). This association of Vulcan and Genius offers 'an excellent insight into the complex system of checks and balances by which the world of the *Roman* is held together and made to conform to the will of the higher power represented by Genius' (p 290). Jean excludes from his conclusion Alanus' poetic sense of natural order as a type of Grace, but is careful to undermine claims of secular experience to an intrinsic value of its own. 'What is clearly affirmed is that the proliferation of conflicting points of view overlies the rock and loam out of which any transcendent aspiration must necessarily spring' (p 291).

156a — *Chaucer and the Poets: An Essay on Troilus and Criseyde.* Ithaca: Cornell University Press, 1984.
Ch 1, 'Love Psychology: The *Troilus* and the *Roman de la Rose*, pp 53–86: In his synthesis of the *Filostrato* and *RR*, Chaucer's psychological analysis of the experience of courtly love is 'far more rigorous, and closer in spirit to both Jean de Meun and Boccaccio' than C.S. Lewis, with his emphasis on Guillaume de Lorris' tonal influence, allows (p 54). Chaucer's Pandarus qualifies the courtly love situation in a way comparable to Jean's qualification of Guillaume (pp 61–65). Wetherbee juxtaposes the genius of Pandarus and the narrator as artists, and contrasts the imaginative responses of Pandarus and Troilus to love. 'In effect, Pandarus and Troilus embody two different aspects of the imaginative faculty as medieval psychology understood it' (p 76). Governed by appetite, the Pandaric imagination reduces a stimulus 'to ingenuity, machination in the interest of possession'; moved by aesthetic impulses, Troilus' imagination attempts to approximate the ideal (p 76). 'Troilus is seduced and betrayed by the very beauty that arouses him to ecstatic vision' (p 82). He is most 'intensely conscious of Criseyde's paradisal aspect when most strongly subject to her physical attraction. There is nothing in literature that approximates the moment in which Troilus rises to the eloquence of

Dante's Saint Bernard, only to "fall away" into the welcoming arms of Criseyde' (p 83).

157 White, Beatrice. 'Medieval Mirth,' *Anglia*, 78 (1960), 284–301.
Most popular jokes in the Middle Ages have as their subject either sex or stupidity (p 299). 'With reference to jokes about sex it is obvious that ... the body should eventually seem ridiculous and come to furnish inexhaustible material for laughter both joyous and derisive ... If it is seen from this angle then the *Roman de la Rose*, that "Breviary of the aristocracy," reveals itself as a preposterous and extravagant caper on the brink of obscenity' (p 300).

158 Wood, Chauncey. '*La Vieille*, Free Love, and Boethius in the *Roman de la Rose*.' *Revue de Littérature Comparée*, 51 (1977), 336–42.
Wood discusses La Vieille's defense of free love which misappropriates analogies from Boethius on birds and cages — 'facile sophistries ... not designed to convince us but rather to show the shallowness of La Vieille's position' (p 341). Jean knows Boethius' distinction between men and plants and animals, wherein men are free to choose a false good, and suffer the consequent confusion. 'It may be that in the Middle Ages, when less was read than today, proportionately more was remembered, so that it should not strain our credulity to imagine a medieval reader of the *Roman de la Rose* distinguishing between proper and improper quotations of Boethius' (p 342).

159 Zumthor, Paul. 'Autobiography in the Middle Ages?' *Genre*, 6 (1973), 29–48. [Translated by Sherry Simon].
Zumthor postulates three distinctions in autobiography: an opposition between *I* and *you*; an opposition between person and non-person; and a neutralization of the opposition between fictional narration and history. 'The pronoun *I*, obviously conditioned by a certain cultural model, must surely have undergone a radical change between the twelfth century and that of Jean-Jacques ... Medieval story tellers did not make as clear a distinction between an account of real events and fiction as did those of other periods' (p 29). There are very few medieval literary texts in which one does not find an *I*, whether as the speaker of all that is said or, in the second degree, as a speaker in his own person within the text. The distinction between real and fictional is less important to medieval writers than the opposition between teaching and non-teaching. Zumthor differentiates between narratives intended to be sung (ie, narrative song and sung narration) and narratives not intended to be sung (short texts like exemplum or nouvelle, and romances from which an allegorical *I* can be isolated). Guillaume's *RR* generates a sustained tradition of this latter group (the allegorical *I*), providing 'a model whose influence no "literary" discourse of the twelfth, thirteenth, or fourteenth centuries could

entirely avoid' (p 37).

160 — 'Narrative and Anti-Narrative: *Le Roman de la Rose*.' *YFS*, 51 (1974), 185–204. [Translated by Frank Yeomans]
After defining notions of emblem, symbol, and personification, Zumthor juxtaposes narrative strategies in the two parts of *RR*, differentiating three functions of the allegory: didactic (or explicative), deictic, and narrative. Jean de Meun takes up 30 of the 47 figures Guillaume de Lorris had used, and introduces 44 more into the 'allegorical reality' of the first part, thus infringing upon 'its integrity, upon its existential purity' (p 201). Zumthor sees a distrust of pure narrative increasing into the fifteenth century.

🌶 Part II: Boece de Consolacione

Introduction

> No philosopher was so bone of the bone and flesh of the flesh
> of Middle-age writers as Boethius. Take up what writer you
> will, and you find not only the sentiments, but the very
> words of the distinguished Roman.
>
> Richard Morris (**162**, p ii)

Although Morris' rhetorical assertion leans eloquently toward
exaggeration, with reference to Chaucer it is altogether true. There is
not one of Chaucer's major works which does not owe a major debt to
'the distinguished Roman.' Boethius and his commentators are to
Chaucer's philosophical perceptions as the *Roman de la Rose* and the
later French love poets are to his literary craftsmanship — that is,
they are all-pervading. To the Middle Ages Boethius was not just a
philosopher; he was a dramatic personality. And, for Chaucer, he was
a poet. The poet within the philosopher Boethius, with his rich sense
of metaphor and dramatic form, appealed as much to Chaucer as the
philosopher in the poet, who composed such beautiful meters as
Consolatio I.m.1 (weeping in exile), I.m.2 (the anxious mind which
once roamed freely the heavens); II.m.5 (the former age), II.m.7 (ubi
sunt), II.m.8 (Hymn to Love); III.m.6 (gentilesse), III.m.9 (Hymn to
the Maker), III.m.11 (on recollection), III.m.12 (Orpheus); IV.m.1
(soaring wings of philosophy), IV.m.6 (concord through mutual love);
V.m.3 (on knowing and not knowing). Such poems were always in
Chaucer's head, affecting his decisions both as a poet and a
philosopher.

The parallels between the sensibilities of Chaucer and Boethius
are truly striking, especially when one considers that they lived in very
different societies, in different parts of the world, and a millenium
apart. In their public lives both were dedicated civil servants, working
closely with the highest officials in the government. Chaucer was not,

of course, as powerful a political counselor as Boethius, nor was the
state of England as great as Theodoric's empire. But tradition revered
Chaucer, nonetheless, as a counselor to kings, praised him for his
wisdom, and depicted him in manuscript drawings (much as Boethius
was depicted) as a guide showing others the way. Insofar as he was
remembered at all for his public life, Chaucer, like Boethius, was
esteemed not for his political savvy as a clever courtier, but rather for
his moral sagacity.

But it is not simply high-minded diplomatic service which reveals
the similarity of their temperaments. Both men loved academic
learning, even, perhaps, for its own sake. Boethius was the more
learned — *magister officiorum* to Theodoric and, as it turned out, to
all of medieval Europe. Boethius set out to translate into Latin all the
writings of Plato and Aristotle. Although he did not complete his
undertaking he did manage to supply the West with many of its
textbooks, textbooks which were studied for the next thousand years.
Chaucer admired that scholarship, grew up on it, and emulated it both
in earnest and with good humor.

When we think of Chaucer and Boethius together our thoughts
turn instantly to the English poet's translation of the *Consolatio*. But
Boethius was more to Chaucer than philosophical spokesman from
life's prison. He was Boethius the musician, the arithmetician, the
geometrician, and the astronomer. At various places in the Chaucer
canon the poet reveals awareness of all sides of the great old scholar.
Like Boethius, Chaucer's interests reach deeply into all the arts. He
shares with Boethius a love of Plato and Aristotle, and even though he
does not always know them firsthand, as the philosopher did, he thinks
and writes as if he did.

Both men possessed acute powers of theoretical observation. But
at the same time both were fascinated by technology and the practical.
In a famous letter of Cassiodorus to Boethius (see **273**, pp 2–3), the
Senator requests in the name of Theodoric the Emperor that Boethius
provide information on the making of a water clock and sundial which
might be presented to the Burgundian King. One is reminded of
Consolatio I.m.2, where Boethius recalls how in his youth he travelled
the 'hevenliche pathes' of the sun and stars and moon, how he sought
the causes of things and 'comprehendid al this by nombres' (**7**, p 322).
One is also reminded of Chaucer, whose scientific interests sent his
mind running along the same heavenly paths and who could calculate
time and seasons to the admiration of even twentieth-century
astronomers. Chaucer is not known to have made or written treatises
on the waterclock, but he did write a treatise on the astrolabe and
possibly another on the equatory, a device for calculating the positions
of the planets, which is surely as complex as a waterclock. Cassiodorus

was filled with awe at what the wise Boethius could do and at the style in which he did it. And so were Chaucer's contemporaries and subsequent admirers awe-filled toward him — 'O Socrates plains de philosophie,' the French poet Eustache Deschamps addresses him; Thomas Usk speaks of him as 'the noble philosophical poet in English'; and to Thomas Hoccleve he is 'universall fadre of Science' and 'heire in philosophy to Aristotle in our tongue' (Spurgeon, 428, vol 1, p 8, pp 21–2; vol 3, p 16). Something of this same admiration must lie behind Richard II's appointing him Clerk of the King's Works in 1389, an appointment which might have utilized his engineering abilities more than his craftsmanship in poetry.

Chaucer and Boethius are similar in other ways as well. Both were profoundly committed to humanistic values, to the value of old books, and to a therapeutic sharing of the knowledge of the ancients with future generations. Both were teachers and translators, concerned with translating ideas as well as words. Boethius translated Aristotle, Nicomachus, Euclid, and Porphyry in hope of preserving for posterity what he deemed the best of the ancients. So too was Chaucer a translator, bringing new corn from the fields of old books. Students have often felt that Chaucer's account of the Clerk in the General Prologue to the Canterbury pilgrimage has an autobiographical ring to it — 'gladly wolde he lerne and gladly teche' (*GP*, l 308). Indeed, Chaucer is most didactic and clerkish when translating his old 'totorn' books. *Boece* was not translated simply for Chaucer's own pleasure. He cites it first and foremost among the works of edification for which he would be remembered in his Retraction, giving it priority even over his translation of saints' lives. His other translations likewise reveal didactic intentions — the *ABC* written apparently as a meditation for Blanche the Duchess, and his *Treatise on the Astrolabe*, composed for the instruction of 'lyte Lowys my sone.' Didactic intent abounds in Chaucer. His moral balades willingly offer good counsel. Didactic purpose is even apparent in the *Canterbury Tales*, especially in the two prose sections, the *Tale of Melibee*, which some have seen as counsel to Richard on the value of peace, and the *Parson's Tale*, whose plain instruction is given an eminence beyond that of the other tales by its placement at the conclusion of the pilgrimage where it transforms the Canterbury journey from a social to a spiritual event. Like his Clerk, Chaucer was a teacher in the tradition of the *'grant translateur par excellence,'* the *magister officiorum* himself.

Finally, we find a likeness in the profound recognition of the complexity of language as a vehicle for communication which Chaucer and Boethius share. Philosophy instructs Boethius in the problems of calling things by the wrong names (II.pr.6) and in the multiplicity and ambiguity of language (III. pr.10–pr.11), where several words may define the same thing, a thing which remains, nonetheless, greater than the sum of its parts; she also instructs him in the power of ideas in words, their playful quality which can make labyrinthine circles that hold errant ideas — a 'hous of Dedalus, so entrelaced that it is unable to ben unlaced' (*Boece*, 7, p 357). Both of these essentially linguistic attitudes appealed strongly to Chaucer, who frequently talks about the sly and deceptive nature of words as well as their precision and the great labor required in yoking words and ideas exactly. Chaucer's effort to make words cousin to the deed is nowhere more clearly demonstrated than in the *Boece*, where he toys with alternate readings and studies Jean de Meun's translation as well as the Latin text and commentaries in his attempt to parse the subtleties of Boethius' ideas. To some modern readers, many of Chaucer's glosses in *Boece* have seemed redundant or self-evident. But we must remember that he was raised in a society which was accustomed to subtle distinctions, whether in scholastic or legal logic, which could find satisfaction in differentiating between near synonyms and amusement in the dividing of some indivisible essence in at least a dozen ways. His *Boece* is the first prose work in English to develop precise technical vocabulary.

Scholars at the beginning of the twentieth century tended to conclude that Chaucer came to know Boethius well sometime during his middle years. Skeat 163, working on the assumption that once Chaucer knew something he repeated it verbatim several times over, concluded that Chaucer did not study the *Consolation* until the mid-1370's, and that it was not until he translated it in 1381–3 that its influence became pronounced in such works as the *KnT* and *T&C*. Jefferson 189 takes a similar view, finding no direct influence of Boethius on an early work like *BD* that could not be explained by Boethian adaptations in the *Roman de la Rose* or the *dits* of Machaut. More recently, however, as more Boethian influences have been pointed out even in works as early as *BD*, it has seemed evident that Chaucer knew Boethius thoroughly from the outset. That Chaucer drew more heavily on Boethian thought after he had completed his translation is certainly understandable, however. It will always be necessary to consider works like *T&C, KnT*, and *Boece* as a group, since they belong to the same phase of Chaucer's intellectual development.

As an independent literary effort Chaucer's translation of *Boece* has received a mixed response from modern readers. Nineteenth-century classicists, who liked their Catullus pure and, like Gibbon, saw everything after Augustus and Trajan as a decline, found little worthy of attention in Boethius, let alone in corrupt medieval translations by men who knew little Latin grammar and no Greek. (Gibbon, it should be noted, had a great admiration for Boethius, however; see 162.) When Chaucer's translation was compared to such

Latin editions of the *Consolatio* as those of Obbarius **218** and Peiper
219 the medieval translator was found to be woefully incompetent as a
Latinist. His reputation was only partially cleared when it was argued
by Liddell **197** and others that Chaucer worked with a French
translation, probably Jean de Meun's. The discovery of a French
source excused some of his blunders since they were perpetrated by
someone else, but made him the more culpable for having had to use a
crib. When it was demonstrated that he worked with a Latin text as
well as the French translation he was doubly damned — first for
having used the French and then, since he had the Latin text handy,
for not having corrected Jean's errors. Oddly, no one seemed bothered
by Jean's having made the errors in the first place; he remains a
learned man. Perhaps German and English classicists at the turn of
the century expected less from the French.

Recent scholars have been more tolerant of Chaucer's impurities,
acknowledging that the manuscripts he worked with were not the same
as Peiper's and allowing that even the best Latinists of the fourteenth
century made 'glaring' mistakes. None of them had our grammar
books or glossaries or carefully prepared editions. Chaucer's ability as
a Latinist can only be judged when we know precisely which Latin ms
or mss he worked with. It may even be that his ability as a Latinist or
French linguist is not the most important issue. It seems likely that
Chaucer was less interested in Jean's translation as a crib than he was
in studying it as a translation, for Jean, too, was a philosophical poet.
It is true that he follows Jean's syntax more closely in translating
Book I than in the rest of *Boece*. But that should not be taken as an
indication that his Latin was getting better as he went along. Rather
it suggests that he was becoming more engaged in the ideas he was
exploring and working more independently with them. Moreover,
Jean's translation is fascinating. He too recognized subtleties in the
text which he tried to get at through expansions and doublings of
words. Chaucer often follows him, especially when the expansions
enlarge upon the innuendoes of an idea. Chaucer learned much about
Boethius from Jean. There are, nevertheless, many instances in which
he does not follow Jean's expansions or makes expansions of his own.
More work remains to be done in this area of study to show ways in
which Chaucer understood Boethius with considerable subtlety and
also changed him to fit his own perceptions, though Machan's recent
book **199b** goes far in showing the way.

Bernard L. Jefferson **189** was the first modern scholar to find
merit in Chaucer's translation and to appreciate the poet's work.
Jefferson's study was limited by the fact that he did not have access to
a full transcription of Jean's translation. (He saw only samples
transcribed from Bibliothèque Nationale ms fr. 1097). More recently

the studies of Dedeck-Héry (176–79) have made possible closer comparison of Chaucer's translation with its French antecedents — if not the precise ms, at least one quite similar. Work has also been done by Barnet Kottler 194 to bring us closer to the Latin text Chaucer knew, and E.T. Silk 211, 241 has supplied important material on the tradition of the Latin commentaries. No ms or group of mss has been found which can explain all the curiosities of Chaucer's translation, however; it may well be that many of the glosses are entirely Chaucer's own.

The style of *Boece* has been generally scorned. A.C. Baugh's assessment — 'formless and undistinguished' — is typical (170). Recently a few studies have attempted to understand the style in terms of contemporary standards for translation from Latin into the vernacular. James Cline 174 did important groundwork in this area, though Ralph W.V. Elliott 180, 181 has made the most eloquent appeals on Chaucer's behalf, to suggest that Chaucer used the translation to experiment with language as he grew in his mastery of English expression. Any definitive statement of Chaucer's style in *Boece* must await the appreciation of such studies on *translatio* as those by Kelly 191, Machan 199b, and Nims 202, however, as well as a reappraisal of the expectations of prose in fourteenth-century England and France.

I have divided my bibliography into studies of *Boece*, discussions of Boethius, and Boethian influences on Chaucer. Research in the general area of Boethian studies has been greatly facilitated by Luca Obertello's recent endeavor (268), the second volume of which is devoted entirely to an annotated bibliography. The annotations are in Italian.

Editions

161   *Chaucer's 'Boece' Englisht from 'Anicii Manlii Severini Boethii Philosophiae Consolationis libri quinque.'* Edited from MS Cambridge University Library Ii.3.21, by F.J. Furnivall. Chaucer Society Publications, 1st series, no. 75. London: Trübner, 1886. [Dedicated to Henry Bradshaw, 'in his day the best Chaucer Scholar in England.'] The ms dates from ca 1420; Furnivall regards it as the best of the English *Boece* mss, with BL Addit. ms 10340, which Morris had edited (162), as the next best. Furnivall considered printing a parallel text edition with the Latin on the facing page, but 'I hadn't time'; besides, Peiper's Latin edition is available 'for about 2s.' (p v). This ms

includes the insertion of *FA* and *Fortune* after Book II.m.5 (pp 36–8).

162 *Chaucer's 'Boece' Englisht from Boethius's 'De Consolatione philosophiae.'* Edited from B.M. Additional MS 10340, collated with Cambridge University Library MS Ii.3.21, by Richard Morris. Chaucer Society Publications, 1st ser., no. 76. London: Trübner, 1886.
This edition was first printed in 1868 for EETS. Its introduction is eloquent in its praise of Boethius the man: 'surely we who read him in Chaucer's tongue, will not refuse to say that his full-circling meed of glory was other than deserved. Nor can we marvel that at the end of our great poet's life, he was glad that he had swelled the chorus of Boethius' praise; and "of the translacioun of Boece de Consolacioun," thanked "oure Lord Ihesu Crist and his moder, and alle the seintes in heuen" ' (p ii). Morris lists numerous passages from Boethius in Chaucer's poetry and compares them with their source. 'Had I had an opportunity of examining the Cambridge MS carefully throughout before the work was so far advanced, I should certainly have selected it in preference to the text now given to the reader' (p xvi). Addit. MS 10340 is 'written by a scribe who was unacquainted with the force of the final -*e* ' (p xvi). As appendix to the Introduction Morris prints Gibbon's account of Boethius, 'a man of fine genius,' 'the last of the ancients,' whose *Consolation* was 'a golden volume not unworthy of the leisure of Plato or Tully, but which claims incomparable merit from the barbarism of the times and situation of the author' (pp xvii–xx).

163 Skeat, W.W., ed. *Oxford Chaucer.* 1894/1899. Vol 2, pp 1–151. See **2.**
Skeat's text is based on Cambridge ms Ii.3.21, 'certainly the best extant authority' (p xlvi), which he collated with BL ms Addit. 10340, Caxton, and Thynne. He also consulted the Latin text of Obbarius (**218**) and the English text in Cambridge ms Ii.1.38 ('I now wish that I had collated it throughout' p xlvii). His introduction (pp vii–xlviii) dates the translation 'without fear of mistake' (p vii) in 1381–83, comments on Boethius' life (pp vii–xii), provides a synopsis of the *Consolation*, and discusses its influence, with special attention to Walton's verse translation (pp xiii–xix). Skeat discusses the style and manner of Chaucer's translation as well as evidences of Boethius in Chaucer's poetry (pp xix–xxxvii). The Boethian material in *BD* seems to depend on *RR:* 'in all probability, Chaucer, in 1369, was not very familiar with Boethius in the Latin original. And this accounts at once for the fact that he seldom quotes Boethius at first hand, perhaps not at all, in any of his earlier poems, such as the Complaint unto Pite, the Complaint of Mars, or Anelida and Arcite, or the Lyf of St. Cecilie' (p xxi). He probably began studying it in earnest ca 1375, under the inspiration of Jean de Meun. Skeat reminds the reader that Chaucer translated with 'no access to a convenient and well-arranged Latin

Dictionary, but only to such imperfect glossaries as were then in use. Almost the only resource, unless he had at hand a friend more learned than himself, was to guess' (p xxii). Some mistakes 'were almost inevitable'; 'we must not always infer that emendation is necessary, when we find in his text some curious error' (p xxii). The remainder of Skeat's introduction (pp xxxvii–xlviii) deals with mss and editions.

164 Liddell, Mark, ed. *'Boece.'* In *The Globe Chaucer.* Ed. A.W. Pollard *et al*, 1898/1928. See 3. Pp 352–437; xl.
Liddell bases his text on ms Cambridge Ii.1.38, with departures according to Addit. 16165, Harleian 2421, Bodley 797, Hengwrt 393, Cambridge Ii.3.21, Addit. 10340, Salisbury 13, Auct. F.3.5, and Caxton. He also consults Jean de Meun's translation in BN ms fr. 1097. Liddell's collations lead him to classify *Boece* mss in two groups. He follows the orthography of his basic text except where the few Northern forms peculiar to it have been changed to Chaucer's spelling. Chaucer's Latin scholarship 'was by no means adequate to the task, a deficiency which he probably felt himself, for he makes very free use of an existing French version now commonly ascribed to Jehan de Meung' (p xl).

165 Thynne, William, ed. *The Works of Geoffrey Chaucer.* 1905. See 4. [Introduction by W.W. Skeat]
Skeat notes that *Boece* was first printed by Caxton, who added an epitaph for Geoffrey Chaucer. Thynne includes the epitaph as a conclusion to his edition. 'Caxton's text is of great value, as it represents an excellent MS, now lost; and Thynne's reprint is so close that it is likewise of much value, and not infrequently corrects some of the best extant MSS' (p xxxiii).

166 Robinson, F.N., ed. *Works.* 1957. See 7. Text, pp 319–84; notes, pp 797–810, 903–5.
Robinson follows Liddell's mss classification, adding Thynne to Group A and noting that the two groups have only minor textual differences. He favors Cambridge Ii.1.38 as his basic text, with collations from Addit. 10340, Cambridge Ii.3.21, Caxton, and Thynne. He also draws upon Liddell for comparisons with the OF text. His Latin citations are from Peiper's edition 219. Robinson would date *Boece* shortly after 1380. Chaucer's translation, 'though painstaking, is diffuse and sometimes very free' (p 797). (Robinson did not, it should be noted, have access to Jean de Meun's translation as did Liddell 164). His notes, like Skeat's, are more extensive than those of other editions.

167 Fisher, John H., ed. *Complete Works.* 1977. See 11. Text, pp 813–903; textual notes, pp 970–71.
Fisher bases his text on Cambridge Ii.3.21, as did Skeat, using Cambridge Ii.1.38, Caxton, and Addit. 10340 for correction.

Cambridge Ii.3.21 includes a Latin text which must be close, as Skeat maintained, to the version Chaucer worked from; it also contains the best text of *FA*, appended to *Boece* II.m.5. Fisher emphasizes the weaknesses of prose style in *Boece* : 'When we compare the elegant rendering of Boethian dicta in Chaucer's verse with their fumbling expression in the prose translation, we can hardly believe that they are by the same person' (p 815).

168 Boyd, Beverly Mary, ed. *Chaucer according to William Caxton: Minor Poems and Boece, 1478.* Lawrence, Kansas: Allen Press, 1978.
The edition includes Caxton's texts of *PF* (in Caxton known as *Temple of Brass*), *AA, Boece, Truth, Fortune, Scogan, Purse, John* [*really Henry*] *Scogan's Ballade* which quotes the whole of Chaucer's *Gentilesse,* and verses 'Wyth empty honde' and 'Whan feyth failleth.' Boyd discusses John Shirley and the value of Caxton's edition, which is deserving of ms status (pp xi–xix). There are no radical differences between Caxton's *Boece* and the text as it appears in other A mss. The one Shirley ms of *Boece* belongs to the same group as Caxton's edition. 'Since Caxton is thought to have been a dealer in books as well as a printer, some of the manuscripts from which his editions were printed may have come from his own shop' (p xviii). Nothing is known of his compositors, though something is known of their method and its effect on the text. Only one copy of Caxton's quarto containing *AA* is known; seventeen copies of his *Boece,* excluding fragments, survive, however. Boyd's edition includes textual notes.

169 Pace, George B. and Linda E. Voigts. 'A "Boece" Fragment.' *SAC,* 1 (1979), 143–50.
A binding fragment, *Fragmenta Manuscripta* no. 150, University of Missouri-Columbia, bears portions of *Boece,* II.m.7 (verso twenty-two lines, recto twenty-one lines). A.I. Doyle dated the fragment as 'beginning of the fifteenth century,' contemporaneous with the Hengwrt and Ellesmere *CT* mss (p 145). Ralph Hanna says it belongs to the genetic group Addit. 10340 and Salisbury 13 (ie, the B group). It is the only *Boece* ms in North America.

Discussions of Chaucer's *Boece*, with Entries also on Jean de Meun's *le Livre du Confort*

See also **23**, **34** and **55**.

170 Baugh, A.C. 'The Middle English Period: Chaucer.' In *A Literary*

History of England. Ed. A.C. Baugh. New York: Appleton-Century-Crofts, 1948. Pp 249–63.
Chaucer's prose in *Boece, Astrolabe*, and the prose tales 'is formless and undistinguished' (p 255).

171 Burnley, J.D. *Chaucer's Language and the Philosophers' Tradition.* Cambridge: D.S. Brewer; Totowa, N.J.: Rowman and Littlefield, 1979. Burnley discusses Chaucer's conceptual and philosophical vocabulary for such topics as *tyrant, wisdom, philosopher, heart, reason, beyond reason,* and *gentilesse.* Frequently Boethius stands behind Chaucer's philosophical language in treating all of these topics. A short list of words which Chaucer associates with 'the philosopher' includes *tranquillite, pees, quiete, reste; constance, ferme, stable, stedfast, sad; pacience; suffisaunce* (pp 72-3). See Burnley's index for verbal clusters pertaining to the other topics.

172 Chisnell, Robert E. 'Chaucer's Neglected Prose.' In *Literary and Historical Perspective of the Middle Ages.* Ed. Patricia Cumminis and Charles W. Connell. Morgantown: West Virginia University Press, 1982. Pp 156–73.
More extensive use of *Boece* should be made in the teaching of Chaucer's poetry. Knowledge of his prose is essential to a full appreciation of his thought.

173 Cipriani, Lisi. 'Influence of *Romance of the Rose* on Chaucer.' 1907. See **90.**
Cipriani argues for influence of *RR* on Chaucer's translation of *Boece* (p 565). Robinson calls her argument very dubious: 'The parallels she cites are mostly without significance' (**7**, p 797).

174 Cline, James M. 'Chaucer and Jean de Meun: *De Consolatione Philosophiae.*' *ELH*, 3 (1936), 170–81.
Cline reviews the case for associating the French translation of the *Consolatio* in BN MS fr. 1097 with Jean de Meun: The ms includes a dedicatory epistle by Jean to Philip IV; extracts from the epistle are collected in BN Lat 8654 under the rubric: 'Ici sunt pluseurs notables de la translacion du livre Boece de Consolacion qui mestre Jehan de Meun translata en francois'; linguistic tests by Langlois **196** argue that the translation is in the dialect of Jean's authenticated writings. But, the *same* preface occurs before BN fr. 1096, also a translation of the *Consolatio*, but not one entirely in prose, rather in prose and verse. The latter is a freer and more intelligible translation; 1097 exhibits the same redundancy and obscurity evident in Chaucer's translation (pp 171–2). Cline examines internal evidence in the preface to determine which text it best fits. The preface makes three assertions: 1) that the translation was made at the king's command; 2) that Jean is to render *fully* the sense of the original (*plainement la sentence*) without

following the Latin too closely (*sens trop ensuivre des paroles du Latin*); 3) that if he were to translate too closely (*mot à mot*) the version would be unintelligible. This rubric might seem to fit 1096 better than 1097, with its awkward phrasings which seem to be more 'word for word.' But *mot à mot* does not mean a literal translation; nor does *plainement* mean free translation. To illustrate thirteenth- and fourteenth-century usage of such ideas Cline cites prefatory remarks in the Wyclif Bible (second recension) on translating according to sense, not merely to gloss, ' "so that the sentence be as opin, either openere, in English as in Latyn; and if the lettre mai not be suid in the translating, let the sentence euere be hool and open," — that is, *full — plainement*' (p 176). The translator says he will render ablative absolutes as English clauses, participial constructions as clauses connected with *and*, and relative clauses as principal clauses connected with a coordinate conjunction. Hence, 'Whanne rightful construccioun is lettid bi relacion, I resolue it openli' (p 177). He then cites examples. Cline points out that this medieval theory of open translation is what we would call literal translation, 'a translation as close to the original as can be accomplished without doing violence to English idiom. But it is in no sense synonymous with our idea of free translation' (p 178). MS 1097 follows this scheme of open translation; so does Chaucer. 'However his extravagance may be regarded today, it is proper to observe that in his time, Chaucer used the conventions of open translation with moderation. If he did not always make a virtue of necessity, he made no evil of it. And lesser men did. Once the idea became current that a certain degree of expansion was good they grew enthusiastic. As translation *mot à mot* erred on the side of too much condensation, open translation went to the other extreme of unnecessary fulness; almost every Latin phrase became an English clause, whether advisedly or not' (p 180).

175 Cropp, Glynnis M. 'Quelques Manuscrits Méconnus de la Traduction en Prose de *La Consolatio Philosophiae* par Jean de Meun.' *Scriptorium*, 33 (1979), 260–66.
In preparing his edition of the *Livres de confort de philosophie*, V.L. Dedeck-Héry **176** ignored four early manuscripts of good quality: Bruxelles, Bibl. Royale, 10394–414 and 11199; Madrid, Bibl. Nac., Vitr. 23–13; Paris, Bibl. de l'Arsenal, 738. A fifth ms, Glasgow, Univ. Lib., Gen 1227, is difficult to date, but includes Jean de Meun's prologue. Cropp fits the mss into Dedeck-Héry's *a* and *b* stemma of mss and concludes: 'De ces cinq manuscrits, quatre n'ont pas encore été signalés dans des recensements de mss des traductions françaises de la *Consolatio*. Nous âvons donc apporté un complément d'information à la fois à ces recherches générales et à nos connaissances du *Livres de*

confort de philosophie de Jean de Meun. Il est certain que d'autres mss de traductions de la *Consolatio* restent encore méconnus' (p 266). See also Glynnis M. Cropp, 'A Checklist of Manuscripts of the Medieval French Anonymous Verse-Prose Translations of the *Consolatio* of Boethius,' *NQ*, n.s. 26 (1979), 294–96; and Noel Harold Kaylor, Jr., 'An Additional Checklist of Manuscripts of the French Anonymous Verse-Prose Translation of the *Consolatio* of Boethius,' *NQ*, n.s. 28 (1981), 196–97.

176 Dedeck-Héry, V.L. 'Jean de Meun et Chaucer, Traducteurs de la Consolation de Boèce.' *PMLA*, 52 (1937), 967–91.
Noting the difficulty English philologists have had in assessing Chaucer's translation of Boethius, Dedeck-Héry compares the additions and glosses of Jean's and Chaucer's translations to determine more precisely Chaucer's debt to the French source. There are many examples of additions and glosses in Chaucer which are not found in the French text. There are more than ample proofs that he used Jean, however: viz, phrasing and stylistic resemblances, similar ways of dealing with difficult Latin passages, and treatment of ablative absolutes, participles, gerunds, adjectives, and tense. But the most important proof is Chaucer's repetition of Jean's errors. (Dedeck-Héry lists approx. seventy-five instances.) It seems likely that Chaucer also used a commentary like that of Guillaume de Conches or Nicholas Trivet. 'Nous pouvons affirmer que Chaucer, en traduisant la Consolation de Boèce, s'est servi de la traduction française et que, bien qu'il n'ait employé celle-ci ni exclusivement ni d'une façon suivie, sa dette envers Jean de Meun est considérable' (p 991).

177 — 'The Manuscripts of the Translation of Boethius' *Consolatio* by Jean de Meung.' *Spec*, 15 (1940), 432–43.
Dedeck-Héry uses Chaucer's translation as part of his apparatus for classifying the French mss. He notes, however, 'his translation cannot, of course, be put on the same footing as the manuscripts, inasmuch as it is not based entirely on the French text and as, on the contrary, it deliberately often shuns it and changes it in order to remain closer to the Latin original. But where Chaucer unmindfully omits to look at the Latin text, his translation can be useful to us' (p 435). In the seventeen mss studied (none of which is Jean's original) there are two main branches. The branch with which Chaucer's translation is associated is closer to the original and is headed by the fourteenth-century BN MS fr.1097, which 'permits us to deduce the original more easily than the others' (p 443). Fragment BN Lat. 8654N, f 48, helps disencumber 1097 of clerical errors.

178 — 'Le Boèce de Chaucer et les manuscrits français de la *Consolatio* de J. de Meun.' *PMLA*, 59 (1944), 18–25.

The ms Chaucer worked with belongs to the *a* group of mss (see **177**). The connections between ms Besancon 434 and ms Rennes 2435 derive from a ms related to the fragmentary ms Bodl. Rawl. 641, which shows the most peculiar readings reproduced in Chaucer. It is likely that Chaucer's source ms, like Rawl. 641, also contained a Latin text of the *Consolatio* and a Latin commentary.

179 — 'Boethius' *De Consolatione* by Jean de Meun.' *MS*, 14 (1952), 165–275.
This posthumous publication of Dedeck-Héry's edition of Jean de Meun's *Consolatio* is based on MS Paris, BN fr. 1097, with clerical errors, mistakes in readings, elisions and omissions corrected by its twin ms, Chantilly 284, the fragmentary BN Lat. 8654B, and others of the seventeen mss the editor worked with (see **177**). Ms comparisons in the textual notes to this edition are extensive. In his introduction to the edition Alex. J. Denomy observes: 'The editor deliberately included all variants, however minute, to provide the machinery for one day determining the definite Latin manuscript and French commentary that Chaucer used in his translation ... Within the text in italics are printed words, phrases and sentences that have no corresponding Latin equivalent in the original. In general these are tautological in character, doublets to reinforce or explain the meaning, explanatory notes and glosses' (p 166). [In personal correspondence dated May 21, 1982, Traugott Lawlor informs me that his and Ralph Hanna's collation of the Besancon MS proves Denomy's claim that D-H included 'all variants' to be 'emphatically not true.']

179a Dolson, Guy Bayley. *The Consolation of Philosophy in English Literature*. Cornell University Dissertation, 1926.
A comprehensive study of works in English influenced by Boethius' *Consolation*. Includes general discussion of Chaucer's and Walton's translations. In preparing the dissertation Dolson published several essays on the Boethian tradition, including: 'I.T. — Translator of Boethius,' *AJP*, 42 (1921), 124–6 (I.T. is John Thorpe, not John Thorie); 'Boethius' *Consolation of Philosophy* in English Literature during the Eighteenth Century,' *Classical Weekly*, 15 (1922), 124–6 (four 18th century translations and strong interest by Dr. Johnson); 'Imprisoned English Authors and the *Consolation of Philosophy* of Boethius,' *AJP*, 43 (1922), 118–9 (James I of Scotland, Thomas Moore, John Leslie); 'Southey and Landor and the *Consolation of Philosophy* of Boethius,' *AJP*, 43 (1922), 356–8 (*Imaginary Conversations* is strongly influenced by Boethius); and 'Did Caxton translate the *De Consolatione Philosophiae* of Boethius?' *AJP*, 47 (1926), 83–6 (the myth is unfounded; Caxton's *Boece* is Chaucer's).

179b Donner, Morton. 'Derived Words in Chaucer's *Boece:* The Translator

as Wordsmith.' *ChauR*, 18 (1984), 187–203.
Discusses 'how, when, for what purpose, and to what effect Chaucer
either chose new adoptions or used contemporary patterns of word
formation to meet the demands of translating Latin into English' (p
187). Out of the 2700 or so different words that appear in *Boece*, 'some
200 are new adoptions from French or Latin and more than 150 are
new derivations formed on contemporary English patterns ... There
are reasonable grounds for considering most of [the adoptions and
derivations] innovative' (p 187). Chaucer is particularly shrewd in his
use of affixation to create new words and in his invention of gerunds
and participles. 'The paucity of conversions in *Boece*, like the
abundance of gerunds and participles, signals a quality of Chaucer's
writing that has long been recognized and admired by serious students
of his work, his respect for language' (p 202).

179c   Eckhardt, Caroline D. 'The Medieval *Prosimetrum* Genre from
Boethius to *Boece*.' *Genre*, 16 (1983), 21–38.
Defines the *prosimetrum* tradition Chaucer might have known and
considers why Chaucer rejected it in his translating of *Boece*. Perhaps
Chaucer, following Dante's discussion in the *Convivio* of the apparent
guilelessness of prose, chose to write, as he says in the *Astrolabe*, in
'naked wordes,' in a style that is 'rewde' rather than 'curious,' in order
that the ideas might be more clear, as the two speakers in *Boece* face
the 'ultimate dilemmas of the universe with a passionate desire for
clarification' (p 32).

180   Elliott, Ralph W.V. 'Chaucer's Reading.' 1969. See **103**
Before condemning Chaucer's failure to read his originals aright, we
must understand the physical circumstances of his reading and know
what text he used — certainly not the purified texts reconstructed by
modern editors. Chaucer was an astonishingly learned man working in
three foreign languages: 'Few great English writers display so patently
an intellectual indebtedness to the work of lesser men than Chaucer
does to Jean de Meun and to Boethius' (p 52). There is not a major
poem of Chaucer's which does not draw on Boethius, and the
philosopher is direct inspiration for many of the minor ones. Although
the *Boece* translation impregnates Chaucer for life with Boethian
philosophy, he uses the ideas creatively and integrally to his own
purpose, especially in *T&C, KnT*, and *NPT* where the *Consolation*
'fertilised and ordered his thinking' (p 53).

181   — *Chaucer's English*. London: André Deutsch, 1974.
Ch 3, 'I Speke in Prose,' pp 132–80: *Boece* is probably 'Chaucer's first
excursion into prose' (p 153). Critical opinion is wrong in dismissing it
as second-rate. Though there is a looseness and diffuseness, as
Robinson points out (**166**), there are also 'many passages of firm

syntactical cohesion, of carefully controlled diction, of active lexical
inventiveness, and of genuine poetic sensibility' (pp 153–54). Chaucer's
principles on the art of translating seem to agree with those of John
Purvey, a close associate of Wyclif, especially in dealing with
constructions like the ablative absolute. Often in his expansions
Chaucer strives to clarify the Gallicisms he uses. There are about 150
coinages and borrowings which appear only in *Boece*. 'That Chaucer
was experimenting with words seems incontrovertible if we consider
the types and morphemic structures involved, the use of certain words
for rhetorical or rhythmic effect, alliteration, for example, as well as
for the immediate contextual meaning required, and, perhaps most
significant, the valuable practice *Boece* afforded for further lexical
inventiveness in *Troilus and Criseyde* and the *Canterbury Tales* ...
Boece was an invaluable linguistic practice ground' (pp 160–61).
Elliott analyzes III.m.11, lines 1–12 in terms of 'unmistakable poetic
rhythm' modelled on the Latin line. 'If we are content to accept *Boece*
as an uneven work, we are all the more gratified by the many passages
of smoothly flowing, idiomatic, and at times poetic, prose' (p 165).
The translation of *Boece* came at a strategic moment in Chaucer's
poetic career. 'It provided him with a ready-made framework within
which he could experiment with words and phrases, rhythms, and
sentence patterns quite different from those in the "poetry" that lay
behind him. It enabled him also to come to grips with Boethius's
thought, by laying it bare, examining it at leisure, expanding it,
turning it over, as it were, with the help of a flexible style and a
growing word power. When he returned in his subsequent poems to
render some of Boethius's passages again, this time in verse, the result
is all the better for the trial run in prose. It is easy to dismiss the
prose as immature, heavyhanded, even ugly, compared with the
succinctness and pleasing movement of most of the verse, but it is just
as easy, and critically no more helpful, to dismiss the Eagle or the
Goose for not being more like Chauntecleer. The point of contrasting
passages from *Boece* with corresponding passages in the poems is not
to render the former absurd by comparison, but to illustrate Chaucer's
growing mastery of English expression' (p 168).

182 Fehlauer, Friedrich. 'Die englischen Übersetzungen von Boethius *De
Consolatione Philosophie.*' In *Normannia, Germanisch-Romanische
Bücherei.* Zweiter Band. Berlin: Emil Felber, 1909. Pp 1–112.
Fehlauer reviews English translations and adaptations of the
Consolatio by King Alfred; the Old English translator of the *metra*
into alliterative lines; Chaucer (pp 31–48); John Walton (1525 edn; the
translation was done ca 1410); George Colville (1556); Elizabeth I
(1593); John Bracegirdle (1609); Thomas Challoner (ca 1563); Richard

Graham, Viscount Preston (1680?); Ridpath (for George II, ca 1785), W.V. Cooper (1902); and H.R. James (1906). Fehlauer offers information about the translator or occasion of the translation, includes comparative excerpts, observations on the form of translation employed, and concludes with a brief discussion of the consequences of the numerous translations. The section on Chaucer reviews arguments on the date of translation, its sources, its style ('Chaucer ist nicht eigentlich Prosaiker, sein Prosastil ist ziemlich schwerfällig, während seine Verse schön leichtflüssig sind und auch die Sprache in der gebundenen Form eine viel anmutigere ist' [p 37]), vocabulary, and errors. Fehlauer compares *FA* with Chaucer's translation of II.m.5 and the Latin original (pp 46–7). He discusses the relationship of Walton's translation to Chaucer's (pp 51–61).

183 Fischer, Olga. 'A Comparative Study of Philosophical Terms in the Alfredian and Chaucerian Boethius.' *Neophilologus*, 63 (1979), 622–39. The traditional view that OE was an impoverished language and that ME made up for these deficiencies by extensive borrowings from the French is examined through a comparison of the Alfredian and Chaucerian translations of Boethius. Alfred did not aim for a literal translation ('What was important to him was that his readers should have no difficulty in understanding his text' [p 625]); Chaucer's aim was to 'adhere to the Latin text as strictly as possible.' In order to accomplish this Chaucer makes extensive use of loanwords from the French when precise English equivalents are not available. In doing so, however, he 'is not always very discriminating' (p 632), and many of these equivalents 'were not in real use, but probably mere on-the-spot adaptations' (p 633). Another kind of carelessness is shown in Chaucer's translation — he 'does not really distinguish between the different senses a word can have in either Latin or French. He simply takes over the loanword with all its senses, some of which soon became obsolete' (p 633). Of 225 terms examined in Fischer's sample, Chaucer uses native terms for only fifty. On the other hand, Alfred manages to provide adequate translations for almost all these terms by means of native words. 'It can in no way be maintained that all the new loanwords used after the Norman Conquest were needed to fill linquistic or cultural gaps in O.E.' (p 639).

184 Hammond, Eleanor Prescott. *Bibliographical Manual.* 1908. See **36**. Lists mss and printed editions. The references to *Boece* in *Adam, LGW*, and the *Retraction*, the constant evidence of Chaucer's familiarity with the *Consolatio*, and the note of Shirley MS Addit. 16165 ('Boicius de consolacone prosed in Englisshe by Chaucier') confirm the title and authenticity of the work. Conjectures on the date of *Boece* range from 1373 to 1384. Hammond lists other translations of

the *Consolation* and includes notes on Chaucer's translation and its source.

185 — 'Boethius: Chaucer: Walton: Lydgate.' *MLN*, 41 (1926), 534–5. The error in translating 'somnos dabat herba salubres' (II.m.5) as 'sleeping contentedly on the grass' rather than sleeping after a vegetable diet originates in the OF translation, then comes into Chaucer in *Boece* and *FA*, is picked up from Chaucer by Walton in the fifteenth century, and finally crops up in the 1609 translation. In Bk III m.12, *occidit* (was undone) is translated by Chaucer who follows Jean's 'et fu morte' as *killed*; so too by Queen Elizabeth and the 1609 translation. An admirable Boethian passage occurs in Lydgate, *Fabula Duorum Meratorum* (lines 734–46), which is 'both more compact and more vigorous than the prose of Chaucer ... so much so that it would be especially interesting to know how Lydgate became possessed of it, — also, how much Boethius-knowledge it represents' (p 535).

186 Hittmair, Rudolf. *Das Zeitwort Do in Chaucers Prosa*. Wiener Beitrage zur Englischen Philologie, LI. Wien und Leipzig: Wilhelm Braumüller, 1923.
Although Hittmair occasionally draws upon the *Astrolabe, Melibee*, and *ParsT, Boece* is his main source of primary examples. He contrasts Chaucer's use of *do* with its use in Alfred's redaction and in the translations of Boethius by Walton and Queen Elizabeth (pp 105–22).

187 Hollander, John. ' "Moedes or Prolaciouns" in Chaucer's *Boece*.' *MLN*, 71 (1956), 397–99.
Prolaciouns (II, pr. 1), which has no equivalent in the Latin sources has a specific musical meaning [nb, *Prolacioun* does not appear in the OF either — R. Peck]. The term *tonus* was reserved for church modes, which had little connection with Greek octave scales. In the fourteenth century the *Ars Nova* of Machaut gave *modus* an entirely different meaning. Instead of designating obsolete scales it referred to rhythm. *Tempus* indicates a ratio of whole to half; in perfect time three half notes make up a whole, while in imperfect time two halves make a whole. *Modus* indicates a ratio between quarters and halves; three if major, two if minor. *Prolatio* indicates eighths to quarters, triple if major and duple if minor. To Chaucer's audience, then, *modus* in a musical context would indicate a rhythmic pattern rather than a tonal one. *Prolaciouns* is thus a gloss to make sure that *moedes* is understood in right context (p 398). Chaucer's mistake indicates that 'he knew and understood at least the notation of the music of the fourteenth century. It is a mistake that only a late medieval musician might tend to have made' (p 399).

188 Hussey, S.S. 'The Minor Poems and the Prose.' 1970. See **42**.
'It is possible that Chaucer knew the book [*Consolatio*] quite well

before settling down to translate it — parts of the *Romaunt* owe a
good deal to Boethius' (p 247). Hussey provides a synopsis of *Boece*;
he finds the prose style 'sometimes diffuse, with glosses which at times
illuminate but now and then merely irritate' (p 249).

89 Jefferson, Bernard L. *Chaucer and the Consolation of Philosophy of
    Boethius.* Princeton, N.J.: Princeton University Press; London:
    Oxford University Press, 1917. Rpt New York: Gordian Press, 1968.
    Originally a Princeton University Doctoral Dissertation (1914), this
    study sets out to show the full indebtedness of Chaucer to the
    Consolation of Philosophy. Ch 1, 'The Translation,' pp 1–46,
    comments on the sources, inaccuracies, and style of *Boece.* Jefferson
    notes that Chaucer used a French translation and Trivet's commentary
    as sources. Since he did not have access to BN fr. 1097 Jefferson
    worked with transcribed passages which Liddell supplied, the excerpts
    in Langlois' essay (**196**), and the fragments of Trivet published in
    Peterson (**203**). Thus his list of 'errors' is based principally on
    comparison with the Latin. Chaucer does not always understand
    historical allusions; he misses the finer shades of meaning by losing the
    force of Latin conjunctions, prepositions, and pronouns, and he often
    translates interrogatives as declaratives, misapplies or ignores negatives
    to reverse the Latin meaning, becomes so literal that the English has
    little or no significance, and mistakes case relationships. Part of the
    fault may be due to the poor Latin text he was working with; and part
    may be misunderstandings in the French text. Chaucer's vocabulary is
    highly Latinized, especially in difficult passages, many of the words
    appearing for the first time in written English. His style is
    characterized by a conspicuous lack of sentence unity and coherence,
    excessive use of *and* and *that*, monotonous repetition of nouns, and
    diffuseness. (*Boece* is half again as long as the original.) Nevertheless,
    some passages are skillfully composed, 'marked by a fullness, a sense of
    measure and proportion.' *Boece* lacks 'any idea of a precise application
    of mechanical principles such as come later to characterize the prose of
    John Lyly; yet Chaucer, gifted with a sensitive ear, feeling the spirit of
    his original, has reproduced its enthusiasm, its dignity of expression,
    and, as best he could, its symmetry of style. His translation is the
    translation of a poet' (p 46). Ch 2, 'Influence of the *Consolation* on
    Chaucer's Thought: Providence,' pp 47–80, considers many of
    Chaucer's favorite Boethian themes — Fortune, destiny, chance,
    gentilesse, suffisaunce, divine 'purveyaunce,' the bond of love, and
    truth. 'The idea of an overruling Providence seems to have made a
    deep impression on Chaucer at one time in his life. In particular,
    Troilus and the *Knight's Tale* have a decidedly fatalistic background
    and contain long and frequent passages which dwell upon various

questions relating to Providence, especially in its relation to men' (p 68). Jefferson thinks providential themes in *BD* are derived chiefly from *RR* and Machaut's *Remède de Fortune*, rather than directly from Boethius. In *Mars*, *T&C*, *KnT*, *MLT*, *LGW*, and *FrankT* Chaucer draws on Boethian questions of divine justice, the existence of evil in a benevolent universe, and questions of foreknowledge and free will. Ch 3, 'Influence of the *Consolation* on Chaucer's Thought: Felicitee,' pp 81–119, considers man's strongest instinct, the love of happiness, as it is manifested in such Chaucerian creations as the Franklin, January, Hypermnestra, and Criseyde. Jefferson follows Boethius' procedure and begins with the motif of False Felicity, especially as it is manifested in power (*MonkT*), fame (*HF*), and riches (*FA, Sted, Truth, Gent, WBT*, and *KnT*). To explain Chaucer's treatment of true felicity Jefferson discusses *Gent* (pp 94–104) and *Truth* (pp 104–19). Ch 4, 'Influence of the *Consolation* on *Troilus* and the *Knight's Tale*,' pp 120–32, explores the two works most heavily influenced by Boethius. 'Chaucer's thoughts must have been afire with the Boethian philosophy when he worked over these tales from their Italian originals, for always looming up in their background ... are the fundamental Boethian conceptions of fate and human felicity, determining his mental attitude toward the subject' (p 120). Jefferson considers characterization to be Chaucer's primary means of dramatizing Boethian ideas. Criseyde, by a kind of auto-suggestion, becomes false herself, even as she worries about falseness. 'Her tragedy was, that she, beautiful, tender-hearted, womanly in every instinct, had so earnestly sought happiness, and instead of finding it, had, because she knew the world only too well, plunged headlong into an act of unfaith of the very kind that she herself most abhorred and feared, to be the eternal example of unfaithfulness in love. And no one is more conscious of her tragedy than Criseyde herself, as she shows in the plaintive words which mark her last appearance in the poem' (p 129). She is the only person in the poem who has intellectual discrimination to see the falseness of her felicity. Ch 5, 'The Boethian Influence of Detail,' pp 133–66, lists passages in Chaucer's poetry showing Boethian influence.

189a Kaylor, Noel Harold, Jr. 'John Walton's 1410 Verse Translation of the *De Consolatione Philosophiae* in the Context of its Medieval Tradition.' *FCS*, 6 (1983), 121–48.
Walton is not simply a translator of the *Consolatio* but rather is part of a self-conscious tradition of medieval translators. Kaylor summarizes the history of Boethius translation from King Alfred and Provençal to the fifteenth century. Fourteenth-century France produced seven different translations of the *Consolatio* which have survived. Chaucer worked from Jean de Meun's, and Walton worked

mainly from Chaucer's. The 'close similarity between the verses of
Walton and the prose of Chaucer is not isolated, but continuous' (p
140). But Walton understood Boethius well; his translations of
difficult passages are often clearer than Chaucer's. Sixteenth century
printers of Walton regularly change Walton's wording to make it
correspond to Chaucerian words printed by Caxton in 1479 (p 142),
thus sometimes at the expense of Walton's clarity.

189b — *The Medieval Translations of Boethius' Consolation of Philosophy
in England, France, and Germany: An Analysis and Annotated
Bibliography.* Vanderbilt University Dissertation, 1985. Dir. Hans
Schultz.
Chapters on the translations of King Alfred, Notker Labeo, Jean de
Meun, and Chaucer, with discussion of the medieval *Consolatio*
tradition pertaining to each. The bibliography includes about 300
annotated items. Kaylor spent some time at the University of
Regensburg working on this project; the coverage of items in German
is particularly strong.

190 Kean, Patricia. *Chaucer and the Making of English Poetry*. Vol 1:
Love Vision and Debate. London: Routledge and Kegan Paul, 1972.
Kean draws extensively on *Boece* in commenting on Chaucer's use of
Boethius, noting verbal parallels between *Boece* and Chaucer's poetry.
'The *de Consolatione* ... provides the model of a love which is an
essential part of the whole frame of the universe, and which is as
essential to the microcosm as it is to the macrocosm, in that it is
expressed in the pattern of individual births and deaths and of
individual loves' (p 158).

191 Kelly, Douglas. '*Translatio Studii:* Translation, Adaptation, and
Allegory in Medieval French Literature.' *PQ*, 57 (1978), 287–310.
'*Translatio* is a diversified and fundamental characteristic of medieval
composition' (p 291). There are three prominent modes: 1) translation
as such, including scribal transmission; 2) adaptation; and 3)
allegorical or extended metaphorical discourse. '*Translatio* is in fact
rarely only close translation' (p 292). Works like the *Ovide Moralisé*,
Brunetto Latini's *Tresor*, and Jean de Meun's 'brilliant patchwork' in
the *Rose* compiled from heterogeneous sources, utilize all three modes
of *translatio* (pp 291–3). Guillaume's *Rose* uses personification for
purposes of adaptation (pp 299–302).

192 *The Kingis Quair.* This mid-fifteenth-century poem, attributed to
James I of Scotland, draws heavily on *Boece* and Boethian material
from Chaucer. The poet-narrator sits down to read *Boece* and begins
reflecting upon the tragic reversal of Fortune, which leads him to recall
his own story — 'All myn aventure I gan ourhayle' — which is
opposite to that of Boethius. The Boethian philosopher enjoyed

success, then was cast down and imprisoned; the *Kingis Quair* poet begins in prison, but, like Palamon and Arcite or the narrator of Charles of Orleans' ballades, even in his time of misfortune sees the lady whose love he would win and who brings him good fortune. Below are listed the principal editions of *KQ* and two essays which focus on the Boethian material in the poem. [See **510** for a more complete bibliography on *KQ*. See also **64, 556a,** and **645.**]

192a Skeat, W.W., ed. *The Kingis Quair, together with A Ballad of Good Council, by King James I of Scotland.* The Scottish Text Society. London and Edinburgh, 1884.

James may have read *De Consolatione* in Chaucer's translation, though he implies in stanza 7 that he read it in the Latin original (p 58). Skeat notes several borrowings from the *Romaunt* as well as *Boece*, and also from *KnT, BD,* and *LGW.* The poem has more of Gower and Lydgate's gravity and moralizing and 'very little of Chaucer's lightness of heart and humour' (p 94).

192b Lawson, Alexander, ed. *The Kingis Quair and the Quare of Jelusy.* London: Adam and Charles Black, 1910.

Introduction with comments on James I's life, the authenticity of the two poems, and their mss. Sparse notes.

192c MacKenzie, W. MacKay, ed. *The Kingis Quair.* London: Faber and Faber, 1939.

MacKenzie relates the poem to other fifteenth-century Chaucerian poems such as *Temple of Glas, AL, FL,* and *CL,* poems on which 'it would be impossible to overrate the influence of Chaucer' (p 29). In *KQ* the influence is specifically *Boece.*

192d Norton-Smith, John, ed. *The Kingis Quair of James I of Scotland, with Introduction, Notes, and Glossary.* Oxford: Clarendon Press, 1971.

Discusses Charles of Orleans and James I (ca 1422) in confinement in London, with 'leisure to read Chaucer intelligently, together with the opportunity to learn about his poetry from assured sources of transmission; for James, possibly from texts handed down through the royal tutor, poet and friend of Chaucer, Henry Scogan, who had recently died (in 1407); for Charles, from texts perhaps preserved by the Chaucer family and put into his hands by Alice (née Chaucer), Countess of Suffolk, wife of Charles's custodian during the period 1430–6' (p xi). 'The poet's application of Boethius and his *De Consolatione* to his own plight amounts to an individual concern — it is not merely a literary formula with which to preface a poetic adumbration of a certain philosophical view of the human condition. If the eventual solution accorded the poet invites certain parallels with ideas examined in the *De Consolatione* (which was also the fruit of prison and exile), it also suggests crucial differences. The reader is intended to appreciate both' (p xiv). Norton-Smith's notes (pp 51–83) are rich in detailing parallels and differences between *De Consolatione* and *KQ*; also in parallels in wording and detail with the *Romaunt*.

192e McDiarmid, Matthew, ed. *The Kingis Quair of James Stewart.* Totowa, New Jersey: Rowman and Littlefield, 1973.

Discusses earlier editions ('the best of these texts is that of Skeat, for its consistently skeptical and constructive criticism,' p 1), the ms, and the language, date, authorship, and style. 'The *Kingis Quair* is a poetical autobiography' (p 48). What is notably missing from earlier discussions of the poems is an adequate accounting of its author and subject, namely James Stewart (p 49). The poem reviews the 'circular course of experience and learning,' a conception which James Stewart might have found 'in many places, but most conveniently in commentaries on Boethius [eg, the circular diagram of the spiritual life in the 1525 edition of Walton's translation, EETS, pp 369–71], the moralizations in copies of Sacrobosco's *Sphere*, and especially in De Guileville's *Pèlèrinage de la Vie Humaine*' (p 55). Like Boethius or Cresseid in Henryson's *Testament*, the king learns to accept Fortune's whims. 'The main difference in his case ... is that he discovers grace not through reasoning or painful correction, but by a change in Fortune's treatment of him that reveals how unhappiness can introduce happiness, even the greatest that can befall a man. He has seen the two faces of Fortune and found them fair ... What James finally preaches is, effectually, salvation through marriage, finding the love of God in the love of a woman ... It need hardly be said that this is not a "courtly" love of a Troilus for his Criseyde; it has a doctrinal character that is more easily related to the known importance for the author of the event that inspired it than to any literary convention' (p 56).

192f Ebin, Lois A. 'Boethius, Chaucer and *The Kingis Quair*.' *PQ*, 53 (1974), 321–41.

The *Kingis Quair* reflects a direct response to rather than an imitation of Boethius' *Consolation* and Chaucer's *T&C* and *KnT*. The author takes up questions of Fortune but answers them in terms quite different from Chaucer. By substituting Minerva for Philosophy he gives a more 'explicitly Christian emphasis' to the theme (p 334). He likewise 'devotes almost as much attention to Boethius as a writer as he does to Boethius as a philosopher' (p 338). The narrator 'learns to overcome Fortune while he remains in this world. Significantly, he learns not from Philosophy but through his journey from youth to maturity, the journey of every man's life, an experience at once more immediate and credible than Boethius'. Finally, in contrast to Boethius, James demonstrates that man's full recognition of Fortune's role comes from all of the kinds of experience accessible to him — in life, in books, in dreams, and in writing' (p 341).

192g   Carretta, Vincent. 'The *Kingis Quair* and the Consolation of Philosophy.' *SSL*, 16 (1981), 14–28.
Challenges those critics who view *KQ* as a courtly love poem. 'In order to have Boethius sanction courtly love as he supposedly does in the *Kingis Quair*, a gross distortion of the *Consolation* is necessary. But this distortion will remain as long as the poem is read as one of courtly love told by a reliable historical figure. I suggest that the author very carefully discredits his narrator-persona's reliability and that Boethius is used not to support this persona but rather as a moral touchstone against which the persona's folly is to be judged' (p 15). The poet read Boethius just as Chaucer and his contemporaries did, as a warning against trust in Fortune. 'In this kind of inverted *Consolation*, the author has presented us with a narrative persona who learns essentially the opposite of what Boethius had learned ... Although his own blindness and ignorance keep him temporarily happy at the top of Fortune's wheel, there should be no doubt that he will be an object lesson of Philosophy's teachings about those who enslave themselves to Fortune's wheel, because, as Fortune herself warns him, "The nature of it is evermore, / After ane hicht, to vale and geve a fall" (st. 172)' (p 24).

193   Koch, John. 'Chaucer's Boethiusübersetzung: Ein Beitrag zur Bestimmung der Chronologie seiner Werke.' *Anglia*, 46 (1922), 1–51.
Chaucer must have translated *Boece* ca 1381, but he could have known Boethius and drawn upon him long before making the translation. The *Consolation* was very well known and available to Chaucer not only in Latin but in several French translations, as well as in literary adaptations (p 2). Chaucer's translation is not very adept. The sentences are heavy ('schwerfällige Umschreibungen' [p 3]), Latinate, and often erroneous. Chaucer misunderstands historical references in his source, but we must remember that he did not have access to our convenient reference works. He had difficulty moving gracefully back and forth between the Latin and the French translation he worked with, which accounts for some of the awkwardness in his translation. He has more errors than one finds in contemporary translations of Ovid, Virgil or Statius. But accuracy was less his goal than conveying the general idea. We recognize everywhere in Chaucer's translation that he was trying to reach a broad audience (p 5). Koch summarizes Boethian influences throughout Chaucer's works and offers an extensive synopsis of the treatise. One cannot say that Chaucer took over Boethius' complete philosophical system; rather he selected bits which fit into his own world view (p 32). He was less interested than

Boethius in criticizing worldly ambition and the vanity of earthly renown, perhaps because of his closeness to court circles. He prefers Trojan mythology to Greek; nor does he share Boethius' pacifistic views. Koch's 'contribution' (*beitrag*) toward determining the chronology of Chaucer's works (pp 33-51) is based upon an examination of the degree of Boethian influence in each, following roughly the principle that greater Boethian influence suggests closer proximity to *Boece*. He ranks eighteen Chaucerian works which draw upon the *Consolation*, excluding *BD*, on grounds that its Boethian matter comes from French sources, *ClerkT*, on grounds that its Boethian matter comes from Petrarch, and *ParsT*, because its philosophical matter is too diffuse. He also excludes the Boethian lyrics because they are deliberately based on the *Consolation* and could have been done at any time after Chaucer became acquainted with Boethius. The top five works of fiction reflecting Boethian matter are *T&C, KnT, MonkT, HF*, and *PF*, in that order. Koch dates *Boece* ca 1381. His intricate argument, which takes into account other factors as well as *Boece*, leads him to conclude that *T&C* was begun in 1382, *PF* in the spring of 1382, *Romaunt* in 1384, *HF* in the winter of 1384–85, *LGW* in 1385–86. *Palamon and Arcite* was begun in the late 1370's, then reworked with Boethian material to become *KnT* ca 1388. The *de casibus* tragedies were begun after 1381 as separate pieces, some of which were written after Chaucer worked with Innocent III; *MonkT* was not finally assembled until after 1385. The link between idleness in *SNT* and the *Romaunt* suggests a date ca 1386. *Mel MerchT*; *WBT* precedes *Bukton* (1396), but post-dates *Gent; Fortune* and *Truth* are from 1386–87. *Truth* is too personal a poem to be addressed exclusively to Vache, as Rickert argues (*MP*, 11 [1913], 209–25). Chaucer's most productive years were 1386–93, after he was displaced from the customs job in the crisis of 1386 (also the year Phillipa died), a time when he may have returned to the *Consolatio* for personal reasons and concentrated on his writing.

194 Kottler, Barnet. *Chaucer's Boece and the Late Medieval Textual Tradition of the 'Consolatio Philosophiae.'* Yale University Dissertation, 1953.
Kottler makes extensive collations of twenty-three late mss (mostly fourteenth-century) with spot collations of an additional twenty-two mss in an effort to shed light on the Latin text of the *Consolatio* which Chaucer might have used. By Chaucer's day a new vulgate version with certain new readings which had driven out older readings influences all mss, though the crossing over is so heterogeneous that it is not possible to make discreet classification of the traditions. Ch 1 reviews previous scholarship. Silk's dissertation on Cambridge Ii.3.21

(211) is pivotal; so too the work of Dedeck-Héry on BN fr. 1907
(176–79). The question is not whether Chaucer did in fact use a
Latin and a French text but, rather, which mss did he use. Silk's table
of comparisons to demonstrate Chaucer's dependence on a Trivet text
lacked a control factor. 'Chaucer could not have relied exclusively
upon the text as quoted in the Trivet commentary' (p 13). Silk's
'unique' readings are not unique but are shared by most late mss. The
value of lists of Chaucer's errors in such studies as those of Stewart
212, Skeat 163, Liddell 197, Fehlauer 182, and Jefferson 189 is
'contingent upon our knowledge of the nature of the text available to
Chaucer' (p 14). Ch 2 is devoted to mss. No complete list of Boethius
mss exists; of later mss of the thirteenth through the fifteenth centuries
none has been published at all. Kottler derived his list of forty-five
mss from printed catalogs of major collections in England, France,
Italy, and the U.S.A. Ch 3, 'The Textual Tradition,' notes that though
there are over four hundred mss of the *Consolatio* there is a lapse of
three centuries between the Ur-Text and the earliest known mss. A
review of attempts by Engelbrecht, Peiper, Weinberger, Schepss, and
Klingner to unravel mss relationships points to the deficiencies in all
schemes both for early and late ms traditions. In later traditions some
erroneous vulgatization gets cleaned up but also 'innumerable
accretions of glosses and commentaries' get worked in (p 59). Ch 4
discusses textual variants. Ch 5, 'The Nature of Chaucer's Latin Text,'
demonstrates that the distinction between a Trivet and non-Trivet
text must be abandoned: 'The existence of the later vulgate tradition
means that some readings are virtually common to the whole tradition
... It seems clear that this new reading could hardly have been
avoided by Trivet or by Chaucer' (p 153). The nature of Chaucer's
Latin text cannot be defined by discrete classification since that is
prevented by continual crossing. Some mss do *tend* to reject new
readings in preference to the old. Chaucer is of the new tradition,
though sometimes he seems to maintain old readings; in other places
he follows Jean de Meun. 'No manuscript among those studied here
contains all the readings necessary to account for Chaucer's rendering'
(p 170). This does not mean that Chaucer used more than one Latin
ms, however; rather it suggests the likelihood of a lost ms which would
contain all the readings of his rendering. Silk's Cambridge Ii.3.21 is
the closest known, though not the one (p 174). Many of the variants
are of no use in determining Chaucer's Latin source because there is
no way of adjudicating between claims of the Latin and French
sources. Though some of Chaucer's 'errors' are traceable to his Latin
source, it remains evident that many appear to be his responsibility.
Moreover, 'in the matter of omissions, most of the relevant passages or
works have not been omitted in the manuscripts studied' (pp 174–5).

195 — 'The Vulgate Tradition of the *Consolatio Philosophiae* in the Fourteenth Century.' *MS*, 17 (1955), 209–14.

By the fourteenth century a new vulgate tradition of Boethius mss had been established. 'Clearly the solution to such a specific problem as the extent of Chaucer's reliance on the translation of Jean de Meun [and his commentators] depends upon our knowledge of the state of the texts they used' (p 213).

195a Krapp, George Philip. *The Rise of English Literary Prose*. New York: Oxford University Press, 1915. Rpt New York: Frederick Ungar, 1963.

Comments briefly on Chaucer's four prose works. 'Chaucer was not temperamentally an experimenter or innovator ... He seems to have felt no impulse, therefore, to invent prose for English literature' (p 4). His 'scholarship was not always sufficient to save him from blunders' in the *Boece*; its main defects are 'crudity and awkwardness, even at times obscurity, of expression, due to imperfect adaptation of thought to the English idiom' (p 5).

196 Langlois, Ernest. 'La Traduction de Boèce par Jean de Meun.' *Romania*, 42 (1913), 331–69.

Langlois contends that the prose translation of Boethius ms BN fr. 1097 is the work of Jean de Meun. The dialect is Jean's and the translation is prefaced by a dedicatory epistle from Jean to Philip IV on the purpose of the translation. V.L. Dedeck-Héry (**176**, p 969) finds Langlois' argument to be 'prouvé irréfutablement.'

196a Lawler, Traugott. 'Chapter 14: Chaucer.' In *Middle English Prose: A Critical Guide to Major Authors and Genres*. Ed. A.S.G. Edwards. New Brunswick, N. J.: Rutgers University Press, 1984. Pp 291–313.

Surveys critical assessments of Chaucer's prose style in *Boece*, *Astrolabe*, *Equatorie*, *Pars T*, *Mel*, and *Retraction*, comments on textual authority, and supplies a bibliography.

197 Liddell, M.H. 'Chaucer's Translation of Boece's *Boke of Comfort*.' *Academy*, 48 (Sept. 21, 1895), 227.

Liddell compares Chaucer's *Boece* (Skeat's text); Jean de Meung BN MS fr. 1097; Lat. 18424; fr. 1098; and Obbarius' Latin text to show 'striking similarites' between the English and French translations in Book I. 'There are, on the other hand, divergences enough to exculpate Chaucer from the charge of having merely translated Jehan de Meung's French without ever having looked at the Latin original. The most natural explanation of the similarities is that Chaucer had before him as he worked his predecessor's version, and drew largely from it, translating word for word in the difficult passages, in the others altering the French to suit his ideal of fitness and accuracy. In his alterations ... he very often blunders; for Jehan de Meung's

version certainly possesses a fluency, beside which Chaucer's
translation is cramped and stilted' (p 227).

197a — 'Chaucer's Boethius Translation.' *Academy*, 49 (March 7, 1986),
199–200.
Bodleian ms Auct. F.3.5. is a paraphrase of *Boece* Bk I.

198 — 'One of Chaucer's Sources.' *Nation*, 64 (Feb. 18, 1897), 124–5.
'There are many passages in Chaucer's translation where he does not
slavishly follow Jehan de Meung, but displays a scholarship
surprisingly independent for one who knew so little of the rudimentary
principles of Latin grammar. For, despite many assertions to the
contrary, the *Boece* shows mistakes numerous enough and great
enough to condemn as unfounded any aspirations its author may have
had to be considered a good Latin scholar, even when judged by the
standards of his time. How, then, did he manage to translate the
difficult metres whose subject-matter is often tortuous with scholastic
logic, and whose language is recondite with frequent reminiscences of
Virgil's Georgics?' (p 125). The solution lies in the commentaries
which grew up about such texts that 'embrace pretty much all the
learning of the time that had the slightest connection with the subject
in hand' (p 125). Liddell finds similarity between Chaucer and a
commentary wrongly attributed to Aquinas, and shows the influence of
such commentaries on Boethian passages in *T&C, KnT, HF*, and *GP*.

199 Lowes, John Livingston. 'Chaucer's *Boethius* and Jean de Meun.'
RomR, 8 (1917), 383–400.
'This article is concerned with one thing, and one thing only — the
demonstration of Chaucer's uses, in his own translation of *Boethius*, of
the French version which is best represented by MS. B.N. fr. 1097' (p
383). Lowes reviews scholarly opinion on Chaucer's relationship with
the French text, noting that Liddell's study (**197**) has been ignored,
then sets out an interlined comparison between BN fr. 1097 and *Boece*
V.pr.vi, 182–222. 'The chances against coincidence as the source of
such a series of correspondences in word order alone would run into
the millions' (p 392). Lowes also studies passages from fr. 1097 cited
by Langlois **130** and the comparable way in which both medieval
poets translate in prose the metres of Boethius (pp 393–6). Chaucer's
dependence upon Jean de Meun is unmistakable, but it is also clear
that he had the Latin text before him. For example, in one instance he
translates three lines from the Latin, then inserts a translation of
Jean's translation as a gloss (p 397). Lowes reiterates the need for a
parallel text edition with the French, such as Liddell announced, which
would make more evident the extent Chaucer's prose style and
vocabulary are influenced by the French (p 399).

199a Machan, Tim William. 'Forlynen: A Ghost Word Rematerializes.'

N&Q, 31 (1984), 22–4.
The term 'forlyven' in modern editions of Boece III, pr 6, should read 'forlynen.' Rather than a nonce word, the term is simply derived from OE *forlignier*, in Chaucer's source (cf Walton's translation). The error derives from a misreading of *v* for *n* in the mss. 'Chaucer is not, as *MED* suggests, the only writer to use *forlynen* in the sense "to degenerate"; he is the first to use *forlynen*. The ghost word in *OED* is in fact a real word' (p 24).

99b — *Techniques of Translation: Chaucer's Boece.* Norman, Oklahoma: Pilgrim Books, Inc., 1985.
Machan explores the 'mechanics of Chaucer's translation techniques' in *Boece* (p 3), the origins of its lexicon and syntax, and the essential conditions necessary to account for its style. Ch 2, 'Words,' pp 11–57, compares Latin (**222**), French (**179**), and English (**166**) texts, along with fifteenth-century Latin-English and English-Latin wordlists, in an effort to determine the range of lexical techniques Chaucer employs in responding to the meaning of his sources. Chaucer uses three techniques in establishing his lexicon: substitution of native words for source words; circumlocutory expression; and adoption of source words into English with derived forms (p 41). In glossing Latin Chaucer usually works within the tradition suggested by medieval wordlists, though there is no evidence that he used any particular one. Even so, *Boece* has the highest ratio of any Chaucerian work of nonce words, neologisms, and derived words. Chaucer has difficulty with Latin idioms, but so does Jean de Meun, which 'may indicate that the translation of idioms was in general uncertain in the Middle Ages' (p 23). Chaucer's use of doublets, calques, nonce words and neologisms, lexical and syntactic derivitives, glosses, and double translations reflects a keen desire for accuracy in netting Boethius' ideas. His manipulation of language manifests a 'philologist's joy in experimenting with words and their structures' (p 55). Ch 3, 'Syntax,' pp 59–84, attempts to determine how Chaucer 'responds to the grammatical problems and syntactic subtleties of Latin and French' (p 61). Through comparative juxtaposition of texts, Machan studies Chaucer's treatment of 'grammatical shibboleths' such as ablative absolutes and participial constructions, the influence of Latin and French on his syntax, and his techniques 'to alter or clarify the syntax of his originals' (p 61). Chaucer's aim is 'clearly to stay as close as possible to the Latin and French while still composing intelligible English' (p 62). Chaucer uses 'a philologist's knowledge of the complete syntactic resources of his own language in order to translate the syntactic structures of his sources' (pp 82–3). Ch 4, 'Style,' pp 85–110, argues that 'aesthetic considerations are incidental in

Chaucer's procedure' and that the features of Chaucer's style are 'limited to the expression of meaning' (p 87). 'One of the most striking characteristics of Jean's translation is its wordiness. Although *Boece* may be "diffuse," it is diffuse with a purpose, to express the ideas of the *Consolation*' (p 94). Whether using glosses, double translations, cleft sentences, doublets or other forms of expansion, Chaucer is primarily concerned with 'close but intelligible translation. What Chaucer writes is conditioned not by artistic considerations but a concern for meaning: to express intellectually complex or idiomatic Latin and French in English' (p 107). Ch 5, 'The Implications of Chaucer's Technique,' pp 111–24, argues that *Boece* was left unrevised and that in its present form it 'was not intended for the general public' (p 124). Signs of incompleteness are numerous. It lacks a preface. Moreover, 'Chaucer is most "creative" in the philosophically simplest Books of the *Consolation*.' The farther he got into the treatise, 'the more perfunctory' he became; such a change in technique leads one to believe that '*Boece* did not undergo final revision ... that Chaucer, for whatever reason, hurried through the last half ... but intended to return to it and supply it with the same lexical ingenuity as he did in the first half' (pp 115–6). The several 'as thus' and 'or this' passages are double translations and suggest notes by the translator to himself (p 121). Ch 6, 'Towards an evaluation of Chaucer as Translator,' pp 125–31, suggests that 'writing *Boece* was in part a way for Chaucer to examine language as language' (p 127), affirming Machan's theory of the deep philological streak in the poet which crops up in the *Boece*. Machan's bibliography on medieval translation techniques, pp 149–56, includes several Latin-English and English-Latin word lists.

200 Manzalaoui, Mahmoud. 'Chaucer and Science.' In *Geoffrey Chaucer*. Ed. D.S. Brewer. London: Bell, 1974. Pp 224–61.
'Boethius' *Consolatio* is ... a model which Chaucer rarely equals. Boethius' easy and majestic transition from observational detail to poetical description and dramatic involvement in the cosmic or the panoramic picture, is rivalled or surpassed by Dante, but not by the English poet' (p 232).

201 Mersand, Joseph. *Chaucer's Romance Vocabulary*. 1937. See 51
'It is significant that 18.5 percent of the entire Romance vocabulary of *Boethius* occurred for the first time in literary English. This is the largest percentage in any of Chaucer's works and offers incontrovertible evidence of the effect upon Chaucer's vocabulary of a Latin original which he was translating' (p 67).

202 Nims, Margaret F. '*Translatio:* "Difficult Statement" in Medieval Poetic Theory.' *UTQ*, 43 (1974), 215–30.
Translatio recognizes the potential of words for semantic extension and

the potential of things for symbolic or metaphoric interpretation (cf Bede: 'As words are receptive of polysemousness, so things are receptive of multiple signification,' p 218). Such awareness is seen in Cicero's distinction between independent words and words in combination, John of Salisbury's observations drawn from Boethius and Aristotle on the flexibility of words, Alain de Lille's theories of *involucrum*, and Geoffrey of Vinsauf's notions of the mind and face of words. 'So striking is the twelfth and thirteenth centuries' recognition of semantic flexibility that some grammarians, anticipating twentieth-century speculation, dismissed the very possibility of metaphor by holding that all the meanings given to a word in a speech act to become extensions of the word's literal meaning' (p 217). In conclusion Nims considers Chaucer's use of clusters of metaphors in the *Romaunt, BD, HF*, and *CT* in ways similar to Geoffrey of Vinsauf's recommended usage.

02a Oizumi, Akio. 'The Romance Vocabulary of Chaucer's Translation of Boethius's *De Consolatione Philosophiae.*' Doshisha University, *Jimbungaku*, Studies in Humanities, 108 (1968), 57–78; and 109 (1969), 64–95.
Classified listings of all romance words in *Boece*.

203 Petersen, Kate O. 'Chaucer and Trivet.' *PMLA*, 18 (1903), 173–93.
Ample evidence gives Trivet's commentary an important place among the sources of Chaucer's Boethius. A comparison of *Boece*, the Latin text (Peiper **219**), Trivet's commentary (Addit. MSS 19585 and 27875), and a Pseudo-Aquinas commentary (1497 edn) reveals more than 370 cases in which a word, phrase, or entire gloss in Trivet's commentary finds a literal English equivalent in Chaucer's *Boece*. About three hundred of the correspondences may be found also in the Pseudo-Aquinas compilation but in about seventy cases the latter fails to give as close a correspondence with Chaucer's text as Trivet does. Chaucer must have used a Latin text of the *Consolatio*, a French prose translation, and 'very probably' Trivet's Latin commentary (p 189). Perhaps his ms was one like BN MS Lat. 18424, which has Latin text plus Trivet's commentary.

04 Robbins, Rossell Hope. 'Chaucerian Apocrypha.' In *A Manual of the Writings in Middle English*. Ed. Albert E. Hartung. New Haven: Connecticut Academy of Arts and Sciences, 1973. See vol 4, p 1065.
On 'Scogan's Moral Balade,' Robbins observes, 'Lines from works of "my mayster Chaucer" — *Wife of Bath's Tale, Boethius*, and the *Monk's Tale* — are freely quoted , as well as Chaucer's *Gentilesse* ... complete, between lines 105 and 125. The poem falls into the traditions of instructions to the estates and advice to young people.'

05 Saintsbury, George. *CHEL*. 1908. See **62**.

Boece is 'literature within and without' (p 212). Faults have been found with Chaucer's translation. 'But one of the last things that some modern scholars seem able to realise is that their medieval forerunners, idolators of Aristotle as they were, appreciated no Aristotelian saying so much as that famous one "accuracy must not be expected" ' (p 213).

206 Schlauch, Margaret. *English Medieval Literature and Its Social Foundations*. Warsaw: Panstwowe Wydawnictwo Naukowe, 1956.
Schlauch discusses central Chaucerian themes originating in Boethius. (pp 237–40). 'The *Consolatio* had been the work of a man gifted with literary talents, an earnest (if not very original) thinker in philosophy, a writer who was also a diplomat and — within limits — a statesman. In short, there were analogies between the careers and interests of Boethius and Chaucer, which made the translation of the *Consolatio* a very congenial task for the English poet' (p 238). *Boece* spans the breadth of Chaucer's works and interests, from the lyrics marked by philosophical reflectiveness to the scientific and technological interest revealed in the *Astrolabe*. In a work like *Mars* one encounters a 'lighter' version of the issues of both *Boece* and the *Astrolabe* (p 240). See also **423** and **424**.

207 Schmidt, A.V.C. 'Chaucer and the Golden Age.' *EIC*, 26 (1976), 99–115.
'Both the over-correctness and the inaccuracy of the *Boece* are less interesting and much less significant than the genuinely poetic tendency to specificity to be found in such phrases as "the gobbetes or the weyghtes of gold" for *auri pondera*' (p 107). Boethius drew details from Ovid to add concreteness of imagery and *gravitas* of tone to his treatment of the former age. So does Chaucer (pp 107–8).

208 Science, Mark. 'A Suggested Correction of the Text of Chaucer's Boethius.' *TLS*, Mar. 22, 1923, pp 199–200.
There are nearly one hundred instances in which Walton has incorporated Chaucer's language into his translation. In several passages Walton has given 'a metrical rendering of Chaucer's prose rather than a translation direct from the original Latin' (p 199). On the basis of Walton, then, Science argues for *forlynen* rather that *forlyven* in III, pr.vi, lines 27–9, as translation of *dégénérare*, to be derived from OF *for-ligner*; an OF translation in BN Lat. 18424 supports this reading (p 200). See Machan **199a**.

209 Shirley, Peggy Faye. 'Fals Felicite and Verray Blisfulnesse: Alfred and Chaucer Translate Boethius's *Consolation of Philosophy*.' *DAI*, 38 (1977), 1417A–18A. University of Mississippi Dissertation. Dir. Tommy Joe Ray.
A very general discussion which finds Chaucer's translation more 'accurate' than Alfred's.

210 Shoaf, R.A. 'Notes Toward Chaucer's Poetics of Translation.' *SAC*, 1 (1979), 55–66.

'To initiate recovery of Chaucer's poetics of translation it is necessary to isolate and describe his attitude to the past and especially his attitude to the past-ness of language itself' (p 56). Though Chaucer was fluent in at least four languages and derived literature from all of them it might be said that the language he was actually translating was that of past literary conventions. A translation is 'literally a missaying' (p 58), a violation of authority. Chaucer was keenly aware of the limitations of language and the fact that he had to modify it and adapt it to his own unique forms. 'Language is not a stable given; it is a mutable inheritance ... at once arbitrary and the phenomenon of the ideal' (pp 61–2), paradoxical and discontinuous with life itself. Medieval poetry 'begins to explore this paradox and this discontinuity at least as early as the twelfth-century Latin lyric' (p 62). Because of this discontinuity 'Chaucer's attitude toward traditions and the conventions his poetry inherited was that of a translator. He violated the authority of conventions that confused *vox* and *res*' (p 64). As poet Chaucer spends most of his career between 'the self-validating and self-perpetuating conventions of poetry and the intellectual quest for truth through rational discourse in prose. This margin is the locus of the Boethian problematic: Philosophy evicts the Muses but Boethius continues to sing' (p 65). Chaucer 'missaid' the past in order that it might have new meaning for the present (p 66).

211 Silk, Edmund Taite. 'Cambridge MS. Ii.3.21 and the Relation of Chaucer's Boethius to Trivet and Jean de Meung.' Yale Graduate School Dissertation, 1930.

Silk believes that 'Chaucer was constantly dependent upon the Latin commentary of Nicolas Trivet' (p 61). His argument explores the relationship of Chaucer, Jean de Meun, and Trivet (pp 1–62), and includes seven appendices: A) a transcription of Cambr. Univ. Lib. MS Ii.3.21 (pp 63–551); B) Excerpts from Trivet's commentary found in BN Lat. 18424 and MS Vat. Lat. 563 (pp 552–626); C) Excerpts from Jean de Meun's translation of Boethius, BN fr. 1097 (pp 627–47); D) Excerpts from Bodleian MS Rawl. G 41, containing a twelfth-century *De Consolatione Philosophiae* with fifteenth-century annotations in Latin, and a passage from Jean de Meun (14th century) beginning at Bk I.m.1, and continuing to I.pr.4 (pp 648–54); E) Excerpts from Guillaume de Conches' Commentary on III.m.11, BN MS Lat. 1430 (pp 655–58); F) Excerpts from William Whetely's commentary on III.m.11 New Coll Ox. MS 264 (pp 659–64); G) Excerpts from William of Aragon's commentary, Cambr. MS Ii.3.21 (pp 665–76). Chaucer may have had access to eight or more Latin commentaries (but see

Minnis 261p). His translation differs from the French in several important ways: his phraseology often reproduces that of the Latin more closely than the French does; Chaucer is often more accurate than Jean de Meun; at the same time he is 'not infrequently' less accurate; he has introduced peculiarities and obscurities of expression which he might have avoided by consulting the French version; he coins some 65 new English words on the model of Latin words in Boethius where the French has entirely different words; he often shows that he follows a Latin text different from that which Jean followed; he has some 174 glosses amounting to about 300 lines of text which are wanting in the French version (p 8). Chaucer often uses two words to translate one from the Latin; so too does the French, but not always the same two (p 16). This is not to say, however, 'that Chaucer's translation is entirely dissimilar to that of Jean de Meung, or that Chaucer made no use of the French work. It would be absurd to undertake any such demonstration. There are instances in many ... passages in which the wording of the English and the French are almost identical' (p 13). But there are many instances which indicate that Chaucer frequently translates the Latin very closely and in so doing receives no assistance from the French. Some of his glosses are simply the French rendering, but it is 'unsafe to conclude that Chaucer has borrowed a given gloss from Jean de Meung until it is ascertained that he cannot have borrowed it from Trivet' (p 32).

212 Stewart, Hugh Fraser. *Boethius: An Essay*. Edinburgh: W. Blackwood, 1891.
Stewart would date Chaucer's intimate knowledge of Boethius from ca 1369 when he wrote *BD*, though *Boece* was translated later. The translation is filled with 'promiscuous mistakes' (p 224); 'its inaccuracy and infelicity is not that of an inexperienced Latin scholar, but rather of one who was no Latin scholar at all' (p 226). Chaucer's prose is strenuous — 'a desperate wrestle' with the language. 'The restrictions of metre were indeed to him as silken fetters, while the freedom of prose only served to embarrass him; just as a bird that has been born and bred in captivity, whose traditions are all domestic, finds itself at a sad loss when it escapes from its cage and has to fall back on its own resources for sustenance' (p 227). Chaucer's poetic renditions of Boethian matter are altogether praiseworthy, however; in the poems, 'with what clearness and precision does the argument unfold itself, how close in the reasoning, how vigorous and yet graceful is the language' (p 228).

213 Thompson, Patricia. 'Wyatt's Boethian Ballade.' *RES*, 15 (1964), 263–67.
Wyatt's poem is an adaptation of Bk III.m.5, 6, and 3. Though it is

generally assumed that he used Chaucer's translation he certainly was capable of doing his own. Boethius was part of university curriculum, and Wyatt was a university man (p 263). Walton in his translation consistently consults the Latin, though he uses Chaucer too and often plagiarizes his phrasing. But there is nothing common to Chaucer and Wyatt which is not also in Boethius. Wyatt's debt to Chaucer, nonetheless, is there, but not to the *Boece*. Rather it is to Chaucer's moral ballades, of which the poem is 'a formal imitation' (p 266). There is 'every evidence of compatibility between Chaucerian and early Tudor moral lyric. That Wyatt should compose a Boethian ballade is most natural, and, in following Chaucerian precedent he was not, like Spenser, consciously archaizing. The Chaucerian tradition was as yet unbroken. But there is no need, on that account, to assume that Wyatt also depended on *Boece*' (p 267).

214 Wild, Friedrich. *Die sprachlichen Eigentümlichkeiten der wichtigeren Chaucer-Handschriften und die Sprache Chaucers.* Wiener Beiträge zur englischen Philologie, XLIV. Wien und Leipzig: Wilhelm Braumüller, 1915.

Wild's pronunciation study mentions the *Astrolabe* but does not use it as a source for his study of Chaucer's speech characteristics because Skeat's edition contains too many normalizations to be useful or reliable. Instead he concentrates on two texts of *Boece* (Cambridge Univ. Lib. ms Ii.3.21 and BL Addit. 10340) as his prose sources along with numerous mss of *CT* and *T&C*. Wild studies the pronunciation (spelling) of over 1100 words in various mss.

215 Wilson, Herman Pledger. 'Chaucer as a Prose Writer.' *DA*, 16 (1956), 2154. University of Tennessee Dissertation. Dir. Roscoe E. Parker.

Wilson studies *Boece, Mel, ParsT*, and *Astrolabe* to determine characteristics of Chaucer's style, stylistic relationships of his with other English prose, and his place in the continuity of English prose. Chaucer's prose is both literary and practical; it had 'significance to his contemporaries.'

216 Wimsatt, James I. 'Chaucer, Fortune, and Machaut's "Il m'est avis".' In *Chaucerian Problems and Perspectives: Essays Presented to Paul E. Beichner.* Ed. Edward Vasta and Zacharais P. Thundy. Notre Dame University Press, 1979. Pp 119–31.

In Chaucer's *Boece* II. pr.1, the phrase 'the felefolde *colours* and deceytes of thilke merveylous *monstre*' is indebted to 'Il m'est avis,' line 13: 'monstre envolepe de boneur' (pp 122–3). Cf the Latin: 'multiformes illius prodigii fucos.' Wimsatt demonstrates that Machaut's poem is heavily indebted to Boethius (p 120–8). Chaucer must have known the poem prior to translating *Boece*.

217 Witcutt, W.P. 'Chaucer's Boëthius.' *American Review*, 8 (1936),

61-70.

The greatness of Boethius — for King Alfred, Chaucer, and for us — is his ability to crystalize the inherited wisdom of the ages. Chaucer and Alfred both 'knew of and faced the alternate to belief in God — our "Darwinian" chance; ... it was no news to them that this world was not the center of the universe, but an insignificant planet, set in the vastness of space' (p 62). Boethius ponders the greatest of questions — 'the end of man' — with such sophistication that he speaks to everyone. All moderns should be required to read Chaucer's *Boece* to see how deeply it 'belongs to *us*' (p 63). One is always surprised at the modernity of Boethius (p 67). 'Perhaps our children will return to the high sanity of Boëthius, and drink from the well at which Chaucer drank. Perhaps the book and translation will be read when the books of the modern prophets have long since been done away with by long and dark eld, both them and their authors. At least we hope so' (p 70).

217a Wülcker, R.P. 'Aus Englischen Bibliotheken.' *Anglia*, 2 (1879), 354-87.

In discussing mss in Salisbury and London Wülcker shows that the *Boece* in Salisbury ms 113 is a copy of BL ms 10340 (pp 372-3).

Latin Editions of *De Consolatione Philosophiae*

218 *Anicii Manlii Severini Boethii De consolatione philosophiae libri quinque.* Recensuit Theodor Obbarius. Jena: Hochhausen, 1843.
The prolegomena includes chapters on Boethius' life and writings (pp vii-xxvii), his religion and philosophy (pp xxvii-xlvi), and on the codices and editions of the *Consolatio*. Obbarius comments on twenty-two mss and seven incunabula editions. Bibliographical notes compare ms readings.

219 *Anicii Manlii Severini Boetii Philosophiae consolationis libri quinque. Accedunt ejusdem atque incertorum opuscula sacra.* Recensuit Rudolfus Peiper. Bibliotheca Scriptorum Graecorum et Romanorum Teubneriana. Leipzig: Teubner, 1871. .
Peiper chooses the ninth-century ms Tegernseensis Clm 18765 as his basic text which he collates with thirteen other mss, in consultation with others besides. The prolegomena provides a life of Boethius; elegaic verses commemorating Boethius by Rabanus, Gerbert, and others (pp xxxv-xli); a survey of commentaries on the *Consolatio* (pp xli-xlvi); comments on the sacred writings; interpretations of the *Consolatio* in the high Middle Ages; and imitations of the *Consolatio*

from Martianus Capella through the fifteenth century (pp lvi–lix).

220 *Anicii Manlii Severini Boethii De Consolatione philosophiae libri quinque.* Recensuit Georgius D. Smith. London: Burns Oates and Washbourne, 1925.
Besides an introduction with chapters on the life and religion of Boethius, this text includes appendices on *Providentia et fata, De mundo perpetuo,* and *Praecipua quae de Boethio habentur testimonia.* The bibliography (pp 188–200) is divided into sections on his life, religion, editions and commentaries, translations, composition, philosophy, and works imitating the *Consolatio.* Also Smith includes indices on Boethian references in Dante (pp 201–3) and on memorable items in the *Consolatio* (pp 204–25). Notes include cross references to sources, influences, and commentaries; notations on metrics.

221 *Anicii Manlii Severini Boetii De consolatione philosophiae.* Recensuit Guilelmus Weinberger. Corpus Scriptorum Ecclesiasticorum Latinorum. Wien: Hoelder-Pichler-Tempsky; Leipzig: Akademische Verlagsgesellschaft, 1934.
Prolegomena (pp v–xxxi) considers the circumstances of the *Consolatio*'s composition, its sources, interpreters and commentators, its eighty-four codices (seven of which are discussed in detail) and the early editions.

222 *Anicii Manlii Severini Boethii Philosophiae Consolatio.* Edidit Ludovicus Bieler. Corpus Christianorum: Series Latina XCIV. Turnhout: Brepols, 1957.
The Latin introduction considers Boethius' life and writings and provides a rationale of the edition, useful bibliography, a list of important mss and their dates together with information on the use made of each by Weinberger and Peiper, and a list of printed editions. Bieler's indices list scriptural allusions in the *Consolatio* and classical sources. He also includes an alphabetical listing of first lines of the meters. Bieler works with thirteen more mss than Weinberger **221** did, and fifteen more than Peiper **219**. Green **228** calls this 'the now standard critical edition' (p v).

Selected Modern English Translations

223 Walton, John, trans. *Boethius: De Consolatione Philosophiae (c. 1410).* Ed. Mark Science, with introduction, notes, and glossary. London: Oxford University Press, 1927.
Science collates sixteen of nineteen mss and three extant printed copies

of the 1525 edition. The Introduction describes the nineteen mss, discusses their interrelationships, date, authorship, Walton's method of translation, language, versification. Science uses Lincoln Cath. ms A.4.11 as his basic text, supplemented by BL ms Royal 18.A.xiii. Walton's translation is greatly indebted to Chaucer in that Walton used a Latin original and Chaucer's translation as well. But the debt was increased in the hands of the printers, who corrected Walton by referring to *Boece*. A large number of alterations in the 1525 printed edition are due to Chaucer's translation. That edition also shows many instances of modernizing Chaucer's words, which were already becoming obsolete.

- Review by Helen T. McMillan Buckhurst, *RES*, 5 (1929), 341. 'The most interesting fact which emerges from this analysis [of mss] is the importance of the early printed edition' and the role of Thomas Richard, printer, in altering ms readings 'in order to bring them into line with Chaucer's version' (p 341).

224 *Boethius' Consolation of Philosophy, translated from the Latin by George Colville, 1556*. Ed. Ernest Belfort Bax. Vol 5 in the Tudor Library Series. London: David Nutt, 1897.
Bax's Introduction (pp vii–xx) comments on Boethius' life and works. Colville's prose translation 'is one of the finest specimens we could desire of the rugged, terse, vigorous English of the sixteenth-century. It is especially free from the euphemisms that characterize some of the Elizabethian writers' (p xx). Colville dedicates his translation to Queen Mary. In his prefatory remarks he claims to have translated from 'a very olde prynte.' He includes a summary of the *Consolatio*'s argument, with comments on 'theodoryk Kynge of the gotes,' and a prologue on fortune and the transitory nature of life. His text includes a running summary in the margins, which Colville claims his Latin text had as well. He identifies the speaker of each section without identifying the prose-meter divisions.

225 *Queen Elizabeth's Englishings of Boethius, De Consolatione Philosophiae, A.D. 1593, Plutarch, De Curiositate (1598), and Horace, De Arte Poetica (1598)*. Ed. Caroline Pemberton. Early English Text Society, o.s. 113. London: Kegan Paul, Trench, Trübner, & Co., 1899.
The unique ms, partly in the Queen's hand, is in the Public Record Office. According to Camden, 'At Windsor she amused herself with translating Boethius's *De Consolatione*, 1593, as she had at Enfield done the like favour to Ochinus Sermon' (p vii). Pemberton's 'Forewords' discusses the Queen's learning, her knowledge of Latin and Greek, and cites contemporary accounts of her miraculous speed in translating the work (one account says she completed it in twenty four hours; another says twenty seven hours). Pemberton notes that it is

impossible that she could have translated that swiftly, though she sometimes dictated, but also notes that her translation is 'tolerably exact and generally very literal' (p x). The Boethius translation adds most to the Queen's reputation as a scholar; her Plutarch is bad, and her Horace worse (p xi). Pemberton juxtaposes Elizabeth's translation with Chaucer's (pp xiii–xiv), to show that Chaucer's is much longer than the Queen's. She made use of Chaucer's translation, however, in the making of her own, as Pemberton's running notes make clear. Elizabeth's meters are in verse. The prosae are in prose.

226 Boethius. *The Theological Tractates.* Trans. H.F. Stewart and E.K. Rand; and *The Consolation of Philosophy.* Trans. I.T. (1609), revised by H.F. Stewart. Loeb Classical Library. Cambridge, Mass.: Harvard University Press; London: Heinemann, 1918. Rev/1926.
Latin texts with English translations on facing pages. Rand's note on the text indicates that he has used the apparatus in Peiper's edition (219) for the Latin texts, though he has also depended on his own collations and has often followed the opinions of August Engelbrecht, *Die Consolatio Philosophiae des Boethius* in the *Sitzungsberichte* of the Vienna Academy, cxliv (1902), 1–60. The five theological tracts included in the volume are *De Trinitate, Utrum Pater et Filivs et Spiritvs Sanctvs de Divinitate Svbstantialiter Praedicentvr, Quomodo Substantiae In Eo Quod Sint Bonae Sint Cum Non Sint Substantialia Bona, De Fide Catholica,* and *Contra Eutychen et Nestorium.*

227 — *The Consolation of Philosophy,* trans. W.V. Cooper. In *The Consolation of Philosophy: Boethius, Thomas À Kempis, Sir Thomas Browne,* with intro. by Irwin Erdman. Modern Library. New York: Random House, 1943, pp 3–120.
Cooper's prose translation does not mark the *prosa/metrum* divisions. The volume includes *The Imitation of Christ* and *Religio Medici.* Erdman's introduction gives a synopsis of each work and discusses briefly its philosophical-religious-personal qualities.

228 — *The Consolation of Philosophy,* trans. Richard Green. Library of Liberal Arts. Indianapolis: Bobbs-Merrill, 1962.
Green's prose translation is based on the critical edition by William Weinberger in the Corpus Scriptorum Ecclesiasticorum Latinorum 221, with cross-checking against Bieler's edition (222). 'My purpose in this translation has been to provide students and the general reader with an accurate version of this famous medieval book in modern, idiomatic English' (p v). Green attempts to preserve the figures and metaphors wherever possible; thus his decision to present the *metra* in prose. The edition includes an introduction, with sections on the author, the poet as philosopher, and the philosopher as poet; selected bibliography, summary, and index.

228a The Consolation of Philosophy, trans. V.E. Watts. Hammondsworth
and Baltimore: Penguin, 1969.
Watts' Introduction comments on Boethius' life and writings, the
circumstances under which the Consolation was written, its genre, and
Boethius' Christianity. The translation is based on Weinberger's
edition (221).

Concordance and Commentaries on
De Consolatione Philosophiae

229 Cooper, Lane. A Concordance of Boethius: The Five Theological
Tracts and the Consolation of Philosophy. Publication no. 1 of
Medieval Academy of America. Cambridge, Mass., 1928.
The concordance is based on the Loeb Classical Library edition 226,
with its five tracts.

230 Courcelle, Pierre. 'Étude critique sur les commentaires de la
Consolation de Boèce (IXe–XVe siècle).' Archives d'histoire doctrinale
et littéraire du moyen âge, 14 (1939), 5–140.
Chapter 1, on Carolingian commentaries, pp 12–51, includes
discussions, excerpts and comparisons of the commentaries of
Remigius of Auxerre, the Second Vatican Mythographer, John Scotus,
the anonymous commentator of St. Gall, Asser, Alfred, Vatican
Latinus 3363, Notker, and the Provençal commentator, with special
emphasis on the influence of Remigius on subsequent commentaries.
Ch 2, 'Les diverses interpretations carolingiennes,' pp 52–76, considers
attitudes toward Boethius' orthodoxy among Carolingian
commentators, who Christianize the Consolatio. 'Ce serait une erreur
de croire que les commentateurs carolingiens, abusés par les textes de
chroniques qui présentent Boèce comme un martyr de la foi, n'ont pas
été surpris par le caractère "laïque" de la Consolation et les résonances
païennes des théories qui y sont soutenues' (p 52). Discusses
anonymous Paris Latin 10400, Bovo de Corvey, anonymous ms of
Einsiedeln 302, the reviser of Remigius, and Adalbold of Utrecht. Ch
3, on twelfth-century commentators (pp 77–94), emphasizes the high
esteem with which Boethius was regarded and comments on the
commentaries of Guillaume de Conches, anonymous Reginenses 72 and
244, the anonymous ms of Erfurt, anonymous Vatican Latinus 919
(which bears many ties with Guillaume de Conches' commentary), and
anonymous of the Tables of Marseille. Ch 4, on the commentaries of
the fourteenth and fifteenth centuries (pp 95–144), considers Nicholas

Trivet, Tholomaeus of Asinariis, Pierre of Paris, William of Aragon,
Thomas of Wales or Marquard (?), Pierre d'Ailly, Regnier de Saint
Tron, Guillermius de Cortumelia, Denis de Lewis, Arnoul Greban, and
Josse Bade d'Assche. Boethius provided the Middle Ages with 'un
ferment d'humanisme. Mais par un curieux retour, c'est au moment où
l'humanisme triomphe que Boèce sera dèlaissé' (p 118). Appendix lists
mss of various commentaries (pp 119–40).

231 — *La Consolation de philosophie dans la tradition littéraire:
antécédents et postérité de Boèce.* Paris: Études Augustiniennes, 1967.
Courcelle's comprehensive study of the *Consolation* as a medieval text
is arranged according to the matter of *Consolation* itself. *PREMIÈRE
PARTIE: Le personnage de Philosophie* (Livre I) consists of three
chapters: Ch 1, 'La Description de Philosophie par Boèce,' pp 17–28,
discusses peculiarities of Boèce's description of Philosophie; in his eyes
she is 'la sagesse humaine à son degré de perfection; elle sait tout ce
que l'homme a pu et puet apprendre par l'exercice de la raison, mais
cela seulement. Au reste, la ressemblance de la raison humaine avec
l'Intelligence divine ne doit pas nous étonner; car pour Boèce l'une
reflète l'autre: la vraie philosophie est, à ses yeux, ce que les hommes
les plus sages ont su reconnaître en eux de divin' (p 22). The
consolation will be for Boèce 'un vrai cours de métaphysique' (p 19).
Courcelle notes several curious features of Boethius' approach to
philosophy, eg, his treatment of the Aristotelian definition of man in I,
pr.6 (pp 26–7), where he modifies the definition to focus on the
narrator's forgetting the immortal part. Ch 2, 'Alcuin et la tradition
littéraire du IXe au XIIe siècle sur Philosophie,' pp 29–66, cites
numerous Boethian passages in the writings of Waldram, John
d'Orleans, Gautier de Spire, Alain de Lille, Hugo de Trimberg,
Audradus Modicus, Hrotsvitha, Saxo, Rodbert de Corbie, Hildebert de
Lavardin, Philippe de Harvengt, Albert de Stade, Pierre le Chautre,
Henri de Settimello, Adelard of Bath, Pierre de Compostelle, Bernard
Silvestris, St Bernard, and others. Behind their admiration lies the
approval and design of Alcuin in the Prologue to his *De grammatica,*
which sets out guidelines on instruction in the liberal arts.
'L'introduction d'Alcuin est en réalité ... un va-et-vient perpétuel, des
sources profanes — principalement la *Consolatio Philosophiae* de
Boèce — à l'Écriture sainte' (pp 33–4). Courcelle discusses 'l'audace et
l'originalité' of Alcuin's 'christianisée' of the *Consolatio.* Eg, Alcuin
relates Philosophy's scepter to a flower branch (symbol of the stock of
Jesse) and the echelons between *pi* and *theta* on her robe to Jacob's
Ladder (pp 36–47). Alcuin's interpretations and way of glossing the
text dominated the imaginations of scholars commenting on the
treatise for the next four centuries. Ch 3, 'Les images de Boèce et

Philosophie,' pp 67–99, discusses the portrait representations of
Boethius in mss, scenes of his life, representations of Philosophy,
dialogues between Boethius and Philosophy, and their company with
the Muses. *DEUXIÈME PARTIE: Le Personnage de Fortune et ses
biens* (Livres II et III.1–8) likewise has three chapters: Ch 1, 'La
description de Fortune par Boèce,' pp 103–111, considers her fickle
character and her value as an instructor, but also the difficulty of
explaining evil fortune in a benevolent universe. Ch 2, 'De la Fortune
antique à la Fortune médiévale,' pp 113–39, considers the origins of the
idea of Fortune and her goods (especially in Aristotle, Cicero,
Macrobius); her literary iconography in Horace, Ovid, Seneca,
Pseudo-Plutarch, Tacitus, Tibullius, Ausonius, Claudian; and her
subsequent representation in medieval texts. Ch 3, 'Les images de
Boèce et Fortune,' pp 141–58, considers ms representations of Fortune
and her wheel and Fortune and her goods. *TROISIÈME PARTIE: Le
Souverain Bien et la Mal* (livre III, pr.9 à IV, m.4) also has three
chapters: Ch 1, 'Les doctrines de Boèce et leurs sources,' pp 161–176,
considers influences on Boethian ideas, namely from the *Timaeus*,
Chalcidius, Proclus, Ammonius, Iamblichus, Plotinus, and St
Augustine. Ch 2, 'La prière de Philosophie dans les textes littéraires
jusqu'au XIIe siècle,' pp 176–84, discusses growing admiration of and
commentaries on III.m.9, which relate the passage to Genesis and the
beginning of John's gospel. Courcelle's discussion includes comments
on St Thomas Aquinas' and Dante's attitudes toward the prayer-like
hymn: 'On ne s'étonnera pas, avec de tels antécédents, de voir Dante
placer son *Paradis* sous le signe du *Te cernere finis* [III.m.9.v.27]
boécian; il semble s'être assimilé très intimement cette Prière et
n'hésite pas à mettre le vers de Boèce sur le même plan que le verset
de saint Jean relatif à la vie éternelle' (p 184; cf Dante, *Epistle* XIII
[10] and John 17.3). Ch 3, 'Les illustrations,' pp 185–99, considers
representations of Boethius and Philosophy in prayer. Eg, Bodl. Digby
174, fol. 11r, which shows Boethius on the left of an enthroned Christ
who is recognizable by his cruciform nimbus, his five wounds, and the
orb between his feet, but who, like Philosophy, holds a book and has a
torn robe, all surrounded by sun, moon, and stars (cf I.m.5). The
illustrations of III.m.9 usually show Boethius in prayer, sometimes
with Philosophy likewise praying at his side as they behold the
resplendent light (eg, Cambridge Trin. Lib. ms 12, fol.44v). Courcelle
also discusses illustrations of other prayers, namely that of unpunished
persecutors in IV.pr.1, mythological scenes, and nine drawings of
Philosophy supplying wings and flight for the soul (IV.m.1).
QUATRIÈME PARTIE: Les Rapports de Dieu et du monde (Livre IV
pr.5 à V, fin), in two chapters: Ch 1, 'Les doctrines de Boèce et leurs
sources,' pp 203–31, considers Boethius' sources for his theory of

providence and destiny, foreknowledge, free will (especially Proclus, Ammonius, Aristotle, and Simplicius), and the perpetuity of the world. Ch 2, 'Les Illustrations,' pp 237–8, is devoted especially to mythlogical figures in the latter part of the *Consolatio*, figures of chance (V.pr.1), divine foresight (V.pr.6), and varieties of animals (V.m.5). *CINQUIÈME PARTIE: Controverses d'écoles autour de la 'Consolation'*, in four chapters: Ch 1, 'Identification des commentaires carolingians (IXe–Xe siècles), pp 241–74, locates the tradition in Remi d'Auxerre, the second Vatican Mythographer, John Scot, the anonymous commentator of St. Gall, and various early French and English adaptations. Ch 2, 'Les diverses interprétations carolingiennes,' pp 275–99, discusses the commentaries of anonymous of St. Gall, Remi d'Auxerre, anonymous of *Parisinus latinus* 10400, anonymous of *Bruxellensis* 10066–77, Bovo of Corvey, anonymous of *Einsiedlensis* 302, the reviser of Remi, and Adalbold of Utrecht. Ch 3, 'Les commentaires du XIIe siècle,' pp 301–15, considers Guillaume de Conches, anonymous of *Reginenses* 72 and 244, anonymous of *Erfurtensis* Q 5, anonymous of *Monacensis* 14689, anonymous of *Vaticanus latinus* 919, and the anonymous of the *Tables de Marseille.* Ch 4, 'Les commentaires de XIVe et XVe siècles,' pp 317–32, considers Nicholas Trivet, Tholomaeus of Asinariis, Pierre de Paris, William of Aragon, Pseudo-Thomas Aquinas (William Whetley, Thomas of Wales, or Marquand?), Pierre d'Ailly, Regnier de Saint-Trond, Pietro da Muglio, Giovanni Travesio, Guillermus de Cortumelia, Denis de Leewis, Arnoul Greban, and Josse Bade d'Assche. The 'Conclusion,' pp 333–44, summarizes the book's argument. Courcelle doubts that Boethius had direct access to many ancient texts but rather had to work through Proclus and his school, Porphyry, and so on (pp 334–5). APPENDICES on portrayals of the tyrant in Boethius (pp 347–53); the cosmic vision of Boethius and St Benoit (pp 355–72); the text of Alcuin's Prologue to his students (pp 373–5); and three French translations of *Cons. III.m.9.* The book has 132 plates (several with multiple scenes), an extensive bibliography, and tables of mss of commentaries, proper names, key phrases in *Consolatio*, and mss illuminations.

232 Dwyer, Richard A. 'The Appreciation of Handmade Literature.' *ChauR*, 8 (1973–74), 221–40.
Manual transmission of texts often results in active scribal participation in their aesthetic refinement. Dwyer examines the process by comparing thirteen medieval French translations of the *Consolatio* whose scribes revise, compile, edit and assimilate one another's work in truly medieval reinterpretation of the Latin original. The translations of Pierre de Paris (ca 1305) and Renaut de Louhans

(ca 1315) humanize the intellectual rigor of Boethius with anecdotes about repentant thieves and proud scholars, to reflect popular taste and understanding of the philosopher.

233 — *Boethian Fictions: Narratives in the Medieval French Versions of the Consolatio Philosophiae.* Cambridge, Mass.: The Medieval Academy of America, 1976.
Dwyer discusses half a dozen French versions of the *Consolatio* which 'freely diverge from the Boethian text' by adding narrative interpolations (p 2) and which 'taken collectively exhibit aspects of the popular medieval uses of Boethius' (p 17). Compared to these versions Jean de Meun's translation is 'one of the least interesting' (p 3). Between the Carolingian period and the end of the fifteenth century, about three dozen commentaries were written. 'The *Consolatio Philosophiae*, in truth, seems to be a kind of apocalypse in which the envisioned personification of purely Human Wisdom restores the narrator's mental health by a guided course of Neoplatonic metaphysics, a course raised to almost sacramental dignity by the resources of late Latin rhetoric and poetics' (p 4). Early commentaries glossed Philosophy as Wisdom of God and Christ himself, though after the third book they had trouble with the Neoplatonism. Remigius was the first to make a coherent reconciliation between the Christian and Neoplatonic by using Chalcidius' translation of the *Timaeus* as part of his apparatus (p 6). Adalbold, Bishop of Utrecht (d. 1027), wrote a commentary on Bk III.m.9, which showed others the way. William of Conches (ca 1125) brought the defense of Boethius' Platonism to its apogee. Other commentators of the twelfth century follow William. Trivet stresses the Aristotelian vein, playing down the Platonism. No acceptable romance version of the *Consolatio* was available prior to that of Jean de Meun. Pierre de Paris wrote an inferior prose version with glosses in the early fourteenth century; though inferior by one standard (accuracy) it offers an exemplary instance of medievalization. Ch 1, 'The Earth is Made to Speak,' pp 19–32, considers the rhetorical appeal of the *Consolatio*, the use of mythology and pre-Christian history to exemplify moral points. Though Philosophy seems to have a low opinion of the Muses, the commentators emphasize 'refreshment as the function of Boethius's poetry' in Philosophy's songs. The function of the prose sections is more restricted to rational dialectic, with forms limited to catechism, syllogism, and dialogue, none of which are found in the verses. 'The verses might be said, then, to constitute modes of knowing and discoursing alternative to those central to speculative philosophy, and this is a far cry from diverting decoration or even what Sir Philip Sidney called "a medicine of cherries" ' (p 22). Though the prose and verse are linguistically distinguished as 'two modes of

knowing and discoursing, the notion of reminiscence ... shares
something with that of abstract reasoning ... The function of allusion
is to set the memory going, turning over its riches until the desired
truth is reclaimed. A highly developed poetry of allusion is essentially
non-narrative inasmuch as the narrative links are left to be supplied by
the memories and imaginations of all those initiated into the rhetorical
arcana' (p 23). The translators often attempt to play Memory and fill
in the gaps, though their display is often erroneous and incongruous.
Ch 2, 'King on a Wheel,' pp 33–49, discusses the commentator's
responses to Dame Fortune and the exempla of her fools. The Croesus
story was a favorite. Those interested in narrative structure stress the
tragedy; those interested in psychology stress fortune (p 40). Remigius
invents Phania, the daughter, to set off the motif of pride (cf William
of Conches' gloss). Jean de Meun's Phania is a Boethian miniature of
Fortuna, albeit courteous and an embodiment of gentilesse. Renaut de
Louhans' commentary turns Perses into a king in place of Cyrus to
have him soon defeated by Paulus who, with his broader vision, weeps
for him as he defeats him. 'The replacement of Boethius' simple,
irrational agency by a medieval one, highly motivated by notions of
Justice, has resulted in increased attention to human qualities, even in
the personifications. The victims are more carefully drawn and the
mediating automata more delicately articulated, because it is human
psychology that is beginning to rule both earth and heaven' (pp 48–9).
Ch 3, 'The Tempting Integument,' pp 51–65, considers treatments of
the Orpheus myth. (See pp 54–5 on William of Conches' glosses.)
Anonymous of Meun, very solicitous of his reader, adds 'a long
unmoralized account of the story of Arion and the dolphin,' which he
draws from Vincent's *Speculum Historiale* 4.109, then returns to
Orpheus, drawing on William of Conches, and then adds the Ixion
story. Instead of attempting to harmonize accounts from Fulgentius,
Vincent, and others, 'he simply exhausted the interest each had for
him and then moved on' (p 59); Tantalus becomes a figure of anger
and covetousness; Ixion and Tytius figures of Pride; Orpheus, of sloth.
Dwyer contrasts the amateurish structure of the Anonymous' narrative
with Henryson's *Orpheus*. Ch 4, 'A Legacy for Common Profit,' pp
67–87, discusses metrical influence of the meters on commentators.
The earliest commentary exclusively on the meters is by Lupus of
Ferrieris (mid-ninth century). The earliest translations are exclusively
in prose; later the translations become occasions for metrical
experimentation. Renaut de Louhans uses 8-line stanzas for his
prologue and Bk I (except for one meter), then uses couplets for Bks
II–V, except for two stanzaic interpolations. Attempts were even made
to turn the *Aeneid* into alternating prose and verse (p 68). In
conclusion Dwyer relates the rhetorical structures of such translators

to Robert Jordan's thesis on inorganic art (*Chaucer and the Shape of Creation*, 1967), to sum up their addiction for eclecticism and the encyclopedic (pp 86–7). An appendix includes: 1) Anonymous Burgundian on Calixto; 2) Renaut de Louhans on Croesus; 3) Anonymous of Meun on Croesus; 4) Anonymous Burgundian on Orpheus; 5) Anonymous of Meun on Judgment of Paris; 6) Anonymous Benedictine's revision of Renaut de Louhans on Orpheus; 7) Renaut de Louhans' version of Bk I m.2; 8) Anonymous Benedictine's version of Bk I m.2; 9) Pierre de Paris on Alcibiades; 10) Anonymous Benedictine on the Inconstant Scholar; 11) Renaut de Louhans' stanzas on Death.

233a Frakes, Jerold C. 'The Ancient Concept of *casus* and its Early Medieval Interpretations.' *Vivarium*, 22 (1984), 1–34.

Relates Germanic and Anglo-Saxon concepts of *wyrd* and *weas* to Aristotelian-Boethian notions of *casus* as differentiated from *fortuna* and *fatum*, especially in the glosses by Notker.

233b —— 'Die Rezeption der neuplatonischen Metaphysik des Boethius durch Alfred und Notker.' *Beiträge zur Geschichte der deutschen Sprache und Literatur*, 106 (1984), 51–74.

On epistemological restrictions in Boethian metaphysics.

234 Gilbert of Poitiers. *The Commentaries on Boethius*. Ed. Nikolaus M. Häring. Toronto: Pontifical Institute of Mediaeval Studies, 1966.

Häring's introduction (pp 1–47) reviews the theological controversy surrounding Gilbert, his censure by St Bernard, and his brilliance as a theologian. 'Gilbert of Poitiers is too great and important a scholar to be shrugged off as an obscurantist. In fact, his equal is not to be found in Latin theology from St Augustine to the most celebrated theologians of the thirteenth century' (p 4). 'It took history some seven centuries to arrive at the simple truth that in order to judge Gilbert's teaching one should begin with an unprejudiced examination of his writings' (p 9). Häring provides a descriptive bibliography of the thirty-nine mss used in his edition. The text of Gilbert's commentary in the mss is so remarkably uniform that 'it is difficult to divide them into meaningful groups or to draw up a *stemma* on the strength of significant variants' (p 34). Moreover, Gilbert is so painstaking in his commentary that it is possible to reconstruct the text of Boethius he used; he 'clearly endeavoured not to omit a single word' (p 43). Häring prints the texts of the commentaries (pp 49–364), along with appendices which include Gilbert's *De Sancta Trinitate, De Bonorum Ebdomade*, and *Contra Euticen et Nestorium*. The edition also includes a select bibliography of writings related to Gilbert and his school and indices of authors and sources used by Gilbert, persons named, and a glossary.

235 *Excerpta Valesiana*. Ed. J. Moreau and V. Velkov. Leipzig: Teubner, 1968.

The Anonymous Valesianus, writing at Ravenna as a near-contempory of Boethius and Cassiodorus, provides the earliest details of Boethius' execution.

36 Gruber, Joachim. *Kommentar zu Boethius De Consolatione Philosophiae.* Berlin: Walter de Gruyter, 1978.
The Introduction, pp 1–48, reviews briefly the life and canon of Boethius, the literary tradition of the *Consolatio* — its 'prosimetrische' form, its poetry, its kinship to popular philosophy, consolation literature, dialogue, and protreptic traditions — the sources and the uniqueness of the treatise, and its transmission. The Commentary, pp 49–416, proceeds systemmatically, section by section, book by book, glossing ideas, vocabulary, phrases, and concepts in terms of meanings, sources, and philosophical, rhetorical, and traditional associations.

237 Jourdain, Charles. 'Des Commentaires inédits de Guillaume Conches et de Nicholas Triveth sur la Consolation de la philosophie de Boèce.' *Notices et extraits des manuscrits de la Bibliothèque Impériale,* 20, ii (1862), 40–82.
After a brief discussion of the interests of Guillaume de Conches and Nicholas Trivet and the best mss in which their commentaries occur, Jourdain provides an extract from MS de Troyes 1381 of Guillaume's comments on the *pi* and *theta* passage of I.pr.1 (pp 72–4), a passage which includes Guillaume's division of *Scientia* into *Eloquentia* and *Sapientia*; of *Eloquentia* into *Grammatica, Rhetorica, Dialectica*; of *Sapientia* into *Theoretica* and *Practica*; of *Practica* into *Ethica, Economica, Politica*; of *Theoretica* into *Theologica, Mathematica, Physica*; of *Mathematica* into *Arithmetica, Musica, Geometrica, Astronomia*; of *Musica* into *Instrumentalis, Humana, Mundana*; of *Musica Humana* into *Melica, Metrica, Rithmica*; and of *Metrica* into *Diaconica, Enarmonica,* and *Cromatica.* The second excerpt is of Guillaume's commentary on III.m.9 (pp 75–80), on 'l'ame du monde et de l'âme humaine.' The third excerpt is from Guillaume's explication of the myth of Orpheus in III.m.12 (pp 80–1). The last extract is on the elements of knowledge in IV.pr.4 (pp 81–2).

238 Klinger, Friedrich. *De Boethii Consolatione Philosophiae.* Zurich and Dublin: Weidmann, 1966.
A study in Latin of the structure of the *Consolatio,* with special attention given to II m.8, III m.9, and IV m.6. Klinger comments on the historical sources of Boethian ideas (Cicero, Stoicism, Platonism, St Augustine, Iamblichus, and Proclus), and contrasts the rationales of Books IV and V.

239 Minio-Paluello, L. 'Les traductions et les commentaires aristotéliennes de Boèce.' *Studia Patristica,* 2 (1957), 358–65.
Reviews theories of Boethius' access to Aristotle and surveys principal

commentaries which accompany the texts on logic in the Middle Ages and early Renaissance. 'Une édition nouvelle des ouvrages de Boèce devra contenir entre autre: 1. texte des *Catégories*, deux rédactions; 2. commentaire aux *Catégories* avec lemmes incomplets; 3. texte du *De interpretatione*, une ou deux rédactions; 4. deux commentaires au *De interpretatione* avec lemmes incomplets; 5. texte des *Analytiques Premiers*, deux rédactions; 6. commentaire aux *Analytiques Premiers*; 7. texte des *Topiques*, une ou deux rédactions; 8. texte des *Réfutations Sophistiques*, une ou deux rédactions. Une édition de ces textes devra être basée sur les manuscrits et non pas sur les éditions imprimées; seuls les commentaires au *De interpretatione* (mais non pas le texte continu et les lemmes) pourront être reproduits de l'édition de Meiser, avec peu de retouches' (p 365).

240 Scheible, Helga. *Die Gedichte in der Consolatio Philosophiae des Boethius.* Heidelberg: Carl Winter, 1972.
Part I, pp 8–171, offers a systemmatic commentary on the thirty nine *metra* of the *Consolatio*, with additional discussion of the opening two poems and the sequence of poems in Bk III.3–7. Part II, *Das philosophische System der Consolatio Philosophiae*, consists of two chapters, one on the Boethian 'Weltbild,' which considers Boethian notions of God as creator and upholder of the universe; God's eternality, immutability, and supreme goodness; the Cosmos, with its elements and stars and foundation in ordinance; and the soul as an essence between God and the Universe (pp 174–96). The second chapter of Part II, *Der Mensch*, considers Boethian anthropology (psychology), epistemology, and ethics (pp 197–216).

241 Silk, Edmund T. 'The Study of Boethius' "Consolatio Philosophiae" in the Middle Ages.' *Transactions of the American Philological Association*, 62 (1931), xxxvii–xxxviii.
An abstract of Silk's Yale dissertation. 'Just as what St Jerome, Ambrose, or Augustine said about the Bible eventually almost equaled in importance what the Bible said itself, so from the ninth to the fifteenth century the works of commentators on the *Consolatio* gradually acquired an importance almost overshadowing that of the utterances of Boethius himself' (p xxxvii). The student would approach the treatise through a commentary where strange words, Greek quotations, unfamiliar and difficult scientific, religious or philosophical matters, and allusions to pagan mythology and Roman history would be explained. Silk names some of the better known commentators but notes that the body of the mss yet to be surveyed before the histories of commentaries can be complete is immense.

242 — *Saeculi Noni Auctoris in Boetii Consolationem Philosophiae Commentarius.* Rome: American Academy in Rome, 1935.

This commentary is found in three fragmentary mss (Bodleian MS
Digby 174, which preserves the greater part of the commentary; Paris
BN Lat. 15104, which includes part of the commentary on Bk III and
most of it on Bk V; and the Laurentian codex MS 78.19, containing
Vita III, attributed to Johannes, and interspersed with excerpts from
the commentary). Silk tentatively attributes authorship to Johannes
Scottus, on grounds that the commentary bears the imprint of his
personality and contains doctrines strikingly like his views. The
commentary was written before the close of the ninth century, and is
the primary source for Remigius of Auxerre's commentary. It would
seem that Rand was correct in thinking that a lost commentary by
Scottus lay behind that of Remigius. Silk's introduction (pp ix–lxi)
describes the commentary, which begins with a brief life of Boethius,
then accounts for his literary models and purpose, comments on his
style (scarcely inferior to Virgil or Cicero), provides an etymology on
his name and titles, and explores the allegorical and semi-dramatic
features of the treatise. After an aside directed against those who
think the Muses to be goddesses, the commentator begins the task of
exposition, as one philosopher interpreting another. He knows Plautus,
Cicero, Virgil, Sallust, Juvenal, Persius, Suetonius, and Solinus.
Augustine is his favorite Church father though he also draws on
Jerome, Claudian, Boethius' commentary on Porphyry, Orosius,
Martianus Capella, *Timaeus* commentators, Gregory Nazianzus,
Isidore, and Fulgentius. Silk's Introduction also discusses theological
and philosophical views of the author, the date of the treatise, and the
mss. In an appendix he compares the work with the derivative
commentary of Remigius (especially the comments on Bk III.m.9)
which shows Remigius to be inferior both as a scholar and as teacher.

- Review by E.K. Rand, *AJP*, 57 (1936), 338–41. Rand reviews the
  search he himself began for the lost commentary of John the Scot
  of which his disciple Remigius of Auxerre made use, and praises
  Silk and his good luck in finding it. In his assessment of John's
  commentary Rand observes: 'The commentary is a masterpiece of
  construction by one who thoroughly understands the work he is
  explaining. The commentator is versed in Greek, in rhetoric, in
  dialectical method and in the seven liberal arts ... The
  commentary of Remigius is revealed as a sheer appropriation' (p
  339). So closely does Remigius follow the language of the
  comments which he appropriates from John that Silk might have
  used him more frequently, especially at either end of the
  commentary, to supply what is missing of John's text.

- Review by Jacob Hammer, *AHR*, 42 (1937), 722–3: 'a
  conservative and well-arranged text, with a good critical

apparatus in which due consideration is given to the Insular features of the manuscripts' (p 723). Hammer finds Silk's comparisons of John with Remigius to be particularly valuable.

Boethius: The man and his work (selected)

243 Bark, William. 'The Legend of Boethius' Martyrdom.' *Spec*, 21 (1946), 312–17.

'If Boethius died a martyr, it must follow that the Arian Theodoric was a persecutor and that opposition to Arianism was a matter of considerable importance in his Italy. Actually this is an oversimplification and consequently a misinterpretation of history' (p 312). Boethius' downfall is well-documented in the *Liber Pontificalis* and *Anonymous Valesianus* as well as the *Consolatio*. 'Only after several centuries had passed did men begin to see in him a martyr who died for his religion, and not until the later Middle Ages did the legend become well established' (p 313). Early sources are not clear on religious persecution as cause of his execution. Rand **276** supported the persecution theory on the basis of Boethius' 'alleged opposition to Arianism' in the *Opuscula Sacra* (p 315). But Arianism is mentioned only twice in the *Opuscula*: the issues there are the Monophysites, Sabellians, and Manichaeans. 'The writings of Boethius offer no evidence of attacks on Arianism' (p 317). Theodoric knew that Boethius was orthodox and accepted that fact before heaping honors on him. He had granted toleration to Catholics for years. 'To stir fear and indignation fierce enough to drive Theodoric to the extremity of judicial murder, in despite of his whole policy of toleration, Boethius surely would have had to do more than observe that the Arians did not interpret the Trinity as the Catholics did' (p 317). Arianism was not a lively issue at this time. The real cause of Theodoric's enmity was fear of imperial aggression with which Boethius was suspected of being linked. With the removal of the religious issue, so too is the case for martyrdom removed.

244 Barrett, Helen Marjorie. *Boethius: Some Aspects of His Time and Work*. Cambridge: University Press; New York: Macmillan, 1940.

An introduction to Boethius, with chapters on the state of Western Europe in the fifth century and Theodoric the Ostrogoth, Boethius' scholarly interests, his relationship with Theodoric, and his fall from power, with a careful review of the charges against him and his likely motives. Chapters are also devoted to the *Consolation*, its philosophical background, Boethian views on temporality and eternity, his theological writings, and his Christianity. Barrett rejects Usener's theory that the *Consolation* is based on an abridgement of the lost Aristotelian *Protrepticus* 286 to argue that it is an original work, influenced by Platonic, Aristotelian, Stoic, and Neoplatonic thought, and that it really was composed in prison. 'In connexion with the question of Time and Eternity, as with so many other problems of thought, Boethius's principal debt was to Plato' (p 123).

- Review by E.K. Rand, *Spec*, 16 (1941), 350–1. Noting the important distinction between *fides* and *ratio* which Boethius and Barrett both acknowledge, Rand wonders why Barrett is perturbed over the lack of specific Christian assertion in the *Consolatio*. Why should there be Christian assertion 'if the plan of his work was to set forth *ratio* rather than *fides?* We may assume that he said his prayers, saw his confessor, and died a Christian death — so far as Theodoric allowed him' (p 350).

- Review by C.S. Lewis, *MAE*, 10 (1941), 29–34. Lewis wishes Barrett had been more consistent in her skeptical attitude toward evidence drawn from Cassiodorus (p 29) and questions her notion that Boethius equates evil with nothing, as if nothing were zero. Rather, evil, though not a thing, 'consists always in the depravation of some *thing*, which, in being so depraved, departs from its true nature ... and therefore, in a sense, tends towards nothingness. Evil consists not in being, but in failing to be; it is privative, defective, parasitic' (p 30). Lewis also questions Barrett's use of *present* as if it can be employed only where there has been a *past* and will be a *future*. 'But most fortunately *present* is the opposite, not only of *past* and *future*, but also of *absent*; nor is it a mere pun to remind ourselves that we also call a gift a "present" ' (p 31). The *Consolatio* is less personal than Barrett would have it be, though not less true. The fact of physical prison has little relevance. (The metaphor is of considerable importance, however). On the lack of specific Christian reference in the treatise Lewis observes: 'If I remember aright, Thomas More in prison made a resolution to woo his mind "little by little" ' from the world. In logic each step of argument is finished before the next is taken; but in life everything is always beginning over again. There is nothing really irrelevant in discussing things preparatory to conversion twenty years after you have been converted; for continual re-conversion is, perhaps, the nearest most mortals come to stability ... Boethius' mind had long been occupied on the general philosophical case for the religious life, which he may have designed either for a work on its

own, or as the introduction to a larger work on Christian
theology. He began to execute it after his disgrace, and perhaps
in prison. His motive was neither to distract his mind nor
primarily to console himself, but to edify and instruct the human
race — to deliver his message' (pp 33–4). Lewis would include *De
Fide* among the genuine works.

245 Bolton, Diane K. 'The Study of the *Consolation of Philosophy* in
Anglo-Saxon England.' *Archives d'histoire doctrinale et littéraire du
moyen âge*, 44 (1977), 33–78.
Study of Boethius revived in the Carolingian Renaissance. The
Consolatio was 'one of the earliest classical texts to be discovered and
studied, probably by the Englishman, Alcuin, who had been head of
the episcopal school at York ... In 790 Alcuin listed the books in York
Library, mentioning Boethius by name but in a context which suggests
that he was referring to one of the translations of Aristotle rather than
to the *Consolation of Philosophy*. But Alcuin had read and absorbed
the *Consolatio* by the time that he wrote his *Grammatica*' (p 34).
Bolton traces the development of commentaries between Alcuin's day
and Alfred's, dividing Anglo-Saxon mss with commentaries into four
categories: Remigius types, Trinity College ms 0.3.7 types, Paris BN
ms lat.6401A types, and Cambridge Univ. Libr. ms Kk. III.21 types.
After discussing various glossings of allusions to classical mythology
Bolton appends a description of fourteen Anglo-Saxon Boethius mss
(Appendix I, pp 51–60) and excerpts from various Remigian mss of
mythological glosses (Appendix II, pp 60–78).

246 Bommarito, Domenico. 'Boezio e Dante nella Tradizione Protrettica.'
Northwestern University Dissertation. Dir. Mario Trovato. *DAI*, 40
(1979), 3336A. [Italian Text]
Ch 1 considers Boethius' use of the *Protrepticus* tradition of Aristotle,
Cicero, and Iamblichus as it is reconstructed by such classical
philologists as Ingemar Düring, *Aristotle's Protrepticus Studia Graeca
et Latina Gothoburgensia* XII, 1961), and traces protreptic thematics
from Boethius to Dante. Ch 2 confronts the phenomenon of Boethius'
poetry in his philosophical treatise and analyzes the variety of his
meters to clarify how poetry can be framed in the philosophical
schemes of the new Christian poetics. An understanding of the true
significance of *musica* in Boethius is necessary for an understanding of
Dante's poetics, in which poetry is rhetorical fiction set to music, a
theory consonant with that of Boethius' *De Musica*. Ch 3 analyzes
similar uses in Boethius and Dante of classical myth and metaphor in
the Christian protreptic tradition, with special attention given to
Ulysses and *virtus*, Circe and bestial metamorphoses, Orpheus and the
activity of wisdom, the sun and the divine presence, the flight of *mens*

to God and the return home, and Boethian figures of light and
illumination in Dante. Ch 4 explores the concept of God in the two
authors to reveal no substantial diversity between their conceptions of
divine essence, even though their works are of diverse times.

47 Bonnaud, R. 'L'education scientifique de Boèce,' *Spec*, 4 (1929),
198–206.
Taking off on Rand's appeal for canonization of Boethius **276**,
Bonnaud stresses the difficulty of separating religion and politics in the
sixth century. Boethius was attracted to education and the need for
classical learning, especially Neoplatonic thought, but also Aristotle
and the sciences. It was in the latter areas that Boethius' impact on
the Middle Ages was greatest, rather than as a religious figure. Both
sides on questions of nominalism owed him a debt: 'Mais le plus beau
titre de gloire de Boèce est d'avoir servi de base aux disputes sur le
problème des Universaux ... Notre philosophe a ainsi apporté sa
contribution à la création des sciences expérimentales et c'est lui qui a
fourni les premiers arguments aux empiristes' (p 203). Bonnaud notes
Boethius' importance to the arts of music and arithmetic and reviews
the debts of medieval poets to him, especially Jean de Meun, Christine
de Pisan, and Jean Gerson. 'L'importance considérable de Boèce me
paraît justement consister en ce qu'il servit de pivot entre les deux
états d'esprit, en participant profondément à la science profane et à la
foi chrétienne, et dans au autre sens, en préparant par sa dialectique et
ses travaux scientifiques l'avénement de la science expérimentale' (p
206).

48 Bower, Calvin. 'Boethius and Nicomachus: An Essay Concerning the
Sources of *De institutione musica*.' *Vivarium*, 16 (1978), 1–45.
Working from the assumption that Boethius drew upon explicit
sources and that he was a competent translator who, in his *De Musica*,
proceeded as he had done earlier with Nicomachus' *De Arithmetica*,
Bower concludes: 'Boethius chose the two most viable theorists known
to him, Nicomachus and Ptolemy, served as moderator between them,
and translated their basic ideas into Latin. The text of Ptolemy has
survived intact, but we may still read the lost treatise of Nicomachus
in the first four books of Boethius' *De institutione musica*' (p 45).

49 Brogard, Roger. 'L'Harmonie des spheres selon Boèce.' *Spec*, 4 (1929),
206–13.
Brogard compares Boethius' views on the harmonic sequence of the
spheres with those of his alleged source, Nicomachus, noting a
difference in the placement of Mercury and Venus, a difference
Brogard then reconciles.

50 Cappuyns, Dom M. 'Boèce.' In *Dictionnaire d'histoire et de
géographie ecclésiastiques*, 9 (Paris: Librairie Letouzey et Ané, 1937),

348–79.
Dom Cappuyns' biography of Boethius is often cited by other scholars. It includes discussion of Boethius' family, his public service, his trial, exile, and death, the cult which grew up surrounding his 'martyrdom,' his Christianity, his writings on the quadrivium, his philosophical writings (translations, commentaries, and treatises), as well as a summary of his characteristic doctrines and their subsequent historical interests. Includes a bibliography.

250a Chadwick, Henry. *Boethius: The Consolations of Music, Logic, Theology, and Philosophy*. Oxford: Clarendon Press, 1981.
Chadwick places Boethius' life and intellectual achievements in the setting of his own 'turbulent and tormented age' (p v), emphasizing Boethius' debt to the late Platonists of Athens and Alexandria and Neoplatonic and Augustinian influences, especially on the Christian tractates. Ch 1, 'Romans and Goths,' pp 1–68, details the complex conflicts between the Eastern and Western branches of the Church and Theodoric, with excellent comments on Pope Symmachus, John the Deacon, the Acacian and Laurentian Schisms, Boethius' role in politics, and the collapse of religious-political toleration in the later years of Theodoric's reign. Ch 2, 'Liberal Arts in the Collapse of Culture,' pp 69–107, considers Boethius' treatises on Arithmetic and Music, their sources, and their ties to late Roman traditions. Ch 3, 'Logic,' pp 108–173, offers a sophisticated discussion of Boethius' understanding and development of definitions and theories of logic, interpretation, contingencies, propositions, and hypothetical syllogisms. Ch 4, 'Christian Theology and the Philosophers,' pp 174–222, vigorously lays out the contents, sources, and historical controversies to which the five theological tractates pertain. Ch 5, 'Evil, Freedom, and Providence,' pp 223–253, analyzes the ideological structure of the *Consolation*, differentiating Boethius' movement from Stoic moralism to Platonic transcendence, commenting on his theories of reminiscence and natural theology as well as Augustinian elements within his theory of foreknowledge, free will, providence, and fate. Chs 4 and 5 are particularly thoughtful in their sensitive delineation of the religious Boethius. Ch 6, 'Presentation and Transmission,' pp 254–57, is an afterword on manuscript traditions. The bibliography (pp 258–84) is excellent, including a discussion of editions of the Boethian canon.

251 Chenu, M.D. *Nature, Man, and Society in the Twelfth Century: Essays on New Theological Perspectives in the Latin West*, selected, edited and translated by Jerome Taylor and Lester K. Little. Chicago: University of Chicago Press, 1968. Originally published as *La théologie au douzième siècle*. Paris: J. Vrin, 1957.

'The Platonism of the *Timaeus* and of Boethius' (pp 64–79): The connection between the *Timaeus* and Boethius was intimate in the High Middle Ages. *Consolatio* III.m.9 was regarded as summary of the *Timaeus*. Ancient mss of the Latin version of *Timaeus* contain numerous passages from Boethius in their margins (pp 64–5). 'Though one can speak of the Augustinianism of Boethius, and though the author of the *Consolation* contributed to an Augustinian reading of the *Timaeus* ... it is nonetheless true that he read the works of Plato with other eyes than Augustine's, with greater scholarly fidelity and without that religious and philosophical transformation to which the Christian doctor subjected them. In truth, Boethius, even in his lofty spiritual aspirations, remained a man formed by the school — the school of Ammonius of Alexandria, which made him a follower of Proclus as distinct from other strains of Neoplatonism — and he retained the learning, the techniques, and the methods of the school. Yet he was far from being weak in personality; he showed this in his curiosity, his preferences, his interiorized convictions, his nobility. His extraordinary success throughout the Middle Ages testifies indisputably to his personal appeal' (pp 72–3). Boethius platonized Aristotle. The immediate effect of his yoking Plato and Aristotle together was 'to divide the life of the mind into two levels [intellect and reason], irreducible despite their permanent connection' (p 75). Boethius' influence upon metaphysics was decisive: he 'reigned in schools wherever metaphysical analysis of creation nourished the contemplation of God, as it had in his theological *opuscula*' (p 76). In treating the composite condition of created things his influence was 'Neoplatonic insofar as it stressed the primacy of the One, but Aristotelian in its treatment of everything involving form' (p 76). Moreover, 'Boethius gave the natural sciences their statute of autonomy'; he was, until St Thomas, 'the great authority for a systematization of knowledge differentiated according to its objects' (p 77). Boethius was thoroughly a man of the Latin West. His platonism was distinct from that of pseudo-Dionysius (also a disciple of Proclus) and from that of Augustine. He achieved one of the most intelligent adaptations of the *Timaeus* and pushed far along 'the Christianization of the providence of the God-demiurge. The famous metre, *O qui perpetua*, of *Consolation* III, m. 9, possessed great religious depth, despite the ostensible naturalism of its terminology' (p 78). See Chenu's index for numerous other references to Boethius.

52 Collins, James. 'Progress and Problems in the Reassessment of Boethius.' *Modern Schoolman*, 23 (1945/46), 1–23.
Surveys scholarship on the place of Boethius in the history of logic (pp 5–8), in the history of mathematics and music (pp 8–16), and in the

history of theology (pp 16–22). Stresses the need for a comprehensive treatment of Boethius, one in which the historian of medieval philosophy works 'in continued cooperation with students in allied fields who have studied other aspects of this many-sided mind' (p 23).

253 Coster, Charles H. 'The Fall of Boethius: His Character,' *Annuaire de l'institute de philologie et d'histoire orientales et slaves*, 12 (1952), 45–81.
The fall and punishment of Boethius are tied to Arian persecutions instituted by Justinian. Coster places Boethius' death as late as 526.

254 Courcelle, Pierre. *Late Latin Writers and Their Greek Sources*. Trans. Harry E. Wedeck. Cambridge, Mass.: Harvard University Press, 1969.
Courcelle discusses the mainstream of Hellenism through Macrobius, St Jerome, Augustine, Boethius, Cassiodorus, and early monasticism. Ch 6, 'The East to the Rescue of Pagan Culture: Boethius,' pp 273–330, considers the centrality of Boethius to the transmission of Hellenic thought in the Middle Ages, with special emphasis on his scientific works, his works on logic, Neoplatonism in the *Consolatio*, Boethius' Christianity, and Symmachus' course of studies and his failure. 'While Hellenic culture was dying in Africa and Gaul in the sixth century, it produced a veritable literary renaissance in Italy during the reign of Theodoric' (p 273). Courcelle's discussion is particularly adept in exploring Boethius' sources. He supports arguments on the orthodoxy of Boethius' Christianity but warns against emphasizing 'excessively the Christianity of Boethius' thought' (p 319). Boethius works with Neoplatonic sources knowing that they are Neoplatonic; the *Consolatio* is 'his real philosophical testament' (p 319), propounding 'a purely rational theology' (p 322). Above all 'he wanted to keep separate in his books the domain of reason and the domain of faith' (p 321). When Theodoric broke with Byzantium it was 'natural for Boethius to be the first victim,' for he had come to embody the Hellenistic revival. With his death and that of Symmachus 'it was Greek culture that was on the point of disappearing' (p 330).

255 de Rijk, L.M. 'On the Chronology of Boethius' Works on Logic,' *Vivarium*, 2 (1964), 1–49, 125–62.
Reviews chronologies and methods of dating by Usener, Rand, McKinlay, Brandt, Kappelmacher, and Shiel; then establishes his own approach based on terminological and doctrinal peculiarities and references in Boethius' works. De Rijk deduces the following chronology:

Boethius' birth	c 480
In Porphyrii Isogogen, editio prima	c 504–05
De syllogismis categoricis libri duo	c 505–06

Liber de divisione	between 505–09
In Porphyrii Isogogen, editio secunda	c 507–09
In Aristotelis categorias, editio prima	c 509–11
In Aristotelis Perihermeneias, editio prima	not before 513
In Aristotelis Perihermeneias, editio secunda	c 515–16
Possible second edition of *In categorias*	after 515–16
De syllogismis hypotheticis libri tres	between 516–22
Trans. of *Topica, Sophistici elenchi, Analytica priora, Analytica posteriora*	not after 520
In Ciceronis Topica Commentaria	before 522
Commentary on Aristotle's *Topica*	before 523
De topicis differentiis libri quattuor	before 523
The so-called *Introductio*	early 523
Scholia on Aristotle's *Analytica Priora*	early 523
Death	524

255a De Vogel, Christine J. 'Boethiana.' *Vivarium* 10 (1972), 1–40.
De Vogel challenges Courcelle's views that the *Consolatio* is essentially
pagan in its Neoplatonism to insist upon its essentially Christian
character. There are no passages in the *Consolatio* that could not have
been written by an orthodox Christian working within Christian
literary traditions, and there are many passages which are explicitly
Christian and could not have been written by a pagan Neoplatonist.
There is one explicit biblical citation along with many phrases that
have biblical resonances. Fleming (110a) refers to this essay as 'the
most closely reasoned [on the subject of the *Consolatio's* orthodoxy]
and the keenest in its sensitivity to the literary nature of the
Consolatio' (p 42). See also De Vogel, 'The Problem of Philosophy and
Christian Faith in Boethius' *Consolatio*,' in *Romanitas et
Christianitas: Studia Iano Henrico Waszink*. Ed. W. den Boer *et al.*
Amsterdam: North-Holland, 1973. Pp 357–70.

256 Dronke, Peter. 'L'Amor che move il sole e l'altre stelle.' *Studi
Medievali*, 6 (1965), 389–422.
The idea that love powers the motion of the heavens found in *Inferno*
1.38, 1.74, and *Paradiso* 27.111, 30.52, comes to Dante through two
main channels — *Consolatio* II.m.8 and Aristotle's *Metaphysics*
1072b,3. The background of the Boethian idea is complex — a
combination of mythic, poetic, and conceptual elements. Dronke's
essay isolates 'what is most relevant to a *cosmological* conception of
love' (p 391), discussing Aphrodite in classical literature (Sophocles,
Euripides, Plato, Parmenides, Empedocles, Lucretius, the Orphic
tradition, Apuleius, Proclus, Plotinus) and in the medieval
commentaries on that tradition (John Scotus Erigena, William of
Conches, and Bernard Sylvestris). He concludes by comparing

Chaucer's invocation to Venus (*T&C*, III.1–49) to Boccaccio's.
Chaucer turns 'Boethius' metaphysical statements into an exultant
hymn of praise and at the same time an intimate prayer' (p 421).
Boethius similarly influences Troilus' song (III.1744–71): 'To give
Troilus such a song, instead of Boccaccio's verses, is also a feat of
dramatic transformation. Chaucer's Troilus is extraordinarily unlike
Boccaccio's, unlike any lover, in fact, of ancient or medieval romances.
This hypersensitive, brooding intellectual, who has an intense personal
devotion to a metaphysical principle, who prays for grace to love as
the "holy bond of thynges" in the same glowing words that Dante uses
in prayer to the Madonna, this lover who can feel the problem of free
will as keenly as his own separation from his beloved — what
celebration of the joy of love could be more dramatically right for him
than this?' (pp 421-2). By drawing upon both traditions Chaucer
'expresses his vision of the interdependence of human and divine love;
and this was his own vision, as was Dante's of "l'amor che move il sole
e l'altre stelle" ' (p 422).

257   — 'Boethius, Alanus and Dante.' *RF*, 78 (1966), 119–25.
On the sources of *Paradiso* 33.94–6, especially the idea of *letargo*.
Dante's mode of lethargy suggests a condition of inspired ecstatic
vision, in contrast to the lethargy of *Consolatio* I. pr.2 ('a pathological
somnolence or coma requiring medical treatment' [p 122; cf p 119]), or
the Boethian restatement of lethargy in *Anticlaudianus*. Dante's
treatment seems without precedent. But the ecstasy of the vision itself
is strongly Boethian, especially *un punto solo*, which is like Boethius'
comparison of eternity to a point and time to a line stretching to
immense length. 'Boethius' eternity is not before time, or longer than
time: it is a quality of being, not a quantity, a fullness *tota simul*, in
which length is meaningless' (p 125). For Dante, as for Boethius, 'the
punctum, the transfigured moment, is incommensurable with any span
of time. Anywhere outside that *punctum* lethargy would be a defect or
disease: it would be objectless. Only here self-forgetfulness finds a
perfect object, lethargy is *maggior*' (p 125).

257a   Duclow, Donald F. 'Perspective and Therapy in Boethius'
Consolation of Philosophy.' *Journal of Medicine and Philosophy*, 4
(1979), 334–343.
Duclow examines the *Consolation* as an exercise in psychotherapy.
The healing comes through Neoplatonic insights attained 'by
progressing through a series of perspectives' (p 335). At the end,
Boethius' external situation has not changed, but the attitude of the
persona has: 'no longer a lethargic patient, he has come to an
introspective acceptance of his situation' (p 342). By accepting
suffering and anxiety as characteristics of the human condition, the

persona transcends temporalities for a vision of the divine center. 'The act of writing the *Consolation* both sprang from and reinforced this healing process' (p 342).

258 Dürr, Karl. *The Propositional Logic of Boethius*. Studies in Logic and the Foundations of Mathematics, eds L.E.J. Brouwer, E.W. Beth, and A. Heyting. Amsterdam: North-Holland Publishing Company, 1951.

Discusses sources of 'De Syllogismo Hypothetico' (including the document of the School of Ammonius), the effects of Boethius' propositional logic in the early scholastic period, and then, after commenting on 'metascience' and 'metalanguage,' analyzes the 'De Syllogismo Hypothetico' and a section of Boethius' commentary on Cicero's *Topics*.

259 Economou, George Demetrios. *The Goddess Natura in Medieval Literature*. Cambridge, Mass.: Harvard University Press, 1972. Pp 28–52.

In his discussion of the philosophical background to his topic Economou cites Boethius' fourfold definition of Nature in *Contra Evtychen* and the influence of *Timaeus* and Plotinus on Boethius. Ch 2, 'Boethius and the Poetic Background,' pp 28–52, considers philosophical nature in the *Consolatio*. 'The irregularities and vicissitudes of man's life are owing to his failure to follow nature and her greatest gift to him, reason' (p 29). Economou draws on the commentaries of pseudo-John Scotus Erigena and William of Conches to expand upon Boethian attitudes toward nature. 'William defines Genius as natural concupiscence, who desires whatever he believes is good, whether it is or not ... a definition that underscores the fact that the responsibility for sexual conduct lies with the individual. Alan of Lille and Jean de Meun would make radically different uses of this definition in their characterizations of Genius' (p 37). 'The *Consolation* is much more than a philosophical document; it is a great work of literature' (p 37). In Boethius' personification of Natura she becomes creator, nourisher, shaper, presiding power over generation and increase, the whole world; she is the charioteer who holds the reins of the world in her hands (pp 40–1). Boethius' metaphoric conception of Nature stands as a primary source for subsequent treatments throughout the later Middle Ages.

260 Friedman, John Block. *Orpheus in the Middle Ages*. Cambridge, Mass.: Harvard University Press, 1970. Pp 86–145.

Ch 4, 'Oraia-phonos and Eur-dike in Hell,' pp 86–145, shows how the view of Orpheus and Eurydice as complementary parts of man's soul — reason and passion — develops first in Boethius' *Consolatio* and then in allegorical commentaries on Boethius and Ovid. Boethius' interpretation was so influential 'that we could hardly consider

medieval attitudes toward Orpheus without referring to it' (p 90). For
Boethius, Orpheus is a key exemplum, the man who has almost gained
spiritual enlightenment, looks back to material concerns, and loses all
the excellence he gained. The *Consolatio* and its glosses and
commentaries enjoyed remarkable popularity, especially in the schools.
Its psychological interpretation of the Orpheus story marks one strain
of the Orpheus tradition. The sixth-century African commentator
Fulgentius took a somewhat different approach to the Orpheus story
— more rhetorical, though still allegorical — by studying the
etymology of Orpheus (*oraia-phonos* = *best voice*), Eurydice (*eur-dike*
= *profound judgment*), and Aristaeus (*aristo* = *best*). The Boethian
and Fulgentian approaches remain more or less distinct throughout the
Middle Ages, with the Boethian, concerned with the spiritual progress
of the soul, being the more prominent. Boethius' version of the story
in *Consolatio* Bk III m.12 combines details from both Ovid and Virgil
to create a kind of parable. He is 'the first Latin writer to develop an
ethical allegory from the story ... and the effect of his version on
subsequent conceptions of the legend cannot be overemphasized' (p
93). Friedman traces the overall plot of the *Consolatio* to show how
the monitory exemplum fits in and is appropriately placed. He also
discusses ways in which the commentaries develop accretions, citing
Remigius, who seems to be responsible for working Aristaeus (who is
not mentioned by Boethius) into the Boethian allegory (pp 97–102);
Notker Labeo, an eleventh-century German commentator who
amplified the seriousness of Orpheus' fall (pp 102–4); William of
Conches, a twelfth-century expositor 'who has the necessary
philosophical training to understand his original and who at the same
time has sufficient imagination to make his text seem contemporary'
(pp 104–9); Nicholas Trivet, who substitutes his own Aristotelianism
for William's Platonism, draws on Bernard Silvestris and the Vatican
Mythographers, and whose work influenced Henryson (pp 109–14); and
Peter of Paris (ca 1309) whose commentary is 'remarkable chiefly for
what he did not know about the subject' and who adds a happy
ending (pp 114–8). Friedman notes that commentators on Ovid, like
Bersuire, often echo the Boethian commentators, especially William of
Conches (p 128). There are also Boethian influences in *Sir Orfeo*.

261 Gibson, Margaret, ed. *Boethius: His Life, Thought and Influence*
Oxford: Basil Blackwell, 1981.
Fourteen essays, Introduction, Epilogue, Index of Manuscripts, and
seventeen plates, some of which are provided with short notes, in
commemoration of the fifteen-hundreth anniversary of the birth of
Boethius. The book is divided into three sections: Part 1: Boethius'
Life and Circumstances (pp 13–69); Part 2: The Scholastic Writings

(pp 71–234); and Part 3: The *De Consolatione Philosophiae* (pp 235–409). The essays are annotated herewith in the order in which they appear in the volume.

261a Albinia de la Mare. 'Frontispiece: BL MS Lansdowne 842A.f.lv.' Pp xvii–xix. De la Mare describes the title page to two volumes of Boethius, ca 1475–85, in the hand of Tommaso Baldinotti of Pistoia, apparently for Lorenzo de Medici.

261b Henry Chadwick. 'Introduction.' Pp 1–12. Comments on Boethius' historical importance as a spiritual guide to laymen. Comments briefly on the canon and its historical context, and Boethius' imprisonment at Pavia. 'Boethius' mind is retrospective ... soaked in Plato and Aristotle and in their Neoplatonic exegetes ... Yet the opuscula and dialectical treatises injected an essential ingredient into the formation of scholastic theology and philosophy, and the music and arithmetic long remained to educate medieval men ... If tragedy had never overtaken him and if he had never written the *Consolation of Philosophy* charged from start to finish with intellectual and moral passion, no doubt his influence on posterity would have been greatly reduced, but it would still have been far from negligible' (p 12).

261c John Matthews. 'Anicius Manlius Severinus Boethius.' Pp 15–43. In his telling of Boethius' imprisonment and execution by torture and beating Matthews prefers 'the more circumstantial account of the *Excerpta* [Valensiana II.85–7] to the plain and differing statement in the *Liber Pontificalis* (p 38, n.1). Matthews discusses the mosaic fresco in Theodoric's palace at Ravenna, as described by the ninth-century chronicler Agnellus, the relationship of Theodoric's court protected by marshland to Rome, the Senate's relationship to barbarian emperors from 380 onwards, Boethius' distinguished ancestors and their role in the arts, the Christianization of the Roman patricians and the absorption of classical training into Christian tradition in the fifth and sixth centuries, and Boethius' part in furnishing and presiding over lavish festivities of state. Boethius' political involvements with Constantinople were intricate. 'The failure of Theodoric's gesture in promoting Boethius and his sons, the execution of Boethius and the decline of Theodoric's government which this initiated, were all stages leading to the reunification of the empire by Justinian' (p 29). The commitments of Boethius and Cassiodorus (who succeeded him as *magister officiorum* differed profoundly. They were descended from different traditions — Boethius from a senatorial tradition, and Cassiodorus from an imperial one (p 31). Cassiodorus' role in Theodoric's court provides an interesting study of the intricacies of Boethius' downfall. 'In his own age, and certainly in his own mental and emotional horizons, Boethius was still very much a Roman senator and a representative of the ancient world' (p 38).

261d Helen Kirby. 'The Scholar and his Public.' Pp 44–69. Considers intellectual life in sixth-century Italy, beginning with Cassiodorus' founding of the double monastery at Vivarium, his writing of the *Institutiones* there, his comfort with an intellectual life that embraced Cicero, Aristotle, and Plato as well as Christian theology, and his concern for secular education (pp 44–50). Such learned men as Cassiodorus, Boethius, Symmachus, Ennodius, Martianus Capella, Vettius Agorius Basilius Mavortius, and Macrobius suggest an intellectual vigor that is hardly aware of an impending dark age. But it is a mistake to think of this group as a sixth-century Hellenistic Renaissance, as Courcelle does (254, pp 274–5), given the sense of continuity which such writers manifest. The 'renaissance theory,' which links Boethius somewhat desperately to a few sources which he hoped to preserve, does a disservice to his 'powers of independent thought' (p 61). 'Boethius' motives in embarking upon his intellectual projects were not as grandiose as has sometimes been argued' (p 59). Rather than relying heavily on Ammonius, for example, Boethius may have been working from a common fund of sources which Ammonius likewise drew upon (p 61).

261e Jonathan Barnes. 'Boethius and the Study of Logic.' Pp 73–89. Considers Boethius' translations, commentaries, and treatises on peripetetic logic. 'Boethius took immense pains over his translations' (p 76). He was not an original logician, nor did he pretend to be. But he understood the complexity of translation and was 'fully conscious of the shortcomings of his Latin style' (p 77). He was not simply a translator of scholia, however. 'He was out to present Greek logic to a Latin audience; he knew what that audience would require; and both the general tenor of the commentaries and some of the detailed annotation were planned by Boethius himself for his own readers' (p 80).

261f Osmund Lewry, O.P. 'Boethian Logic in the Medieval West.' Pp 90–134. Traces descent of Boethian texts on logic to Alcuin, who revives the teaching of Boethius, a practice then carried on by his student Hrabanus Maurus and Hrabanus' student Walafrid Strabo. In the ninth century Boethian logic flourishes under the tutelage of John Scottus Erigena and Remigius of Auxerre; in the tenth and eleventh, under Notker Labeo, Iso of St Gall(?), Gerbert of Aurillac, Abbo, Garlandus, Lanfranc, Roscelin, and Peter Damian, as ms production increases. Lewry provides charts of mss from the eighth to the sixteenth century for the *Perihermeneias* the *Isagoge* and its commentaries, and the *Praedicamenta*. Considers later computators like John of Salisbury, Abelard, Adam of Balsham, Roger Bacon, and

Robert Kilwardby, and explores ways in which Boethian logic was used in university curricula. Examines taxation lists of texts available for copying, as well as lemmata and other allusions, to trace sphere of Boethian influence; also examines frequency with which commentators mention Simplicius and Ammonius in conjunction with Boethius. Illustrates how rhetoric displaces logic in importance in the fifteenth and sixteenth centuries, as Valla and others prefer Cicero and Quintilian to Boethius.

61g John Caldwell. 'The *De Institutione Arithmetica* and the *De Institutione Musica*.' Pp 135–54. Places Boethius at the end of a long tradition in arithmetic. 'Boethius' competence in dealing with the highly technical mathematical literature of the Greeks is unquestionable' (p 142). 'His work on music is much the more original of the two treatises,' however (p 134). Perhaps its chief significance for its time is that 'it presented, or rather revived, Pythagorean theory for Latin readers' (p 143). What was its intended audience? Certainly Boethius 'was not in the business of writing simple handbooks for beginners. He seems to have wished to gloss over no difficulty for the sake of feebler minds than his. It is a difficult book today, and it will have been difficult in the early years of the sixth century. The educational system of the ancient world was still nominally intact, but contemporary readership of this book can only have been small. By one of those curious accidents of history it was to be of the most profound significance in the development of Western musical thought from Carolingian times on; and that is the real importance of Boethius for musical history' (p 143). Bk I is justly the most admired. Its tone is vividly rhetorical. Boethius 'was himself no mean poet, and the metra of the *De Consolatione* can hardly be considered the work of one who had earlier neglected the art' (p 146). Some of his poems survive in *De Consolatione* mss, others in mss of miscellaneous poetry 'with neumes (a primitive type of musical notation, the remote ancestor of our modern system) indicating the tunes to which they might be sung ... Some [of the notations] may be adaptations of liturgical melodies' (p 147). It is not clear whether Boethius himself was a performing musician, but 'he may have had a practical knowledge of performance ... He was a poet, and he conceived poetry as a musical phenomenon, not merely metaphorically nor merely in its rhythmic and metrical aspects, nor even merely through the recognition of speech as an aspect of vocal music; but as a potential vehicle for real song, of which his own poems are perhaps a perpetually incommunicable example' (p 148).

61h David Pingree. 'Boethius' Geometry and Astronomy.' Pp 155–61. A stemmatic study of early geometry mss. 'Boethius was not the only translator of Greek texts belonging to the quadrivium in the late fifth and early sixth centuries — a conclusion toward which the Verona fragments of Euclid seem also to point. Thereby the argument that M [an eighth-century ms of at least the Definitions, Postulates, and Axioms of Euclid's *Elements* I–V, which was copied at least twice at Corbie and which seems to be the ancestor of several of the earliest mss] most probably represents Boethius' translation because we know of no other translator loses some of its force, though Boethius certainly remains the chief suspect' (p 159).

261i Alison White. 'Boethius in the Medieval Quadrivium.' Pp 162–205. There is little sign of systematic instruction in the quadrivium in Theodoric's time. But by the tenth century the Boethian texts for *De Arithmetica* and *De Musica* were established. A sure sign that an author is becoming standard reading is the appearance of abbreviated forms of his texts. White cites the increasingly elaborate introductions to the texts which even include glosses on Boethius' name (said to mean 'helper of many') and explanations of his titles (pp 168–9). White devotes a section of her essay to the importance and creativity of Gerbert of Aurillac in advancing the study of arithmetic and music (pp 169–74) and another to glossators and educators in the eleventh to thirteenth centuries in various later mss. 'Increased concern with the quadrivium meant even closer attention to the standard authors; it [the twelfth century] was an age, *par excellence*, of the commentary' (p 178). The latter part of the essay considers the roles of Hugh of St Victor, Thierry of Chartres, Grosseteste, Roger Bacon, Simon Bredon, etc, in quadrivial studies.

261j John Mair. 'The Text of the *Opuscula Sacra*.' Pp 206–13. The five treatises had a lively influence on Carolingian and scholastic theology. Mair concurs with Victor Schurr [**279**, pp 105–227] that Tractate V against the teachings of Nestorius and Eutyches was the first to be written. It is 'the most original of Boethius' theological essays' (p 208). Boethius decisively takes the part of the Eastern bishops 'over an issue upon which Pope Symmachus had refrained from comment' (p 210). Of the tractates on the Trinity, Tractate II preceded I. 'Notwithstanding the notable contributions of Rand, Schurr, Cappuyns and others, the study of the Tractates still proceeds at a fairly low level of certainty' (p 211).

261k Margaret Gibson. 'The *Opuscula Sacra* in the Middle Ages.' Pp 215–34. 'Boethius' prose has a hard clarity of expression that may seem more objective than Augustine's, and ... brief. Such qualities ... commended the *Opuscula* as teaching texts, and it was principally in the schoolroom that they were to survive: as useful to the eclectic scholars of the ninth century as to the sophisticated professionals of

twelfth-century Paris and fifteenth-century Cracow' (pp 214–5).
Gibson explores influence of the tractates by tracing direct borrowings
from the text. Alcuin seems to have steered clear of Boethius as a
theologian (p 215), but his students did not. Carolingian mss of the
Opuscula are numerous. Above all the tractates provided a guide to
terminology any schoolmaster could use. One of the earliest schools in
which the tractates were read seriously was Corbie (nb, Hadoard and
Ratramnus, who was one of the first to be at home with them). 'But
the man who had the intellectual bent to use the *Opuscula Sacra* was
John Scotus Eriugena' (p 219). In the eleventh and twelfth centuries
the tractates were discussed alongside the *logica vetus*. 'Indeed, they
alone kept theology on the curriculum' (p 220). Abelard, Peter
Lombard, Hugh of St Victor, Thierry of Chartres, and Gilbert of
Poitiers draw upon them. They were studied in the context of
Sentence-literature after Peter Lombard and Robert of Melun
discouraged their formal exposition.

2611   Anna Crabbe. 'Literary Design in the *De Consolatione Philosophiae*.'
Pp 273–4. After considering the genre ('a multicolored garment' [p 237]
which 'parallels no genre precisely yet is like almost all' [p 238]), the
person and function of Philosophy (a Sophia figure 'as comprehensive
as a lifetime's reading might make it' [p 239]), and the details and
direction of the philosophical argument of the *Consolatio* (an
argument derived from three main constituents — Greek and Roman
philosophy and Latin poetry) with its strong appeal to reason, Crabbe
explores literary connections between the *Consolatio* and Cicero,
Seneca, and Platonism, but, more important, the work's affinities with
Ovid and Augustine. Crabbe draws parallels between exile motifs in
the *Consolatio* and Ovid's exile poetry, especially the *Tristia* and *Ex
Ponto* (nb, 'the poet's unwilling change of subject matter to the elegy
of lament' [p 246], the chameleon-like muses, premature age and a
death-wish, the power of philosophy to console, the treachery of
fortune and the power of adversity to show one his true friends).
'Boethius is indulging in a display of cultivated literary wit that will
extend some way into the work, and which is little short of playful' (p
247). The driving away of the harlot muses perhaps owes something to
Propertius' elegies where Cynthia arrives home early to discover her
lover sharing his couch with a couple of inferior prostitutes, whom she
drives out (pp 249–50). But Augustine is even more influential than
Ovid or Propertius (cf *De Ordine*, the *Dialogues*, and the
Confessions), especially on the issue of degenerative-regenerative
effects of poetry. 'Augustine and Boethius stand side by side in any
treatment of early autobiography as the only Latin examples more
concerned with matters spiritual than temporal' (p 256). Boethius was

surely well aware that his *Consolatio* must inevitable challenge the
Confessions. The two share much — Neoplationism, a strong emphasis
on memory and the problem of forgetting oneself, the search for
remedies, etc. But there are basic differences in tone. 'Augustine
thinks of God in terms of a personal relationship and his *Confessions*
received embarrassed criticism on that account. Boethius' religion is
the complete antithesis, coldly impersonal, abstract and theoretical to
a degree, even when ... he is extolling divine amor' (p 261).

261m   David Ganz. 'A Tenth-Century Drawing of Philosophy Visiting
Boethius.' Pp 275–7. Discussion of BL Harley 2688, f 22v, of
Philosophy with her ladder putting the Muses to flight.

261n   Jacqueline Beaumont. 'The Latin Tradition of the *De Consolatione
Philosophiae*.' Pp 278–305. 'There is barely a library in Europe
without at least one copy of the *De Consolatione Philosophiae*, and
although the list of identified manuscripts of both text and
commentary is long, it is not exhaustive. Of those which are known,
many have still to be fully studied. Modern editions of some of the
most important commentaries have still to be prepared. A firm
chronology, particularly for the earliest period, has not yet been
established' (p 278). Boethius was little studied between the time of
his death and the 8th century. Alcuin appears to be the one who
introduced his work into Northern Europe, but he did so extensively,
urging Boethian ideas and terminology upon others. The first
commentary to which a name is attached is that of Servatus Lupus of
Ferriers (ca 862). Early scholars, commentators, glossers, and
borrowers quarry Boethius for phrases, allusions, and ideas to
embellish their own work or for eclectic observation and moralizing. 'It
was not an understanding of his work which was required, but the
application, piecemeal and out of context, of thought, images and
elegant phrasing which gave added point to the work of the moment'
(p 282). Beaumont challenges Courcelle 231 for having over-simplified
the history of the commentaries (pp 283–9); his 'assessment may
require some reappraisal when the complexities of the many Remigian
manuscripts have been fully explored' (p 285). Beaumont reviews the
history of the commentators, emphasizing the importance of Remigius
and his revisers. In the tenth century Bk. III m. ix 'became something
of a cause celebre' (p 293). 'The diversity of attitudes displayed in the
interpretation of this one section of the work [by Bovo of Corvey, the
Anonymous of Einsiedeln, the Anonymous of Brussels and, in the next
century, by Adalbold of Utrecht] is an indication of the lively interest
taken in studying and understanding the works of pagan classical
antiquity throughout the tenth century' (p 295).

261o   Christopher Page. 'The Boethian Metrum "Bella bis Quinis" ': a new song from Saxon Canterbury.' Pp 306–11. 'We have no difficulty in imagining a medieval scholar bent over glosses to the *Consolatio* of Boethius in a library, or construing the text in a classroom; it is not so easy to picture a cantor rising from the study of a metrum to sing it for the enjoyment of his fellows in the cloister or refectory. Yet increasingly manuscripts are coming to light which reveal how often this must have happened. Boethius was certainly one of the poets that composers of chant chose to set. By the ninth century we find metra from the *Consolatio* extracted from their source and set down with musical notation amongst battle-songs, hymns, planctus and lyrics in a monastic musical repertory at St Martial de Limoges' (p 307). Page focuses his study on ms Auct. F 1.15 of the Bodleian, produced at St Augustine's, Canterbury, ca 1000, which includes, with neumes, 'Carmina qui quondam' (I m.i), 'O stelliferi' (I m.v), 'Si quantas rapidis' (II m.i), 'Omne hominum genus' (III m.vi), 'Huc omnes pariter' (III m.x), 'Quisquis profunda' (III m.xi), 'Felix qui potuit' (III m.xii), 'Vela Neritii' (IV m.iii), 'Quid tantos iuvat' (IV m.iv), and 'Bella bis quinis' (IV m. vii). Melodies notated in staffless neumes were not always interpreted in the same way. Often only a few lines have neumes, the assumption being that 'the melody is to be repeated until the end of the text is reached' (p 308).

61p   Alastair Minnis. 'Aspects of the Medieval French and English Traditions of the *De Consolatione Philosophiae*.' Pp 312–61. Minnis concentrates on the vernacular translations of Jean de Meun, Chaucer, and Walton, attempting to reconstruct what each translator worked with in the making of his translation. Jean first made extensive use of Boethius in the *Roman de la Rose*. In his translation of the *Consolatio* entitled *Li Livres de Confort*, Jean drew upon a 'longer version' of William of Conches' commentary or a compilation based on William of Conches rather than William of Aragon or Remigius of Auxerre. Minnis compares treatments by Jean and various commentators of the narrative of Nero's slaying of Seneca and of Croesus, king of Lydia, and his daughter Phanie, both of which stories appear in *RR* as well as *Li Livres*. The raw material for such stories is to be found in the commentaries, William of Conches' being the most relevant. Chaucer's treatment of such stories in *MonkT* draws on *RR*, Boethius, and Trevet, though some details of his Nero tale perhaps come from Vincent of Beauvais' *Speculum Historiale* or Boccaccio's *De Casibus Virorum Illustrium*. Chaucer used *Li Livres de Confort* along with a Latin text in *Boece*. 'The extrapolations which do not derive from Jean are from Trevet's commentary, and no other. Some of Chaucer's glosses may resemble those of William of Conches, but this is only because Trevet had incorporated material from the earlier commentary into his own. Moreover there is nothing in Chaucer's *Boece*, nor indeed in any other Chaucer passage based on Boethius, to suggest that he knew either William of Aragon's commentary or William Wheteley's commentary. We are fortunate that, in the *Boece*, Chaucer's additions to the original text are quite extensive, and therefore provide an adequate basis for satisfactory comparison of the different commentaries' (p 341). Chaucer must have worked from a manuscript which included Trevet, so that when he read the one he also read the other. Walton drew on Chaucer. Minnis includes appendices on 'Chaucer's list of the labours of Hercules' and 'Trevet's Prologue and Walton's *Prologus Super Librum Boecii*' (21-30).

261q Nigel F. Palmer. 'Latin and Vernacular in the Northern European Tradition of the *De Consolatione Philosophiae*.' Pp 362-409. Palmer sets out criteria by which the use of the vernacular *Consolatio* texts can be assessed and then considers two later medieval German translations, the Münster fragments, with their interlinear lexical glosses, and the Oxford ms Hamilton 46, a partial rendering of Books III-V dated 1465, 'an extreme example of the presentation of translation as commentary' (p 382). 'For some readers the translations will have granted access to a difficult text which they aspired to read, but which was beyond them in the original. For others the use of a vernacular text will have been a means to gain greater familiarity with a text they already knew, and at the same time to bring this learning out of the study into the parlour. The encounter with Boethius in the vernacular was a step towards seeing his teaching — on fortune and adversity, on true happiness, his theory of knowledge — in the context of real life' (pp 371-2). Includes an appendix of excerpts from the German mss and an appendix by Anthony Grafton on 'The Dutch Tradition' (p 398).

261r Anthony Grafton. 'Epilogue: Boethius in the Renaissance.' Pp 410-5. 'The early humanists were not quite sure what to make of Boethius ... The *Consolatio*, though clearly a masterpiece of a sort, was couched in a peculiar combination of literary genres and an unfamiliar brand of Latin prose. No classic of Latin literature made the humanists more uneasy' (p 410). Petrarch uses him frequently; so too Erasmus. By mid-sixteenth century Boethius was firmly established in the canon of classics. Scaliger wrote of him: 'I feel that few are comparable to him. Valla teaches him to speak Latin; but Boethius teaches Valla to be wise' (*Poetices libri* VII, 1581 edn, p 285, as cited by Grafton, p 413).

261s Malcolm Godden. 'King Alfred's Boethius.' Pp 419-24. *Consolation* seems to have been 'little known, if at all, among the Anglo-Saxons before the time of Alfred, though there is a flourishing interest after his time' (p 419). Perhaps the king's Welsh adviser Asser introduced him to the text. Trevet consulted the Alfredian translation in the early fourteenth century (p 420). Godden summarizes scholarship on Alfred's sources, his interests, and subsequent textual history.

261t M.B. Parkes. 'A Note on ms Vatican, Bibl. Apost., lat. 3363.' Pp 425-7. Mid-ninth-century ms from Loire Valley imported into British Isles where interlinear and marginal glosses were added by a late ninth-century insular hand originating from Wales, South-West England, or Cornwall. Some metra have neumes on beginning verses. The ms was in Southern England in the 10th century when it was corrected and had further glosses added by other hands, one of which was St Dunstan's. Dunstan works with mss and glosses which must have been in England at that time.

261u Diane Bolton. 'Illustrations in Manuscripts of Boethius' Works.' Pp 428-37. 'Early English and German manuscripts often receive full-page illustrations, fourteenth-century manuscripts frequently have French or Italian miniatures, and lavish fifteenth-century manuscripts tend to be of French or Flemish provenance. The thirteenth century was, with some exceptions, usually a time of the plain schoolbook' (p 428). Fine manuscripts were often commissioned for great patrons. Bolton considers some mss Courcelle missed, surveys illustrated mss for the *Consolatio*, the Logical Works, the Quadrivium, and the Opuscula Sacra.

262 Krappe, Alexander Hoggerty. 'Two Mediaeval Derivatives of Boethius' *De Consolatione philosophiae.*' *Leuvensche Bijdragen*, 18 (1926), 1-6. *Consolatio* II, m.7, 'a variant of the *ubi sunt* theme, could not fail to impress the mediaeval mind, imbued as it was with the conviction of the inconstancy of all things terestrial ' (p 2). It reappears in amplified form in the prologue to Wace's *Roman de Rou* (vv. 1-62), though Wace ('mediaeval intellectual' that he 'doubtless was') adds the passage on the importance of the chronicler 'without whom even the most glorious deeds of the past would be doomed to oblivion' (p 4); and in Richard of London's *Itinerarium peregrinorum et Gesta regis Ricardi*, where the chronicler draws certainly on the passage in Wace's prologue and perhaps directly on Boethius as well, 'although it is not possible to prove it' (p 6).

263 Laistner, Max Ludwig Wolfram. *Thought and Letters in Western Europe. A.D. 500-900.* London: Methuen, 1931/rev 1957. Pp 85-91. Laistner emphasizes the range of Boethius' contributions to Western thought. 'Boethius provided the scholars of succeeding generations with a technical terminology and many definitions which became classic and were ultimately approved and taken over by the Schoolmen. It would be fascinating to speculate on the development of medieval thought which might have resulted had Boethius lived to

complete his task of making the entire corpus of Aristotelian and
Platonic writings available in Latin dress' (p 87). Laistner is disposed
to include *De fide catholica* with Boethius' genuine works. There is no
question about Boethius' orthodoxy (p 88), though his death was not
martyrdom. 'Political fear, not religious animosity of an Arian prince
towards a Catholic senate, was responsible for the severity of Boethius'
punishment' (p 86).

263a Lerer, Seth. *Boethius and Dialogue: Literary Method in the
Consolation of Philosophy*. Princeton: Princeton University Press,
1985.
Lerer outlines the tradition of literary and philosophical dialogue in
antiquity and the early Middle Ages to show how Boethius established
in most of his writings, but especially in the *Consolation*, a consistent
persona in the guise of a reader and writer beset by the impediments of
cultural decline, perpetually challenged by his difficult intellectual tack
of revitalizing texts at a time when Latin was becoming a fossilized
language. Boethius gives voice to a persona (himself assembled out of
tropes and literary conventions), whose life is charted not through
events experienced but rather through texts read, such as Cicero's
Tusculan Disputations, Augustine's *Soliloquia* and *De Magistro*, and
Fulgentius' *De Continentia Virgilianae*, texts for professional students
and out of which the *Consolatio* took shape. Lerer draws on the
critical approaches of Said and Fish in establishing his method of
critical assessment of the older literatures. The heart of the book is an
extended analysis of the dialogue's progress in the *Consolation*. See
also Seth Lerer, 'Boethian Silence,' *M&H*, 12 (1984), 97–125.

264 McKinlay, Arthur Patch. 'Stylistic Tests and the Chronology of the
Works of Boethius.' *Harvard Studies in Classical Philology*, 18 (1907),
123–56.
McKinlay finds striking divergences in Boethius' style in different
periods of his writing. On the basis of comparisons in Boethius' use
and placement of adverbs, conjunctions, and particles, McKinlay
argues that *De Arithmetica* was written after the influence of
translation began to affect Boethius' style and that *De Musica*
probably was done about the same time that he worked on the *Topica*
Neither are among his earliest writings. *Ars Geometria* is most likely
spurious; but McKinlay would 'hesitate to deny the *De Fide* on
stylistic grounds (p 153).

265 Manitius, Maximilianus. *Geschichte der lateinischen Literatur des
Mittelalters*. 3 vols. Munchen: Beck, 1911. Rpt 1965.
A brief life, bibliography, and annotated summary of Boethius'
writings on the quadrivium, philosophy, and theology, with notation
on important mss (vol 1, pp 22–36).

265a   Masi, Michael, ed. *Boethius and the Liberal Arts: A Collection of Essays.* Utah Studies in Literature and Linguistics, Vol. 18. Berne: Peter Lang, 1981.

An interdisciplinary effort to explore Boethius' impact on the full range of the Liberal Arts in the Middle Ages. Includes Myra L. Uhlfelder, 'The Role of the Liberal Arts in Boethius' *Consolatio*,' pp 17–34, with an appendix on the meters of the *Consolatio* as structural and thematic bonds; Eleonore Stump, 'Boethius and Peter of Spain on the Topics,' pp 35–50, which describes Boethius' method of logic and charts the process by which that method was lost; Fannie J. Lemoine, 'The Precious Style as Heuristic Device: The Function of Introductions to the Arts in Martianus Capella and Boethius,' pp 51–65, on Boethius' use of ornamentation in his introduction to the *De Arithmetica* as well as in the *Consolatio*; Pearl Kibre, 'The Boethian *De Institutione Arithmetica* and the Quadrivium in the Thirteenth Century University Milieu at Paris,' pp 67–80, which considers the popularity of *De Arithmetica* and its influence on various writers from Sacrobosco and Jordanus Nemoriarius to Grosseteste, Roger Bacon, St Bonaventure, Albertus Magnus, and Vincent of Beauvais; Michael Masi, 'The Influence of Boethius' *De Arithmetica* on Late Medieval Mathematics,' pp 81–95, on the extraordinary increase of influence of Boethian mathematics between 1200 and 1600; Ubaldo Pizzani, 'The Influence of the *De Institutione Musica* of Boethius up to Gerbert D'Aurillac: A Tentative Contribution,' pp 97–156, which argues against an organic and coherent corpus of Boethian writings on the quadrivium, suggesting that *De Musica* was a late work whose history does not get linked with that of the *De Arithmetica* as a major arts text until after the Carolingian Renaissance; Calvin M. Bower, 'The Role of Boethius' *De Institutione Musica* in the Speculative Tradition of Western Thought,' pp 157–74, which places Boethius' *De Musica* in a context of other music treatises in the Sixth Century, then traces its increasing importance from the Ninth Century onward upon theory as opposed to traditional *cantus* training; Julia Bolton Holloway, '*The Asse to the Harpe:* Boethian Music in Chaucer,' pp 176–86, which, after tracing the trope back to Ur, ca 2600 B.C., suggests that Chaucer uses the figure in *T&C* as commentary on both Troilus and Pandarus, who mouth Boethian ideas but do not hear their true meaning; Menso Folkerts, 'The Importance of the Pseudo-Boethian *Geometria* during the Middle Ages,' pp 187–209, which considers the scanty evidence pertaining to an authentic Boethian *Geometria* and then shows the dissemination and impact of both on the Middle Ages; and Pierre Courcelle, 'Boethius, Lady Philosophy, and the Representation of the Muses,' pp 211–18, a translation by Susanne Strom of **231**, pp 90–99, discussing fifteen illustrations from various *Consolatio* mss.

265b —— *Boethian Number Theory*. Atlantic Highlands, N.J.: Humanities Press, 1983.

A translation of *De Institutione Arithmetica*, with discussion of Boethius' number theory and its influence on iconography, music, cathedral architecture, and literature.

266 Means, Michael H. *The Consolatio Genre in Medieval English Literature*. University of Florida Humanities Monograph, no. 36. Gainesville: University of Florida Press, 1972.

Means outlines the consolatory elements, apocalyptic elements, and educational features of the *Consolation* as they reappear in *RR*, Dante, *Pearl*, *CA*, *Piers Plowman*, Lydgate's *Reason and Sensuallyte*, the *KQ*, and Hawes's *Pastime of Pleasure*. He also sees a tinch of Boethius in Alanus' *De Planctu Naturae* and Spenser's *Ruines of Time*; in *Wynnere and Wastoure* and the *Parlement of the Thre Ages*; in *Mankind* and *Everyman*; and in Chaucer's dream visions.

267 Nitzsche, Jane Chance. *The Genius Figure in Antiquity and the Middle Ages*. New York and London: Columbia University Press, 1975. Pp 42–64.

Although Boethius does not speak directly of a genius figure, his commentators do. Bernardus Silvestris based his notion of the four descents of man upon Guillaume de Conches' glosses on the *Consolation* (pp 45–55). 'Guillaume introduces Genius to amplify his tropological interpretation of the Orpheus and Euridice myth related by Philosophy in Boethius' *De Consolatione*. Euridice, wife of Orpheus (wisdom or eloquence), represents natural concupiscence or *genius* ... [*naturalis concupiscentia*] which is joined [*coniuncta est*] to each one of us: for no one, not even a child one day old, can exist in this life without it. From which again the poets imagined that there was a certain god, namely the *genius*, who is born with each one of us and dies. Whence Horace: *deus albus et ater mortalis in unumquodque caput*. Genius is natural concupiscence. The marriage of Orpheus and Euridice represents the union of the soul (with its inherent passions and desires). In effect, the two figures illuminate the consequences of the natural descent —— the imprisonment of the soul in the inferior body at birth' (pp 46–7). Boethius is also a factor in the development of theories of the artificial descent; he stands at the head of such dream vision writers as Alanus, Guillaume de Lorris, Jean de Meun, Deschamps, Marot, Machaut, the Pearl poet, Chaucer, and Gower, in whose works 'an instructive guide paralleling the demonic intermediary leads the dreaming protagonist, beset with anxieties, into self-knowledge or truth' (p 63).

268 Obertello, Luca. *Severino Boezio*. Accademia Ligure di Scienze e Lettere. 2 vols. Genoa, 1974.

Vol 1 consists of four parts: 1) *La Vita* (pp 1–153), with discussion of
the prominence of the family into which Boethius was born, his youth,
the religious controversy of his day, his relationship with Theodoric
and the Empire, his fall, the incrimination and process of the
condemnation, his exile and death, and his fame in posterity; 2) *Le
Opere* (pp 155–382), with discussion of Boethius' program of work, his
scientific writing, translations, commentaries, writings on dialectic,
rhetoric, and theology, the chronology of his works, and their
transmission; 3) *Le Fonti* (pp 383–562), with discussion of Greco-Latin
tradition of education and of philosophy, Nicomachus, Porphyry,
Iamblichus, the Schools of Athens and Alexandria, and of Boethius'
use of earlier Latin thought; 4) *Il Pensiero* (pp 563–781), with
discussion of Boethius' views on the grades of speculative knowledge;
predication, categories, and reality; his doctrine of Being; his views of
nature and the existence of God; his theories of eternity, fate,
providence, the problem of evil; and Boethius as a Christian thinker.
Vol 2 consists of three parts: 1) an annotated bibliography (pp 9–226)
of editions and translations of Boethius' works, studies of his life, his
career, his thought, his works, their textual tradition, and his value as
a man of letters; linguistic studies, his sources and the sources of his
thought, his treatment of fortune, and studies on translations of the
Consolatio (which includes a separate section on English translations);
2) *Bibliografia Generale* (pp 227–49); 3) *Il Pensiero antico e medievale:
fonti e studi critici* (pp 251–308). The bibliographies and the first
volume are both well-indexed. Bibliographical entries are arranged
chronologically, often beginning with fifteenth- and sixteenth-century
entries, providing full coverage of French, German, Spanish, and
English scholarship, as well as Italian and Latin.

269 Patch, Howard Rollin. *The Goddess Fortuna in Medieval Literature.*
Cambridge: Harvard University Press, 1927.
Patch explores attitudes toward Dame Fortune from ancient times
through the Middle Ages, with special attention devoted to her
activities and cults, her dwelling place, and her famous wheel.
Boethian influence dominates the medieval view. This work is the
culmination of several other studies by Patch on the Goddess Fortuna.
See also his 'The Tradition of the Goddess Fortuna: In Roman
Literature and the Transitional Period,' *Smith College Studies in
Modern Language*, 3, iii (1922), 131–77; 'The Tradition of the Goddess
Fortuna: In Medieval Philosophy and Literature,' *Smith College
Studies in Modern Language*, 3, iv (1922), 179–235; and 'Fortuna in
Old French Literature,' *Smith College Studies in Modern Language*, 4,
iv (1923), 1–45. Boethius offers the Middle Ages a compromise
between pagan acceptance of the goddess and Christian annihilation of

her.

270 — 'Fate in Boethius and the Neoplatonists.' *Spec*, 4 (1929), 62–72.
The idea that Fate makes the world go round is found in Proclus,
though without a sense of man's being involved with that process by
his own submission or any notion of God at the center of Fate's orbit
(pp 65–6). Boethius supplies the notion that whatever departs farthest
from the first mind becomes most deeply enmeshed in fate. He
harmonizes with Proclus the idea that the center of the circle is at
rest, an idea he found in Plotinus which places God at the very heart
of the universe. 'The more the soul is freed from things corporeal and
thus, according to both Proclus and Plotinus, from Fate, the more it
may attain to that centre of stability and simplicity which, according
to Plotinus, is Providence, or God. Here is that "hinge of all things,"
which means freedom and, for Boethius, consolation, but lacking in
that more ecstatic, if intellectual, mysticism which is found in Plotinus,
and which would be out of place in the *Consolatio Philosophiae*. With
an inspired eclecticism ... Boethius utilized his sources, joining the
two schemes in form and significance in a masterly fashion and with
rich expression, later to be equalled in skill only by Dante' (pp 71–2).

271 — 'Consolatio Philosophiae, 4, m.6, 23–4.' *Spec*, 8 (1933), 41–51.
This passage is one of at least five which treat of the concord of the
universe, the Love that rules the sun and stars. The idea comes to
Boethius through Thales, Anaximenes, Pythagoras, Heraclitus, the
Stoics, *Timaeus*, and also Aristotle's *De Caelo*. Proclus and Plotinus
draw on Plato and Aristotle in their dealing with the idea. Boethius
treats the idea also in *De Trinitate* II.8–9, and *Contra Eutychen* I.43–4,
both of which passages are unmistakably Aristotelian in derivation.
'Neoplatonism sometimes brings us back to Aristotle' (p 46).

272 — 'Necessity in Boethius and the Neoplationists.' *Spec*, 10 (1935),
393–404.
By exploring the process by which Boethius' theory of conditional
necessity is first thought of then elaborated, Patch would throw light
on the structure of the *Consolatio*. By Bk V Boethius is ready to deal
with the great theme of divine providence and human free will. 'It
reveals a fine symmetry in the work as a whole to remember that in
the last analysis what opens the way for such a conclusion is the
Aristotelian theory of contingency. Free will is surely the richest and
the strangest of the gifts of Fortune' (p 404).

273 — *The Tradition of Boethius: A Study of His Importance in Medieval
Culture*. Oxford and New York: Oxford University Press, 1935. Rpt
New York: Russell and Russell, 1970.
'As a scholar Boethius was fitted to gather up the best of the old, and
as Christian and in a sense a martyr to adapt it to the apprehension of

succeeding ages' (p 2). In his Introduction Patch discusses attitudes toward Boethius held by his contemporaries, surveys the scope of his canon, and stresses the originality of the *Consolatio* as well as its literary and philosophical ties. 'His method ... was that of a student and a philosopher; never that of an imitator.' 'The Neoplationists led men to the worship of intellect; Boethius brought them to God' (p 5). 'Like Plato, Boethius had the mind of a poet with which to take his flights, and like Aristotle a rational conscience for ballast' (p 6). Ch 1, 'Tradition and Legend,' pp 8–19, considers legends that grew up after his death about the martyrdom, as well as the political events of Boethius' latter years. Ch 2, 'Medieval Thought,' pp 20–45, stresses the importance of Boethius in all areas of medieval thought, both philosophical and theological. Boethius was especially popular in intellectual circles as evidenced by the great number of commentaries. Even women studied the *Consolatio* (p 31). His most far-reaching contribution to learning sprang from his commentary on a sentence in Porphyry, out of which grew 'the great controversy among the schoolmen which divided them into so-called realists and nominalists' (p 35). Boethius supplied the textbooks in all the arts throughout the medieval period (pp 36–41). Patch notes his influence on Jean de Meun; so too on others: 'Deschamps never seems quite to get away from his memories of Boethius. But it is impossible to arrive at a complete estimate of his influence on writers like Dante and Chaucer' (p 43). Ch 3, 'Translations of the Consolatio,' pp 46–86, comments on King Alfred, Notker Labeo, the Provencal Boèce, Simund de Friene, Jean de Meun, Chaucer, John Walton, George Colville, Sir Thomas Chalonier, Queen Elizabeth, and I.T.; Patch also notes Samuel Johnson's interest (p 46). For Chaucer, 'no work seems to have had such a profound or at least far-reaching effect ... as the *Consolatio* ... The influence of Boethius is pervasive and almost at all times tangible' (p 66). Of *Boece* and Chaucer's moral balades Patch observes: 'The prose is not without its music; one feels only that in the verse, apart from the question of details from other sources and metrical fluency, the poet shows a freer hand and feels more at home' (p 69). Patch compares *FA, Fort,* and passages from *T&C* and their Boethian sources. Ch 4, 'Imitations and Influence,' pp 87–113: Boethius learns his allegorical method from Martianus Capella. His influence on Alanus de Insulis, Bernardus Silvestris, Adelard, Jean de Meun, Machaut, Deschamps, and Albertano of Brescia, many of whom also had direct bearing on Chaucer, is enormous. So too on subsequent Chaucerians like Charles of Orleans, the author of *KQ*, Gerson, and More. 'Conclusion,' pp 114–23, summarizes Boethius' importance: 'If the doctrine of the *Consolatio* had a profound effect in Chaucer's case, I believe that the form of it had in Dante's. The dialogue between the prisoner and Lady Philosophy prepared the way for Dante's instruction conducted by Beatrice and by Virgil' (p 121). Patch includes a bibliography (pp 171–91), and seven plates from mss of the twelfth-fifteenth centuries depicting Boethius and Philosophy, Fortune, the Arts, the Muses, etc.

- Review by Lane Cooper, *MLN*, 53 (1938), 222–4: Patch does not do justice to Boethius' influence on Dante. Cooper challenges his assertion on the origin of the realist-nominalist contoversy. Patch defends his position in *MLN*, 53 (1938), 398.

- Review by Richard McKeon, *MP*, 34 (1936), 197–8: 'The tradition of Boethius which Professor Patch traces is that of the author of the *Consolation of Philosophy*. The Boethius who as author of the theological treatises contributed richly to the terminology and 'sentences' of the Middle Ages, the Boethius who as translator and author of logical treatises was quoted with Aristotle and Porphyry throughout centuries of logical inquiry and debate and whose commentaries, themselves glossed, guided an almost endless series of commentaries, the Boethius who as author of *De arithmetica* and the *De musica* contributed to the fundamental texts on which the growing medieval interest in the quadrivium was based, all appear in more abbreviated form and usually in statements derived from secondary sources' (p 197). McKeon praises the notes and bibliography and 'the great value of his book in bringing together compendiously so many aspects of a many-sided figure' (p 198).

- Review by E.T. Silk, *Spec*, 11 (1936), 425–7. Patch scarcely comes to grips with the breadth of Boethian influence on later generations. Moreover, his book is deficient in 'charting the course that research should take' (p 426). Especially, more attention should be given to the commentaries, many of which have not been published.

274 — 'The Beginnings of the Legend of Boethius.' *Spec*, 22 (1947), 443–5.
In answer to Bark **243** Patch traces the legends of Boethius' martyrdom back to their earliest sources. At least as early as the mss containing the *Vitae*, and presumably then, much earlier, the stand taken by Boethius against Theodoric was interpreted as that of opposition to a tyrant. 'Nor can it be fairly supposed that in the sixth century the conduct of Theodoric had only a political significance for the people' (p 443). Paul the Deacon (8th century), the Dialogues of Gregory the Great (7th century), the tombstone in Pavia, and Procopius (very soon after Boethius' death) all present him as a martyr. Boethius and Symmachus were put to death on grounds that

they were setting about a revolution, because they practiced
philosophy and were mindful of justice. 'Once and for all it is made
clear that even to a skeptic like Procopius the author of the *Consolatio*
was a martyr. What must he have been therefore in the minds of his
Catholic friends? His execution was not perhaps made public; but can
it be doubted that among people in the neighborhood of Pavia he was
regarded as a Christian martyr? The fact is that in tone and almost in
substance the passage in Procopius is like that in some of the *Vitae* as
well as that in Alfred's preface' (pp 444–5).

275 Rand, Edward Kennard. 'On the Composition of Boethius' *Consolatio
Philosophiae.' Harvard Studies in Classical Philology*, 15 (1904), 1–28.
Usener's study 286 has 'done more than any single publication toward
restoring Boethius to his rightful place among the Christian
theologians' (p 1). But Usener errs in attempting to discredit the
Consolatio as a personal work — a mere translation of Aristotle's
Protreptikos and some Neoplatonic source, to which a lame
introduction (ie, Bks I–II, pr.4) and some feeble poems have been
added. The *Consolatio* is a highly original work which is carefully
structured. Though the treatise has its ups and downs, the former are
not all in the prose sections, nor the latter all in the meters. 'Boethius'
skill as a versifier is generally recognized; may it not be that a poet
who invented eleven varieties of strophe shows occasional originality of
phrase and conception as well?' (p 5). The first book is in no way
inferior to the rest of the treatise. It is 'the opening act in a
metaphysical drama; it presents in pictorial form, a speculative
problem which the following books are to solve' (p 8). Book II is the
second act of the drama, the applying of gentle remedies. 'There is
certainly no marked inferiority of either conception or arrangement in
this section as compared with those that follow' (p 9). Book III applies
stronger medicine as the argument becomes more complex. There is no
need to assume some interpolated source that Boethius must be
working from. 'Is it not as reasonable to assume a modicum of
originality on the author's part, to credit him with a general plan and
theory of his own, which he illustrates by citation or adaptation from
various works familiar to him?' (p 12). There is 'nothing particularly
Neoplatonic in Boethius' solution' to the problem of divine
foreknowledge and free choice. 'Cognition depends not on the qualities
of the known but on the capacity of the knower, and may be either
sensus, imaginatio, ratio, or *intelligentia* — an ascending scale
(IV.pr.4)' (p 22). Books IV and V are 'not a reworking of a
Neoplatonic text, but a criticism of Neoplationism and the most
original part of the *Consolatio*' (p 24). Usener goes too far in
attempting to reduce Boethius' philosophy to 'a safe insignificance' (p

25). The *Consolatio* is 'more than a patchwork of borrowed texts' (p 25); nor is it a mere pastime or 'the diversion of an idle hour.' It throbs with feeling: 'the lonely thinker starts with a real fact, his bitter experience, and with that constantly in view works out a satisfying theodicy' (p 25). The *Consolatio* is 'the work of a Christian theologian who holds fast to the distinction between *fides* and *ratio*. Boethius is trying by the unaided effort of the reason to establish a theodicy for which revelation has its own proofs, and for this reason, inevitably, recurs to the utterance of the schools and not the councils' (p 27). The conclusion is the same as that of theology, however. 'The fundamental aim of the work is to make the language of philosophy approach as closely as possible to the meaning of faith; for Boethius was neither a Pagan, nor a cold eclectic, nor a dilettante reviser of others' texts, but the first of the scholastics' (p 28).

276 — *Founders of the Middle Ages*. Cambridge, Mass.: Harvard University Press; London: Oxford University Press, 1928. Pp 135–80. Chapters on the Church and pagan culture, St Ambrose the mystic, St Jerome the humanist, Boethius the first of the scholastics, the new poetry, the new education, and St Augustine and Dante. Ch 5, pp 135–80, places Boethius in the context of his time and considers his noble temperament. 'One feels a repressed emotion in Boethius. He has absorbed poetry, as Plato had done, only in a more sombre fashion; his prevailing mood is nearer to Dante's than to Plato's. He has not Plato's divine gift of comedy' (p 140). Rand discusses the breadth of Boethius' intellectual ambitions, his precise vocabulary, his textbooks and his theological writings, and then offers an analysis of the *Consolation* (pp 159–79). He concludes by reviewing the case for Boethius' sainthood. 'I wish that someone influential with the Holy See would present a new petition in favor of St Severinus or St Boethius, for, if I have stated the facts about him, the logic of the case seems inexorable' (p 180).

276a Reiss, Edmund. *Boethius*. Boston: Twayne, 1982. A general study with chapters on Boethius as a master of the arts, an explorer of language, a concerned Christian; also, the question of his martyrdom, the argument of *Consolatio*, the form and method of the *Consolatio*, and the Boethian legacy. Reiss's discussion of the audience of the theological tractates is of particular interest. So too his suggestion that the names of Boethius' false accusers in Book I of the *Consolatio* (Basilius, Opilio, and Gaudentius) are symbolic, implying Power, Wealth, and Pleasure (pp 88–94). Regarding the absence of explicit Christian doctrine in the *Consolatio* he suggests: Had Boethius lived longer, he might well have followed his *Consolation of Philosophy* with a *Consolation of Theology* (p 154).

277 Sandys, John Edwin. *A History of Classical Scholarship.* 3 vols. Cambridge: University Press, 1903/rev 1906. Vol I, pp 251–8.
Sandys emphasizes the tension between Aristotelian and Platonic elements in Boethius' writings, to which the later medieval writers responded, usually following the Aristotelian Boethius. Sandys declares the *Consolatio* a theist rather than Christian work. He emphasizes it influence on Dante (p 258).

77a Scarry, Elaine. 'The Well-Rounded Sphere: The Metaphysical Structure of *The Consolation of Philosophy.*' In *Essays in the Numerical Criticism of Medieval Literature.* Ed. Caroline D. Eckhardt. Lewisburg, Pa.: Bucknell University Press, 1980. Pp 91–140.
Intricate analysis of circular structures in the *Consolatio* to illustrate Boethius' 'attempt to attain the gift of godlikeness by participating in a simple unity of form and substance' (p 93). Scarry considers technical elements such as personification, verse prose, and book divisions, progressions through cognitive heirarchy, and manifestations of analogical binding within the work which enable one to see, 'as though with the eye of Insight, the whole of the work in a single glance' (p 136). The spherical structure is intended to be, like Plato's perfect cosmos in the *Timaeus,* in and of itself a guiding companion. 'Boethius, his name so close to the Greek word for helper, created a work meant to be — even in the most extreme crises of isolation — a consolation, acquaintance, and friend' (p 137).

278 Schmidt-Kohl, Volker. *Die neuplatonische Seelenlehre in der Consolatio Philosophiae des Boethius.* Beiträge zur klassichen Philologie, no. 16. Meisenheim am Glan: Anton Hain, 1965.
Schmidt-Kohl considers such platonic concepts as the cave, the body as prison of the soul, material fetters, and exile in the *Consolatio*; such antinomies as One-Many, fragmentation-integration, inner-outer, light-darkness, seeking-finding, forgetting-remembering; mythic schema such as the descent, clothing exchange, the divine spark, wandering in exile, drunkenness and somnolence, the ascent; and various topoi pertaining to man's appointed nature.

279 Schurr, Viktor. *Die Trinitätslehre des Boethius im Lichte der 'skythischen Kontroversen'.* Paderborn: Ferdinand Schöningh, 1935.
A work which began as a comparison of Boethius' and Augustine's doctrine on the Holy Trinity comes to the conclusion that the *Opuscula Sacra* are not youthful effusions but the product of Boethius' mature philosophic thought. Schurr provides convincing proof of Boethius' debt to Augustine, but also to Aristotle in technique. Boethius' position on universals was never precisely defined. His *De Trinitate* is concerned with a late stage of the 'Scythian controversy,' in which Maxentius and Dionysius Exiguis sought to mediate between

the monophysitism of the East and the conservatism of Rome on
questions of the Divine Passion. Arianism is not the issue for Rome at
this time. The doctrines held by Boethius and the Scythiac
theologians were designed to effect a harmony between the Eastern
and Western Churches. There were thus political as well as theological
aspects to the controversy. It is the political issue which got Boethius
into trouble and led to his downfall, a fact which may weaken the
claim of martyrdom (pp 222–3).

• Review by E.K. Rand, *Spec*, 11 (1936), 153–6. Rand develops
  Schurr's discussion of the East-West controversy and Boethius'
  role in effecting a harmony to praise Schurr's work but also to
  qualify the conclusion: 'It is clear that Boethius' theology, an
  innocent thing in itself, led to his downfall ... Such fervor,
  displayed in 512, revealed to Theodoric a Boethius quite different
  from the apparently calm and detached philosopher whose
  counsel he had followed in matters of state, and when in 523
  Boethius took sides on what ... had become a question veritably
  burning he may have at once thereby signed his own
  death-warrant and gained a martyr's crown' (p 156).

280 Shiel, James. 'Boethius' Commentaries on Aristotle.' *MRS*, 4 (1958),
217–44.
'Our view of Boethius the translator of scholia is not quite in harmony
with all that scholars have written about him. It dulls the praise of his
vast scholarship; for where he mentions works of Aristotle other than
the logic, he is just translating references among his Greek scholia, so
that all his knowledge of Aristotle seems to derive from this one codex
of the Organon' (p 243). Moreover, he probably worked at home rather
than travelling to Alexander and Athens, as once was thought. 'There
was nothing to hinder him from translating an annotated Organon in
his beloved *bibliotheca* far removed *(longe positus)* from either
Alexandria or Athens' (p 244). All this does not diminish his greatness.
'There is a patriotic nobility about his motives,' as Cassiodorus
pointed out. 'Our study of him as a translator emphasizes anew his
remarkable function of transmission: through him Aristotelian logic,
the equipment of Neoplatonic paganism, is carried into the Christian
Church to be eventually part of its armour of faith' (p 244).

281 — 'Boethius the Hellenist.' *History Today*, 14 (1964), 678–86.
A general assessment of the significance of Boethius in his day and for
later generations. Illustrated with 6 plates, including one of a 4th
century ivory panel of a woman of the Symmachi household (the line
which produced Boethius' wife Rusticiana), a 13th century
illumination of Boethius in prison, and a photograph of the tomb of
Boethius in the crypt of San Pietro Ciel d'Oro, the church where St

Augustine is also buried.

82 Stewart, Hugh Fraser. *Boethius.* 1891. See **147.**
Stewart's essay was recipient of the Hulsean Prize at Cambridge in
1888. Ch 1, pp 1–14, reviews the question of Boethius' Christianity.
Ch 2, pp 15–54, provides a stirring account of Theodoric's purging of
Odovacar's household as he conquered Rome, and a review of Boethian
biography. Boethius' father had been a trusted servant of Odovacar.
Ch 3, pp 55–80, offers a synopsis of the *Consolation* with comments on
form, style, and its relationship to its sources. The treatise is neither
Boethius' confession of faith nor a tacit rejection of Christianity, but
rather a fairly systematic summary of Boethius' metaphysics. Ch 4, pp
81–107, discusses Boethius' views on God, the Universe, Fortune,
chance, evil, psychology, free-will and predestination in the
Consolation. Ch 5 offers a synopsis of the five theological treatises and
considers individual arguments for and against their authenticity.
Steward emphasizes their imitative qualities: Boethius' 'best energies
were spent on adapting the writings of the Greek philosophers to the
requirements of Roman readers. And if in philosophy he was content
to take his stand on Plato and Aristotle, why in the theology should he
be deemed too proud to stoop to ask help of Augustine?' (p 118). Ch
6, 'On Some Ancient Translations of Boethius' Last Work,' pp
160–240, includes discussion of Boethian matter in *Beowulf,* Alfred's
adaptation, the Provençal 'Boèce,' Notker, Simun de Fraisne, Jean de
Meun, Pierre de Paris, Jean de Cis, Renaut de Louhan, Chaucer, John
Walton, and several Italian, Greek, Spanish, and German adaptations.
Ch 7, pp 241–57, considers briefly the importance of Boethius to
medieval schoolmen. Appendix A: a synopsis of mss of the Theological
Treatises (pp 255–9); B: passages in Chaucer based on the *Consolatio*
(pp 260–70).

83 Sullivan, Mark W. *Apuleian Logic: The Nature, Sources, and
Influence of Peri Hermeneias.* Amsterdam: North-Holland Publishing
Company, 1967.
Ch 6, 'The Influence of the *Peri Hermeneias,*' pp 170–208, considers
Martianus Capella, Cassiodorus Senator, Isidore of Seville, Alcuin and
Charles the Great, Dunchad, Pseudo-John Scotus Erigena, and
Remigius of Auxerre, and textual transmission and influences from the
ninth to the twelfth Centuries. Ch 7, '*Conclusion,*' pp 209–30, explores
the relationship of Boethius' *De Syllogismis Categoricis* to the *Peri
Heremeneias.* After reviewing the argument of J. Isaac, O.P., *Le Peri
Hermeneias en Occident de Boèce a Saint Thomas* (Paris: J. Vrin,
1953), which leans toward the notion that Boethius and Apuleius drew
upon a common source, Sullivan concludes that it is 'probable that
Boethius borrowed *directly* from Apuleius' (p 227), using the *Peri*

Hermeneias as source for much of the philosophical Latin diction that he used as well as some explanations. There are important differences between the two treatises, however. 'Boethius treats subjects in a much fuller way than Apuleius does' (p 223) and employs many technical terms not used by Apuleius — eg, *affirmatio, negatio, affirmativa, negative, subalterna, subcontraria, contradictoria, syllogismus, terminus, major extremitas, minor extremitas, medius terminus, figura*, etc (p 224).

284 Taylor, Henry Osborn. *The Medieval Mind: A History of the Development of Thought and Emotion in the Middle Ages.* 2 vols. London and New York: Macmillan, 1911. Vol I, pp 88–102, 188–90, 300–2.
Taylor discusses Boethius, along with Cassiodorus, Gregory the Great, and Isidore, as a 'Latin transmitter' (I, 88–93), referring to him as 'an antique-minded man, whose love of knowledge did not revolve around "salvation" '(p 90). In Boethius' literary endeavors 'one sees a veritable love of intellectual labour and a love of the resulting mental increment' (p 92). In his discussion of 'Conversion of the North,' Taylor comments on Alfred's adaptation of the *Consolatio* and his great love of Boethius as an example and kindred spirit, trying to save what is best and to be remembered in good works (pp 188–90).

285 Thorndike, Lynn. *A History of Magic and Experimental Science.* New York: Columbia University Press, 1923. Vol I, pp 616–22.
Thorndike emphasizes the importance of Boethius' works in the advancement of medieval scientific thought. 'His constant rhapsodizing over the stars and heavens would lead [Christians] to regard the science of the stars as second only to divine worship. Indeed, his position is the usual one in the subsequent Middle Ages' (p 622).

286 Usener, Hermann. *Anecdoton Holderi. Festschrift zur Begrüssung der XXXII Versammlung deutscher Philologen und Schulmanner zu Wiesbaden.* Leipzig: Teubner, 1877.
Working from Alfred Holder's discovery of a Cassiodorus fragment which ascribes *De Trinitate* and other theological writings to Boethius, Usener demonstrates that the *Opuscula Sacra* are authentic Boethian works, thus settling to a considerable extent the dispute over his Christianity. To explain the absence of explicit Christian reference in the *Consolatio* Usener argues that II.pr.4–IV.pr.6 is mainly a translation of Aristotle's *Protreptikos*, while the remainder is the translation of a lost Neoplatonic work. It may even be that Boethius found the two combined already in a single source. The poems are Boethius' own addition and that which precedes II.pr.4 is a make-shift introduction; both the meters and the introduction are inferior, make-do work. Usener finds Boethius' *De Differentiis Topicorum* to

be, comparatively, Boethius' most independent work (p 41). See Rand's appraisals of Usener's arguments in **275, 276**.

287 Wetherbee, Winthrop. *Platonism and Poetry in the Twelfth Century: The Literary Influence of the School of Chartres.* Princeton: Princeton University Press, 1972. Pp 74–82.

Boethius has a prominent role throughout Wetherbee's discussion of Platonism and the pursuit of wisdom in the twelfth century. In Ch 2, 'Philosophy and Experience,' pp 74–82, he focuses on Boethian metaphors which dominate the psychology of twelfth-century literature. 'The twelfth century was in many respects an *aetas boethiana* ... Of all the *auctores* it was Boethius who most nearly rivaled the authority of Plato' (p 74). Boethius' purpose is 'more psychological than Plato's, his cosmology more simply a source of metaphor, and his use of mythology and other imagery more integrally bound up with his intention of writing' (p 74). The *Consolatio* provides a link between abstract use of *integumenta* in *Timaeus* and the role of such figures in poetry (p 75). Wetherbee concentrates his discussion on Boethian use of nature, prison, and journey imagery to explore states of mind. 'Rhythm is as important as reason in the development of Boethius' theme, and the dialectical movement of the *De consolatione* is not only in the dialogue of Philosophy with the prisoner, but in a larger dialogue between rational argumentation and poetry' (p 77). This is seen especially in poems like that on Orpheus (III.m.12), 'in which the pursuit of freedom and wisdom is dramatized in mythological terms' (p 79). Wetherbee emphasizes the darker side — the unresolved side — of the *Consolation*, which is conveyed through metaphor and the emotional progression of the narrator's questions. Read as a work of imaginative literature 'the dialogue seems to me more convincing as a dramatization of the psychological experience of the attempt, than as an exposition of the means of such transcendence' (p 82). The dramatic tensions of the *Consolatio* provided a model for the twelfth-century poets. 'It was largely through exploiting the contrast between the deep and often somber seriousness of Boethius and the optimism of the far more fanciful and abstract allegory of Martianus Capella that the Chartrian poets expressed their sense of the human condition' (p 82).

287a Wiltshire, Susan Ford. 'Boethius and the *Summum Bonum.*' *Classical Journal*, 67 (1972), 216–20.

Compares structure of the *Consolation* to that of classical drama, with Book 3 as the *peripeteia*, framed by poems on *amor*. The *summum bonum* described in III.pr.10, is a preethical vision, a concept of the ideal good, identified with God, but 'argued through dialogue, illustrated and enlarged through poetry, and presented with the powerful effect of drama' (p 220).

288 Wright, F.A. and T.A. Sinclair. *A History of Later Latin Literature from the Middle of the Fourth to the End of the Seventeenth Century.* London: Routledge; New York: Macmillan, 1931. Pp 80–90. 'Boethius was put to death for his political views and was not victim of Theodoric's religious persecution. He is to be regarded as the heir not of St Stephen but of Cato' (p 82). 'The *Consolatio* is one of the great things in world literature' (p 82), comparable to *Pilgrim's Progress* as prison literature which has consoled many generations of readers. Because of the lack of explicit Christian reference in the *Consolatio*, 'one is tempted to ask whether Boethius had abandoned his faith' (p 86).

Boethian Influence on Chaucer (Selected)

[Boethian influence is so pervasive in *Troilus*, the *Knight's Tale*, the *Man of Law's Tale*, the dream visions, and the Moral Balades that a complete bibliography of the philosopher's influence on the poet would virtually reduplicate the other bibliographies. The selection here points to several of the more thorough and explicitly Boethian studies, covering a variety of approaches.]

289 apRoberts, Robert P. 'The Boethian God and the Audience of *Troilus*.' *JEGP*, 69 (1970), 425–36.
In *T&C*, Criseyde's departure is 'a fated event,' her behavior 'part of the destinal pattern which controls the fate of Troy' (p 425). In Boccaccio, chance is the culprit. Yet Chaucer stages his drama in such a way that free will is preserved. Troilus rightly believes that God's foreknowledge gives necessity to all events, but he is wrong from the Boethian view in believing that this necessity is causal, precluding man's free choice (p 433). Chaucer creates a sense of inevitability which puts the reader in the position of the Boethian God watching 'Criseyde play out her part with free will and yet do what he knows she is to do. Like that God he possesses a knowledge of her future action and this knowledge does not make Criseyde sin — she sins of her own free will' (p 436).

290 Bachman, William Bryant, Jr. 'Idealistic-Materialistic Opposition as an Informing Principle in Chaucer's Philosophical Narratives.' *DAI*, 36

(1976), 6696A. Syracuse University Dissertation, 1975. Dir. Paul
Theiner.
Augustinian and Boethian influences on Chaucer's philosophical
narratives have long been recognized. The narratives, however, do not
translate the idealism of the philosophers into their art. Rather
Chaucer responds 'critically to the idealistic posture of Boethius'
Consolation of Philosophy, and ... what most informs his more
philosophical poetry is a tension produced by the idealistic demands of
the *Consolation* and the materialistic demands of the experiential
world.' *T&C* generates 'a dialectical presentation of the medieval
problem of love ... a modal tension that is ultimately resolved in
fideism.' The *KnT* emphasizes even more than *T&C* the force of
experiential knowledge to generate 'a deterministic tragedy.' Bachman
examines 'the theodicy of the *Franklin's Tale* in terms of the Boethian
relationship between perception and evil,' an opposition which
questions both Boethian and experiential realities, and views *NPT* in
terms of perceptual relativism which 'opposes the *Consolation's*
demand for non-experiential perception.' *ParsT*, primarily
Augustinian and decidedly idealistic, forms 'an opposition to the
materialism of what has preceded it in the Canterbury Tales. This
opposition provides the informing principle in the philosophical unity
of the Tales.'

291 Carriere, Jeanne Louise. *Boethian Narrative Structure in
Fourteenth-Century English Literature*. University of California, Los
Angeles Dissertation, 1975. Dir. Henry A. Kelly. See also, *DAI*, 36
(1976), 5273 A.
Chapters on the Latin *Consolatio* and Boethius, Gower's *CA, Pearl,
BD*, and partial usages of Boethian narrative structure in *HF, PF*, and
T&C. Carriere argues that the *Consolatio* produced a literary genre;
'not only its philosophical content, but its pattern of expression as well
was repeated' (p vii). The pattern consists of 'a dramatic dialogue in
which a misguided narrator is corrected, soothed, and educated by a
superior figure in a two-part reasoned dialectic, the purpose of which is
not so much consolatory as instructional. The end of the guiding
figure's instruction is an insight into a truth which reaches beyond
reason' (p vii).

292 Chamberlain, David. 'The Music of the Spheres and *The Parlement of
Foules*.' *ChauR*, 5 (1970), 32–56.
Chaucer discusses four types of music in the Boethian tradition —
musica mundana, musica humana, musica instrumentalis, and *musica
divina*, the language of which pervades the *Consolation* and Chaucer's
poem in such metaphors as accord, proportion, harmony, and the
pervasive number metaphors. *PF* is dominated by sevens — the 7

spheres, the 7-line 70 syllabled norm of the stanzas, the 700 minus-one line length of the poem — all of which function as signs and means of order, like that carefully explored in the *Consolatio*. *PF* is a 'learned poem.' Most of its 'music can be recognized and interpreted only in terms of medieval ideas, but when recognized it serves to enrich, clarify, and intellectualize the poem' (p 56).

293 — 'The Nun's Priest's Tale and Boethius' *De Musica*.' *MP*, 68 (1970), 188–91.
A refutation of Dronke **299** who thinks Daun Russell's allusion to *Boece* (*NPT*, 3291–3303) to be a satiric jab at Boethius' *De Musica*. 'It is really quite unlikely that Chaucer would have disagreed with Boethius' idea that reasoned knowledge in art is superior to physical skill or instinct' (p 188). Between the years 1000 and 1400 the regard for Boethius' *De Musica* was at its zenith. 'Within mathematics, the special provinence of music was all numerical proportioning, and Chaucer shows respect for "sciences touching nombres and proporcioun," as he calls them at the beginning of his *Astrolabe*. In rejecting Boethian hierarchy in music, he would actually have been rejecting the whole medieval tradition of the liberal arts' (p 189). Tracing music metaphors through the *Consolatio*, Chamberlain shows that Chaucer would indeed have considered Boethius among those that 'kan synge,' not apart from them as Dronke proposes. The fox twists Boethius' ideas maliciously, while Chaucer and the Nun's Priest use them benevolently to amuse readers. 'Within typical pithiness and subtlety ... Chaucer draws on the whole medieval tradition of music ... as well as on his beloved *Boece*, to laugh gently once again at Chauntecleer and all his kin, this time for singing with *heart* and feeling in recklessness and not with *head* and reason in wisdom' (p 191).

294 — 'Philosophy of Music in the *Consolatio* of Boethius.' *Spec*, 45 (1970), 80–97.
'When Boethius first sketches his memorable classification of music, he promises to say more later about *musica mundana* and *humana*, but he does not do so in *De musica* itself' (p 80). Scholars have thought he never returned to the subject, but, Chamberlain argues, the *Consolatio* is that return. After discussing Boethius' views on the origin, definition, and classification of music, Chamberlain demonstrates how the classifications operate throughout the *Consolatio*, going far beyond *De musica* in developing the philosophic purposes of music. Music is not only the substance as well as the instrument of ethics, 'it is also the substance as well as the instrument of metaphysics' (p 97).

295 Cherniss, Michael D. 'Jean de Meun's Reson and Boethius.' *Romance*

Notes, 16 (1975), 678–85.
Although the overall literary strategy of the *Roman* bears some
similarity to that of the *Consolation*, quantitatively and qualitatively
the two are too radically different for easy analogies to have more than
superficial validity. One section, however, the second appearance of
Reson at the outset of Jean de Meun's continuation, repays detailed
comparison. Jean doubtless expected his reader to recognize in the
dialogue between Amant and Reson 'a kind of parody of the
Consolation' (p 680) in which Reson equates with Philosophy and
Amant with the despairing narrator. Using Jean de Meun's preface to
his translation as a guide to the poet's understanding of what the
allegory in the *Consolation* entails, Cherniss analyzes the dispute in
RR to show that Amant ends up being no Boethius or lover of Reson.
Jean's 'parody of the Boethian dialogue emphasizes the moral and
intellectual distance between the philosophical Boethius and the
sensual Amant' (p 685).

296 Crampton, Georgia Ronan. *The Condition of Creatures: Suffering and
Action in Chaucer and Spenser*. New Haven: Yale University Press,
1974. Pp 15–16, 39, 111.
The book examines the *agere et pati* (deed and pathos) topos as a
shaping force in the dynamics of literature. 'Boethius uses various
versions of *agere et pati* in the *Consolation of Philosophy*. It would be
difficult to name a more influential book through the Middle Ages, a
more likely conduit' (p 15). Crampton cites Bk IV. pr.4, where the
agere-et-pati distinction is especially prominent as the *doer* of a crime
is said to be more wretched than the *sufferer* of the wrong. Lady
Philosophy even argues that wicked men are more happy when
punished than they would be in evading punishment. Chaucer usually
translates Boethius' varied expressions for the antinomy as *do* and
suffer, once using *rescyveth* and *dooth* where Boethius used *accipientis*
and *inferentis* (pp 15–6). Following Boethius, Chaucer works within a
framework of oppositions. Reason generally equates with action and
passion with suffering. Any literate medieval or Renaisance man would
know the *topos* from schoolboy days (p 39). Crampton devotes two
chapters to the operation of the idea in the *KnT*, and two to the
Faerie Queene.

297 Curry, Walter Clyde. *Chaucer and the Mediaeval Sciences*. Oxford:
Oxford University Press, 1926/rev London: Allen and Unwin, 1960.
Pp 241–98.
Ch X, 'Destiny in Troilus and Criseyde,' pp 241–98, derives Chaucer's
notion of destiny primarily from Boethius and goes on to comment on
Boethius' use of astronomy.

298 Dieckmann, Emma M. ' " ... Moore Feelynge Than Had
Boece, ... ".' *MLN*, 53 (1938), 177–80.
The point of the joke in the fox's remark is 'not flattery, but irony' (p
177). 'The cold, mathematical, treatment of music by Boethius had
been questioned by many as early as the eleventh century' (p 180).
But see **293**; also **299**.

299 Dronke, Peter. 'Chaucer and Boethius' *De Musica.*' *NQ*, 13 (1966), 92.
The fox's reference in *NPT* to Chauntecleer's having more feeling in
music 'than hadde Boece, or any that kan synge,' is a jab at the
philosopher's ranking of the critic above performers or composers.
'This was all very well for Boethius the critic. Chaucer the poet could
not take it solemnly. With a single deft touch he intimates that on this
point he found Boethius as insensitive, as quaintly wrong-headed, as
most of us would today. To be explicit, one might paraphrase the
words he gives to the Fox: 'Besides you are musically more sensitive
that the great critic himself — not to mention any mere performer.'
Yet this is to overemphasize. The effect is achieved far more delicately
than that by means of the caesura ... It is the little pause, the
pretended hesitation, that gives the flicker of humour away' (p 92).
See **293** and **298**.

300 Dunleavy, Gareth W. 'The Wound and the Comforter: The
Consolation of Geoffrey Chaucer.' *PLL*, 3 (Summer Supplement,
1967), 14–27.
The *Consolatio* was a staple in Chaucer's intellectual diet, useful in
developing subthemes of gentilesse, truth, the elusiveness and fickleness
of power, fame, and fortune, and pervasive wound-and-comforter
motif. 'The Boethian outlook must have stayed his sides, helped him
preserve his own integrity and devoutness while serving masters who
may have been both politically and personally obnoxious to him' (p
16). His relationship to the *Consolatio* is more personal and more
philosophical than that of Dante. The wound-comforter motif first
appears in *ABC*, then *BD* with its 'close to 300 general and verbal
influences from the *Consolatio*' (p 24), then in *T&C, Mel*, and *ParsT*.

301 Economou, George D. *The Goddess Natura in Medieval Literature.*
1972. See **101**.
Ch II is devoted to 'Boethius and the Poetic Background' (pp 28–52).
Boethius presents Nature 'as kind of certifex presiding over creation'
(p 33). Commentaries on the *Consolatio* like those of Pseudo-John
Scotus Erigena and William of Conches 'provide useful indication of
the Boethian contribution to and influence on the shaping of the figure
of Natura' (p 34). William's commentaries, especially, show Chartrian

fascination with the world of nature. The *Consolatio* reaffirms and clarifies several of the major classical concepts of Nature.

02 — 'Chaucer's Use of the Bird in the Cage Image in the *Canterbury Tales.*' *PQ*, 54 (1975), 679–84.
Relates the bird-in-cage image in *MancT* (H 163–74), *SqT* (F 607–20), and *MilT* (A 3221–6) to *Boece* III m.ii. Jean de Meun also appropriated the image from Boethius for La Vieille's argument on female rights and appetites in *RR* lines 13941–66 (Langlois' text). Chaucer adapts both Boethius' and Jean's use of the image to new and provocative effects. In *SqT* he brings the application full circle by comparing the bird to a bird. 'Chaucer felt free to play with the image and in a way that reveals the precision and complexity of his literary adaptations and allusions' (p 683).

03 Elbow, Peter. 'Two Boethian Speeches in *Troilus and Criseyde* and Chaucerian Irony.' In *Literary Criticism and Historical Understanding: Selected Papers from the English Institute*. Ed. Phillip Damon. New York and London: Columbia University Press, 1967. Pp 85–107.
Chaucer's craft is such that the reader's response to Troilus' long speech on free will in Bk IV and Criseyde's briefer one on happiness in Bk III progresses in three stages: 'First we agree with them; then we are led to disagree and see them ironically; yet in a third step we come to see an irony in that very irony, and agree again more profoundly with the speeches than we had at first ... Both positions somehow remain affirmed ... What haunts in Chaucer is his ability to mean both — to have it both ways. The final problem — that of Chaucerian irony — is that there is no joke' (p 86). Elbow notes Pandarus' quick entrances after such speeches and the narrator's interfering comments which complicate the perspective. Criseyde would be autonomous, characteristically asserting her control by refusing the favor asked while granting a smaller one of her choosing. Eventually we come to see her as a 'profound instance of unfree behavior.' With Diomedes 'she is perfectly sincere in her actions; she is not playing coy games. The matter lies deeper. Her wielding of agency and control serves actually to hide from herself the fact that she will always give in to a certain amount of importunity and shrewdness — the qualities of Troilus and Pandarus which Diomedes so happily combines. This is not a random characteristic in her; Chaucer identifies it as "pite" (V, 824), one of the highest courtly virtues. It is the suffering, in the end, of both Troilus and Diomedes that eventually wins her. Always she "means well" (eg, V, 1004). Thus, her bemusement at the end is genuine: she does not know how it all happened and does not feel it is her doing' (p 94). The ending moves the reader to a third perspective, carrying 'detachment beyond mortality where we cannot follow. We

understand the ending perfectly well, and may even feel vicariously what it says; yet still we are left weeping below' (p 105).

304 — *Oppositions in Chaucer.* Middletown, Conn.: Wesleyan University Press, 1975.

Both Chaucer and Boethius 'have an ingrained tendency to see oppositions everywhere, but to deal with them in such a way that both sides remain affirmed' (p 13). Chaucer may have learned the habit of thought from Boethius, though the practice of studying questions through oppositions was deeply ingrained in medieval rhetoric and scholasticism. Ch 1, 'Boethius' *The Consolation of Philosophy*,' pp 19–48, considers sources of the pattern for Boethius, especially in Plato, and describes many oppositions, polarities, and contrarieties which Boethius works with in the *Consolatio*. The model that Boethius uses for transcending oppositions is hierarchical — 'in effect, the cave is contained by or is a subset of the sky' (pp 43–4). Elbow devotes separate chapters to *T&C*, *KnT*, and *NPT*. Ch 5, 'Freedom and Necessity in Chaucer,' pp 113–30, considers Chaucer's fascination with the fundamental Boethian dichotomy to show how Chaucer transcends the opposition at many points in his poetry. Ch 6, 'Irony Relinquished,' pp 131–42, considers Chaucer's use of an ironic narrator and examines those moments when he moves beyond that kind of opposition. The concluding chapter, 'The Value of Dialectic,' pp 142–61, relates the use of dialectic to 'making' (p 145), a method which calls attention to epistemology and questions of time and progression.

305 Eldredge, Laurence. 'Boethian Epistemology and Chaucer's *Troilus* in the Light of Fourteenth-century Thought.' *Mediaevalia*, 2 (1976), 49–75.

Eldredge examines Troilus as a thinker, knower, and perceiver in light of Boethius and the intellectual background of epistemological thought in Chaucer's time. Troilus' limited success in knowing the nature of love reflects skeptical trends in the universities which Chaucer's learned friends would have recognized and which Chaucer has counterpointed against Boethian epistemology to affirm, in the end, an old truth. In contrast to Ockham's position on the contingency of the world which seems to separate it irrevocably from God, Boethius allows man's higher faculties the possibility of perceiving in 'a single stroke of the mind' (p 57) an instantaneous mode of perception traditionally reserved for God. 'But Boethius is more Platonist than Christian in the *Consolation of Philosophy*, and Lady Philosophy exhorts everyone to strive to attain the heights of divine perception, for therein lies the greatest freedom of the will' (p 57). There is a type of relativism in Boethius' thinking, however, which is contingent upon the perspective from which the mind attempts its perceptions. 'It is not important whether Troilus can provide us with a discourse that eliminates all the dichotomies between heaven and earth. What is important is that in physically rising to a point in the eighth sphere, Troilus provides us, the readers, with an analogue to Lady Philosophy's advice to strive to see with our highest faculty' (p 65). The moral of the poem is thus larger than the epilogue, 'but it is only by seeing the nature of the epistemological processes in the poem that a reader can grasp all the implications of that moral' (p 66).

307 Gardner, Averil. 'Chaucer and Boethius: Some Illustrations of Indebtedness.' *University of Cape Town Studies in English*, 2 (1971), 31–8.
Gardner reviews works bearing the most direct stamp of Boethius — the five Boethian balades, *T&C, KnT*, and *WBT*, though he does not discuss the latter two. *FA* and *Fort* are the most closely tied to Boethius. *Fortune* 'contains in short space, in spirited verse, all that is said of Fortune in the *Consolatio*' (p 32). *Truth* and *Gent* do not correspond exactly to any single passage in Boethius but are akin in thought to Philosophy's teaching. To demonstrate Boethian matter in *T&C* Gardner follows one theme, that of the effect of the heavenly powers on the lives of men, noting many lines drawn directly from Boethius. He concludes by commenting briefly on Troilus' speech on determinism in Bk IV. 'The obvious answer to those who seek to prove Chaucer's determinism is that Troilus is not Boethius. He is a hot-headed young man who has not attained that state of mind in which it would be possible for him to be consoled by philosophy' (p 37). Nonetheless, the speech is too long. 'Chaucer has sacrificed dramatic consistency to his anxious wish to be faithful to each step of the Boethian argument' (p 37).

308 Gaylord, Alan T. 'Uncle Pandarus as Lady Philosophy.' *Papers of the Michigan Academy of Science, Arts, and Letters*, 46 (1960), 571–95.
'The part Pandarus attempts to play is intended by Chaucer, though not by Pandarus, as a parody of the philosophical counsel offered to Boethius. Although it is assumed that such a parody provides a humor based upon an audience's ability to distinguish between the real thing and its travesty, between vision and expediency, between reason and chop logic, it is nevertheless quite possible that not everyone would recognize all of the Boethian parody. Yet even short of that, it is still probable that close attention to nothing but the surface of the poetry could discover the same kind of sophistry and ludicrous illogic that the parody serves to satirize' (p 572). Pandarus' arrival at the side of the weeping Troilus, his demand for confession, and his solicitous friendship are all inversions of Philosophy's behavior in the *Consolatio*. His call for Troilus to awake from his 'litargie' is a specific reference to

I.pr.2. His physician and medicine metaphors also derive from Boethius along with the discussion of Fortune and Pandarus' crooked reasoning as he encourages Troilus to take advantage of her wheel. 'Once Pandarus has invited Troilus to step onto the wheel and once he has established Criseyde as an image of true felicity, his counsel has played its part and his practical aid must now begin. Thus the element of parody is no longer as intense as it was earlier, although the satirical note continues, piping gently through Pandarus' full assumption of a priestly role' (pp 588–9). But Pandarus' mode of healing is 'falsely homeopathic, since the remedies he offers only serve to intensify and complicate the woes Troilus suffered originally' (p 593).

309 — 'The Role of Saturn in the *Knight's Tale.*' *ChauR*, 8 (1973–4), 171–90.
Saturn should be interpreted, within the traditional scheme of moralized astrology in Chaucer's day, as a sign for necessity which short-sighted men impose on themselves. He is an astrological adjunct to the Boethian themes of providence, destiny, free will, and love which Chaucer has built into the poem. But he is not the destructive element *per se.*

309a Gilbert, A.J. 'The Influence of Boethius on the *Parlement of Foules.*' *MAE*, 47 (1978), 292–303.
PF follows a Boethian course of 'a rational enquiry into what is essentially irrational' (p 292). Much of the poem's terminology is Boethian as well as its attitudes toward dream, nature, and the will.

310 Gordon, Ida L. *The Double Sorrow of Troilus: A Study of Ambiguities in Troilus and Criseyde.* Oxford: Clarendon Press, 1970. Pp 24–60.
Boethian matter is prominent throughout this study. Ch 2, 'Ambiguity and Boethius,' pp 24–60, traces many features of Chaucerian irony to the *Consolatio* with its dichotomies of true and false goods and the juxtaposition of temporal and eternal perspectives. Chaucer surpasses other authors in his ability to use philosophical matter comprehensively and coherently (p 26). Gordon traces several Boethian topics which are inherently ambiguous (felicity, love, consolatory medicines, fortune, determinism, and free will) through *T&C*, demonstrating Chaucer's ability to exploit such ambiguity for further ambiguity.

311 Halverson, John. 'Aspects of Order in the *Knight's Tale.*' *SP*, 57 (1960), 606–21.
Halverson suggests three hierarchic aspects of order operative in *KnT*: the order of nature, the order of society, and the divine order of the cosmos. Natural order is manifested chiefly in the seasonal references,

death and life cycles, and in the marriages. Social order is epitomized
by the noble life with its valor, piety, courtesy, wisdom, chivalry,
honor, and liberality. The divine order is Boethian: the prison is like
that of Boethius; so too the process of mental growth which moves
doubt and pessimism to serene optimism, culminating in Theseus'
insight into the 'First Moevere' and 'faire cheyne of love.'

312 Hirshberg, Jeffrey Alan. ' "Cosyn to the Dede": *The Canterbury Tales*
and the Platonic Tradition in Medieval Rhetoric.' *DAI*, 38 (1978),
6741A–42A. University of Wisconsin Dissertation, 1977. Dir. Jerome
Taylor.
Noting that Chaucer quotes Boethius but cites Plato as his authority
that words must be 'cosyn to the dede,' Hirshberg traces the topos 1)
epistemologically from Plato, Augustine, Thierry of Chartres, and
Alain de Lille to the late medieval speculative grammarians; 2)
'sociopolitically' from Isocrates to Gower and Chaucer (in *Sted*); 3)
escatologically in Langton and Gower; and 4) hermeneutically from
Sallust to William of Conches, Geoffrey of Vinsauf, and Jean de Meun.
Boethius draws on the *Timaeus*, consistently associating with ideal
rhetoric metaphors of medicine, music, and memory. Words rightly
used create images of eternal truth even within the microcosm.
Against this ideal rhetoric Boethius sets flattery and the corrupting of
words. Hirshberg considers Boethius' views in relation to those of
Augustine and later commentators like William of Conches and
Nicholas Trivet, then brings the trope and its Boethian tradition to
bear on *MancT* and *ParsT* along with other tales.

313 Huber, John. 'Troilus' Predestination Soliloquy: Chaucer's Changes
from Boethius.' *NM*, 66 (1965), 120–5.
Differences between Troilus' speech and Boethius suggest that
'Chaucer is attempting to emphasize Troilus's eagerness to shun
responsibility by denying the very possibility of human freedom' (p
120). His qualifying phrase 'by necessite' (IV.1050, 1057) is not
justified by any of the versions noted in Latin editions. The Middle
English *Boece* poses problems, however. Richard Morris' text, based
on BM ms Addit. 10340 (**162**) shows the same double translation of
the Latin 'necesse est' as *T&C*. Morris, Furnivall, and Skeat note that
the second 'by necessity' is a gloss in Cambridge Univ. Lib. ms Ii.3.21.
Robinson omits the second 'by necessite' without noting any variants.
'Until textual criticism accounts for the variations in *Boece* ... one
can fall back on Chaucer' general accuracy as a translator, both of
Boece as a whole and of the greater part of Troilus' soliloquy, to
conjecture that the 'by necessite' of line 1057 is calculated to surprise
the reader' (p 124).

314 Lawler, Traugott. *The One and the Many in the Canterbury Tales.*
Hamden, Conn.: Shoe String Press, 1980.
Although Lawler treats 'the one and the many' primarily as a
rhetorical concept, he does touch on its philosophical implications
occasionally. His hope is 'to improve our understanding of the
wholeness and oneness' of the *CT*, to 'provide a single large
perspective from which to understand many problems which trouble
all readers' (p 30). He suggests Boethius and St Paul as possible
sources for Chaucer's notions of unity within multiplicity (pp 27–30)
and uses Boethian attitudes toward process and closure to explain
Chaucer's plan for concluding the *CT* (pp 119–20).

315 Lumiansky, R.M. 'Chaucer's Philosophical Knight.' *Tulane Studies in
English*, 3 (1952), 47–68.
In a detailed study of the suitability of *KnT* to its teller Lumiansky
finds the knight to be of a philosophical disposition, doctoring up his
chivalric romance with Boethius. Lumiansky notes seventeen specific
passages in which he borrows from Boethius to stress destiny and its
workings in the universe. 'The Boethian influence is so pervasive as
virtually to control the action' (p 57).

316 McAlpine, Monica E. *The Genre of Troilus and Criseyde.* Ithaca and
London: Cornell University Press, 1978.
Boethius does not lend his authority to the old *de casibus* theory of
tragedy, though Fortune's use of that definition in *Consolatio* II, pr.2,
is often projected upon him. '*De Casibus* tragedy is a genre that
remains innately and radically committed to worldliness even as it
laments the frustrations of man's power in this world' (p 31).
Boccaccio followed the old view of the genre which Chaucer takes off
on in the *MonkT*. But in *T&C* Chaucer moves more deeply and is
more truly Boethian. He discovered in the *Consolatio* an alternative
definition founded not on the 'dedes of Fortune' but on the deeds of
people, who act and suffer with the consequences of their action. Thus
'Troilus' career is a Boethian comedy, while Criseyde's career is the
authentic Boethian and Chaucerian tragedy. At the crucial moments
Troilus makes morally enhancing choices, but Criseyde, in one
instance, makes a morally degrading choice' (p 33). Chaucer thus uses
the *de casibus* tragedy as a foil, a 'contrarie,' in order to present more
probingly his own perception of Boethian tragedy. McAlpine devotes
chapters to 'The Tragedy of Fortune and the *Consolation of
Philosophy*,' pp 47–85, in which she examines the tension between
Fortune and Philosophy and clarifies the true nature of Boethian
tragedy; 'De Casibus Tragedy: Boccaccio and Chaucer,' pp 86–115, in
which she examines in detail the vision of the *Monk's Tale* and its
generic limitations; ' "Litel myn tragedye": The Narrator of *Troilus*

and *Criseyde*,' pp 116–47, in which she shows how Chaucer
manipulates the 'contrarie' through the narrator's inept responses to
the immediate situations of the plot; 'The Boethian Comedy of
Troilus,' pp 148–81, in which she explores the progress of Troilus'
feelings; and 'The Boethian Tragedy of Criseyde,' pp 182–217, in
which she argues for 'Criseyde's worth in her own right, apart from
Troilus' even though Criseyde is left in 'tragic unfulfillment' (p 217).
'The task of verifying the narrator's claim that *Troilus and Criseyde* is
a tragedy is a demanding and exacting one. It requires us to reject one
concept of tragedy and to evolve another, while simultaneously trying
to come to terms with two complex protagonists' (p 218).

317 McCall, John P. 'Five-Book Structure in Chaucer's *Troilus*.' *MLQ*, 23
(1962), 297–308.

The structure of *Troilus* imitates the five-book structure of Boethius'
Consolation. In the first books of each, Troilus and Boethius suffer the
'same illness, react in similar ways, and turn to the aid of learned
physicians who claim they can cure them of their woes' (p 298). The
comparison is, of course, 'up-so-doun,' the plots diametrically opposed.
The second books of each reveal the workings of Fortune. The plot in
T&C is less closely tied to the *Consolation* here than elsewhere, but
the book draws heavily on Boethian ideas, nonetheless. Philosophy
begins with 'lyghte and meneliche remedies,' then 'litel strengere
medicynes.' So too does Pandarus begin with little favors before
applying stronger. The third books of each are devoted to happiness
and the applying of stronger medicines still in healing the malady. Bk
III of *T&C* draws extensively on Bk III of *Boece* for metaphors of
felicity. Boece is led step by step to comprehend the essence of true
and perfect good, while Troilus is led by stages to fulfillment of a
partial and transitory good. *T&C* IV turns joy to woe and dramatizes
Lady Philosophy's arguments concerning weakness of 'schrewes.' The
argument on free will and predestination in *T&C* IV comes from
Boece V, though its place and dramatic significance is explained in IV,
pr.6, 24–9. McCall emphasizes the contrast as *Boece* IV ends with its
sights on heaven (IV. m.7, 63–72) while Troilus is discovering hell on
earth (IV, 1695–1701), wracked by doubts about human freedom and
divine providence. In the fifth books we are now dealing openly with
opposites, though the solution in *T&C* is precisely that furnished by
Boethius. *Troilus* is primarily a historical tragedy, one that dramatizes
a man's systematic subjection to Fortune and the awesome
consequences of that subjection ... The themes and the form of the
tragedy are consistently permeated by the philosophy and the art of
Boethius, so that in significant ways we can say that the *Consolation*
and the *Troilus* are companion pieces which 'go hand in hand'

[Jefferson **189**, p 130]. And while Boethius' work is a *comoedia* and Chaucer's a tragedy, both embody the same ultimate vision of man's human and divine relationships to eternal truth' (p 308).

318 Masiu, Michio. 'Chaucer's Tenderness and the Theme of Consolation.' In *Studies Presented to Tauno F. Mustanoja on the Occasion of his Sixtieth Birthday. NM*, 73 (1972), 214–21.
Reading Chaucer's works chronologically one gradually becomes aware of a tendency toward 'emotional internalization,' especially in the form of consolation or comfort in death or courtly love relationships (p 214). Masiu compares the delicacy of sorrow in *BD* to the old Japanese 'a-wa-re,' a state in which the heart feels deeply a personal and social hierarchy (p 216). Such feeling with its 'subtle double function of consolation' is found in *T&C* as well, with its Boethian influences. *T&C* ends with 'the consolation of Christianity,' a step beyond the consolation of philosophy. 'Chaucer has from the depth of his heart felt that this soul's pilgrimage toward heaven may deserve the reward for Troilus' 'trouthe' and 'gentilesse' (p 221).

319 Mogan, Joseph J., Jr. *Chaucer and the Theme of Mutability.* The Hague and Paris: Mouton, 1968.
Mogan traces the concept of mutability through Boethius and Augustine to Chaucer; he devotes the better part of a chapter to its presence in *Boece*, then comments upon its recurrence in Chaucer's Boethian balades (pp 54–93).

320 Norton-Smith, John. *Geoffrey Chaucer.* London: Routledge and Kegan Paul, 1974.
Discusses Boethian influences, especially as a source for Chaucerian imagery, in *HF* (pp 40–4, 51, 60–1), *LGW* (p 68), *KnT* (pp 102, 128, 132), *MilT* (pp 141–2), *T&C* (pp 160–70, 192–5, 209), and for Chaucer's view of measure and moderation (pp 230–5).

321 — 'Chaucer's Boethius and *Fortune*,' *Reading Medieval Studies*, 2 (1976), 63–76.
[I have not seen this essay.]

322 Owen, Charles A., Jr. 'The Significance of Chaucer's Revisions of *Troilus and Criseyde.' MP*, 55 (1957), 1–5.
Chaucer inserts the nineteen stanza soliloquy of Boethian material into Bk IV to call attention to the problem of free will and to represent Troilus' internal struggle. He 'wanted to focus attention at this point on Troilus and show Criseyde's departure as more clearly dependent on Troilus' decision. The soliloquy further performs the function of internalizing the action ... so that we shall be aware of the characters as sentient human beings struggling against their own

ignorance and a hostile world to think their way through their problems' (p 4). The passage is comparable to Criseyde's solitary reflections in her chamber in Bk II.

323 Patch, Howard Rollin. 'Troilus on Predestination.' *JEGP*, 17 (1918), 399–423.
The soliloquy on determinism in Bk IV shows Troilus' failure to accept responsibility. The fatalistic view is an extension of his self-pitying humility. As he tries to argue philosophically he confuses himself. 'Chaucer shows amazing power in keeping the dramatic effect and the psychology of his character true' (p 420). The monologue is beautifully adapted to the scene in which Troilus convinces himself that 'I've never had a chance.'

324 — 'Chaucer and Lady Fortune.' *MLR*, 22 (1927), 377–88.
After a brief survey of medieval attitudes toward Fortune, Patch comments on the role of Boethian Fortune in *BD, HF, Fortune, KnT, T&C, MonkT, MLT,* and *NPT*.

325 — 'Troilus and Determinism.' *Spec*, 6 (1931), 225–43.
Part of the problem in dealing with determinism lies in the fault of the term itself, which involves both an intellectual and aesthetic concept. Fatalism in moral tragedy is very different from the spectacle of the action of irresponsible puppets (p 227). 'While the Greeks had a sense of destiny, they were able to sustain the paradox of fate and free will, so well recognized and discussed in the Middle Ages. The critic's enthusiam [for freedom of thought, action, love, etc.] shows the instinctive revolt almost anyone feels at any kind of moral slavery' (p 228). The difficulty of dealing with fatalism in art occurs when the mind rejects the paradox as a contradiction (p 229). 'The solution ... lies partly in the fact that man may suffer worldly tragedy and yet, like Job, win spiritual victory' (p 230). Boethius resolves the problem by putting the question into the perspective of eternity, 'where Divine foresight is unlimited, and parallel lines are at last to meet' (p 230). To imagine *T&C* as an argument embodying determinism destroys the character of both Criseyde and Troilus and presents 'a new Chaucer, and one that we have never met hitherto' (p 238). The Boethian vision is not deterministic. 'The Epilogue no more contradicts the mood of the poem than various tendencies of human nature in one person contradict one another; on any other terms every Christian would have to be a complete ascetic and every Catholic a puritan. It is an aspect of Chaucer's greatness and his breadth that he can enter as heartily into the love affair as into the vision of the limitation of earthly things and the supreme value of lasting idealism' (p 240). That interpretation which harmonizes all the parts is the one nearest the intention of the

author. 'Chaucer's head was where it should be, and he did not
cultivate sentimental art at the expense of common sense' (p 243).
Includes plate of Boccaccio and six-armed Fortuna, from ms Royal 14.

326 Payne, F. Anne. *Chaucer and Menippean Satire.* Madison: University
of Wisconsin Press, 1981.
Payne expands the fourteen-point definition of Menippean satire in
M.M. Bakhtin, *The Problems of Dostoevsky's Poetics,* trans. R.W.
Rotsel (Ann Arbor, 1973), to twenty one points, noting that most
critical responses to Boethius' *Consolation* and its tradition have been
simplistic. Ch 3, 'The Consolation of Philosophy as Menippean Satire,'
pp 55–85, relates Boethius' 'Menippean *summa*' to such works as
Seneca's *Apocolocyntosis,* Petronius' *Satyricon,* and Apuleius' *Golden
Ass.* Chaucer 'saw Boethius' work not only as a textbook for classical
philosophy but also, and much more important, as the culmination
and fulfillment of an ironical mode of containing and assessing the
realities of human thought and experience' (p 58). As in other
Menippean satires, the 'character' Boethius 'is the obvious butt of the
protagonist's joke' (p 68). The tragic sense that pervades the
Consolation is 'that common to the Menippean dialogue, the
knowledge that man is not provided with images or words that are
adequate to contain his electrifying inklings of reality' (p 80). The
Menippean thrust of the *Consolation* is the same as it is in Lucian:
'the protagonist's views prevail but ... with the ironic awareness that
the supernatural protagonist's freedom is Other, not available to man,
who though he can imagine it, cannot experience it, except as he
writes to contain it' (p 82). The *Consolation* is full of 'reduced
laughter' (p 83), providing 'an archetypal image of man's struggle to
come to terms with chaos and certainty, freedom and limitations' (p
84). 'The befuddled "I" embodies the human awareness of the
inescapability of chaos' (p 85). Payne also includes a chapter on
Lucian as Menippean satirist, and two chapters each on *T&C, NPT,*
and *KnT,* which emphasize Boethian influences on Chaucer's sense of
wit and irony, his use of dialogue and imagery, his manipulation of
genres, his sense of human limitation and the endless quest, and his
treatment of man's aggressions and the parodoxical pleasure and pain
in freedom of thought.

327 Peck, Russell A. 'Theme and Number in Chaucer's *Book of the
Duchess.*' In *Silent Poetry: Essays in Numerological Analysis.* Ed.
Alastair Fowler. London: Routledge & Kegan Paul, 1970. Pp 73–115.
BD is the drama of a soul overwhelmed by grief, struggling to reorient
itself. 'Its general formula for mental restitution is Christian; its
specific formula is Boethian' (p 73). The opening forty-three lines, like
the first *metrum* of *Boece,* establish the dilemma of a frenzied mind,

overwhelmed by 'sorwful ymagynacioun,' unable to get hold of itself. As in Boethius, the mental sickness is presented as an unnatural condition, a problem of forgetting and misdefinition. The dreamer's decision to read is comparable to Boece's decision to write. Both lead to a means of taking counsel, a physician who helps the bereaved person within the narrator's being to discover his wound, that is, the source of his grief. In *BD* the counsel comes in the dream itself as the dreamer, who would help the Black Knight to heal the heart which lies sick inside him, repeatedly asks basic questions which precipitate the Black Knight's rehearsing of his grief three times over until he reveals and accepts plainly the cause — the death of the good faire White. As in Boethius, the immediate source of grief seems to be evil fortune, but soon the therapy moves to deeper issues — definitions of suffisaunce and a more true remembering of the nature of events. The positioning of the questioning dreamer beside the grieving Knight is icono-graphically similar to the appearance of Philosophy at the corner of Boece's bed. Peck compares the dialogue in the dream to 'the longe moevynges of his thoughtes' which Boethius speaks of in III m.xi, which must be drawn into 'a compas' if the distraught person is to regain his sense of wholeness (pp 79–80, 89). That circle is achieved in the home image of the conclusion, with the dreamer's waking and writing his dream.

328 —, ed. *The Confessio Amantis*, by John Gower. New York: Holt, Rinehart & Winston, 1968, pp xi–xxix.
The structural model behind Gower's *Confessio* and such poems of consolation as *Pearl, Sir Orfeo, KQ, BD*, and Dante's *Divine Comedy* is Boethius' *Consolatio*. 'In each the primary subject is the narrator's restless state of mind; the plot is his search for repose' (p xi). The plot normally follows four stages: 1) an opening description of the narrator's spiritual inertia — a restlessness, illness, forgetfulness or psychological turmoil; 2) an act by the distracted narrator which precipitates a change of scene and the encountering of new characters who are likely to be projections of some part of himself or of his environment; 3) an ensuing discussion, dialogue, or debate with the new characters in which the topics of concern are explored and which leads to a redefinition of the narrator's sense of being; 4) a climactic moment when the disturbed persona will waver, 'then achieve a final revelation which will bring about his return, usually to home' (p xii). See also Russell A. Peck, *Kingship and Common Profit in Gower's Confessio Amantis* (Carbondale: Southern Illinois Univerity Press, 1978), pp 29–35, which discusses the process in further detail.

329 — 'Chaucer and Nominalist Questions.' *Spec*, 53 (1978), 745–60.
One reason for Chaucer's great interest in Boethius is the

philosopher's concern with the efficacy of will, a topic which fascinated fourteenth-century philosophers like Duns Scotus, William of Ockham, and Robert Holcot (p 747). Chaucer's strong interest in Boethius may have fed his apparent concern with nominalistic questions, especially speculation on the philosophical relationship between language and perception which originates as a topic in the *Consolatio*, where Philosophy's therapy is largely an elaborate word game that uses words against words to break down old verbal assumptions, and then uses new words and mental pictures 'to construct a new psychological dwelling place' (p 747 n. 15). In *BD* Chaucer's metaphor of a 'whit wal or table' to describe the intellect perhaps owes something to Ockham, though the poet certainly knew the idea also from *Cons.* V m.4, 17–9 (p 751). His use of *Boece* in *HF*, lines 964–82, to illustrate the inability of the human intellect to concentrate and recognize its proper place (pp 754–5), and his use of the Boethian problem of simultaneously knowing and not-knowing in *PF* (lines 120–68; cf V m.3, 42–56), point to Chaucer's subtle understanding of nominalistic issues which originate in Boethius (pp 756–7).

330 Piehler, Paul. *The Visionary Landscape: A Study in Medieval Allegory.* London: Edward Arnold, 1971.
This study explores nine propositions: 1) that medieval visionary allegory involves a process of psychic redemption closely resembling modern psychotherapy; 2) that the content and structure is derived from the ancients; 3) that the major element is dialogue; 4) that it employs rational and symbolic forms; 5) that it is extraordinarily complex in its modes and comprehensiveness; 6) that its 'seminal images' are analytic; 7) that the fundamental quest is for a principle of authority; 8) that the major allegorical poets regard themselves as part of a cumulative tradition; 9) that the genre wanes in the fifteenth century for various reasons. Piehler uses Boethius to define the seminal images of the tradition (pp 21–30). Ch 3, 'Boethius,' pp 31–45, contrasts the *Consolation* to Platonic dialogues, noting that in Plato the 'emphasis is on the development of the idea rather than of the individual' (p 33). Piehler relates Lady Philosophy as an allegorical figure to earlier Christian personifications of *Mater Ecclesia* (p 36), which in part reflects Boethius' shift into an individual psychological quest. 'The dialogue represents the movement of a doctrine, a body of ideas, from a position almost external to the mind, to a point where the ideas have become part of the equipment, even the constitution, of the mind itself' (p 35). Boethius dwells upon the idea of cosmic alienation as a state of mind. His kind of allegory and symbolism forms the basis of the later visionary tradition. Ch 4, 'Alain's Vision of Nature,' pp 46–68, also draws extensively on

Boethius for purposes of comparison. Other chapters deal with
Landscapes of Vision (sacred places, psychology of landscape in terms
of wilderness and city, sources of allegorical landscape); Landscape and
Dialogue, with discussion of the *Roman de la Rose*, Dante, and *Pearl*.
The book makes some use of Jung and Freud.

331 Presson, Robert K. 'The Aesthetic of Chaucer's Art of Contrast.'
EM, 15 (1964), 9–23.
Among numerous varieties of antithesis in Chaucer, Presson notes the
juxtaposition of the Monk's tragedies and *NPT*, where Boethius is
used for antithetical effects (pp 16–21). 'The antithesis, although
primarily a device of emphasis, is clearly an indication of the way
Chaucer saw experience' (p 23).

332 Robertson, D.W., Jr. 'Chaucerian Tragedy.' *ELH*, 19 (1952), 1–37.
Chaucer finds his definition of tragedy in *Cons*. II, pr.2. He would
have understood the *Consolatio* to be a Christian document in which
Fortune and her gifts are inferior to God. To love the uncertain and
transitory rewards of the world is to subject oneself to their
fluctuations. To love God is to acquire freedom and peace of mind.
'We cannot say ... that the victim or "hero" of a Chaucerian tragedy
is either the victim of chance or the victim of an inevitable destiny.
Like the speaker in the *De consolatione*, he is the victim of his own
failure' (p 4). 'It is from charity that all virtues arise. Thus the *De
consolatione* develops in a systematic way, but in the guise of a
philosophical dialogue, the contrast between the two loves, charity and
cupidity, which is the cornerstone of medieval theology' (p 6–7).
Robertson applies these premises to *T&C* to show how the principal
characters invert the inner hierarchy of sapientia, scientia, and the
senses to doom themselves in cupidity. Their fall has political
overtones, for the destruction of a man is the destruction of a city
when we consider that every man builds either Babylon or Jerusalem
within himself and that Babylon is doomed to fall (p 14).

333 Rowe, Donald W. *O Love, O Charite! Contraries Harmonized in
Chaucer's Troilus*. Carbondale: Southern Illinois University Press,
1976.
Rowe views *T&C* as a harmony of contraries. Ch 1, 'The Dynamic
Principle of the Troilus,' pp 3–56, stresses the importance of
opposition and debate in medieval thought and traces the idea of
concordia discors in Chaucer's familiar sources, especially Boethius
and his commentators (viz, *Boece* III m.12, and II m.8). In *T&C* we
encounter 'a world where people speak in "ambages," words "with two
visages"; thus, it is appropriate that the narrator invokes Janus, the
god with two faces, to guide Pandarus' (p 46). Ch 2, 'Psychological

and Sacramental Characterization,' pp 57–91, emphasizes the
symbolism in the poem, 'dissimilar similitudes' whereby corruptible
love imitates incorruptible love but is not the same. The argument
here draws heavily on patristic writers. Ch 3, 'The Marriage of Heaven
and Hell,' pp 92–120, begins with Bernardus Silverstris' discussion of
two Venuses, then focuses on the divine-earthly oppositions in the
consummation scene in Bk III. 'Though Troilus seizes Criseyde like a
hawk, his repeated tendency to ascend in song recalls Boethius' image
of a bird in a cage, an image of the soul, bound to the flesh but forever
seeking its true home' (p 117). Ch 4, 'Tragedy and Comedy,' pp
121–51, discusses *Boece* III m.11, 27–32, on the 'two roundes' of the
World-Soul (p 147) to demonstrate how Troilus' history mirrors the
divine comedy, uniting both circles 'as he falls into this world to
experience its tragedy before returning to the heights from which he
fell, the sphere of the fixed stars, the true home of the soul. His course
is ultimately a spiral, as he is turned one way by God's circumscribing
love, just as the planets are turned by the divine motion of the fixed
stars, at the same time that his own cupidity turns him in the opposite
direction, just as each of the planets has its contrary circular motion.
Thus it is that God harmonizes contraries in man and in the cosmos:
"O Love, O Charite!" ' (p 151). Ch 5, 'Chaucer and his Narrator,' pp
152–72, draws an interesting parallel between the narrator of *T&C*
and Boethius at the beginning of the *Consolatio* (both in a kind of
helpless state, imprisoned by fate). The authors use the device to keep
the audience simultaneously at a distance and involved in the
dilemma, that is, engaged in two contrary ways of knowing.

334 Ruggiers, Paul G. 'The Unity of Chaucer's *House of Fame*.' *SP*, 50
(1953), 16–29.
Ruggiers suggests that the man of great authority who appears at the
end may be less a mystery than he at first seems. The carefully
constructed poem is thematically consistent. Chaucer combines
Boethian ideas of fame and fortune in Part I. In Part II he uses
Boethian terms to provide the scientific and theological basis of an
orderly universe in which the transcient flights take place. The man of
great authority at the end of Part III may well be Boethius himself,
who would appear to make 'a sane and dispassionate pronouncement
incorporating the theme of the untrustworthy fortunes of love into the
larger picture of the instability of fame in general, a pronouncement
voicing the conviction that only disillusion must result from an abuse
of the passions and the folly of trusting the inconstant goddesses' (p
28).

335 — 'Towards a Theory of Tragedy in Chaucer.' *ChauR*, 8 (1973–4),
88–99.

After briefly discussing Boethian tragedy of Fortune in the *MonkT*, the recurring problem of destiny, and the Boethian notion of predestination, Ruggiers concludes: 'Chaucer's achievement in his major works has been to hold in balance the two sides of the Boethian dichotomy: man is free to choose, but the choices are foreseen and foreknown' (p 96).

336 Ruud, Jay. 'Against Women Unconstant: The Case for Chaucer's Authorship.' *MP*, 80 (1982), 161–4.
The mirror image of lines 8–10 derives from *Boece* V. m.4. ll. 6–19. Since the poet seems familiar not only with the Boethian passage but also with Chaucer's gloss on it [or the source of that gloss), Chaucer's authorship of *AWU* is 'somewhat less "doubtful"' than has been claimed' (p 164).

337 Steadman, John M. *Disembodied Laughter: Troilus and the Apotheosis Tradition*. Berkeley: University of California Press, 1972.
Steadman makes extensive use of Boethius in his discussion of Troilus' flight to the eighth sphere where earth becomes only a point. Ch 4, 'Boethian Monologue and Prophetic Dream,' pp 66–83, considers Neoplatonic flight analogues in which flight serves as a form of consolation. 'Troilus's laughter at death and human grief alike has reduced to insignificance the last grounds for complaint against the providence and just dispensation of the gods' (p 83). Ch 5, 'Felicity and Mutability: Boethian Framework of the Troilus,' pp 84–111, argues that 'the flight stanzas themselves represent a fusion of Boethian *topoi* with the apotheosis motif of the poets and the pneumatology of Stoic and Neoplatonic philosophers' (pp 85–6). A footnote on p 86 cites eleven studies on the problems of sources of Boethian doctrine (Stoic, Platonic, Aristotelian, Christian). 'It was difficult for a poet to take Boethius piecemeal. Though the *Consolation* would hardly meet Husserl's conditions for philosophy as *strenge Wissenschaft*, it is nevertheless a closely reasoned, tightly structured work centering upon the vision of an eternal good as true felicity and culminating in the idea of divine providence as an eternal present. To detach a single concept, such as Boethius' Fortune, from the whole and develop it in isolation from its original context could violate the integrity of this system and distort the concept thus isolated' (p 93). Steadman draws parallels with Dante to conclude that Chaucer's affirmative 'comic' ending complements rather than contradicts the negative example of his tragedy. The Boethian matter is 'precisely the sort of commentary that Strode and Gower might have expected' (p 106). Troilus' final insights come close to those of the Boethian philosopher and scholastic theologian (p 139).

338 Stroud, Theodore A. 'Boethius' Influence on Chaucer's *Troilus.*' *MP*,
49 (1951–2), 1–9.
T&C extends the principle of Fortune's turning wheel; viewed in
relation to the *Consolatio* the poem 'has a significantly allegorical
cast' (p 1). Boethius was a basic stimulant to Chaucer's creative
imagination. It is as if 'he sought to exemplify the philosophical stages
of the *Consolatio* somewhat as Dante did for Aquinas' hierarchy of
sins' (p 2). Troilus is a Boethius driven by the alternations of Fortune,
at first well-nigh demented by his sudden loss of freedom. In the love
affair he beholds first the false goods of Fortune, then, with Criseyde's
loss 'more egre medicynes.' His interminable period of frustration
prepares the reader emotionally for his reward of viewing the world
sub specie aeternitatis. He differs from *de casibus* heroes in that 'he
actually gropes for the *De contemptu mundi* lesson' (p 4). Criseyde
reflects a deeply rooted pessimism 'as she inquires how man can ever
be truly happy' (p 7).

338a Schweitzer, Edward C. 'Fate and Freedom in *The Knight's Tale.*'
SAC, 3 (1981), 13–45.
'Arcite's death is not only just but poetically inevitable' (p 13).
Chaucer's precise use of astrological and medical details pertaining to
the disease *amor hereos*, which the poet presents in the manner of
Arnald Villanova as *amor furiosus*, suggests that Saturn and the fury
that startles Arcite's horse dramatize the consequences of human
choice rather than fatalism. Arcite's 'wrastling for this world,' figured
in Emelye, 'axeth a fal,' which he gets. 'The very imperfection of the
world proves the existence of a higher perfection against which
imperfection can be measured' (p 39). Chaucer uses 'Boethius'
Consolation to turn apparent contradictions between universal order
and particular disorder into 'significant paradox' (p 45).

339 Wetherbee, Winthrop. 'Some Intellectual Themes in Chaucer's
Poetry.' In *Geoffrey Chaucer.* Ed. George D. Economou. New York:
McGraw-Hill, 1975. Pp 75–91.
Designed for undergraduates first encountering Chaucer, this essay
provides a comprehensive survey of the principal intellectual strains in
Chaucer's poetry. Wetherbee emphasizes the influences of Macrobius,
Boethius, Jean de Meun, and fourteenth-century philosophers
(Ockham, Bradwardine, Wyclif). His discussion of Boethius (pp 82–6)
concentrates on *Troilus* and *KnT*, suggesting that it is the
combination of Boethian *contemptus mundi* and affirmation that
Chaucer finds so appealing and true to his own almost
antiphilosophical views in later life.

340 Wood, Chauncey. *Chaucer and the Country of the Stars.* 1970. See

350. Pp 22–36, *passim.*
Boethian views qualify Chaucer's attitude toward astrology (pp 22–36). The prominent debate on will in Chaucer's writings is not whether free choice exists but rather whether it can be explained (p 22). 'Boethius does admit more astral influence than St. Augustine, and it is perhaps because of his influence that so many humanists of the later Middle Ages accepted more celestial influence than they might have otherwise' (p 34). Wood comments on similar Boethian influences on Boccaccio and Dante (pp 41–3), and remarks occasionally on Boethian ideas in *Mars, MLT*, and *FrankT*.

❧ Part III: The Treatise on the Astrolabe

Introduction

If surviving manuscripts are any indication of a work's popularity, *The Treatise on the Astrolabe* was for two hundred years after Chaucer's death deemed one of his most important compositions. It survives in more than two dozen manuscripts, more than there are of *Troilus and Criseyde* or any of Chaucer's other compositions except for the *Canterbury Tales*. Much of Chaucer's fame as a mathematician and philosopher owes its credence to the existence of the *Astrolabe*. From the beginning the work was valued for its charming style — 'Bred and Mylk for Childeren,' as several early scribes entitled it. But it was also valued for its scientific instruction. Thomas Speght observes in the introduction to his 1598 edition of the *Astrolabe:* 'This booke ... standeth so good at this day, especially for the Horizon of Oxford, as in the opinion of the learned, it cannot be amended.' Though Gabriel Harvey seems confused in sharing Chaucer's glory with Lydgate, his honest amazement — even chagrin — at Chaucer's learnedness owes much to the *Astrolabe* as well as *Boece:* 'Others commend Chawcer & Lidgate for their witt, pleasant veine, varietie of poetical discourse, & all humanitie: I specially note *their Astronomie, philosophie* and other parts of *profound or cunning art.* Wherein few of their time were more exactly learned. It is not sufficient for poets to be superficial humanists: but they must be exquisite artists, and curious uniuersal schollars' (Spurgeon, **428**, vol 1, p 127).

There can be little doubt as to the authenticity of the treatise. It is ascribed to Chaucer in many of the manuscripts and by Lydgate who, in the Prologue to Book I of *The Fall of Princes,* says that Chaucer made 'a tretis, full noble and off gret pris, upon thastrabre' for 'his sone, that callid was Lowis.' Several studies have shown that Chaucer's treatise is based in part on a Latin translation of Messahala's *Compositio et Operatio Astrolabii* and that it draws also upon Sacrobosco's *De Sphaera.* Other studies have emphasized the independence of Chaucer's work and that he drew upon his own practical knowledge of the subject. *The Treatise on the Astrolabe* is incomplete. It consists of the famous Prologue addressed to 'lyte Lowys my sone,' in which Chaucer explains why he writes in English, challenges some of the conclusions drawn in other treatises he has read, and announces the five-part division of his plan. Part I explains how to use the instrument. This section differs markedly from its source which begins with instructions on making the instrument. Part II, which depends heavily on Messahala, consists of a series of 'conclusions' (problems) for the user of the astrolabe to practice. The treatise breaks off mid-sentence at the end of conclusion 40, though some mss include several additional conclusions.

The Prologue indicates that Part III was to include diverse tables of longitudes and latitudes of fixed stars, tables on the 'declinacions of the sonne' and on the longitudes of 'citees and townes,' tables for telling time 'and many anothir notable conclusoun after kalenders of the reverent clerkes, Frere J. Somer and Frere N. Lenne.' Both Somer and Lynn were well-known Oxford astronomers. Part IV was to explain 'the moevyng of the celestiall bodies with the causes,' especially the daily movements of the moon 'from houre to houre' in every sign according to 'thyn almenak.' This part was also to include a table explaining when the moon and any planet will arise. Skeat suggests that conclusions 44 and 45 found in some mss of Part II may have been intended for this fourth section of the treatise. Part V was to be an introduction 'after the statutes of oure doctours' in which 'a gret part of the generall rewles of theorik in astrologie' would be taught. All the tables of the treatise are to be based on the latitude of Oxford. Some critics have suggested that Chaucer completed some of the tables for Part III. Skeat 342 asserts that Parts IV and V were never written.

Why Chaucer did not finish the work has been cause for speculation, especially among scholars at the beginning of this century. Some argue that Chaucer became bored with the project; others remind us that Chaucer habitually left work unfinished. Some wonder if little Lewis died; others suggest that part of the ms has been lost. More recently some have considered whether *The Equatorie of the Planetis*, with its calendar, was to have been part of the project. Or perhaps the *Equatorie* was by someone else and pre-empted work Chaucer was planning. Many *Astrolabe* manuscripts include diagrams; one (Cambr. Dd. 3.53) has more than sixty. With two notable exceptions (Gunther 346 and Fisher 351) printed editions do not reproduce the diagrams. *The Treatise on the Astrolabe* was included in the editions of William Thynne (1532, 1542, 1551), John Stowe (1561), and Thomas Speght (1598, 1602). During the seventeenth century not only was Chaucer less read, but the astrolabe ceased to be the indispensable tool it once was for time-telling, navigation, surveying, and the calculation of planetary positions. Thus Chaucer's *Astrolabe* and his reputation as a mathematician fell into oblivion until the great revival of interest in Chaucer and philology in the latter half of the nineteenth century. Nonetheless, the treatise was included in the reissue of Speght in 1687, in John Urry's edition of 1721, and in Chalmers' edition of 1810. In 1870 A.E. Brae published the first scholarly edition of the *Astrolabe* **341**. His work remains a significant contribution and is frequently cited by subsequent scholars even though it was superseded almost immediately by Skeat's important edition of 1872 (**342**). After Skeat's edition the *Astrolabe* has been regularly printed with Chaucer's other works, although it remains the least read portion of the Chaucer canon. It would appear that scholars are more pleased with knowing that it is there than with studying it.

In the early part of the twentieth century a few scholars, however, found salient matter if not in the text itself at least in matters related to it and devoted considerable attention to the *Astrolabe* in their efforts to fill gaps in Chaucer's biography. Not only is the *Astrolabe* one of the few Chaucerian works which specifies a precise date — 'the year of oure Lord 1391, the 12 day of March at midday' — but it also is addressed to 'lyte Lowys my sone.' Just who Lewis was has raised a host of conjectures. Since there are no birth, baptismal, or death records of a Lewis Chaucer, some have thought he must be another Lewis, perhaps the son of Chaucer's friend Sir Lewis Clifford; others have argued that he is indeed Chaucer's son. This contention has raised a further controversy over the identity of Lewis' mother. Could it be Cecilia de Chaumpaigne who on May 1, 1380, released the poet from liability *de raptu meo*? (That works out just right: a child of that alleged union would be at the 'tendre age of 10 yer' in 1391, the year in which the *Astrolabe* was most likely written.) Others have held that if the child bore the name of Chaucer he must surely be the son of Chaucer's wife Philippa. Some have argued, on the other hand, that there was no real little Lewis at all, that he is simply a rhetorical device which Chaucer cleverly uses to engage his reader in an abstruse subject. (Cf Chaucer's Manciple, the poet John Gower, and the poet-counselor Henry Scogan, who all use the device 'my son' as a form of address from the instructor to his student.) 'Diverse folk diversely they demed,' Chaucer's Squire says, and so it seems, at least in this matter.

Aside from the biographical questions it raises, the *Astrolabe* has been of great interest to philologists studying Chaucer's language. Since it is more loosely related to its sources than translations like the *Tale of Melibee* or *Boece*, scholars have felt that it reveals more accurately Chaucer's native speech patterns, even though it deals with a scientific topic. Early in this century, several German philologists searched the text for examples of morphology and syntax. More recently it has enjoyed a modest prominence in stylistic studies of Chaucer's prose. Since Brae's edition, the *Astrolabe* has been used to demonstrate Chaucer's interest in astrology and to help explain the many astronomical allusions in his poetry. Some scholars have suggested that Chaucer himself was a practitioner of the art; others have drawn upon the *Astrolabe* to show that he eschewed the art, but loved the science.

In the past two decades Chaucer's treatise has begun again to figure prominently in biographical studies, not so much as a window into Chaucer's family life or intó his theories of education, but rather as an avenue toward his philosophical interests. Such discussions tend to link Chaucer to circles of academics at Oxford, especially at Merton College. Although some monumental works in the history of science were published earlier in this century, this area of research is only recently coming into its own. There tends to be a marked up-grading of Chaucer's worthiness as a scientist, especially after Derek Price's publication of the Peterhouse manuscript of *The Equatorie of the Planetis*, which mentions Chaucer in a marginal note and is most likely related to Chaucer in some way. Studies like those of Thomas Lounsbury at the end of the last century, which condescendingly exposed the inadequacies of Chaucer's mastery of the Roman classics and tended to look upon the poet as an intellectual lightweight, have been replaced by careful textual and source studies which tie Chaucer's ideas and practices to the best of those at Oxford, noting that Chaucer's errors are likely to be the errors of his historical period rather than his own stupid blunders. Occasionally essays even suggest that he corrects and moves beyond what he found in his sources.

Since the publication of the *Equatorie*, with its instructions on making such an instrument, several essays have been devoted to the making of an astrolabe, noting that Chaucer's treatise was not simply addressed to little Lewis, but to Lewis with an astrolabe suspended from his thumb. With renewed interest in Chaucer the mathematician several studies have appeared explaining medieval astronomy and emphasizing the prominence of astrological lore in many of Chaucer's writings; they also point out how exact and knowledgeable that lore is. The full range of studies of this sort may be found in Peter Brown's annotated bibliography on Chaucer and the Sciences, in a later volume of this series. I shall restrict myself here to those items which make some use of the *Astrolabe* in their analysis. Thus I do not include all discussions of astronomical imagery in Chaucer. Astrological studies which do not pertain to the *Astrolabe* will be included in volumes devoted to their particular contexts (*KnT, MilT, MLT, NPT, FrankT,*

T&C, and so on).

I have divided this bibliography into three sections: a list of editions; an alphabetical listing of discussions on or related to the *Astrolabe*; and a highly selective list of background works on medieval astronomy.

Editions of the *Treatise on the Astrolabe*

See also **4**, **10**, and **523** for Thynne's editions of the treatise.

341 Brae, Andrew Edmund, ed. *The Treatise on the Astrolabe of Geoffrey Chaucer*. London: J.R. Smith, 1870.
The text is based on three late mss in the British Library — Sloane 261, Sloane 314, and Addit. 23002. Brae also uses Thynne's printed edition, which was based on a manuscript (now lost) similar to Brae's other sources. He provides a convincing argument for the attribution of ms Sloane 261 (his basic text) to Walter Stevins (ca 1555). He calls the treatise 'the most interesting of Chaucer's works' (p 1) and links its composition to Chaucer's 'preparative study' while working on astronomical phenomena in the *Canterbury Tales*. An appendix reprints Brae's earlier essays on astronomy in the *GP*, the Parson's prologue, and on other astronomical topics like 'prime,' 'the Carrenare,' and 'shippes opposteres.'

342 Skeat, Walter W., ed. *A Treatise on the Astrolabe, addressed to his son Lowys, by Geoffrey Chaucer*. London: N. Trübner, 1872.
Skeat describes sixteen mss which he divides into two classes: 1) Cambridge Univ. Lib. Dd. 3.53 (A); Bodleian ms E Museo 54 (B); Bodleian ms Rawlinson, Misc. 1370 (C); Bodleian ms Ashmole 391 (D); ms Bodley 619 (E), which bears, like (B), the title 'Brede and Milke for childeren' and contains marginal corrections and additions in Latin from Messahala; Corpus Christi College, Cambridge, ms 424 (F); Trinity College, Cambridge, ms R. 15.18 (G); and Cambridge Univ. Lib. ms Dd. 12.51 (P). In class 2) Skeat includes BL ms Sloane 314 (H); BL ms Sloane 261 (I), which was Brae's principal text; Bodleian ms Rawlinson Misc. 3 (K); BM ms Addit. 23002 (L); St John's College, Cambridge, ms E.2 (M), containing Latin rubrics to the conclusions and several variant readings which Skeat includes in his notes; Bodleian ms Digby 72 (N); and Bodleian ms Ashmole 360 (0). To this second group Skeat adds Thynne's edition of 1532. Bodleian ms Ashmole 393 (Q) he leaves unclassified. Skeat uses Camb. Univ. Lib. ms Dd. 3.53 (A) as his copy text; the manuscript has been

'diligently "rubbed and scraped" by the hand of a corrector who well
knew what he was doing' (p viii). The ms contains over sixty
drawings, although Skeat does not reproduce them. He does, however,
include six of his own which show the parts of an astrolabe and their
movements. The unfinished condition of the treatise reflects Chaucer's
irregular habits of composition. Some sections of Part II may have
been intended for the projected Part IV, which was never written.
Skeat is the first modern commentator to stress that Messahala's
Compositio et Operatio Astrolabie, numerous copies of which were
available in medieval England, was Chaucer's principal source. He uses
Cambridge ms Ii.3.3 of Messahala for his notes and appends a portion
of the Latin text to his volume. Skeat estimates on the basis of title
headings in Part II that Messahala's treatise accounts for about
two-thirds of Chaucer's treatise. The remaining third probably comes
from some sort of 'general compendium of astronomical and
astrological knowledge' (p xxv). He notes that mss of Messahala are
not all alike and that 'it is clear that Chaucer not only took what he
liked, but rearranged his material after his own fashion' (p xxvi).
Early printed editions are full of errors and absurdities: 'After a
careful examination of the old editions, I came to the conclusion that
the less I consulted them the better' (p xxvi). He praises Brae's
edition, however, and says he would have abandoned his work when
that edition appeared, except for the fact that Brae 'expended his
labour upon very inferior materials' and is thus 'sometimes misled by
the badness of those mss to which alone he had access' (p xxvii; pp
xxvii–xxxi summarize Brae's errors). Skeat draws heavily on Brae's
introduction, however, in his summary of what light the *Astrolabe*
throws upon the interpretation of other passages in Chaucer's writings,
including the *GP, KnT, MilT, MLT, SqT, FrankT, NPT, Pars Prol,
PF* and shorter poems (twenty-nine passages in all). Skeat's text
includes a running paraphrase and commentary at the foot of the
page, twenty-seven pages of critical notes, and a glossary.

343 Skeat, Walter W., ed. *Oxford Chaucer.* 1894. See **2**. Vol 3, pp
lvii–lxxx; 175–241 + 6 plates.
This is essentially the same text and apparatus as the 1872 edition,
though it does include some corrections and silent emendations (See
442, p 246, n.4). The critical notes are somewhat shorter, however,
because of Skeat's decision not to list spelling alterations as he did in
the earlier edition. Skeat discusses eight additional mss but does not
classify them: BL ms Egerton 2622 (R); BL ms Addit. 29250 (S); ms
Phillipps 11955 at Cheltenham (T); ms Bodley 68 (U); Bodleian ms E
Museo 116 (W); and 'a ms at Brussels, no. 1591' (X). [See Pintelon
349 on this last ms.] The single volume edition (Oxford, 1894) deletes

the running commentary and most of the notes.

344 Liddell, Mark H., ed. *The Globe Chaucer.* 1898/1928. See **3**, pp liii–liv, 638–58.

Working with eighteen mss Liddell revises Skeat's classification, setting five mss apart as the more authoritative of both types and choosing as the basis for his text ms Bodley 619, which 'bears evidence of having been written by an Astronomer of Merton College' (p liii). Liddell's introduction stresses the 'ripeness of scholarship, certainty of style, clearness of judgment' of this later work by Chaucer. 'There is little of that uncertainty which characterises the *Boece*, and no infelicities of idiom or mistakes in construing the Latin' (p liii). Liddell follows Skeat in stressing the work's connection with Messahala. Chaucer 'either did not live to complete it or tired of his work and abandoned it' (p liii).

345 *The Complete Works of Geoffrey Chaucer,* with an Introduction by Thomas R. Lounsbury. 2 vols. New York: Thomas Y. Crowell, 1900. Vol 1, pp 439–64.

Includes the text of Skeat's 1872 edition, without notes or identification of editor or source.

346 Gunther, Robert William Theodore, ed. *Chaucer and Messahalla on the Astrolabe.* Vol V, *Early Science in Oxford.* Oxford: Oxford University Press, 1929, 1932.

This is the first published version of a complete text *with diagrams.* The volume includes an edited text and facsimile of Bodleian ms Ashmole 391, a modern English translation of the text, and a facsimile of Messahalla's *De Compositione Astrolabii* (Camb. Univ. Lib. ms Ii.3.3), with an English translation. Gunther collates Ii.3.3 with the late and shorter Bodleian ms Ashmole 1796 and also includes a few readings from ms Ashmole 1522. The volume contains brief prefaces on the value of Chaucer's treatise (pp v–viii) and on Messahalla (pp 133–6). Of the astrolabe itself Gunther says: 'in many of its forms the astrolabe can still claim to be one of the most valuable educational instruments. 1) It is a beautiful piece of workmanship, having a basis of beauty and order in mathematical curves. 2) It is concrete and meant to be handled. 3) It can be taken to pieces and put together again by a boy of 10, and so is superior to a watch or clock. 4) It will provide an introduction to great and worthy fields of investigation — the heavens and the earth, geography, longitude and time, latitude, etc. 5) It will serve to illustrate much of the great scientific work done by the ancients. In short, the Astrolabe contains material for an education from the nursery to the University, and Chaucer was very fully alive to its great and manifold utility' (pp v–vi).

- Review in *TLS*, March 27, 1939, p 263. Praises the work of so distinguished an authority as Gunther and applauds the great service rendered to Oxford and 'the archeology of science.'

347 Kalusa, Max. *Chaucer-Handbuch fur Studierende.* Leipzig: Bernhard Tauchnitz, 1915/1927.
Includes the Prologue to the *Astrolabe*, pp 207–8.

348 Robinson, F.N., ed. *The Works of Geoffrey Chaucer.* 1933/rev 1957. See **7**, Pp 544–63; notes, pp 867–72, 921–3.
Gives listing of twenty-five mss, twenty-two of which were described by Skeat. The three additional mss are all found in the United States and are identified as *Plimpton*, after the collector George A. Plimpton; *Penrose*, after its owner Boies Penrose of Philadelphia; and *Harvard*, after the university library where it makes its home. Derek Price examined the Penrose and Harvard mss and suggested to Robinson by letter that they perhaps represent 'a missing link between the two main groups' of mss (p 921). Robinson follows Liddell and uses Bodley 619 as his basic text which he compares throughout with Skeat's Camb. Univ. Lib. Dd. 3.53 and the Class 2 readings of Thynne and Brae.

349 Pintelon, P. *Chaucer's Treatise on the Astrolabe, MS 4862-4869 of the Royal Library in Brussels.* Rijksuniversiteit te Gent, Werken uitgegeven door de Faculteit van de Wijsbegeerte en Letteren, no. 89. Antwerp: De Sikkel; The Hague: Nijhoff, 1940.
A facsimile edition with introduction and notes. Includes a fresh description of the twenty-two mss of the *Treatise* cited in Skeat. The Brussels ms belongs to the same group as Camb. Univ. Lib. ms Dd 3.53 and Rawlinson, D.913, that is, to the group Skeat held to be the best representatives of Chaucer's original. A foreword by Prof. van Langenhove, who directed Pintelon's work as a dissertation in 1935, explains that in 1939 Pintelon was killed in an automobile crash, leaving his work unfinished: 'Hij was een fijngevoelig man. Hij leefde niet nutteloos' (p ix).

- Review by Simonne d'Ardenne, *Moyen Age*, 51 (1941), 206–9: 'La présentation de l'édition facsimilé est admirable et rendra de grands services à tout spécialiste de l'oeuvre chaucérienne' (p 207). It is 'regrettable,' however, that more attention was not given to the notes and introduction.

- Review by Simonne d'Ardenne, *English Studies*, 24 (1942), 125. 'The present edition gives the impression of something immature, a rough draft of what might otherwise have been a great book.'

350 Willoughby, E.F. *Chaucer's Treatise on the Astrolabe: MS 4862-4869 the Royal Library in Brussels.* Antwerp: De Sikkel, 1940. [Cited in Griffith. I have been unable to locate this volume or to determine its relationship to Pintelon **349** which was issued the same year by the same publisher.]

351 Fisher, John H., ed. *Complete Poetry and Prose of Chaucer.* 1977. See
11. Pp 905–34.
Text based on ms Cambridge Dd.3.53 (A), with corrections and
variants from Bodley 619 (B), Bodleian ms Rawlinson D.913 (C), and
Harvard (Z). This is the only popular edition to include illustrations:
the twenty-two figures which Fisher prints are from R.T. Gunther's
edition of Cambridge MS Dd.3.53 **346**. Fisher calls the Prologue to
the *Astrolabe* 'one of our few examples of Chaucer's free compostion in
prose. It shows that he could do better than *Boece*, but it still lacks
the assurance of his verse' (p 907). Fisher believes that the enigmatic
colophon which mentions 'N. Strode' perhaps gives us 'some clue as to
who introduced Chaucer to the mysteries of astronomy' (p 907). This
edition of Chaucer's *Works* also includes *The Equatorie of the Planetis.*

Scholarly Discussions on or Related to the
Treatise on the Astrolabe

352 Anon. 'The Astrolabe.' *Bodleian Quarterly Record*, 2 (1919), 238.
The Bodleian Library possesses two astrolabes; the one at Merton
College which dates from about 1390 must be very like that which
Chaucer gave to little Lewis.

352a Basquin, Edmond A. 'The First Technical Writer in English: Geoffrey
Chaucer.' *Technical Communications* (Third Quarter, 1981), pp 22–24.
Praises Chaucer's skills as a technical writer.

353 Bennett, J.A.W. *Chaucer at Oxford and at Cambridge.* Oxford:
Oxford University Press; Toronto: Toronto University Press, 1974.
Ch 3, 'The Men of Merton,' pp 58–85, is especially useful in defining
the context of Chaucer's interest in astronomy, its teachers and its
implements. 'One by one every astronomical trail in Chaucer leads us
to Oxford, and in Oxford to Merton' (p 75). Discusses possible links
between the *Astrolabe* and the *Equatorie* (pp 75–8). See also **464**.

- Review by Robert B. Burlin, *Queen's Quarterly*, 82 (1975), 636:
  'One would like to know much more about the climate of thought
  which encouraged the transition from "pure scholasticism to
  natural science as we understand it." Chaucer's "philosophic
  mind" was undoubtedly formed in some part by these university
  men and there is much in the shape of his thinking and imagining
  that remains historically unlocated. We will have to await many
  more editions such as Synan's Campsall before an adequate
  assessment of the "Merton mentality" in the late fourteenth

century becomes feasible.'

- Review by E. Talbot Donaldson, *MLR*, 71 (1976), 626–7: 'it should be noted ... that Bennett's chapter on the men of Merton is a superb tribute to the intellectual attainment of that college in Chaucer's day' (p 626).

- Review by Joseph E. Grennen, *Thought*, 51 (1976), 110–1: 'The chapter entitled "The Men of Merton" will in the long run probably serve Chaucerians even better than the particular annotations of the two tales, since it strongly suggests, despite Bennett's own caution, that a knowledge of the works not only of such scholars as Bradwardîne and Strode, specifically mentioned by the poet, but also of lesser known figures like Heytesbury, Dumbleton, Swineshead, and William Reed, may be a necessary part of the intellectual baggage of future critics of Chaucer' (p 111).

354 Braddy, Haldeen. 'Chaucer, Alice Perrers, and Cecily Chaumpaigne.' *Spec*, 52 (1977), 906–11.
There is some evidence that Alice Perrers' surname was 'Chawpeneys,' an anglicization of Chaumpaigne. William Chaumpaigne had one wife named Agnes and another named Alice. It is not altogether clear which wife was mother of Cecily, but probably Alice, the late spouse, was stepmother. Braddy thinks Alice, the 'often mated stepmother of Cecilia, served as the living prototype of the often married Alice of Bath' (p 910), and suspects that her son Geoffrey Perrers was fathered by the 'elvyssh' Geoffrey Chaucer, who also may have enjoyed the stepdaughter Cecily's favors at Aldgate (p 911). Little Lewis was the son of Philippa, however (p 910).

355 Brewer, Derek. *Chaucer and His World*. London: Eyre Methuen, 1978. Pp 53–63, 207–7.
In discussing Chaucer's schooling, Brewer notes the scattering of arithmetical terms throughout Chaucer's works and suggests that study might have begun for the poet at about age 10, as it did for little Lewis (p 62). 'It is mathematics, and not theology or rhetoric, that Chaucer associates with the universities ... Dozens of realistic details suggest that Chaucer knew Oxford town and its inhabitants better than Cambridge and we cannot deny him closer knowledge of the university, or at any rate of people in it' (p 206). His *Astrolabe* and his use of astronomical tables link him to Oxford, as do Ralph Strode, Walter Burley, and John Somer. Brewer notes that Somer had an astronomical calendar made for Joan of Kent, who 'does not normally figure in the history books as an intellectual, but if not she, at least her circle, which contained so many of Chaucer's friends, took an intelligent interest in astronomical matters' (p 206). [See John H.

Fisher's review, cited below under Gardner **375**.]

356 — *Chaucer in His Time.* London: Longman, 1973. Pp 139–45.
Notes that the first recorded use of the idea of 'the King's English'
occurs in Chaucer's *Astrolabe* (p 141; cf Robinson, **7**, p 868, note to
lines 56 ff). Brewer suggests that both the *Astrolabe* and *Equatorie* are
'products of the Merton school of mathematics and astronomy that
flourished especially in Oxford in the middle of the century. (In that
he wrote these works in English he is also a remarkable pioneer in his
own right.)' (p 141).

357 —, ed. *Chaucer: The Critical Heritage I: 1385–1838.* London:
Routledge and Kegan Paul, 1978. See pp 104–6, 148–9.
Walter Stevins (ca 1555) names himself in the Dedication of BL ms
Sloane 261 as the writer of this copy of Chaucer's *Astrolabe*. Brewer
includes Stevins' note 'To the reader' in which he explains how he has
corrected corruptions and false places in the text, errors doubtless
made by scribes before him, 'leauing to worthie Chawcer his due praise
for this worke.' He hopes that lovers of 'wittie Chawcer do accepte my
good will and entente' (pp 105–6). *Henry Peacham* (1622) calls
Chaucer 'an excellent Mathematician, as plainly appearth by his
discourse of the Astrolabe to his little sonne *Lewes*' (p 149).

358 Brusendorff, Aage. *The Chaucer Tradition.* 1925. See **25**.
Reiterates his theory that Cecilia Chaumpaigne was little Lewis'
mother (pp 176–77n).

358a Carter, Tom. 'Geoffry Chaucer: Amateur Astronomer?' *Sky and
Telescope*, 63 (1982), 246–47.
An active amateur astronomer, rather than merely curious about
astronomical lore, Chaucer apparently made observations on his own.
Astrolabe is a rare example of '14th-century English popular scientific
writing' (p 246), the style closely parallel to today's popular scientific
writing. The Chaucer 'signature' in the *Equatorie* may be by the poet,
in which case we have two 'amateur' Chaucerian works; or it may be
by someone else referring to the poet, in which case he was well known
as an astronomer; or it may not refer to Chaucer at all (p 247).

359 Cowling, George H. *Chaucer.* London: Methuen, 1927. Pp 22–3.
Cowling develops speculations surrounding the rape of Cecilia
Chaumpaigne (p 22–3). 'Possibly it was for her that Chaucer wrote
The Life of St. Cecile. Who shall say?' (p 24).

360 Cross, J.E. 'Teaching Method, 1391: Notes on Chaucer's Astrolabe,'
English, 10 (1955), 172–5.
Noting Chaucer's appeal in the Prologue 'to every discret persone that
redith or herith this litel tretys,' Cross stresses the lecture style of
Chaucer's prolixity, his plain language ('nakid wordes'), and compares

the familiar admonitions, reiterations, descriptive adverbs, and 'friendly consideration for his little student' to oral techniques of 'classroom teaching.' Chaucer works on the principle that 'examples teach more than precepts' (p 174).

361 Curry, Walter Clyde. 'Chaucer's Science and Art.' *Texas Review*, 8 (1923), 307–22.
Announces the need for such a work as **362** and explains what the rationale of such a work should be. 'Chaucer was himself no scientist, and since he was not interested, as a scientist, in either astrology or geomancy or alchemy or physiognomy, he cannot be praised or blamed for either knowledge or ignorance' (p 307). In his poetry he always makes 'scientific astrology a handmaiden to his literary art' (p 320).

362 — *Chaucer and the Mediaeval Sciences*. 1926/1960. See **297**.
Although Curry deals primarily with alchemy and medicine, he gives consideration throughout to astrology and reviews physiognomical and astrological treatises known in Chaucer's day. No specific discussion is devoted to Chaucer's *Astrolabe*.

363 Donaldson, E. Talbot. 'The Manuscripts of Chaucer's Works and their Use.' In *Writers and Their Background: Geoffrey Chaucer*. Ed. Derek Brewer. London: G. Bell & Sons, 1974; Athens, Ohio: Ohio University Press, 1975. Pp 85–108.
Suggests the reason so many *Astrolabe* mss survive is 'because scientific translations were not so avidly read as creative works and hence did not suffer the wear-and-tear that must have destroyed many manuscripts of Chaucer's literary productions' (pp 93–94).

364 Eade, J.C. " 'We ben to lewed or to slowe": Chaucer's Astronomy and Audience Participation.' *SAC*, 4 (1982), 53–85.
Eade examines ways in which Chaucer called upon his reader's mental agility and elementary acquaintance with astronomy to show how passages customarily regarded as 'fiercely difficult, if not impenetrable' (p 53) yield to orderly analysis once their technical apparatus has been mastered. Comments on *alnath*, the *Parson's Prologue*, and *MerchT*, but concentrates on *FrankT*, *Mars*, and *MLT*.

365 Eisner, Sigmund. 'Building Chaucer's Astrolabe,' *Journal of the British Astronomical Association*, 86 (1975), 18–29, 125–32, 219–27.
Eisner provides instructions on how to make an astrolabe so that we can respond to the subtleties of Chaucer's treatise as 'litell Lowys' might have done: 'With an astrolabe in one's hands one can perform the identical computations done by medieval astronomers, and even though they believed in a geocentric universe they were not particularly bad astronomers' (p 18). Eisner's cardboard model includes both a Julian and Gregorian calendar, a calculating device for

twelve important Chaucerian saints' days, a shadow scale, and a scale for determining the unequal hours. Includes an annotated bibliography on astrolabes (pp 226–7).

366 —— 'Chaucer's Use of Nicholas of Lynn's Calendar,' *E&S*, 29 (1976), 1–22.
Discusses what is known of Nicholas of Lynn and describes his calendar. One table unique to Nicholas enables its consultant to tell time by means of the ratio of shadows to a man six feet tall. Chaucer apparently uses this table several times in the *Canterbury Tales*. In the *Astrolabe* Chaucer indicates that he will use Lynn in Part III: but what he says he will use does *not* appear in Nicholas' calendar, which has neither stellar tables nor terrestrial longitudes.

367 —— ed. *The Kalendarium of Nicholas of Lynn*, trans. by Gary MacEoin and Sigmund Eisner. The Chaucer Library. Athens: University of Georgia Press, 1980. [See **506** on the purpose of Chaucer Library editions.]
Lynn 'flourished at Oxford in the late fourteenth century, he was a Carmelite friar, and he wrote a calendar. Beyond these bare facts we can say with some assurance that he walked in an environment conducive to his own expertise. Anything beyond these assertions is speculation' (pp 4–5). He was remembered as a mathematician and explorer by Bale, Gerardus Mercator, and Hakluyt in the Renaissance. Eisner's Introduction (pp 1–56) traces the origins of the medieval *Kalendarium*, 'which modern readers would call an almanac' (p 5), which normally included saint's days, sunrises and sunsets, twilights, new and full moons, solar and lunar eclipses, planetary information, dates of moveable feasts, 'medical information including proper times for phlebotomy or bloodletting, and astrological information pertaining to all of the above' (p 7). Lynn's calendar was composed in 1386 and dedicated to John of Gaunt. It is divided into a prologue, the months of the year, astrological tables and charts, and canons (the 'how to' section) on a dozen different topics ranging from shadow scales to eclipses, moon cycles, feasts, and medicinal matters. Eisner summarizes the tables and canons (pp 11–29) and notes Chaucer's use of the *Kalendarium* for time calculation in *MLT, NPT*, and *ParsT* (pp 29–34). Lynn's calendar survives, 'in greater or lesser completeness' (p 9), in fifteen mss (pp 34–47). Eisner's edition and translation (pp 57–223) is based on Bodleian ms Laud Misc. 662 (L), a late fourteenth century ms which includes Metonic cycles from 1387–1462. There is no specific evidence that Chaucer did not see L' (p 35).

367a —— 'Chaucer as a Technical Writer.' *ChauR*, 19 (1985), 179–201.
Chaucer's pedagogical skills shine in his technical writing as he instructs with clarity and in memorable ways. In *Astrolabe* 'Little

Lewis' serves well as 'an audience persona,' ie, 'any intelligent and uninformed person' (p 61). Eisner compares Chaucer's technical prose with Richard Wallingford's translation of the Latin *Exafrenon* (ca 1385) and anonymous translations of Nicholas Lynn and Walter Anglus (ca 1400) to illustrate Chaucer's writing genius. *Astrolabe* and *Equatorie* are similar in tone, use of metaphor, and wording. 'Although definitive proof is unavailable, the more one looks at the *Equatorie*, the more difficulty one has in challenging the view that it is Chaucer's' (p 186). Chaucer regularly explains terms, amplifies descriptions, and uses similies, vocatives, and first and second person pronouns, as other technical writers of the time rarely do. In drawing upon Messahala, 'Chaucer gently refines his source when he translates ... He translates word for word when he chooses but never hesitates to amplify or explain as that need occurs. The inescapable conclusion is that Chaucer as a translator adapts his material to a purpose that includes explication, clarity of exposition, and foremost attention to the requirements of the listener or reader' (p 198).

168 Eitle, Hermann. *Die Satzverknüpfung bei Chaucer.* Anglistische Forschungen, no. 44. Heidelberg: Carl Winter, 1914.
Eitle bases his analysis of conjunctions and grammatical problems in linking clauses mainly on the *CT* (the six-texts edition), but he does include some examples from the *Astrolabe* and *Boece* (see index). No comments on style.

69 Elliot, Ralph W.V. *Chaucer's English.* 1974. See **181**.
Ch 3, 'I Speke in Prose,' pp 132–80, includes a section (pp 132–43) on the *Astrolabe*. 'What Chaucer thought of his prose writings *qua* prose is ... difficult to determine except in the case of the *Astrolabe*. The pose of modesty and incompetence so familiar from the poems reappears ... as the self-styled "lewd compilator" whose *endityng* is *rude*, and whose English is *light*. *Lewd* Chaucer certainly was not; certainly not in 1391 or thereabouts when the astrolabe was being written at the same time as some of the *Canterbury Tales*' (p 133). *Rude* means artless, without ornament; *light* means easy, straightforward. Elliot compares an *Astrolabe* passage with its Latin source to stress the simplicity of Chaucer's vocabulary and the suppleness of his syntax. Chaucer relies heavily on recurring patterns of clauses beginning with *and, but, tho*, relative pronouns, and simple imperatives. Elliot discusses Chaucer's use of technical words which appear here for the first time in English and 'unexpectedly' in Chaucer's poems (pp 136–40).

70 Elmquist, Karl Erik. 'An Observation on Chaucer's Astolabe,' *MLN*, 56 (1941), 530–4.
Noting two instances in which Chaucer's text addresses a general

audience, Elmquist sees three possibilities of intent: 1) the work was designed for Lewis, though it was expected that others might read or hear it; 2) though originally intended for Lewis it was thought of in the end as a literary production for a wider audience; or 3) it was intended from the beginning as a literary translation similar to the *Boece*, but cast into the conventional form of a piece of private instruction.

371 Emden, A.B. *A Biographical Register of the University of Oxford to A.D. 1500.* 3 vols. Oxford: Clarendon Press, 1957.
Includes entries both for Geoffrey Chaucer and Lewis Chaucer (I, 396–7). Gives Lewis' birthdate as ca 1381. 'As Chaucer's *Astrolabie* was written 30 yrs. after his friend mag. Ralph Strode (q.v.) was fellow of Merton Coll., his son Lewis could not have been under the tutorship of Strode at Oxford; moreover, Strode died when Lewis Chaucer was about 6 yrs. of age.' Emden cites Skeat, Brusendorff, Lydgate, and Manly in discussing the Camb. Univ. Lib. ms Dd. 3.53 colophon, which cites 'N.' Strode as Lewis' Oxford tutor.

372 Farnham, W.C. 'The Dayes of the Mone.' *SP*, 20 (1923), 70–82.
The Dayes of the Mone (ms Harleian 2320), a day by day lunary of admonitions on appropriate behavior, reflects the powerful attraction astrology held for the medieval mind and bears on Chaucer's knowledge of such matters. The lunary suggests what time is good for buying and selling or for bloodletting or surgery; what sicknesses are likely or what the effects of the stars on a child born on that day might be — all with reasons (usually biblical). Farnham prints the text, but Laurel Braswell, in correspondence dated Sept. 8, 1981, notes that it is 'very bad and riddled with errors.' Braswell's edition of fifteen Middle English lunaries is forthcoming in the Middle English Text series, Heidelberg: Carl Winter. A thorough discussion of this type of work (including several texts) may be found in Max Förster, 'Vom Fortleben antiker Sammellunare im englischen und in Volkssprachen,' *Anglia*, 67 (1944), 1–171.

373 Freedman, William A. 'Geoffrey Chaucer, Technical Writer.' *Journal of the Society of Technical Writers and Publishers*, 7 (1961), 14–5.
Following Warren Deck's rules for technical writing — clarity, organization, direct instruction, proper division of presentation, analysis of audience, simplicity of style — Freedman extols Chaucer's skill as a technical writer in the *Astrolabe*. [The essay first appeared in the *General Electric Review* (July, 1955).]

374 Frieshammer, Johann. *Die sprachliche Form der chaucerschen Prosa: Ihr Verhältnis zur Reimtechnik des Dichters sowie zur Sprache der älteren londoner Urkunden.* Studien zur englischen Philologie, 42. Halle: Max Niemeyer, 1910.
Frieshammer uses eight mss of *Mel* and *ParsT*, two of *Boece* (ms

Camb. Univ. Lib. Ii.3.21 and BL ms Addit. 10340), and Skeat's edition of the *Astrolabe* as sources for his linguistic study.

375 Gardner, John. *The Life and Times of Chaucer*. New York: Knopf, 1977.

Gardner sees the *Astrolabe* as supplementary evidence that Chaucer 'probably did get at least some training at university level and became later the personal friend of several Oxford scholars' (p 88). He then toys with Skeat's suggestion that little Lewis might have been mothered by Cecily Champain, 'the baker's daughter,' but concludes that more likely the mother was Philippa, since Lewis grew up with Chaucer's name. It was not unusual in families like Chaucer's to start the advanced education of the child early; possibly Chaucer may also have written a work on the *Sphere* for Lewis as an introduction to the *Astrolabe*. Clearly, Chaucer was 'ambitious for his children' (p 271).

- Review by John H. Fisher, *SAC*, 1 (1979), 170–7, along with a review of Brewer's *Chaucer and His World* 355: 'Neither author does justice to the learned side of Chaucer's personality, evidenced in the translation of Boethius and the astronomical treatise(s)' (p 173).

376 Garrod, H.W. 'New Life Records of Chaucer.' *TLS*, October 11, 1928, p 736.

Strode the poet and Ralph Strode were 'two distinct persons.' Nor was Ralph Strode a Merton fellow, though the 'N. Strode' of the Cambridge ms colophon probably was. Perhaps Thomas Chaucer's interest in Merton is related to Lewis' having been there. A long tradition calls the astrolabe in the Merton College Library Chaucer's.

377 Goldschmidt, Ernst Philip. *Medieval Texts and their First Appearance in Print*. Supplement to the Bibliographical Society's Transactions, no. 16. London, 1943.

Mentions the difficulty of forming opinions on the interdependence of European treatises on the astrolabe. 'When I was confronted with the four Western texts side by side [Chaucer, Robertus Anglicus, Andalo di Negro, Prophacius Hebraeus] it proved impossible to determine their relationship to each other without referring to the Arabic prototypes ... Neither Messahallah's nor Al Zarquali's texts are printed in Arabic at all' (p 120). See pp 24–7 on first printed editions of Boethius.

378 Grimm, Florence M. *Astronomical Lore in Chaucer*. University of Nebraska Studies in Language, Literature, and Criticism, no. 2. Lincoln, 1919. Rpt New York: AMS Press, 1970.

Grimm treats medieval astronomy and Chaucer's knowledge of it in general terms. Ch 1, 'Astronomy in the Middle Ages,' pp 3–9, is a cursory review of the history of the Ptolemaic system. Ch 2,

'Chaucer's Scientific Knowledge,' pp 9–12, notes that Chaucer displays detailed knowledge of astronomical lore in *Astrolabe*. Ch 3, 'Chaucer's Cosmology,' pp 12–27, classifies astronomical lore in Chaucer according to references to the celestial spheres, their harmony, the cardinal points and regions of the world, heaven-hell-purgatory, and the four elements. Ch 4, 'Chaucer's Astronomy,' pp 27–51, catalogues Chaucerian references to the sun, moon, planets, and galaxy. Ch 5, 'Astrological Lore in Chaucer,' pp 51–78, mentions several astrological references in *CT* and *Scogan*, but finds Chaucer less systematic than Milton or Dante in his use of astrology. 'Chaucer's attitude toward the philosophical aspects of astrology is hard to determine because in most of his poems he takes an impersonal ironic point of view towards the actions he describes or the ideas he presents ... But one is tempted to think that he, like Dante, thought of the heavenly bodies in their spheres as the ministers and instruments of a Providence that had forseen and ordained all things' (p 78).

- Review by Howard Rollin Patch, *MLN*, 35 (1920), 128. Written as a convenient manual for the beginning Chaucerian, much of Grimm's material is no more than résumé of scholarly opinion or a collection of Chaucer's own allusions. More attention should have been given to Chaucer's immediate predecessors. Patch objects to Grimm's speaking of the period as 'the long dark centuries of the Middle Ages,' to suggest that there may have been more light than Grimm has seen.

379 Hammond, Eleanor Prescott. *Bibliographical Manual*. 1908. See 36. Lists the eighteen mss first described by Skeat, the printed editions (Thynne, Stow, Speght, Urry, Chalmers, Brae, Skeat, and Liddell), and discusses various titles bestowed upon the treatise in the manuscripts, its authenticity, its sources, and its date (pp 359–60).

380 Harvey, S.W. 'Chaucer's Debt to Sacrobosco.' *JEGP*, 34 (1935), 34–8. Chaucer's treatise is compiled from several sources: Messahala's *Compositio et Operatio Astrolabii* furnishes only the framework, not about two-thirds of the treatise as Robinson 348 claims. Chaucer often combines material from both Messahala and Sacrobosco. He uses Messahala for headings to the conclusions in Part II, which makes that source seem more prominent than it is. Analysis of one section shows that seven lines derive from Messahala, thirty-nine from Sacrobosco, with nineteen probably Chaucer's own (p 36). The comparisons give 'a clear idea of the method used by Chaucer in combining his borrowings from Sacrobosco with the outline he drew from Messahalla. They likewise indicate the extent of his debt to Sacrobosco. Yet their greatest interest is the proof they furnish that Chaucer carried over into his scientific prose writings the same methods he employed in his

best poetical work. He was capable of seeing things in splendid perspective, as became a great artist, and also of unerringly selecting the essentials from a mass of detail, as became a true scientist' (p 38).

81 Hodgson, Phyllis. *Chaucer: The Franklin's Tale.* London: Athlone, 1960.
Appendix IV: 'Astronomy, Astrology, and Magic,' pp 125–36, discusses the structure of the universe, motions of heavenly bodies, measurements of their positions, judicial astrology, and magic. 'Chaucer's lucid and precise statements in *The Astrolabe* and probably in *The Equatorie of the Planetis* leave no doubt of his own mastery of astronomy and astrology' (p 135).

82 Houseman, Percy A. 'Science in Chaucer.' *Scientific Monthly*, 38 (June 1934), 561–4.
Houseman laments the neglect of Chaucer in modern times but admits that some of his themes are 'unseemly, judged by the standards of good taste of today' (p 561). But his 'Rabelaisian robustness is properly balanced by the truly religious spirit in which he often writes, and by the catholicity of his vision. In his love of everything in the world — the rocks, the trees, the sunrise and the common man — he stands second to none' (p 561). Although the *Astrolabe* is unfinished it provides 'an elaborate description of a very intricate instrument and its astronomical uses ... That Chaucer's ten-year-old son, for whose edification the work was intended, could ever have comprehended a single word of it, is past belief' (p 562).

83 Hulbert, James R. 'Chaucer's Romance Vocabulary.' *PQ*, 26 (1947), 302–6.
Hulbert feels that 'the technical vocabulary of the *Treatise on the Astrolabe* and the *Canon Yeoman's Tale* should be omitted' from linguistic studies like that of Joseph Mersand 51 on the introduction of romance vocabulary into English 'because we have little or no earlier writing on such subject matter. English alchemists and astronomers must have used such terms well before their appearance in Chaucer's books. Moreover, they are not part of a general literary vocabulary' (p 304). Hulbert concludes, in opposition to Mersand: 'Chaucer did not introduce into English any considerable number of French or Latin words not in use in the London speech of his time' (p 306).

84 Hussey, S.S. 'The Minor Poems and the Prose.' 1970. See 42.
Discusses the astrolabe and briefly outlines the origin of such treatises as Chaucer's *Astrolabe* and the *Equatorie* (pp 250–3). Stresses the charm and clarity of Chaucer's prologue and the 'occasional direct intervention of the teacher' (p 251). 'It is not fanciful to imagine that a small portable model [of an astrolabe] gave intense pleasure to the

little boy, about whom we know nothing certain' (p 252). The spelling
and phonology of *Astrolabe* are remarkably consistent.

385 Jambeck, Thomas J. and Karen K. Jambeck. 'Chaucer's Treatise on
the Astrolabe: A Handbook for the Medieval Child.' In *Children's
Literature: The Great Excluded.* Ed. Francelia Butler and Bennett A.
Brockman. Journal of the Modern Language Association Seminar on
Children's Literature and the Children's Literature Association, no.
III. Storrs, Connecticut: [np], 1974. Pp 116–22.
Traditionally, social historians have rejected the notion that there
existed in the Middle Ages a concept of the child or a concomitant
theory of his education (eg, Philippe Aries, *Centuries of Childhood*).
Chaucer's treatise proves the contrary. The Jambecks discuss
Chaucer's methods of making an abstruse subject manageable. They
compare Chaucer's vocabulary with Messahala's to show how
painstakingly Chaucer avoids easy Latinate cognates (eg, *semicirculos*
— 'halve circles'; *considerare* — 'loke; *solsticium hyemale* — 'the
lowest point where the sonne goth in wynter'). 'Lewis' native
experience controls Chaucer's exposition; the father domesticates the
fussy erudition of the expert to the child's homelier vocabulary' (pp
118). Chaucer syntax is relatively simple: at the center of his technique
is 'the abiding principle that the child, however untutored, is able to
grasp the most elusive abstraction if it is assimilated to the constructs
of his own experience' (p 121). Though the treatise has been called
'bred and Mylk for Childeren,' it 'can hardly be characterized as a sop
to a childish whim, for there is no stooping to demeaning play' (p
122). The *Astrolabe* confirms the popular assessment of a 'learned
Chaucer' by its scientific content; but 'the measure of Chaucer's
seriousness can be taken more clearly from his keen interest in his
pupil's cognitive ability which, in turn, informs the treatise with a
conception of the child striking in its modernity' (p 122).

386 Karpf, Fritz. *Studien zur Syntax in den Werken Geoffrey Chaucers.*
Wiener Beiträge zur Englischen Philologie, no. 55. Wien und Leipzig:
Wilhelm Braumüller, 1930.
Uses *Astrolabe* to exemplify Chaucer's prose syntax.

387 Karpinski, L.C. 'Augrim-Stones.' *MLN*, 27 (1912), 206–9.
In glossing *MilT* A.3210, Karpinski notes that in the *Astrolabe*
Chaucer refers to an arithmetical counter similar to the abacus which
uses stones as markers. The word *augrim* is probably related to
algorism.

388 Kean, Patricia Margaret. *Chaucer and the Making of English Poetry.*
1972. See **190**.
Uses *Astrolabe* to support an astrological reading in *T&C* (pp 166–8).

89 Kittredge, George Lyman. 'Lewis Chaucer or Lewis Clifford.' *MP*, 14 (1917), 513–8.
Challenges Moore's spreading the composition of *Astrolabe* from 1387–92 (402). A few months is enough time to compose so short a treatise; 1391 accordingly is the date. Sir Lewis Clifford's son Lewis died in October of that year. 'We may conjecuture ... that it was the sudden death of Lewis Clifford the younger that made Chaucer drop his pen in the middle of a sentence when the *Astrolabe* was still far from completion' (p 514). Kittredge discusses the friendship of Chaucer and Sir Lewis Clifford, noting that Sir Philip la Vache was Clifford's son-in-law. The phrase 'my son' was a term of endearment common in courtly literature (cf numerous instances in courtesy books, John Russell's *Book of Nurture*, Gower's *Confessio Amantis*, and Henry Scogan's moral balade addressed to Prince Hal and his brothers who are referred to as 'my noble sons'). The age of young Lewis is not known. He could have been born any time between 1373 and 1387.

90 Koeppel, Emil. 'Chauceriana.' *Anglia*, 14 (1892), 227–33.
Suggests that Chaucer did penance for his rape of Cecilia Chaumpaigne, from whence sprang little Lewis, by writing 'The Lyf of S. Cecile' (p 233).

91 Kohl, Stephan. *Wissenschaft und Dictung bei Chaucer: Dargestellt hauptsächlich am Beispiel der Medizin.* Frankfurt am Main: Akademische Verlagsgesellschaft, 1973.
Part I, pp 13–188, considers Chaucer's knowledge of medicine and alchemy in his presentation of *CYT* and *PhysT*; of astrological medicine and dream theory in Pertelote and Pandarus' medical analyses of dreams; and of astrology and horoscopes in *MilT* and *FrankT*. Pp 184–8 are devoted to *Astrolabe* and its evidence of Chaucer's knowledge of the science but disbelief in the art. Part II considers Chaucer's poetical uses of science in his early dream visions (pp 189–217); love-sickness, its treatment and moral dimensions in *T&C* and *KnT* (pp 218–308); and Chaucer's use of physiological material in the moral realism of his portraits in *GP* and in further characterization of the Monk, Prioress, Pardoner, and Friar within the framework of the tales, and also in his portrayal of Malyn, Alisoun, and Thopas within the tales (pp 309–84). Some attention is given to Chaucer's portraits in light of *Porträttradition* (pp 371–7). Bibliography, pp 385–401.

92 Kunitzsch, Paul. *Typen von Sternverzeichnissen in astronomischen Handschriften des zehnten bis vierzehnten Jahrhunderts.* Wiesbaden: Otto Harrasowitz, 1966.
Distinguishes seventeen types of star lists from Western Europe from the tenth to fifteenth centuries and classifies them in two groups

according to whether they were directly or indirectly translated from Arabic. Kunitzsch attributes the type of list which usually accompanies 'Messahalla' to Maslama, a near contemporary of the ninth century. The Arabic sources for all lists derive from Spain. Kunitzsch traces one list from Lupitus of Barcelona (tenth century) to Hermannus Contractus (*De utilitatibus Astrolabii*) from whence it was widely disseminated into such works on the astrolabe as those by Ascelinus of Laon (early eleventh century), Adelard of Bath (mid-twelfth century), John Sacrobosco (thirteenth century). Another hybrid type accompanying Pseudo-Messahalla spreads into every corner of Europe from the thirteenth century on. The list of seventy-two stars accompanying one copy of Chaucer's *Astrolabe* is such a hybrid. The lists have marginal value in establishing dates for the composition of some astrolabe treatises.

- Review by Patrick McGurk, *MAE*, 37 (1968), 233–4: appends and classifies (according to Kunitzsch's scheme) star lists in eleven additional manuscripts. 'A most useful book: one day the convolutions of fifteenth- and sixteenth-century star lists will be unravelled' (p 234).

- Review by David Pingree, *Spec*, 42 (1967), 742–3: notes that Kunitzsch's title is misleading, that several of his mss are fifteenth-century and that the last catalogue he uses is dated ca 1430. Pingree notes that all the catalogues are 'intended for the makers and users of astrolabes or quadrants ... which severely limits the number of stars that can be usefully included' (p 742). The shortest of Kunitzsch's lists is seventeen stars; the longest, seventy-two. The average is thirty-four.

393 Langhans, Victor. 'Die Datierung der Prosastücke Chaucers.' *Anglia*, 53 (1929), 235.
Argues for 1391 as the date of the *Astrolabe's* composition. See **389**.

394 Lipson, Carol. ' "I N'am But a Lewd Compilator": Chaucer's "Treatise on the Astrolabe" as Translation.' *NM*, 84 (1983), 192–200. Lipson examines the relationship between Chaucer's 'Treatise' and Messahala's instructions for the use of the instrument in order to determine whether or not Chaucer has merely translated Messahala as many scholars have noted (see, for example, the notes of Robinson's edition **7**). While Messahala assumed the reader's familiarity with scientific terms, Chaucer is careful to provide 'clear and simple definitions,' as well as 'visual clues as to size, shape, appearance, or function' of parts of the instrument (p 195). Chaucer also added a lengthy discussion of the relation of the astrolabe to astrology. 'None of this was in Messahala' (p 196). Of the twenty-one sections in Chaucer's description, only two (sections 4 and 18) 'have any real similarity to the Messahala piece in wording and detail.' Lipson points out that in 1935 S.W. Harvey 380 suggested that Chaucer actually depended upon Sacrobosco and drew very little from Messahala. But in truth *Astrolabe* is not a translation of either source. 'Of the three sections Chaucer completed, none of the preface, virtually none of the description, and about one fifth of the instructions section can be said to translate Messahala. Only isolated sections translate Sacrobosco's work, and in these Chaucer generally weaves the fragments into a new whole. Mainly the treatise is Chaucer's prose handling, and the success or failure of the prose construction rests with Chaucer and not with the sources' (p 199).

5 Loomis, Dorothy Bethurum. 'Constance and the Stars.' In *Chaucerian Problems and Perspectives: Essays Presented to Paul E. Beichner*. Ed. Edward Vasta and Zacharias P. Thundy. Notre Dame: Notre Dame University Press, 1979. Pp 207–20.
Loomis argues that the Tale of Constance offered Chaucer 'the perfect opportunity to set forth and justify his belief in astrology' (p 207). The intricate astrological references in *MLT* reflect Chaucer's interests, not 'the lawyer's misunderstanding of destinal forces' (p 207). 'There can be no doubt about Chaucer's interest in astrology, nor of his competence as an astronomer. *The Astrolabe* may have been child's play to a fourteenth-century man of scientific interest ... but it was still being praised by Gabriel Harvey in the sixteenth century and by Thomas Hearne in the eighteenth for its accuracy. And it has been called ... "the earliest first-class scientific work in our language" ... If indeed Chaucer was the author of *The Equatorie of the Planetis* ... he appears there not as a casual amateur but as a serious student of astronomy' (p 209). Chaucer had access to William Rede's gift of scientific books to Merton where he might have studied the Neoplatonic astronomy cultivated at Chartres and the writings of Grosseteste and Aquinas, as well as commentaries on Boethius. He does not always agree with accepted views but in his disagreement he writes 'as an astronomer and not as a philosopher' (p 217). *MLT* does not indicate any 'scepticism about astrology on Chaucer's part. What it does show ... is that God is lord of the heavens and can miraculously intervene to prevent the direst effects of astral influences' (p 217).

McFarlane, K.B. *Lancastrian Kings and Lollard Knights*. 1972. See 566. Pp 139–85, 207–11.
Discusses Sir Lewis Clifford at length. Imagines his son to be 'little Lewis' (p 183).

Madeleva, Sister M. *A Lost Language and Other Essays on Chaucer*. New York: Russell and Russell, 1951.

Ch 14, 'A Child's Book of Stars,' pp 81–100, includes a text of the prologue and an enthusiastic appraisal of the treatise and the circumstances of its composition. 'Of all facts and conjectures upon the domestic life of Chaucer, these are among the happiest' (p 89). 'One is thoroughly ready to study stars on such an invitation as: "Yf thou wilt pleye this craft with the arisyng of the mone, loke thow rekne wel hir cours houre by houre." This is a very pattern of a "compleat angler" in the deep pools of the sky, a fourteenth century Walton of the stars' (p 91). 'Nowhere does the *Astrolabe* suffer the constraints of a literal translation; nowhere does it betray the Latinity of its origin. Occasionally through the easy, facile flow of the teacher's exposition thrills the quiet beauty of the poet's prose' (p 98).

398 Manly, John M. 'Litel Lewis My Sone.' *TLS*, June 7, 1928, p 430. Historical records relating to Carmarthen Castle (Wales) mention a Lewis Chaucer along with Thomas Chaucer. The documents are important in that 1) they establish 'the reality of a Lewis Chaucer'; 2) they show him in close association with Thomas and in a junior position. 3) Because of the office assigned Thomas it is likely that he is the poet's son; 4) this Thomas, like Geoffrey Chaucer, was active in the Bridgewater district; 5) since Lewis was not a common name, perhaps Chaucer's son was godson of Sir Lewis Clifford, 'soldier and statesman who certainly brought to the poet from France poems from Eustace Deschamps' (p 430). Manly theorizes that Lewis may have been killed in the Welsh campaign immortalized by Shakespeare.

399 Manzalaoui, Mahmoud. 'Chaucer and Science.' 1974. See 200. Medieval science covers three types of disciplines: the empirical and useful; pseudo-scientific physiognomy, dream lore and judicial astrology; and the occult and geomancy. Chaucer was interested in all three types, but especially the empirical. 'It is a measure of Chaucer's interest in astronomy that he should have produced a simple exemplar of the scientific treatise, in a language which a young boy could follow. It is nonetheless an unexpected use of his talents' (p 233). Manzalaoui notes the 'homely vigour' of passages like I.19, 1–5, which compare the 'kervyng overthwart the almykanteras' to the crooked 'clawes' of a spider or a 'wommans calle' (hairnet). He notes that in his abjuration of judicial astrology in the *Astrolabe* Chaucer seems to have in mind distinctions between types of medieval science, although in his poetry such distinctions are deliberately blurred. Manzalaoui takes to task critics who try to do too much with Chaucer's astronomical allusions: Wood 442 is too much 'a Robertsonian'; North's datings (406) 'are distinctly unconvincing' (p 242). 'In Chaucer studies, one man's ingenuity is another man's dottiness' (p 243).

400 Masi, Michael. 'Chaucer, Messahala, and Bodleian Selden Supra 78.'

Manuscripta, 19 (1975), 36–47.
Masi suggests that Selden Supra 78, which came to England from
Spain in the mid-fourteenth century, may have been a principal source
for Chaucer's astronomical work(s). It contains 1) *Centum Verba
Ptolemi*, with commentary by Hali; 2) Alabicius, *Introductorius ad
Iudicia Astrologiae*, tr. Johannes Hispalensis; 3) Messahala, *De
Compositione et Utilitate Astrolabii*; 4) *Tractatus de Sphera Solida et
de Astrolabio Spherico*; 5) *Canones Azarchelis sive Regule super
Tabulas Astronomie*, tr. Gerardus Cremonensis (1303); 6) *Theorica
Planetarum*, usually ascribed to Gerardus Cremonensis; 7) *Tabulae
Teletanae*, with one table for the latitude of Cremona. Masi has
examined films of 180 Messahala mss. There are important differences
between Chaucer's *Astrolabe* and its source: Unlike Messahala, which
tells how to construct an astrolabe, Chaucer's Part I restricts itself 'to
a mere description of a constructed instrument with an account of its
parts and how they function. This material appears to be written by a
person well-acquainted with the instrument's use and seems to owe
little to textual sources, either Messahala's or any other known treatise
on the astrolabe. It is in Part II of the treatise that close kinship is
obvious. Chaucer lists forty operations or "conclusiouns" that may be
performed with the astrolabe. Of these, all but ten are taken from the
treatise of Messahala' (p 40). The order varies in Messahala mss
though most follow that found in Gunther's edition (Cambridge ms
Ii.3.3). In none of the mss does the sequence of operations coincide
precisely with Chaucer's. 'We may assume that the present order of
operations in ... Chaucer's treatise represents Chaucer's own
arrangement of the material' (p 41). Even when translating, Chaucer
deletes or adds varying amounts of material. 'The only explanation is
that ... Chaucer himself ... understood the operation of the
instrument and was capable of making additional comments on its use'
(p 41). Two interpolations in Chaucer's text correspond to a gloss
unique to this ms and suggest that he worked with this precise source,
though he probably worked with others as well. Masi cites Kunitzsch's
idea that Messahala may not in fact be the original author, but also
notes a difficulty in that argument (p 51 [see 392]).

401 Metlitzki, Dorothee. *The Matter of Araby in Medieval England.* New
Haven: Yale University Press, 1977.
'Chaucer's Scientific Imagery,' pp 73–92, stresses the precision and
detail of Chaucer's scientific imagery which 'can only be probed within
the rigorous frame work of Arabic learning' (p 74). Metlitzki
emphasizes that the *Astrolabe* is a compilation, not a translation. 'It is
likely that Chaucer, with his special relationship to the kingdom of
Leon and Castile through the wife of John of Gaunt, was acquainted

with the astronomical writings of the famous Alfonso X, with whom he shared so absorbing an interest' (p 77).

- Review by Charles Burnett, *RES*, 29 (1978), 332–3: remarks upon the large number of Arabic translations found almost exclusively in England. 'Many of the Arabic translations become the *koine* of Medieval European science, and as they worked themselves into the general scientific diet of the medieval scholar it is perhaps no longer meaningful to call them "Arabic" ... Latin Averroists and Avicennists were no more "Arabic" than Marxists are "German" ' (p 333).

- Review by John H. Fisher, *JEGP*, 76 (1977), 539–41: 'The sketches of the contributions of Walcher, prior of Malvern, Adelard of Bath, Robert of Keton, Daniel of Morley, Roger of Hereford, Alfred the Englishman, Roger Bacon, and Michael Scot in transmuting Arabic documents into Latin (so often with the assistance of Mozarabic translators), are extremely well done' (p 540).

- Review by Russell A. Peck, *Criticism*, 20 (1978), 68–70: affirms as plausible Metlitzki's speculation that Chaucer's trip to Spain in 1366 may have enabled him to gather material of the kind that went into his *Astrolabe*. 'It *may be* that Chaucer had been involved with study at Oxford during the four or five years prior to 1366 [the so-called blank years in the Life Records] and that his reasons for the trip to Spain were more academic than courtly, though under the auspices of the court' (p 69).

402 Moore, Samuel. 'On the Date of Chaucer's Astrolabe.' *MP*, 10 (1912), 203–5.
The reference to March 12, 1391, is 1392 by our reckoning. But the treatise was not composed all at once. Lynne's calendar was composed in 1386; thus we may accept 1387 as a reliable *terminus a quo* for the prologue and Part I. Part II was probably written in 1392. See Kittredge's objection **389**.

403 Mori, Yoshinobu. 'Chaucer to Tenmon Senseijutsu.' *Eig*, 120 (1974), 261–2, 324–5, 373–5. [Notes on Chaucer and astrology.]

404 Nagucka, Ruta. *The Syntactic Component of Chaucer's 'Astrolabe.'* Zeszyty Naukowe Uniwersytetu Jagiellońskiego, 199 (Kraków), Prace Językoznawcze Zeszyt, 23. Cracow: University Jagielloniensis, 1968. An empirical test of Chomsky's theory of syntax applied to a historical text. Nagucka chooses the *Astrolabe* for analysis because it is 'the most independent of Chaucer's prose works in the sense that it does not follow any known foreign sources' and because it is 'composed in simple language' (pp 10–1). Naguska analyzes basic sentences, grammatical transformations, and morphological processes. Argues against such assertions that the language of Middle English is full of confusion, blendings, anomalous and antigrammatical constructions; such criticisms are 'limited to surface structure.' 'The word order of the ME sentence, which has attracted a great deal of attention, does not, if analysed against the background of a deep structure, seem so free and flexible as some traditional linguists claim. That on the surface there are certain word organizations which show that an extensive reordering is permissible does not mean that a sentence has not an inherent and grammatically restricted structure' (pp 111–2).

405 North, John D. 'The Astrolabe.' *Scientific American*, 230 (January, 1974), 96–106.
Identifies the parts of an astrolabe and shows with stereographic diagrams how it works. Includes excellent color pictures of a twelfth-century Persian astrolabe, a thirteenth-century Moorish astrolabe (front & back), and seventeenth-century Spanish mariner's astrolabe. Discusses the history and use of the instrument: its main use is to tell time, but it can tell several kinds — sidereal time, solar time, the unequal hours — and can also be used for casting horoscopes, calculating heights of mountains and depths of wells, navigating, and surveying in general. 'Like a modern electronic computer, the astrolabe of the Middle Ages was a source of astonishment and amusement, of annoyance and incomprehension. Imprecise as the astrolabe may have been in practice, it was undoubtedly useful ... The instrument might have been used, more often than not, in the dark, but "dark" is hardly the word to describe the age in which it was so widely known and so well understood' (p 106).

406 — 'Kalenderes Enlumyned Ben They.' *RES*, 20 (1969), 129–54, 257–83, 418–44.
'None appears to have realized fully the extent to which astronomical and astrological thought penetrate Chaucer's work ... By simple astronomical means, upward of twenty more or less precise dates can be deduced from a dozen of Chaucer's works' (p 129). 'Chaucer gave two methods of computing the houses in his *Treatise on the Astrolabe*, which should at least have convinced some of his commentators that the task was not to be entered upon lightly' (p 135). North refutes the theory that Ralph Strode of Merton College was tutor to Chaucer's 'son' Lewis in 1391; Strode was dead by 1387 [see **371**]. The Cambridge ms Dd. 3.53 colophon which mentions 'N. Strode' as Lewis' tutor must be inaccurate: 'Since "N" is an easy mistake for "R" in reading a fourteenth- or fifteenth-century hand, the fact that no Oxford Strode with the initial "N" has turned up in records should not be the cause of dismay. It should rather be taken as a second reason

for the rejection of the evidence of the Cambridge colophon' (p 134n).
North notes that Chaucer probably worked from Nicholas Lynne's
tables (p 423). 'Chaucer was very familiar with the astrolabe. He
knew rather better than most of his latter-day commentators how to
determine the point of the compass at which a planet sets on the
western horizon' (p 270). His calculations in the poems are often very
precise. Chaucer was 'at first imbued with a deep sense of the
plausibility of astrology' (p 442) which later faded. North notes an
absence of Chaucerian astronomy after 1393–4. Perhaps the reason is
the growing disillusionment with judicial astrology which Chaucer
mentions in the *Astrolabe* (p 437). All of Chaucer's calculations are
from the first half of the year, which may reflect Chaucer's use of
Ovid's *Fasti*, of which only the first six books (Jan. 1 — June 30) have
survived. The *Astrolabe* was apparently part of a greater project,
which, if completed, would have taken many years (pp 432–3).

407 — 'Kalenderes Enlymyned Ben They': Some Astronomical Themes in
Chaucer. Oxford: Museum of the History of Science, 1969.
Publication in a single volume of the three parts first published in *RES*
406.

- Anon. Review in *TLS*, Oct. 20, 1970, p 1140: praises North's
  essay. 'Chaucer, rejoicing in a Nabokovian ingenuity, played in his
  poems some remarkable games that he could hardly have
  expected his audience to appreciate, though analogous with the
  extraordinary numerological patterns of other medieval and
  Renaissance poetry.'

- Review by A.J. Meadows, *JHA*, 2 (1971), 45: 'The main interest
  in these papers ... is perhaps less in questions of dating, than in
  the allegorical interpretations, which are generally very
  convincing ... The investigations as a whole have the orderly
  development (and the fascination) of a scholarly detective story.'
  See also **399** and **427**.

408 Ovitt, George J. 'A Late Medieval Technical Directive: Chaucer's
Treatise on the Astrolabe.' In *Proceedings: 28th International
Technical Communication Conference of the Society for Technical
Communication*, E78–E81, May 20–3, 1981. Pittsburg, Pennsylvania.
[I have not seen this item.]

409 Owen, Charles, Jr. 'A Certein Nombre of Conclusions: The Nature
and Nurture of Children of Chaucer.' *ChauR*, 16 (1981), 60–75.
Although a portion of the title of Owen's essay derives from *Astrolabe*
mss, the content of the essay does not.

410 Parr, Johnstone, and Nancy Ann Holt. 'The Astronomy-Astrology in
Chaucer's *Complaint of Mars*.' *ChauR*, 15 (1981), 255–66.

Neugebauer's *Tafeln (1914)*, now computerized, is applied to astronomical positionings in *Mars* to conclude that 'if the poem is analyzed and annotated correctly, Chaucer reflected with considerable accuracy the actual transits of the planets between February 14 and early May (or possible September) of 1385' (p 263). The phrase *voide cours* and Mercury's *chevache* are explained. 'Being as aware of and as knowledgeable about astrology as Chaucer was, he could easily have heard or read of the advent of the exact conjunction of Venus and Mars in mid-March 1385 in advance of the time the conjunction took place — especially if the astrologers of the day made any unusual predictions' (p 263). We do not know exactly which tables were used by John Somer or Nicholas Lynne, the astronomer Chaucer mentions in *Astrolabe*.

411 Peavler, James Martin. *Chaucer's 'Natural' Astronomy.* University of Missouri dissertation, 1971. Dir. George Pace.
A short dissertation (111 pages) which speaks in general terms about astronomical references in Chaucer's works. Ch 1, *'Introduction,'* commonplace knowledge of astronomy in Chaucer's time; Ch 2, *'Chaucer's Astronomy I,'* distinctions between natural and judicial astronomy; Ch 3, *'Chaucer's Astronomy II,'* on planets and astrological influences; Ch 4, *'Astronomical time in Chaucer,'* how Chaucer used stars to tell time; Ch 5, *'Conclusion.'* There is little to show that Chaucer was an original thinker on astronomical matters, but much to show that he became an expert on the astronomical knowledge of his time. Peavler uses the *Astrolabe* frequently to support his points and finds it especially useful in establishing Chaucer's definitions of terms like 'natural' and 'artificial' day, 'conclusion,' 'tortuous,' 'roote,' 'center,' 'constellation,' 'face,' 'mansion,' 'zodiac,' 'signs,' 'arc of day,' 'celestial equator,' 'ecliptic,' 'tropic,' 'zenith,' 'horizon,' and 'meridion.'

412 Plimpton, George A. *The Education of Chaucer, Illustrated from the Schoolbooks in Use in his Time.* London: Oxford University Press, 1935.
Ch 4, pp 126–34, is devoted to scientific texts which Plimpton had in his personal ms collection, which included Chaucer's *Astrolabe* (see Robinson 7). Plimpton prints photographic plates of interesting pages in his collection, such as a thirteenth-century ms page of Boethius' *Arthmetica*, a page from Walter Burley's translation of Aristotle's *Nichomachian Ethics* (1391) with a portrait of Aristotle in the initial, a tower of knowledge from the *Margarita Philosophica* showing the stages of medieval education, and pages from treatises on astronomy including one from Chaucer's *Astrolabe*. See also pp 93–114, on higher education.

413 Price, Derek J. 'Chaucer's Astronomy.' *Nature*, 170 (1952), 474–5.

Refers to Chaucer's *Astrolabe* as 'still to-day the best work in the English language on this extremely important medieval instrument which served both for observation and as an ingenious calculator for determining the positions of the stars at any time' (p 474). Argues that the newly discovered '*Equatorie of the Planetis*, together with its accompanying sets of astronomical tables, goes far to providing those missing sections' of the *Astrolabe* (p 474). Price suggests that Chaucer first wrote a set of tables and his projected outline, then modified his plan as the work proceeded. He then abandoned the project because it ultimately became too complex.

414 — 'The Equatorie of the Planetis – I.' *TLS*, Feb. 29, 1952, p 164. The *Astrolabe* 'stands out most significantly as proof of a singular interest in that science for which fourteenth-century England had become pre-eminent through the efforts of the "Merton School" of astronomer-physicians.' With the discovery of the *Equatorie*, the *Astrolabe* is no longer alone. The *Equatorie* was written at the close of 1392, immediately subsequent to the *Astrolabe*. 'The close relationship of this text to the "Astrolabe" is confirmed by a general similarity in style, treatment, and terminology.' Both works contain an unusual style of dating. 'It must be sadly admitted that the brilliant son, godson, or literary invention, "litel Lowis" of the work on the astrolabe does not appear in the Peterhouse manuscript. Perhaps the author may have intended to write him into a finished version.' (See **473**)

415 — 'The Equatorie of the Planetis – II.' *TLS*, Mar. 7, 1942, p 180. A continuation of Price's Feb. 29 announcement of the discovery of the *Equatorie* ms. Like the *Astrolabe*, the *Equatorie* draws upon Messahallah. See **474**.

416 Prins, A.A. 'The Dating of the Canterbury Tales.' In *Chaucer and Middle English Studies in Honour of Rossell Hope Robbins*. Ed. Beryl Rowland. Kent, Ohio: Kent State University Press, 1974; London: Allen & Unwin, 1974. Pp 342-7.
Discusses the problem of reconciling astronomical dates of the *GP* and the Intro. to *MLT*. There need be no inconsistency if it is assumed Chaucer does not refer to the zodiacal sign but to the constellations of fixed stars. 'Formerly astrologers always took the influence of the larger fixed stars into account and they were perfectly familiar with the differences between the two zodiacs and the precession of the equinoxes. Chaucer would probably have dealt with the subject in the *Astrolabe* if he had finished that treatise' (p 343).

417 Reisner, Thomas A., and Mary E. Reisner. 'Lewis Clifford and the Kingdom of Navarre.' *MP*, 75 (1978), 385–90.
Discovery in the Chamber of Accounts of the Royal Navarrese Archives, Pamplona, of an unpublished and miscatalogued document

helps fill the hiatus between Clifford's French imprisonment and ransom in 1352 and the next record of 1377. Dated Dec. 27, 1355, under Clifford's seal in Bayona, the document may shed light on Chaucer's mission to Spain in that year. The Reisners doubt that Chaucer was involved in the Battle of Nájera, though Clifford probably was. The document helps explain many of the later intimate connections Clifford had with the royal household.

418 Robertson, D.W. Jr. *Chaucer's London.* New York: John Wiley, 1968. Pp 98–101.
Discusses rape in late fourteenth-century England, and argues against Chaucer's guilt of any sexual abuse. 'Chaucer did not rape or otherwise molest Cecily and then force her to make a false statement' (p 100).

419 Root, Robert Kilburn. *The Poetry of Chaucer.* 1900/1922. See 61.
Ch 5, 'Boethius and the Astrolabe,' pp 80–6, draws observations on the *Astrolabe* mainly from Skeat. 'Since the work has no literary value save that of clear exposition, and since the modern reader is little likely to attempt its perusal, it is not necessary to discuss it further, except to call attention to the charming character of the introductory sentences addressed by the author to his little son' (p 86). Root compares Chaucer to Dante and Milton in his use of 'the clock of the starry heavens' to tell time. 'The crowning proof of the poet's astronomical attainments is furnished by his *Treatise on the Astrolabe*' (p 23).

420 Rye, Walter. 'Chaucer and his son Lewis.' *TLS,* June 28, 1928, p 486.
Manly's argument that Lewis and Thomas Chaucer were employed in the Welsh wars is faulty (see 398). Lewis is indeed Chaucer's son, but Sir Lewis Robsart was his namesake, not Sir Lewis Clifford.

421 Saintsbury, George. *CHEL.* 1908. See 62.
Chaucer's *Astrolabe* is 'an excellent piece of exposition — clear, practical and to the purpose; and, in spite of its technical subject, it is, perhaps, the best prose work Chaucer has left us. But, after all, it is a scientific treatise and not a work of literature' (vol II, p 212).

422 Saunders, H.N. *The Astrolabe.* Teignmouth, Devon, 1971.
Saunders' booklet tells how to construct and use astrolabes. Included are problems solvable only if one has an astrolabe with which to work.

423 Schlauch, Margaret. 'Chaucer's Prose Rhythms.' *PMLA,* 65 (1950), 568–89.
After discussing classical oratory and thirteenth-century Latin prose styles, Schlauch observes that 'Chaucer varies the types of rhythms and the amount of cadence in his prose writing to fit the readers or auditors for whom it was intended. For his rather free adaptations of cadence he did not require strict formal training in Latin *ars*

dictaminis' (p 579). Less formal than Melibee or Boethius, the style of the *Astrolabe* reveals almost no concern for *cursus* and may be designated *stylus humilis* (p 584). Although one finds modifications like *planus anglicus* in Chaucer's other prose, freedom from the restrictions of traditional Latin prose style is seen especially in the prologue to the *Astrolabe* 'with its sparing cadences and unobtrusive rhythms ... as successfully adapted to its purpose and reader as ... the loftier, more consciously wrought texts to theirs' (p 589).

424 — 'The Art of Chaucer's Prose.' In *Chaucer and Chaucerians.* Ed. Derek S. Brewer. University of Alabama: University Press, 1966. Pp 140–63.

'Chaucer's prose works fall within more than one literary genre' (p 143). The *Astrolabe* is of 'the plain style of scientific exposition' (pp 143–8). Its Prologue is 'a rare example of independent Chaucerian composition in prose' which 'explicitly declares the principle that style should be adapted to a reader's age and capacities' (p 143). 'The discourse is made as informal as possible within the limitations imposed by subject matter and purpose' (p 144): *ie*, few periodic sentences, a prevailing paratactic syntax, 'recurrent use of vocatives, apostrophes, first and second person pronouns, etc., as a means of establishing a direct relationship with his pupil' (p 147). The tone is that of 'a good schoolmaster patiently emphasizing a point' rather than 'a rhetorician bent on achieving the effects of mannered prose' (p 145).

425 Sedgwick, Henry Dwight. *Dan Chaucer: An Introduction to the Poet, His Poetry and His Times.* Indianapolis: Bobbs-Merrill, 1934. Pp 221–2.

Argues that little Lewis 'is a mere fiction to serve for an introduction and to justify the simplicity of the author's exposition ... The treatise is obviously meant for publication, and the suggestion that it was written for a little boy might tempt readers, who otherwise would be fearful of a dry and tedious disquisition, as indeed it seems to me to be' (pp 221–2).

426 Skeat, W.W., ed. *Oxford Chaucer.* 1894/1899. See 2, pp xxxii–xxxiii. Concerning the deed dated May 1, 1380, wherein Cecilia Chaumpaigne released to Chaucer all rights of action against him *de raptu meo*, Skeat observes, 'It may mean that Chaucer was accessory to her abduction, much as Geoffrey Stace and others were concerned in the abduction of the poet's father; or it may be connected with the fact that his "little son Lowis" was ten years old in 1391, as we learn from the Prologue to the Treatise on the Astrolabe' (vol I, p xxxiii).

427 Smyser, Hamilton M. 'A View of Chaucer's Astronomy.' *Spec*, 45 (1970), 359–73.

Notes that ME literature does not warrant an assumption of a widespread enthusiasm for or understanding of the rudiments of astronomy. Yet Harry Bailly performs time-telling feats accurate to within two minutes. Chaucer's interest, unique in ME poetry, was shared by some in the court: Lynne made a calendar for Gaunt, and Somer made one for Joan of Kent. But few in the court had Chaucer's understanding of the zodiac: 'Chaucer mastered it, partly because he had a strong scientific bent, as is evident already in the *House of Fame*; partly, I suspect ... because he believed firmly in the possibility of astrological prediction, so firmly that he was not content simply to take his predictions from almanacs, but sought the skill to reckon ascensions for himself' (p 361). Smyser suggests that Chaucer's interest in astrology grew in the 1380's, along with his increased use of Boethian matter. Perhaps Dante influenced Chaucer's use of astronomy, but their methods are quite different: Dante's astronomy tends to be visual; his English heir is Milton. 'Chaucer's use is quantitative, more technical, in a sense more accurate, and it is never stylized' (p 370). Smyser challenges many of North's interpretations (406) by noting that the astronomical observations sometimes occur in Chaucer's sources.

428   Spurgeon, Caroline F.E. *Five Hundred Years of Chaucer Criticism and Allusion: 1357–1900*. 3 vols. Cambridge: Cambridge University Press, 1925.

Spurgeon includes nine entries on the *Astrolabe:*

1. John Lydgate, Preface to the *Fall of Princes* (1430):

> And to his sone / that Callyd was 'lowyes,'
> he made a tretees / ful noble and of greet prys
> Vpon thastrelabre / in ful notable fourme
> Sette hem in Ordre / with ther dyuisions
> mennys wittes / taplyen and confourme,
> To Vndirstonde / be ful expert Resons
> Be Domeffyng / of sondry mansyons,
> The Roote Out sought / at the assendent
> To-fforn or he gaff / ony Iugēment.   (vol I, p 38)

2. Walter Stevins, 'To the Reader' (1555). An account of Stevins' efforts to correct errors as he recopies his new ms of the *Astrolabe* (BM Sloan 261). Stevins would leave 'to worthie Chawcer his due praise for this worke.' (vol I, p 92–3)

3. Sloane ms 314, an *Astrolabe* ms (ca 1560) which bears the heading '1391. Sr Jeffery Chawseres worke.' (vol I, p 95)

4. Brian Twyne, *Antiquitatis Academiae Oxoniensis Apologia* (1608), which praises Chaucer as a perspicacious mathematician for his *Astrolabe*. (vol I, 180–1)

5. John Seldon, *Illustrations* (1612), notes that the *Astrolabe*, 'chiefly learned out of Messahalah,' shows that 'it is plaine hee [Chaucer] was much acquainted with the Mathematics.' (vol I, 186)

6. Henry Peacham, *The Compleat Gentleman* (1622), calls Chaucer 'an excellent Mathematician, as plainly appeareth by his discourse of the Astrolabe to his little sonne Lewis.' (vol I, p 197)

7. Egerton ms 2622, f. 50 (ca 1680–90) mentions *'A Treatise of ye Fabrique and use of ye Astrolabe*, written by ye famous Clerke Sr Geffery Chaucer Kt.' (vol I, p 255)

8. Robert Henry, *History of Great Britain* (1781), calls the *Astrolabe* 'a work which discovers an extensive knowledge in astronomy, with an admirable faculty of communicating that knowledge to a child only ten years of age.' (vol I, p 460)

9. James Orchard Halliwell-Phillipps, *Archaeologia*, 29 (1842), 374–5, argues that the *Astrolabe* is ultimately from a Sanscrit original; Nicholas Strode was tutor to Chaucer's son as the Cambridge colophon shows. (vol II, p 227)

429 Steele, R. 'Chaucer and the "Almagest".' *Library*, series 3, 10 (1919), 243–7.
Traces the Wife of Bath's two citations of Ptolemy to Gerard of Cremona's translation where they are found in the introductory note by the translator 'which hardly any medieval reader would distinguish in quotation from the text itself' (p 244). They are also found in Walter Burley's *De vita et moribus philosophorum*; Chaucer's presentation corresponds better with Burley than with Gerard's original.

430 Tatlock, John S.P. 'Astrology and Magic in Chaucer's *Franklin's Tale.' Anniversary Papers by Colleagues and Pupils of George Lyman Kittredge.* Boston: Ginn, 1913, pp 339–50.
Finds Chaucer's attitude toward astrology and magic to be 'precisely that which we find in many other mediaeval writers than Chaucer, both literary and theological' (p 350).

431 — *The Scene of the Franklin's Tale Visited.* Chaucer Society, Ser. 2, no. 51, London & Oxford, 1914, pp 17–34.
Working from the discussion of influences, zodiac signs, and ascencions in the *Astrolabe*, Tatlock sees Chaucer to be greatly interested in astrology and in general believing 'there was a good deal in it, though his view probably varied from time to time' (p 33). 'But more than this, that coolly prosaic work the *Astrolabe* accepts such astrological notions as the properties of various planets and zodiacal signs (I.21), the influence of each sign on a particular part of the human body (*ibid*), the presiding of each planet over certain hours of the day

(II.12), the (at least possible) general influence of the planets on man (I.21). The work was to have included still more of astrology, such as the "dignities" of planets, and other *useful things* (Prol., end). Would Chaucer have deliberately misled "lyte Lowys my sone"?' (p 23). The attack on judicial astrology at the end of the *Astrolabe* may reflect a change of view (p 27) or a disapproval of pseudo-science; 'yet it would be very risky to assert that at any time he had no belief whatever in any of its claims' (p 27).

432 Thorndike, Lynn. *The Sphere of Sacrobosco and Its Commentators.* Chicago: University of Chicago Press, 1949.
Texts, translation, and commentary on one of the *Astrolabe's* principal sources.

433 Ussery, Huling E. *Chaucer's Physician: Medicine and Literature in Fourteenth-Century England.* Tulane Studies in English, no. 19. New Orleans: Tulane, 1971.
Ussery discusses relationships between astrology and medicine (pp 105–7). Although Chaucer disclaims belief in 'judicial astrology' in his *Astrolabe,* 'I see no reason to doubt his belief in "electionary astrology," and I think most historians of science would agree with me' (p 106).

434 Veazie, Walter B. 'Chaucer's Text-Book of Astronomy: Johannes de Sacrobosco.' *University of Colorado Studies, Series B: Studies in the Humanities,* 1 (1940), 169–82.
Apparently Chaucer had been giving 'litel Lowys' lessons in the sphere before introducing him to an astrolabe, using Sacrobosco's *Sphaera* as his text. Veazie discusses Sacrobosco's other writings as well as *The Sphere,* noting that Sacrobosco might have been a source for some of Chaucer's material on Aristotle and geometry.

435 Watts, P.R. 'The Strange Case of Geoffrey Chaucer and Cecilia Chaumpaigne.' *Law Quarterly Review,* 63 (1947), 491–515.
The deed of release *'de raptu meo'* was discovered in Close Roll of 3 Ric 2 (dated 1 May 1380) by Floyd and was announced by Furnivall in *Athenaeum* 29 Nov. 1873. Watts surveys critical responses to the document, returning frequently to the considered judgments of Furnivall. Skeat was the first to connect the 'rape' with Lewis' birth. J.W. Hale picked up the speculation in *DNB* (vol X, p 162). However, 'nothing but vague supposition is adduced to support these conjectures' (p 493). Watts discussed the laws pertaining to rape and comments on the distinctions between rape and forced rape; also he notes that pregnancy was indicative of mutual consent. The *meo* seems to refer to Chaucer, and *raptu* seems to mean rape. It is doubtful that Chaucer got off because influence placed him above the law, for why then would there be any document at all? If there were no charge there would be no need for guarantees to clear of subsequent

claims by Cecilia. The most logical legal explanation seems to be that Cecilia was pregnant.

436 Waugh, W.T. 'The Lollard Knights.' *Scottish Historical Review*, 11 (1913), 55–92.
Waugh discusses Lewis Clifford (pp 58–63), Richard Stury, Thomas Latimer, John Montague, Sir John Clanvowe, Sir William Neville, Sir John Cheyne, John Trussell, John Peche, and Reginald Hilton, and provides details on the prominence of Clifford in Gaunt's affairs. All these knights were friends to the Duke; all hated the clergy, supported poor priests, and welcomed Lollard attacks on the church. Waugh discusses charges levelled against them in the chronicles of Knighton and Walsingham.

437 Wedel, Theodore Otto. *The Mediaeval Attitude toward Astronomy, particularly in England.* Yale Studies in English, no. 60. Oxford, 1920.
See esp. 'Astrology in Gower and Chaucer,' pp 132–56.
'Judging from the references to astrology apart from those in his *Treatise on the Astrolabe*, Chaucer subscribed to all the doctrines of the science as it was taught in his day. Judicial astrology, in so far at least as it undertook to define the individual's inclinations according to the configuration of the stars at birth, is nowhere condemned' (pp 148–9). Wedel thinks Chaucer 'deliberately' ignored the late fourteenth-century debate on 'the subject of free will and stellar influence' (p 148). References to astronomical influences on the body in Chaucer's poetry show that he espoused 'such notions' (p 151), but was forced to call them impious when 'writing in cold prose' where he must 'disclaim a belief in the more doubtful portions of the science, because he was writing to "lyte Lowys my sone" ' (p 152). See Wood **442** for a detailed analysis of the limitations of Wedel's views.

438 Wilson, Baxter D. 'The Astrolabe and Medieval English Life.' *Popular Astronomy*, 57 (1949), 155–70.
A concise history of the instrument and a discussion of its uses (eg, to determine positions of stars and planets at a given time, to enable an engineer to measure the width of a river or height of a tree or depth of a well, or to help a customs agent to calculate tides, a seaman to navigate, or a gunner to find the desired range). 'It was probably during his time as Clerk of the King's Works that Chaucer grew very familiar with the instrument' (p 164), though he might have also used it on his continental journeys and in calculating horoscopes. Wilson thinks that Chaucer knew the Merton astrolabe and imagines that Lewis was at Oxford (p 169).

439 Wilson, Winifred Graham. 'Chaucer's Astrolabe.' *Life and Letters Today*, 37 (1943), 75–81.
A general essay which emphasizes Chaucer's skill as a teacher. Wilson

thinks 'litel Lowys' was studying mathematics at Oxford 'under the tutorship of that most eminent philosopher Master N. Strode' (p 75). Offers some discussion of Messahalla, especially his observations on such terms as 'astrolabium' and 'zodiacus.' But see North [406 p 134] on the Cambridge ms colophon which refers to son Lewis, Oxford, and 'illius nobilissimi philosophi magistri N. Strode.'

440 Winny, James. 'Chaucer's Science.' In *An Introduction to Chaucer*. Ed. Maurice Hussey, A.C. Spearing, and James Winny. Cambridge: Cambridge University Press, 1965. Pp 153–84.
Stresses Chaucer's 'wide knowledge of intellectual matters ... displayed most convincingly in ... *Boece* and the *Treatise on the Astrolabe*' (p 153). His poetry shows 'breadth of reading and of scientific interests such as a few modern writers might possess ... He is the poet not merely of medieval English society, but of the intellectual life of the time' (p 154). Much of Winny's discussion is devoted to the range of astronomical materials — from astrology to geography — which Chaucer so deftly uses. 'Much in medieval life must have been grim and uncomfortable; but against this the scientific beliefs of the age offered a sense of intimate involvement in a universal design which gave shape and purpose to man's experience. We may feel ourselves participating in this intellectual assurance when we read Chaucer's poetry' (p 184).

441 Wood, Chauncey. 'Chaucer and Astrology.' In *Companion to Chaucer Studies*. Ed. Beryl Rowland. New York: Oxford University Press, 1968/rev 1979. Pp 176–91/rev, pp 202–20.
Reviews succinctly the most useful background studies on astrology, then summarizes various essays and studies on Chaucer's use of astrological materials. Includes a selected bibliography of eighty-eight items, many of which are assessed in the essay.

442 — *Chaucer and the Country of the Stars: Poetic Uses of Astrological Imagery*. Princeton: Princeton University Press, 1970.
Frontispiece of front and back sides of a late Gothic astrolabe, plus thirty-three plates of zodiac illustrations, horoscopes, planetary deities, and other astronomical lore. Ch 1, 'Chaucer's Attitude toward Astrology,' pp 3–50, places Chaucer 'quite high among the skeptics on the mediaeval scale of belief in astrology' (p 51). Challenges views of Tatlock 431, Wedel 437, and Thorndike 460 on Chaucer's acceptance of judicial astrology. Chaucer's characters frequently raise questions of determinism; the real issue, however, concerns the relationship of free will, merit, and grace in salvation, not horoscopes. Chaucer works subtly within Boethian and Augustinian definitions of free will and the will's independence from the stars. His views are like those of Deschamps, Petrarch, and Boccaccio. 'The emphasis here on Boethius

and Oresme as touchstones for later writers has been necessitated to redress the balance effected by earlier scholars who mistakenly felt that medieval men either vacillated in their views, or, in admitting some fraction of astrology, were hinting that they would accept the whole openly if it were not for the fear of reprisal' (p 43). Ch 2, 'The Conventions and Possibilities of Astrology,' pp 51–102, stresses that astrological images in both literature and art must be examined in their immediate contexts in order to determine their usage properly. 'Chaucer characteristically draws upon extant conventions only to vary their themes, to use them in new contexts, or to appropriate them with such skill of execution that they become fresh and poetically vital rather than artistically desiccated' (p 51). His models for literary uses of astronomical imagery derive from Dante and Boccaccio, especially in *KnT* and *T&C*. Chs 3–4 examine astrological imagery in *Mars, WBT, MLT, FrankT*, and *ParsT*. The book concludes with an appendix on 'The Workings of Astrology: "Brede and Milke for Childeren," ' pp 298–305, which explains the basic elements of medieval astrology and astronomy. See also **340**.

- Review by John North, *RES*, 22 (1971), 471–4: 'Mr. Wood is right to press the point that Chaucer's characters are not Chaucer, but wrong to overlook so consistently the fact that Chaucer's attitudes might have undergone considerable change between the time when he cast his first horoscope and the time of composition of the *Treatise on the Astrolabe*' (p 472). North also questions whether what Wood sees as parody and humor might not instead reveal Chaucer's involvement in the possibilities of astrology. 'The new book presents an argument in terms as strong as any reasonable critic would wish to use for claiming that Chaucer was a skeptic in his view of astrology' (p 474).

- Review by John M. Steadman, *JEGP*, 71 (1972), 113–6: 'As Professor Wood correctly perceives, the contrast between Chaucer's own lack of "feith" in judicial astrology and the opinions expressed by his *dramatis personae* creates a potentially ironic situation which he may consciously exploit for the purpose of "undercutting" his narrators or the protagonists of his tales, or both' (pp 115). 'These arguments presuppose a highly literate and sophisticated audience, sensitive to Chaucer's variations from his sources and quick to recognize their ironic implications for this techniques of characterization' (p 116).

- Review by R. MacG. Dawson, *Dalhousie Review*, 50 (1970), 271–3: 'a poetic approach, rather than a technical one, but at the same time it is firmly rooted in the works of the medieval astrologers' (p 271).

143 — 'Medieval Astronomy and Astrology.' In *The Literature of Medieval England*. Ed. D.W. Robertson, Jr. New York: McGraw-Hill, 1970, pp 10–23.
A concise introduction to medieval astronomy which contrasts its assumptions with those of modern day astronomy. Illustrated with zodiacal diagrams and reproductions of medieval cosmological models. Differentiates between pure and judicial astronomy.

A Select Bibliography of Background Studies in Astronomy and Related Matters

44 Abrams, John. 'The Development of Medieval Astronomy.' In *By Things Seen: Reference and Recognition in Medieval Thought*. Ed. David L. Jeffrey. Ottawa: University of Ottawa Press, 1979. Pp 187–209.
Abrams traces astronomy from the Greeks through Ptolemy to the High Middle Ages (Sacrobosco, Bacon, Oresme), and considers the relationship of astronomy to other arts.

45 Allen, Don Cameron. *The Star-Crossed Renaissance: The Quarrel about Astrology and Its Influence in England*. Durham, North Carolina: Duke University Press, 1941.
Cites instances in which Chaucer's name or literary characters are associated with astrology or alchemy in Renaissance literature.

46 Allen, Richard Hinckley. *Star Names and Their Meanings*. New York: G.E. Stechert, 1899.
Provides ancient, medieval, and Renaissance glosses and etymologies on astronomical names, with chapters on the Solar Zodiac, Lunar Zodiac, Constellations, and Galaxy. Indices of general astronomical names, Arabic names, Greek names, astronomical references in the Bible, and a partial list (9 pages) of authors, authorities, and books of reference cited.

47 Boll, Franz, and Carl Bezold. *Sternglaube und Sterndeutung*, 1917/rev ed. by W. Gundel. Leipzig: Teubner, 1931.
A survey of the importance, development, and methods of astrology. Hans George Gundel appends a bibliography to the 1931 edition (pp 231–5).

48 Carmody, Francis J. *Arabic Astronomical and Astrological Sciences in Latin Translation: A Critical Bibliography*. Berkeley and Los Angeles: University of California Press, 1956.

Invaluable in helping to sort out differences in the numerous Latin
translations with confusingly similar titles.

449 Coopland, G.W. *Nicole Oresme and the Astrologers: A Study of his
Livre de divinacions.* Cambridge, Mass.: Harvard University Press,
1952.
Analyzes the views of one of Chaucer's contemporaries. Wood 442
notes that Books 8 and 9 of Oresme's *Le Livre de divinaciouns* were
transcribed with additions by Eustache Deschamps as *Demoustracions
contre sortileges.*

450 Dillon, Bert. *A Chaucer Dictionary: Proper Names and Allusions,
excluding Place Names.* Boston: G.K. Hall, 1974.
Originating in Dillon's Duke Dissertation, 'A Dictionary of Personal,
Mythological, Allegorical and Astrological Proper Names and
Allusions in the Works of Geoffrey Chaucer' (1972), the book
systematizes and records names and their sources in Chaucer's
writings to indicate the poet's intellectual and poetic concerns,
borrowings, recurrent interests, treatment of sources. The names are
given descriptive heads followed by lists of occurrences.

451 Duhem, Pierre. *Le Système du monde: Histoire des doctrines
cosmologiques de Relation a Copernis.* 10 vols. Paris: A.E. Herrmann,
1913–59.
The definitive study of medieval astronomy.

452 Förster, Max. 'Vom Fortleben antiker Sammellunare in englischen und
in andern Volkssprachen.' *Anglia,* 67 (1944), 1–171.
Discusses characteristics of lunaries in Latin, Old English, Middle
English, and continental vernacular languages. Prints several
examples.

453 Gunther, R.T. 'Astrolabe.' In *Encyclopedia Britannica,* 14th Edition,
vol II, pp 574–5. London and New York, 1929.
The best of the encyclopedia articles on this topic.

454 MacNeice, Louis. *Astrology.* New York: Doubleday, 1964.
A popular survey of the topic; some color reproductions of medieval
astrological illustrations. Tables brought up to date (1964).

455 Orr, Mary Acworth [Mrs. John Evershed]. *Dante and the Early
Astronomers.* London: Wingate, 1956.
Part I traces the history of astronomy from ancient times to Dante.
Part II considers popular astronomy in Dante's time, astronomy books
used by Dante, and astronomical matters in Dante's writings. Orr
makes no specific mention of Chaucer.

456 Robbins, Rossell Hope. 'English Almanacks of the Fifteenth Century.'
PQ, 18 (1939), 321–31.

Surveys Middle English almanacs, and reproduces from St John's
College, Cambridge, ms 135, a typical, previously unpublished example
in Middle English couplets of an *Erra Pater* or *Prognostication of
Esdras* type of almanack, which calculates from the day of the week on
which Christmas or New Year falls, and which covers one week.
Robbins also prints two unpublished Latin prognostics from BM ms
Egerton 1995, which speculate on the amount of sunshine and wind
prevailing from Christmas Day to Epiphany.

457 Sarton, George. *Introduction to the History of Science.* 3 vols in 5.
Washington, D.C.: Carnegie Institution of Washington, 1927–48.
See esp. vol II, pt. 1, pp 20–1, 114, and 167–75 on the history of
translations of scientific treatises from the Arabic.

458 Saxl, Fritz, and Hans Meier. *Verzeichnis astrologischer und
mythologischer illustrierter Handschriften des lateinischen Mittelalters.*
Heidelberger Akademie der Wissenschaften. 3 vols in 4. Heidelberg: C.
Winter, 1915–53. Rpt Nendeln/Liechtenstein: Krause-Thomson, 1978.
Discusses and prints mythological and astrological illuminations in mss
throughout Europe. Volume III is devoted to mss in England. A
supplement to this monumental study is Patrick McGurk, *Catalogue of
Astrological and Mythological Illuminated Manuscripts of the Latin
Middle Ages: IV. Astrological Manuscripts in Italian Libraries (Other
than Rome).* London: Warburg Institute, 1966.

459 Talbot, Charles H. *Medicine in Medieval England.* London:
Oldbourne, 1967.
Makes frequent references to Chaucer. See esp. Chapter 5, 'Medical
Education,' pp 64–71, which deals with the teaching of medicine at
Oxford and Cambridge. See also Talbot and E.A. Hammond, *Medical
Practitioners in Medieval England* (London: William Clowes, 1965).

460 Thorndike, Lynn. *A History of Magic and Experimental Science.* 8
vols. New York: Columbia University Press, 1923–58.
Vols 1 and 2 trace the origins of astrology from Egyptian, Chaldean
and Greek sources from beginnings to the thirteenth century. Vols 3
and 4 deal with the fourteenth and fifteenth centuries. See esp. I,
697–718, 'Gerbert and Arabic Astrology,' which includes discussion of
several early works on astrolabes.

461 Weisheipl, J.A. 'Curriculum of the Faculty of Arts at Oxford in the
Early Fourteenth Century.' *MS*, 26 (1964), 142–85.
Weisheipl discusses the study of sciences, noting that not all medieval
science was tied to the universities. Some fell under the provenance of
the guilds. But 'the academics of antiquity and the universities of the
Middle Ages prided themselves in transmitting the liberal arts and the
speculative sciences as worthy of study in their own right and as

preparatory to the specialized study of theology, law, and medicine' (p 143). Weisheipl discusses undergraduate and advanced curricula and schedules of lectures. For specifics on the study of astronomy, see pp 172–3; for natural philosophy, pp 173–5.

Part IV: The Equatorie of the Planetis

Introduction

In December, 1951, after studying the contents of Peterhouse ms 75 in the Perne Library, Cambridge, Derek Price concluded that the catalogue attribution of an *Equatorie of the Planets* to Simon Bredon could not be correct: The *Equatorie* in this unique ms, like Chaucer's *Astrolabe*, contains a precise date: Dec. 31, 1392. [Bredon died in 1372.] Moreover, its author states: 'This cercle wole I clepe the Lymbe of myn equatorie, that was compowned the Yer of Crist 1392 complet, the last meridie of Decembre' (Fisher, **11**, p 938, lines 25–8). The 'lymbe' is the perimeter of the face of the instrument, which is to be graduated for calculations. Probably the sense of the passage is that the equatorie is constructed to make calculations based on that date, not that the 'lymbe' itself was made on that day. Nonetheless, 1392 must be the approximate date of compostition of the treatise, since there is no other reason for designating that date. Simon Bredon had been dead for twenty years.

Who then might the author be? Chaucer's intense interest in astronomy at precisely this time and his announcement in the prologue to the *Astrolabe* (1391) that he wished to undertake many astronomical projects, including the making of tables, make the poet an obvious candidate for authorship. Price resisted jumping to this conclusion, but his investigations pointed in a single direction: there can be little doubt that Chaucer was somehow associated with this work. *The Equatorie* makes specific reference to the *Treatise on the Astrolabe* more than once, almost as if it were designed as a companion piece. Furthermore, its style is reminiscent of the *Astrolabe*; its dialect is identical, the vocabulary is similar. Like the *Astrolabe*, the *Equatorie* includes a mention of John Somer, the Oxford astronomer. One fascinating feature of the manuscript is that it is a working draft. Its many corrections and revisions strongly suggest that it is almost certainly a holograph. With the discovery of Chaucer's name in a marginal comment on the radix (computational base) of the tables, the

evidence seemed overwhelming. In the Feb. 29, 1952, *TLS*, Price
announced the discovery of what might well prove to be 'a hitherto
unknown work by Chaucer' (p 164). This was welcome news to
Chaucer scholars; Price's discovery showed that hidden treasure
awaited the diligent researcher even in these later days.

An equatorie works on principles similar to an astrolabe, although
it is a larger and more complex instrument. The beginning of the
treatise explains that the larger the instrument the smaller the
fractions of the arcs can be; accordingly, the size corresponds directly
to the accuracy of calculations. A large, well-constructed equatorie can
make possible computation of the positions of the planets without the
use of tables. The instrument lacks the elegance and simplicity of an
astrolabe, which often might be elaborately decorated with fine metal
work; it is also more ungainly and formidable in its several intricate
parts, which require a good mathematician to operate. Price notes
that no equatorie has survived intact, although two incomplete
examples of the actual instrument (one at Merton) have been traced.

With the publication of Price's edition of the *Equatorie* in 1955,
scholarly work on the treatise became more possible. Initially scholarly
arguments demonstrated if not proof of Chaucer's authorship at least
the absence of obstacles to such a conclusion. The only spoiler has
been John North 471, the noted London astronomer, who has
identified grisly black rocks in an otherwise happy harbor — rocks
which, to my knowledge, no tregetour has completely removed. But
still, in the effort to relate the work to Chaucer, there seems to be
ample room for navigating, despite North's 'foul confusion.' His
doubts have simply made the sport more intriguing.

I have divided the bibliography into two short sections. The first
presents the two editions of the *Equatorie*; the second, an alphabetical
list of essays on or relating to it. For a list of background works on
medieval astronomy see the third part of the *Astrolabe* bibliography.

Editions of the *Equatorie of the Planetis*

462 Price, Derek J. *The Equatorie of the Planetis*, ed. from Peterhouse ms
75.1, with a linguistic analysis by R.M. Wilson. Cambridge:
Cambridge University Press, 1955.
'There is ... nothing in this book which can by itself be accepted as
definite proof of authorship; there is, however, a mass of lesser
evidence which has the cumulative effect of suggesting that this is a
Chaucer holograph' (p xv). Ch 1, 'Introduction,' pp 3–5: The

Equatorie 'must be regarded as a companion work to the Treatise on the Astrolabe' (p 3). 'If we accept a hint contained in the *Astrolabe* that Chaucer had previously written a treatise on the "Solid Sphere," the three works together would make a very suitable and complete treatise on the basic theory and the instrumentation of medieval astronomy' (p 4). The *Equatorie* must derive from a Latin treatise, perhaps one by Simon Bredon, a Merton astronomer who died in 1372. Ch 2, 'Provenance and Physical Description of the Manuscript,' pp 6–16: The ms came to Peterhouse between 1418–1542 and was bound with Trivet, *Expositio super Aug. de ciuitate dei*, and Vegetius, *De re militari*. Fols 1–70 include two sets of tables; 71–78, the equatorie treatise. The nineteenth-century binding was removed so that Price could examine the 'radix Chaucer' note; the *Equatorie* was then rebound as a separate volume, Peterhouse ms 75.1; the other treatises were returned to the former binding (now ms 75.2). Ch 3, 'Transcript and Facsimiles,' pp 17–46: Fols 71v–78v. The text is diplomatically transcribed: 'Editorial interference with the transcription has been kept to the minimum permitted by normal typography. Even obvious errors in the manuscript have been retained, and the original punctuation has been reproduced as closely as possible' (p 17). Ch 4, 'Translation,' pp 47–61. Ch 5, 'Notes to the Text,' pp 62–74: The text uses typical Arabic rhetorical formulas to describe an ideal instrument (90 holes, 6' diameter, etc) which the author modifies out of practical necessity to portable size (24 holes, 1–2' diameter) (p 67). 'The closing section is completely false, for it contains the supposition that Caput is restricted to one half of the zodiac, and Cauda to the other half. In point of fact both nodes rotate through the entire zodiac, making a complete revolution in the draconitic period of approximately 18.6 years' (p 74). The ending, though lacking an *explicit*, is 'sufficiently logical to bring this section to a satisfactory close' (p 74). Ch 6, 'The Astronomical Tables,' pp 75–92: Alphonsine, adjusted to London. The 'Radix Chaucer' note specifies days for 1392. The Tables themselves contain some notes on determination of the ascendancy of planets. One contains a query for 17–22 May 1379, on which Price observes, 'If the author is Chaucer, and the inquiry is drawn from his experience, it would be of great interest to identify the querent who had been expressly promised a kingdom. It is tempting to think it might be John of Gaunt; certainly in 1379 he had just concluded an alliance with the King of Portugal, whereby he was to be invited to come to Lisbon with a fleet and army in pursuit of the Kingdom of Castile' (p 90). Ch 7, 'The Ptolemaic Planetary System,' pp 93–118: 1) Preamble; 2) General Foundation of the Theory; 3) Sun; 4) Venus, Mars, Jupiter, Saturn; 5) Mercury; 6) Moon; 7) Alfonsine 'precision'; 8) Technical Terms of Ptolemaic Astronomy, as found in the Text; 9)

Accuracy of the theory and the Equatorie; 10) Calculation of
Planetary Positions. Ch 8, 'History of the Planetary Equatorium,' pp
119–36: 'The instrument described ... shows many features ... found
in the Merton instrument but not elsewhere' (p 130). Ch 9,
'Paleography': 1) Contractions, 2) Punctuation. Ch 10, 'Linguistic
Analysis' (by R.M. Wilson): Vocabulary: 11 words found earlier only
in Chaucer; 24 words common to *Astrolabe*, where they make their
first appearance. Wilson affirms the likelihood that this ms is a
holograph and that it may be Chaucer's. 'There is certainly nothing in
the language or style of the *Equatorie* which is definitely against
Chaucerian authorship. On the contrary, there are certain facts which
offer some support to such a theory; and if none of them is particularly
striking by itself, taken together they may well have some significance,
though the exact value of this is perhaps more difficult to determine'
(p 148). Ch 11, 'Ascription to Chaucer,' pp 149–66. Price enlarges the
'Radix Chaucer' signature, then superimposes it upon an enlargement
of a Chaucer signature in a P.R.O. document (1378), which Manly
thought to be a Chaucer holograph. Even greatly enlarged the two
signatures appear virtually identical. Ch 12, 'Glossary and Three
Appendices,' pp 167–206: 1) Cipher Passages in the Manuscripts; 2)
Compositio Equatorii Secundum Johannem de Lineriis; 3) Specimen of
the Middle English Scientific Texts.

- Review by Curt A. Zimansky, *MLN*, 71 (1956), 70–7: Rather
  than having worked with a Latin source, the author composed an
  original piece based on the use of his own instrument. 'That we
  are dealing with a Chaucer holograph is possible, and may be
  actually the simplest hypothesis' (p 74). Almost certainly the
  astrolabe treatise referred to is Chaucer's. 'One remarkable
  passage at the end of the manuscript (f 64v) is clearly the work of
  a believer in judicial astrology. The handwriting may be that of
  the author of the *Equatorie* text itself, working at a different time
  or using a different pen' (p 75).

- Review by Robert W. Ackerman, *PQ*, 35 (1956), 220–3: Reviews
  the three principal conjectures for Chaucerian authorship and
  concludes that the strongest piece of evidence is the 'Radix
  Chaucer' marginalia.

463 Fisher, John H., ed. *Complete Poetry and Prose of Geoffrey Chaucer.*
1977. See 11. Introduction, pp 936–7; text and notes, pp 938–48.
Text based on ms Peterhouse 75.1 as edited and translated by Price
462. Capitalization and punctuation have been added and abbreviated
articles and prepositions expanded. The three diagrams of the ms are
included. Notes include glosses and commentary.

Discussions on or related to the *Equatorie of the Planetis*

See also **381, 384, 395, 413-415.**

464 Bennett, J.A.W. *Chaucer at Oxford and at Cambridge.* 1974. See **353.** Pp 75-8.

Suggests that the name under the 'Leyk' erasure in the first line identified by Price as 'Leyners' (ie, John of Linières, a famous astronomer of Paris who invented an equatorium) might be an error for Lenn (Lynn). 'The *Leyk* of the *Equatory* and the *Lenne* of the *Astrolabe* may thus be one and the same authority' (p 78).

465 Brewer, Derek S. *Chaucer and His World.* 1978. See **355.**

Whether the *Equatorie* is by Chaucer or not, 'what is important is to recognize the large place that astronomy held in Chaucer's interests for its own sake in his own life'; Chaucer used astronomical lore for 'adornment, wit, structure, motivation, even philosophy' (p 206).

466 Eisner, Sigmund. 'Chaucer's Use of Nicholas of Lynn's Calendar.' *E&S*, 29 (1976), 1-22.

Disagrees with Bennett **464** that 'Leyk' in the *Equatorie* could be an error for Lynn (p 3). See **366** and **367.**

467 Herdan, G. 'Chaucer's Authorship of *The Equatorie of the Planetis:* The Use of Romance Vocabulary as Evidence.' *Language*, 32 (1956), 254-9.

Recognizing that the percentage of Romance words in Chaucer's writings changes significantly with the length of the text (Herdan takes his comparative statistics on Romance vocabulary from Joseph Mersand **51**), Herdan predicts that the Romance vocabulary of a work such as the *Equatorie* containing about 6048 words should be $10 \log 10$ $6048 = 37.8\%$. In fact, Romance words in the *Equatorie* constitute 37% of the vocabulary. 'The agreement between observation and expectation, or between fact and theory, is so striking that without going further into the question of statistical significance we may conclude that by the token of Romance vocabulary the *Equatorie* is to be regarded as a work by Chaucer' (p 258).

468 — *Language as Choice and Chance.* Groningen: P. Noordhoff, 1956. See pp 18-22.

Argues again that the vocabulary of the *Equatorie* suggests Chaucerian authorship. See **467.**

469 Hussey, S.S. 'The Minor Poems and the Prose.' 1970. See **42.**

Outlines briefly the origin of such treatises as the *Astrolabe* and the

Equatorie, and reviews arguments of attribution of the *Equatorie* to Chaucer. Concludes that authorship is uncertain (pp 251–2).

470 Kennedy, E.S. 'A Horoscope of Messehalla in the Chaucer Equatorium Manuscript.' *Spec*, 34 (1959), 629–30.
The horoscope cast for 17–22 May 1379 in the margin of the *Equatorie* derives from Messehalla, where a horoscope is cast on behalf of someone asking whether or not he will receive a kingdom promised him 23 May 791. Both the *Equatorie* and *Astrolabe* also draw extensively on Messehalla.

471 North, John D. 'Kalenderes Enlumyned Ben They.' 1969. See **406**, pp 432–5.
On the question of authorship, Price's edition raises three main issues: a) Was Chaucer the author of the text, tables, both or neither? b) Is the ms in large part a Chaucer autograph? c) If Chaucer is neither the scribe nor the author, 'what is the significance of the note written against some astronomical tables in the same hand as the *Equatorie* text, and containing Chaucer's name?' (p 433). If the hand *is* Chaucer's, why would he refer to himself by surname? The note implies that 1392 is the date Chaucer 'took as his standard of reference' (p 434). There are other radices on the same page, one 1393 and another 1395, all in the same hand as the 'Radix Chaucer.' 'It is not ... impossible for an astronomer to revise the radix from which he works; but had Chaucer done so he would not have characterized his *first* as "Radix Chaucer," and left the others unattributed. We notice, furthermore, that there is even a radix 1400 elsewhere referred to in the same hand. It is thus hard to see how this hand can be Chaucer's' (p 434). Perhaps the author used Chaucer's tables. Also there are important differences between the *Equatorie* and the *Astrolabe:* a) differences in vocabulary (eg, *Astrolabe:* bordure, backhalf, Algomeyse; *Equatorie:* lymbe, bakside, Algomeiza); b) *Astrolabe* gives angles only to degrees, with named signs; *Equatorie* gives angles to degrees and minutes, with numbered signs. Perhaps this is because the *Astrolabe* was designed for a boy, 'but in that case at least the *Equatorie* cannot be regarded as the missing *Theorike*' (p 434); c) the cross reference to an astrolabe treatise in *Equatorie* is not necessarily to one in English; d) the tables for *Equatorie* are for London and are Alfonsine. 'So far as I know there is no evidence for Chaucer's having been familiar with the Alfonsine tables' (p 435).

472 Onions, C.T. 'The Equatorie of the Planetis.' *TLS*, Mar. 7, 1952, p 173.
Notes the representation of the Anglo-Saxon *y* by *e* in *enches* in the page of *Equatorie* printed in Price's original notice (*TLS*, Feb. 29, 1952) to be consistent with southeastern forms in Chaucer's canonical

works where it can be established by rhyme: eg, *keste* for *kiste*, as past tense of kiss, which Chaucer will rhyme with *reste* or *wiste*. The author of *Equatorie* 'was thus obviously familiar with such local forms with *e*, if they were not indeed an element of his native speech.' Such forms offer 'at least an initial clue to its probable area of origin.'

473 Price, Derek J. 'The Equatorie of the Planetis — I.' *TLS*, Feb. 29, 1952, p 164.
Price's initial announcement of his discovery of the ms in Perne Library of Peterhouse, Cambridge. See the introduction to this section of the Bibliography and item 414 for details on this announcement.

474 — 'The Equatorie of the Planetis — II.' *TLS*, Mar. 7, 1952, p 180.
A continuation of the Feb. 29 announcement. Discusses the handwriting and notes a likeness sufficient 'to strike the eye at once' to a signature in Exchequer bills for 1377 [sic. 1378?]. Discusses the name 'Leyk' which has been erased by scraping. Has tried to read it with infrared photography and ultraviolet light but without much success. Possibly it refers to Costa ben Luca (d. ca 912). Discusses the equatory itself and the instructions for constructing it. See also 415.

475 — 'The Equatorie of the Planetis.' *Journal of the S.W. Essex Technological College*, 3 (1952), 154–68. [I have not been able to obtain this essay.]

476 — 'Chaucer's Astronomy.' *Nature*, 170 (1952), 474–5.
Develops theory of Chaucer's authorship of *Equatorie* on the basis of the 'radix Chaucer' signature and the P.R.O. signature of 1378. 'The *Equatorie of the Planetis* provides us with the only account in English of this device, and focuses attention on an important medieval astronomical instrument the very existence of which had been almost forgotten' (p 475). 'The construction of a facsimile of Chaucer's instrument has shown that results may be read to an accuracy of about five minutes of arc, and to this order of fineness the Ptolemaic theory serves well' (p 474).

476a Samuels, M. L. 'Chaucer's Spelling.' In *Middle English Studies Presented to Norman Davis in Honour of his Seventieth Birthday*. Ed. Douglas Gray and E. G. Stanley. Oxford: Clarendon Press, 1983. Pp 17–37.
Applying eleven criteria to thirteen late fourteenth-century sources, Samuels provides strong support for the view that 'the *Equatorie* is in Chaucer's own spelling' (p 28). It seems, in fact, to be the best exemplar that we have of Chaucer's spelling, which 'increases the likelihood that the *Equatorie* is an authentic and autograph work of Chaucer' (p 35). The *Equatorie* is thus of value to editors wishing to provide a text with authentic Chaucerian spelling. 'The *Equatorie* is a

short text which could not provide a model complete enough for the wide-ranging lexis of Chaucer's major works' (p 35). *Boece* and *Astrolabe* are longer but they contain 'layers of language' and are less suitable as models. Until a consensus is established from all three texts 'probably the nearest an editor could get at present to Chaucer's spelling would be to take a consensus of Hengwrt-Ellesmere and Corpus Christi Coll. Cambridge 61 and then, wherever feasible, to alter spellings in the directions indicated by the *Equatorie*' (pp 35–36).

477 Schlauch, Margaret. 'The Art of Chaucer's Prose.' 1966. See 424. Pp 148, 162–3.
'The general stylistic characteristics of the *Astrolabe* are found here [in the *Equatorie*] also. Some of them are tempered or more sparingly used, as is to be expected in a work addressed to the general adult public, not dedicated to an individual, a beloved child' (p 148). Many of the devices, such as the use of the first and second person, characterize medieval scientific writing and are not unique to the *Astrolabe* or the *Equatorie*. 'But it may be said that in composing the *Astrolabe* and the *Equatorie* (if it is his) he [Chaucer] made felicitous use of such devices as were already familiar in scientific writing' (p 148) — eg, pleonasm, tautological pairs, parataxis, simple imperatives, anaphora.

478 Spencer, William. 'Are Chaucer's Pilgrims Keyed to the Zodiac?' *ChauR*, 4 (1970), 147–70.
Although this essay does not specifically mention the *Equatorie*, it concentrates on the planets and their houses. Spencer argues that the order of pilgrims in the GP follows the sequence of signs of the zodiac with the disposition of each pilgrim being dominated by the planet which rules in each sign. The likelihood of such a pattern 'makes sense in terms of what we know about the man and his age' (p 169).

479 Wilson, R.M. *The Lost Literature of Medieval England*. London: Methuen, 1952/1970.
Mentions the *Equatorie* discovery to illustrate that 'such discoveries, though rare today, are by no means unknown' (p 237). The cover illustration to the University Paperback edition of 1972 reproduces the Peterhouse ms 75.1, f 73v diagram of the face of the *Equatorie*.

Part V: The Lost Works

Introduction

The list of writings incorporated into the Prologue to the *Legend of Good Women* F 405-30 mentions Chaucer's having made a 'gret while' ago 'Origenes upon the Maudeleyne.' In the G-text Chaucer mentions having made another work as well, 'the Wreched Engendrynge of Mankynde, / As man may in pope Innocent yfynde' (G. 414-5). Neither work is known to survive, so both presumably have been lost. Since the 'Wreched Engendrynge' is not mentioned in the F-text, which presumably was written earlier than the G-text, it seems that Chaucer must be referring to a work he has recently completed (or at least undertaken). The 'Maudeleyne,' on the other hand, was evidently an early effort; the way in which Chaucer speaks of it suggests that it may have been lost even in his own lifetime.

In the Retraction to the *Canterbury Tales* he mentions a third work, 'the book of the Leoun' (X [I] 1086), which is likewise a mystery. Like the 'Maudeleyne,' the *Book of the Leoun* seems to have been written in the distant past, almost beyond the reaches of the poet's memory, as he recalls it 'and many another book, if they were in my remembrance.' Perhaps it was written for some occasion or for some person and once presented or given, was, like so much of fourteenth-century art, quite literally beyond recovery. Chaucer also mentions having written 'many a song and many a leccherous lay,' some of which are also presumed to be lost.

Scholars have made various attempts to reclaim the lost poems, or at least to reconstruct what they might have been. Some have held that less is lost than at first appears, that we possess most of the lyrics (483) and that the 'Wreched Engendrynge' is an allusion to the Prologue to the *Man of Law's Tale* which is based on a passage in Innocent III's *De Contemptu Mundi* 480. The *Book of the Leoun* may refer to Machaut's *Le Dit dou Lyon* or perhaps to poems by Eustache Deschamps or Jean de Condé which bear similar titles and which Chaucer may have translated or drawn upon in constructing an early

poem like the *Book of the Duchess*. It should be noted, however, that
the *Book of the Duchess, Parlement of Foules, Hous of Fame* and
Legend of Good Women are all separately specified in the Retraction,
along with *Troilus* and the *Canterbury Tales*. Evidently Chaucer is
referring to an independent work. Professor Robbins suggests that
some of the lost lecherous lays may have been written in French (see
484). Professor Wimsatt discusses a ms of French poems which might
conceivably be Chaucer's, or at least like Chaucer's had he written
French poetry (see **485**).

General Studies on the Lost Works

See also **479**.

480 Brusendorff, Aage. *Chaucer Tradition*. 1925. See **25**. Pp 426–33.
'The Lost Works,' pp 426–33, considers 'Origines upon the
Maudeleyne,' 'Wreched Engendring of Mankynde,' 'Book of the
Leoun,' and the many lays, songs, complaints, roundels, and virelays,
mentioned in Chaucer's book lists, suggesting possible sources for
each, and noting other external evidence of their existence.
Brusendorff suggests that in the 'Maudeleyne' Chaucer probably took
'somewhat the same line as that pursued in his *Lyf of Seint Cecile*' (pp
426–27). He doubts that his 'prose paraphrase of Pope Innocent II's
[sic] famous treatise' was completed 'since the terms in which Chaucer
refers to the work would seem to show that he had not translated more
than the first seven chapters of the work, which alone treat 'of *The
Wreched Engendring of Mankynde*.' There is absolutely no proof of the
theory that Chaucer continued his work a good deal further, then
broke off, and used his translation for the poetical paraphrases of bits
of the papal treatise in the Man of Law's Prologue and Tale' (pp
427–8). The *Book of the Leoun* can hardly be a translation of
Machaut's *Dit dou Lyon*; rather it is more likely to have been a
paraphrase of a work like Deschamps' *Traictie du mauvais
gouvernement de ce royaume*, a satire against the political situation in
France ca 1380–2. 'Chaucer may have adapted it to suit the disorderly
state of affairs in England about 1397–9; several features of the poem
must have been of especial interest to him, such as the long passage on
Free Will (lines 1048 ff,) and the narrative of Coronis (lines 2751 ff, cf
MancT). At any rate it is far more probable that Chaucer modelled a
work of his old age on a satirical piece by Deschamps than on a
specimen of Machaut's love poetry, the taste for which he had
outgrown long ago' (p 430). Other lost works may include the Ceys

and Alcione mentioned in *LGW*. Some once thought the reference in Gower's *CA* to Chaucer's having made 'his testament of love' referred to a poem by that title (nb, the inclusion of Usk's treatise among his works). But probably the line is rather a gentle hint to Chaucer 'that he might do worse than follow Gower's example and compose a great work treating of Love — a hint which Chaucer seems very properly to have resented in spite of the pretty compliment immediately preceding the lesser poet's too officious suggestion' (p 431). Brusendorff cites several nineteenth-century speculations on these lost works which I have not included in this bibliography.

481 Clemen, Wolfgang. *Chaucer's Early Poetry*. Trans. C.A.M. Sym. London: Methuen, 1963.
Probably Chaucer wrote many conventional poems which have not come down to us after the pattern of Machaut in the first decade of his productive period (pp 171–2). Probably many of the lost poems were free translations like the *ABC* and *Venus*, the value of which in Chaucer's development 'can hardly be exaggerated; for here we often have a creative type of translation that leads on to something new' (p 173).

482 Maynard, Theodore. *The Connection Between the Ballade, Chaucer's Modification of It Rime Royal, and the Spenserian Stanza*. Washington, D.C.: Published Catholic University of America Dissertation, 1934.
We can only speculate upon the fate of the 'mery songs and lecherous lays' Chaucer claims in the *Retraction* to have written. He 'may have destroyed them in later life, because he disapproved of them on moral grounds ... [Or he] may not have thought them worth keeping. And this merely because he was ashamed of their artistic immaturity' (p 50). He does refer to them with pride in *LGW*. Whatever they were they must have been modelled on Machaut, Deschamps, and Froissart. Since the Chaucerian ballades which survive are frequently from his mature years, the lost ones must be of his youth (p 62).

483 Moore, Arthur K. 'Chaucer's Lost Songs.' *JEGP*, 48 (1949), 196–208.
Moore argues that the many songs and lecherous lays which Chaucer mentions in the *Retraction* and the Prol to *LGW*, lyrics to which Gower and Lydgate also appear to refer, may not be lost. When we consider the many songs intercalated in the narrative poems — songs like the balade for Alceste in *LGW*, the Black Knight's songs in *BD*, and the various songs in *Troilus* — the number of Chaucer lyrics exceeds thirty, which is certainly ample to justify his early reputation as a lyric poet.

484 Robbins, Rossell Hope. 'Geoffroi Chaucier, Poète Français, Father of English Poetry.' *ChauR*, 13 (1978), 93–115.

Noting the polish of an early work like *BD* and the fact that Chaucer's known lyrics are mainly written after the poet was past forty, Robbins argues that Chaucer must have established himself as a palace poet in his younger days by writing poems which have not survived. These poems may well have been written in French.

485 Wimsatt, James I. *Chaucer and the Poems of 'Ch' in University of Pennsylvania ms French 15.* Cambridge: D.S. Brewer, 1982.
Fifteen of the 310 French lyrics in this late fourteenth century codex have the initials 'Ch' neatly inserted between rubric and text. The initials seem to indicate authorship. There are no obvious candidates among contemporary French poets. Could 'Ch' be Chaucer? 'A number of features of the manuscript do indeed indicate that the "Ch" lyrics might have been composed in English court circles when Chaucer was in his first years of court service in London; that is, in the decade beginning in 1357 or a bit earlier. Nevertheless, he would be a bold scholar indeed who would claim outright that "Ch" stands for Chaucer. For while the works display a measure of wit and skill within the limitations of the fashionable forms, they are not consistently outstanding. If they bear comparison with some of Chaucer's love lyrics, they hardly show the genius of his mature narratives, and one can find in them but few specific foretokens of his English poetry' (p 1). Wimsatt reviews the mode of the poems, which follow the highly artificial conventions of the Old French trouvere tradition as they had been modified in the early fourteenth century — love subject matter but cast in the complex *formes fixes* of ballade, chant royal, lay, virelay, and rondeau. Ten of the fifteen lyrics are three-stanza ballades, four are five-stanza chants royaux, and one is a rondeau. 'The dry facts about the metrics provide some solid information about "Ch" ' (p 3). The poet writes after it was the fashion to be a musical composer (near mid-century) and before it was the practice to include envoys, as in the mature Deschamps (ca 1370). Five of the poems are built around personification allegories; another six, around literary reference to such ladies as Esther, Thisbe, Phyllis, Guinevere, etc; and the other four turn around single conventional images such as the imprint of the lady's eyes inside the poet's heart. Wimsatt notes several interesting similarities of theme with Chaucer's poems, ranging from *T&C* and *AA* to *BD* and *Pity*. Wimsatt edits the fifteen poems, with translation on the facing page. The ms as a whole has many connections with Chaucer and his circle. Granson seems to have had a part in the putting together of the ms. 107 of the poems are by Machaut, who exerted by far the greatest influence on Chaucer; 27 are by Granson, whom Chaucer called the 'flower' of French poets; several are by Deschamps, with whom Chaucer exchanged poems; others are

by Grimace, Nicole de Margival, Philippe de Vitry and Jean de le
Mote. Nicole and Jean have been seen as influencing Chaucer's work.
The 'Ch' poems are spread out between texts 235 and 276,
interspersed with Granson lyrics. Wimsatt discusses each of the known
contributors to the anthology and provides texts and translation for a
balade by Philippe de Vitry (#62), and a response by Jean de le Mote
(#63), which is further evidence of the coherence of the anthology. It
is remarkable that Froissart is not included in the ms, though several
Froissart-like pastoureles are. Wimsatt prints the five balades of
Granson found in the ms (appendix A), an exchange between Jean
Campion and Jean de le Mote (appendix B), a bibliography, and a list
of the contents of the ms. Pennsylvania ms French 15 is 'by far the
most interesting extant anthology of fourteenth century French lyrics'
(p 78): the quality of selection is high, the range of subject and forms
is wide, and the arrangement of texts reflective of a sensitive reader of
literature, perhaps Granson or another friend of Chaucer.

Individual Lost Works

'Origines upon the Maudeleyne'

486 Garth, Helen Meredith. *Saint Mary Magdalen in Medieval Literature.*
Johns Hopkins University Studies in Historical and Political Science,
vol 67, no. 3. Baltimore: Johns Hopkins University Press, 1950.
Emphasizes basic characteristics of the Magdalen tradition — her
symbolism and general importance in the Middle Ages. Includes
extensive bibliography.

487 Hammond, Eleanor P. *Bibliographical Manual.* 1908. See **36**. Pp
433–4.
'Lamentation of Mary Magdalen,' of which no mss are known, was
printed by Pynson in 1526, and subsequently reprinted in the
blackletter editions of Thynne and Speght, and, later, by Urry, Bell,
Anderson and Chalmers, either as Chaucer's 'Maudeleyne' or as a
poem imputed to Chaucer. Tyrwhitt rejected the poem. Bertha M.
Skeat, who edited the poem in a Zurich dissertation (1897), suggests
that the author was a nun and would date the poem ca 1460–80.

488 Jennings, Margaret. 'The Art of the Pseudo-Origen Homily: *De Maria
Magdalena.*' *M&H*, 5 (1974), 139–52.
Explores the synthesis of homiletic, scriptural, rhetorical, dramatic,
and mystical patterns of the Pseudo-Origen masterpiece, which

originates in the late twelfth or early thirteenth centuries, and which perhaps was Chaucer's source. The original stands at the pinnacle of the *modus antiquiis* in sermon construction. The work is 'a magnificent expression of the Christian humanism of the Middle Ages. Its major character is fully and humanly drawn with a consistent personality, adequate motivation, and plausible response' (p 149).

489 Malvern, Marjorie M. *Venus in Sackcloth: The Magdalen's Origins and Metamorphoses.* Carbondale: Southern Illinois University Press, 1975.
Discusses Gnostic and Apocryphal traditions as well as ancient pagan sources as background to the flowering of the cult of Magdalen and various 'lives' of the erotic penitent saint in the Middle Ages. Treats extensively her iconography and representation in the fine arts (20 plates), and devotes two chapters to her impact on medieval drama (pp 100–25). Concludes with twentieth-century treatments of the story.

490 McCall, John P. 'Chaucer and the Pseudo-Origen *De Maria Magdalena:* A Preliminary Study.' *Spec*, 46 (1971), 491–509.
Pseudo-Origen's *De Maria Magdalena* enjoyed great popularity and wide circulation between the thirteenth and sixteenth centuries. Of the fourteen earliest mss four are anonymous, which suggest that in its earliest form no author was known. Two early mss ascribe it to Anselm of Canterbury, another to Gregory the Great. But apart from these few 'the homily is consistently assigned to Origen'; ms evidence thus 'overwhelmingly supports the conclusion that this is the original for Chaucer's "Orygenes upon Maudeleyne" ' (p 493). The homily was apparently used for Easter Thursday and also for the Feast of Mary Magdalene (July 22); this explains why it exists in two forms. There is no clear reason why it was assigned to Origen. The exegesis of the biblical text is unlike Origen's allegorical method: 'the stylistic, figurative, and rhythmic intricacies of the Latin text contrast sharply with Origen's usual simplicity and clarity' (p 494). Chaucer may have seen *De Maria Magdalena* in a devotional miscellany containing works by Bernard such as those on the Virgin, which Chaucer apparently knew, or in a ms containing Innocent's *De Miseria Humanae Conditionis.* Chaucer was not only a great translator but also a great user of translations; moreover, he regularly worked from more than one version when others were available. Several French translations of the homily exist from the fourteenth century; also Italian, German, Provençal, Spanish, Portuguese, Flemish, and in the sixteenth century, English. Chaucer's interest in the sermon was thus not unique; 'he was one among many' (p 496). The homily is lively, dramatic, full of pathos and human understanding, not so much a commentary on John 20:11–8 as a dramatization with a moral. McCall summarizes the

treatise, with swatches of translation and commentary, and appends a checklist of Latin mss, mss of translations, and printed editions of translations.

490a Mycoff, David A., ed. *A Critical Edition of the Legend of Mary Magdalena from Caxton's Golden Legende of 1483.* Salzburg Studies in English Literature: Elizabethan and Renaissance Studies, ed. James Hogg. 92:11. Salzburg: Institut für Anglistik und Amerikanistik, Universität Salzburg, 1985.
Part 1, 'Patristic and Medieval legends of Mary Magdalene,' deals with types and categories of the legend, its development and transmission through Latin texts, and Middle English Magdalen legends, with appendices on textual affiliations between the *Speculum historiale*, the *Legenda aurea*, and the South English legendary. Part 2, 'Caxton's Legend of Mary Magdalene,' pp 95–115, is a textual introduction on early printed editions, a system for classification of variants, and discussion of variants. The edition (pp 116–47) includes extensive notes (pp 149–86). Part 3 (pp 187–256) consists of appendices: (1) a critical edition of Caxton's legend of Mary of Egypt, (2) a transcription of Middle French legends of Mary Magdalene and Mary of Egypt (*Légende dorée*).

491 Oram, Karen Alexandra. 'Stylistic Ornament in Three Fifteenth-Century English Legends of Mary Magdalene: A Study in Flamboyant Styles.' Catholic University of America Dissertation, 1981. Abstracted, *DAI*, 42 (1981), 714A.
Oram considers such features of flamboyance as schematic parallelism, aureate clusters, rhyme and alliteration in Osbern Bokenham's 'Lyf of Marye Maudelyn' (1447), William Caxton's 'Lyf of Seynt Marye Magdalene' (1483), and the ms Digby 133 *Play of Mary Magdalene* (late fifteenth century).

492 Robbins, Rossell Hope. 'A Middle English Prayer to St. Mary Magdalen.' *Traditio*, 24 (1968), 458–64.
In the massive sweep of in-depth research on hymns and prayers to St Mary Magdalen, one little Middle English poem in Harley ms 667, from the second half of the fourteenth century, has been overlooked. It is 'the sole versified prayer [in English] to this saint before 1500' (p 458). It relates only vaguely to the European Latin tradition. 'Verse prayers to saints are not very common in Middle English' (p 462).

493 Saxer, Victor. *La Culte de Marie Madeleine en Occident des Origines à la fin du Moyen Âge.* Cahiers d'archéologie et d'histoire, No. 3. Paris: Société des fouilles archéologiques, 1959.
A comprehensive study of the Magdalen cult with extensive bibliography.

494 Szövérffy, Joseph. '*Peccatrix Quondam Femina:* A Survey of the Mary Magdalen Hymns,' *Traditio,* 19 (1963), 79–146.
Szövérffy traces the well-established tradition of Mary Magdalen hymns through one hundred and sixty poems. His comments on recurring motifs and on other studies of the Magdalen literature are extensive. This study is a good starting point for a novice in the field.

495 Woolf, Rosemary. 'English Imitations of the *Homelia Origenis de Maria Magdelena.*' In *Chaucer and Middle English Studies in Honour of Rossell Hope Robbins.* Ed. Beryl Rowland. London: George Allen and Unwin Ltd, 1974. Pp 384–91.
Woolf investigates English imitations of the *Homelia* and problems involved in such imitation, especially problems pertaining to the differing treatments of Magdelena in John and the Synoptic Gospels. 'One thing is certain: Chaucer's *Origenes upon the Maudeleyne* kept very close to its original. To recast it as a narrative of the Resurrection or as a life of Mary Magdalene would have required a theological acuity entirely alien to Chaucer, whilst the device of extracting the *planctus* seems more characteristic of the decline and close of the Middle Ages when vernacular complaints of the Virgin were especially in vogue' (p 389). Chaucer probably wrote the piece in prose. There is much in the Latin work to attract the young Chaucer, but he probably translated the work because he was asked to do so, in which case he wrote not simply to please a patroness but also undertook 'a work of fashion' (p 390).

'Wreched Engendring of Mankynde'*

[*Since virtually all of the studies below are part of a single controversy, for the sake of convenience I have arranged the items chronologically.]

496 Brown, Carleton. 'An Holy Medytacion — by Lydgate?' *MLN,* 40 (1925), 282–5.
'An Holy Medytacion,' printed by MacCracken as one of Lydgate's minor poems (670), is 'almost a verbal translation of a Latin poem *De Humana Miseria Tractatus* (Trinity College Dublin ms E.2.33). The Latin poem, a political satire in rhythm and in substance an imitation of the celebrated Apocalypsis Goliae, was probably composed by an Englishman during the reign of Henry III. The English adaptation inserts many didactic amplifications (lines 63–6, 69–72, 74–110, 115–8, 136–46, 154–6, 166–80). Evidence supporting Lydgate's authorship is slim. The poem is in couplets instead of the stanza form Lydgate regularly used in his shorter poems. It appears in only two mss, both

by Shirley. In Trin. Coll. ms R.3.20 it occurs between *Anelida's Compleynt* and Occleve's *Letter of Cupid*, with no indication of authorship (p 284); in Ashmole 59, which was transcribed after 1447 when Shirley was eighty years of age, the ascription reads: 'Here nowe folowethe an holy meditacon made by the Religious man Lidegate Daun Johan, the munk of Bury.' This ms also ascribes 'Quia amore langeo' and a macaronic poem to the Virgin to Lydgate, neither of which is by him. Brown finds un-Lydgatean rhymes in the poem as well. 'Neither external nor internal evidence, therefore, appears to give ground for assigning the *Holy Medytacion* to the Monk of Bury. But I can not feel that in removing this poem from his canon we are seriously impairing the lustre of Lydgate's poetic laurels' (p 285).

497 — 'Chaucer's *Wreched Engendring*.' *PMLA*, 50 (1935), 997–1011.
The source of 'An Holy Medytacion,' *De Miseria Humana Tractatus*, is based on Innocent III's *De Contemptu Mundi*. The poem cannot be by Lydgate for various linguistic reasons. But it could be by Chaucer. The rhymes 'are characteristically Chaucerian' (p 1005), the spelling and idiom is right, and it occurs with other Chaucer poems in the mss. 'Having once recognized Chaucer's authorship of the poem, one need feel no hesitation in cancelling the unfortunate heading given it by Shirley ... and identifying it as ... "Of the Wreched Engendring of Mankinde" ' (p 1009). The springtime description of the beginning of the poem with its 'haunting Chaucerian quality' (p 1010) is not an imitation of the Canterbury Prologue; 'instead of being an echo, [it] becomes an adumbration' (p 1011). Possibly Chaucer composed the poem before he came under the direct influence of *De Contemptu Mundi*.

498 Tatlock, J.S.P. 'Has Chaucer's *Wretched Engendering* Been Found?' *MLN*, 51 (1936), 275–84.
Challenges Brown's thesis **497**: 'Vocabulary is a parlous thing to meddle with in argument' (p 278). The verse of *'An Holy Medytacion'* is too regular to be Chaucer's, its rhymes too 'commonplace,' too 'easy and cheap' (p 278). Chaucer's reference to a translation of *Wreched Engendring* 'implies distinctly that is was in prose, that it was a genuine translation, and that it was from Innocent's *De Contemptu Mundi*' (p 284). The *Medytacion*, on the other hand, is a loose translation of a work only indirectly related to Innocent, in couplets interspersed with pious invention 'during which the phrases of the greatest of early English poets repeatedly sprang to mind' (p 279). Brown claims the work to be early Chaucer, but it is in decasyllabic couplets, not the octosyllabics of early Chaucer, which would suggest something around 1386, not earlier (p 279). All of 'Chaucer's formally religious works are without exception rather close translations or at

least in substance entirely borrowed' (p 281). The *Medytacion* has too much pious interpolation to qualify as Chaucer's. 'It is a trifle of a paradox that Mr. Brown, after drily remarking in 1925 that the *Meditation* is no great loss to Lydgate, in 1935 is ready to claim it is good enough for Chaucer' (p 280).

499 Dempster, Germaine. 'Did Chaucer Write "An Holy Medytacion"?' *MLN*, 51 (1936), 284–95.
There are strong reasons against Brown's argument **497**: 1) Generation was surely the main subject of *Wreched Engendring*, but that topic is 'almost completely left aside' in *Meditation* (p 286). 2) Other writers contemporary with Chaucer use not only as many 'identical rime-pairs' as Chaucer but many more than did the author of *Meditation*, thus invalidating the argument that use of rhyme-pairs suggests Chaucer. 3) The frequent occurrence of 'Chaucerian phrases' is undermined by the fact that *Meditation* 'can hardly be said to be written in Chaucer's *style*' (p 287). 4) The scattering of Chaucer pieces throughout the Trinity ms 'warns us at once against assuming that Shirley had any reason for placing *An Holy Medytacion* near Chaucerian pieces' (p 289). Shirley is gossipy and if he had any hint of Chaucerian authorship it is likely he would have mentioned it. That he says the poem is Lydgate's 'does not speak in favor of Chaucer' (p 289). There are other more general objections to Chaucerian authorship. The monotonous treatment of topics reflects not Chaucer but rather an ecclesiastic who is, 'if not a professional preacher, at least a moralizer by inclination and practice' (p 291). The poverty of invention speaks against Chaucer also; contrast the poem with *ABC*. There are many instances of syntax, phrasing, and vocabulary which 'sound un-Chaucerian'; Brown's 'characteristically Chaucerian phrases' bear the 'clearest earmark of imitative work' (p 293). The poet must have been a preacher with 'good intentions, an inactive brain, and not over-intense emotions' (p 294) who liked Chaucer and strove to imitate him.

500 Brown, Carleton. 'An Affirmative Reply.' *MLN*, 51 (1936), 296–300.
The un-Chaucerian qualities cited by Tatlock **498** and Dempster **499** are due to Shirley's 'eccentric spellings.' 'Engendering' is always 'connected with man's wretched state consequent upon Adam's sin,' not merely procreation (pp 298–9). Cf *Pricke of Conscience*, which abridges details pertaining to procreation. The absence of such material in *Meditation* 'merely serves as evidence of Chaucer's good taste' (p 300).

501 Fischer, W. *AB*, 47 (1936), 291–2; Dorothy Everett, *YWES*, 17 (1936), 70–2.
Reviews of the Brown-Tatlock and Dempster debate.

502 Webster, Mildred. 'The Vocabulary of "An Holy Medytacion".' *PQ*, 17 (1938), 359–64.
Analysis of vocabulary 'adds weight to the argument that the poem is Chaucer's' (p 359). Considers Chaucerian words, inflectional forms, and non-Chaucerian words. Only .6% of the words may be considered non-Chaucerian in that they do not occur in the Chaucer concordance, but some of these are 'translation words and others are suited to the context' (p 363). So small a percentage is entirely consistent with Chaucerian practice. With Gower, Occleve, and Lydgate the number of non-Chaucerian words varies from 1.05% to 3.25% (average 1.98%, or three times as great as that of *An Holy Medytacion*) (p 364). The average new words for other Chaucerian poems is .605%, 'almost exactly that of the poem in question' (p 364).

503 Dempster, Germaine. 'Chaucer's *Wretched Engendering* and *An Holy Meditation*.' *MP*, 35 (1937), 27–9.
Dempster's essay was read by Tatlock and 'can be taken as our joint work' (p 27n). The first part of the argument dissociates *Holy Meditation* from Innocent. 'About one (scattered) quarter of the poem is somewhat like Innocent's treatise; nothing in the other three quarters has any kind of resemblance to anything in it' (p 27). Dempster then returns to the problem of meaning in the title of Chaucer's treatise. 'If words mean anything, "wretched engendering" means conception and gestation' (p 28). The *Meditation*, on the other hand, is not only not about procreation but expressly refuses to discuss it. Moreover, *LGW* implies that Chaucer's work was in prose. Chaucer never wrote in couplets in his early career. Moreover, the style of *Meditation* never recalls Chaucer by its 'vigor, freshness, or variety, but only by easily borrowed phrases that make the *Meditation* Chaucerian to the same extent as an overdose of pearls and pretty feathers impart a Rembrandt character to some portraits by followers of Rembrandt' (p 29). There is no shred of support for the conjecture of Chaucerian authorship of *Meditation*, 'a good deal against it, and not the slightest objection to the *Meditation* having been written by an admirer of Chaucer' (p 29).

504 Brown, Beatrice Daw. 'Chaucer's *Wreched Engendrynge*.' *MP*, 35 (1938), 325–33.
Mrs. Brown's essay has been read by her husband Carleton 'and can be taken as our joint work' (p 325n). Mrs. Dempster's restatement of old arguments 'contains assertions so vehement as to call for examination' (p 325). Her argument that mss contain not 'the slightest presumption in favor of Chaucer' is wrong. Trin. Coll. Camb. ms R 3.20 'is not a haphazard miscellany, and the manuscript arrangement makes it evident that Shirley gave attention to the grouping of his material' (p

326). The poem appears second in a group of seven poems of which
the first, fourth, fifth, sixth, and seventh are ascribed to Chaucer and
known to be by him. Moreover, Mrs. Dempster's assertion that
Chaucer 'never wrote couplets before the late eighties' requires revision
of the handbooks on Chaucer of forty years' standing! Tatlock himself
argued that the *Palamon* was early and in couplets (p 326). Dempster
objects that the style never recalls Chaucer's vigor and freshness, but
that depends on what one compares it with. The *Meditation* shows
more variety than *Ariadne*. Moreover the rhyme-pairs are distinctive
and Chaucerian. On the 'overdose of pearls and pretty feathers' thesis,
'subjective reporting of this kind is anyone's game'; it should be noted
that the 'borrowed' phrases come from 'a surprisingly wide range of
Chaucer's work. The powers of selection and association presupposed
by these results seem inconsistent with the primitive psychology
attributed by Mrs. Dempster to Chaucer's sedulous ape' (p 329). The
lines in *LGW* which Mrs. Dempster says state that *Wreched
Engendring* is in prose were added to the G-Prologue. The 'in prose'
phrase refers to *Boece* in the F-text. 'It seems overliteral ... to apply
the former context to the new insertion and infer that the added item
must have been a prose translation' (p 330). Mrs. Brown concludes by
defending the interpretation of 'wreched engendring' as a metaphor of
the fallen state of man, insisting that no medieval writer would have
understood the phrase in 'the narrowly restricted sense in which Mrs.
Dempster takes it' (pp 331–2).

505 Lewis, Robert Enzer. 'What Did Chaucer Mean by *Of the Wreched
Engendrynge of Mankynde?*' *ChauR*, 2 (1968), 139–58.
The syntax of the *LGW* passage does suggest that *translated* and *in
prose* refer syntactically to both *Boece* and *Wreched Engendrynge*.
Moreover, the sense is that the work may be found in the writings of
Pope Innocent, among his works rather than in the *De miseria
humane conditionis*. Nonetheless, after discussing meanings of *miseria,
conditionis, wreched,* and *engendrynge*, Lewis concludes that the title
could be Chaucer's way of translating *De miseria humane conditionis*.
The varieties of titles of Innocent's work in the 360 mss is striking. *De
miseria humane conditionis* is the more popular title in mss in the
British Isles. Manuscript titles often reflect the content of the first
chapter, not the whole work, although it is meant to refer to the whole
work. Brown was wrong in thinking that Chaucer refers to a work
derived from Innocent, and Tatlock and Dempster wrong in thinking
that the work must be a translation of just the first five chapters.
Chaucer used at least eight chapters of Innocent's treatise in *MLT* and
PardT, yet not a single one of these passages is from the first five
chapters of the treatise. The evidence seems to be that in adding the

mention of the treatise in the revised prologue of *LGW* Chaucer means 'to indicate that he made a translation of the whole *De miseria humane conditionis*'; it would have been in prose and made between 1385–95. 'More than this one cannot say' (p 158).

506 Lotario dei Segni (Pope Innocent III). *De Miseria Conditionis Humanae*, ed. Robert E. Lewis. The Chaucer Library. Athens: University of Georgia Press, 1978.
The purpose of the Chaucer Library editions is 'to present the works that Chaucer knew, translated, or made use of in his writings in versions that are as close as possible to those that were in existence, circulating, and being read by Chaucer and his contemporaries' (p xi). Lewis consulted 688 mss of *De Miseria* and collated 208, including all mss of English provenance. He chooses Lansdowne 358 as his copy text, a manuscript 'typical of the kind in existence and circulating in Britain during the Middle Ages' (p 51). His introduction includes discussions of date, authorship, the treatise's contents, its popularity and influence, Chaucer's indebtedness to it in *CT*, and the question of whether he translated some of it as *Wreched Engendrynge*. It is possible that Chaucer did translate it exactly as he says he did, probably after 1390 and before 1394–5 (pp 17–31). Lewis' edition prints the Latin and modern English translation on facing pages; it includes extensive notes on mss readings and on marginal glosses.

- Review by Daniel Silvia, *SAC*, 2 (1980), pp 167–72. 'I am at a loss to say who could find this book of use. It purports to be neither what Innocent wrote nor what Chaucer read. The elaborate and extensive apparatus does not in any reasonably simple way provide retrievable information. The text itself is based on a manuscript [Lansdowne 358] that has no authority of any kind ... It is still not clear whether Chaucer used *De Miseria* or instead got his materials from some other source. This edition calls into question whether it is feasible to expect that we can recover all of Chaucer's library' (p 172).

Book of the Leoun

507 Dear, F.M. 'Chaucer's *Book of the Lion.*' *MAE*, 7 (1938), 105–12. Noting that Froissart refers to Lionel, Duke of Clarence, as 'Monseigneur Lion,' Dear conjectures that Chaucer's poem might have been 'an occasional piece for Lionel, in whose service he was during the years 1357–60, and perhaps longer' (p 105). There are no known personal references to Lionel in any of Chucer's works, though there are references to all other patrons — Gaunt, Richard, and Henry. To

assume that Chaucer's poem was merely a translation of Machaut's poem is 'too simple an explanation to be adequate, since Chaucer always showed originality and purpose in combining even those passages which followed close to his models' (p 106). In the Retraction it is grouped with poems like *PF* and *BD*. Dear summarizes Machaut's *Dit dou Lyon*, where 'allegorically the lion represents the type of perfect lover, just as the ugly beasts round about represent the flatterers and slanderers' (p 112). Probably the poem was written 'to celebrate Lionel's marriage, consecrated at Milan, June 5, 1368, or perhaps the signing of the marriage treaty which had taken place at Windsor with some ceremony on 25 April. Then the lion could easily have represented Lionel, ie, the perfect lover, and the lovely lady, Violante, who was young and beautiful. And since, according to Hardyng, Lionel was brave and handsome, and exceedingly tall of stature, it would have been quite suitable to identify him with the majestic king of beasts' (p 112).

508 Langhans, Victor. 'Chaucers Book of the Leoun.' *Anglia*, 52 (1928), 113–22.

The *Book of the Lion* may have been lost even before Chaucer died. Since Tyrwhitt the poem has been considered an early work, based perhaps on Machaut's *Dit dou Lyon*. Langhans doubts that its source need be restricted to that work, however. Probably it was written about the time of *BD*, when Machaut's influence on Chaucer was great. Brusendorff 480 argued that it might be a late work, a political satire based on Deschamps. But Langhans says that is unlikely, since Chaucer so seldom expresses political opinions, especially in old age. Chaucer classifies it with his sinful works, which he would not have done had it been a satire propounding social reform. Besides, it would be difficult for a late work of Chaucer to disappear. An early work might well have been lost, however.

✎ Part VI: The Chaucer Apocrypha

Introduction

The Chaucer Apocrypha is at present the most neglected area of Chaucer and fifteenth-century studies. It is also the most chaotic. But that very choas makes it potentially one of the richest areas for investigation. Consisting of those works not by Chaucer but which were once associated with his name, the poems and tales of the apocrypha have suffered a curiously paradoxical fate: having once enjoyed an unwarranted esteem by having been included in the blackletter editions of Chaucer in the sixteenth and seventeenth centuries, they then were beset with scurrilous opprobrium, as editors, beginning with Tyrwhitt, plucked them of their false glories and cast them out. Once so chastened and flung aside, their curse has been a chilly oblivion. Since they are neither one thing or the other, few literary judges have given them so much as a literary hearing.

Yet once looked at apart from questions of Chaucerian authorship and the implied accusations of presumption, or worse, lack of craft or imagination, this very considerable body of literature may be seen to have many excellences and curiosities which will amply reward the attention of scholars — historians as well as men of letters — in years to come. Indeed, the reclamation has already begun by such perceptive British scholars as Derek Pearsall, in his editions of *The Flower and the Leaf* and *The Assemblie of Ladies* 645, and V.J. Scattergood, in his *Works of Sir John Clanvowe* 622. Excellent work has likewise recently appeared on Lydgate [see especially 668, 673, 674, 676], which has helped somewhat to free him from the deadly witticisms of Saintsbury 677. Ethel Seaton's curious book on Sir Richard Roos 679, though eccentric in its mad pursuit of anagrams, double acrostics, and territorial rights over most of the literary acreage of the fifteenth and early sixteenth centuries, contains several moraines of eclectic research which will benefit judicious scholars attempting to explore the taste, fashions, audiences, and acquaintanceships of the great households which patronized Chauceriana. Anthony Jenkins' edition of the *Isle of Ladies* **663** and Russell Fraser's *Court of Venus* **641** have also helped fill major gaps and will greatly facilitate the mapping of paths through the quagmire. But perhaps most useful of all at this stage is Richard Firth Green's recent study, *Poets and Princepleasers* **557**, which provides a detailed survey of the courts that produced and admired 'Chaucerian' poetry.

To be done right, the Chaucer Apocrypha should have a separate volume in the *Chaucer Bibliographies* all to itself. By including it here we revisit upon it the crimes of our fathers by viewing it merely as an addendum to Chaucer. Worse, because of limitations of space, time, and patience, I am unable to provide a complete or even comprehensive coverage. At best the following selection is an acknowledgement of some important work in this area, with hints at directions students might wish to consider for further study. I have divided this bibliography into six parts: 1) crucial reference works which define the Chaucer Apocrypha and represent the most comprehensive surveys of work done in this area; 2) facsimile editions of manuscripts and of early printed editions; 3) studies of Chaucer's audience in the fourteenth, fifteenth, and sixteenth centuries; 4) general studies pertaining to the Apocrypha; 5) spurious additions to the *Canterbury Tales*; 6) miscellaneous works and authors. I have included little material on the Scottish Chaucerians, since that has been for several decades a well-defined and researched area apart from the English Chaucerians. In a comprehensive study of the Chaucer Apocrypha, Henryson's *Testament of Cresseid* would enjoy a more prominent place than I have allowed (see **686–734**); so too the *Kingis Quair* (see **192–192g**) and, though not Scottish, the balades of Charles of Orleans, all of which are intimately affiliated with the Chaucer Apocrypha. In lieu of more thorough treatment in this bibliography I direct readers to the following researches of Florence H. Ridley on Henryson and *KQ:*

509 Ridley, Florence H. 'Middle Scots Writers.' In *A Manual of the Writings in Middle English: 1050–1500*. Vol 4. New Haven: the Connecticut Academy of Arts and Science, 1973. Pp 961–1060; 1123–284. The description of Henryson's works appears on pp 965–88, with *Testament of Cresseid* on pp 976–8. See **688**.

510 — 'Middle Scots Writers.' In *A Manual of the Writings in Middle English: 1050–1500*. Vol 4. New Haven: The Connecticut Academy of Arts and Science, 1973. Pp 961–1060; 1123–84. The description of James I and *The Kingis Quair* appears on pp 961–5. 'The evidence for James I's authorship consists of the poem's autobiographical content, its title and colophon in the unique manuscript, Bodleian 3354, and John Major's attribution to the king of a poem about his queen.

However, an autobiographical pose may be assumed by any poet for
the creation of any story. The evidence of ms Bodleian 3354 cannot be
accepted as conclusive for it was compiled about 1490, thus not by
anyone who could have vouched personally for James' authorship; and
of the twelve poems which it contains one has an illegible signature,
five are correctly, five incorrectly attributed to Chaucer, and *The
Kingis Quair* to James' (p 965). It is impossible to evaluate Major's
testimony accurately since its source is unknown. The 'most telling
evidence against' James' authorship is 'the failure of people whom one
might expect to acknowledge the king's poetic ability' (p 964). The
bibliography for *KQ* (pp 1124–35) is divided according to MSS,
Editions, Selections, Modernizations, Textual Matters, Language,
Versification, Date, Authorship, Sources and Literary Relations, Other
Scholarly Problems, Literary Criticism, and Bibliography. On *KQ* see
also **192–192g**.

Comprehensive Reference Works on the Chaucer Apocrypha

511 Skeat, W.W., ed. *Chaucerian and Other Pieces, being a Supplement to
the Complete Works of Geoffrey Chaucer, in six volumes.* Volume VII.
Oxford: Oxford University Press, 1897.
This is the first attempt to separate the apocryphal and spurious into
a separate, scholarly edition which would preserve them according to
their own merits. Although the works have all been appended to
Chaucer's canon, Skeats warns that 'appended' be understood
advisedly, since it is not true that all the non–Chaucerian works in the
blackletter editions were attributed to Chaucer. Thynne marked 'In
Praise of Peace' as Gower's, Scogan's 'Balade' is attributed to Scogan,
the 'Letter to Cupid' is dated 1402, though Chaucer is known by the
editor to have died in 1400, the 'Testament of Cresseid' speaks of
Chaucer having written his *Troilus*, and so on. Skeat's edition includes
useful notes on individual items, discussion of mss and earlier editions,
comments on authorship, and résumés of the items. The following
works are included: Thomas Usk, *Testament of Love; Plowman's Tale;
Jack Upland*; Gower's *The Praise of Peace*; Thomas Hoccleve, *The
Letter of Cupid, To the Kinges Most Noble Grace*, and *To the Lordes
and Knightes of the Garter*; Henry Scogan, *A Moral Balade*; John
Lydgate, *Complaint of the Black Knight* (or *Complaint of a Loveres
Lyfe*), *Flour of Curtesye, Balade in Commendation of our Lady, To

*my Soverain Lady, Ballad of Good Counsel, Beware of Doubleness,
Balade Warning Men to Beware of Deceitful Women,* and *Three
Sayings*; Richard Ros, *La Belle Dame Sans Mercy*; Robert Henryson,
Testament of Cresseid; Clanvowe, *Cuckoo and the Nightingale* (or *Book
of Cupid, God of Love*); *Envoy to Alison; Flower and the Leaf* and
Assembly of Ladies (by a lady); John Lydgate, *A Goodly Balade* and
Go Forth, King; The Court of Love; A Virelai; John Walton,
Prosperity; Leaulte Vault Richesse; Sayings printed by *Caxton*; and
Balade in Praise of Chaucer.

512 Hammond, E.P. *Bibliographical Manual.* 1908. See **36.**
Ch 5, 'Verse and Prose Printed with the Work of Chaucer,' pp 406–63:
Hammond catalogues all doubtful works as well as apocryphal works
in her alphabetical listing. For each item she supplies notes on mss,
printed editions, authenticity, title, and other addenda. The items
include: Alison; Assembly of Gods (Lydgate?); AL; Ballad(s) marked
as Chaucer's in Shirley's ms Adds. 16165; BC; Ballad in
Commendation of our Lady; Ballad of Pity, or Complaint to his Lady;
Beryn; Beware; CBK (Lydgate); Chastity; Chronicle made by
Chaucer; CD; CMF; CML; CL; Craft of Lovers; CN; Doubleness
(Lydgate); Eight Goodly Questions with their Answers; Fairest of Fair;
FL; FC; Gamelyn; Go Forth, King; How Mercurie with Pallas Venus
and Minarva Appered to Paris of Troie, He Slepying by a Fountain; If
It Befall; I have a Lady; In Feuerere; Isle of Ladies; It Cometh by
Kynde; It Falleth for a Gentleman; JU; John Gower unto the Worthy
and Noble King Henry IV (In Praise of Peace); LBD; Lamentation of
Mary Magdalen; Leaulte Vault Richesse; Letter of Cupid (Hoccleve);
Letter of Dido to Aeneas; MB; Moral Proverbs of Christine; Mother of
God (Hoccleve); Mother of Nurture; Newfangleness (*AWU*); Nine
Ladies Worthy; Of Their Nature; O Merciful; O Mossie Quince; Ora
pro Anglia Sancta Maria quod Thomas Cantuaria; Pilgrim's Tale;
PlowT; Poems Supposed to be Written by Chaucer During his
Imprisonment; Praise and Commendation of Geoffrey Chaucer; Praise
of Women; Prophecy; Prosperity (Walton); Prov; Remedy of Love;
Romaunt; Sayings of Dan John (Lydgate); Scogan unto the Lords and
Gentlemen of the King's House; Since I from Love; Story of Thebes,
or, Siege of Thebes (Lydgate); Ten Commandments of Love; TC; TL;
To the Kings Most Noble Grace and to the Lords and Knights of the
Garter (Hoccleve); To My Sovereign Lady; Ros; Utter Thy Language
(Lydgate); Virelay; Wicked Tongue (Lydgate); WN.

513 Robbins, Rossell Hope. 'The Chaucerian Apocrypha.' In *A Manual of
the Writings in Middle English: 1050-1500.* Ed. Albert E. Hartung.
New Haven: Connecticut Academy of Arts and Sciences, 1973. Vol. 4.
Pp 1061–1101; 1285–1306.

'Some one hundred miscellaneous poems have been either ascribed to
Chaucer in fifteenth- and sixteenth-century manuscripts, or printed
with or as Chaucer's in the black-letter editions of the sixteenth
century, or linked to Chaucer by later scholars in the eighteenth and
nineteenth centuries' (p 1061). Robbins divides these poems into those
now accepted as by Chaucer; spurious Canterbury tales; poems by
Lydgate, Hoccleve, Gower, Henryson; Usk's prose *Testament*; and
other poems of the Chaucerian apocrypha. His discussion concentrates
on the later category and considers 1) the influence of John Shirley; 2)
other mss containing Chaucerian Apocrypha besides those of Shirley;
3) black-letter editions of Chaucer with Chaucerian Apocrypha; 4)
later editions of Chaucer with Chaucerian Apocrypha; apocryphal love
lyrics; and 5) courtly love aunters. Robbins discusses fifty-six
individual items all of which are cross-referenced with the
Brown-Robbins *Index of Middle English Verse* (New York: Columbia
University Press, 1943) or its Supplement (Robbins and Cutler,
Supplement to the Index [Lexington: University of Kentucky Press,
1965]). The love lyrics he devotes special attention to include The
Lover's Mass [Index 4186]; Balade to his mistress, fairest of fair [Index
923]; Balade and Envoy to Alison [Index 2479]; A Goodly Balade to his
Lady Margaret, or, Mother of Nurture [Index 2223]; To My Sovereign
Lady [Index 99]; Epistle to his Mistress, signed Chaucer [Index 1838];
Praise of Margaret the Daisy [Index 1562]; Warwick's Virelai [Index
1288]; Virelai [Index 267]; Earl Rivers' Virelai on Fickle Fortune
[Supplement 3193.5]; O Merciful and O Merciable [Index 2510]; The
Lover's Complaint against Fortune and his Lady [Index 564]; The Lay
of Sorrow [Index 482]; CMF [Index 231]; CML [Index 2626]; The Nine
Ladies Worthy [Index 2767]; The Judgment of Paris [Index 3197]; The
Describing of a Fair Lady [Index 1300]; O Mossie Quince [Index 2524];
Beware of Deceitful Women [Index 1944]; Balade against Hypocritical
Women [Index 2661]; A Praise of Women [Index 228]; The Remedy of
Love [Index 3084]; Balade by Chaucer [Index 1635]; The Plowman's
Song [Index 2611]. Courtly love aunters to which Robbins devotes
individual attention include: CL [Index 4205]; Birds' Praise of Love
[Index 1506]; Birds' Devotions [Index 357]; The Ten Commandments of
Love [Index 590]; The Parliament of Love [Index 2383]; The Court of
Venus [not in Index of Supplement]; The Craft of Lovers [Index 3761];
How a Lover Praiseth his Lady [Index 4043]; Supplicacio Amantis
[Index 147]; LBD [Index 1086]; O Bewtie Pereles [Index 2386]; For He
is True [Index 823]; AL [Index 1528]; FL [Index 4026]; IL [Index 3947];
Letter of Dido to Aeneas [Supplement 811.5]; The Example of Virtue
[Supplement 3954.8]; The Pastime of Pleasure [Index 4004]; The
Comfort of Lovers [Supplement 3357.5]; The Castell of Pleasure [Index
3811]. Robbins' commentaries regularly include résumés of the work

under consideration. He reminds the reader of the similarities between
love lyrics in the Chaucer Apocrypha and other fifteenth-century court
lyrics: 'To complete the picture of fifteenth-century courtly love
poetry, therefore, it is essential that the appropriate sections of the
chapter on Lyrics be consulted' (p 1074). Robbins' bibliography (pp
1285–1306) is thorough; it is subdivided according to the categories of
the introduction mentioned above and includes separate listings with
some annotation for individual poems cited under apocryphal love
lyrics and courtly love aunters. This is a major study and should be
the starting point for researching the Apocrypha.

Facsimile Editions of Manuscripts

514 *The Bannatyne Manuscript, compiled by George Bannatyne, 1568.* 4
vols. Printed for the Hunterian Club, 1896. Rpt New York: Johnson
Reprint Corporation, 1966.
The Bannatyne ms, which contains much of Henryson and Dunbar,
includes two Chaucerian pieces in a Scots dialect (#70, f 67a,
'Sumtyme this Warld so Steidfast was' vol II, pp 181–2; and #224, f
230a, 'The Song of Troyelus: Gif no luve is, O God, quhat feill I so' vol
III, pp 668–9, the latter consisting of five stanzas), and the following
additional eight poems which are attributed to Chaucer, usually by
the signature 'Finis quod Chaucier': #44, f 45b, 'Qwhylome in Grece,
that nobill regioun' vol II, p 123; #278, f 258a, 'Schort Epigrammis
aganis Wemen,' namely 'Gif all the erth war perchmene scribable' vol
IV, p 755; #279, f 258b, 'This work quha so sall sie or reid' vol IV, pp
755–8; #286, f 263a, 'O wicket Wemen, wilfull and variable' vol IV, p
768; #296, f 269a, 'The Lettre of Cupid: Cupeid, unto quhois
commandiment' vol IV, pp 783–98; #297, f 275a, 'All tho that list of
wemen evill to speik' vol IV, pp 799–804; #306, f 281a, 'Quhat menth
this? quhat is this windir Vre?' vol IV, pp 817–22; and #354,
'Quhylome in Grece that nobil regioun,' which is a duplicate of #44.

515 *Bodleian Library MS. Fairfax 16,* ed. John Norton-Smith. London:
Scolar Press, 1979.
A facsimile edition, with introduction (pp vii–xxi), of a 'nearly
perfectly preserved' ms (p vii) consisting of five parts recopied as a
whole from booklets of poetry of courtly experience concerned with
'sophisticated morality and the trials and tribulations of *fin amors* —
those concepts and imaginative experiences which reflect the social
and literary refinements of the "lettered chivalry" of the time' (p vii),

with a beautiful full page color illumination for Chaucer's *Mars* from
the hand of the Abingdon Missal Master. 'The bookseller who made
up Fairfax 16 made it up "to order", according to choices offered to
John Stanley [1400–1469, a gentleman employed in the service of
Henry V and Henry VI as Sheriff of Anglesey, Captain of Carnarvon,
Sergeant of the Armoury of the Tower, and Usher of the Chamber as
well as serving as MP for Surrey and as JP]. Stanley did not choose
single works or authors but booklets containing authors or works
possibly in already existing saleable copy or ready to be copied up
from resident display booklets' (pp vii–viii). Booklet I (ff 15r–186v)
includes *Mars*, *Venus*, Lydgate's 'Complaynte of a louers Lyfe,' *AA*,
Clanvowe's 'The Boke of Cupide god of Loue' (*CN*), *Truth*, Hoccleve's
'Epistle to Cupid,' 'Ragman's Roll,' *LBD*, Lydgate's *The Temple of
Glass*, *LGW*, *PF*, *BD*, 'The Envoy to Alison,' 'The Chaunces of the
Dyce,' and *HF* followed by three blank pages. This is the authoritative
text of *HF*. Booklet II (ff 187r–201v) includes *Pity*, *ABC*, *Fortune*,
Scogan, *Purse*, *Bukton*, a proverbial couplet, *Sted*, *AWU*, Lydgate's
Fall of Princes II.4432–8, 'Four Things that Make a Man a Fool' by
Lydgate?, 'On the Mutability of Man's Nature,' 'Complaint against
Hope,' *CD*, Hoccleve's 'Balade to Henry V for Money,' Lydgate's
'Doubleness,' and Lydgate's 'Prayer for King, Queen and People.'
Booklet III (ff 202r–305v) consists of Lydgate's *Reason and Sensuality*;
Booklet IV (306r–313v), of 'How a Lover Praiseth his Lady.' Booklet
V (ff 314r–29v) includes 'Venus Mass' and a collection of twenty
ballads, complaints, and letters of uncertain authorship except for
Charles of Orleans' 'O thou ffortune whyche hast the gouernaunce.'
Norton-Smith suggests that 'the idea of collections of Chaucer's minor
poems probably arose in the mid-fifteenth century' (p ix). He lists *CD*
as 'author unknown': 'The repetitious grammatical sequences (clogged
with relatives) and the total lack of plot-structure, concrete imagery
and literary allusiveness proclaim it not to be Chaucer's' (p xxviii).

516 *Manuscript Tanner 346: A Facsimile.* [Bodleian Library]. Introduction
by Pamela Robinson. The Facsimile Series of The Works of Geoffrey
Chaucer. Vol I. Ed. Paul G. Ruggiers and Donald M. Rose. Norman,
Oklahoma: Pilgrim Books; Suffolk, England: Boydell-Brewer, 1980.
An anthology of court poetry consisting of four booklets written in the
mid-fifteenth century by three scribes. Booklet I (ff 1–75), begun by
scribe A and completed by scribe B, contains *LGW* (ff 1r–40v);
Hoccleve's *Lepistre de Cupide* (ff 41r–48v); Lydgate's *A Complaynt of
a Loveres Lyfe* (ff 48v–59r); *AA* (ff 59v–65r); *Mars* (ff 65r–69v); *Venus*
(ff 69v–71r); *Pity* (ff 71r–73r); *A Lover's Plaint*, beginning 'As ofte as
syghes ben in herte trewe' (ff 73r–74v); *A Complaint for Lack of Sight*
(ff 74v–75v). Booklet II (ff 76–101), in the hand of scribe C, contains

Lydgate's *The Temple of Glas* (ff 76r–97r); Clanvowe's *CN* (ff 97r–101r); and *Envoy to Alison* (ff 101r–101v). Booklet III (ff 102–19), begun by scribe C and completed by scribe B, contains *BD* (ff 102r–19v). Booklet IV (ff 120–31), in the hand of scribe A, contains *PF*. 'The earliest owner of the ms who can be identified with any plausibility is John Greystoke, who died in 1501' (p xix). Robinson's introduction discusses the contents of the ms, date, foliation and collation, ruling, layout, handwriting, abbreviations, punctuation, corrections and annotations, decoration, binding, and the history of the ms.

517 *Manuscript Bodley 638: A Facsimile.* Introduction by Pamela Robinson. The Facsimile Series of The Works of Geoffrey Chaucer. Vol 2. Ed. Paul G. Ruggiers and Donald M. Rose. Norman, Oklahoma: Pilgrim Books; Suffolk, England: Boydell-Brewer, 1982.
A late fifteenth-century verse anthology which is missing the first quire, which may have contained *Mars, Venus*, and the missing first 467 lines of *Complaint of a Lover's Life* (cf 1st booklet of Fairfax 16). The ms seems to have been for some time in the possession of a grammar school, which may have used it as a text (pp xxxvii–xl). 'The manuscript is written by a single scribe who signed himself Lyty or Lity ... He wrote texts, headings, running titles, and learned apparatus ... in a mixed hand and the colophons in a Bastard display script' (p xxviii). The ms includes several works by Chaucer including *AA, Pity*, Prol to *LGW* (F version), *PF, BD, HF, ABC, Fortune, CD* and miscellaneous other works: Lydgate's 'Complaynte of a Loueres Lyfe' (lacking lines 1–467 of printed editions ff 1r–4v); Clanvowe's 'The boke of Cupide god of loue' (*CN*) (ff 11v–16r); 'The Temple of Bras' (Lydgate's 'Temple of Glass'; ff 16v–38r); Hoccleve's 'The lettre of Cupide god of loue' (ff 38v–45v); 'The chaunce of the Dyse' (lacking lines 295–336 of printed edition; ff 195r–203v); 'The Complaynte ageyne hope' (ff 209v–212r); 'Ragmanys Rolle' (ff 214v–218v); and 'The Ordre of Folys' (lacking lines 41–8 and 57–176; ff 219r–219v). Robinson agrees with Norton-Smith (515) that anthologies of Chaucer's verse probably did not arise until mid-fifteenth century 'when Shirley began publishing his verse anthologies' (p xxxv).

518 *St. John's College, Cambridge, Manuscript L.1: A Facsimile.* Introduction by Richard Beadle and Jeremy Griffiths. The Facsimile Series of The Works of Geoffrey Chaucer. Vol 3. Ed. Paul G. Ruggiers and Donald M. Rose. Norman, Oklahoma: Pilgrim Books; Suffolk, England: Boydell-Brewer, 1983.
The ms includes *T&C*, in a hand of the second quarter of the fifteenth-century, and a copy of Henryson's *TC* (ff 121v–128v) in an early seventeenth-century hand 'from a contemporary printed edition

[Speght] and inserted ... after the last book of the *Troilus*, giving evidence of the abiding interest of the story' (p xix). The ms is crucial to Root's three stages theory of the evolution of *T&C*, a theory based on the notion that Chaucer added Boethian material to the poem after its initial composition (see pp xxvii–xxix). The seventeenth-century scribe of Henryson's *Testament* does not identify him as author. He concludes the poem 'Explicit Liber Troili & Creiseidos.'

519 *The Findern Manuscript: Cambridge University Library MS. Ff 1.6.* Introduction by Richard Beadle and A.E.B. Owen. London: Scolar Press, 1977. Rpt 1978.

A facsimile edition of a late fifteenth- early sixteenth-century ms thought to have been compiled at Findern, southwest of Derby. A number of names appear in margins and on blank leaves which 'suggest a network of family and social relationships amongst a circle of north midland gentry ... The construction of the ms itself gives weight to the view that it was most probably an informal product of a well-to-do country house of the period' (p viii). Several leaves are missing, some having been cut out. The contents includes Gower's *CA* v.5921–6052 (part of Tale of Tereus), *CA* iv.1114–1244 (Amans on Idleness), *CA* iv.1245–1466 (Tale of Rosiphelee), *Pity*, 'A Lover's Plaint' in Lydgate's manner ('As ofte as syghes ben in herte trewe'), 'A Complaint for Lack of Sight' in Lydgate's manner, 'A Lover's Plaint' ('I may woll sygh for greuous ys my payne'), 'Without Variance' ('Where y haue chosyn stedefast woll y be'), 'A Lover's Plaint' ('Ye are to blame to sette yowre hert so sore'), *CN*, 'The Lover Wishes His Lady Recovery,' *PF*, *CA* i.3067–3425 (Tale of Three Questions), 'The Parliament of Love,' 'The Rule of Fortune,' a gnomic tag ('Pees maketh plente'), 'Feigned Love,' 'The Seven Deadly Sins' ('As I walkyd apon a day'), *Purse*, Complaint from *AA*, Tale of Thisbe from *LGW*, *Venus*, 'A Love Song' ('My woo full hert this clad in payn'), Hoccleve's *Lepistre de Cupide* (missing 20 stanzas), *CA* iv.2746–2926 (against Somnolence in prologue to Tale of Ceix and Alceone), *CA* viii.271–846 (part of Tale of Apollonius), *Sir Degrevant*, 'Cronekelys of seyntys and kyngys of yngelond,' 'The Emperour of Allmyen he Beryth goold an Egyll,' *LBD*, 'A Love Cycle' ('Welcome be ye my souereine'), 'A Slighted Lover's Complaint' ('Some tyme y loued as ye may see'), 'Desire to Serve His Mistress' ('Sith fortune hath me set thus in this wyse'), 'A Pledge of Loyalty' ('Now wold I fayne sum myrthis make'), 'A Lover's Distress' ('Alas alas and alas why'), 'The Vicissitudes fo Love' ('Alas what planet was y born undir'), 'A Lover's Plaint' ('Continuance / Of remembraunce'), 'Fortune Has Cast Me From Weal to Woe' ('My self walkyng all Allone'), 'The Delivered Lover' ('Som tyme y louid so do y yut'), 'A Love Song' ('ffor to preuente'), 'The Rancour of this Wicked

World,' 'An Orison to Our Lady by the Seven Joys,' 'A Prayer of the
Holy Name,' Lydgate's 'The Wicked Tongue,' 'Ther is no mor dredfull
pestelens' (a composite text including three stanzas from Lydgate's
Fall of Princes and three from *T&C*), 'Tied with a Line' by John
Halsham (?), 'Seven Wise Counsels,' Lydgate's 'A Complaint, for Lack
of Mercy,' 'Love's Sorrow' ('This ys no lyf alas that y do lede'), 'A
Complaint against His Mistress' ('My whofull herte plonged yn
heuynesse'), 'Desire to Serve' ('Euer yn one with my dew
attendaunce'), 'A Petition to His Mistress' ('Yit wulde I nat the causer
faryd a-mysse'), 'A Balade' ('Veryly / And truly'), 'A Lover's Plaint'
('As in my remembrauns non but ye Alone'), Lydgate's 'The Pain and
Sorrow of Evil Marriage' (imperfect), 'How myschaunce regnyth in
Ingeland; Capitulo xxvij,' 'A compleint vnto Dame Fortune; Capitulo
xxviij' (probably connected with the previous entry), 'The
complexions' ('Off yefftis large in loue hayth gret delite'), Lydgate's 'A
tretise for lauandres,' Alexander-Cassamus fragment (lines 1604–1977)
translated from *Les Voeux du Paon*, 'Complainte against Fortune' in
the manner of William de la Pole, Benedict Burgh's 'Chaunge not thi
ffreende that thou knowest of oolde' from *Cato Major*.

520 *The Poetical Works of Geoffrey Chaucer: A Facsimile of Cambridge
University Library MS GG.4.27.* 3 vols. With introductions by M.B.
Parkes and Richard Beadle. Norman, Oklahoma: Pilgrim Books,
1979–80.
'The manuscript is the only surviving example of a fifteenth-century
attempt to collect Chaucer's major poetical works in one volume:
Troilus and Criseyde, The Canterbury Tales, The Legend of Good
Women, and the Parliament of Fowls were copied consecutively, each
new item beginning in the middle of a quire. These are followed by the
early version of Lydgate's Temple of Glass and its accompanying poem
La Compleyn. The only independent quire contains three of Chaucer's
minor poems and two other lyrics. The Collection was originally
decorated and illustrated on a lavish scale' (vol 3, p 1). The ms now
begins with the independent quire which includes *ABC, Scogan, Truth,
The Bird's Praise of Love* ('In may whan every herte is lyght'), 'De
amico ad Amicam,' and 'Responsio.' The copies of *T&C* and *CT* are
both mutilated. After the Lydgate entries at the end (which are not
identified as being by Lydgate), an early seventeenth-century drawing
based upon the 1598 edition of Speght has been added, along with
Gentilesse, remarks on Hoccleve, Chaucer's portrait and genealogy and
other commendations of Chaucer, *Testament of Cresseid*, the
Retraction, Speght's glossary, *Purse*, and *Adam*. The ms came into the
possession of Joseph Holland ca 1600.

Early Printed Editions containing Apocryphal Works

521 Boyd, Beverly Mary, ed. *Chaucer according to William Caxton: Minor Poems and Boece, 1478.* See **168**.
Boyd prints three Caxton texts: First, a unique quarto copy consisting of only twenty-four leaves, lacking a gathering at the end, which includes *PF* (identified as 'the temple of bras' in the Explicit); a verse treatise ascribed to 'Iohn Gkogan' (should be Henry Scogan), which quotes the whole of *Gent;* 'Wyth empty honde men may no hawkes lure,' which Caxton does not label as Chaucer's ('he may or may not have realized that it is based on a proverb, which the Poet quotes twice: in the Wife of Bath's prologue [III:415], and in the Reeve's Tale [I:4134]' — p xi); 'The good counceyl of chawcer' (*Truth*); 'Balade of the vilage [sic. for 'visage'] without peyntyng' (*Fortune*); and three stanzas of *Scogan*, at which point the booklet breaks off. [The BLC lists a 1477? copy with these contents as well as a 1478? copy.] Boyd's second text is also a unique copy of a Caxton quarto in ten leaves, which includes *AA, Purse,* and a poem beginning 'Whan feyth failleth in preestes sawes,' which some mss attribute to Chaucer under the title of 'A Prophesy,' but which Caxton does not specify as Chaucer's. The third Caxton text which Boyd includes is *Boece,* printed in folio, of which seventeen copies (excluding fragments) survive.

522 Pynson, Richard, printer to the kynges most noble grace. [Blackletter edition, without title page.] London in Fletestrete, [1526?]
'Here beginneth the boke of Fame / made by Geffray Chaucer: / with dyuers other of / his workes.' Besides *HF,* Pynson includes *PF,* which begins under a woodcut above which is the heading 'The Assemble of Foules'; *LBD,* with the heading: 'This boke called la bele Dame Sauns mercy was translate out of French into Englysshe by Geffray Chaucer flour of peotes [sic] in our mother tong,' and an envoy 'de limprimeur' of six seven-line stanzas unique to Pynson [see Hammond **36**, pp 432–33, for a reprinting of the envoy]; *Truth,* headed 'Ecce bonum consilium Galfredi Chaucer contra fortunam'; 'Moral prouerbes of Christyne' [probably translated from the French by Earl Rivers]; 'The complaynt of Mary Magdaleyne' [probably by Lydgate]; 'The letter of Dydo to Eneas'; and 'A lytell exortacion, howe folke shulde behaue them selfe in all companyes' [by Lydgate].

523 Geoffrey Chaucer. *The Works 1532* [Thynne] *with supplementary material from the Editions of 1542, 1561* [Stow], *1598* [Speght] *and 1602.* A facsimile edition with Introduction [unpaginated] by Derek S. Brewer. London: The Scolar Press, 1969. Rpt 1974.

[See 4 for Skeat's 1905 facsimile edition of Thynne.]
Thynne's edition, 'the first serious attempt to gather together all of
Chaucer's productions,' was printed at London by Thomas Godfray,
and contains forty-four items, including a Preface by Sir Brian Tuke,
secretary to Henry VIII, and two tables of contents. At the end of the
second table appear three Chaucerian poems, none of which are
authentic: Eight Goodly Questions with their Answeres (beginning
'Sometyme in Grece that noble region'); To the Kynges Most Noble
Grace / and to the Lordes and Knyghtes of the Garter (actually by
Hoccleve); and Three Sayings (beginning 'Whan faithe fayleth in
preestes sawes'); all three were first printed by Caxton. CT ('The
seventh time printed and a relatively poor text. Of the woodcuts, the
Knight and the Squire are, according to Skeat, new; the others are
repeated from the editions of Caxton'); Romaunt ('The fullest text
available and the first edition'); T&C ('fourth time printed, but an
independent text'); The Testament of Creseyde ('An Anglicised text of
independent value of the Scottish poem of the late fifteenth-century by
Robert Henryson. The gap in the foliation ... shows that the poem
must have been inserted as an afterthought'); LGW; A Goodly Balade
of Chaucer (beginning 'Mother of norture'; the unique textual
authority); Boece (a close reprint of Caxton); BD (entitled 'The
Dreame of Chaucer'; first edition and of independent authority — the
only authority for lines 31–96); Bukton; PF (entitled 'The Assemble of
Foules'); FC ('by Lydgate, according to John Stow in 1561. The only
authority'); Pity (first edition and an independent text); LBD ('by Sir
Richard Ros, written soon after 1450'; first printed here); AA (first
printed by Caxton); AL (fifteenth century anonymous poem);
Astrolabe (first edition); CBK ('By Lydgate. Previously printed by
Wynkyn de Worde in an undated quarto'); A Preyse of Women
(beginning 'Altho ye lyste of women euyl to speke'); HF (independent
authority); TL (by Usk; Thynne's text is the sole authority); The
Lamentatyon of Mary Magdaleyne (previously printed by Pynson);
The Remedy of Love (beginning 'Seyng the manyfolde inconvenyence,'
a sixteenth-century anonymous poem; sole authority); The Complaynt
of Mars and Venus (Mars and Venus linked; previously printed by
Julian Notary, but Thynne has some independent value); The Letter
Of Cupyde (Hoccleve; first edition); A Balade of Commendation of our
Lady (a conflation of two poems, the first addressed to the Virgin
Mary, the second a secular poem to an earthly lady, beginning 'I haue
none englysshe conuenyent & digne,' entitled by Skeat 'To my Soverain
Lady.' 'Both are presumed to be by Lydgate — for the latter this text
is the only authority. Its twenty-first line is the first line of Chaucer's
'Merciles Beaute.'); Johan Gower / Unto the Worthy and Noble Kynge
Henry the Fourth (entitled by Skeat 'The Praise of Peace'); CN (first

edition, of some independent authority); 'O leude booke with thy foule rudeness' (entitled by Skeat 'Envoy to Alison.' 'The first letters of the lines of the final Envoy spell out the name ALISON'); Scogan / Vnto the Lordes and Gentylmen of the Kynges House (known as 'A Moral Balade,' containing complete text of *Gent*); *Sted* (first edition, of independent authority); *Truth* (printed by Caxton, Wynkyn de Worde, and Pynson, but of some independent authority); Balade of the Village without Paynting (*Fortune*; '*Village* in the title is a further corruption of Caxton's *Vilage* misprinted for *Visage*'); *Scogan* (from Caxton); Go forth kyng / rule the by sapience ('By Lydgate. Several times previously printed'); *Purse* (from Caxton); Chaucer vnto the Kynge (last stanza of *Purse*); Consider wel euery Cyrcumstaunce (probably by Lydgate, entitled by Stow 'A Balade of Good Counsel'); Epitaphium Galfridi Chaucer ('A Latin elegy on Chaucer, written by Stefano de Surigo, an Italian Humanist scholar, of the order of the Humiliates, licentiate of Milan University, a poet Laureate who taught Latin Eloquence at Oxford [1454–ca 1471] and at various Continental universities. First printed by Caxton [by whom the last four lines were probably written] in his edition of Chaucer's *Boetius*, 1479').

EDITION of 1542. Two issues; a reprint of Thynne's 1532 edition except that *PlowT* (which may have been printed previously separately by Godfray) is added, immediately after *CT*.

EDITION of 1550. A bookseller's reprint of Thynne; *PlowT* is placed before *ParsT*.

EDITION of 1561. Two issues, each printed by John Kyngston for John Wight. Edited by John Stow. 'Many of Stow's additions were taken from an ms in Trinity College Cambridge (R.3.19), which he once owned, but the bulk of the book is a reprint ... of the 1550 edition.' Brewer reproduces in facsimile the new woodcuts and all Stow's additions, which include: The Prologues and beginning of *KnT*; A Saiying of Dan Ihon (beginning 'Ther bethe four thinges that maketh man a foole'), another beginning 'Ther bene four thinges causing gret folye,' and a Balade de Bon Consail (beginning 'If it be fall that God the list bisite'), all by Lydgate; A balade of good counseile translated out of Latin verses in to Englishe, by dan Ihon lidgat cleped the monke of Buri (beginning 'Consyder well euery circumstance'); A balade in the Praise and commendacion of master Geffray Chaucer for his golden eloquence (early fifteenth century); *Gent* (now printed separately); A Prouerbe agaynst Couitise and Negligence (*Prov*, so-called by Skeat, who deemed them genuine); *AWU* (uncertain authorship); Here Foloweth a Balade ... Dispraise of Women (by Lydgate); The Craft of Louers ('In the last stanza the date MCCCXLVIII is given as the time of the poem, but Trinity College, Cambridge, ms.R.3.19 gives it as 1448, with Stow's marginal note that

Chaucer died in 1400'); A Balade, Of their Nature (beginning 'Of their nature they greatly them delite'); The X Commaundements of Loue; The IX Ladies Worthie; Alone Walkyng (sometimes called 'Virelai'); A Ballade: In the Season; A Ballade: O Mercifull (partly from Lydgate's 'Court of Sapience'); Here foloweth How Mercurie with Pallas (known as 'The Judgement of Paris'); A Balade Plesaunte (beginning 'I haue a Ladie where so she bee'); An other Balade (beginning 'O Mossie Quince hangyng by your stalke'); A Balade, Warnyng Men to Beware of Deceitptfull Women ('Attributed to Lydgate by Skeat, but rejected by Schirmer'); Lady; A Balade declaring that Wemens Chastite; CL (anonymous, early 16th century); Adam; Here beginneth the Prologue of the Storie of Thebes (previously printed by Wynkyn de Worde, ca 1500, but first printed with the works of Chaucer here).

EDITION of 1598. Ed. Thomas Speght. 'There has been some attempt to improve the accuracy of the text, and helpful editorial matter has been added,' viz a glossary, a life, and prefatory matter including a letter from Francis Beaumont 'to his very louing friend, T.S.' commending Speght's scholarly contribution and expressing his own love of Chaucer as a writer of comedy. Speght also adds several works to the Chaucer canon: Chaucers dreame ('The Isle of Ladies.'); 'Fairest of faire, and goodliest on liue' ('The twenty-nine lines beginning thus comprise several scraps of anonymous fifteenth-century verse, of which the three seven-line stanzas, constituting a balade, are Lydgatian in style'); and FL (sole authority).

EDITION of 1602. Ed. Thomas Speght. Acknowledges help on this revised edition from Francis Thynne (see 523a), who supplied him with more materials, better glosses, and helped to correct the text by reference to old copies. The irregularities of meter, Speght says, are more likely to be the fault of the scribe than of Chaucer. New items in this edition, which Brewer prints in facsimile, include ABC; Jack Upland (previously printed by John Gough, ca 1536); an expanded glossary, etc.

EDITION of 1687. Not represented in facsimile here since it is essentially a reprint of 1602. Preliminary pages, signed J.H., explain that Chaucer has been sent abroad into the world again 'in his old dress,' by the desire of 'many learned and worthy gentlemen.' J.H. says he has attempted to find the ms of The Pilgrim's Tale said in Speght's 'Life of Chaucer' (1602 edition) to have been seen in the library of Mr. Stow, but without success.

523a Thynne, Francis. Animaduersions and Corrections of some imperfections of impressiones of Chaucers workes (sett downe before tyme, and nowe) reprinted in the yere of oure lorde 1598. Ed. G.H. Kingsley, 1856. Revised by F.J. Furnivall. Early English Text Society,

Original Series, no. 9. London: Oxford University Press, 1875. Rpt 1965.

Thynne's *Animadversions* on Speght's edition corrects several of Speght's mistakes regarding his father William Thynne's 1532 edition of Chaucer, noting especially problems pertaining to censorship and Cardinal Wolsey created by the *Plowman's Tale* and the *Pilgrim's Tale*. According to Francis, William Thynne first showed a one column edition of Chaucer, which included the *Pilgrim's Tale*, to the king, to whom the edition was dedicated; 'when kinge henrye the eighte had redde, he called my father unto hym sainge, "Williame Thynne! I dobte this will not be allowed; for I suspecte the Byshoppes will call the in questione for yt" ' (p 9). Although the king promised to protect William from prosecution, nonetheless William had to remove the *Pilgrim's Tale* from the two column 1532 edition. Even the *Plowman's Tale* was denied its rightful printing until the 1542 edition, after Wolsey's death. According to Francis' uncle, Sir John Thynne (the builder of Longleat House, an owner of Chaucer manuscripts, and a member of Parliament at the time), Parliament would have condemned Chaucer altogether 'had yt not byn that his woorkes had byn counted but fables' (p 10). Francis defends the authenticity of the *Pilgrim's Tale*, which never did appear in a black-letter edition; like the Canon's Yeoman, who does not appear in the General Prologue either, the Pilgrim was to have been one of several pilgrims who 'did overtake' the pilgrimage along the way. Francis claims that his father, upon his death, passed on to him 'some fyve and twenty' Chaucer MSS, some of which were subsequently stolen, and others given away (p 12). One manuscript was 'subscribed in diuers places withe "examinatur Chaucer" ' (p 6). Thynne also notes fifteen mistakes in Speght pertaining to Chaucer's family and its historical context, eighteen corrections in the glossary, and twenty-seven corrections in textual annotations. Most of these corrections are sound and receive the admiration of Furnivall. Henry Bradshaw, whose note Furnivall prints (pp 75–76), argues that a one column edition of William Thynne's Chaucer never existed, that Francis must be recalling an edition of the *Court of Venus* printed between 1536–1540 under the name of Chaucer which may have been seen by Bale and reported to John Thynne. Furnivall considers possibilities that Francis may be telling the truth about the one column edition, however (pp xlii–xliii).

The Kingsley Preface to this volume (pp vii–xvii) includes short lives of William and Francis Thynne, along with comments on the hard lives of antiquarians in that time: 'Poor John Stowe, with his license to beg, as a reward of the labour of his life, is a terrible proof of how utterly unmarketable a valuable commodity may become' (p x). Furnivall's *Hindwords* (pp xx–cxliv) discusses William Thynne's life, his grants from Henry VIII, his duties as Clerk of the Kitchen, his service at Anne Boleyn's coronation, his will, his edition of Chaucer, and the *Pilgrim's Tale* (pp xlii–xlvi). His discussion of Francis Thynne's life reprints most of the pertinent documents along with extracts of Francis' numerous writings. The appendices to the volume include an edition of the *Pilgrim's Tale* (pp 77–98), the prologue to the *Plowman's Tale*, and an extract from the *Court of Venus*. Thynne's *Animadversions* is dedicated to Sir Thomas Egerton, Lord Ellesmere.

524 Dryden, John. *Fables Ancient and Modern, translated into Verse from Homer, Ovid, Boccace, and Chaucer; with Original Poems.* London: Jacob Tonson, 1700.
Includes modernizations of 'Palamon and Arcite or the Knight's Tale in three Books,' 'The Cock and the Fox: or the Tale of the Nun's Priest from Chaucer,' 'The Flower and the Leaf: or the Lady in the Arbour. A Vision out of Chaucer,' 'The Wife of Bath her Tale,' and 'The Character of A Good Parson: Imitated from Chaucer and Inlarg'd.' To which is added the original of Chaucer's *KnT*, *NPT*, 'The Floure and the Leafe as it was written by Geffrey Chaucer,' and *WBT*.

525 *The Works of Geoffrey Chaucer Compared with the Former Editions and many valuable MSS. Out of which, Three Tales are added which were never before Printed.* Ed. by John Urry, student of Christ-Church, Oxon. Deceased; Together with a Glossary by a student of the same College [Timothy Thomas]. To the Whole is prefixed the Author's Life, newly written [by John Dart; corrected and enlarged by William Thomas], and a Preface, giving an Account of this edition [by Timothy Thomas]. London: Bernard Lintot, between the Temple Gates, 1721.
In his Preface Timothy Thomas notes that the three new Tales Urry alludes to must be *'The Coke's Tale of* Gamelyn, the *Merchants Second Tale,* or *The History of* Beryn, and the Adventure of the Pardoner and Tapster at the Inn at Canterbury. Though the latter is not properly a Tale, but an Account of the Behaviour of the Pilgrims, and particularly of the *Pardoner,* at their Journey's end, and a kind of Prologue to a set of Tales to be told in their Return, it was not judged proper to make any Alteration in that part of the Title Page, lest it should be thought that any thing is omitted in this Edition, which was intended by Mr. Urry' (fol.k.3). Thomas accepts *Gamelyn* as Chaucer's but of the other two additions he observes: 'It may (perhaps with some shew of reason) be suspected that *Chaucer* was not the Author of them, but a later Writer, who may have taken the hint from what is suggested in vv.796 of the *Prologues,* that the Pilgrims were to tell Tales in their Return homewards; but as to that the Reader must be left to his own Judgment. But supposing they were not writ by our Author, we are however obliged to *Mr. Urry's* diligence for finding out

and publishing two ancient Poems, not unworthy our perusal, and they have as good a right to appear at the end of this Edition, as Lidgate's Story of *Thebes* had to be printed in former ones' (fol K.4–L.1). In his review of mss Thomas observes, 'It may be proper here once for all to advertize the Reader, that the *Plowman's* Tale is not in any of the mss which Mr. Urry describes, nor in any other that I have seen or been informed of' (fol F.1). The Life of Chaucer in this edition (by John Dart and William Thomas) praises Chaucer as 'a compleat Master' of the 'Elegiack kind of Poetry' as 'appears plainly by his *Complaint of the Black Knight*, the Poem called *La belle Dame sans mercy*, and several of his Songs' (fol F.1). The chronology is as follows: 'The *Court of Love* was written while he [Chaucer] resided at *Cambridge*, in the eighteenth year of his age. / The *Craft of Lovers* was written in the year of our Lord 1348, which was the twentieth year of his age; and it is probable the Remedy of Love was written about that time or not long after. / The *Lamentation of* Mary Magdalen, taken from *Origen*, was written by him in his early years. And perhaps *Boethius de Consolatione Philosophiae* was translated by him about the same time. / The *Romaunt of the Rose* ... seems to have been translated by *Chaucer* while he was at court, and about the time of the Rise of *Wicklyffe's* Opinions, it consisting of violent Invectives against the Religious Orders. It is left imperfect at the end, and there are some *Lacuna's* in other places of it. / The *Complaint of the Black Knight*, was written (as some do conjecture) during *John* of *Gaunt's* Courtship with *Blaunch*; and Chaucer's *Dreme* is supposed to be written upon account of the Duke of *Lancaster's* Marriage ... The *Book of* Blaunch *the Duchess*, commonly called *The Dreme of Chaucer*, was written upon the Death of that Lady ... *Of the Cuckow and Nightingale* ... seems by the Descriptions to have been writ at *Woodstock* ... Several other Ballads are ascribed to him, some of which are justly suspected not to have been written by him; as that beginning *O Mossie Quince*, etc. and that beginning *I have a Ladie*, etc. which must needs be written long after his time ... The *Testament of Love* was written in his Troubles, in the latter part of his Life. / The Song beginning *Fly fro the prese*, etc. was written on his Death-bed. / The *Testament* and Complaint of Creseide, are by Bale and Pits (after Leland) ascribed to Chaucer: But as to the Author of them, the Reader may be referred to the Note prefixed to them [which refutes their authenticity]' (fol F.1–4).

526 Tyrwhitt, Thomas, ed. *The Canterbury Tales of Chaucer, to which are added An Essay on his Language and Versification, and an Introductory Discourse, together with Notes* [and a Glossary]. 4 vols. London: T. Payne, 1775 [Glossary added as vol 5, 1778.] Second

Edition. 2 vols. Oxford: The Clarendon Press, 1798.
[Although Tyrwhitt's edition of *CT* includes no apocryphal works, his
'Introductory Discourse' and 'Notes' comment extensively on the
Chaucer canon and were of greatest importance in the initial sorting
out of authentic Chaucer from the non-genuine. Urry's Chaucer **525**
was the most inflated of any Chaucer text ever published (thus its
value for research in the Chaucer Apocrypha). Tyrwhitt objects to
Urry not only for including so much 'rubbish,' however, but also for
his manipulation of Chaucer's language: 'The strange licence, in which
Mr. Urry appears to have indulged himself, of lengthening and
shortening Chaucer's words according to his own fancy, and of even
adding words of his own, without giving his readers the least notice,
has made the text of Chaucer in his Edition by far the worst that was
ever published' (I, p xiii). Tyrwhitt admires Timothy Thomas'
'modest and sensible Preface,' however, as well he might, for Thomas
makes the first good effort to establish a sound grammar, a
pronunciation of Chaucer's verse which scans, and a better method for
establishing the text. In my annotation of Tyrwhitt, I comment only
on those passages which bear upon the Chaucer Apocrypha. My
gleanings are based upon the two volume Second Edition of 1798.] In
the 'Abstract of the Historical Passages of the Life of Chaucer' (i, pp
xvii–xxv) Tyrwhitt cites *TL* as proof that Chaucer was born in
London and *CL* as proof that he studied at Cambridge, but warns:
'This is by no means a decisive proof that he was really educated at
Cambridge; but it may be admitted, I think, as a strong argument
that he was not educated at Oxford; as Leland supposed, without the
shadow of a proof' (I, p xvii). Tyrwhitt notes from *Astrolabe* that
Chaucer had a son called Lowis: 'We must be cautious however, in
such an examination, of supposing allusions which Chaucer never
intended, or of arguing from pieces which he never wrote, as if they
were his. We must not infer from his repeated commendations of the
Daysie-flower, that he was specially favoured by Margaret, Countess of
Pembroke; and still less should we set him down as a *follower* of Alain
Chartier, because his Editors have falsely ascribed to him a translation
of one of Alain's poems' — ie, *LBD* (I, pp xxiii–xxv). Tyrwhitt rejects
Gamelyn (see **609a**) on lack of sound ms evidence. So too *PlowT*, for
which there is not 'the least ground of evidence, either external or
internal, for believing it to be a work of Chaucer's' (I, p 112). At the
conclusion of his edition Tyrwhitt appends 'An Account of the Works
of Chaucer ... and of those Other Pieces which have been improperly
intermixed with his in the Editions' (II, pp 525–34). He notes that the
Romaunt was probably one of Chaucer's earliest works, the printed
text of which has 'many gross blunders' which 'may be corrected by
comparing it with the Original' (II, p 525). He wonders that *CL* is not

mentioned in *LGW*, 'but notwithstanding the want of that testimony in its favour, I am induced by the internal evidence to consider it as one of Chaucer's genuine productions. I have never heard of any ms of this poem' (II, p 526). He considers *CBK* to be genuine but does not 'wish much confidence to be given to the conjecture ... that this poem relates to John of Gaunt' (II, p 527). The supposed plan prefixed by Speght to *Chaucer's Dreme* [suggesting that the poem pertains to Blanche's marriage to John of Gaunt] 'is mere fancy; but there is no ground for doubting the authenticity of the poem itself' (II, p 527); *FL* was also printed for the first time by Speght, 'but I do not think its authenticity so clear as that of the preceding poem [*Chaucer's Dreme*]. The subject, at least is alluded to by Chaucer in LGW. 188–94' (II, p 527). *CN* is genuine, though the Ballade attached to the end in printed editions does not belong and is not by Chaucer (II, p 528). The only other apocryphal work which Tyrwhitt deems authentic is *TL* (see 685). After thus commenting on Chaucer's genuine works, Tyrwhitt specifies those works in the blackletter editions whose true authors can be identified: *Testament and Complaint of Criseide*, by 'Robert Henrysone'; *The Floure of Courtesie*, by Lydgate; *LBD*, by Sir Richard Ros; The Letter of Cupid, 'by Occleve'; John Gower *Unto the Noble King Henry the 4th*; Sayings of Dan John (Lydgate); Scogan *Unto the Lordes and gentelmen of the Kynges house*; and 'A balade of goode counseil, translated out of Latin,' 'A balade maid in the preise, or rather dispreise, of women for their doubleness,' and 'A balade warning men to beware of deceitful women,' all three by Lydgate, along with his 'Ballade in Commendation of our Ladie.' Anonymous compositions contradicting the strongest internal evidence for authenticity, like *PlowT, Gamelyn, JU*, and 'The Continuation of the Canterbury Tales' (ie, the episode with the Pardoner and the Tapster), should be deleted. Finally, 'I have declared my suspicion ... that the "Lamentation of Marie Magdalene" was not written by Chaucer; and I am still clearer that the "Assemblee of Ladies," "A Praise of Women," and the "Remedie of Love," ought not to be imputed to him. It would be a waste of time to sift accurately the heap of rubbish, which was added, by John Stowe, to the Edit. of 1561. Though we might perhaps be able to pick out two or three genuine fragments of Chaucer, we should probably find them so soiled and mangled, that he would not thank us for asserting his claim to them' (II, p 533).

[Despite Tyrwhitt's precautions, early nineteenth-century biographers of Chaucer drew heavily from apocryphal works which still adhered to the canon for biographical clues, especially *CL, TL, FL*, but also others even though Tyrwhitt had rejected them. Let the contents of one popular mid-nineteenth edition suffice to indicate what the canon

looked like at the time that modern Chaucer studies under the
guidance of Furnivall and the Chaucer Society were just getting
underway.]

527 Morris, Richard, ed. *The Poetical Works of Geoffrey Chaucer.* With
memoir by Sir Harris Nicolas. The Aldine Edition of the British Poets.
6 vols. London: G. Bell and Daldy, 1866.
Vol 4 includes as part of Chaucer's canon *CL, CN*, and *FL*; vol 5
includes *Chaucer's Dream.* Vol 6 (*Romaunt* and Lesser Poems)
includes, besides authentic Chaucer, 'Complaynte of a Lover's Lyfe; or
The Complaint of the Black Knight' (681 lines beginning 'In May,
when Flora, the fresshe lusty quene'); 'A Goodly Ballade of Chaucer'
(64 lines beginning 'Mother of norture, best beloved of alle'); 'A Praise
of Women' (175 lines beginning 'Altho that lyste of women evyl to
speke'); 'Prosperity' (8 lines beginning 'Right as povert causith
sobirnesse'); 'Leaulte Vault Richesse' (8 lines beginning 'Warldly joy is
onely fantasy'). Also, as poems of doubtful authorship like *Prov* and
MB, Morris includes 'Virelai' (40 lines beginning 'Alone walkynge');
'Chaucer's Prophecy' (13 lines beginning 'Qwan prestis fayling in her
sawes'); and 'Incipit Oratio Galfridi Chaucer: Orisoune to the Holy
Virgin' (140 lines beginning 'Moder of God, and virgyne undefouled').

Chaucer's Audience of the Fourteenth, Fifteenth, and Sixteenth Centuries

See also **544, 547, 554, 557, 568, 579.**

528 Bennett, Henry Stanley. 'The Author and his Public in the Fourteenth
and Fifteenth Centuries.' *Essays and Studies by Members of the
English Association*, 23 (1937), 7–24.
In the fifteenth century a new clientele was slowly forming; English
was more and more the language of all forms of discourse. Various
kinds of schools multiplied. A man like John Shirley 'saw that there
was a public who were scarcely rich enough to commission books to be
written or to be copied for their exclusive use, but who, nevertheless,
were eager to read whatever they could get hold of, especially the
works of certain authors whose fame was a matter of common report'
(p 19; cf pp 19–21). This new reading public was not satisfied merely
by borrowing books. 'All the mass of undistinguished writing, so
boring and so dead to those whose souls adventure only among
masterpieces, was the material on which a new body of lovers of

literature was nourished, and who were crying out for fuller satisfaction when Caxton returned to England with his books "in preente" ' (p 24).

529 Bennett, J.A.W. 'Those Scotch Copies of Chaucer.' *RES*, 32 (1981), 294–96.

John of Ireland (fifteenth-century teacher of philosophy at the University of Paris) mentions *T&C* IV.953–1085 in his *Meroure of Wisdom*. (He also knows the *Parson's Tale*.) Evidently more Scots than Henryson and Dunbar knew Chaucer in the fifteenth century. Ireland ascribes Hoccleve's 'Moder of God and Virgin Wndefauld' to Chaucer, perhaps because of its similarity in tone to Chaucer's *ABC* and in language and meter to Custance's prayer to the BVM in *MLT*. The *Meroure* includes three Latin Marian poems by Ireland. 'The rather pedestrian style of the prose *Meroure* hardly prepares us for the metrical and stylistic virtuosity of these Latin pieces, which display Ireland as a practising poet. His eulogy of Chaucer's verse was heartfelt, not conventional; and as a philosophical writer in the vernacular he stands next in line to Hilton, Usk, and Pecock' (p 296).

29a Berry, Reginald John. 'Chaucer Transformed: 1700–1721.' *DAI*, 40 (1979) 231A. University of Toronto Dissertation.

Surveys who read what editions in the later 17th and early 18th centuries. Differentiates moral and popular traditions represented especially by Dryden's Preface to *Fables*, where he draws heavily on Speght's edition for his earnest attitudes, and Pope's early Chaucerian poems, namely his 'Tale from Chaucer,' 'May and Januarie,' and 'The Wife of Bath Her Prologue,' all of which illuminate Pope's keen sense of irony. Gay, Betterton, and Prior follow Pope, but by the time of Urry (1721) the scholarly and popular traditions come together again 'in the polite world of the common reader.'

29b Clogan, Paul M. 'Chaucer and Leigh Hunt.' *M&H*, n.s. 9 (1979), 163–74.

In his copius and astute critical comments on Chaucer, Hunt initiated a kind of technical analysis of Chaucer's writings. He is one of the first to attempt an analysis of irony, humor, and narrative techniques and to associate poetry with the idea of music' (p 164). Hunt admired Chaucer's descriptions of nature, especially *CN* with its 'spotless treatment, as well as sentiment' (p 172), and *FL*, which he called a 'beautiful poem,' 'eminently chaste and reserved, and its moral ... the triumph of manly and womanly virtue over idle dissipation' (p 172). Hunt saw Dryden's Chaucerian tales to be inferior to the originals, even in versification. He follows Godwin's biography of Chaucer for the details of Chaucer's life. For Hunt, Chaucer is strong in both fancy and imagination, 'the strongest imagination of real life, beyond any writers but Homer, Dante and Shakespeare,' and 'in comic painting inferior to none' (p 168).

529c Doyle, A. I. 'English Books In and Out of Court from Edward III to Henry VII.' In *English Court Culture in the Later Middle Ages*. Ed. V.J. Scattergood and J.W. Sherborne. London: Duckworth, 1983. Pp 163–81.

Discusses who made and owned various important mss, especially of works by Chaucer, Gower, Lydgate, and Wyclifite writers in the late fourteenth and fifteenth centuries. Considers lending and exchanging of books. 'The inn may often have been as important in this traffic as the palace' (p 179).

530 Gaertner, Otto. *John Shirley: Sein Leben und Wirken*. Halle: Von Ehrhardt Karras, 1904.

Ch 1, 'Shirleys Leben,' pp 5–16, is derived mainly from church records, Stow, Tanner's *Bibliotheca Britannico-Hibernica*, Pollard's entry in the *DNB*, Annals of the Shirley family in the Counties of Warwick and Derby (1841), and the Shirley mss. Ch 3, 'Shirleys Handschriften,' pp 17–28, describes the contents of Harl 78, Harl 2251, Harl 7333, Trinity College Cambridge R.3.20, Addit 16165, Ashmole 59, and Addit 5467. Ch 4, 'Die Werke im Ms Additional 5467,' pp 29–57, considers in greater detail the contents of the ms, devoting special attention to its translations. Ch 5, 'Shirleys Bedeutung für die englische Literatur,' pp 58–62, reviews the importance of Shirley as a transmitter of texts and as an index to early fifteenth-century London taste. 'Anhang,' pp 63–79, includes 'Prologe of the Kalundare of this litelle booke,' 'The Cronycle made by Chaucier,' and several excerpts from books of manners in Shirley mss.

531 Hallmundsson, May Newman. 'Chaucer's Circle: Henry Scogan and His Friends.' *M&H*, 10 (1981), 129–39.

Discusses Shirley's heading attached to his ms of Scogan's 'Moral Balade' and the relationship of Davis John and Thomas Chaucer to the occasion 'in the Vyntre' when the poem was presented. Scogan may have been affiliated with the London Pui. The 'Moral Balade' was written about the same time as Hoccleve's *La Male Regle*; the two works have several similarities. Lawrence Bailly, Simon Gaunstede, and Roger Elinham were mutual friends of both Scogan and Hoccleve. 'Scogan came of a noble family in Norfolk. He served as the king's esquire under Richard II and as tutor to the sons of Henry IV, for whom he wrote *A Moral Ballad*. His associates were connected with the court and included members of the royal family as well as various knights of the king's chamber [men like Clifford, Neville, and Stury] ... The Chaucer circle also included others who, like Scogan, had originally come from Norfolk, such as the merchant Hugh Fastolf, the king's butler John Payne, and two of Hoccleve's colleagues in the

Privy Seal, James Billyngford and Roger Elinham. The existence of such a "Norfolk group" within the Chaucer circle offers an interesting speculation concerning Scogan's early connections with Chaucer and his friends' (p 135).

532 Hammond, Eleanor P. 'A Scribe of Chaucer.' *MP*, 27 (1929–30), 27–33.
Discusses a fifteenth-century scribe other than Shirley whose work is found in at least six books containing Chaucer, Hoccleve or Lydgate poems. The scribe had access to Shirley's volumes and sometimes picks up work even in the middle of a tale. 'How can we account for him except as a professional employed in a *scriptorium* or a publishing business, where many codices were in stock to furnish bases for reproduction?' (p 29). He seems to puzzle over tale order in *CT* mss. 'It is impossible ... to feel that each of his variants is derived, that it has any source than his self assertion, his indifference to verbal fidelity' (p 31). It is remarkable that so many of Shirley's mss stayed together and reached Stow's hands. 'Something had kept the Shirley manuscripts together between Shirley's death and Stow's purchase; and while that something was operative, a mass of verse of Edward VI's reign was transcribed into a secondary set of volumes, along with copies from one or two Shirley volumes. Several of these derivative collections, and at least one of the Shirley codices used in their construction, were later owned by Stow. We cannot be far astray if we assume that this protective and reproductive agency was a commercial one' (p 32). Several watermarks of the codices support the theory. Includes plates of six pages showing the hand of the scribe where he takes over from other scribes.

532a Hudson, Anne. ' "No newe thyng": The Printing of Medieval Texts in the early Reformation Period.' In *Middle English Studies Presented to Norman Davis in Honour of his Seventieth Birthday*. Ed. Douglas Gray and E.G. Stanley. Oxford: Clarendon Press, 1983. Pp 153–174.
Considers why and how sixteenth-century reformers so frequently resorted to medieval mss in their reform propaganda. 'All evidence points to a remarkable conservatism in the sixteenth-century handling of medieval material' (p 171). Discusses ms and publication history of *PLT* and *JU*, along with other Wycliffite works like *Lanterne of Lyght* and *The Wycket* and several plowman poems. Hudson identifies a third medieval ms (Bodl. 703), which contains a Latin redaction of *JU* which Heyworth does not mention in his edition (665).

533 Lenaghan, R.T. 'Chaucer's *Envoy to Scogan*: The Uses of Literary Conventions.' *ChauR*, 10 (1975–6), 46–61.
Discusses circumstances of civil servants in the 1390s.

534 Mathew, Gervase. *The Court of Richard II*. London: John Murray,

1968.
Background to the society out of which the Chaucer Apocrypha
developed. Chapters on International Court Culture, the English
Court, Life at the Court, the Royal Palaces, Court Art and Aesthetics,
Thomas Usk and Thomas Hoccleve, Geoffrey Chaucer, John Gower,
Piers Plowman, Provincial Art, Social Ideals and the Social Structure,
the Influence of the Magnates, Chivalry, the Heroine and Marriage,
Conflict of Loyalties, the King's Policies, the Revolution, and Henry
the Fourth.

535 Owen, Charles A., Jr. 'The *Canterbury Tales:* Early Manuscripts and
Relative Popularity.' *JEGP*, 54 (1955), 104–10.
The tales most frequently excerpted from the *CT* in the fifteenth
century are *ClerkT* (6 times), *PriorT* (5), and *Mel* (5). The frequency
of anthologizing the moral and religious pieces suggests a shift in
literary taste. 'Chaucer's poems appear surrounded by Lydgate's' and
'Gower and Chaucer advance to the Elizabethan period with almost
equal reputations ... Chaucer's early readers, probably confined to the
court circle in which he moved, were a more discriminating group than
the wider audience his tales reached as the fifteenth century advanced'
(p 110).

535a Patterson, Lee W. 'Ambiguity and Interpretation: A Fifteenth-
Century Reading of *Troilus and Criseyde.*' *Spec*, 54 (1979), 279–330.
A fifteenth-century treatise for women religious called by its compiler
Disce mori includes an extended discussion of carnal love that is
explicit in its reference to *T&C* (a stanza is quoted). The work draws
on a popular thirteenth-century handbook for nuns, David of
Augsburg's 'De compositione,' whose discussion of fleshly affections
the compiler applies to *T&C*, a work which he accepts quite literally as
a fully real and accurate depiction of human conduct. He quotes some
of the poem's most beautiful verses. 'That he does so in order to
condemn love means not that his response is inconsistent but that his
hermeneutic is sophisticated. For (unlike David of Augsburg) he seeks
not to disarm the text but to arm the reader, and he accomplishes this
by locating the poem in a context that allows its reading to be at once
safe and loving' (p 330).

536 Pearsall, Derek. 'The Chaucer Circle.' In *Old English and Middle
English Poetry*. London: Routledge and Kegan Paul, 1977. Pp 194–7.
'For Chaucer's real sources of nourishment, for his audience, his circle,
we have to look beneath the surface glitter of the royal court, to the
multitude of household knights and officials, foreign office diplomats
and civil servants who constitute "the court" in its wider sense, that
is, the national administration' (p 194). Pearsall comments briefly on
the Lollard Knights, Simon Burley, Henry Scogan, Thomas Hoccleve,

Thomas Usk, Ralph Strode, Thomas Bradwardine, and the Almonry School at St Paul's.

537 — 'The Troilus Frontispiece and Chaucer's Audience.' *YES*, 7 (1981), 68–74.
Discusses ms Corpus Christi 61's relationship with Anne Nevill and the Beauforts. Emphasizes the folly of trying to identify all the individuals in the picture or of thinking that it represents an actual occasion. To suggest that it represents Chaucer's usual audience is misleading. 'We might do well to look beyond the entourage of king and nobility for Chaucer's audience, to the multitude of household knights and official, career diplomats and civil servants, who consitiute the "court" in its wider sense, that is, the national administration and its metropolitan milieu' (p 73).

538 Silvia, Daniel S. 'Some Fifteenth-Century Manuscripts of the *Canterbury Tales*.' In *Chaucer and Middle English Studies in Honour of Rossell Hope Robbins*. Ed. Beryl Rowland. London: George Allen and Unwin Ltd, 1974. Pp 153–63.
Sixteen fifteenth-century mss contain Chaucerian tales which were excerpted from *CT* either as examples of moral pieces or as courtly works. Such a practice reflects not simply the popularity of those tales but mainly the reading taste of the time. The most frequently anthologized tale is that of the Clerk (six times), followed by *PriorT* and *Mel* (five times each). No other tale appears in isolation more than twice. In some mss the tales are not even identified as Chaucer's but seem to be valued, along with works by Lydgate and other moral writers, primarily for their sententious matter. In ms Hn 'the heading "Prouerbis" for the Melibeus can hardly be the product of literary awareness' (p 160). See also Robert A. Pratt, 'The Importance of Manuscripts for the Study of Medieval Education as Revealed by the Learning of Chaucer,' *Progress of Medieval and Renaissance Studies*, Bull. no 20 (1949), 43–51, who makes a similar point, without emphasizing the choice of isolated tales as a telling sign of individual taste or the unique placement of such anthologized tales in moral or courtly contexts.

539 Strohm, Paul. 'Jean of Angoulême: A Fifteenth-Century Reader of Chaucer.' *NM*, 7 (1971), 69–76.
Jean makes many comments on individual Canterbury Tales in Paris BN ms fonds anglais 39. 'Certainly, Jean does not represent the taste of the whole of Chaucer's circle. Chaucer needed and had Scogans and Buktons too. But even in his own day Chaucer must have had a mixed audience with mixed reasons for enjoying his work' (p 76).

540 — 'Chaucer's Audience.' *Literature and History: A New Journal of the Humanities*, 5 (1977), 26–41.

Chaucer's principal audience was composed of the 'lesser gentry.' His 'circle of literary acquaintance' embraced 'people of similar standing and people just to either side of him on the social scale' (p 31), including Clanvowe, Clifford, and Vache, as well as Scogan and Bukton. Chaucer 'would have regarded himself as a gentleperson addressing other gentlepersons rather than as a bourgeois poet deferring to a royal audience' (p 33). Strohm discusses Chaucer's 'poetics of juxtaposition' and the kind of audience attracted to thematic tensions in Chaucer's poetry. 'These were people who would have gained through their social situation a capacity for the kind of complexity of response which Chaucer's poetry requires ... In all, these were people who not only lived with uncertainty and change, but stood to benefit from it' (p 39). Chaucer's 'assertion of the relativity of traditional values' would have been especially attractive to such an audience.

541 — Chaucer's Fifteenth-Century Audience and the Narrowing of the "Chaucer Tradition".' *SAC*, 4 (1982), 3–32.
Few of Chaucer's primary audience (men like Sturry, Clifford, Clanvowe, Montagu, Vache, Scogan, Bukton, Gower, Strode, Usk, and Hoccleve) outlived him, and fewer still were active after his death. This initial audience was small but seems to have appreciated his innovative power. In the fifteenth-century his audience was more broadly dispersed, but more narrow, conservative, and genteel in its literary taste. Strohm discusses the dispersion of Chaucer manuscripts in the fifteenth century, noting the popularity of tales of obeissance. John Shirley typifies the taste of the time in promoting a 'backward-looking quality' (p 21). 'The works popular in the fifteenth century fulfill rather than deny the general horizon of generic expectations with which the audiences would have approached them' (p 26). The narrowing of aesthetic expectation was not due to political chaos or lack of individual geniuses or worn out literary traditions. 'Artists do not exhaust traditions, nor do traditions exhaust themselves'; rather, the change occurs in 'the capacity of audiences to appreciate the full range of Chaucer's tradition and in the capacity of new artists, working without public esteem or encouragement, to perpetuate that tradition' (p 32).

541a — 'Chaucer's Audience(s): Fictional, Implied, Intended, Actual.' *ChauR*, 18 (1983), 137–45.
First of four essays on 'Chaucer's Audience: A Symposium,' presented to the New Chaucer Society, April 16. 1982, in San Francisco. Strohm places the various kinds of Chaucerian audience within the context of recent theoretical criticism of 'audience.' The other essays in the symposium include: Richard Firth Green, 'Women in Chaucer's

Audience,' *ChauR*, 18 (1983), 146–54; R. T. Lenaghan, 'Chaucer's Circle of Gentlemen and Clerks,' *ChauR*, 18, (1983), 155–60; and Patricia J. Eberle, 'Commercial Language and the Commercial Outlook in the General Prologue,' 18 (1983), 161–74. None of the essays consider the Chaucer Apocrypha as Chaucerian 'audience.'

542 Tout, T.F. 'Literature and Learning in the English Civil Service in the Fourteenth Century.' *Spec*, 4 (1929), 365–89.
Much of the literature of late Medieval England was produced by civil servants, but literary historians often fail to take account of the differences (especially in terms of education) between the civil servant and a learned clerk. The education of a civil servant was 'technical rather than humanistic. Its object was not to widen the mind, but to give a man the tools of his trade' (p 369). Civil servants with literary interests may be divided into three classes: those who were educated at a university before entering state service; those who 'posed as patrons of learning, friends of learned men, collectors of libraries, benefactors of universities, or pious founders of academic colleges' (p 369); and, 'men who themselves made solid contributions to literature' (p 369). After reviewing briefly the careers of Richard de Bury and Thomas Bradwardine, among others, Tout turns his attention to Chaucer. Scholars have not fully appreciated the importance of the civil service in Chaucer's literary career. His 'excellent education' was the 'education which the household of a king, or one of the greater magnates, could give to its junior members' (p 382). J.M. Manly's suggestion (*Some New Light on Chaucer*) that Chaucer was educated in the Middle Temple must be dismissed for lack of evidence. Tout reviews records concerning Chaucer's civil service positions and concludes that although Chaucer's career was 'chequered' 'it gave him the leisure to write what the world will not willingly let die' (p 387).

543 Whiting, B.J. 'A Fifteenth-Century English Chaucerian: The Translator of *Partonope de Blois*.' *MS*, 7 (1945), 40–54.
The translator of *Partonope de Blois* should be added to the roster of those who read Chaucer with discrimination and retentiveness. Whiting documents sixty-four instances of specific indebtedness, plus ten shared proverbs and several instances where circumstances rather than words likewise suggest indebtedness.

543a Yeager, R.F. 'Literary Theory at the Close of the Middle Ages: William Caxton and William Thynne.' *SAC*, 6 (1984), 135–64.
Yeager examines Caxton and Thynne's literary choices and principles of critical selection in their Chaucer editions and discusses the categories of apocryphal materials they include. Both 'read more than they printed' (p 139). 'What seems to have mattered most to Caxton was the message of the literary work, not the metrics' (p 146).

Although he may have 'trafficked unabashedly in what his customers liked,' he 'strove to shape his productions to reflect a serious, if bourgeois, literary theory' (p 147). For Thynne *LGW* seems to have been a central Chaucerian text. Many of the apocryphal poems he includes are tied to it in tone and allusion — 'amorous, gentle, naive, and without irony' (p 164). Yeager comments in passing on a large number of apocryphal lyrics; he also provides an interesting speculation on the date of Chaucer's death, later than 1400, at least as Thynne might have perceived it.

General Studies Pertaining to the Apocrypha

544 Ainger, Alfred. *Lectures and Essays.* 2 vols. New York: Macmillan, 1905. Vol 2, pp 136–51.
Ainger reviews critical responses to Chaucer, from the flurry of activity surrounding him in the fifteenth century, the Scottish Chaucerians, then Sidney, Spenser, Daniel, Shakespeare, and Milton. After a fading of reputation in the Stuart era, Chaucer again became a major poet for Dryden and then the romantic writers — Scott, Wordsworth, Coleridge, Southey, Keats, and later Tennyson and Morris — all of whom were 'devoted Chaucerians' (p 141). Ainger notes that while the poets admired Chaucer, 'the general reading public (even of those who thought they liked poetry) seems to have held aloof' (p 142). It is in the later nineteenth and twentieth centuries that Chaucer has again recovered a broad audience. Credit must be given to the scholars preparing the new texts and working out a well-ordered canon. This movement began with a small band of poets, headed by R.H. Horne (author of *Orion*) who, in 1841, addressed themselves to the task of 'modernizing' Chaucer. The group included such distinguished lights as Wordsworth, Elizabeth Barrett, and Leigh Hunt. 'But what Wordsworth and his allies failed to see was that, although their versions of Chaucer were done with poetic skill and real reverence for the author's text ... they could not preserve the essential charm of the original' (p 145). The successful direction has been the presenting of Chaucer on his own. 'Burns stands alone among modern poets as of a genius markedly akin to Chaucer's' (p 147). Chaucer's fame, like that of the names 'conserved in the shade' of *HF*, has endured well. With all the renewed interest in Chaucer, 'we will earnestly hope that he will never become, like Hamlet, "too much i' the sun" ' (p 151).

545 Alderson, William L., and Arnold G. Henderson. *Chaucer and*

Augustan Scholarship. University of California English Studies, no. 35. Berkeley, Los Angeles, London: University of California Press, 1970. Includes chapters on antiquarian backgrounds: the edition of 1687; Dryden's *Fables* (1700), which included *FL*; Urry's edition (1721); and Morell's edition (1737). Discusses problems of the Chaucer canon in the early eighteenth century and includes fifty pages of allusions to Chaucer and his works between 1551 and 1800 not found in Spurgeon 582. Includes an appendix on the Morell-Entick controversy, but lacks an index.

- Review by H. Neville Davies, *Yearbook of English Studies,* 2 (1972), 245–6: 'A full-scale history of Chaucer's reputation and the strange vicissitudes of his text is a scholarly feat of the future. In it Alderson and Henderson will play a part' (p 246), though they leave many gaps.

546 Baugh, A.C. *A Literary History of England.* New York: Appleton-Century, 1958. Pp 288–99.
Baugh entitles his chapter on the fifteenth century 'Ebb Tide' (the drama is presented in a separate chapter). He stresses the continuing tradition of *RR* as well as Chaucer and Gower. He finds *FL* to be 'somewhat lacking in substance ... little more than a tableau gracefully described' (p 293); *CN* is probably by Thomas Clanvowe; *AL* is 'not very logically planned' (p 293); *LBD*'s preface and opening lines 'are such as Chaucer might have devised, but he never could have carried on the tiresome and long-winded debate' (p 292). Baugh devotes some attention to spurious Canterbury tales, Lydgate, and Hoccleve. Prose romances, Malory, the ballad and Robinhood materials are given more positive treatment in a chapter headed 'Looking Foreward' (pp 300–12).

547 Bennett, Henry Stanley. *Chaucer and the Fifteenth Century.* Oxford History of English Literature. Oxford: Clarendon Press, 1947.
General discussion of Chaucer's London, the extravagant court, literary taste, and religion, with brief comments on the *Beryn* passage in which Pardoner and Miller explicate the windows in Canterbury Cathedral (pp 17–8) and anonymous 'Chaucerian' satires such as the *Complaint of the Plowman, Song Against the Friars,* and *JU* (p 21; see also pp 155–7); Chaucer's biography and canon (pp 29–95); and social and political background of the fifteenth century (pp 96–104). Chapter V, pp 105–123, is a revision of **528**. Ch VI: Fifteenth-Century Verse (pp 124–76) stresses the vigor of non-courtly, non-Chaucerian verse (pp 124, 151–65). The courtly poets, on the other hand, were overwhelmed by 'a crushing weight of tradition,' a 'degradation of verse ... brought about by this progressive in-breeding'; 'whatever vitality Chaucer had imparted to his themes and metrical patterns was utterly exhausted

during the century' (p 125) as court writers 'slavishly followed
traditional forms and themes, and clutched eagerly at any device
which they thought might help them' (p 126). Such failure is seen
especially in Lydgate, Hoccleve, and Hawes, each of whom Bennett
discusses separately. The best of the courtly poems are found in the
Chaucer Apocrypha — *CN* (p 131), *LBD* (p 132), and *FL* and *AL* (pp
133–6). The unknown author of *FL* 'was a poet of distinction' (p 133),
who writes 'a pleasing little morality: the blacks are not really very
black, while the whites are not too self-conscious of their virtues. It
marks the beginning of a change: the appeal seems no longer to be to
ecclesiastical or "courtly" standards, but rather to a commonsense
morality which might commend itself to the changing age it sought to
amuse and instruct' (p 134). *AL* suffers from heavy-handed allegory.
'Despite some memorable passages, much observation, and a sense of
dialogue, the *Assembly* remains a museum piece' (p 136). Bennett also
gives some attention to John Capgrave, John Walton, John Russell,
Peter Idly, and the Scottish Chaucerians (pp 165–76). Chronological
Tables of Bibliography, with sections on individual fifteenth-century
authors and anonymous works, pp 219–318.

548 Blake, Norman F. 'Late Medieval Prose.' In *The Middle Ages*. Ed.
W.F. Bolton. *History of Literature in the English Language*. London:
Barrie and Jenkins, 1970. Vol I, pp 371–402; see especially pp 385–9.
Considers Chaucer's influence, partly through *Boece* but through his
poetry too, upon writers like Usk who abandon the simplicity of native
alliterative prose to imitate French styles, with inflated, Latinate
vocabulary and heavy syntax. 'Usk's work is important because it
shows that Chaucer was immediately regarded as a model, and that
his style was emulated by prose-writers as much as by poets' (p 387).
Comments also on *JU* and *Friar Daw's Reply* (p 388).

549 Bonner, Francis W. 'Genesis of the Chaucer Apocrypha.' *SP*, 48
(1951), 461–81.
The Chaucer apocrypha grows out of confusion about Chaucer's canon
and biography which he himself creates by listing works not known.
'The fact that Chaucer was renowned in his own day and during the
fifteenth century as the chief English poet of love and was supposed to
have composed a large body of love poetry very probably influenced
his early editors to assign to him many 'unclaimed' compositions of
that genre' (p 465). Gower's reference to Chaucer's 'testament of love'
is responsible for the Usk attribution. Shirley's comments have helped
in fixing the Chaucer canon (p 468). Most of the 'more that
three-score pieces of the Chaucer apocrypha make their first
appearance in manuscripts of the fifteenth century' (p 469) and were
probably attributed to Chaucer by later editors solely because they

'happened to be contained in manuscripts which also contained works
generally recognised as authentic' (p 471). Bonner discusses Stowe's
additions, sixteen of which are spurious, and comments on five groups
of mss which contributed to the genesis of Chaucer apocrypha. The
fact that the works of Gower and Lydgate were often grouped with
Chaucer's probably accounts for the frequent coupling of Chaucer's
name with the other two poets (p 479).

550 — 'Chaucer's Reputation during the Romantic Period.' *Furman
Studies*, 34 (1951), 1–21.
Bonner begins with a fabricated statement of Chaucer's formidable
attacks on the corruptions of the clergy in the *PlowT* and *JU*, and his
powers of description of rural objects in *FL*, all of which errors appear
in the assessments of Chaucer by Leigh Hunt, Charles Cowden Clarke,
William Godwin, Washington Irving, Henry David Thoreau, and
others. Tyrwhitt, in 1775–8, inaugurated a new era in the history of
Chaucer's reputation by expelling from the Chaucer canon as spurious
TC, *FC*, *LBD*, *Letter of Cupid*, *PlowT*, *Gamelyn*, *Beryn*, *JU*, etc. He
left in, however, *TL*, *CL*, *CBK*, *IL*, *FL*, and *CN*. The romantic period
not only accepted many non-Chaucerian works as authentic, it also
delighted in and embellished the many legends of the Chaucer
biography. Some objected to 'the freedom which Godwin had allowed
his imagination in dealing with the facts of Chaucer's life. No one,
however, pointed out that Godwin's "facts" were drawn largely from
spurious literature, and fictitious accounts such as the one based on the
Testament of Love [which Chaucer supposedly wrote in prison] were
left without correction by the critics' (p 11). The picture of Chaucer as
'a champion of human rights, suffering great hardships for his ideals,
intrigued other Romantics' besides Godwin; Hazlett, Charles Cowden
Clarke, Thomas Campbell, and Robert Southey all admired the
idealistic Chaucer (pp 11–2). Thinking Chaucer several times unjustly
imprisoned for his political beliefs, Isaac D'Israeli gave a 'colorful and
impassioned account of Chaucer's noble attempts for the causes of
Lancaster, Wyclif, and the commons' (p 12). Chaucer's reputation as a
political reformer was paired with the idea of him as a fervent religious
reformer, especially in works like the *PlowT* and *JU*. 'The Romantics
are practically unanimous in the belief that he — as Leigh Hunt
phrases it — "took pleasure in exposing the abuses of the church," and
most of them were confident that Chaucer zealously espoused the
cause of "his friend" Wyclif' (p 14). *CBK*, *CN*, and *FL* contributed to
his reputation as a nature poet, which also appealed greatly to the
Romantics, some arguing that *FL* was one of his 'most charming
productions' (p 16). Bonner discusses evaluations of *FL* by R.H.
Horne, Henry Todd, Godwin, Leigh Hunt, Scott, Wordsworth, Thomas

Campbell, Keats, Shelley, Southey, and Elizabeth Barrett, who preferred it to all of Chaucer's poems (pp 16–20). *CN* was also greatly admired. Some felt, as did Isaac D'Israeli, that 'the "Canterbury Tales" are but the smallest portion of Chaucer's works!' (p 21).

550a Brown, Peter. 'Is the "Canon's Yeoman's Tale" Apocryphal?' *ES*, 64 (1983), 481–90.
Norman F. Blake, ed., *The Canterbury Tales by Geoffrey Chaucer*, edited from the Hengwrt Manuscript, York Medieval Texts, second series (London, 1980), pp 6–10, argues that *CYT*, which is not found in the Hengwrt ms (the first complete Chaucer collection and thus, according to Blake, the most authoritative), is by an imitator of Chaucer and is thus apocryphal. Brown reviews the case, noting the considerable body of criticism linking *CYT* with *SNT*. To avoid the pitfalls of such comparisons, Brown examines the poem as if it were an independent work, a meritorious procedure in and of itself, a model which might well be followed in the examining afresh of all the Chaucerian Apocrypha 'which, like paintings once thought to be genuine and subsequently shown to be fakes, have for too long been consigned to the limbo-land of criticism. If such issues are broached the debate about the authenticity of the *Canon's Yeoman's Prologue* and *Tale* promises to be far-reaching in its implications' (p 490).

551 Brusendorff, Aage. *Chaucer Tradition*. 1925. See 25.
Comments on many poems of Lydgate, Hoccleve, and Clanvowe ascribed to Chaucer, and focuses on *Ros, MB, AWU*, and *CN* as spurious poems (pp 433–44).

552 Chiarenza, Frank John. 'Chaucer and the Medieval Amorous Complaint: A Study in the Evolution of a Poetic Genre.' *DAI*, 31 (1970), 2337A. Yale Dissertation, 1956.
The first part of the dissertation explores the tradition of literary love games 'for which Ovid provided the rules of play' and which 'continued through the lyrics of the goliards as a frolicsome resignation to the popular maxim *amor vincit omnia.*' Discusses *complainte d'amour, salut d'amour*, Provençal *canso*, French *chansor*, Italian *canzone*, Spanish *contiga*, and German *Minnesang*. The second part concentrates on Chaucer. No specific discussion of the Chaucer Apocrypha.

552a Downer, Mabel Wilhelmina. 'Chaucer Among the Victorians.' *DAI*, 43 (1982), 1537A. CUNY Dissertation. Dir. Wendel Johnson.
The Victorians looked on Chaucer as one who exposed the ills of medieval society, but also as an innovator in his use of language and his skill in characterization. His earthiness and bawdry provided a mixed response. Each of the critics tends to define his own literary values and limitations through Chaucer.

553 Edwards, A.S.G., and J. Hedly. 'John Stowe, *The Craft of Lovers* and T.C.C. R.3.19.' *SB*, 28 (1975), 265–8.
Stowe derived his edition of *The Craft of Lovers* from Trinity College Cambridge ms R.3.19, although he may have consulted 'at least one of the other manuscripts' (either BL Addit. ms 34360 or BL ms Harl. 2251). 'It also seems that in one case he employed his editorial role to suppress evidence that conflicted with his wish to attribute the poem to Chaucer' (p 267). Speght took his text from Stowe; thus neither black-letter edition has independent value.

554 Eliason, Norman E. 'Chaucer's Fifteenth Century Successors.' *MRS*, 5 (1971), 103–21.
'Judicial appraisal of these much maligned poets has long been wanted' (p 103). Chaucer students should see what his near contemporaries admired in him, namely, his poetic craftsmanship. They praise his 'aptness,' his freshness, his conciseness, his polish. Eliason discusses Lydgate, Shirley, Hawes, and Skelton, who fail because they aim too low or too high; but they offer 'a practical judgment deriving from first hand experience, not theoretical judgment deriving from treatises on rhetoric' (p 111). 'Their failure to match the felicity of Chaucer's versification is not surprising, for few English poets have been able to. But their failure to match its simplest element, the meter, and its most conspicuous trait, its regularity, is something of a puzzle' (p 112). It must be that the language was changing as the century advanced, and 'Chaucer's meter could not be understood aright' (p 112). The irregularities of Skelton and Wyatt are 'obviously not unintentional' (p 113); once Chaucer's 'imitators believed that metrical irregularity was warranted by their model, they extended the practice more and more, so that by the end of the century, Chaucer's meter could not be appreciated at all' (p 114). 'Chaucer's canniness in relying on this obsolescent -*e* and his cunning exploitation of it were evidently appreciated by Gower, who follows the same practice of keeping -*e* and avoiding it as the meter requires, but were lost on Hoccleve and Lydgate. They were a generation younger than Chaucer and Gower, and to them this -*e* must have seemed archaic. Instead of a sound still current in London speech ... it had become passé ... Their rather helter-skelter employment of -*e* certainly shows that it proved a hindrance rather than a help in their meter' (p 115). The earlier disappearance of -*e* in the North freed the Scottish Chaucerians from the problem.

555 Fox, Denton. 'Chaucer's Influence on Fifteenth Century Poetry.' In *Companion to Chaucer*. Ed. Beryl Rowland. Toronto: Oxford University Press, 1968. Pp 385–402. [This essay was not included in the revised edition of 1979.]

The fifteenth century is 'the great *terra incognita* of English
Literature' (p 385). Chaucer's influence was great, but not as profound
or baleful as some have thought. 'The same forces that worked on
Chaucer ... also worked independently on the fifteenth-century poets'
(p 386). Chaucer is usually grouped with Gower and Lydgate as a
symbolic representative of a continental, learned, non-alliterative, and
highly rhetorical style. 'Aureate poetry' was probably more the result
of study of Latin poetry and its rules of ornamentation than Chaucer.
Chaucer's influence on fifteenth-century metrics needs to be reassessed.
Lydgate's meters, for example, are not due to a misunderstanding of
Chaucer's line; rather, he 'knew very well what he was about, and
intentionally combined iambic pentameter with accentual verse as a
sort of flourish' (p 390). But Chaucer did popularize regular meter and
the rhyme royal stanza. Fox emphasizes the importance of Lydgate to
the century; it was the romantics who first began to scorn him.
Though a first impression of Lydgate might be, 'How Chaucerian,' a
second and more accurate view would be, 'How un-Chaucerian' (p
393). Chaucer's great works had only 'a superficial and desultory
influence on Lydgate's matter' (p 393). Lydgate and other
Chaucerians draw more on the allegorical method of the dream vision
than the narrative techniques of *T&C* and *CT*. Also the complaint was
a favorite form; but for both complaint and allegory the French
sources which had influenced Chaucer and courtly society continue to
be the dominant influence, along with Chaucer. Chaucer's position is
more that of explorer and patron saint than 'a model misunderstood
and blindly imitated' (p 400). Bibliography, pp 400–2.

556   Gray, Douglas. 'Later Poetry: The Courtly Tradition.' In *The Middle
       Ages*. Ed. W.F. Bolton. *History of Literature in the English Language*,
       London: Barrie and Jenkins, 1970. Vol I. Pp 312–70.
       A general survey of literature from Chaucer's time to the early
       sixteenth century, with consideration of court culture and such poets
       as Gower, Lydgate, the 'Chaucerians' (pp 325–30), Hawes, Barclay,
       Skelton, anonymous *fine amour* lyrics (pp 341–9), ballads, and
       fifteenth-century Scots poets. In *FL* the reader finds 'close to the
       splendid surface, the pageantry and pastime of courtly life' (p 327); *CL*
       is a 'witty' and 'lively' poem with vivid descriptive writing and 'joieuse
       recreation' (p 329).

556a   *Oxford Book of Late Medieval Verse and Prose*, ed. Douglas Gray.
       Oxford: Clarendon press, 1985.
       Includes *KQ, TC*, Hoccleve's *Letter of Cupid*, and excerpts from *FL*
       and *LBD*.

557   Green, Richard Firth. *Poets and Princepleasers*. Toronto: University
       of Toronto Press, 1980.

Green's purpose is 'to shed some light on the condition of authors
employed in the households of late medieval kings and princes, and to
elucidate both the kind of life they led and the kind of work, literary
and otherwise, expected of them' (p 4). Specific attention is given to
Chaucer, Usk, Clanvowe, Scogan, Hoccleve, Roos, Banester, Ashby,
Hawes, Skelton, Gower, Lydgate, Shirley, and Caxton, as well as the
households with which they were associated. Ch 1, 'The King's
Familia,' pp 13–37, draws extensively on Edward IV's *Liber Niger*,
various registers, poems, and books of manners to determine
constituents of the extended 'family' of a courtly household — their
offices, obligations, expectations, and rewards. Ch 2, 'The Camera
Regis,' pp 38–70, considers that household within the household, the
inner familia where aristocratic taste was formed and where the court
poet had his hearing. Within this group court games and
entertainments served an important role in the sophisticating of leisure
time. Eg, Henry VII was said to have valued Stephen Hawes as a
groom of the chamber for 'his facetious discourse and prodigious
memory, which last did evidently appear in this, that he could repeat
by heart most of our English poets, especially Jo. Lydgate, a monk of
Bury, whome he made equal in some respects with Geff. Chaucer' (p
68). Chaucer himself seems not to have been 'a fully fledged member
of the camera regis, for whenever the lists draw the distinction
between squires (or valets) of the chamber and those of the household
he is invariably included under the latter category' (p 68). Great
households employed secretaries like Alain Chartier, Martin le Franc,
George Ashby, John Shirley, Richard Holland, William of Worcester,
and William Peeris (p 69). If not authors in their own right they
owned books, wrote or translated books, served as historians, and
fostered court literature. Ch 3, 'A Lettered Court,' pp 71–100,
explores education within the paterfamilia. Literacy of servants was
highly valued. 'Broadly speaking, the court provided an education in
two areas: "noriture," the art of genteel behaviour, and "lettrure,"
basic scholastic accomplishment' (p 73). Green considers the value of
books to such households (cf aristocratic bibliophiles like Duke
Humphrey) and the fashion of book-collecting (pp 91–100). Books
were often kept in chests, and were thus transportable. Henry VII is
the first king known to have possessed a formal library with librarian.
Ch 4, 'The Court of Cupid,' pp 101–34, contrasts court minstrels of
the Middle Ages with the literary entertainment of the later period. 'If
the old minstrel literature was a literature of performance, the new
courtly verse might by characterized as a literature of participation ...
The essential mystery had gone out of the story-teller's role; no longer
could he exploit the theatrical possibilities of a privileged position to
manipulate the response of an admiring audience. Chaucer's literary

abilities gave him an entry into an aristocratic society thoroughly
conversant with the conventions binding the poet's imaginary world
and confident in its role of literary arbiter' (p 111). The very intimacy
of court circles required a conventional manner for reasons of social
decorum. What angered Chartier's readers of *LBD* 'was not the
inherent absurdity of a lover driven to his death by the heartlessness of
his mistress, but the impropriety of presenting a mistress so lacking in
pity as to allow such a thing to happen. It is an extraordinary paradox
that Chartier should have been branded as anti-feminist for creating a
heroine who asserts her right to make up her own mind: death from
thwarted desire can hardly have been any more common in Chartier's
day than our own, yet when the lady, with what appears to us to be
admirable common sense, refuses to treat her suitor's protestations
seriously ... she is condemned as unnatural by polite society, and her
creator is pilloried for his unchivalrous treatment of womankind' (p
114). Green considers evidences and complexities of courtly games as
they pertain to the game of love (pp 115–24), commenting on *FL* and
AL to emphasize the influence of *RR*. 'That poets in the late middle
ages should have worked so striking a transformation on the traditional
metaphor of love as service suggests how strong an imaginative
influence the actual court exerted upon them — an influence which
cannot be adequately explained in terms of the relationship between
audience and performer. The shift from lover-as-servant to
servant-as-lover shows how far the court had come to seeing in the *cour
amoureuse* a formalized and idealized expression of its own way of life,
and though the poet might collaborate in this social fiction, he could
not be said to direct it' (p 125). Increased interest in poetry as part of
the sophisticated love game brought little direct benefit to individual
poets. 'The vocation of minstrel, if it had conferred no great prestige
and commanded few lavish rewards, had at least provided its
practitioner with a recognized skill for which his employers were
willing to offer material encouragement; the household poet, on the
other hand, practised an avocation which he shared with his superiors,
and he would have been not only presumptuous, but also ill-advised,
to seek direct recognition for it' (p 127). Green comments on begging
poems and the compiling of anthologies from poems which circulated
on loose leaves or in unpretentious booklets. He challenges the notion
of Hammond 36 and Brusendorff 25 that Shirley was proprietor of a
circulating library or commercial scriptorium (pp 131–3); rather he
seems to have been a gentleman who lived in fashionable quarters
among other people of means. Ch 5, 'An Adviser to Princes,' pp
135–67, emphasizes the role of education served by the translators,
'historians,' and poets. Every major court writer translated or
compiled works of the *Secretum Secretorum* type. 'Boethius' work

must have been read by medieval princes with a kind of personal involvement which it is perhaps difficult to conceive of today. It was after all only those who had something to lose in the world who were exposed to Fortune's malice ... and for such men Boethius' teaching had a particular relevance' (pp 146–7). If the *Consolatio* was too abstruse for the majority of its aristocratic readers then they might turn to the *de casibus* tradition. Even if the king himself did not fall, his servants might: Richard II might be humiliated; Usk loses his life (p 148). Green notes the prominence of instructional literature in the vernacular (especially French) and the importance of Berkeley Castle as a center of English translation (pp 154–5). 'Few men in the middle ages would have understood our reticence about giving advice' (p 161). 'It was probably to such works as *Boethius* and *Melibee* rather than to love allegories like the *Parliament of Fowls* that Chaucer would have owed his advancement' (p 166). Ch 6, 'The Court Apologist,' pp 168–202, considers the poet as propagandist. Green notes the increasing emphasis on Chaucer as a rhetorician in the fifteenth and sixteenth centuries (pp 177–8), and Henry IV's desire to get Christine de Pisan as propagandist and the role of Gower in that regard (pp 179–83). Afterword, pp 203–11; bibliography, pp 225–38.

- Review by Nicholas Jacobs, *SAC*, 4 (1982), 154–9: 'Green's thesis is compellingly argued, and, though lovers of medieval literature who have recreated the Middle Ages in their own image may find its conclusions at first sight dispiriting, it should, by encouraging a reconsideration of much neglected fifteenth-century literature, eventually refresh our understanding of the period' (p 157). Green has not altogether 'refuted the arguments for an increasing middle-class element in fifteenth-century English literary culture,' however (p 158). 'By no stretch of the imagination could all the activity involved' in such writings as diverse as *Wynnere and Wastoure, Sir Launfal, Piers Plowman,* and the mystery cycles 'be fitted into Dr. Green's categories' (p 159). His claim for the overwhelming cultural dominance of the aristocracy must be modified in light of other evidence.

557a — 'The *Familia Regis* and the *Familia Cupidinis.*' In *English Court Culture in the Later Middle Ages.* Ed. V.J. Scattergood and J.W. Sherborne. London: Duckworth, 1983. Pp 87–108.
Discusses Charles VI's *cour amoureuse* and the literature it and other *familia Cupidinis* influenced. Comments on *AL, FL, LBD, LGW,* and *RR* in such settings. Who were the ladies of whom the court poet went in fear? Mainly, they were imaginary. The king's household was virtually all male, 'and the queen's establishment was largely so' (p 98). The love courts were fictional elaborations, 'literary

embellishments' of a 'closed, predominantly masculine, and self-consciously literary society which preened itself before the flattering looking-glass of the *familia Cupidinis*.

558 Hammond, Eleanor Prescott. 'The Nine-Syllabled Pentameter Line in some Post-Chaucerian Manuscripts.' *MP*, 23 (1925), 127–52.
What Chaucer's metrical practices were can only be known through the scribes. Could the idiosyncrasies of the scribes be recognized and separated, the residuum might not be Chaucer but it would at least be a step nearer to him than the report of the codices (p 130). Hammond notes the occurrence of a nine-syllabled pentameter line in early mss of Chaucer, Hoccleve, and Lydgate, a line which is headless, broken-backed, or lacking an unaccented syllable at the verse-pause. The practice varies from one ms to another. We need to identify the idiosyncrasies of each scribe. Eg, the Fairfax 16 scribe was 'a steady, well-behaved workman' who seems to have been insensitive and indifferent to the value of *-e* in his transcriptions (p 131). 'The Shirley and the Selden codices were written by men who were reading their texts in the large, not word by word, as does the professional copyist — men who objected in theory to the nine-syllabled line and who had no scruples, in practice, against emending it' (p 151).

559 — ed. *English Verse between Chaucer and Surrey, being Examples of Conventional Secular Poetry, exclusive of Romance, Ballad, Lyric, and Drama, in the Period from Henry the Fourth to Henry the Eighth.* Durham: Duke University Press; London: Cambridge University Press, 1927.
This verse anthology concentrates on what is not readily obtainable by the student. Includes selections from Walton's *Boethius*, Hoccleve, Lydgate, Burgh, Shirley, Harding, Ripley, Hawes, William Nevill and Robert Copland, Barclay, Skelton, Cavendish, Morley, and several anonymous authors. The selection is designed for the advanced student interested in tracing links from Chaucer to Spenser. The introduction considers political turmoil of the period, growing nationalism, the growth of education, courtly and bourgeois sensibility, imitation of Chaucerian prosody, and continental influences. 'Every vulgarity, every pedantry, every vice, every upleap of vigor, every dignity of Englishmen is poured into the alembic of Shakespeare' (p 37).

560 Hench, Atcheson L. 'Printer's Copy for Tyrwhitt's Chaucer.' *SB*, 3 (1950–1), 265–6.
The Aldeman Library of the University of Virginia possesses a fragment of a black-letter Chaucer annotated by Tyrwhitt. 'Nearly all the matching fragments of the volume, also annotated, are in the British Museum' (p 265). The thousands of marginal annotations reveal 'the painstaking devotion of a great scholar to his task ... The

volume deserves and awaits close study' (p 266). [Tyrwhitt, it is to be remembered, was the first editor to sift out 'the heap of rubbish' added by Stow, though he defended several apocryphal works such as CL, TL, IL, FL, CN, and 'Virelay.' See **526**]

561 Jack, Adolphus Alfred. *A Commentary on the Poetry of Chaucer and Spenser.* Glasgow: Maclehose and Jackson; Boston: Macmillan, 1920. Ch 3, 'The Chaucer Apocrypha and Imitations,' pp 117–40: Jack remarks on *Gamelyn* ('better lost some suppose,' though it 'goes in a jaunty folk metre' p 121); *CBK*; *CN* ('a pretty poem Chaucer might conceivably have written'; 'the poem, though short, is too long' p 122); *CL* ('if Chaucer wrote it, it has come down to us in a late transcription' p 123); *AL*; and *FL* (a poem with 'virility' and also 'a gentle softness in the describing without Chaucer's stiffness behind the pretty,' its lines 'characteristically feminine' p 125). In his adaptations of Chaucer, Dryden surpassed his original as is 'admitted even by Dr. Skeat' (p 126). 'Indeed Dryden, the first great poet to lend his genius to the task of translating Chaucer, has never received, for this particular work, adequate acknowledgement ... The poem is as Chaucer might have written could we suppose him to have lived in Dryden's day' (pp 127–8). Jack discusses other less successful adapters — Pope, Wordsworth, Swinburne; 'in Wordsworth there was nothing of the sly' (p 131). Successful imitations of Chaucer from earlier times include the *KQ* and some writings of Henryson and Dunbar.

562 Leonard, Frances McNeely. *Laughter in the Courts of Love.* 1981. See **131**.
Ch 3, 'Laughter in the Courts of Love,' pp 57–105, explores fifteenth- and early sixteenth-century court poetry of the tradition of Chaucer and Gower, with extended comments on *CA, Golden Targe, Bouge of Court*, and *CL*. Ch 4, 'The Pilgrimage of Love,' pp 105–31, gives special consideration to Gavin Douglas' *Palice of Honour* ('a brilliant and busy poem ... that does not wear well over a series of close readings' p 107), Stephen Hawes' *The Pastime of Pleasure*, and *King Hart* (a poem sometimes attributed to Gavin Douglas).

563 Lewis, C.S. 'The Fifteenth Century Heroic Line.' *E&S*, 24 (1938), 28–41.
Because of its odd number of feet and lack of a medial break 'the decasyllabic line stands at a much further remove than almost any other metre from the natural modes of rhythmical human behaviour, whether in song or dance or shout' (pp 29–30). Regardless of whether Chaucer 'caught the music of the modern decasyllabic and intended his countrymen to hear this music in his own verse,' it is doubtful that his audience understood the line (p 31). 'If Chaucer was in fact introducing the tune of Spenser, Milton, and Tennyson, then he was

introducing a new thing for which French poetry furnished only a hint,
and to which French poetry would hardly at all have opened the ears
of his contemporaries' (p 32). The heroic measure of such works as
Lydgate's *Assembly of Gods*, Barclay's *Ecloge*, and Hawes' *Pastime of
Pleasure* seems to be 4-stress. And, indeed, some lines in Chaucer read
'more naturally as Fifteenth-Century Heroics' (p 38). On the other
hand, 'there are hundreds of lines in Chaucer that demand pure
decasyllabic reading' (p 38). It must be remembered that 'the French
decasyllabic, being unaccented, was no metre at all to English ears' (p
40). Evidently later generations tried to read Chaucer as a 'rough
four-beat line' (p 41).

564 — *Allegory of Love*. 1936. See 132.
Ch 6, *Allegory as the Dominant Form*, pp 232–967, emphasizes the
dominance of allegory between Chaucer's death and the poetry of
Wyatt, with special attention to Lydgate's dream visions; *KQ, CN,
LBD, FL, AL*; the allegories of Dunbar ('the first completely
professional poet in our history,' p 251); Douglas and Hawes; William
Nevill's *Castell of Pleasure* ('the nadir of the whole genre' p 253), and
such Renaissance efforts as *The Pastime of Pleasure, Court of
Sapience, Court of Venus*, and *Palice of Honour*. [See also 625.]

565 Licklider, Albert H. *Chapters on the Metric of the Chaucerian
Tradition*. Baltimore: J.H. Furst, 1910.
A 1907 Johns Hopkins dissertation reassessing theories of metric in the
Chaucer tradition, with consideration given to syllabic articulation,
accentuation, arsis-thesis variation in Chaucer, Gower, Lydgate,
Hoccleve, Hawes, and the Scottish poets. The last chapter relates the
methods of accentuation of Sir Thomas Wyatt to the Chaucer
tradition. 'In general one may say they loaded so much that was
clumsy, artificial, and tawdry upon Chaucer's line that they
completely obscured its beauty' (p 12). 'Chaucerian tradition has
metrical regularity' (p 32), but the Chaucerian lines Renaissance
readers encountered in mss were 'not so smooth as our excellent
modern editions make them' (p 33).

566 McFarlane, K.B. *Lancastrian Kings and Lollard Knights*. Oxford:
Clarendon Press, 1972.
Discussion of John Cheyne, Sir Thomas Latimer, Sir Lewis Clifford,
Sir Richard Sturry, John Montagu, Sir William Nevill, and Thomas
Clanvow, including some consideration of their interests in books.
Mentions Thomas Clanvow as possible author of *CN*, though Sir John
Clanvow is the more likely candidate (p 184). Appendix B (pp 230–2)
on Sir John Clanvow. Appendix C (pp 233–8) on Henry V's books.

567 Mason, Harold Andrew. *Humanism and Poetry in the Early Tudor
Period*. London: Routledge and Kegan Paul, 1959. Pp 158–71.

Chaucer changes the direction of interest in poetry; his contribution
which the tradition followed is 'merely artifice, the elaboration of the
stanzas into patterns' (p 160). There is hardly a line among his
followers that might not be found in other poems of this type. As
author of courtly love poems Chaucer 'seems to have taken the first
step down the slippery slope that led to the utter banality of most of
the similar poems written after him. For, once the forms had been
provided, anybody could string together the tags into the semblance of
a poem' (p 163). 'Can we doubt that if we had *all* the songs sung at
court between Chaucer and Wyatt we should be able to shew that
every word and phrase used by Wyatt was a commonplace and had
been used by many of his predecessors?' (p 171).

568 Miskimin, Alice S. *The Renaissance Chaucer*. New Haven: Yale
University Press, 1975.
Ch 8, 'The Renaissance Chaucer: From Manuscript to Print,' pp
226–61, considers the Chaucer Spenser would have known in a period
of Renaissance confusion over Chaucer's texts and canon. 'The effect
of successive enlargements of the canon of Chaucer's poems and of
irreversible evolution in the spoken language, of which men were
aware, is that literary imitations became increasingly indistinguishable
from their older originals' (p 233). 'Skelton could distinguish Chaucer
from Lydgate as few readers could' (p 234); but by Speght's 1602
edition almost 40 percent of the published Chaucer was spurious (p
257), which would make it virtually impossible for even the most
sensitive Renaissance reader handicapped by linguistic barriers, to
discern the true Chaucer. Moreover, 'no selection, no matter how
judicious, of "typical" pseudo-Chaucerian pieces from the mass
inflation of the canon in the sixteenth century could be adequately
representative, in range of content, quality, and style, of the thickening
and blurring effects brought about by their aggregate inclusion. To say
the pseudo-Chaucerian poems are redundant and their effect reductive
is true, but it is not true enough' (p 258). In commenting on the
apocrypha Miskimin finds it 'of interest chiefly by association' (p 230).
She notes Chaucer's ability to mock poetic diction in *Ros* and *MB*, but
neither of these witty lyrics were printed until the twentieth century (p
235). Instead it was the Chaucerian poetic language of *Pity, Lady*, and
Mars — 'soberly formal, untainted by irony, and not leavened by wit'
— that was kept 'artificially alive by poets for another century' (p
235). The resulting verse is marred by aureate diction, 'baffling
randomness' in the use of -*e* and -*en*, arbitrary spelling, crippled
rhythms, and 'deliberately awkward metrical archaisms' (pp 236–7).
C.S. Lewis thought *CL* an amazing performance (*English Literature of
the Sixteenth Century*, p 240), but, 'in my opinion, that so turgid and

mindless an allegory should be taken for Chaucerian love poetry is
somewhat more to be deplored than applauded' (p 231). Speght's
addition of *JU* is 'perhaps the least defensible and most puzzling of all
the Chauceriana' (p 253). Miskimin discusses the reformer's Chaucer
(pp 255–7), reviewing Francis Thynne's account of censorship in the
days of Henry VIII. See 523a. By the end of the century 'Chaucer
was presented as a precursor of their own Renaissance, valuable for
moral wisdom, excusably obscene in wit, and preeminently a love poet
of the vanished Courts of Love and chivalry which Tudor and
Elizabethan court pageantry revived in masquerades' (p 260).

569 Moore, Arthur K. *The Secular Lyric in Middle English*. Lexington:
University of Kentucky Press, 1951. Pp 124–54.
Moore considers the Chaucerian lyric mode and its effects. 'The lyric
impulse in Chaucer and most of his disciples, acknowledged or
otherwise, is admittedly weak, but the excess of defects in their shorter
poems is partially owing to the decline of the trouvères and to the
fragmentation of the whole art in the practice of fourteenth-century
French poets, who abandoned musical accompaniment and extirpated
metrical and emotional license' (p 125). Such poetry is anemic, its
prime motive always ulterior, and its surface drama inconsequential (p
128). Chaucer's imitators — Lydgate, Hoccleve, Charles of Orleans,
William de la Pole — are more feeble than he, admiring artificial
diction and trying 'with little success to imitate it' (p 137). Regarding
fifteenth-century poetry in general, 'it is probably correct to say ...
that the merit of the verse increases in direct ratio to the distance of
its removal from the influence of that *vers de société* which Chaucer
and Gower first imported from France' (p 154).

570 Owings, Jr., Frank N. 'Keats, Lamb, and a Black-letter Chaucer.'
PBSA, 75 (1981), 147–55.
In a letter of 3 May 1818, Keats gives a 'huzza' for having obtained a
black-letter edition of Chaucer; in a letter of 9 December 1832, Charles
Lamb also claims to have possessed one. Lamb's copy is now in the
Lilly Library, Indiana University, Bloomington, Indiana. In view of the
fact that Lamb obtained several of Keats' books, it is likely that
Lamb's copy once belonged to Keats. Keats' 'La Belle Dame Sans
Merci' was first published in Leigh Hunt's *Indicator* (10 May 1820),
with a note by Hunt citing Alain Chartier's poem as inspiration for
Keats' title. Roos' version of Chartier's poem is included in the 1598
black-letter edition.

571 Pearsall, Derek. 'The English Chaucerians.' In *Chaucer and
Chaucerians*. Ed. Derek Brewer. London: Nelson, 1966. Pp 201–39.
Chaucer cast a long shadow, but we should not let that 'blind us to
the real qualities of the English Chaucerians' (p 201). Lydgate has

been 'a ready target for the long line of English men of letters who have preferred wit to honesty, the plausible sneer to the painstaking effort at appreciation' (p 204). Discusses such Chaucerian influences on Lydgate as the complaint, the *Romaunt*, and other dream visions. 'Lydgate's learning was not as extensive as it looks. It is 'mostly culled from Ovid and Chaucer,' but his insatiable appetite for facts and names marks him very much a man of his age' (p 214). There is some influence of *ABC* and *SNT* in his religious poetry, but mainly he turns to non-Chaucerian traditions in his religious verse. Discusses also Hoccleve, Clanvowe, Charles of Orleans, Hawes, Capgrave, Cavendish, Burgh, and Barclay, and comments on *KQ, FL, AL, IL*, and *CL*. 'When poets begin to imitate Chaucer consciously, as Spenser does, because they think him a great poet and worthy of imitation, the Chaucer tradition, properly so called, has ended, and history of Chaucer criticism begins' (p 239).

572 Prasad, Prajapati. 'The Order of Complaint: A Study in Medieval Tradition.' *DA*, 25 (1966), 3930. University of Wisconsin Disseration, 1965. Dir. Helen C. White.
Traces material of love complaints from Virgil and Ovid to fourteenth-century England, culminating in Chaucer and Gower. Does not look beyond 1400.

573 Robbins, Rossell Hope. 'A Late-Sixteenth-Century Chaucer Allusion (Douce ms 290).' *ChauR*, 2 (1967), 135–7.
Robbins prints a hitherto unpublished sixteenth-century poem (twelve quatrains of doggerel praise), beginning with an apostrophe to Britain which has lost its 'Tullie,' then 'passing into an indirect account of Chaucer's burial' (p 135). The poet would have Chaucer's verse engraved in gold and set in marble: 'Alyue he learning did encrease'; he was 'a pierles poet ... subiect yet to fate, / his soule a heauenlie poet in mearth / Lyues, whith coelestiall state' (p 137).

574 — 'Dissent in Middle English Literature: The Spirit of (Thirteen) Seventy-six.' *M&H*, 9 (1979), 25–51.
This essay provides useful background material to that Renaissance tradition which viewed Chaucer as a reformer. Robbins discusses 1) the pervasiveness of the Three Estates theory in Middle English literature, especially in such writers as Gower, Hoccleve, Langland and 'in the near propaganda of Peter Idley and Lydgate' (pp 28–34); 2) the latent political dissent in the religious reforms of Wyclif and his followers (pp 34–6); 3) the 'head-on but short-lived protest of John Ball and the Peasants' Revolt against the Estates Theory' (pp 28, 37–8); and 4) various Middle English poems which nibble away at the *status quo* by various forms of satire (pp 38–40). 'In certain respects Middle English literature itself, by its very existence, advocated

dissent. It is in the vernacular. To break away from Latin or French and use English was a major act of rebellion ... The vernacular destroyed the intellectual and political control of the aristocrats of church and state. With the vernacular, ordinary people could approximate the knowledge and skills of the ruling class' (p 40).

575 — 'The Vintner's Son: French Wine in English Bottles.' In *Eleanor of Aquitaine: Patron and Politician*. Ed. William W. Kibler. Austin: University of Texas Press, 1976. Pp 147–72.
'Chaucer and the Chaucerians: 1370–1530,' pp 161–6, emphasizes the continuing dominance of French taste imported by Chaucer in fifteenth-century English court poetry and discusses new French models, like Alain Chartier's *LBD*, which become influential. 'There were many more, probably not translated directly, but all building up that reservoir of tradition that vivified the followers of Chaucer. These poets are now little read, even by *romanistes*, but I would suggest that minor French writers of the fifteenth century might be worth investigating further for influence on Middle English palace poetry' (p 165).

576 — 'The Structure of Longer Middle English Court Poems.' In *Chaucerian Problems and Perspectives: Essays Presented to Paul E. Beichner*. Ed. Edward Vasta and Zacharias P. Thundy. Notre Dame: University of Notre Dame Press, 1979. Pp 244–64.
Over the past fifty years the Middle English *dits amoureaux* have received little attention. The reasons are several: 'One is embarrassingly obvious: these are not major poems' (p 244). Secondly they are relatively inaccessible. A third reason is the lack of appropriate criticism. Nothing can remedy the first deficiency. The second will be remedied when Robbins' 'forthcoming anthologies' are published. The present essay lays out groundwork to remedy the third deficiency by describing the design and construction of the longer court love letters as an aid in understanding and appreciating them. There is no essential difference between the longer and the shorter love lyrics in ms preservation; they were 'composed under the same social conditions, for intellectual and social diversion and amorous dalliance among a miniscule elite group' (p 245); the short lyrics fall into two main genres (*salut d'amour* and *complaint d'amour*) and the longer poems are 'simply literary and social exercises extending the salutation and complaint.' The elongation is achieved by 'surrounding them or embedding them in formal set pieces, minor genres, themes, topics or figures' (p 245). Neither the long or short poems bear much resemblance to reality. Neither the wars nor even everyday concerns of the aristocracy are discussed. The basic form of the *saluts d'amour* 'consists of a brief celebration of the lady, for her beauty (the *effictio*)

and personality (the *notatio*), sometimes little more than a series of anaphora or a catalogue of delights' (p 247). Many are couched as epistles. The form works within the boundaries of its conventions. 'In the same way that today anybody who is anybody has a psychiatrist, the fifteenth-century man-about-court had a mistress. In neither case was any cure expected — "al was for nought"; but it's fun, conspicuously expensive, satisfies the ego, and allows for one-upmanship ... To show you, I'll write a *salut d'amour* or maybe a *complaint d'amour*, because she says she doesn't love me. But even if by granting favors my mistress thereby removed the cause of complaining I would never celebrate her surrender. So whether she shows pity or not, I'll go on writing my complaints. It's all part of a ritual game' (p 248). Noting the devices agglutinated in stretching the core of the *salut d'amour* into a love ditty, Robbins describes the composition of *How a Lover Praiseth his Lady, The Lover's Book,* and *The Parlement of Love* (pp 251–3). To describe extended complaints he considers *The Supplicacio Amantis, The Temple of Glass,* and *AL* (pp 253–9). Robbins notes that the longer poems were frequently pillaged for extrapolable stanzas for shorter lyrics or to stand by themselves as separate poems (pp 259–60). 'If we try to judge these English court poems, both the short lyrics and the longer *dits amoureux,* by standards of high seriousness, they will be found wanting. On the other hand, if we regard them as ephemeral, occasional pieces, designed to please for the moment, to provide an escapist interlude from a harsh society, "to make your hertes gaye and lyght," then we may appreciate them as eminently fitting to their function in palace and court circles' (p 260).

577 — 'The Middle English Court Love Lyric.' In *The Interpretation of Medieval Lyric.* Ed. W.T.H. Jackson. London: Macmillan; New York: Columbia University Press, 1980. Pp 205–32.
Emphasizes the courtliness and occasional nature of the more than three hundred short lyrics and the thirty or so longer love poems. This body of Middle English literature is 'probably the most neglected genre in English' (p 208). Ignorance of the genre obscures links between Chaucer and Spenser. The essay sets out seven guideposts to help the modern reader to know what to expect in exploring such poetry.

578 Saintsbury, George. 'The English Chaucerians.' In *CHEL.* 1908. See 62. Vol 2, pp 225–53.
'The influence of Chaucer upon English poetry of all dialects, during the entire century which followed his death, and part, at least, of the next, is something to which there is hardly a parallel in literature' (p 225). Discussion includes Lydgate [see 677]; Hoccleve [see 662]; Oldcastle, Burgh, Ashby, Bradshaw, Riply, Norton, and Bokenham;

Beryn; PlowT ('sufficiently disposed of with Tyrwhitt's label of
"rubbish," ' p 245); *LBD* ('a heavy thing, showing the characteristic, if
not the worst, faults of that *rhétoriqueur* school, of which Chartier was
the precursor, if not the actual leader' (p 247); *CN* ('The poem is one
of great attractiveness — quite independently of the fact that Milton
evidently refers to it in an early sonnet' p 247); *AL; FL* (The
argument that it is by a woman is no more valid than that the Wife of
Bath's prologue is. 'The great charm of the piece is a certain nameless
grace of choice, arrangement and handling of subject,' p 249. 'There is
a singular brightness and freshness over it all, together with a power of
pre-Raphaelite decoration and of vivid portraiture ... Indeed, outside
of Chaucer himself and the original beginning of Guillaume de Lorris
in the *Roman de la Rose*, it would be difficult to find anything of the
kind better done,' p 250); and *CL* (written after the 'period of
staggers,' this early Renaissance poem has its prosody under control,
but like its predecessors, uses a 'community of goods in the matter of
phraseology'; the poet, if a Cambridge clerk as its 'Philogenet' claims,
is one of a 'nest of singing birds that even the university of Spenser,
Milton, and Dryden cannot afford to oust,' pp 250–1).

579 Scattergood, V.J. *Politics and Poetry in the Fifteenth Century:
1399–1485*. London: Blandford Press, 1971.
Ch 2, 'Political Verse in Medieval England,' pp 13–34, surveys the not
inconsiderable volume of political verse, emphasizing how little we
know about the circumstances of its composition. Considers the
writings of Gower, Hoccleve, Lydgate, Ashby, Ryman, and anonymous
verse. Discusses patronage ('every type of medieval verse was a
commodity which could be purchased' p 18), but also executions of
propagandists who fell into the power of their patron's enemies, and
the enacting of laws to suppress political verse. Much political verse
that survives does so in out of the way places (flyleaves, blank leaves of
mss, etc). Most verses published as 'bills' have disappeared, though
their authors may have been drawn and quartered. Ch 2, 'Nationalism
and Foreign Affairs,' pp 35–106, considers antagonism toward the
Scots and the French and patriotic verses pertaining to conflicts with
those peoples. Ch 4, 'Domestic Affairs I: 1399–1442,' pp 106–36, Ch 5,
'Domestic Affairs II: 1442–55,' pp 137–72, and Ch 6, 'Domestic Affairs
III: 1455–85,' pp 173–217, consider *Mum and the Sothsegger* and other
literature surrounding the overthrow of Richard II; political poems of
Hoccleve and Lydgate pertaining to the latter part of Henry V's reign
and John Oldcastle; Duke Humphrey's employment of 'historians' and
poets (especially Lydgate) to celebrate the military achievements of
himself and his brother, and verses on his death and on William de la
Pole, Duke of Suffolk, with his sensational fall from power and his

brutal death; and propagandist verse on the later years of the War of
the Roses. Ch 7, 'Religion and the Clergy,' pp 218–63, surveys
anti-Lollard verse and verse such as 'Why I Can't be a Nun,' *JU* and
Friar Daw's Reply, the *Croxton Play of the Sacrament*, and poems by
Hoccleve and Lydgate crying out against religious abuses of the day.
Chapters 8–10 (pp 264–377) pertain to literature commenting on
society at large — its theoretical basis (estates theory) and moral
responsibility (courtesy books, advice to princes); its efforts at
effecting reform dealing with lawlessness, unjust taxation and
agricultural oppressions (*London Lickpenny*, Peter Idley's *Instructions
to his Son*, *The World Upsidedown*, *Libelle of Englyshe Polycye*,
Regement of Princes, *Treatise of a Gallant*, *Childe of Bristowe*, *Money
Money*, *A Trade Policy*, *Corruption of Public Manners*, etc); and
verses of social protest. The book provides an informative survey of
political events and social attitudes of the period.

580 Southall, Raymond. *The Courtly Maker: An Essay on the Poetry of
Wyatt and his Contemporaries*. Oxford: Basil Blackwell, 1964.
The middle chapters on the Devonshire ms, *T&C* as a Point of
Departure, the Public World of Courtly Love, the Recalcitrant
Universe, the Psychology of a Courtier, the Inimitable Translator, and
Harmony of Numbers, contain various matters which pertain to the
Chaucerian tradition.

581 Spearing, A.C. *Medieval Dream-Poetry*. Cambridge: University Press,
1976.
Ch 4, 'The Chaucerian Tradition,' pp 171–228, considers use of the
dream genre in Lydgate, *Temple of Glass*; Clanvowe, *CN; KQ*; Scottish
dream-prologues; Dunbar; Skelton, *The Bowge of Court*; Douglas, *The
Palice of Honour*; and Skelton, *The Garland of Laurel*. 'There is an
important distinction to be drawn between those writers who
understood what Chaucer was doing in his work and those who did
not. The former responded to the creative principles of Chaucer's
dream-poems, imitated those, and sometimes took them further in
directions implied but not completed by Chaucer's work; the latter —
a far more numerous class — imitated only the external forms of his
poems, without responding to their inner spirit ... It is the intelligent
ones that provide the best poems, and also, incidentally, help us best
to understand what Chaucer was doing in his dream-poetry. To read
Chaucer through the eyes of an intelligent late-medieval poet, who
studied him not in an academic spirit but as a master who could point
out new creative possibilities, can be an illuminating experience' (p
171). Spearing uses Lydgate's *Temple* to illustrate 'unintelligent
imitation of Chaucer' (p 171), where Chaucerian matter is there
'simply because Lydgate had liked it in Chaucer and wanted to add to

the glittery effect of his own poem' (p 173). Lydgate's use of the narrator reveals that he 'was completely insensitive to this aspect of Chaucer's poetry' (p 174). 'The poem offers a mixture of religiosity and illicit passion, which will give the desired emotional satisfaction only if we allow ourselves not so much to dream as to daydream' (p 176). In fact much of the dream-poetry of the Chaucerian tradition might better be called 'daydream-poetry.' *CN* deliberately combines day-dreaming and dreaming for subtle effect (pp 176–81). The poem is only 290 lines long, 'but, on its miniature scale, it indicates a sensitive reading by Clanvowe of Chaucer's dream-poems, and a lively understanding of the irony they persistently direct against the dreamer-narrator, by making the poem express only his personal, biased point of view, even while it implies the possibility of other points of view' (p 180). Clanvowe had 'a real grasp of the dynamic of the Chaucerian dream-poem ... It was to be a long time before another English follower of Chaucer was to see so fully the implications of his master's reshaping of the dream-poem. Perhaps no other English poet before Skelton was a really intelligent reader of Chaucer's dream-poetry' (p 181). The Scottish poets made highly perceptive and creative uses of Chaucer's forms, however. Spearing discusses *KQ*'s intelligent use of Boethian material from Chaucer (pp 181–7).

582 Spurgeon, Caroline F.E. *Five Hundred Years of Chaucer Criticism and Allusion, 1357–1900.* 3 vols. Cambridge: University Press, 1925. Volume 1 gives fairly complete coverage of references to Chaucer and his work up to the year 1800. Volume 3 includes additional references which the first volume missed and presents early references in languages other than English (mainly Latin and French). The introductory essay discusses the fluctuation of Chaucer's reputation during the first half-millenium of his history, discusses various qualities ascribed to Chaucer, the evolution of his biography, and various scholars who have explored his history. Spurgeon breaks the history of Chaucer criticism down into six stages: 1) enthusiastic and reverential praise which lasts to the end of the fifteenth century; 2) universal acknowledgment of his genius in the form of imitation in Scotland up into the sixteenth century, and, in England, admiration of his role as a social reformer and exposer of vice and folly; 3) admiration of writers in the late sixteenth century who see him as obsolete and difficult, his style as rough and unpolished, his versification imperfect; 4) the low point when in the seventeenth century his language seems an unknown tongue and knowledge of his versification entirely disappears; 5) the period of 'modernizations,' beginning with Dryden's *Fables* in 1700; 6) the period of scholarly study and appreciation beginning with Tyrwhitt in 1776, then onto the establishing of the Chaucer Society in 1868 and,

on further, to Skeat's 'final scholarly complete edition' in 1894.

583 Thompson, [R.] Ann. *Shakespeare's Chaucer: A Study in Literary Origins.* Liverpool: Liverpool University Press; New York: Barnes and Noble, 1978.
In her introduction (pp 1–15) Thompson stresses Chaucer's reputation for learnedness in the Renaissance and comments on *PlowT* and *JU* as 'Chaucerian' pieces that contributed to his reputation. Ch 2 considers uses of Chaucer by dramatists other than Shakespeare, prior to 1625. Ch 3 considers uses of Chaucer in *Romeo and Juliet* and *Midsummer Night's Dream.* Ch 4 focuses on *Troilus and Cressida*, and Ch 5 on *Two Noble Kinsmen.* Concludes that for Elizabethan and Jacobean writers Chaucer was a major poet — an 'English Homer.' That they frequently draw on *T&C, KnT*, and *CT* indicates 'firstly that they did not think of him primarily as a funny (even bawdy) poet as many people do today, but as a serious romantic writer, and secondly, that they did not regard these non-naturalistic medieval romances as impossibly archaic and undramatic' (p 216).

- Review by D.W. Robertson, Jr. *Shakespeare Quarterly*, 31 (1980), 441: Thompson handles the subject 'in a readable and sometimes deft style'; 'her conception of "Boethian philosophy" seems frequently superficial, and she accords Chaucer's Troilus and Criseyde, as well as Shakespeare's Romeo, more sympathy than I think they deserve, or at least more than would have been accorded them by their original audiences.'

584 Wright, H.G. 'Thomas Speght as a Lexicographer and Annotator of Chaucer's Works.' *ES*, 40 (1959), 194–208.
Speght's is the first edition to include a glossary. He made use of Latin and Greek authors and, in the 1602 edition, also Francis Thynne's *Animadversions* (1599), though there are instances in which he remains independent of Thynne. Sometimes he glosses the obvious in a most interesting way. The glossary was a boon to those who perceived Chaucer to be a great writer but needed guidance to understand him. Pope probably used the third edition of 1687.

Spurious Tales

See also 55 (Lydgate's *Tale of Froward Maymond*); 641 (*Pilgrim's Tale*); 619 (Hoccleve's *New Ploughman's Tale*); and 667, 669, and 676 (*Siege of Thebes*).

Tale of Beryn

585 *The Works of Geoffrey Chaucer*. Ed. John Urry. 1721. See **525**.
Urry is the first to print *Beryn*, which he places, along with 'The Mery
Adventure of the Pardonere and Tapstere at the Inn at Canterbury,' at
the end of the volume, after the *Romaunt, Boece, Astrolabe*, dream
visions, and lyrics, just prior to the Glossary. His edition of Chaucer
does not include Lydgate's *Seige of Thebes*, nor does it make any effort
to link the two new pieces to the Tales. In the short preface to the
two, the editor (presumably Timothy Thomas) notes that they are
'taken out of a ms. borrowed from the Honourable Lady Thinn's; and
not to be met with in any of the other mss which Mr. *Urry* had
perused: So that if the sense and measure of the Verses are not so
perfect here as in the other Tales, it must be attributed to the want of
mss upon the authority of which all the other corrections are chiefly
grounded. The Verse in all probability is of the same kind with that of
Gamelyn, and were it to be found in as many mss might no doubt be
as easily compleated, but having no other besides the forementioned,
the Reader must be content with only a faithful Transcript of it out of
that ms.' (p 594). [*Beryn* was reprinted by Bell in 1782; by Anderson,
with a disclaimer of its authenticity, in 1793; by Chalmers as a 'Poem
imputed to Chaucer' in 1810; and by Wright in 1847. See **587** for
Furnivall's Chaucer Society Publication.]

586 Bashe, E.J. 'The Prologue of the *Tale of Beryn.' PQ*, 12 (1933), 1–16.
'The *Beryn* Prologue should furnish us with knowledge of what a
nearly contemporary poet believed Chaucer was trying to delineate in
each of his characters ... The *Beryn*-writer is not stupid and he wrote
within half a century of Chaucer's death' (p 2). He understands well
the characters of the Knight, Host, and Pardoner.

586a Bowers, John M. '*The Tale of Beryn* and *The Siege of Thebes:*
Alternative Ideas of *The Canterbury Tales.' SAC*, 7 (1985), 23–50.
After reviewing modern arguments which view *CT* apocalyptically as
a one-way journey, Bowers investigates the alternative ideas of two
early fifteenth-century readers who responded to Chaucer in different
ways from each other but both conceived of the journey
philosophically and structurally as a two-way journey. The Beryn
poet's grasp of Chaucer's characterizations and narrative strategies is
subtly detailed as he invests the 'pilgrims with more dramatic vitality
than they display in Chaucer's own links' (p 50). 'The Beryn poet was
concerned not so much with the spiritualized pilgrimage as with the
secular, nonreligious, and even grossly irreverent quality' of Chaucer's
frame story (p 30). Bower discusses the Northumberland ms which
places several of Chaucer's tales on the return journey that *Beryn*

introduces, concluding with *Pars T* which is apparently told at a
'thropes end' near London. Lydgate's conception of the pilgrimage is
less realistically detailed. He perceives of a journey of circularities, not
just from London to London but from fiction to fiction, 'a historical
fabric composed of countless repetitions' (p 47). 'The ending of his
Thebes encourages the reader to begin *The Canterbury Tales* anew, for
the simple reason that they are worth re-reading' (pp 48–49).

587　*The Tale of Beryn with A Prologue of the Merry Adventure of the
Pardoner with a Tapster at Canterbury.* Ed. F.J. Furnivall and W.G.
Stone. Chaucer Society Publications, Second Series, 17, 24. London:
N. Trübner, 1887.
Edited from the Duke of Northumberland's ms 55, f. 180 ff, where it
appears after *CYT.* 'The [unique] MS. is often faulty in metre, and is
not a correct copy of the original poem' (p xi). The edition includes a
1573–9 map of the road from London to Maidstone and Boxley, the BL
ms Sloan 2596 drawing of Canterbury, and a three-column foldout
drawing of the road from London to Canterbury from Ogilby's *Roads*
(ca 1675). The second part of the volume is an English abstract by
W.A. Clouston of the French original behind *Beryn (L'Histoire du
Chevalier Berinus)*, plus Persian, Indian, and Arabian versions and
variants. An appendix summarizes the continuation of the *Romance of
Berinus* which the author of the spurious tale did not include (pp
121–74). Notes and glossary, pp 175–238.

SUMMARY OF BERYN:

　Prologue (lines 1–732): Upon arriving at Canterbury the
Pardoner flirts with Kit the Tapster who, after accepting a groat for
reassurance, agrees to spend the night with him. After visiting the
Cathedral the pilgrims split up while the Pardoner lingers behind at
the tapstry in hope of having his 'hole entencioun.' Kit has other
plans, however, and puts him off until later that night. The Pardoner
gives her more money, which she uses for a private feast 'of the beste
gouse' with her paramour. When the Pardoner arrives he discovers he
has been bearded. There is a brawl. The Pardoner gets bloody cheeks,
is bitten by a Welsh dog, and is forced to sleep in the dog's litter.
Next morning he is first up, pretending to be merry, as the pilgrims set
out on their return journey. The Host comments on the beautiful
morning, but hesitates to draw lots for tale-telling for fear that some
'semybousy' sleepy head might get the fall. The Merchant courteously
volunteers, however, and tells the *Tale of Beryn.*
　Tale (lines 733–4024): Faunus, a rich Roman Senator, is delighted
that his wife Agea bears him a son, Berinus. The child receives

anything he asks and grows up a wastrel. His dying mother calls for him, but he pays no heed. Then Fortune becomes his tutor. Faunus remarries, and Beryn is told he will have to stand on his own two feet. Upon running out of clothing, he begins to lament his dead mother. He goes to her tomb, loses his wits, then, after declining a reconciliation with his father, becomes a merchant, giving up his heritage for five ships of merchandise. A storm carries his fleet off course to a town where everyone is false. The Burgess, a steward, the Provost, a blind man, a woman with a baby, and a catchpoll all swindle him, and he is to be brought to court. He decides to flee, but a hundred year old cripple named Geffrey runs him down and insists on helping him at the trial, providing that Beryn will convey him back to Rome. Geffrey cleverly turns the swindlers' devices against them and wins all Beryn's goods back twofold. Beryn weds the fair daughter of Isope, a neighboring Duke. The tale ends with a Latin couplet indicating that a Canterbury monk (*Filius ecclesie Thome*) wrote the tale.

588 Kittredge, G.L. *Chaucer and his Poetry*. Cambridge, Mass.: Harvard University Press, 1915.
In discussing the variety of relations between the pilgrims Kittredge notes that the author of *Beryn* did not mistake *CT* as a volume of disconnected stories, but saw the work as 'micro-cosmography, a little image of the great world' (p 158).

588a Kohl, Stephan, 'Chaucer's Pilgrims in Fifteenth-Century Literature.' *FCS*, 7 (1983), 221–36.
Both Lydgate and the Beryn-poet, in writing their continuations of CT, do so from a cultural perspective different from Chaucer's. The moralistic cultural norms of the Middle Ages no longer regulate the actual practice of their age. Chaucer's irony, which depends upon moral assumptions, will not work for them in their more uncertain times (pp 234–5). 'The narrator of the Beryn Prologue never condemns his pilgrims for their worldly preoccupations. Whatever sin or fraud they commit, to him it is just another amusing incident' (p 226). Cleverness rather than morality is the norm. In Chaucer the pilgrims set out desiring reform; in Beryn they are 'an unreformed and unreformable lot' (p 229). There is satire in the Beryn prologue, 'but it turns against Chaucer the moralist, not against the pilgrims' worldly concerns ... The narrator ... is no longer bound to the norms of the Middle Ages, but identifies himself completely with the non-cultural practice of his day' (p 229). In the Prologue to the *Siege of Thebes* the effect is similar: the way of the world holds sway. The host has become a fiendish intimidator. The 'pilgrims have all abandoned their religious principles under the powerful influence of their devilish governor' (p 233). Lydgate's prologue, with its timid and uncertain narrator, 'reads

like a melancholic report on the end of medieval culture' (p 234).

589 McIntosh, Helen Marie. *The Literary Background of the Tale of Beryn.*
University of Chicago Dissertation, 1932. See also, Abstracts of
Theses, Humanistic Series, 9 (1930-2), 461-4.
Background of *Beryn* may be seen in early folk literature like *The
Book of Sindibád*, the Indian story 'The Merchant and His Son'
(Ratnatschûda of Dschnânsâgara), and an exemplum of the thirteenth
century in Tours ms 468, though none of these could have been a
direct source. The French source of the English poem is extant in BN
777 (B_7), BN 15097 (B_{15}), Arsenal 3343, and Vienna 3436, the textual
relationships of which McIntosh discusses. Although the English poem
is fundamentally a translation of the French *Roman*, the English
author makes obvious attempts 'to increase the realism of the tale and
adapt it to the tastes of his readers. Of the 3290 lines of the story,
1216 are without definite parallel in the source' (p 462). The English
adaptation uses more dialogue and direct discourse to heighten effects,
and 'a definite, though perhaps futile, attempt is made to represent
Beryn as deserving his ultimate good fortune' (p 464).

Tale of Gamelyn

GAMELYN EDITIONS

590 *The Works of Geoffrey Chaucer.* Ed. John Urry. 1721. See 525.
Urry was the first to print *Gamelyn* as the *Cook's Tale.* He introduces
the Tale with the following preface: 'So many of the mss have this
Tale, that I can hardly think it could be unknown to the former
Editors of this Poet's Works. Nor can I think of a Reason why they
neglected to publish it. Possibly they met only with those mss that
had not this Tale in them, and contented themselves with the Number
of Tales they found in those mss. If they had any of those mss in
which it is, I cannot give a Reason why they did not give it a Place
amongst the rest, unless they doubted of its being genuine. But
because I find it in so many mss, I have no doubt of it, and therefore
make it publick, and call it the Fifth Tale. In all the mss it is called
the Cooke's Tale, and therefore I call it so in like manner: But had I
found it without an Inscription, and had been left to my Fancy to have
bestow'd it on which of the Pilgrims I had pleas'd, I should certainly
have adjudg'd it to the Squire's Yeoman; who tho as minutely
describ'd by Chaucer, and characteriz'd in the Third Place, yet I find
no Tale of his in any of the mss. And because I think there is not any
one that would fit him so well as this, I have ventur'd to place his

Picture before this Tale, tho' I leave the Cook in the Possession of the Title' (p 36). In his Preface to the volume Timothy Thomas comments on mss variations, wishing the Tale had been more carefully collated. He does not question its authenticity, however. [Although Thomas Tyrwhitt, *The Canterbury Tales of Chaucer* (526), rejected *Gamelyn*, the tale was included by John Bell, *The Poetical Works of Geoffrey Chaucer* (London, 1782) and by Robert Anderson, *The Poetical Works of Geoffrey Chaucer* (London, 1793), though Anderson added a disclaimer of its authenticity. In the nineteenth-century it appeared in Alexander Chalmers, *The Works of Geoffrey Chaucer* (London, 1810), Thomas Wright, *The Canterbury Tales* (London: Percy Society, 1847), Robert Bell, *Poetical Works of Geoffrey Chaucer* (London: J.W. Parker, 1854), and the Appendix to Fragment-A of Frederick J. Furnivall, *A Six-Text Print* of Chaucer's *Canterbury Tales* (London: Chaucer Society, 1868–77). See Hammond, **36**, pp 425–6. A translation appears in F.J. Harvey Darton, *Tales of the Canterbury Pilgrims* (see **592** below).]

591 Skeat, W.W., ed. *Oxford Chaucer*. 1894/1900. See **2**. Text: vol IV, pp 645–67; Notes: vol V, pp 477–89; Glossarial Index: vol IV, pp 347–58. Skeat's edition of *Gamelyn* first appeared in the Oxford edition of 1884, which was revised and included with the *Complete Works of Chaucer* **2** as an appendix to the A-Fragment. The tale is found only in *CT* mss. Skeat uses Harleian ms 7334 as his foundation text which he collates with six others. Corpus Christi College (Oxford) ms 198 and Lansdowne ms 851 are nearest to Harl. 7334. Skeat's notes are the most extensive of any printed edition. See comments on Skeat's edition in **593** and **594**.

592 *Tales of the Canterbury Pilgrims, Retold from Chaucer and Others by F.J. Harvey Darton.* With Introduction by F.J. Furnivall and Illustrations by Hugh Thomson. London: Wells Gardner, Darton & Co., 1906.
Darton divides the tales into a five day journey ending at Canterbury with *ParsT*. He includes *Gamelyn* as the *Cook's Tale* and completes *SqT* with 'The Story of Cambuscan Bold,' from Spenser, and 'The Fierce Wars and Faithful Loves,' by an eighteenth-century writer who supplied an ending. Darton also includes 'The Chequer of the Hoop' (ie, the Adventures of the Pardoner and the Tapster) as the account of what happened at Canterbury, then adds a redaction of Lydgate's 'The Destruction of Thebes' in three parts (Edippus the Parricide; The Treachery of Ethoicles; & The Doom of Thebes), and the Merchant's Second Tale (ie, the *Tale of Beryn*). Thomson's illustrations are quite handsome.

593 French, Walter Hoyt, and Charles Brockway Hale, eds. *Middle English*

Metrical Romances. 2 vols. Englewood Cliffs, N.J.: Prentice Hall, 1930. Rpt New York: Russell and Russell, 1964. Vol 1, pp 209–35. French and Hale use the text of Harleian ms 7334, from Furnivall's edition in *The Harleian ms 7334* (London, 1885). They note other mss and recommend Skeat's edition 'for copious notes, some of which have been used here' (p 209).

594 Sands, Donald B., ed. *Middle English Verse Romances.* New York: Holt, Rinehart and Winston, 1966. Pp 154–81.
Sands uses the text from French and Hale 593 which he introduces and glosses. Introduction considers relationship of *Gamelyn* to the Robin Hood ballads, historical analogues, and some of the literary qualities of the poem. Since the tale is associated with both Shakespeare and Chaucer it is 'perhaps the most widely known of all romances of the Matter of England' (p 154). It usually was placed just after the Cook's Prologue and abortive tale of Perkyn Revelour and in some mss is called 'The Cook's Tale of Gamelyn.' 'Undoubtedly Chaucer knew about it, was probably going to rework it (for the Yeoman and not the Cook), but never touched its bumpy seven-stress-per-line verses. Whatever Chaucer might have done with it, his product most certainly would lack the forthrightness it now possesses' (p 154).

595 Daniel, Neil, ed. *The Tale of Gamelyn: A New Edition.* Indiana University Dissertation 1967. Dir. Alfred David. See also *DAI*, 28 (1967): 2241a.
The *Tale* is preserved in twenty-five fifteenth-century mss. Daniel follows Corpus Christi 198 (ca 1410–20) in matters of orthography and syntax unless otherwise noted. His editorial procedures are modelled on Kane, *Piers Plowman A-Text*, with variant readings noted at the foot of the page. He praises Skeat's edition of 1884 as the only prior attempt to establish a critical text. Skeat's text is 'highly readable and on the whole accurate and scholarly' (p 1). Daniel's introduction discusses mss and publication history, fourteenth-century outlaws, stories populated by outlaw types, the poem's literary associations, its moral values, versification, and language. Explanatory notes, pp 110–49; bibliography, pp 150–6.

GAMELYN CRITICISM

596 Bullough, Geoffrey. *Narrative and Dramatic Sources of Shakespeare.* Vol 2. London: Routledge and Kegan Paul; New York: Columbia University Press, 1958.
Bullough discusses *Gamelyn* as a source for *As You Like It* (pp 143–8). Lodge must have known the poem when he wrote *Rosalynde*; Shakespeare may also have known it, though the poem was not printed

until 1721. Bullough summarizes the plot of each of the three works, noting parallels.

597 Daniel, Neil. 'A Metrical and Stylistic Study of *The Tale of Gamelyn.*' In *Studies in Medieval, Renaissance, American Literature: A Festschrift Honoring Troy C. Cranshaw, Lorraine Sherley, and Ruth Speer Angell.* Fort Worth: Texas Christian University Press, 1971. Pp 19–32.

Gamelyn does not fit the prosodic system of Chaucer or *Piers*, but falls somewhere between, using both alliterative patterns and rhymes as well as 'compound' or 'dipodic' rhythms (p 24). The lines do not fit exactly into four- or seven-stress patterns. 'By far the largest category is made up of lines which are metrically ambiguous' (p 27). The conclusion to be drawn seems to be that the poem can be read in any way the reader wants to read it. 'The key to the reading of *The Tale of Gamelyn* is in its oral nature' (p 28). Nb, its frequent references to its audience. Daniel argues that the most reliable text of any poem is the best single ms (in this case Corpus Christi 198) rather than a composite made up from a variety of mss. In the matter of metrics the editor's unconscious prejudices concerning prosody are more likely to confuse than clarify the text (p 30). 'Prosodic analysis does not generally discover the meter of the poem; instead it provides a meter for the reader which, if it fits, does not violate the language of the poem. And of course we can never know what the audience of the fourteenth century would have heard or liked to hear' (p 31).

598 Dunn, Charles W. 'Gamelyn,' under 'Romances Derived from English Legends.' In *A Manual of the Writings in Middle English: 1050–1500,* New Haven: The Connecticut Academy of Arts and Science, 1967. Vol 1, pp 31–3; pp 220–2.

Includes all references in Wells, *Manual of the Writings in Middle English* and its nine supplements, 'except erroneous, worthless, or irrelevant items' (p 5), plus additional items up to the date of publication (ie, 1966).

599 Ebbutt, Maud Isabel. *Hero-Myths and Legends of the British Race,* with fifty-one illustrations by J.H.F. Bacon and others. Myth Series. London: Farrar, 1931.

An anthology of heroic tales 'to guide the modern seeker through the labyrinths of the mediaeval mind' (p xvii), with general introduction on the geographic and political milieu of the tales. *Gamelyn,* pp 204–24, includes a brief introduction identifying the 'wicked brothers' theme and commenting on the tale's literary influence, followed by a lively prose abridgment of the story, with four plates by W.H. Margetson entitled 'Go and do your own baking,' 'Lords, for Christ's sake help poor Gamelyn out of prison!' 'Then cheer thee, Adam,' and

'Come from the seat of justice.'

600 Hibbard, Laura. *Mediaeval Romance in England. A Study of the Sources and Analogues of the Non-cyclic Metrical Romances.* Oxford: Oxford University Press, 1924. Pp 156–63.
Discusses *Gamelyn's* appearance in sixteen Chaucer mss. Emphasizes the local character of the poem. 'It is difficult to believe that it emanates from any French original' (p 157). *Gamelyn* shares much with folk origins, though it is developed 'with the literalness of life' (p 158). '*Havelok* draws clearly on romance tradition, *Gamelyn* on everyday realities' (p 159).

601 Kaeuper, Richard W. 'An Historian's Reading of *The Tale of Gamelyn.*' *MAE*, 52 (1983), 51–62.
'The violence in the tale is peculiar to XIVth-century England' (p 52). *Gamelyn's* characters do not come from the chivalric courts of French romances; rather they come from 'the amorphous social level of minor landowners, lesser knights and retainers — those who might at most hobnob with the prior of a nearby religious house and know the sheriff, but whose horizons are essentially local' (p 53). Kaeuper ransacks PRO plea rolls to produce numerous situations similar to those in the tale, ranging from disturbances of the peace and corrupt sheriffs to gangs of outlaws and kangaroo courts; the specific incidents and the tone of the historical records are remarkably like those in the tale. In both people are beginning to have hopes in the possibility of the King's justice and thus are the more disappointed by its failure. 'This amalgam of outraged idealism and pure pragmatism with regard to the law is a salient characteristic of the *Tale of Gamelyn*' (p 59). The people wanted more of the King's justice but know 'from bitter experience how badly it was working in the countryside, how easily it was swayed, how often litigation had to be supplemented by a laying on of hands which was far from apostolic. So they flocked to the King's courts, kept a good cart staff at hand, and listened with great delight to a tale like that of *Gamelyn*' (p 60).

602 Keen, Maurice. *The Outlaws of Medieval Legend.* London: Routledge and Kegan Paul, 1961. Pp 78–94.
Considers *Gamelyn* in the context of historical outlaws and social unrest. 'How it came to be included among Chaucer's tales is unexplained. It may be that he intended to remould it, and put a new version of it into the mouth of his Plowman or some other rustic character, and that being found among his papers it was taken for his own. But, however it came about, it is to the accident which associated the story with the name of the greatest English medieval poet that we owe its survival' (p 78). 'Neither Chaucer the satyrist nor Chaucer the writer of romance would have had much sympathy with

the fierce and angry author of this poem' (p 88).

603 Leach, Henry Goddard. *Angevin Britain and Scandinavia.* Harvard Studies in Comparative Literature, vol 6. Cambridge, Mass.: Harvard University Press, 1921. Pp 335–55.

Gamelyn is 'a rattling good poem' (p 353), similar in tone and style to *Havelok.* It probably comes from Lincolnshire, along with other outlaw legends.

604 Rogers, Franklin R. 'The *Tale of Gamelyn* and the Editing of the *Canterbury Tales*,' *JEGP*, 58 (1959), 49–59.

Gamelyn is found exclusively in *CT* mss. Most of the twenty-five ms copies belong to group c or d classifications of CT mss, the earliest — Harley 7334 (*Ha₄*), Corpus Christi 198 (Cp), and Lansdowne 851 (La) — dating ca 1410. It is found also in Petworth (Pw) and Egerton 2863 (*En₂*) ca 1420–50. The four earliest mss all show some dialect mixture (Midland, but with significant numbers both of Kentish and southwestern forms). The Kentish forms probably represent work of a Kentish copyist. *Ha₄* and Cp may be from the same shop at the same time. La may be from the same shop but copied a little later. The descent probably began with a North Midland original that passed through defective Kentish copies to Pw and La exemplars, which were also the dual sources for *Ha₄* and Cp. By the second decade of the fifteenth century three distinct versions of *Gamelyn* were in existence. Scribes often connected the tale to the preceding Cook's fragment with transitions like (La): 'Fye therone it is so foule I will nowe tell no forthere / For schame of the harlotrie that seweth after / A vilany it were thare of more to spell / Bot of a knighte and his sounes my tale I wil forthe tell' (p 57).

605 Saintsbury, George. In *CHEL.* 1908. See **80.** Vol 2, pp 221–4.

Following Skeat's suggestion **591** that *Gamelyn* lay among Chaucer's papers Saintsbury speculates on what the result of a Chaucerian rehandling of the tale might have been like. 'One need not weep that Chaucer let *Gamelyn* alone. He would have given us a delightful story, but the story is full of delight for competent readers as it is. If he had made it into "riding rime" it would not have been better, as such, than its companions. If he had made it into anything else it might have been a doubtful gain. And, lastly, the copy might, as in so many other cases, have killed the original. Now, even for more Chaucer, of which we fortunately have so much already, we could not afford to have no *Gamelyn*, which is practically unique' (p 224).

606 Shannon, Edgar R., Jr. 'Medieval Law in the *Tale of Gamelyn*.' *Spec*, 26 (1951), 458–64.

Comments on the poem's delight in physical violence, its strong anti-clerical bias, and the presentation of such folk customs as wrestling matches and feasts. 'But the most significant historical feature of the tale is its exact portrayal of the functionings of mediaeval English law' (p 458), such matters as the holding of land in fee simple, questions of primogeniture, the role of the sheriff, outlaws and wolf's head, mainprise, bail, and trial by jury. *Gamelyn* seems filled with force and disorder, but 'the author was well-versed in the law of his day and ... the poem mirrors accurately and in some detail the uncertain, though gradually developing, processes of justice in the fourteenth century' (p 463).

607 Snell, F.J. *The Age of Chaucer.* London: Bell, 1901/rev 1906. Pp 1–6. Supports Lindner's theory (*ESt*, 2 [1879], 94–114, 321–43) that *Gamelyn* is 'exceptionally antique' (p 3). In *Gamelyn*, no mention is made of Robin Hood, which suggests that 'Robin had not yet attained the universal popularity and pre-eminence among outlaws that was afterwards his' (p 3).

608 Thiébaux, Marcelle. 'The Medieval Chase,' *Spec*, 42 (1967), 260–74. A detailed historical account of hunting, attitudes toward it, supplies, and the event itself. Mentions *Gamelyn* in connection with anger against shrieval administrators who enforced forest laws (p 262).

609 Tyrwhitt, Thomas. 'An Introductory Discourse to the *Canterbury Tales*.' In *The Canterbury Tales of Chaucer.* See **526**. 'As it is sufficiently certain that the *Cokes* Prologue and the beginning of his Tale are genuine compositions, they have their usual place in this Edition. There was not the same reason for inserting the story of *Gamelyn*, which in some mss is annexed to the *Cokes Tale*. It is not to be found in any of the mss of the first authority; and the manner, style, and versification, all prove it to have been the work of an author much inferior to Chaucer. I did not therefore think myself warranted to publish it a second time among the Canterbury Tales, though as a Relique of our antient Poetry, and the foundation, perhaps, of Shakespeare's *As you like it*, I could have wished to see it more accurately printed, than it is in the only edition which we have of it' (I, p 88).

The Plowman's Tale

[After an independent printing by Godfray (ca 1532–5), *PlowT* was first printed with Chaucer's poetry in Thynne's 1542 edition (see Brewer's facsimile of this printing [**523**]), where it was appended after *ParsT*; then in 1551 it was placed before *ParsT*, where it remained in subsequent black-letter editions until Tyrwhitt. (See Hammond **36**, pp 444–6, on its publication history and relationship to *Pierce the*

Ploughman's Crede.) Skeat dates the poem 'after 1396' (511, p xxxiv).
The argument placed before the Tale in Speght (1598) reads: 'A
complaint against the pride and couetousnesse of the cleargie: made no
doubt by Chaucer with the rest of the Tales. For I haue seene it in
written hand in Iohn Stowes Library in a booke of such antiquity, as
seemeth to haue beene written neare to Chaucers time.' It was
commonly thought that the tale was left out of the editions of Chaucer
prior to 1542 because of its offensive and scandalous assault on friars
and monks. (See the penciled note on the first page of the 1542 edition
in Brewer's facsimile; the idea is reasserted in Urry's 1721 edition
[525].) Despite Tyrwhitt's verdict against the Tale's authenticity
(526, I, p 112); the editions of Bell (1782), Anderson (1782), Chalmers
(1810), Chiswick (1822), and Aldine (1845) included it, and in
nineteenth-century biographies it remained one of the primary proofs
of the reformer Chaucer's Wyclifite sympathies (see Bonner 550).]

610   *The Works of Geoffrey Chaucer.* Ed. John Urry. 1721. See 525.
In the apology printed as headnote to *PlowT*, Urry notes that neither
the Prologue nor Tale is in any of the mss 'that I have seen, nor in any
of the first Printed Books; Caxton and Pynsent [sic.], I presume, durst
not publish it: The former printed this Poet's Works in
Westminster-Abbey, and both before the abolition of Popery; and the
mss being before that, I fancy the Scriveners were prohibited
transcribing it, and injoyn'd to subscribe an Instrument at the end of
the Canterbury Tales, call'd his Retraction. So that if this Tale had
not been carefully collected and preserv'd in Master Stowe's Library, as
the Editor of Islip's 1602 Book says he has seen it, in a hand of near to
Chaucer's time for Antiquity, in all likelyhood it had been lost' (p 178).

611   Aston, Margaret. 'Lollardy and the Reformation: Survival or Revival?'
History, 49 (1964), 149–70.
Lollard texts included such works as *ABC ayenst the Clergye, An ABC
to the Spiritualte, The Praier and Complaynt of the Ploweman unto
Christ,* and *The Complaint of the Plowman* or *The Plowman's Tale,*
the last of which ends up in early editions of Chaucer's works. No ms
version of *PlowT* survives, though a fourteenth-century Lollard poem
may have been its basis (p 158). Discusses publication of the tale in
Thynne's second edition (1542) and also publication of *JU*, with its
scurrilous and vituperative attack on the friars which convinced John
Foxe later in the century that Chaucer was 'a right Wiclevian, or else
there was never any' (p 160). Some discussion of Bale, Leland, and the
dissolution of the monasteries.

612   Bradley, Henry. 'The Plowman's Tale.' *Athenaeum*, 12 July 1902, p 62.
Although *PlowT* is a product of the sixteenth century, it is a recasting
and massive expansion on two different occasions of a

fourteenth-century poem, of which only a fragment remains. Its prologue is 'a rather clumsy attempt to provide a quasi-Chaucerian framework for a piece that was certainly not originally written as a Canterbury Tale.' The prologue was probably written by the person who prepared the first edition for the press. The tone of the two interpolations (lines 205–28 and 717–1268) is that of the Reformation. The remaining 94 stanzas seem to be later fourteenth century. The two successive sixteenth-century expansions adapted the poem 'to the needs of contemporary controversy.'

613   Elliott, Thomas Joseph. 'Complaint as a Middle English Genre: A Survey of the Tradition Culminating in the School of *Piers Plowman*.' *DAI*, 31 (1971), 4116A. University of Michigan Dissertation, 1970. Dir. Donald B. Sands.
Focusing on complaint as social protest, rather than religious complaint or the lover's lament, Elliott differentiates complaint from satire, noting that complaint normally uses satiric devices as the occasion for the execution of more basic purposes. One sub-group of 'songs' on the evils of the age, which Elliott designates as the school of *Piers Plowman*, includes *Wynnere and Wastoure, Parlement of the Thre Ages, Pierce the Plowman's Crede, Jack Upland, Friar Daw's Reply, Upland's Rejoinder, The Plowman's Tale, Mum and the Sothsegger, The Crowned King*, and *Death and Liffe*. 'The Plowman Group represents an attempt to provide a narrative base for complaint without abandoning the traditional monologue structure. Devices such as dream/vision, allegory, and débat were probably deliberate means chosen by the authors for the adaptation of complaint; they are thus not simply derivations from contemporary popular poems such as *Le Roman de la Rose*.' Such works of social protest suggest that 'the dominant myth [of the late Middle Ages] is not that of a Golden Age in the past but rather a future Utopia which men will build for themselves in this world.'

614   Irvine, Annie S. 'A Manuscript Copy of *The Plowman's Tale*,' *University of Texas Studies in English*, 12 (1932), 27–56.
An early sixteenth-century ms of the *Plowman's Tale* was bound into a copy of the 1532 edition of Thynne now found in the University of Texas library. Collation reveals that the ms could not have been copied from any edition later than 1542 (the edition in which the tale was first printed). It seems likely that the ms must have been copied from some other ms source in existence at the time. It may possibly have been prepared especially for the volume in which it is now bound.

614a Kerling, Johan. *Chaucer in Early English Dictionaries: The Old-World Tradition in English Lexicography Down to 1721 and Speght's Chaucer Glossaries*. Germanic and Anglistic Studies of the

University of Leiden, vol. 18. Netherlands: Leiden University Press; Boston: Kluwer, 1980.
Includes an appendix on 'Chaucer, *The Plowman's Tale*, and Henry VIII.'

615 Skeat, W.W., ed. *Oxford Chaucer*. 1897. See **511**. Vol 7. Text, pp 147–90; Introduction, pp xxxi–xxxv; Notes, pp 484–92.
Skeat uses the 1542 edition as the best and his sole authority. He draws several comparisions between *PlowT*, which is in rime royal, and *Pierce the Ploughman's Crede*, which is in alliterative verse. 'Both these pieces are written in a spirited style, and are of considerable interest for the light which they throw upon many of the corrupt practices of the monks, friars, and clergy. The Crede is directed against the friars in particular, and reflects many of the opinions of Wyclif, as will easily appear by comparing it with Wyclif's works' (pp xxxiv–xxxv). Skeat comments on the Pelican-Griffin allegory, suggesting connections between *PlowT* and Spenser and Dryden.

615a Swart, Felix. 'Chaucer and the English Reformation.' *Neophil*, 62 (1978), 616–19.
How did *PLT* and *Pilgrim's Tale* become associated with Chaucer? Although there is little evidence firmly linking Chaucer with Wycliffite activities, perhaps a group of Wycliffite mss circulated with those by Chaucer. No trace of such early copies remains, however. Swart reviews censorship and regulation of the book trade in the early 16th century. *PLT* and *Pilgrim's Tale* were attached to Chaucer by protestant propagandists so that they might slip by the censors. 'Both *Tales* are clearly based on older material, and could be clever forgeries or retouched, but substantially genuine, medieval poems. But whatever they are, there can be little doubt as to the intended effect of their appearance in print: Chaucer was to support the English Reformation posthumously. Ironically, two interlopers among his Canterbury pilgrims helped to defeat the spirit of their St. Thomas, whose shrine was closed in 1538' (p 618).

616 Wawn, Andrew N. 'The Genesis of *The Plowman's Tale*.' *Yearbook of English Studies*, 2 (1972), 21–40.
'Of all the apocryphal works ... *The Plowman's Tale* distorted the poet's subsequent reputation more decisively than any other' (p 21). From 1542 until Tyrwhitt excised it from the canon 'the poem created and then sustained the impression that Chaucer was England's most significant pre-Reformation protestant poet' (p 21). The Plowman had the distinction of being awarded two apocryphal tales, Hoccleve's *Miracle of the Virgin and the Sleeveless Garment* **619**, which was added to a Northumberland ms by a scribe or patron who wished to minimize the fragmentary state of *CT*, and the Tale of the Pelican and

Griffin. Bradley 612 raises questions on the genesis of *PlowT* which
are worth pursuing. The vocabulary throughout the poem suggests a
date no later than 1450, thus supporting 'a *prima facie* case for a
much earlier date of composition for nearly all of the poem than the
date suggested by Bradley' (p 27). Wawn notes a few forms first
appearing between 1435–45, but also several datable allusions to
historical events and current fashions which trace back to the late
fourteenth century, like *crokettes* (hair fashion, ca 1393), *longe pykes*
on priests' shoes (days of Anne of Bohemia), and *preestes pokes* (a
kind of sleeve not referred to after the beginning of the
fifteenth-century). Also there seem to be references to the Great
Schism and to material comparáble to that of the *Crede* (ca 1393),
which may be by the same author. There are many similarities
between Lollard doctrine and that of the Pelican, especially with the
views of the Lollard William Thorpe in his examination by Archbishop
Arundel in 1407. The evidence is strong that the poem comes from the
early fifteenth century; there is 'no evidence at all' to support
Bradley's view of sixteenth-century interpolation in lines 86–700 and
717–1269. However, lines 1–52, 205–27, with their absence of rhyming
refrains probably are interpolations of sixteenth-century origin. There
is evidence that a protestant tract (ca 1546) knows a *PlowT* which did
not have a prologue (p 36). It could be that the same interpolator was
responsible for the prologue and the other stanzas. The debate was
probably included in its original form by the sixteenth-century
interpolator (p 39). But there are other interpolations as well. 'The
debate and the material relating to monks and secular canons, in the
form which we now have both of them, were probably the work of
another Lollard writer who came across the original poem and wished
both to extend the range of the poem's assault on the clergy and also
perhaps to modify such ambiguities and infelicities of expression as
may have existed in the original form of debate' (p 39). Most of the
Lollard tracts seem to have been written before 1425. The *PlowT*
must have originated from the same period. The debate section must
have been expanded by a Lollard interpolator writing not long after
preparation of the original poem. This expanded version then survived
into the sixteenth century, 'at which time it was furnished with both a
Prologue and lines 205–28 and, thus equipped, was ready to take on its
new role of Henrician propaganda and Canterbury tale' (p 40).
Though the version finally printed is rambling and repetitious, it
displays 'a remorseless energy and generates a strong impression of the
poet's immense conviction and total commitment to the cause which
sustained him' (p 40). Wawn's footnotes contain many references to
Lollard tracts and related literature.

617 — 'Chaucer, Wyclif, and the Court of Apollo.' *ELN*, 10 (1972), 15–20.

'Most revered and persuasive of all ancient English voices cited in the protestant cause was that of Geoffrey Chaucer, the belief in whose authorship of the Lollard *Plowman's Tale* had been firmly established in the minds of the Elizabethan and Jacobean reading public during the years following its initial absorption into the Chaucer canon after 1542' (p 15). Vaughan's *The Golden Fleece* (1626) presents Chaucer as an enthusiastic Lollard in Wyclif's cause, even picturing Wyclif as 'the distinguished disciple of that arch heresiarch Chaucer!' (p 17). *Fleece* presents Scotus, as Chaucer's opponent. 'Vaughan went to considerable trouble in preparing the portion of the *Plowman's Tale* which was to be printed' (p 18) in his anthology, selecting his passages carefully. 'A whole range of seventeenth- and eighteenth-century writers were happy to subscribe to the more general tradition of Wyclif's influence on Chaucer' (p 20), the *PlowT* providing the main impetus for such testimony. 'If ... both Chaucer and Wyclif could have read of themselves in the first part of *The Golden Fleece*, one may be forgiven for believing that Chaucer at least would, like the Griffin in the tale he never wrote, have "grynned as he were wode" (line 1269)' (p 20).

618 — 'Chaucer, *The Plowman's Tale*, and Reformation Propaganda: The Testimonies of Thomas Godfray and *I Playne Piers*.' *BJRL*, 56 (1973–4), 174–92.

Hoccleve's *Miracle of the Virgin and the Sleeveless Garment* may have been grafted onto CT as *PlowT* in the Christ Church ms 'on the initiative of an individual scribe or at the request of a particular patron. One thing is certain — having met the needs of the moment, the first *Plowman's Tale* was subsequently rewarded with oblivion' (p 174). But fame and notoriety characterize the life of the second *PlowT* (Pelican and Griffin) in Thynne's 1542 edition. Apparently the poem was first printed ca 1536 by Thomas Godfray independently of CT, however, because the *Pilgrim's Tale*, an anti-monastic poem ca 1536–8, borrows lines from it (pp 175–6). Thomas Godfray, along with T. Berthelet who collaborated with Godfray and shared the same printing equipment, was involved at this time with the printing of Henrician propaganda. Nb, 'the belief of the antiquarian Leland, a contemporary of both printers, that the 1532 edition of Chaucer, assigned by the colophon to Godfray's press, was in fact printed by Berthelet' (p 178). Wawn discusses several of the anticlerical tracts, especially *I playne Piers which can not flatter* (ca 1546–7), a complaint against failure to redistribute monastic wealth which draws upon *PlowT* but apparently in a form which had not been provided with the 52-line Prologue identifying the narrator as Chaucer's Plowman. The *I playne* author does know lines 717–1268 of *Plow T*, however, which Bradley in 1902 had argued were an extended Reformation interpolation along with the Prologue. Wawn argues to the contrary that lines 717–1268 'and nearly all the rest of the poem [except for the Prologue] should be thought of as products of the early fifteenth century' (p 188). It is not certain how *Plow T* came into Godfray's hands. King Henry was interested in Wyclif and Lollard ideology and searched libraries for such material (cf J.J. Scarisbrick, 'Henry VIII and the Vatican Library,' *Bibl. d'Humanisme et Renaissance*, 24 [1962], 211–6); 'or perhaps it came to light as a result of information supplied to the authorities by a member of a family or community in whose possession the poem may have been since the early days óf Lollardy in England' (p 191), people like John Tyball and Thomas Hilles who showed the Cambridge Lutheran Dr. Robert Barnes 'certayne old bookis' in a Wyclifite vein.

The Siege of Thebes

See **667** ff.

Tale of The Virgin and Her Sleeveless Garment

See also **618**.

619 *A New Ploughman's Tale: Thomas Hoccleve's Legend of the Virgin and her Sleeveless Garment, with a Spurious Link.* Ed. Arthur Beatty. London: Kegan Paul, Trench, Trübner, 1902.
The tale is found in two mss, Christ Church (Oxford) ms CLII, where it appears near the end of CT after *SqT* and before *SNT, CYT, ParsT* (the rest of the ms includes a fragment of Lydgate's *Tale of the Churle and his byrd* and *The Sege of Thebes*); and in Ashburnham ms 133, where it is included among eleven pieces by Hoccleve. Beatty's edition prints the two mss side by side. His introduction briefly remarks on miracles associated with the Virgin, the fact that the apocrypha gives two different tales to the Plowman, this one having nothing to do with Thynne's 1542 tale of the Pelican and Griffin, and comments on the rime royal stanza used by many of Chaucer's imitators ('Hoccleve perhaps made the most unskilful use of it, for even at his best he was never able to make it more than pedestrian, while at his worst it is very bad indeed' p x). The prologue tells how the Host declares the lot fallen to 'Ploughman Tyler,' who says he will tell how the Virgin rewarded a faithful monk (Christ Church, vv 1–35; Ashbm, vv 1–21). In the tale, the Virgin appears sleeveless to a Monk, instructing him to

say 150 Ave Marias. This he does, and the next day she appears with
sleeves on her garment and the promise that he will be made Abbot of
St Gile. It happens as she promised, and for seven years he teaches the
people her psalter, then dies, to be received into heaven (Christ
Church, vv 36–140; Ashbm, vv 22–126).

Individual Apocryphal Works and Authors

Assembley of Ladies (*AL*)

(See *Flower and Leaf,* below)

Balade of a Reeve

620 Brusendorff, A. *Chaucer Tradition.* 1925. See **25**. Pp 278–84.
Brusendorff prints Shirley's two texts of the poem side by side. 'Since
we have accepted the seven preceding poems as Chaucer's on the sole
authority of Shirley, there is scarcely any reason to doubt his
testimony here' (p 281). Brusendorff cites supplementary internal
evidence that points to Chaucer's authorship as well.

Chaucer's Dreame

(See *Isle of Ladies*)

[This poem beginning 'When Flora the quene of pleasaunce,' first
printed by Speght (1598) from Longleat ms 256, where it is ascribed to
Chaucer, was reprinted by Urry (1721), Bell (1782), Anderson (1793),
Chalmers (1810), Chiswick (1854). The poem was frequently linked
with *CBK* and *BD* as poems pertaining to Blanche, Duchess of
Lancaster, and John of Gaunt. Tyrwhitt accepted it as genuine (**526**,
vol 2, p 527). See **663** for Anthony Jenkins' modern edition of the
poem, under the title *'Isle of Ladies.'* See also Hammond, **36**, pp
429–30.]

621 *The Works of Geoffrey Chaucer.* Ed. John Urry. 1721. See **525**.
'This Dream devis'd by Chaucer, semeth to be covert report of the
Marriage of *John of Gaunt* the King's sonne, with *Blanch* the
daughter of Henry Duke of *Lancaster,* who after long love (during the

time wherof the Poet faineth them to be dead) were in the end by consent of friends happily married: figured by a bird bringing in her bill an hearbe, which restoreth them to lyfe againe. Here also is shewed Chaucer's match with a certain Gentlewoman, who although she was a stranger, notwithstanding so well liked and loved of the Lady Blanch, and her Lord, as Chaucer himself also was, that gladly they concluded a marriage betweene them' (p 572).

Clanvowe (Book of Cupid or Cuckoo and Nightingale) (*CN*)

See also **436, 557, 566, 581, 648.**

622 Clanvowe, John. *The Works of Sir John Clanvowe.* Ed. V.J. Scattergood. Cambridge: D.S. Brewer; Totowa, N.J.: Rowman and Littlefield, 1975.
Introduction, texts, and notes on *Book of Cupid* (*CN*) and the *Two Ways*, with a life of Sir John Clanvowe (pp 25–7), commentary, glossary, and select bibliography on the two texts. 'Clanvowe is constantly associated in the records with men who appear to have formed a prominent group of earnest, secular, intellectual knights who were interested in literature and religion — Lewis Clifford, Richard Sturry, Thomas Latimer, William Nevill, John Montague and John Cheyne ... What distinguishes Clanvowe from the others is that he was a writer of some ability' (p 9). Chaucer, and perhaps Deschamps and Jean de Condé, are Clanvowe's main sources. Discusses mss and date of composition (1386–91). Arguments for Thomas Clanvowe's authorship are unsubstantial. Sir John's attachment to the court is well known. *Two Ways* proves that he was a man of literary ability. He must have known Froissart quite well. Evidence from wills demonstrates that Clanvowe's circle of friends possessed books. 'Evidently they did not find secular and religious tastes in literature incompatible, so it is perhaps not too surprising that the two pieces of writing ... by Sir John Clanvowe differ to such an extent in subject matter' (p 25). He died in 1391. Scattergood's introduction condenses material from his two previous essays, 'The Book of Cupide,' *English Philological Studies*, 9 (1965), 47–83; and 'The Two Ways,' *English Philological Studies*, 10 (1967), 33–56. See also **628.**

622a Garbáty, Thomas, ed. *Medieval English Literature.* Lexington, Mass. and Toronto: D.C. Heath and Company, 1984.
Includes an edition of *CN* based on Skeat, pp 620–29.

623 Hammond, E.P. *Bibliographical Manual.* 1908. See **36.** Pp 420–1.
CN mss: Fairfax 16, Bodley 638, Tanner 346, Selden B 24, Univ. Libr.

Cambr. Ff i, 6. First printed by Thynne as *Cuckoo and Nightingale*, which was followed by editors until Morris used both titles. Fairfax and Bodley mss call the poem 'The boke of Cupid god of loue.' The 'Cuckoo and Nightingale' title comes from Tanner, where 'Of ye Cuckow & ye Nightingale' is added in a later hand. Cambr. Ff has colophon 'Explicit Clanvowe.' Bradshaw seems to have been the first to doubt the poem's genuineness. Tyrwhitt accepted it.

624 Lampe, David. 'Tradition and Meaning in *The Cuckoo and the Nightingale*.' *PLL*, 3 (1967), 49–62.
'The symbolic traditions that attach to the debating birds' determine the poem's meaning and are 'fully consonant with Clanvowe's beliefs as one of the Lollard Knights' (p 50). The narrator of the poem is 'a comic old buffoon-lover' comparable to the narrator in *PF* or January in *MerchT* or John in *MilT*. The cuckoo (ie, cuckold) is 'a symbolic figure which stands for a man who has been the victim of lust's force and who, consequently but blindly, insists that lust or the destructive part of love is all that love is' (p 51). The nightingale is more complex — a figure associated with adulterous love, as in the *Owl and Nightingale*, but also with charity and divine love, as in the *Thrush and the Nightingale*. The poem 'constitutes a statement of the power of the god of concupiscence and a subtly humorous demonstration of the effects of concupiscence upon the narrator' (p 61). The 'proper medicine' for the narrator's condition, namely marriage, is suggested both by symbolism of setting and the blissful actions of the assembled birds (p 57).

625 Lewis, C.S. *Allegory of Love.* 1936. See **132**. Pp 243–5.
The style alone of *CN* is sufficient 'to distinguish this author's talent from Chaucer's. We find in him neither the merits nor the defects of the high style. Despite his airy subject he remains, as a stylist, on the ground: he has not caught from Chaucer the new richness and sweetness of speech' (p 244).

625a McColly, William. '*The Book of Cupid* as an Imitation of Chaucer: A Stylo-Statistical View.' *ChauR*, 18 (1984), 239–49.
'No brief is held for Clanvowe as the author of *The Book of Cupid*'; nor is it by Chaucer. 'The poet's lack of stylistic inventiveness deprived his poem of materials and devices that are distinctively Chaucer's, and their absence ... clearly marks it as a pale — though in one important stylistic aspect a faithful — imitation' (p 248).

626 Robbins, Rossell Hope. 'The Findern Anthology,' *PMLA*, 69 (1954), 610–42.
Suggests that Clanvowe may have been the scribe rather than the author of *CN* (p 630). [Scattergood **628**, p 143, refutes Robbins' suggestion.]

627 Rutherford, Charles S. *'The Boke of Cupide Reopened.'* NM, 78
(1977), 350–8.
Challenges Lampe's reading (624): 'There is no overt indication on
the narrative level of allegorical intent, no explicit signal urging the
reader to delve for hidden meaning' (p 351). The case for Sir Thomas
Clanvowe's authorship is as strong as that for Sir John Clanvowe, the
Lollard; moreover, the correct title — *Boke of Cupide* — points away
from the celebration of married love. 'The very lightness of tone would
seem rather actively to repel the investment of the poem with any
weighty moralistic baggage' (p 351). It is no accident that the poem
was for four hundred years associated with Chaucer. The threads that
bind it to the Chaucer canon range from thematic similarities to direct
quotation — the May 3 vision of Valentine's Day, the narrator's
'poking gentle fun at himself as a means of enlisting the audience's
sympathetic laughter' (p 353), the *jeu d'esprit* tone, the quotations
from *KnT* and *PF*, and devices from French debate poems — all of
which suggest conscious imitation of Chaucer. The resolution is
descriptive rather than prescriptive. 'The very urbanity and
persistence of the manner in which the cuckoo expresses his cynicism is
an index of the strength of his position ... On purely rational grounds
the cuckoo is certainly correct. Love is irrational; it is uncomfortable.
On the other hand, the nightingale, too, is correct in her assertions
about love. It is a source of bliss, of ennoblement' (p 358). There are
elements of all three stock endings for debates in the poem — the
moral ending, the impasse, and the diversion. 'The rational, cynical
cuckoo will never abandon his logically defensible position; nor will the
emotionally committed nightingale abandon her quasi-religious
devotion to love' (p 358). The narrator functions as a third party to
decide the issue, but the question is begged as the other birds,
recognizing the complexity of the issue, refuse to censure the cuckoo,
deferring the answer to a proper parliament on St Valentine's Day.
The virtue of *CN* lies in 'the deftness with which Clanvowe has
caught, imitated and embellished Chaucerian themes and conventions;
in his recognition of the possibilities of using a form based upon logic
to treat a subject as illogical as love; in his distinct characterization of
the contestants through their rhetoric; and in his fortunate decision to
employ all three of the conventional endings of the debate form to
render a decision on a question in which he must also suspend
judgment' (p 358).

628 Scattergood, V.J. 'The Authorship of *The Boke of Cupide.*' *Anglia*,
82 (1964), 137–49.
The poem is among the earliest and best of the English
pseudo-Chaucerian poems (p 137). Reviews authorship arguments:

Skeat, *Academy* 49 (1896), 365–6; Vollmer, *Das Mittelenglische Gedicht 'The Boke of Cupide'* (Berlin, 1898); Kittredge, *MP*, 1 (1903), 13–8; Brusendorff, **25**, pp 443–5; Ward, *MLN*, 44 (1929), 217–26; Utley, *Crooked Rib* (New York, 1970), p 248; Seaton, **679**, pp 388 ff.; Robbins, *PMLA*, 69 (1954), 630. Makes the case for Sir John Clanvowe, b. 1341: 'clearly a distinguished soldier, courtier, administrator and diplomat, and the King ... rewarded him handsomely' (p 148). Would date the poem between 1386–91, when Sir John was 'old and unlusty,' as the poem says.

629 Utley, Francis Lee. 'Dialogues, Debates, and Catechisms.' *A Manual of the Writings in Middle English: 1050–1500.* Ed. Albert E. Hartung New Haven: Connecticut Academy of Arts and Sciences, 1972. Vol 3, section 7, pp 669–745; 829–902.
Utley's survey of the genre places *CN* in the context of other bird debates including *Owl and Nightingale, Thrush and Nightingale,* and two versions of *Clerk and Nightingale* (pp 716–24), under the general heading 'Debates on Love and Women.' Reviews its sources and possible authors (two Sir Johns and Sir Thomas). Provides resumé (p 722). Bibliography on *CN*, pp 883–4, with discussions on mss, Editions, Selections, Modernizations, Textual Matters, Language, Versification, Date and Authorship, Sources and Literary Relations, and Literary Criticism and General References (ca 85 entries.)

Complaint To My Lodesterre (*CML*)

630 Skeat, W.W. *Athenaeum*, Aug. 4, 1894, p 162.
Skeat announces discovery of the poem and prints it. His edition is reprinted in the *Oxford Chaucer* 2, vol 4, pp xxix–xxxii. Skeat notes that *CMF* and *CML* are certainly by the same person who probably wrote them at about the same time. Both poems are found in Harley 7578.

631 Robbins, Rossell Hope. 'The Lyrics.' In *Companion to Chaucer Studies*. Ed. Beryl Rowland. London: Oxford University Press, 1968. Pp 313–31/rev 1979, pp 380–402.
Notes verbal echoes of *CMF* in *CML*. As in *CD* and *Mars*, the lover justifies his right to bewail. His lodestar has become his mortal foe. The final stanza serves as envoy to 'noble seint Valentyne,' concluding with a homely proverb on his frustrations. Robbins comments on ways in which a poet can 'deepen simple complaints' like *BD, CD, Lady, CMF*, and *CML:* 'The simplest device is a narrative frame which of necessity introduces a second character, the poet, who overhears the complainant. On the other hand, if the lover meets his lady, she might

then explain why she is cruel and the complaint would break down and turn into a debate' (p 320/387). It might even evolve into a full-scale dream vision, as in *BD* or *IL*, at which stage 'the complaint shrinks into an interpolated lyric' (p 321/388). See also Robbins' entry **513**, p 1080; bibliography, p 1297. Dates poem ca 1450.

Complaint To My Mortal Foe (*CMF*)

632 Skeat, W.W. *Athenaeum*, July 21, 1894, p 98.
Skeat announces the discovery óf the balade in Harley 7578 and prints the text. Reprinted in his *Oxford Chaucer* 2, vol 4, p xxvi.

633 Hammond, E.P. *Bibliographical Manual*. 1908. See **36**, p 417.
Notes that ms title for *CMF* and *CML* is 'Balade,' in both instances. Kittredge, *Nation*, 1 (1895), 240, calls the poem 'more than doubtful.' Skeat discussed the matter further in *Canon* **64**, p 148.

634 Robbins, Rossell Hope. *Companion to Chaucer*. 1968/1979. See **631**. Includes *CMF* and *CML* in his commentary on Chaucer's lyrics, noting that Skeat includes them with the doubtful poems of Chaucer, though Robinson does not. *CMF* is 'a modified ballade' in which the lover 'begs his "mortal fo, which I best loue and serve" that she "mercy have and routhe." Sandwiched between the direct petitions to his lady are prayers to St. Valentine, Cupid, and Venus to intercede "that to her grace my lady shulde me take" ' (p 320/387). See also Robbins **513**, p 1080; bibliography, p 1297. Dates poem ca 1450.

Court of Love (*CL*)

See also **192, 556, 568, 578**. No modern edition since Skeat **511**.

635 Brandl, Alois. 'Mittelenglische Literatur.' In Hermann Paul, *Grundriss der germanischen Philologie*. Straussburg: K.J. Trübner, 1893. Vol 2, pt 1, pp 609–718.
Suggests that Scogan's blasphemy against the god of love, referred to in Chaucer's *Lenvoy a Scogan*, consisted in writing *CL*, whose scurrilous lines might well have offended the god (p 684). But see **638**.

636 Hammond, E.P. *Bibliographical Manual*. 1908. See **36**. Pp 418–9.
CL is found in only one ms (Trinity Coll. Cambr. R 3, 19). It was introduced into the Chaucer canon by Stow in 1561 and accepted as Chaucer's by Tyrwhitt. It was first rejected by Bradshaw, though considerable debate followed, with Minto, Swinburne, and T. Arnold protesting in favor, and Furnivall, Skeat, and Lounsbury protesting

against. NED dates the poem 1450; Skeat says 1500 is more likely (See Academy [1889, Part I], p 431).

637 Kitchin, George. *A Survey of Burlesque and Parody in England.* Edinburgh: Oliver and Boyd, 1931. Pp 8–20.
'No one can read the animated Bird Matins which end *The Court of Love* without amazement or a sense of scandal. The application of the most sacred ritual of the Church to alien uses was apparently a quite respectable convention! The Church and its services forming, as they did, the whole intellectual and spiritual life of mediaeval man, matter for burlesque or allegorical treatment could hardly be found outside of its activities' (p 6). See also pp 21–2 on the poem as an example of later Chaucerian pieces.

638 Kittredge, George Lyman. 'Henry Scogan.' *Harvard Studies and Notes*, 1 (1892), 109–17.
In response to Brandl's suggestion that Scogan wrote *CL* (see 635), Kittredge shows by linguistic evidence that the poem belongs to the end of the fifteenth century or later, when Scogan had been dead nearly a hundred years.

639 Neilson, William Allan. *The Origins and Sources of the 'Court of Love.'* Harvard Studies and Notes in Philology and Literature, no. 6. Boston: Ginn & Company, 1899.
Neilson outlines the poem, traces the origins of its allegory to medieval and more ancient sources, giving special attention to Provençal writers, Andreas Capellanus, *RR*, Philippe de Remi, Machaut, Deschamps, Froissart, Christine de Pisan, Alain Chartier, René de Anjou, Charles of Orleans, and various other French, German, and Italian authors. English influences may be seen in Grosseteste, Gower, Chaucer, Lydgate, Hoccleve, and Roos; *FL, AL*, James I, Stephen Hawes, and the Scottish Chaucerians. Comments on origins of 'statutes of Love' device (pp 168–212) and use of birds in love poetry (pp 216–27).

640 Robbins, Rossell Hope. 'Chaucerian Apocrypha.' 1973. See 513. Pp 1086–9; 1299–1300.
Placing *CL* in the category 'Courtly Love Aunters,' Robbins comments on its sources, authorship, humor, and critical assessment. 'It is perhaps the most typical poem of the apocrypha' (p 1087). Cites C.S. Lewis' assessment that *CL* 'towers above most Drab Age verse by its sheer accomplishment' (p 1088; cf *English Literature in the Sixteenth Century* [Oxford, 1954], p 240; but see 568 for opposite view). Includes analysis (pp 1088–9) and bibliography of ca 80 items, most before 1900 (pp 1299–1300).

Court of Venus and Pilgrim's Tale

641 Fraser, Russell A., ed. *The Court of Venus*. Durham: Duke University Press; London: Cambridge University Press, 1955.

This anthology of poems survives in three printed fragments, none of which names the author of the poems. It is not known when it was first published, though perhaps by Thomas Gybson, between 1536–9, with a title page attributing it to Chaucer. Bale, *Illustriam maioris Britanniae scriptorum summarium* (1548, 1549, 1557, 1559), lists it among Chaucer's works. It includes the *Pilgrim's Tale* (pp 82–110), a strongly anti-clerical work, which Francis Thynne, son of William, claimed his father had intended to publish in his first edition of Chaucer's works, but was prevented from doing so by Cardinal Wolsey (p 14). Thynne argues that it was to have been given to one like the Canon's Yeoman 'whiche I dobt not wolde fullye appere, yf the pilgrimes prologe and tale mighte be restored to his former light, they being now looste, as manye other of Chaucers tales were before that, as I ame induced to thinke by manye reasons' (p 28; cf **523a**, pp 7–10). Apparently the author of the *Pilgrim's Tale* deliberately archaized and used provincialisms 'in an attempt to give a Chaucerian flavor to his poem and so sneak it past the censors, from whose strictures Chaucer was specifically exempted' (p 18). Once William Thynne had included *PlowT* in his 1542 edition it became almost impossible to question its authenticity or the likelihood of the *Pilgrim's Tale*. 'For if that authenticity were destroyed, Protestant England would lose the moral support of the greatest English poet before the Reformation' (p 28). Fraser's discussion of Chaucer and the censors in the latter part of Henry VIII's reign is detailed. The *Pilgrim's Tale* could not possibly be by Chaucer, most obviously because of its mediocrity, 'far below Chaucer at his worst' (p 28), but also because it mentions the poet by name, alludes to the *Romaunt* by page and line in Thynne's 1532 edition, and also alludes to England's break with Rome in 1534 and the Lincoln uprising of 1536. 'We may say of Chaucer's hypothetical connection with the *Court of Venus*, then, that he certainly did not write *The Pilgrim's Tale*, and that, while poems of his may have been included in the three known editions of the *Court*, internal evidence does not incline us to give any of the poems surviving in the fragments to him. There is a slight possibility that Chaucer was the author of the Prologue to *The Court of Venus*. It is more probable, however, that this work, like *The Court of Love*, is apocryphal, and that the attribution to Chaucer rests on an error, generated perhaps deliberately to escape censorship, and on a confusion with similar works like *The Court of Love* and *The Complaint of Venus*. Chaucer is therefore to be placed among the "uncertain authors" whose poems may have been included in *The Court of Venus*' (pp 30–1).

See also Hammond's entry on *Pilgrim's Tale* [36, pp 443-4].

Envoy To Alison

642 Chewning, Harris. 'The Text of the "Envoy to Alison".' *SB*, 5 (1952), 33–42.
This ballade of 27 lines is extant in Fairfax 16, Tanner 346, and seven of the black-letter editions of Chaucer beginning with Thynne 1532. The extant texts do not produce evidence sufficient to establish an authoritative text (p 41). But the comparative exercise is useful in establishing the relative value of mss and in demonstrating that consecutive agreement of materials within the mss is more significant than scattered ones. 'Minor poems may not be edited safely in isolation from the larger units of text that contain them' (p 42). That is, sequences of materials within the mss provide important information to the editor. In Fairfax *Alison* is preceded by *BD* and followed without *explicit* by 'Balade upon the Chaunse of Dyse.' In Tanner it is preceded by *CN* and followed by a blank page, then *BD*. In Thynne it is preceded by *CN* and followed by 'Scogan unto the lordes.'

See also Robbins' entry on *Alisoun* (513, pp 1075-6, biblio. p 1294).

An Epistle To His Mistress For Remembrance

643 Robbins, Rossell Hope. 'A Love Epistle by "Chaucer".' *MLR*, 49 (1954), 289–92.
Discusses Stowe's twenty additions to Thynne in Chaucer's name, of which five are definitely by Chaucer. Stowe used Trin. Coll. Cambr. 599 (R.3.19), an anthology which attributed many non-Chaucerian poems to Chaucer. But Stowe missed one headed 'Chaucer,' which has subsequently been overlooked: 'An Epistle to his Mistress for Remembrance,' a competent minor poem, no worse and possibly superior to the general run of late fifteenth-century love poetry. In tone and scope it recalls *CD*, though linguistic and scansion tests indicate that it is by neither Chaucer nor Lydgate. The poem incorporates four stanzas of the pseudo-Chaucerian 'Craft of Lovers,' which also appears in the ms and is headed 'This worke was compiled by Chaucer and is caled the craft of louers.' In the last stanza the date of composition is given as 1448, against which Stowe has noted, 'Chaucer died 1400.' The poem which follows 'An Epistle' is also a conglomerate, using one

stanza from 'Craft of Lovers' and four from Lydgate's *Court of Sapience*. Another instance of mixing occurs in this ms at f.170v, 'where Chaucer's *Monk's Tale* is interspersed with selections from Lydgate's *Fall of Princes*' (p 290). Robbins prints the text of 'An Epistle,' which is ten 7–line stanzas long, and begins, 'Lady of pite, for thy sorowes that thou haddest / ffor Jesu thy son, in time of hys passion,/ haue revthe of me that ys most maddest / In love to wryte.'

Flower and the Leaf (*FL*) and Assembly of Ladies (*AL*)

EDITIONS

[See also 556a.]

644 Skeat, W.W. ed. *Oxford Chaucer*. 1897. See **511.** Vol 7: Text, 361–404; Introduction, lxii–lxx; Notes, 529–40.
Skeat follows Speght (1598) for *FL* and Thynne (1532) for *AL*. Many critics would assign *FL* to Chaucer 'merely because they like it' (p lxii). It is hardly possible to separate *FL* from *AL*; 'the authoress of one was the authoress of the other' (p lxii). The reason for the inferiority of *AL* lies chiefly in the choice of subject. 'It was meant to interest some medieval household, but it gave small scope for retaining the reader's attention, and must be held to be a failure' (p lxiii). Both must have been written before 1500. Clothing imagery and ornamental trappings are prominent in both poems; 'surely these descriptions of seams, and collars, and sleeves, are due to a woman' (p lxiv). Also 'characteristic of female authorship is the remark that the ladies vied with each other as to which looked best' (p lxv). 'It is tedious to enumerate how much these poems have in common' (p lxv). But neither can be Chaucer's for reasons of grammar, pronunciation, rime and meter.

645 *The Floure and the Leafe and The Assembly of Ladies*. Ed. Derek A. Pearsall. London and Edinburgh: Thomas Nelson and Sons, 1962. Pearsall bases his text of *FL* on Speght and *AL* on the three extant mss (Trin. Coll. Cambr. R.3.19; BL Addit. 34360; Longleat 258). The editions include textual notes, extensive explanatory notes, and a glossary. Pearsall's introduction traces the history of *FL*'s reputation — its being the glory of Chaucer from Dryden and Pope to Wordsworth, Hazlitt, and Keats — up to its expulsion from the Chaucer canon at the end of the nineteenth century. Skeat's labels of 'tinsel' and 'flashy attractiveness' have died hard. Neither poem has received its due in the twentieth century. *FL* 'is full of echoes, which is one of its many delights; but it is a good deal more than an imitation

of Chaucer: the grace and charm of its evocation of an ideal world, the
serenely sensible view of life implicit in its allegory, the ease and
delicacy of the handling, a pervading sweet reasonableness — all these
will be immediately apparent to any reader, and give it the right to an
independent existence outside an appendix to Chaucer' (p 1). Pearsall
doubts that both poems are by the same person. Nor is the author of
each necessarily a woman. 'There is certainly no need to assume, with
Skeat, that poetesses were so rare in the fifteenth century that they
must be by the same woman ... [But] if both *FL* and *AL* are by the
same woman, then she has shown a rare, not to say unlikely, talent in
projecting two such totally different *personae*' (p 15). Skeat's
speculations attributing the poems to Margaret Neville, Countess of
Oxford, 'are best forgotten' (p 16; cf Skeat **511**, pp 361–79). Marsh's
suggestion of Lydgate as author (**651**) is likewise unsound. There is
much to be said for W.M. MacKenzie's grouping of *FL*, *AL*, *CL* and
KQ (**192c**, p 18). Pearsall would date composition of both poems in
the third quarter of the fifteenth century, with *AL* being the later of
the two. He discussses the cult of the flower and the leaf (pp 22–9),
and comments on the significance of the allegory in *FL*. 'One of the
poet's gifts is to eschew the heavy moralising and stark contrasts of
much of medieval didactic poetry' (p 43). The poem begins as a
courtly game, is then invested with biblical symbolism, and develops
its moral purposes always within the boundaries of the courtly and
chivalric tone (p 46). *AL* has a simpler theme; its machinery is cruder.
'The lightness and freedom of the verse, and the run-on lines and
stanzas, give to the movements of *FL*, at its best, rare spirit and ease.
The metre of *AL* is altogether more regular' (p 64). There is not much
aureation in either poem.

DISCUSSION OF *FL* AND *AL*

[See also **192c**, **547**, **556**]

646 Fisher [Smith], Ruth. '*The Flower and the Leaf* and the *Assembly of
Ladies:* A Study of Two Love-Vision Poems of the Fifteenth Century,'
DA, 15 (1955), 1233. Columbia Dissertation, 1955.
Discusses the two poems as courtly visions. *FL* presents 'a moral for a
dying chivalry: the active and honorable endure, and the idle and
effeminate are easily destroyed.' *AL* analyzes the character of Loyalty,
using abstractions to present a realistic picture of court fashion and
ceremony. The poet 'becomes absorbed by her characters, endowing
them with actions and attitudes which have no relation to their
allegorical purpose. Her interest lies in a realistic description of the
court — its dress, gossip, conversation — not in the allegorical vision

into which convention forces her.' Fisher discusses influences of
Chaucer, Gower, and particularly Lydgate on the poems. Their
background lies in Machaut, Froissart, Deschamps, and Charles of
Orleans, but also in Christine de Pisan, whose works were at this time
in the possession of Anthony Woodville, later Lord Rivers. The
detailed description of the garden in *AL* indicates a specific place —
perhaps the royal court of Elizabeth Woodville, wife of Edward IV, or
a house connected with the House of Suffolk.

647 Hales, John W. 'The Flower and the Leaf.' *Athenaeum*, Mar. 28,
1903, pp 403–4.
Skeat's suggestion that the poem is by Margaret Neville is untenable.
'Is it likely that one christened Margaret would rebuke the Margaret
faction by showing up those who belonged to it as "foolish virgins,"
who thought only of fleeting enjoyment, and were soon overtaken by
disasters of heat and storm against which they had made no
provision?' (p 403). The lady poet here takes the part of the leaf, not
the flower. The point of view in the poem needs explaining, especially
since Margaret was the name of the Queen.

648 Kittredge, G.L. 'Chaucer and some of his Friends.' *MP*, 1 (1903–4),
1–18.
The cult of the flower and the leaf mentioned in *LGW* shows that
'English court society, in the time of Richard II, entertained itself by
dividing into two amorous orders — the Leaf and the Flower — and
by discussing, no doubt with an abundance of allegorical imagery, the
comparative excellence of those two emblems or of the qualities they
typified' (pp 1–2). Cf references in Gower and Deschamps to such
cults. The circle must have included Sir Lewis Clifford and Sir John
Clanvowe, author of the *Boke of Cupid* (*CN*), which Kittredge would
date as early as 1389. The acquaintance of such men with Chaucer
must have been intimate, and 'it is pleasant to know that it was in part
a literary friendship: Clifford brought the greetings of Deschamps to
the English poet, and Clanvowe was Chaucer's poetical disciple' (p 18).

649 Lyons, Thomas R. and Michael J. Preston. *A Complete Concordance
to Two 'Chaucerian' Poems: 'The Floure and the Leafe' and 'The
Assembly of Ladies.'* Ann Arbor: University Microfilms, 1974.
The concordance is based on Pearsall's edition (645). 'Our aim has
been to follow the conservative editorial practices which have, since the
advent of machine-concording, proven themselves most useful. Thus
we have not grouped together related word-forms nor have we
distinguished among homographs. This is a concordance of forms
exactly as it was initially sorted by computer, with the exact
reproduction of single lines quoted as context for all occurrences of all
forms' (p ii). Notes the unusually high percentages of *and* in *FL* (p

iii). In addition to concordances of English Graphic Forms and of Foreign Graphic Forms, the volume includes a ranking list of frequencies for each poem, a reverse index of graphic forms for each, and an index of rhymes.

650 McMillan, Ann. ' "Fayre Sisters Al": *The Flower and the Leaf* and *The Assembly of Ladies.*' *Tulsa Studies in Women's Literature*, 1 (1982), 27–42.
FL and *AL* 'use established traditions in unusual ways to reflect the concerns of women ... Whether composed by the same poet or not, the two poems taken together constitute variations on the theme of chastity as efficacy' (p 28) and belong to a 'tradition of the defense of women' (p 29). McMillan comments on traditional attitudes toward female sexuality, with special reference to Christine de Pisan's *Cité des Dames*, which links chastity and efficacy in women, and the Findern ms. Commenting on the blushing envoy of *FL*, in which the 'little booke' worries who might behold it as it approaches a public audience, McMillan speculates that a comparable 'maidenly shame could have prevented poets, if women, from attaching their names to their work' (p 36). She does not conclude that the author(s) must be female, however, but only that the narrators of the poems understand the concerns of intelligent women, whether in terms of the efficacy of chastity, as in *FL*, or in the longing to burst the bonds of inactivity imposed on women by that ideal, as in *AL*.

651 Marsh, G.L. 'The Authorship of *The Flower and the Leaf.*' *JEGP*, 6 (1906–7), 373–94.
Marsh agrees with Skeat that the Countess of Oxford may have written *AL* (cf 511, pp 361–79); but she would not have been old enough to have written *FL*. That poem need not have been written by a woman. Lydgate seems a more likely candidate for authorship. A vocabulary comparison and parallels in style, subject matter, and versification support his candidacy. *FL* 'is more like Lydgate at his best as an imitator of Chaucer, than it is like any other known work of the fourteenth and fifteenth centuries; and I have seen no other poem, not by Lydgate, which presents so many and such striking resemblances to Lydgate's early work' (p 394).

652 — 'Sources and Analogues of *The Flower and the Leaf.*' *MP*, 4 (1906–7), 121–67, 281–327.
Reviews the popularity of the poem and offers a synopsis. The first source for the central allegory is Orders of the Floure and Leaf as they existed at court. Accessory to the central allegory are the costumes which the courtiers wore — green and white dress with chaplets of leaves and flowers, nightingale and goldfinch paraphernalia for singers, storm and dancing motifs, etc. Oddly enough, the leaf faction's color

seems to be white (purity), and the flower's green (idleness and inconstancy). The general setting and machinery of the poem derive from other springtime poems, from pastourelles to romances and dream visions of French, English, and Scottish origin. The single most influential literary source is Chaucer, then Lydgate. But the author seems to know Deschamps, Machaut, Froissart, and Christine de Pisan as well, and behind all these is the influence of *RR*, perhaps in Chaucer's translation or in the original (p 327).

653 Maynard, Theodore. *The Connection Between the Ballade.* 1934. See **482**.

The 'exquisite' *FL* and *AL* are in rhyme royal and both have a bearing on Spenser. 'There have been people who have preferred these delightful things to anything in Chaucer; and while it is impossible to admit that they are correct, it is easy to understand their point of view' (p 100).

654 Osgood, Charles Grosvenor. *The Voice of England.* New York and London: Harper and Brothers, 1935. Pp 123–24.

FL, 'by the first unmistakable poetess in English Literature,' is an 'exquisite and most tuneful pageant' of the court adorned 'with true feminine subtlety' in its costumes and color schemes (p 124). 'Later, when the Chaucerian music had died out of the language, the poetess wrote a less successful *Assembly of Ladies*, in which the costuming sounds like a glorified society report'; nonetheless, 'the eternal feminine is sweetly discernible' (p 124).

Thomas Hoccleve

See **661** for annotated bibliography of 148 items on Hoccleve. See also **556a** and **619**.

655 *Hoccleve's Works. I. The Minor Poems.* Ed. Frederick J. Furnivall. *EETS*, e.s. 61. London: Kegan Paul, Trench, Trübner, 1892.

Nineteen poems from Phillips ms 8151 (Cheltenham) and five poems from Durham ms III.9. Furnivall's chatty forewords consider Hoccleve's life and dated poems, his love of Chaucer, and anecdotes about copying the texts. An appendix of entries about grants and payments to Hoccleve from the Privy-Council proceedings, Patent- and Issue-Rolls, and PRO, by R.E.G. Kirk is included (pp li–lxx).

656 *Hoccleve's Works. II. The Minor Poems in the Ashburnham ms Addit. 133.* Ed. Sir Israel Gollancz. *EETS* e.s. 73. London: Oxford University Press, 1925.

Ten poems which should have been included in volume I but were not

for want of access to the ms. These two volumes were reprinted as one
volume and revised by Jerome Mitchell and A.I. Doyle. London:
Oxford University Press, 1970.

657 *Hoccleve's Works. III. The Regement of Princes and Fourteen of
Hoccleve's Minor Poems.* Ed. Frederick J. Furnivall. *EETS*, e.s. 72.
London: Kegan Paul, Trench, Trübner, 1897.
Regement of Princes from Harleian ms 4866, the minor poems from
Egerton ms 615. The shorter poems are all religious, many pertaining
to the Virgin Mary. See Hoccleve's praise of Chaucer and the famous
Hoccleve portrait (pp 179–80). Hoccleve says he has included the
portrait so that those who have forgotten Chaucer may bring him to
mind again. He then explains that images are put in churches to make
people think 'on god & on his seyntes' (v. 5000), noting that some
think such images 'erren foule' and should not be made (vv. 5006–8),
but he would himself pray to the 'blessid trinite' and Mary for mercy
'Vppon my maistres soule' (vv. 5010–12).

658 Bornstein, Diane. 'Antifeminism in Thomas Hoccleve's Translation of
Christine de Pisan's *Epistre au dieu d'amours.*' *ELN*, 19 (1981–2),
7–14.
In his 'Letter of Cupid,' Hoccleve subtly alters the profeminist tone of
Christine's poem as Cupid becomes a jester 'whose exaggerated
defense of women is not trustworthy' (p 8). 'Christine's poem has the
tone of the French court, whereas Hoccleve's version has the tone of
the English tavern' (p 8). 'The rhetorical game of insulting women, an
important aspect of anti-feminism, seems to have appealed to
Hoccleve' (p 10). He manages 'to laugh at women while ostensibly
defending them' (p 14).

659 Doob, Penelope B.R. *Nebuchadnezzar's Children: Conventions of
Madness in Middle English Literature.* New Haven: Yale University
Press, 1974.
Ch 5, 'Conclusions: Thomas Hoccleve,' pp 208–231, considers
Hoccleve's fascination — 'one might even say obsession' — with
madness, melancholy, and disease. 'Hoccleve combines considerable
scientific and medical knowledge with traditional moral and religious
attitudes toward madness and disease as punishment for sin and as
earthly purgatory far preferable to the pains of hell' (p 210). Considers
madness motifs in the Tale of Jereslaus' Wife, the Tale of Jonathas
and Fellicula, *Male Regle*, the melancholic man in the Prologue to
Regement of Princes ('a Boethian Everyman, obsessed with earthly
goods and in need of consolation by the Beggar, an equally concrete
and practical spokesman for Philosophy' p 218), and the *Complaint*
and *Dialogue with a Friend* which begin the *Series* (a 'work united by
the theme of the value of suffering and disease which preoccupied

Hoccleve throughout his poetic career' (p 225). Is such material autobiographical? 'If Hoccleve did go mad, I am inclined to think that his insanity was a short but intense fit of depression, something like that which he describes as making him witless in the *Regement*, caused by his inability to reconcile the claims of God ... But the case is not at all clear' (p 226). Many details of the most 'autobiographical' works are literary borrowings and are conventional. Nor is Hoccleve alone among writers of the time in confessing madness — nb, Gower, Langland, and the Pearl-poet. Hoccleve may have used such detail 'to add realism and forcefulness to the topic — the madness of sin — about which he wished to write' (p 229).

660 Matthews, William. 'Thomas Hoccleve.' In *A Manual of the Writings in Middle English: 1050-1500*. Ed. Albert E. Hartung. New Haven: The Connecticut Academy of Arts and Science, 1972. Vol 3, section 7. Pp 746–56; 903–8.
Biographical sketch and discussion of twenty-three items by Hoccleve. Even by the lowly standards of fifteenth-century verse, Hoccleve achieved no great distinction; were it not for his fondness for contemporary allusion and his obsession with himself it would be fair to agree with his own rhetorical estimate of his dullness and poetic inability' (p 754). 'Hoccleve's devotion to Chaucer is one of his endearing traits, but he learned a minimum from his master ... Hoccleve simply lacked the ability to follow in Chaucer's path' (p 755). The bibliography (pp 903–8) is divided into editions, life, text, language, versification, bibliography, plus separate lists for each of fifty-one Hoccleve pieces.

661 Mitchell, Jerome. *Thomas Hoccleve: A Study in Early Fifteenth-Century English Poetic*. Urbana: University of Illinois Press, 1968.
Ch 1, 'The Autobiographical Element,' pp 1–19, considers the relatively abundant material available on Hoccleve both from his personal reminiscences in his poems and from scattered references in the Privy Council Proceedings, Patent Rolls, Pells Issue Rolls, Close Rolls, and Fine Rolls. Some have argued that the 'autobiographical' elements in the poems are conventional, but Mitchell shows that much of the information can be verified by external evidence, noting that indisputably genuine autobiographical passages are exceptional in the poetry of Hoccleve's day. Hoccleve seems to follow the hint of autobiography in Chaucer's *HF* to develop his own autobiographical technique along lines which no other medieval writer had explored, using vivid and memorable specific detail, in such works as *La Male Regle*, the *Regement of Princes*, *Complaint*, and *Dialogue with a Friend*. Ch 2, 'Themes and Genres,' pp 20–56, surveys 13,000 lines of

Hoccleve's verse in terms of Courtly Poetry, Didactic Poetry, Political Poems, Begging Poems, Religious Verse, and Narrative Poetry, and comments on his use of such stock themes as Fortune, youth and age, friendship, the upside-down world, and poetic skill, but also his concern with heresy and women as themes somewhat more unique in their treatment. Ch 3, 'Style,' pp 57–74, relates Hoccleve's techniques to those of his day, especially as advocated by Geoffrey of Vinsauf, making frequent comparison with Lydgate's prolix style. But, unlike Lydgate, Hoccleve does not revel in aureate diction. Ch 4, 'Handling of Sources,' pp 74–96, compares specific passages (eg, *Letter of Cupid* and Christine de Pisan's *Epistre*) to show how Hoccleve expands his material, compiles or rearranges it with individuality and some skill. 'His lively, realistic direct discourse is one of his most important achievements' (p 96). Ch 5, 'Meter,' pp 97–109, argues that the structure of Hoccleve's line, 'if analyzed in terms of more recent ideas on meter, is by no means so crude as many writers have thought' (p 100). There is no 'thwarted stress' at all if the lines are scanned according to Brooks and Warren's method of scansion or read 'rhythmically,' as 'verses of cadence,' according to the method advocated by James Southworth, *Verses of Cadence* (Oxford, 1954). Hoccleve can be accused of thwarted stress 'only if one believes that he was supposed to write iambic decasyllables with an invariable pattern of verse accents' (p 105). Ch 6, 'Hoccleve and Chaucer,' pp 110–23, discusses the *Regement* portraits of Chaucer in BL ms Harl. 4866, f. 91, from which most later portraits derive, and BL ms Royal 17.D.vi. Mitchell prints a photograph of a third portrait (Rosenbach 594), which is little known and almost an exact replica of Harley 4866 (p 116). Hoccleve's claim to have seen Chaucer should not be interpreted as an indication that they were friends: 'if Hoccleve had really known Chaucer and studied under him, surely he would have had more to tell us' (p 118). Nor are Hoccleve's allusions to Chaucer's poetry as frequent as one might expect. 'His frequent use of headless and broken-backed lines places him closer to Lydgate than Chaucer' (p 122). Mitchell's annotated bibliography of 148 items (pp 125–48) is thorough and valuable.

662 Saintsbury, George. 'The English Chaucerians.' In *CHEL*. 1908. See 62. Vol 2, pp 225–53.
Hoccleve, like Pepys, 'has found himself none the worse off for having committed to paper numerous things which anyone but a garrulous, egotistic and not very strong-minded person would have omitted' (p 236). 'He has some idea how to tell a story' (p 237). See also 578.

Isle of Ladies (*IL*)

See *Chaucer's Dreame*, **621** above.

663 *The Isle of Ladies or the Isle of Pleasaunce.* Ed. Anthony Jenkins.
New York and London: Garland, 1980.
This poem of 2235 lines in octosyllabic couplets was first printed by
Speght (1598), who labelled it 'Chaucer's Dream,' thus confusing it
with *BD*. The title stuck until the nineteenth century. Bell's revised
printing of 1878 was the first to relegate the poem to the apocrypha.
Bradshaw gave it the title 'Isle of Ladies' in a note still attached to the
ms in Longleat House. But that title is not apt either. Jenkins agrees
with Ethel Seaton **679** that *Ile of Pleasaunce* is preferable since it
appears in v. 2201 of the poem; however, *IL* has been given such
authority that 'it would be futile to ignore' it (p 6). Thus Jenkins uses
Isle of Pleasaunce as subtitle. The poem is found in two mss and
Speght's black-letter editions. The Longleat ms 256 (mid-sixteenth
century) is more authoritative than BL ms Addit. 10303. The poem
must date from ca 1475. Seaton's suggestion of Richard Roos as
author is unlikely (p 27). After providing a synopsis (pp 31–5) Jenkins
discusses the poem's conventions drawn from *RR* but given 'a new
vitality' (p 43). The poet's 'determination to press on with his
narrative is unusual in the fifteenth century' (p 51). The narrator lacks
sophistication — no 'tricksy naïveté of the Chaucerian narrator' (p
52). 'Pleasaunce' is a key word as the poet's characters 'move serenely
through the island's pleasant landscape' (p 56). Jenkins compares the
poet's treatment of material with *BD, HF, PF*, and fifteenth-century
dream visions, placing it somewhere between *HF* and Gavin Douglas'
Palace of Honour or Skelton's *Bouge of Court*. 'This dream is a
mocking fantasy'; the ancient lady, who might help the lover, does not.
'His lady is an elusive prize, always beyond the horizon' (p 64). Even
after his marriage is accomplished the new moods of joy are tauntingly
deceptive and evaporate into nothingness. 'Emotionally, then, *The Isle
of Ladies* illustrates a breakdown in medieval allegory. The dream is
no longer an adequate way of isolating and working out a personal
problem ... From that mood of yearning frustration, it is only a short
step to the love-sonnets of the next century which were to allow the
unfettered release of inner torment' (p 65).

664 Conroy, Anne Rosemarie. '*The Isle of Ladies:* A Fifteenth Century
English Chaucerian Poem,' *DAI*, 38 (1977), 253A–54A. Yale
University Dissertation, 1976.
Reviews the poem's publication history and reputation. It was popular
in the early nineteenth century and was alluded to by the Shelleys,

Elizabeth Barrett Browning, Thoreau, and Ruskin. Furnivall declared
the work not Chaucer's on the basis of the -y / -ye rhyme test. 'If
anything so definite as a poetic personality may be said to emerge
from the fifteenth-century manuscript collections of Chauceriana such
as Fairfax 16, Longleat 258, and Sir John Paston's inventory of books,
it is the Chaucer of the *Troilus* and the minor poetry. But by 1598,
the social, courtly Chaucer has become the suitable object of
antiquarian interest, whose language must be glossed even as it is
praised. For Thomas Speght, Chaucer is an historical personage firmly
fixed in time and place in the first biography of the poet included in
an edition of his works. Accordingly, the *Isle* is glossed as an account
of the marriage of John of Gaunt to Blanche of Lancaster and that of
Blanche's unnamed waiting woman to Geoffrey Chaucer.' Appendix
on the concept of old age in women.

See also Robbins **513**, pp 1096–7; 1304–5.

Jack Upland

See also **547, 548, 550, 611, 613a.**

665 *Jack Upland, Friar Daw's Reply, and Upland's Rejoinder.* Ed. P.L.
Heyworth. Oxford: Oxford University Press, 1968.
Introduction describes mss, printed editions; speculates on authors,
dates; and comments on language, versification, and editorial method.
Little attention is given to the Chaucer attribution or to discussion of
the literary or historical contexts of the works. The notes (called
'commentary') mainly cite biblical sources. Select bibliography. See
Robbins' review, *NQ*, 215 (1970), 266–7, which challenges Heyworth's
dating of the three pieces.

Lamentation of Mary Magdalen.

See **487, 525, 526.**

Lament of a Prisoner Against Fortune

666 Hammond, Eleanor P. 'Lament of a Prisoner against Fortune.' *Anglia*,
32 (1909), 481–91.

Prints the text of the poem for the first time, from BL ms Harley 7333, f 30b, which apparently is a volume 'copied in large part or entire from lost collections of John Shirley' (p 481). The work is attributed to Chaucer by Speght, who claims to have seen it in a copy of John Stow, 'whose library hath helped many writers' (p 481). The poem is found in Harley 2251 and Addit. 34360, also, both of which are derived from now lost Shirley texts. In both the latter mss the *Lament* is printed as a continuous, integral part of *Purse*. Stow assigned *Purse* to Hoccleve, and so it is printed by the 1602 and 1687 black-letter editions (p 482). But the *Lament* is not printed. Its author is unknown, and it remained unnoticed until the work of the Chaucer Society uncovered it in the late nineteenth century. 'We who are compelled to restrain ourselves from assigning to Lydgate every anonymous piece of work existing in fifteenth century manuscripts may find consolation in the thought that even Chaucer scrupled to send an idea out into the world unless he could bind upon it a name' (p 483).

John Lydgate and The Siege of Thebes

See also **55, 185, 568, 571, 581, 586a, 588a**.

367 Ayres, Robert W. 'Medieval History, Moral Purpose, and the Structure of Lydgate's *Siege of Thebes*,' *PMLA*, 73 (1958), 463–74. 'There is plentiful evidence that Lydgate regarded his material not as fiction but as history, and that his purpose in writing was not so much to tell a story of any kind as it was to teach some moral and political lesson by reference to what he regarded as ancient historical example ... it is the morality which lies at the very heart of Lydgate's purpose, and ... the incidents of the narrative are intended to reveal and illustrate [*enlumyn*] ... that morality' (p 463). From this approach the so-called digressions are seen to be integral and appropriate to their purpose. The Prologue to *Siege* pretends that it is a tale told by Lydgate on the return journey of Chaucer's pilgrims from Canterbury.

368 Ebin, Lois. 'Lydgate's View on Poetry.' *AnM*, 18 (1977), 76–105. Throughout the 145,000 lines of his poetry Lydgate, especially in his digressions, develops 'a new critical vocabulary to define the qualities of good poetry' and 'articulates ideas about poetry, particularly his conception of the poet as craftsman, his belief in the importance of amplification and high style, and his concern with the relation between the language of poetry and the state' (p 76). His critical vocabulary includes such terms as *enlumyn, adourne, embelissche, aureate, goldyn, sugrid, rethorik,* and *elloquence.* 'Although the vocabulary Lydgate develops either is not found in Chaucer's writing or, if used, is introduced with an entirely different meaning, after Lydgate, these terms become the standard critical language of the fifteenth century' (p 88). Lydgate's notion of the role of the poet differs from Chaucer's. 'In contrast to Chaucer who repeatedly questions the relation between appearance and reality, experience and authority in his area and the limitations the poet's craft by its very nature imposes on his effort to create a truthful vision, Lydgate neither doubts the inherent truthfulness of poetry, nor does he question the poet's intentions. In his work, the problems which Chaucer considers so anxiously no longer are apparent — the ability of the poet to mislead by means of his art, the relation between a poet's or narrator's will or "entent" and his use of his craft, the limits of mortal man with his restricted vision as artist. Rather, Lydgate's digressions point to an unfailing assurance that the poet is noble and his writing leads man to truth' (pp 90–1; see note 25 for bibliography on the relative views of Chaucer and Lydgate on truth and rhetoric). Lydgate's view of poetry is not only substantially different from Chaucer's; it is 'a prelude to the formal poetics in English which first appeared in the sixteenth century' (p 105).

668a — 'Chaucer, Lydgate, and the "Myrie Tale".' *ChauR*, 13 (1979), 316–36.
'In contrast to Chaucer Lydgate suggests a possibility for a fruitful tale which is not considered in the *Canterbury Tales* — the mirror or moral speculum — a tale which is beneficial practically as well as spiritually' (p 331). In his prologue to *The Siege of Thebes* Lydgate's assumptions about poetry, the role of the poet, and illustrative character types are deliberately different from Chaucer's. For Lydgate poetry provides 'man with a means of restoring order and harmony to the world ... In contrast to Chaucer's concern about the ambiguity of poetry, Lydgate's transformation of the "myrie tale" suggests his extreme confidence in the power of writing' (p 332). While Chaucer questions the relation between appearance and reality, fiction and truth, and the limitations the poet's craft by its very nature imposes on his effort to create a truthful vision, Lydgate neither doubts the inherent truthfulness of poetry, nor its power to improve men. In his work the problems which Chaucer considers so anxiously no longer are apparent. Rather his treatment of the "myrie tale" reflects his belief that poetry is noble and leads man to truth' (pp 332–33).

669 Lydgate, John. *Siege of Thebes*, Pt. I, ed. Axel Erdmann. Chaucer Society, second series, no. 46. London: Kegan Paul, Trench, Trübner, 1911.
The *Siege* was written when Lydgate was about fifty years old to form an additional link in *CT*. The poet represents himself as falling in with

the pilgrims at their Canterbury inn in mid-April, having come himself
to fulfill his vow to St Thomas for recovery from an illness. 'There is
no doubt that the Prologue was the first portion written of the poem'
(p x). The Tale ends at line 4716, and is derived from the *Roman de
Thebes*. Erdmann uses BM Arundell 119 as the basis of his edition,
with Bodley 776, Addit. 18632, Lord Mostyn's ms and nineteen other
mss being consulted or acknowledged. The notes and introduction,
discussing sources, date, language, prosody, and mss were published
after Erdmann's death as *Lydgate's Siege of Thebes, Pt. II:
Introduction, Notes, Rhyme-Lists, and a Glossary, with Appendix*, by
Axel Erdmann and Eilert Ekwall. *EETS*, e.s., no. 125. London:
Oxford University Press, 1930. This volume includes a frontispiece
illumination of 'The Party of Pilgrims,' with Lydgate gesturing as he
speaks, from Royal ms 18.D.11, f 148v. Appendix discusses Christ
Church (Oxford) ms 152, which had not been included in Erdmann's
original study.

70 MacCracken, Henry Noble, ed. *Lydgate's Minor Poems*. *EETS*, e.s.,
no. 107. London: Kegan Paul, Trench and Trübner, 1911.
Part I consists of 'The Lydgate Canon' and 'Religious Poems'; Part 2
treats Secular Poems (see 671). MacCracken's discussion of the
Lydgate canon considers peculiarities of his rhyme, meter, and style on
the basis of his 160 genuine poems. 'Lydgate in his secular poetry was
a Chaucerian, while in his religious poetry he had a host of imitators.
In the one case I cannot deny that another Chaucerian might have
written almost any one of the poems of the school of the court of love
ascribed to Lydgate. In the other case I cannot deny that an imitator
might have imitated his style so closely as to make his work
indistinguishable from his model's' (p v). But there are linguistic
differences. Though most of his religious and moral poems are of his
old age, 'Lydgate as an old man still writes the language of his youth,
but his imitators cannot find this language in the rapidly changing
state of the tongue' (p vi). 'Lydgate might have changed his style, his
rhyme, his metre for another, had he ever been conscious that another
style, metre, or rhyme was desirable; there is no evidence that he ever
thought so, or that any contemporary ever thought so' (p vi).
MacCracken lists Lydgate's authentic works and also spurious poems
attributed to him including among others, 'Quia Amore Langueo,'
Court of Sapience, Assembly of the Gods, B-Fragment of *Romaunt,
CL*, and *FL*. Prints texts of sixty-nine shorter religious poems, some of
which are 35 pages long.

71 — *The Minor Poems of John Lydgate*. *EETS*, e.s., no. 192. London:
Humphrey Milford, Oxford University Press, 1934.
Part II: Secular Poems (see 670, for Part I); text 're-read' with mss by

Merriam Sherwood. Includes 7 poems in all. No introductory material, explanatory notes, or glossary.

672 McCray, Curtis Lee. 'Chaucer and Lydgate and the Use of History.' *DA*, 29 (1969), 4461A–2A. University of Nebraska Dissertation, 1968. Dir. Paul A. Olson.

Discusses *Siege of Thebes, Troy Book,* and *Fall of Princes* to show how Lydgate uses Chaucer (*KnT* and *MonkT*) to support his own views of history. The argument suggests that both Chaucer and Lydgate expect their audiences to apply morals of the Troy and Thebes stories to the blunders and moral blindness of their own societies.

673 Norton-Smith, John, ed. *John Lydgate: Poems.* Oxford: Clarendon Press, 1966.

Edition of twelve Lydgate poems, with introduction, biographical and textual notes, select bibliography, glossary, and appendix on aureate diction. 'It is the shorter, occasional, poems treating public and private matters that show Lydgate at his best. The chosen poet of many and various estates of the fifteenth century, Lydgate belongs to the world of late medieval polite versifying ... He never achieved the Horatian intimacy, economy, and intelligence of Chaucer's polite verse (the *Envoys* to Scogan and Bukton) yet his artistry is not much inferior to Chaucer's in ... the *Letter to Gloucester*, the *Departing of Thomas Chaucer,* or the *Balade Sente to the Shirrefs Dyner*. Here, in the translating of an everyday event into a compact form, he is the equal of Deschamps or Dunbar. It was Lydgate who created the "mumming" poem ... just as it was Lydgate who invented the "polysyllabic language" of aureate diction. These are the aesthetic facts that matter' (pp x–xi). Lydgate's long religious poems are hard to appreciate at this date. 'The Pilgrimage of the Life of Man ... is unattractive by literary standards of any age' (p xi). There are four tendencies in Lydgate's verse: 1) a Chaucerian style closely modelled on *Pity, AA,* and *T&C*; 2) a flat explanatory style modelled on that of the *MonkT*; 3) a 'later cryptic style, abounding in headless lines, trochaic rhythms, and epigrammatic jerkiness'; 4) a larger, Latinate use of syntax, periods accompanied by 'incessant stylistic experimentation: (i) the extending of the sense of words, especially verbs; (ii) importation of scientific terminology into secular verse; (iii) invention of aureate diction, especially for religious verse; (iv) extensive use of refrains and moral maxims' (pp xi–xii). In his notes Norton-Smith stresses Lydgate's Oxford ties from 1397–1408 to suggest that 'Henry V and Lacy [Bursar of University College and later Dean of the Royal Chapel at Windsor] may well have been the main forces in shaping the direction and style of Lydgate's religious verse' (p 195, n 1).

674 Pearsall, Derek. *John Lydgate*. Charlottesville: University Press of
Virginia, 1970.
Ch 1, 'Critical Approach,' pp 1–21, argues that Lydgate must be taken
on his own terms. His popularity was enormous through the early days
of printing but difficulty of language caused him to fall into obscurity,
just as it did Chaucer. 'The list of "hard words" in Speght's collected
edition of 1602 sounds a kind of knell, and classicising commentators
of the seventeenth and eighteenth centuries speak with patronising
disdain of the roughness of his language and versification, parroting
the cry of "Matter, but no art" or, as one writer puts it, "solid sense"
but "mouldy words" ' (p 3). Lydgate wrote twice as much as
Shakespeare; three times as much as Chaucer: 'there can be no sense
in which this works to his advantage' (p 4). That he wrote a 'Treatise
for Laundresses' is a 'salutary and salubrious reminder of the
comprehensiveness of his range in poetry' (p 5). His poetry is bad not
because of its subject matter but because of his failure to shape,
control, or master his material. In a poem like *Pilgrimage of Man*
(26,000 lines long) 'he merely goes through the motions of versifying in
the most mechanical manner possible' (p 6). Yet his 'expansiveness
clearly forms part of a deliberate poetic style'; he consciously writes
according to 'accepted canons of taste' (p 8). 'Reading Lydgate is in
fact the best possible introduction to Chaucer, for here is the soil from
which Chaucer grew, and the soil to which he returned. Lydgate
profited in a multitude of ways from Chaucer's example, but
nevertheless in all his writing he reasserts medieval traditions and
habits of mind against Chaucer's free-ranging innovations. He throws
into sharp relief not only Chaucer's greatness but also his differentness'
(p 14). Ch 2, 'Monastic Background,' pp 22–48, discusses monastic
library holdings. Lydgate had access to the Bury library with over
2000 volumes, the second largest in the country, surpassed only by
that of Christ Church Canterbury. 'It would sometimes be helpful to
think of Lydgate as a kind of vernacular Trivet or Waleys rather than
as a cloistered Chaucer' (p 38). Ch 3, 'Chaucer and the Literary
Background,' pp 49–82: 'Lydgate owes his very language to Chaucer,
for it is unlikely that English would have been available in 1400 as a
literary language of high status had it not been for Chaucer' (p 49).
Pearsall discusses borrowings from Chaucer of words, phrases, and
contexts, noting that 'Lydgate's own achievement in "fixing" English
as a literary language should not be underestimated' (p 50). He
emphasizes the importance of Shirley to the Lydgate tradition as well
as the Chaucer tradition (pp 73 ff), though his attributions are not
always accurate. Lydgate's canon is 'a matter on which one would like
to keep an open mind' (p 79). Ch 4, 'Courtly Poems,' pp 83–121: 'It is
rarely necessary to go beyond Chaucer for Lydgate's specific

borrowings' (p 84). Frequently he uses the *Romaunt* for lines and ideas; also poems like *Pity, Mars, BD, AA,* and *KnT*; and *Boece.* Chapters 5–8 deal respectively with Troy and Thebes; Laureate Lydgate; Fables and Didactic Poems; and *Fall of Princes.* In the latter poem Lydgate includes his longest allusion to Chaucer with its invaluable list of his works. Ch 9, 'Lydgate's Religious Poetry,' pp 255–92, devotes some attention to *Life of Our Lady,* a poem which needs no 'props for our esteem. It is at once a confirmation of all that is most characteristic in Lydgate and at the same time an incomparable flowering of devotional poetry which stuns expectation. One can see how Lydgate could have come to have written it, but one could not have predicted that he was capable of it. It is certainly one of the finest pieces of religious poetry in English, and its present availability in one scarce and difficult edition is peculiar commentary on our attitudes to Lydgate. It was extremely widely read in its own day, judging from the large number of extant mss (forty-two, of which thirty-seven are more or less complete), more than for any other Lydgate poem except for freaks like the *Dietary*' (p 285).

675 Renoir, Alain, and C. David Benson. 'John Lydgate.' In *A Manual of the Writings in Middle English: 1050–1500.* Ed. Albert E. Hartung. New Haven: Connecticut Academy of Arts and Science, 1980. Vol 6, section XVI, pp 1809–1920; 2071–5.
A brief review of Lydgate's literary reputation, and introduction to 200 items, including a structural description, synopsis, notes on sources and any known circumstances surrounding composition of the work, and mention of the main critical assessments. Bibliography on general treatments of language, versification, authorship, sources and literary relations, literary criticism, and bibliography, and separate lists for each of the 200 Lydgate items in the commentary. The bibliography is partially annotated.

676 Renoir, Alain. *The Poetry of John Lydgate.* Cambridge, Mass.: Harvard University Press, 1967.
Ch 1, 'Opinions about Lydgate,' pp 1–12, surveys attitudes toward the poet from the Renaissance to the twentieth century, making four points which reveal something of modern dispositions about poetry as well as the nature of Lydgate's achievements: 1) with the end of the eighteenth century Lydgate's reputation fell abruptly from that of a great poet to that of a contemptible rhymester; 2) neither those who praised him as a most dulcet spring of rhetoric or who despised him as a compiler of 'laureate drivel' justify their claims with careful analysis of his poetry; 3) during the Renaissance he enjoyed the admiration of men even though they strongly disapproved of his religious calling and subject matter; 4) the most consistent modern charges against him are

prolixity and dullness. Ch 2, 'Opinions Reconsidered,' pp 313–31,
demonstrates that turn of the century critics like Saintsbury 677 who
mocked Lydgate so confidently cannot have looked very closely at the
poetry itself. 'Lydgate can best be understood, not as a strictly
mediaeval Chaucerian, but rather as a poet who immediately followed
Chaucer and wrote during the period of transition between the Middle
Ages and the Renaissance. The qualifications may seem small, but it
will allow us to evaluate Lydgate's production according to its own
merits instead of condemning him for repeatedly falling short of a goal
at which he was not always aiming' (p 31). Ch 3, 'The Period of
Transition,' pp 32–45, argues against a 'sudden Renaissance.' Lydgate
was in many ways closer to the Renaissance than Chaucer. He was an
early humanist; nor was he alone in his love of books and knowledge of
the classics. 'Possibly the most important single man in the history of
early English humanism was Humphrey of Gloucester' (p 42). Renoir
discusses early libraries, listing statistics on library holdings in
Lydgate's day: Bury, 2000+; Christ Church Canterbury, 690; St Paul's
Cathedral, 171; Exeter, 230; Merton College, 1964; Louvre, 916;
Strassburg Minster, 21; Gnessen, 35, etc. Ch 4, 'The Mediaeval
Tradition.' pp 46–60, relates Lydgate's poetry such as *CBK* to *BD*
and *T&C* to show his medieval ties and lack of a sense of breaking
away. Ch 5, 'Classical Antiquity,' pp 61–73, stresses his understanding
of classical antiquity and his encyclopedic love of ancient lore. Ch 6,
'The Paragon of Animals,' pp 74–94, considers his conflicting attitudes
toward women. Lydgate the monk was antifeminist; Lydgate the court
poet was 'avowedly profeminist' (p 83). Ch 7, 'The Nation and the
Prince,' pp 95–109, discusses the *Troy Book*, political poetry such as
the *Debate of the Horse, Sheep, and Goose*, and nationalistic
tendencies in Lydgate which are more congenial to Renaissance than
medieval views. Ch 8, 'Story of Thebes,' pp 110–35, discusses
Lydgate's only major secular work which was composed outside the
patronage system (p 111). His *Troy Book* was a great success; perhaps
he wished to follow it with the other great collection of legends. The
work is loaded with advice on kingly conduct. Writing his *Siege of
Thebes* as a continuaton of *CT* held a threefold attraction for Lydgate:
1) it provided a sort of tribute to Chaucer; 2) the name of Chaucer
would add prestige; 3) the scheme would allow him a new twist on his
favorite theme of affected modesty — the 'uninhibited Host of the
Canterbury Tales [could] boisterously address him as an
inconsequential idiot' (p 114). In the *Siege* Lydgate changes a
medieval French romance into an English Renaissance epic (p 135). Ch
9, 'Another Point of View,' pp 136–43, discusses Lydgate's love of and
experimentation with artificial, Latinate diction (his aureate terms),
re-emphasizing his transitional qualities between medieval and

Renaissance poetics.

677 Saintsbury, George. 'The English Chaucerians.' *CHEL.* 1908. See **62**.
Vol 2, pp 225–53.
Lydgate 'had some humour ... But this humour was never
concentrated to anything like Chaucerian strength; while of
Chaucerian vigour, Chaucerian pathos, Chaucerian vividness of
description, Lydgate had no trace or tincture. To these defects he
added two faults ... The one is prosodic incompetence; the other is
longwinded prolixity' (p 228). '*The Complaint of the Black Knight,* for
long assigned to Chaucer, though not quite worthy of him, is better
than most of Lydgate's poems' (p 233). 'A little Lydgate [if judiciously
chosen or happily allotted by chance] ... is a tolerable thing: though
even this can hardly be very delectable to any well qualified judge of
poetry. But, the longer and wider that acquaintance ... the more
certain is dislike to make its appearance. The prosodic incompetence
cannot be entirely due to copyists and printers; the enormous
verbosity, the ignorance of how to tell a story, the want of freshness,
vigour, life, cannot be due to them at all. But what is most fatal of all
is the flatness of diction ... the dull, hackneyed, slovenly phraseology,
only thrown up by his occasional aureate pedantry — which makes
the common commoner and the uncommon uninteresting' (p 234).

678 Schirmer, Walter F. *John Lydgate: A Study in the Culture of the
XVth Century,* trans. Ann E. Keep. London: Methuen, 1961.
Originally published in German, Tübingen: Max Niemeyer, 1952.
Discusses Lydgate's relation to the Chaucer tradition in his early work
(pp 31–41) and in the *Siege of Thebes* (pp 59–65). Relates Lydgate's
use of the 5-beat line to Chaucer's and discusses his aureate style (pp
70–7), comparing it to that of humanist Latin authors with their
florida verborum venustas ideal. In discussing the Lydgate canon
Schirmer lists works attributed to Lydgate but which he did not write,
including such Chaucer items as *Gent, Sted, ABC,* and *CD,* as well as
MancT, PriorT, and *SNT* (p 275).

Richard Roos: La Belle Dame sans Merci (*LBD*)

See also **556a** and **557**.

679 Seaton, Ethel. *Sir Richard Roos: Lancastrian Poet.* London: R.
Hart-Davis, 1961.
Seaton refers to her book as 'a hybrid of biography, history, "chronique
scandaleuse," cross-word puzzle, history of literature, and "lecture

expliquée" ' (p 9). The argument is based on mss containing *LBD*,
Roos' familiarity with French poets and cryptic tricks, and style and
meter. The first two chapters are devoted to biography of Richard
Roos, fifth son of William, sixth Lord Roos, and Margaret Arundel, of
'the premier barony of England of the fifteenth century' (p 16). Ch 3:
'*La Belle Dame sans Merci*, its transmission and its implications,' pp
80–102, argues that most of the anonymous poems in such anthologies
as Fairfax 16 and the Findern ms, which Seaton calls 'the Roos
scrapbook' (p 90), are by Roos, who wrote anonymously because of his
aristocratic status; with the eclipse of the Lancastrians his name
'became a liability, not an asset, to be concealed rather than claimed
or acclaimed' (p 95). But his name is secretly placed in the poems by
anagrams and acrostics. *LBD*, 'the one authenticated translation by
Sir Richard Roos, gives evidence of a practiced poetic style, and of
familiarity with French poetry in general' (p 102). Ch 4, 'The Corpus
of Roos's Poetry,' pp 103–28, explains the cryptic devices whereby
more than 100 poems are claimed as part of the Roos canon, including
*IL, AL, FL, Parlement of Love, Eye and the Heart, Lover's Mass,
Chance of Dice*; such Lydgate poems as *CBK, CL, Court of Venus*;
many of the poems hitherto ascribed to Wyatt and Surrey; and several
poems once thought to be by Chaucer, including all the fragments of
the *Romaunt, MB, BC, Pity, AA, Mars, Venus, AWU*, and *LGW*.
Seaton's evidence calls into question 'Shirley's trustworthiness' (p 110),
especially as authority for the Lydgate canon, and leaves Roos with 'a
corpus as large as that of Chaucer, but with a very high proportion of
brief lyrics' (p 128). She allows that the loss of Chaucer's lyrics from
his canon 'will cause regret' and that 'alarm and revulsion will
probably greet the claim for *The Legend of Good Women*, and
horrified incredulity the chapter on "The Tudor Aftermath" ' (p 128).
The following eight chapters consider the poet's 'pleasaunce period,'
his early translations ('whether or not Roos merits the name of "grant
translateur," there is not doubt that he becomes skilful in the art' p
276), his ceremonial poems, personal poems, and satirical verse. The
attribution of *Mars* to Roos is based on the poem's connection with a
group of people active in the mid-fifteenth century. 'The willingness of
critics to accept Chaucer's authorship is a testimony to the poem's
excellence and its minor form. It is a trifle, composed in the
half-sympathetic, half malicious spirit as is *The Rape of the Lock*, and
perhaps with a similar purpose, to help smooth over a family scandal'
(p 333). Seaton's explanation of Roos' writing of *AA* solves many of
the cruxes, though not all: 'Corinne still remains unexplained' (p 338).
Regarding *LGW* (pp 340–69), 'there can be no doubt that Chaucer
wrote *a* poem of good women (as he did *a* translation of *Le Roman de
la Rose*) ... But the poem we have and know ... [is not] the poem

Chaucer wrote as he left it. The presence in both the Prologues and all the Legends of many of Roos's anagrams forces me to this conclusion' (p 340). Roos' Alceste is Elizabeth Beaumont. Roos wrote the C-Fragment of *Romaunt* late in his life when he, like Malory, was in prison. In Ch 12, 'The Tudor Aftermath,' pp 442–515, Seaton argues that many of Roos' poems were copied, altered, modernized, and appropriated by Tudor authors. *CL* is his, as are many of the 'uncertain poems' in Tottel, and 'all but a few of the lyrics and shorter poems now attributed to Sir Thomas Wyatt' (p 454).

- Review by H.S. Bennett, *RES*, 13 (1962), 174–8: 'She has energetically searched for and found a mass of genealogical material relating to the family, together with a great deal of historical data concerning the circles in which they moved ... These chapters help us to appreciate more clearly the intricate ways in which the aristocracy and gentry of the fifteenth century were interrelated, a matter which students of literature are more and more coming to recognize is of great importance to them' (p 174). Cites several attacks on her methods of anagrammatizing. She never makes clear 'what are the rules and conventions she is using' (p 175). Bennett tries her apparent system on her same poems for very different results. The 'sampling leaves me with the conviction that there is not firm basis for Dr. Seaton's claim on behalf of Roos' (p 177); it 'remains inconceivable that so outstanding a poet as Roos is claimed to have been should wish to remain anonymous and succeeded in doing so' (p 178).

- Comment by Derek Pearsall, *John Lydgate*, **674**, pp 20–1, n 42: 'This book aims to establish Roos as the major poet of fifteenth-century England by assigning to him much of its anonymous poetry, as well as poems by Chaucer, Lydgate, Wyatt and others. The ascriptions are based on the "discovery" of double acrostic anagrams of unprecedented complexity, and are wholly preposterous.' However, the book is full of incidental good things, and shows a wide knowledge of fifteenth-century literature and mss.

- Comment by Rossell Hope Robbins, *Manual*, **513**, p 1073: Despite Seaton's unfortunate 'penchant to unearth anagrams,' there is much to praise in her learned book, especially 'Seaton's meticulous scholarship in fifteenth-century manuscripts, polite society in the later Middle Ages, English and French sources and analogues, and an apperceptive appreciation of the poems themselves. Any student who ignores her study does so at his own loss.'

680 Timmer, B.J. 'La Belle Dame Sans Merci.' *ES*, 11 (1929), 20–2.
Timmer questions Skeat's assertion [2, vol 1, p 526] that 'Faire
Rewthelees' in *Lady* (line 27) is a translation of the French phrase 'la
belle dame sans merci.' Timmer cannot find the phrase in Machaut,
Deschamps, or Granson. The stock figure of the pitiless woman is
there, but 'no such definite title as *Belle Dame sans Merci*' (p 21).
The figure of the ruthless woman came from Provençe to Northern
France, then to Italy and England. Possibly the phrase comes from
Italy, though Timmer does not find it in Petrarch. Perhaps Alain
Chartier translated the phrase *La Belle Dame sans Merci* from
Chaucer's 'Faire Rewthelees,' though this is not likely. Probably the
two phrases were formed independently of each other (p 22). Or
perhaps 'Faire Rewthelees, the Wise, yknit unto Good Aventure' is a
pseudonym, as Cowling suggested (*Chaucer* [Methuen, 1927], p 106).

Testament of Cresseid (*TC*)

[Because of the extensive bibliography on Henryson's poem, I cite here
only the several recent bibliographies which have sections devoted to
the poem and selected items published mainly since the appearance of
Heidtmann (**682**) and Ridley (**683**).]

BIBLIOGRAPHIES

681 Aitkin, William Russell. *Scottish Literature in English and Scots: A
Guide to Information Sources*. Detroit: Gale, 1982.
Beginnings to 1980, 3956 items in all. Selected Henryson items 254–72
(pp 31–32).

682 Heidtmann, Peter. 'A Bibliography of Henryson, Dunbar, and
Douglas, 1912–1968.' *ChauR*, 5 (1970–71), 75–82.
Seventy-two items on Henryson — editions, books and selected
unpublished dissertations, essays and notes — plus a dozen general
studies of Middle Scots literature.

683 Ridley, Florence H. 'Middle Scots Writers.' In *A Manual of the
Writings in Middle English*, ed. Albert E. Hartung. 1973. See **509**.
Ridley lists seven editions of *TC* from Thynne (1532) to T. Scotts's
1970 Penquin edition, plus sixteen editions of selections from the
poem, and four modernizations. Bibliography on textual matters,
language, versification, date, authorship, sources and literary relations,

other scholarly problems, literary criticism, and bibliography.
See also Florence H. Ridley, 'A Check List, 1956–1968, for Study of
The Kingis Quair, the Poetry of Robert Henryson, Gawin Douglas,
and William Dunbar,' *SSL*, 8 (1970–71), 30–51 (items 45–90 on
Henryson); and Robin Fulton, 'Additions to Florence H. Ridley's
Checklist, 1956–1968,' *SSL*, 9 (1971–72), 169, with two additional
Henryson items.

RECENT EDITIONS

684 Henryson, Robert. *Poems, Selected and edited with an Introduction,
Notes, and Glossary by Charles Elliott*. Oxford: Clarendon Press,
1963/1974.
Includes *TC* and nine other Henryson poems, including *Morall Fabillis*.

685 Henryson, Robert. *The Testament of Cresseid*, ed. Denton Fox.
London: Thomas Nelson and Sons, 1968.
Uses the unique Edinburgh print of Henry Charteris' edition dated
1593 (BL C.21.C14) as the basis for his edition. Thynne's edition of
1532 is next in importance as base text. Anderson's edition of 1663
(Trinity College Cambridge II.12.217) also has some textual authority
as does the stanza in the Book of the Dean of Lismore (ca 1512–1529)
and the three stanzas included in the Ruthven ms (ca 1560). 'The
other surviving mss and prints are completely without authority' (p 2):
the St John's College Cambridge ms L.1 contains a copy of Speght's
1602 edition; the Kinaston ms (Bodleian ms Add. C 287, dated 1639)
bases its *TC* on Speght's 1598 edition and includes Kinaston's Latin
translation in accentual rhyme royal verse. The poem may have been
printed by Chapman and Myller ca 1508, but no copy survives. Such a
copy may have been the base text for Charteris and other early
seventeenth-century century editions, none of which survive. In his
critical introduction Fox considers Henryson's greatest innovation to
be Cresseid's leprosy, 'the central fact of the poem' (p 23). After a
detailed discussion of leprosy as Biblical topos and a medieval
historical and literary phenomenon, Fox suggests that Henryson uses it
as sign of moral corruption. Cresseid's 'leprosy is the inevitable and
proper punishment for a corrupt, unnatural and sinful life' (p 37).
Early in the poem Cresseid is obsessed by a false shame rooted in
pride (p 48); but through her suffering she is redeemed at the end as
she bequeaths her spirit to Diana. The narrator is, like Chaucer's
Januarie, 'a figure illustrating the folly, self-delusion, and sterility of
lust ... St Paul's *vetus homo*, the "Old Man" which represents
unredeemed man, corrupt and concupiscent' (p 55), a votary both of

courtly love and lechery, stupid and passionately involved in his narrative, 'morally imbecilic' in his reaction to Cresseid's plight (p 56).

686 *Henryson*, Selected by Hugh MacDiarmid. Harmondsworth: Penguin Books Ltd, 1973.
MacDiarmid's introduction discusses Scottish poets in general. 'There is now a concensus of judgment that regards Henryson as the greatest of our great makars' (p 13).

687 *The Poems of Robert Henryson*, ed. Denton Fox. Oxford: Clarendon Press, 1981.
The text and apparatus of *TC* are intended to be the same as those in **685**. 'The annotations have been in many places rewritten, and most of the long critical introduction of the earlier edition has been omitted' (p lxxxii, n 3). The introduction to the poem which remains is devoted mainly to Fox's discussion of leprosy and Henryson's astrological pantheon (pp lxxxii–xciv). Bibliography, pp 495–508; excellent glossary, pp 511–596.

SELECTED RECENT CRITICISM

688 Adamson, Jane. 'Henryson's *Testament of Cresseid:* "Fyre" and "Cauld".' *CR*, 18 (1976), 39–60.
The tone of *TC*, with its evocation of cold and the basic human need for warmth, is more complex than discussions of Cresseid's innocence or her alleged guilt allow. Henryson feels out his subject from within to catch Cresseid's panic and despair, her way of conceiving situations, to transform 'her buried sense of guilt into a more tolerable form' (p 49). As in *T&C* the story is less a pattern of fall and retribution than 'one of human frailty and loss, suffering and self defeat' (p 52). Cresseid moves beyond 'slyding courage' to a knowledge of 'the irremediable waste of her life' which evokes pity, compassion, and terror. At the end we are left with the event of her death which itself must speak its own meaning.

689 — 'The Curious Incident of the Recognition in Henryson's *The Testament of Cresseid*.' *Parergon*, 27 (1980), 17–25.
Critics have erred in following M. W. Stearns' interpretation of the encounter of Troilus and leprous Cresseid as a partial recognition scene (*Robert Henryson*, New York, 1949, pp 97-105). Henryson's point is that there is no recognition at all. The leper's glance makes Troilus think of his Cresseid. The memory-image then completely occupies his mind. The gift he gives is for the memory-image, not for his seeing of Cresseid in the leper. Henryson's line that the sight 'deludis the wittis outwardly' means 'eludes the wit's consciousness.'

690 Aswell, E. Duncan. 'The Role of Fortune in *The Testament of Cresseid*.' *PQ*, 46 (1967), 471–87.
The narrator and Cresseid belong to 'a secular universe, not one in which Fortune is seen as an aspect of our partial and imperfect perspective upon divine providence, as Boethius or Gower would have emphasized. Henryson's planet-gods are immanent deities, natural forces, but their dominance is not shown to be counteracted through a belief in God' (p 485). Thus there are no reassuring metaphysical truths nor pagan afterworld. 'Since our life consists solely of impermanence, of dependence upon external conditions and internal states of mind that exist only to change, and since man has so little control over them, each man must strive to retain control over himself' (p 487) and adapt to Fortune. The poem shows us little of Cresseid's inward thoughts, however; rather, we see the adjustments which Fortune imposes both upon her and the narrator. To adjust to circumstance is all they can do.

691 Baglioni, Annalisa. 'Un'apparente incongruenza nel *Testament of Cresseid*.' In *Studi e ricerche di letteratura inglese e americana*. Ed. Claudio Gorlier. Milan: Cisalpino-Goliardica, 1969. Pp 205–16.
Review article of recent criticism.

692 Bennett, J.A.W. 'Henryson's *Testament:* a flawed masterpiece.' *Scottish Literary Journal*, 1 (1974), 5–16.
'I come to criticise Henryson, not to praise him — or rather, I come to criticise the eulogists of his best-known poem who have obscured his faults by encomiums on its "delicate moral balance," its "reflexion of medieval assurance" ' (p 5). Bennett details numerous inconsistencies in the narrative, from the vague topography and faulty characterization to the heavy-handed *moralitas* and tonal ambiguities. 'Of Henryson's capacity to create arresting scenes there is no question' (p 5); it is in the fuzziness of rationale between great moments that the confusion lies. Bennett points to numerous details which Henryson seems to draw from Chaucer without apparently understanding how they functioned in Chaucer or without resolving precisely how they are to function in his own poem.

693 Benson, C. David. 'Troilus and Cresseid in Henryson's *Testament*.' *ChauR*, 13 (1978–79), 263–71.
Benson challenges the usual view of Troilus' magnanimity in his distribution of alms in *TC*. 'It is Cresseid, not Troilus, who is capable of lasting nobility and true generosity' (p 264).

694 Brody, Saul Nathaniel. *The Disease of the Soul: Leprosy in Medieval Literature*. Ithaca: Cornell University Press, 1974.

Considers medieval medical understandings of leprosy, the leper and society, the ecclesiastical tradition, and leprosy in literature. 'Cresseid's leprosy is a particularly suitable punishment for her promiscuity. Not only does it ravage her beauty, but what is more, because leprosy was commonly understood to be a venereal disease, a consequence of lust, it makes her past sinfulness apparent to her and all who see her' (pp 176–77).

695 Chessell, Del. 'In the Dark Time: Henryson's *Testament of Cresseid.*' *CR*, 12 (1969), 61–72.

'The dark time' alludes to the fifteenth century itself and Henryson's very different sensibility from Chaucer's. Chessell stresses the poem's 'overwhelming depth of compassion' (p 64). When the language condemning Cresseid is most fierce, it heightens one's sense of her frailty. 'Henryson quietly makes it perfectly clear that Cresseid is already aware, at some level in her consciousness, of her disease, and that it is the inevitable outcome of her actions, not a melodramatic punishment for blaspheming the gods' (p 66). In her curse of Cresseid, 'Cynthia embodies the disease itself ... [reflecting] both Cresseid's spotted chastity and her spotted face. The image is a horrible one, and Henryson has the tact to leave it to make its own point unaided by explication' (p 67). Much of the power of *TC* lies in the juxtaposition of the courtly world and its medieval gardens with the world of disease into which Cresseid walks, a world all the more pitiable because of its 'emotional second-ratedness' (p 71). *TC* is 'a purgatorial poem, stringent and severe, but tempered throughout by the warmly human compassion of the poet, which is continually making itself felt in his language and imagery and in the very cadence of his verse' (p 72).

696 Craik, Thomas W. 'The Substance and Structure of *The Testament of Cresseid:* A Hypothesis.' In *Bards and Makars: Scottish Language and Literature: Medieval and Renaissance.* Ed. Adam J. Aitkin, Matthew P. McDiarmid, and Derick S. Thomson. Glasgow: University of Glasgow Press, 1977. Pp 22–26.

The final encounter between Cresseid and Troilus 'is the heart of the poem and was its nucleus' (p 22). Henryson satisfied the Chaucerian reader's unfulfilled desire of bringing lovers together again but with heartbreaking effect, 'just as such things are in real life' (p 23). In composing the poem Henryson perhaps worked backward from the meeting: having first thought of Cresseid's leprosy, he then introduced the council of the gods, her blasphemy, Diomeid's desertion, and last of all the introductory account of the wintry circumstances in which the 'tragedie' was written.

697 Craun, Edwin D. 'Blaspheming Her "Awin God": Cresseid's

"Lamentatioun" in Henryson's *Testament.*' *SP*, 82 (1985), 25–41. Cresseid's three highly amplified exclamations of grief stand sharply in contrast to the poem's concise style of the factual record' (p 26) and function as measures of her moral progress. Cresseid initially places the blame for her misfortunes upon the gods, but, 'under the pressure of immediate, external events, continually revises in her laments both her sense of what constitutes loss and her emotional response to it' (p 39). She learns and changes, 'moving beyond the utter delusions of blasphemy and even the fortunal fatalism characteristic of "medieval pagans" ... to a measure of self-knowledge' (p 40).

698 Dean, Christopher. 'Henryson's *Testament of Cresseid*, 188.' *Expl*, 31 (1972), item 21.
Mars' rusty sword in line 188 suggests that he is not only threatening and menacing but 'also somewhat boorish and churlish.'

699 Donaldson, E. Talbot. 'Briseis, Briseida, Criseyde, Cresseid, Cressid: Progress of a Heroine.' In *Chaucerian Problems and Perspectives: Essays presented to Paul E. Beichner.* Ed. Edward Vasta and Zacharias P. Thundy. Notre Dame: University of Notre Dame Press, 1979. Pp 3–12.
Explains why Criseyde was more interesting to medieval writers than Helen of Troy. Comments on Henryson's development of the sexual potential of Cresseid and notes the poet's handling of the narrator, 'rather coarser than anything Chaucer would have done, but nevertheless very effective in establishing the ironies of the narrator's love-sick attitude toward the heroine' (p 9).

700 Ellenberger, Bengt. *The Latin Element in the Vocabulary of the Earlier Makars Henryson and Dunbar.* Lund Studies in English 51. Lund: CWK Gleerup, 1977.
'The Latinate diction of the *Testament* is as high as can be expected in a longish poem, but hardly dense enough to be called aureate on account of frequency' (p 61).

701 Fox, Denton. 'The 1663 Anderson Edition of Henryson's *Testament of Cresseid.*' *SSL*, 8 (1970–71), 75–96.
Discusses the relationship of the Anderson edition to Scottish and English textual traditions, namely the Charteris' edition of 1593 and Thynne's of 1532. The 1663 edition is of the Scottish tradition but has independent authority. Fox reprints the edition, with notes on variants in Charteris and Thynne.

702 — 'Middle Scots Poets and Patrons.' In *English Court Culture in the Later Middle Ages.* Ed. V.J. Scattergood and J.W. Sherborne. London: Duckworth, 1983. Pp 109–27.

Discusses Scots poets from Robert Bruce to the sixteenth century in
an attempt to determine whether they represent a significant literary
group. Henryson, 'the major poet of the century' (p 113), makes
skillful use of Chaucerian prosody both in metrical patterns within his
lines as well as in his stanzas. But he also draws effectively upon the
alliterative tradition (pp 113–116). Middle Scots poets are more
various than their English contemporaries in the fifteenth century in
that they drew on more various traditions and 'were less swamped by
Chaucer and Lydgate than the English poets' (p 125).

702a Friedman, John B. 'Henryson's *Testament of Cresseid* and the *Judicio
Solis in Conviviis Saturni* of Simon of Couvin.' *MP*, 83 (1985), 12–21.
Henryson's astrological winter setting and the role of Mercury come
into sharper focus through knowledge of Simon's poem on the plague
which served as a source for Henryson.

703 Gray, Douglas. *Robert Henryson.* Leiden: E.J. Brill, 1979.
Ch 5, 'What became of Criseyde,' pp 162–208, proposes a judicious
reading of *TC* as a 'medieval tragedy in the Senecan mode' (p 166). In
the poem's opening *chronographia* 'the "old poet" trying to come to
terms with the fading of love and coldness of age is a kind of domestic
foreshadowing, a serio-comic mirror-image of what is to happen in the
poem' (p 168). He functions as a chorus in the tragedy, careful to
stress Cresseid's fatal destenye' and show that she is 'an object moved
by external forces ... the plaything of Fortune' (p 174). An ancient
pattern of tragedy emerges where 'men are helpless before the gods,
and yet are moved by emotions and vices within themselves ...
Henryson is a good enough poet to let the tensions remain' (p 175).
Gray traces the double motivation and double responsibility through
the progression of the narrative, with extensive remarks on the
planetary gods (especially the role of Saturn). 'Henryson's macabre
imagination creates something like the Senecan theatre of the terrible
in the sufferings of his leprous Cresseid' (p 197). Her elaborate
planctus of seven stanzas is 'perhaps Henryson's finest piece of
rhetorical writing, a great tragic *aria* for his heroine at the lowest ebb
of her fortune' (p 197). Her last *planctus* expresses remorse rather
than Christian repentance, a powerful contrast of purity and pollution.
Explicit Christian references are suppressed. 'Those who would impose
neat moral interpretation on the poem would destroy its tragic
pattern, which holds its contraries in tension' (p 208). See **729** for
review article.

704 Hanna, Ralph, III. 'Cresseid's Dream and Henryson's *Testament.*' In
*Chaucer and Middle English Studies in Honour of Rossell Hope
Robbins.* Ed. Beryl Rowland. London: George Allen & Unwin Ltd,

1974. Pp 288–297.

Hanna explains Cresseid's dream in terms of Macrobian dream theory. It is both prophetic and the result of her preoccupation, that is, part *oraculum* and part *insomnium*. But although it has effect in this world, that effect is not due to the fact of the dream itself 'but due to Cresseid's own actions or choices ... Cresseid's disfigurement ultimately stems from her own actions, her own dalliance' (p 295).

705 Harty, Kevin. 'Cresseid and Her Narrator: A Reading of Robert Henryson's *"Testament of Cresseid".*' *Studi Medievali*, 23 (1983), 753–65.

'The poem's narrator, not its author, is the stern moralist, and his moralizing ironically backfires upon himself. At the conclusion ... Henryson grants his heroine a redemption that the narrator is incapable of appreciating or sharing in' (p 753). The resolution is Boethian: Cresseid is allowed the same consolation by Henryson that Chaucer affords Troilus in *T&C*. She rejects 'any easy explanation of or excuse for her leprous state and freely accepts personal responsibility for her past actions and their consequences.' (p 764). The narrator, on the other hand, is cold in all senses of that term — incapable of love, mean-spirited, and spiteful, like Chaucer's Reeve (p 759).

706 Hirsch, Richard S.M. 'A Note on the Use of Leprosy in Henryson's *Testament of Cresseid* and Claudel's *L'annonce faite à Marie*.' *Actaeus* (Brown University), January 1971, pp 17–19.
[I have not seen this item.]

707 Hume, Kathryn. 'Leprosy or Syphillis in Henryson's *Testament of Cresseid*.' *ELN*, 6 (1968–69), 242–45.

Hume challenges Beryl Rowland, *ELN*, 1 (1964), 175–77, who argued that Cresseid's 'seiknes incurabill' was syphilis. Syphilis was not diagnosed as a separate disease until 1493 in Spain and did not achieve formal recognition in Scotland until 1497, at least five years after *TC* was written. Henryson does not link Cresseid's disease with sexual promiscuity. Leprosy is the disease perfectly suited to his artistic purposes in that 'lepers were considered both peculiarly cursed and blessed: cursed in that they were suspected of being heinous sinners, because God thought it fit to punish them so harshly; blessed in that God was evidently taking special interest in the victim by thus offering him a chance to repent and do penance,' which is exactly the situation in Henryson's poem (p 245).

708 Jentoft, C.W. 'Henryson as Authentic "Chaucerian": Narrator, Character, and Courtly Love in *The Testament of Cresseid*.' *SSL*, 10 (1972–73), 94–102.

Henryson's portrait of the narrator of *TC* shows Chaucerian
detachment, with ironic glimpses into the narrator's personality.
Henryson rightly sees Criseyde as the main character of Chaucer's
poem. The portrayal of Calchas is the only real change he makes in
Chaucer's characters. But his most convincing development of a
Chaucerian spirit in his poem lies in his skillful treatment of *amour
courtois*.

709 Kindrick, Robert L. *Robert Henryson*. Boston: Twayne, 1979.
Chapters on Henryson and his times, his use of literary tradition, and
his influence on later poetry, with separate discussions of *The Moral
Fabillis*, *TC* (pp 118–48), *Orpheus and Eurydice* and other shorter
poems. Summarizes critical discussions of *TC* to conclude that
Cresseid belies 'stern moralists' (p 147).

710 Lyall, R.J. 'Henryson and Boccaccio: A Problem in the Study of
Sources.' *Anglia*, 99 (1981), 38–59.
Challenges MacQueen's repeated suggestions (716 and elsewhere) that
Henryson used Boccaccio's *De genealogia deorum* as a source in his
three principal narrative poems. 'The truth is that in the transmission
of such conventional materials the identification of specific sources is
almost impossible' (p 51). In his portrayal of the pagan gods Henryson
seems to draw on several sources and to add embellishments of his own
as he develops and changes traditional sources to achieve specific
effects. We are not likely ever to find a specific source for the
planetary portraits, but if we do it will not be Boccaccio.

711 McDiarmid, Matthew P. 'Robert Henryson in his Poems.' In *Bards
and Makars: Scottish Language and Literature: Medieval and
Renaissance*. Ed. Adam J. Aitken, Matthew P. McDiarmid, and
Derrick S. Thomson. Glasgow: University of Glasgow Press, 1977. Pp
27–40.
Examines Henryson's personal responses in his four most emotive
poems — the pessimism, humanistic imagination, and scholastic terms
of thought, neither quite at home in his own Christian world nor our
materialistic one. In *TC* Henryson creates a sense of judgment against
Cresseid for her leprosy which is more dramatically instructive than
moral. 'Repentance is not in doubt, but there is no peace of mind in
her death; bitter and despairing self-reproach displaces bitter
upbraiding of her gods ... The bleakness of her direction of thought is
what impresses ... something here of the dark vision that Webster's
characters have in their ends' (p 38).

712 — *Robert Henryson*. Edinburgh: Scottish Academic Press, 1981. Pp
88–116.

McDiarmid would date the composition of *TC* ca 1486–90, prior to *The Spektakle of Luf*, which is 'thoroughly derivative' from Henryson for Cresseid's leprosy. Critics err in viewing Cresseid's ailment as venereal disease. That is 'a peculiarly modern debasement of the heroine's situation, quite unevidenced by the text' (p 100).

713 McDonald, Craig. 'Venus and the Goddess of Fortune in *The Testament of Cresseid*.' *ScLJ*, 4 (1977), 14–24.
By exploring Boethian parallels, McDonald shows that 'Cresseid is guilty of misinterpretting the nature of Fortune and its working in human affairs' (p 16). To some extent Venus is 'a projection of the victim's outraged, if incomplete, sense of justice' (p 19). Cresseid's frail nature is strengthened as she is led to see her false positions. Her apparent adversaries, the god and goddess of love, like Fortune in the *Consolatio*, prove valuable teachers. 'As Boethius grows to understand the folly of placing trust in material goods, so Cresseid, even without the tutelage of Philosophia, comes to a greater self awareness through adversity. What Boethius accomplishes through a philosophical treatise, Henryson accomplishes through poetry' (p 23).

714 McNamara, John. 'Divine Justice in Henryson's *Testament of Cresseid*.' *SSL*, 11 (1973–74), 99–107.
The poem suggests that '(1) divine justice has been vindicated in the actions of the pagan gods, (2) the Christian God whom they represent must, by implication, also be just, and (3) whatever God may choose as the ultimate resting place for Cresseid's soul will therefore be just. But since this justice, though itself reasonable, transcends human reason, it must be accepted on faith' (p 107).

715 — 'Language as Action in Henryson's *Testament of Cresseid*.' In *Bards and Makars: Scottish Language and Literature: Medieval and Renaissance*. Ed. Adam J. Aitken, Matthew P. McDiarmid, and Derick S. Thomson. Glasgow: University of Glasgow Press, 1977. Pp 41–51.
Using Russian formalistic and French structuralist techniques McNamara explores the poem's metalanguage through which time, character, plot, and tradition are all maintained by linguistic layering of the experience of the poem. The poet's self-reflective language sustains both theme and action as linguistic phenomena which are kind to Cresseid despite the evils of her fortune. 'The poem redeems the language about her by various formal devices which call attention to language — both its problematic nature as "inuention" and its capacity to serve as vehicle for moral regeneration and instruction' (p 50).

716 MacQueen, John. *Robert Henryson: A Study of the Major Narrative Poems*. Oxford: Clarendon Press, 1967.

Ch 3, *The Testament of Cresseid,* pp 45–93, divides the poem into eight parts and discusses theme, imagery, allegory, and style in each. Henryson adheres to precepts of medieval rhetorical conventions in his use of aureate diction, colloquialism, sententia, parallelism, ambiguity, and courtly imagery. MacQueen devotes considerable attention to alliterative figura and sound patterns within individual stanzas.

717 Mieszkowski, Gretchen. 'The Reputation of Criseyde: 1155–1500.' *Transactions of the Connecticut Academy of Arts and Sciences,* 43 (1971), 71–153.
Reviews background of Shakespeare's Cressida, from Benoît de Sainte-Maure's *Le Roman de Troie* through Henryson, including allusions to her in French and Italian as well as English and Scottish literature.

718 Newlyn, Evelyn S. 'Tradition and Transformation in the Poetry of Robert Henryson.' *SSL,* 18 (1983), 33–58.
Explores Henryson's Chaucer-like ability to transform his sources in 'Robene and Makyne,' 'The Reasoning Betwix Aige and Youth,' and 'The Annunciation.' Mentions *TC* only briefly.

719 Noll, Dolores L. '*The Testament of Cresseid:* Are Christian Interpretations Valid?' *SSL,* 9 (1971–72), 16–25.
The poem addresses a courtly love morality, not a Christian one. Its concern is tragic decay rather than spiritual regeneration.

720 Patterson, Lee W. 'Christian and Pagan in the "Testament of Cresseid".' *PQ,* 52 (1973), 696–714.
The *Testament* is 'a witty compendium of late medieval literary styles,' the sort of poem 'we might expect from a poetic schoolmaster whose other major work is a series of brilliantly simple rhetorical exercises' (p 696). Set in a pagan world, the poem is deliberately Christian. Cresseid is not excluded by the pagan gods because they have changed or changed her; rather she has changed herself. She has destroyed her 'deeper moral attractiveness'; she is excluded 'not because she is ugly but because she is sluttish' (p 698). When she blames the gods for her failure 'she commits blasphemy and the gods punish her with leprosy. But they do *not* punish her for her wantonness nor, most significantly, for her betrayal of Troilus.' (p 699). Her pagan gods concern themselves with simple equivalency rather than complicated justice. But the ethic, very different from Christian forgiveness, grace, and salvation, becomes complicated by the fact that Cresseid does repent. 'Henryson, with fine and subtle chivalry ... allows Cresseid to earn her escape from the world of "all things generabill." He allows her to move from the objective pagan world of crime and punishment to the

subjective world of sin and repentence' (p 703). The punishment of the pagan gods thus serves a larger, more humane justice through the heroine's growing *inwardness*, her 'inner suffering.' Her initial complaint is an attempt to avoid subjectivity. But upon confronting Troilus, she quietly gazes into herself and becomes truly reflective. Her testament, the 'ultimate act of publication, marks the full growth of Cresseid's inner self' (p 712). The poem's movement from pagan externals to moral introspection is essentially Christian. Indeed, 'the nature of Christian experience is its major theme' (p 697).

721 Ramson, W.S. 'A Reading of Henryson's *Testament*, or "Quha Falsit Cresseid?" ' *Parergon*, 17 (1977), 25–35.
Mainly, it has been the critics who have 'falsit Cresseid' by not paying enough attention to the poem's disposition of its content (its use of proportion), its style, and its use of a narrating presence.

722 Richards, Peter. *The Medieval Leper and his Northern Heirs.* Cambridge: D.S. Brewer; Totowa, N.J.: Rowman and Littlefield, 1977. Richards, a medical doctor at St George's Hospital, London, explores the history of leprosy in England and Scandinavia, using literary, medical, graveyard, and pictorial evidence for documentation. Includes excerpts from seventeen written documents (pp 121–65) and forty-six illustrations. *TC* is discussed briefly. 'Cresseid's shattered aspirations, her disfigured body, her despair, and her inescapable death reflect truth far stranger than fiction, a reality which the experience of later centuries corroborates in the smallest detail' (p 8).

723 Ridley, Florence H. 'A Plea for the Middle Scots.' In *The Learned and the Lewed: Studies in Chaucer and Medieval Literature.* Ed. Larry D. Benson. Harvard English Studies 5. Cambridge: Harvard University Press, 1974. Pp 175–196.
Ridley reviews the history of defining the Middle Scots poets as 'Scottish Chaucerians' to point out that the evidence of Scots' indebtedness to Chaucer is surprisingly slim. Although *TC* takes off from *T&C* it is Henryson's originality and poetic skill which is more striking than any dependence on Chaucer. 'For in the *Testament* Henryson did not imitate Chaucer, did not adopt his material or manner or themes. He found in Chaucer's poem a latent idea and the outline of a static character which he proceeded to develop fully in such a way as to illustrate that idea and make it a lesson universally applicable' (p 196).

724 Scheps, Walter. 'A Climatological Reading of Henryson's *Testament of Cresseid.*' *SSL*, 15 (1980), 80–87.
The northerly climate of Henryson's poem is suitable to its chilling

subject matter. According to medieval medical journals, leprosy is especially severe in winter. Given Cresseid's behavior and her removal to Caledonia, her leprosy is 'an entirely suitable punishment' (p 86).

724a Schmitz, Götz. 'Cresseid's Trail: A Revision. Fame and Defamation in Henryson's *Testament of Cresseid*.' In *Essays and Studies 1979*. Ed. Dieter Mehl. Vol. 32, New Series of Essays and Studies Collected for the English Association. Atlantic Highlands, N.J.: Humanities Press, 1979. Pp 44–56.
Rather than blackening Cresseid's character in *TC*, Henryson rescues it from an already popular prejudice long established in literary tradition affecting the repute of a pitiable sinner. The narrator, following Chaucer, staves off Cresseid's slanderers and vindicates her honor against defamation. Henryson's understanding of tragedy is 'thoroughly medieval' (p 52). Cresseid is not an unwitting victim; she knows her errors and accepts her punishment in the end. The severity of the punishment makes her 'the pitiable object of a barbarous sentence' (p 53) and thus forestalls degradation by her slanderers.

725 Schöwerling, Rainer. 'Chaucers *Troilus and Criseyde* in der Englischen Literatur von Henryson bis Dryden.' *Anglia*, 97 (1979), 326–49.
Henryson's adaptation of the story of Troilus and Criseyde reveals a belated humanistic tendency toward the commonplace of *de casibus* tragedy, an almost puritanical religious world view, distinct didactic tendencies appropriate to the educational struggle of the new bourgeois audience for which he wrote, and a renewed sense of native literature.

726 Sklute, Larry M. 'Phoebus Descending: Rhetoric and Moral Vision in Henryson's *Testament of Cresseid*.' *ELH*, 44 (1977), 189–204.
In *TC* the sun never rises although it sets twice. The image of descent underscores the poem's sense of mutability and the destruction of life. Its vision, although sympathetic toward Cresseid on the surface, is ultimately dark, a view conspicuously without charity. The narrator 'leads us into the poem, offers himself as a sympathetic mediator between us and the bleakness of the world he is portraying, condemns while sympathizing, causing us to wonder what his real function in the poem is; then, at the time when a truly charitable mediator is necessary, the time after Cresseid has been struck down and made to confront her misery alone, he disappears from the narrative completely, leaving us to face that misery unmediated until the last line when, having made us witness first hand Cresseid's sorrow and her disintegration, he returns to say that since she is dead "I speik of hir no moir" ' (p 202).

727 Spearing, A.C. 'The Testament of Cresseid and the High Concise Style.' *Spec*, 37 (1962), 208–225.

Although Henryson's attitude toward brevity may have been influenced by Chaucer, where the concept is applied mainly toward weightiness of meaning, his use of *abbreviatio* and *brevitas*-formulas lies mainly outside the ideals of medieval rhetoric and is more akin to that of Erasmus and the Spaniard Juan Luis Vives. His 'high concise style' is part of a self-conscious literary theory which he comments upon within the poem. Spearing contrasts the brevity of *TC* with the prolix style of *T&C*, which up until the epilogue works in a style opposite to that of *TC*. Henryson's poem, truly a medieval tragedy, is presented from the perspective of the eighth sphere, so to speak, a poem of an old man 'free from the magnificently idealizing illusions of the young Troilus' (p 221). Henryson's cognizance of the harsh blended with the charitable is candid: Cresseid is repentant, but there is no suggestion of Christian healing; 'the facts of suffering cannot be so quickly overcome' (p 224). 'Henryson's poem is compassionate, but it is consolatory only in the sense in which any great work of art is so, by its very existence' (p 225).

728 Strauss, Jennifer. 'To Speak Once More of Cresseid: Henryson's *Testament* Re-considered.' *ScLJ*, 4 (1977), 5–13.
Focussing her discussion on the so-called 'pageant' of planetary gods, Strauss analyzes *TC* as a 'getting-of-wisdom' poem, 'its narrative depicting the painful revelation to the protagonist of the nature of personal moral responsibility and the possibility of integrity in a world of time' (p 5). In learning to distinguish between voluntary and inevitable changes in her life Cresseid comes 'to recognise the terms under which she has responsible being. Her acceptance of that responsibility brings her into the fullness of existence, but paradoxically, and tragically, at a time when death has become the only possibility' (p 12).

729 Wordsworth, Jonathan. 'Redeeming the Irredeemable.' *TLS* (Feb. 20, 1981), p 209.
Review article of Gray 703. Praises Gray for skillful treatment of the *Moral Fables*, but wonders that *TC*, 'indisputably Henryson's greatest poem,' should get but a single chapter. *TC* is 'the first work written in English that is in the full, post-Shakespearean sense, a tragedy. In its association of redemptive suffering and final relentless waste of human love and human life, it belongs neither with the crudities of Seneca, nor with the deary late medieval "Fall of Princes," but with *King Lear*.' Henryson uses three Chaucerian tricks in dealing with Cresseid's infidelity: 1) The narrator's refusal to accept responsibility for details of the story; 2) intrusion of the narrator's personal sympathy; 3) offloading of moral responsibility onto fate or Fortune. Henryson takes an astonishing daring step, unheard of in serious

literature before the 19th century, of making his heroine a prostitute who dares to enjoy life, all the while keeping the shock and distaste to a minimum. Wordsworth links the encounter between Troilus and Cresseid to their first knowing encounter in Chaucer. Troilus' throwing of money into her lap has 'a near erotic violence, brought out especially by the harshness of the verb *swak*. The reminder of earlier lovemaking is painful and horribly appropriate.'

Testament of Love (*TL*)

730 Baugh, A.C. 'The Middle English Period (1100–1500).' In *A Literary History of England*. See 170.
TL is 'better known than it deserves to be' (p 268). 'The allegory is full of obscurities which we can hardly hope to clear up, but even if we could, no great service would be done to English literature' (p 269).

731 Bressie, Ramona. 'A Study of Thomas Usk's *Testament of Love* as an Autobiography.' University of Chicago Abstracts of Theses. Humanistic Series, 7 (1928), 517–21.
Summarizes information on Usk's life gleaned from historical records, especially accounts of his informing on John Norhampton, John More, and Richard Norbury, all of whom were convicted and exiled while Usk went free. Later he was indicted for 'appealing' the three, imprisoned for six months, and then executed. He was not an ecclesiastic but a son of a London craftsman and a citizen.

732 — 'The Date of Thomas Usk's *Testament of Love*.' *MP*, 26 (1928), 17–29.
TL is Usk's defense of himself for having 'appealed' Norhampton, More and Norbury — a vindication for his lapse into treason. 'Margarite' is perhaps an abstraction for all that is good in Richard's reign, or, more likely, a figure of the Queen herself. The work seems to draw specifically on *LGW* and all five books of *T&C*. Its date of composition thus appears to be December 1384–June 1385. Usk's first imprisonment was too early for the composition of the treatise, and his second was too brief.

32a Burnley, J.D. 'Chaucer, Usk, and Geoffrey of Vinsauf.' *Neophil*, 69 (1985), 284–93.
Usk echoes an image from *Poetria Nova* when he writes: 'Now I have crossed the sea; I have fixed my Cadiz on the shore' (p 289). Chaucer and Hoccleve also assimilate bits from the rhetorics and *artes poeticae*, but 'their interest in them was not very great' (p 291).

733 Heninger, S.K., Jr. 'The Margarite-Pearl Allegory in Thomas Usk's *Testament of Love*.' *Spec*, 32 (1957), 92–98.
TL is 'one of the most patently derived works in English' (p 92). Usk's virtuoso treatment of the Margarite-Pearl allegory is 'the one island of interest' in the treatise 'to which we can profitably moor our attention' (p 92). Heninger traces pearl symbolism from the Bible, through Rabanus Maurus, the *Legenda Aurea*, and Nicholas of Lyra, and comments on related use of dew and manna imagery. 'Usk has triumphed by incorporating the erotic and the moral elements into the same symbolic complex' (p 97). He resolves 'the dilemma of carnal *versus* spiritual love by assuming the validity of physical symbols' (p 98).

734 Jellech, Virginia B. '*The Testament of Love* by Thomas Usk: A New Edition.' *DAI*, 31 (1971), 6060A. Washington University Dissertation. Dir. Richard M. Hazelton.
A line-by-line transcription of Thynne's text, with punctuation, capitalization, and spelling unchanged except to remove severe confusion. Extensive annotations show literary sources and conventions and connect the apologetical material in the allegory with what we know of Usk's career in London politics. Jellech concludes that Usk did not use Chaucer's translation of Boethius (probably Jean de Meun's, instead), nor does he use *HF* or show acquaintance with *Piers Plowman*. TL is 'more intimately psychological than Chaucer's or Langland's work and, despite obvious obscurities, richer and deeper than Gower's ... We cannot say we know the literature of the fourteenth century until we know the *Testament of Love*.'

735 Lewis, C.S. *Allegory of Love*. 1932. See **132**.
Ch 5, 'Gower, Thomas Usk,' pp 198–231: 'The use of prose for matter the reverse of utilitarian marks a phase in the coming of age of our language' (p 222). Usk is trying to write *Kunstprosa* — colored and tunable with wings like verse, capable of doing in English what Latin does in the hands of Alanus: 'he deserves from posterity more sympathy and indulgence than he has usually received. That his results should be more interesting than beautiful is only what we should expect. But sometimes he succeeds; and many of his failures must be laid at the door of Chaucer's *Boethius* — a radically vicious model which Usk excusably followed because it had, in his time, no rivals' (p 223). Lewis discusses Chaucerian influences on TL and explores Usk's use of ambiguity in his treatment of love (pp 223–8). He challenges Skeat's assertion that Margarite 'never means a live woman, nor represents even an imaginary object of natural human affection' (**511**, p xxix); 'Margaret does not cease to be a woman by becoming a symbol of grace ... Usk treats courtly love as a symbol of divine love;

but, for that reason, he does not cease to treat courtly love' (p 225).
Pp 228–31 are devoted to Usk's prose style. 'Except for certain
passages, Usk hardly deserves to be read twice' (p 230).

736 Matthews, William, ed. *Later Medieval English Prose.* New York:
Appleton-Century-Crofts, 1963.
Includes a selection from *TL* (pp 247–51). Despite *TL's*
autobiographical form and content, the work is 'highly derivative' (p
242). 'The prose-style of this Christian Boethius is unusual for its
time: self-conscious, extravagant, sugared, and obscure, it calls to
mind some of the Elizabethan mannerists. Chaucer's *Boethius* is the
inspiration for its Latinate tinge in syntax and vocabulary and its
balanced structures ... Interesting as it is historically, Usk's prose is
too narcissistic, too incongruent with the matter, to be anything but
irritating' (p 243).

737 Reiss, Edmund. 'The Idea of Love in Usk's *Testament of Love.*'
Mediaevalia, 6 (1980), 261–77.
Usk alters Anselm's illustrations in *De Concordia Praescientiae et
Praedestinationis* to emphasize the term 'love' wherever possible.
Reiss delineates various forms or changes of love in *TL,* from earthly
affection to divine, emphasizing their intimate affiliation with
'Margarete,' the figurative object of the quest. 'The parallel
development of Margaret, from earthly object of desire to principle of
heavenly love, functions as a way of marking the progress and also as a
metonymical designation of the virtue that is the high road to bliss' (p
277).

738 Sanderline, George. Usk's *Testament of Love* and St. Anselm.' *Spec,*
17 (1942), 69–73.
Book III, called by Skeat 'the dullest book of a dull treatise,' hopeless
in its 'lack of order,' may be cleared of the latter charge when
compared to Anselm's *De concordia praescientiae et praedestinationis
nec non gratiae Dei cum libero arbitrio,* upon which it is modeled. Chs
2–4 dealing with the relations of Divine praescience and free choice,
chs 5–7 on free choice and the will in general, and chs 8–9 on the
relations of grace and free choice correspond, in sequence, to three
questiones in Anselm. Usk's most significant and confusing change is
his introduction into Anselm's matter of Margaret, with all her
allegorical variations. 'The fourteenth century in England has
sometimes been pictured as strongly swayed by the theological
determinism of Bradwardine and Wyclif. Usk's translation of a
treatise in which free choice, although reconciled upon predestination
and grace, is firmly upheld, together with the distinct emphasis upon
liberum arbitrium in the C-Text of *Piers Plowman,* suggests that the

orthodox Catholic teaching on the subject of liberty remained as influential as ever in this century' (p 73).

739 Schlauch, Margaret. 'Two Styles of Thomas Usk,' *Brno Studies in English*, 8 (1969), 167–72.
Compares the prose style of Usk's 'Appeal against the non-victualler anti-royal merchants' (1384) and his *TL*. The style of the 'Appeal' is consonant with its purpose and is legal, not literary. It has the ring of authentic speech in some places, with some alliteration and inversion which reflect the demands of effective oratory. In contrast, 'the style of *TL* is throughout distinctly mannered. All sorts of linguistic devices are exploited for planned effect with a frequency probably unparalleled in any other Middle English text' (p 168). Eg, Usk's distinctive use of alliteration, highly rhythmical patterns of *cursus*, repetitions of key words, paired synonyms, colloquial expressions, 'a veritable passion for inverted word order' (p 170), and also vivid images. 'All of these Uskian traits indicate that the author of *TL* laboured to produce a highly-wrought literary effect by the instrumentality of his language. John Lyly was surely no more conscious in his own striving. The "Appeal" on the other hand shows Usk employing a quite different style, more appropriate to his forensic purpose. The contrast indicates that he was aware of the possibility of choice, which is an essential for the practitioner of literary style. His achievement may not have been great, but it is truly significant in the history of English prose' (p 171).

740 — 'Thomas Usk as Translator.' In *Medieval Literature and Folklore Studies: Essays in Honor of Francis Lee Utley*. Ed. Jerome Mandel and Bruce Rosenberg. New Brunswick: Rutgers University Press, 1970. Pp 73–103.
Comparing *TL* to Anselm's *De concordia praescientiae et praedestinationis* Schlauch notes several errors which must be due to the printer or scribe or perhaps to Usk's own eye skips. Usk is quite capable of translating very closely. But the stylistic aspects of his translations are more interesting than the grammatical. 'When he treated his source most freely he evinced most clearly the rhetorical traits characteristic of his original formal writing. He was, in short, a very conscious experimenter in the medium of fourteenth-century English prose' (p 103).

741 Skeat, W.W. *Oxford Chaucer*. 1897. See **511**. Vol 7, pp xviii–xxxi, 1–145.
Thynne, 1532, is the sole authority for the text of *TL*, a text which is 'almost unparalleled' in its 'shameful corrruption': 'Originally written in an obscure style, every form of carelessness seems to have been employed in order to render it more obscure than before' (p xix).

Skeat explains the acrostic whereby the authorship of the work was determined, a sentence hidden letter by letter in the beginnings of the thirty-two chapters to yield: MARGARETE OF VIRTW, HAVE MERCI ON THSKNVI, where THSKNVI is resolved into two words, Thin USK. Bradley had previously hit upon Usk as probable author by study of autobiographical references in the treatise (p xx). Skeat discusses the work's ties with Chaucer and Boethius and offers a synopsis (pp xxix–xxxi).

742 Tyrwhitt, Thomas. 'An Account of the Works of Chaucer.' In *The Canterbury Tales of Chaucer*. 2 vols. 1798. See **526**.
'The Testament of Love is evidently an imitation of Boethius *de consolatione Philosophiae*. It seems to have been begun by our author [Chaucer] after his troubles, in the middle part of the reign of Richard II, and to have been finished about the time that Gower published his *Confessio Amantis*, in the 16th year of that reign. At least it must then have been far advanced, as Gower mentions it by its title' (II.p 530).

Index

Numbers in boldface type indicate authorship or primary entry. 'R' indicates review entry. A boldface number in parenthesis indicates subdivision of the preceding entry outside parenthesis. For example, Lewis 116, **116R**, 116R, **132 (564)** indicates that Lewis is mentioned in 116, that he reviewed 116, and that he is mentioned in another's review of 116; he wrote item **132**, and **564**, a subdivision of 132, is also by him. On the other hand, Cambridge Univ. Lib. Ii.3.3 342, **346**, 400 indicates that the manuscript is mentioned in entries 342 and 400, while **346** is a primary entry, in this instance a facsimile edition of the manuscript.